*Government, War and Society in Medieval Ireland*

*In loving memory of*
J.A.W.
(1912–2008)

# Government, War and Society in Medieval Ireland

ESSAYS BY

Edmund Curtis, A.J. Otway-Ruthven
and James Lydon

*Edited by*

Peter Crooks

FOUR COURTS PRESS

Typeset in 10.5 pt on 12.5 pt Ehrhardt by
Carrigboy Typesetting Services for
FOUR COURTS PRESS LTD
7 Malpas Street, Dublin 8, Ireland
www.fourcourtspress.ie
*and in North America for*
FOUR COURTS PRESS
c/o IPG, 814 N. Franklin St, Chicago, IL 60622.

© the various authors, the editor and Four Courts Press 2008

First published 2008
First paperback edition 2019
A catalogue record for this title is available
from the British Library.

ISBN 978-1-84682-733-4

All rights reserved.
Without limiting the rights under copyright
reserved alone, no part of this publication may be
reproduced, stored in or introduced into a retrieval system,
or transmitted, in any form or by any means (electronic, mechanical,
photocopying, recording or otherwise), without the prior
written permission of both the copyright owner and
publisher of this book.

SPECIAL ACKNOWLEDGMENT

This publication has been generously supported by the
Trinity College Dublin Association and Trust.

Printed in Ireland
by Sprintprint, Dublin.

# Contents

PART 2: WAR



PART 3: SOCIETY



FURTHER READING

# Illustrations

MAPS



FIGURES



TABLES

# Acknowledgments

The appearance of this volume in 2008 coincides with the anniversaries of two defining works of Irish medievalism. It is seventy years since the publication in 1938 of the second edition of *A history of medieval Ireland* by Edmund Curtis. Precisely three decades later, A.J. Otway-Ruthven – Curtis' pupil and successor in the Lecky chair of history at Trinity College, Dublin – published her own *magnum opus* under the same title. This collection is intended, in part, to mark these platinum and ruby anniversaries, and to salute the achievements of the authors, along with those of Otway-Ruthven's successor as Lecky professor, James Lydon, who celebrated his eightieth birthday earlier in 2008. The warmth with which a great many groups and individuals responded to news of this project is a sure sign of the esteem and affection in which these three scholars are still held.

I would like to record here my thanks to the learned societies and publishing houses that gave permission for the essays to be published in this new edition. They are: the Irish Historical Society and the Ulster Society for Irish Historical Studies [*Irish Historical Studies*] (chapters 1, 5 and 6); the Royal Society of Antiquaries of Ireland (chapters 2, 7, 8, 13, 14 and 16); the *English Historical Review* (chapters 3, 17 and 18); the International Commission for the History of Representative and Parliamentary Institutions (chapter 4); the Military History Society of Ireland [*Irish Sword*] (chapters 9, 10 and 11); Irish Academic Press (chapter 12); *Studies* (chapter 19); the faculty of Washington and Jefferson College, PA [*Topic*] (chapter 20); and the Royal Irish Academy (chapter 21). I am grateful to the trustees of the *Irish Times* and the board of Trinity College, Dublin, for permission to publish images of Edmund Curtis and A.J. Otway-Ruthven. The photograph of James Lydon first appeared in *History Ireland*, 3:1 (Spring 1995); my thanks to the photographer, Brigid Fitzgerald, and to Tommy Graham, editor of *History Ireland*, for permission to reproduce the image in this volume.

I am greatly indebted to friends and colleagues who helped at various stages in the preparation of the volume by advising on the selection of essays, assisting in the sleuth work involved in tracking down errant bibliographical references, showing me samples of forthcoming work, and sharing reminiscences of the authors. In particular, I would like to thank Seán Duffy, Robin Frame, Katharine Simms, Bernadette Williams, Maryann Valiulis, Bill Fuge, Stephen

Harrison, Freya Verstraten, Áine Foley and, of course, Michael Adams, Martin Fanning and the team at Four Courts Press. That the volume appears at a relatively modest price is due to a handsome subvention from the Cente for Irish-Scottish and Comparative Studies in Trinity College, Dublin. Finally, to the new Mrs Crooks: for being eternally patient when your medieval co-respondents make unfair demands on my time – thank you.

The greatest pleasure to have arisen from editing these essays was the opportunity to become acquainted with James Lydon – a personal hero of mine. He was enthusiastic about the volume from the first and touchingly modest about having his name associated with 'his heroes' – Curtis and Otway-Ruthven. I am also exceedingly grateful to Dr Salters Sterling for granting permission, in his capacity as executor general of the late Professor Otway-Ruthven, for the republication of her articles, as well as the map of 'Ireland in 1300', which first appeared in A.J. Otway-Ruthven, *A history of medieval Ireland* (London, 1968). Edmund Curtis died without children in 1943; his executor was Cathleen Synge. Unfortunately, it has not proved possible to locate the descendants of Miss Synge, but I trust that Professor Curtis – who was so instrumental in the early development of medieval studies in Ireland – would approve of the current project.

PETER CROOKS

# Note on editorial conventions

It is in the nature of an anthology to be varied in content and style, but the reader is likely to find the essays in the present collection a particularly sundry lot. Each of the three authors has a highly distinctive voice and their inflections are accentuated by the fact that the essays first appeared across a period of some nine decades: the earliest (chapter 17) was published in 1908, the latest (chapter 1) as recently as 1995. Naturally, academic interests and fashions have shifted more than once during that period. Then there is the matter of audience. Most of the essays began life as articles in the journals of learned societies; but some are the texts of public lectures delivered by the authors and, as such, are less austere in tone and do not include comprehensive references.

The unifying feature is subject matter. Each of the essays explores some aspect of the history of the English colony in later medieval Ireland. In deciding which essays should be included in this new edition, my aim was to be representative rather than seek vainly to be all embracing. I looked for essays whose scholarship remains unsurpassed and whose ideas proved seminal to the subsequent historiography. The value of some of the older essays lies in the primary source materials they contain. Selection involves exclusion: I rejected studies with a regional or local emphasis – despite their undoubted importance – in favour of essays that treat of the medieval lordship of Ireland as a whole. The final assemblage inevitably reflects my preferences and, where I have sinned in omitting, I hope readers will not be too offended. When it came to determining the sequence of the essays, I sought to emphasize the authors' common ground by grouping the essays thematically – rather than by author or date of publication – in three sections under the rubrics 'government', 'war' and 'society'.

The essays in the collection have been completely reset. My policy as editor has been to tamper with the texts as little as possible. While I have silently standardized basic conventions governing spelling and punctuation, all place- and personal names are rendered as in the original. Standardization here would have done violence to the texts, many of which are valuable not simply as works of historical scholarship but as historical documents in their own right. One drawback of this approach is that identical personalities crop up in the course of the volume under different spellings.[1] My hope is that, rather than leading

1 Multiple spellings are cross-referenced in the index.

to bewilderment, these 'inconsistencies' are something that can be enjoyed. This 'hands-off' policy does not extend to the critical apparatus. I have retained the numeration of footnotes wherever these appeared as a consecutive series in the original articles. Citation procedures have, however, been standardized throughout. So far as possible, I have given full bibliographical information for all printed authorities. References to materials in manuscript have been changed to provide current reference numbers.[2] In some special instances, my interventions have been more radical and I have supplemented or corrected the information in the footnotes. All such editorial interventions appear in square brackets and begin with the letters 'EN' ('editorial note').

The introduction provides some background on the authors' lives and work. While I hope these sketches are not sentimental, they are certainly appreciative. This is not the venue for hard-nosed historiography. If the collection stimulates critical commentary elsewhere – whether historical or historiographical – I imagine the authors will be well pleased.

2 References are to MSS in the National Archives of the United Kingdom, Kew, unless otherwise specified.

# Abbreviations and conventions[1]

*Admin. Ire.* — H.G. Richardson and G.O. Sayles, *The administration of Ireland, 1172–1377* (IMC, Dublin, 1963)

*Affairs Ire.* — *Documents on the affairs of Ireland before the king's council*, ed. G.O. Sayles (IMC, Dublin, 1979)

*AC* — *Annála Connacht: the annals of Connacht (A.D. 1224–1544)*, ed. A.M. Freeman (DIAS, Dublin, 1944)

*Account roll Holy Trinity* — *Account roll of the priory of the Holy Trinity, Dublin, 1337–1346; with the Middle English moral play 'The pride of life'*, ed. J. Mills (Dublin, 1891)

*AClon* — *The annals of Clonmacnoise, being the annals of Ireland from the earliest period to A.D. 1408 translated into English A.D. 1627 by Conell Mageoghagan*, ed. D. Murphy (Dublin, 1896)

*AClyn* — *The annals of Ireland by Friar John Clyn*, ed. R. Butler (IAS, Dublin, 1849)

*ADowling* — Thady Dowling, 'Annales Breves Hiberniae' in *The annals of Ireland by Friar John Clyn*, ed. R. Butler (IAS, Dublin, 1849)

*AFM* — *Annala rioghachta Eireann: annals of the kingdom of Ireland by the Four Masters, from the earliest period to the year 1616*, ed. J. O'Donovan, 7 vols (Dublin, 1851)

*AH* — *Analecta Hibernica, including the report of the Irish Manuscripts Commission* (IMC, 1930–)

*AHR* — *American Historical Review* (1895–)

*AI* — *The annals of Inisfallen (MS Rawlinson B. 503)*, ed. S. Mac Airt (DIAS, Dublin, 1951)

*ALC* — *The annals of Loch Cé: a chronicle of Irish affairs from A.D. 1014 to A.D. 1590*, ed. W.M. Hennessy, 2 vols (RS, London, 1871; repr. IMC, Dublin, 1939)

*AMacFirbis* — 'The annals of Ireland, from the year 1443 to 1468, translated from the Irish by Dudley Firbisse, or, as he is more usually called Duald Mac Firbis, for Sir James Ware, in the year 1666', ed. J. O'Donovan in *Miscellany of the Irish Archaeological Society* (IAS, Dublin, 1846), pp 198–302

*AMisc* — *Miscellaneous Irish annals, AD 1114–1437*, ed. S. Ó hInnse (DIAS, Dublin, 1947)

*AU* — *Annala Uladh ('Annals of Ulster'), otherwise Annala Senait ('Annals of Senat'): a chronicle of Irish Affairs A.D. 431 to A.D. 1540*, ed. W.M. Henessey and B. MacCarthy, 4 vols (Dublin, 1887–1901)

bar. — barony of

Betham, *Const. Eng. & early parl. Ire.* — W. Betham, *The origin and history of the constitution of England and early parliaments of Ireland* (Dublin, 1834)

Betham, *Dignities* — W. Betham, *Dignities feudal and parliamentary and the constitutional legislature of the United Kingdom* (Dublin, 1830)

*BIHR* — *Bulletin of the Institute of Historical Research* (1923–)

1 The following symbols are used in this list abbreviations to indicate the edition normally cited in this volume: † References are to 1st edition unless otherwise specified. * References are to 2nd edition unless otherwise specified.

| | |
|---|---|
| *BJRL* | *Bulletin of John Rylands Library* (1903–) |
| BL | British Library [formerly British Museum], London |
| —, Add. MS | Additional MS |
| —, Harl. MS | Harleian MS |
| —, Lansd. MS | Lansdowne MS |
| *Black bk Limerick* | *The black book of Limerick*, ed. J. MacCaffrey (Dublin, 1907) |
| Bodl. | Bodleian Library, Oxford |
| Brady, *Revisionism* | C. Brady (ed.), *Interpreting Irish history: the debate on historical revisionism, 1938–1994* (Dublin, 1994) |
| Brooks, *Knights' fees* | E. St John Brooks (ed.), *Knights' fees in counties Wexford, Carlow and Kilkenny, 13th–15th century* (IMC, Dublin, 1950) |
| Bryan, *Great earl* | Donough Bryan, *Gerald Fitzgerald, the great earl of Kildare (1456–1513)* (Dublin, 1933) |
| *Cal. Carew MSS* | *Calendar of the Carew manuscripts preserved in the archiepiscopal library at Lambeth, 1515–74*, 6 vols (London, 1867–73) |
| *CCR* | *Calendar of the close rolls* [...], *1272–*[*1509*], 47 vols (PRO, London, 1892–1963) |
| *CChR* | *Calendar of the charter rolls* [...], *1226–1516*, 6 vols (PRO, London, 1903–27) |
| *CDI* | *Calendar of documents relating to Ireland, 1171–1307*, ed. H.S. Sweetman and G.F. Handcock, 5 vols (PRO, London, 1875–86) |
| *CDS* | *Calendar of documents relating to Scotland* [...], ed. J. Bain, 4 vols (Edinburgh, 1881–8) |
| *CFR* | *Calendar of the fine rolls* [...], *1272–*[*1509*], 22 vols (PRO, London, 1911–62) |
| *Chart. privil. immun.* | *Chartae, privilegia et immunitates, being transcripts of charters and privileges to cities, towns, and other bodies corporate,* [...] *1171–1395* (pr. for RCI, Dublin, 1829–30; published, 1889) |
| *CJRI* | *Calendar of the justiciary rolls of Ireland*, ed. J. Mills et al., 3 vols (Dublin, 1905–56) |
| *CIPM* | *Calendar of inquisitions post mortem and other analogous documents*, 16 vols (PRO, London, 1904–74) |
| Clarke, *Med. representation* | M.V. Clarke, *Medieval representation and consent: a study of early parliaments in England and Ireland, with particular reference to the* Modus tenendi parliamentum (New York, 1936; repr. 1964) |
| Clarke, 'Windsor' | M.V. Clarke, 'William of Windsor in Ireland, 1369–76', *PRIA*, 41:C2 (1932–3), 55–130 |
| *COD* | *Calendar of Ormond deeds, 1172–1603*, ed. E. Curtis, 6 vols (IMC, Dublin, 1932–43) |
| *Colony & frontier* | *Colony and frontier in medieval Ireland: essays presented to J.F. Lydon*, ed. T.B. Barry, R. Frame and K. Simms (London and Rio Grande, 1995) |
| Conway, *Hen. VII & Ire.* | A. Conway, *Henry VII's relations with Scotland and Ireland, 1485–1498; with a chapter on the acts of the Poynings parliament, 1494–5 by Edmund Curtis* (Cambridge, 1932) |
| *CP* | G.E. Cokayne, *The complete peerage of England, Scotland, Ireland, Great Britain and the United Kingdom*, ed. V. Gibbs et al., 12 vols (London, 1910–59) |
| *CPL* | *Calendar of entries in the papal registers relating to Great Britain and Ireland: papal letters* (London, 1893–) |
| *CPR* | *Calendar of the patent rolls* [...], *1232–*[*1509*], 53 vols (PRO, London, 1891–1971) |
| *CPR Ire., Hen. VIII–Eliz.* | *Calendar of the patent and close rolls of chancery in Ireland Henry VIII to 18th Elizabeth*, ed. J. Morrin (Dublin, 1862) |

| | |
|---|---|
| *CR* | *Close rolls of the reign of Henry III*, 14 vols (London, 1902–38) |
| *Crede mihi* | *Crede mihi: the most ancient register book of the archbishops of Dublin before the reformation*, ed. J.T. Gilbert (IAS, Dublin, 1897) |
| *CStM* | *Chartulary of Saint Mary's Abbey, Dublin*, ed. J.T. Gilbert, 2 vols (RS, London, 1884–6) |
| *CT* | *Caithréim Thoirdhealbhaigh*, ed. and tr. S.H. O'Grady, 2 vols (ITS, Dublin, 1929) |
| Curtis, *Med. Ire.* | E. Curtis, *A history of mediaeval Ireland from 1110 to 1513* (1st ed., Dublin and Cork, 1923); 2nd ed. published as *A history of medieval Ireland from 1086 to 1513* (Dublin and Cork, 1938)* |
| Curtis, 'Letters from Ric. II' | E. Curtis (ed.), 'Unpublished letters from Richard II in Ireland, 1394–5', *PRIA*, 37:C14 (1927), 276–303 |
| Curtis, *Ric. II in Ire.* | E. Curtis, *Richard II in Ireland 1394–5 and the submissions of the Irish chiefs* (Oxford, 1927) |
| Davies, *Discovery* | J. Davies, *A discovery of the true causes why Ireland was never entirely subdued* [...] *until* [...] *his majesty's happy reign* (1st ed., London, 1612)† |
| Devon, *Issues* | F. Devon (ed.), *Issues of the exchequer: being a collection of payments made out of his majesty's revenue, from King Henry III to King Henry VI inclusive* (London, 1837) |
| DIAS | Dublin Institute for Advanced Studies |
| *Docs illus. hist. Scot.* | *Documents illustrative of the history of Scotland, 1286–1306*, ed. J. Stevenson, 2 vols (Edinburgh, 1870) |
| *Dowdall deeds* | *Dowdall deeds*, ed. C. McNeill and A.J. Otway-Ruthven (IMC, Dublin, 1960) |
| *DUC* | *The Dublin University Calendar* [annual] |
| Dugdale, *Monasticon* | W. Dugdale, *Monasticon Anglicanum*, ed. J. Caley et al., 6 vols in 8 (London, 1817–30) |
| Edw. | Edward |
| EETS | Early English Text Society |
| *EHR* | *The English Historical Review* (1886–) |
| Ellis, *Original letters* | H. Ellis (ed.), *Original letters illustrative of English history*, 2nd ser., 4 vols (London, 1827) |
| EN | editorial note |
| *Extents Ir. mon. possessions* | *Extents of Irish monastic possessions, 1540–1541* [...], ed. N.B. White (IMC, Dublin, 1943) |
| Fr. | French [Anglo-Norman] |
| Flanagan, *Ir. soc.* | M.T. Flanagan, *Irish society, Anglo-Norman settlers, Angevin kingship: interactions in Ireland in the late twelfth century* (Oxford, 1989) |
| *Foedera* | T. Rymer, *Foedera* [...], ed. A. Clarke and F. Holbrooke, 4 vols in 7 (RC, London, 1816–69) |
| Frame, *Eng. lordship* | R. Frame, *English lordship in Ireland, 1318–61* (Oxford, 1982) |
| Frame, *Ire. & Brit.* | R. Frame, *Ireland and Britain, 1170–1450* (London, 1998) |
| Gerrard, 'Notes' | C. McNeill (ed.), 'Lord Chancellor Gerrard's notes of his report on Ireland [...], 1577–8', *AH*, 2 (1931), 93–291 |
| Gilbert, *Facsimiles* | J.T. Gilbert (ed.), *Facsimiles of national manuscripts of Ireland* [...], 4 pts in 5 vols (Dublin, 1874–84) |
| Gilbert, *Hist. & mun. docs* | J.T. Gilbert (ed.), *Historic and municipal documents of Ireland, A.D. 1172–1320, from the archives of the city of Dublin* (RS, London, 1870) |
| Gilbert, *Viceroys* | J.T. Gilbert, *History of the viceroys of Ireland with notices of the castle of Dublin and its chief occupants in former times* (Dublin, 1865) |

| | |
|---|---|
| Giraldus, *Expug. Hib.* | Giraldus Cambrensis, *Expugnatio Hibernica: the conquest of Ireland*, ed. and tr. A.B. Scott and F.X. Martin (RIA, Dublin, 1978) |
| Giraldus, *Topog. Hib.* | Giraldus Cambrensis, *The topography of Ireland*, tr. J.J. O'Meara (Dundalk, 1951) |
| *Giraldi Cambrensis opera* | *Giraldi Cambrensis opera*, ed. J.S. Brewer, J.F. Dimock and G.F. Warner, 8 vols (RS, London, 1861–91) |
| Hand, *Eng. law* | G.J. Hand, *English law in Ireland, 1290–1324* (Cambridge, 1967) |
| *HBC* | *Handbook of British chronology* (RHS handbook) |
| Hen. | Henry |
| *Hermathena* | *Hermathena: A Series of Papers on Literature, Science and Philosophy by Members of Trinity College, Dublin* (1874–) |
| *HI* | *History Ireland* (1993–) |
| HMC | Historical Manuscripts Commission (Royal Commission on Historical Manuscripts) |
| Holmes, *Good parl.* | G.A. Holmes, *The Good parliament* (Oxford, 1975) |
| Hore, *Wexford* | P.H. Hore, *History of the town and county of Wexford*, 6 vols (London, 1900–11) |
| *HR* | *Historical Research* [formerly *BIHR*] (1987–) |
| IAS | Irish Archaeological Society |
| *IER* | *Irish Ecclesiastical Record* (1864–) |
| *IExP* | *Irish exchequer payments, 1270–1446*, ed. P. Connolly (IMC, Dublin, 1998) |
| *IHD* | *Irish historical documents, 1172–1922*, ed. E. Curtis and R.B. McDowell (London, 1943) |
| *IHS* | *Irish Historical Studies: The Joint Journal of the Irish Historical Society and the Ulster Society for Irish Historical Studies* (1938–) |
| IMC | *Coimisiún Lámhscríbhinní na hÉireann* (The Irish Manuscripts Commission) |
| Ir. | Irish |
| Ir. close roll | Close roll of the Irish chancery |
| *Ir. Geneal.* | *The Irish Genealogist: Official Organ of the Irish Genealogical Research Society* (1937–) |
| *Ir. mon. deeds, 1200–1600* | *Irish monastic and episcopal deeds, A.D. 1200–1600* [...], ed. N.B. White (IMC, Dublin, 1936) |
| *Ir. Jurist* | *The Irish Jurist*, new ser. (1966–) |
| Ir. memo. roll | Memoranda roll of the Irish exchequer |
| Ir. pat. roll | Patent roll of the Irish chancery |
| *Ir. parl.* | H.G. Richardson and G.O. Sayles, *The Irish parliament in the Middle Ages* (Philadelphia, 1952) |
| Ir. stat. roll | Statute roll of the Irish parliament |
| *Ir. Sword* | *The Irish Sword: The Journal of the Military History Society of Ireland* (1949–) |
| ITS | Irish Texts Society |
| *JCHAS* | *Journal of the Cork Historical and Archaeological Society* (1892–) |
| *JGAHS* | *Journal of the Galway Archaeological and Historical Society* (1900–) |
| *JKAHS* | *Journal of the Kerry Archaeological and Historical Society* (1968–) |
| *JLAHS* | *Journal of the County Louth Archaeological and Historical Society* (1904–) |
| *JRSAI* | *Journal of the Royal Society of Antiquaries of Ireland* |
| KR | King's remembrancer |
| L. | Latin |
| *Libelle Eng. polycye* | *The libelle of Englyshe polycye*, ed. G. Warner (Oxford, 1926) |

| | |
|---|---|
| *Lib. mun. pub. Hib.* | *Liber munerum publicorum Hiberniae*, ed. R. Lascelles, 2 vols (London, 1852) |
| *Liber primus Kilkenniensis* | *Liber primus Kilkenniensis*, ed. C. McNeill (IMC, Dublin, 1931) |
| *Lisronagh rental* | 'Rental of the manor of Lisronagh, 1333, and notes on "betagh" tenure in medieval Ireland', ed. E. Curtis, *PRIA*, 43:C3 (1935–7), 41–76. |
| *Llanthony cartularies* | *The Irish cartularies of Llanthony prima and secunda*, E. St John Brooks (IMC, Dublin, 1953) |
| Lydon, *Lordship* | J. Lydon, *The lordship of Ireland in the Middle Ages* (Dublin, 1972; 2nd ed., Dublin, 2003)† |
| Lydon, *Eng. & Ire.* | J. Lydon (ed.), *England and Ireland in the later Middle Ages: essays in honour of Jocelyn Otway-Ruthven* (Dublin, 1981) |
| Lydon, *Eng. in med. Ire.* | J. Lydon (ed.), *The English in medieval Ireland: proceedings of the first joint meeting of the Royal Irish Academy and the British Academy, Dublin, 1982* (RIA, Dublin, 1984) |
| Lydon, *Law & disorder* | J. Lydon (ed.), *Law and disorder in thirteenth-century Ireland: the Dublin parliament of 1297* (Dublin, 1997) |
| Lynch, *Legal institutions* | W. Lynch, *A view of the legal institutions, honorary hereditary offices, and feudal baronies established in Ireland in the reign of Henry II* (London, 1830) |
| Marlborough, *Chronicle* | 'Henry Marleburrough's chronicle of Ireland [1285–1421]', ed. J. Ware in *Ancient Irish histories*, 2 vols (Dublin, 1809), ii, 1–32 |
| memo. roll | memoranda roll |
| NAI | National Archives of Ireland [formerly PROI], Dublin |
| *NHI*, ii | *A new history of Ireland*, ii: *medieval Ireland, 1169–1534*, ed. A. Cosgrove (Oxford, 1987; repr. with bibliographical supp., 1993) |
| *NHI*, ix | *A new history of Ireland,* ix: *maps, genealogies, lists – a companion to Irish history, part II*, ed. T.W. Moody, F.X. Martin and F.J. Byrne (Oxford, 1984) |
| Nicholls, *Gaelic Ire.* | K.W. Nicholls, *Gaelic and Gaelicised Ireland in the Middle Ages* (Dublin, 1973; 2nd ed., Dublin, 2003)† |
| NLI | National Library of Ireland, Dublin |
| Orpen, *Normans* | G.H. Orpen, *Ireland under the Normans*, 4 vols (Oxford, 1911–20; new ed., 4 vols in 1, Dublin, 2005)† |
| Otway-Ruthven, *Med. Ire.* | A.J. Otway-Ruthven, *A history of medieval Ireland, with an introduction by Kathleen Hughes* (London, 1968; rev. ed., 1980)† |
| *ODNB* | *Oxford dictionary of national biography: from the earliest times to the year 2000*, ed. H.C.G. Matthew and B.H. Harrison, 61 vols (Oxford, 2004) |
| par. | parish of |
| *Parls & councils* | *Parliaments and councils of mediaeval Ireland*, ed. H.G. Richardson and G.O. Sayles, 1 vol (IMC, Dublin, 1947) |
| *Parl. writs* | *Parliamentary writs and writs of military summons*, ed. F. Palgrave, 2 vols in 4 (RC, London, 1827–34) |
| *Peritia* | *Peritia: Journal of the Medieval Academy of Ireland* (1982–) |
| *Pipe roll 14 John* | 'The Irish pipe roll of 14 John', ed. O. Davies and D.B. Quinn in *Ulster Journal of Archaeology*, 3rd ser., 4, supp. (Jul. 1941) |
| *PKCI* | *A roll of the proceedings of the king's council in Ireland* [...], *1392–93*, ed. J. Graves (RS, London, 1877) |
| pl. | plate(s) |
| Pollock and Maitland, *Hist. of Eng. law.* | F. Pollock and F.W. Maitland, *The history of English law before the time of Edward I*, 2 vols (Cambridge, 1895; 2nd ed., 1898)* |
| *P&P* | *Past and Present: A Journal of Scientific History* (1952–) |

| | |
|---|---|
| *PPC* | *Proceedings and ordinances of the privy council of England*, ed. N.H. Nicolas, 7 vols (London, 1834–7) |
| *PRIA* | *Proceedings of the Royal Irish Academy* (1836–) |
| PRO | Public Record Office, London [now included within TNA] |
| PROI | Public Record Office of Ireland, Dublin [now NAI] |
| PRONI | Public Record Office of Northern Ireland, Belfast |
| Quinn, 'Bills and statutes' | D.B. Quinn, 'The bills and statutes of the Irish parliaments of Henry VII and Henry VIII', *AH*, 10 (1941), 71–169 |
| *RCH* | *Rotulorum patentium et clausorum cancellariae Hiberniae calendarium, Hen. II–Hen. VII*, ed. E. Tresham (RCI, Dublin, 1828) |
| RC(I) | Record Commission (of Ireland) |
| *Red bk Kildare* | *The red book of the earls of Kildare*, ed. G. Mac Niocaill (IMC, Dublin, 1964) |
| *Red bk Ormond* | *The red book of Ormond* [...], ed. N.B. White (IMC, Dublin, 1932) |
| *Reg. Alen* | *A calendar of Archbishop Alen's register,* c.*1172–1534*, ed. C. McNeill (RSAI, Dublin, 1950) |
| *Reg. All Hallows* | *Registrum prioratus Omnium Sanctorum juxta Dublin*, ed. R. Butler (IAS, Dublin, 1845) |
| *Reg. Gormanston* | *Calendar of the Gormanston register*, ed. J. Mills and M.J. McEnery (RSAI, Dublin, 1916) |
| *Reg. Kilmainham* | *Registrum de Kilmainham: register of the chapter acts of the hospital of Saint John of Jerusalem in Ireland, 1326–1339* [...], ed. C. McNeill (IMC, Dublin, 1943) |
| *Reg. Mey* | *Registrum Iohannis Mey: The register of John Mey, archbishop of Armagh, 1443–1456*, ed. W.G.H. Quigley and E.F.D. Roberts (Belfast, 1972) |
| *Reg. St John the Baptist* | *Register of the hospital of S. John the Baptist without the Newgate, Dublin*, ed. E. St John Brooks (IMC, Dublin, 1936) |
| *Reg. St Thomas* | *Register of the abbey of St Thomas the Martyr, Dublin*, ed. J.T. Gilbert (RS, London, 1889) |
| *Reg. Swayne* | *The register of John Swayne, archbishop of Armagh and primate of Ireland, 1418–39*, ed. D.A. Chart (Belfast, 1935) |
| *Reg. Tristernagh* | *Register of the priory of the blessed Virgin Mary at Tristernagh: Registrum cartarum monasterii B.V. Mariae de Tristernagh*, ed. M.V. Clarke (IMC, Dublin, 1941) |
| *Rep. DKPRI* | *Reports of the deputy keeper of the public records in Ireland* (Dublin, 1869–) |
| *Rep. HMC* | *Reports of the Royal Commission on Historical Manuscripts* (London, 1870–) |
| *Rep. RCI 1811–15* | *Reports from the commissioners appointed by his majesty to execute the measures recommended in an address of the house of commons, respecting the public records of Ireland: with supplements and appendices*, i: *rep. 1–5* (RC, London, 1811–15) |
| RHS | Royal Historical Society, London |
| RIA | Royal Irish Academy, Dublin |
| Ric. | Richard |
| Richardson and Sayles, 'Ir. revenue' | H.G. Richardson and G.O. Sayles, 'Irish revenue, 1278–1384', *PRIA*, 62:C4 (1962), 87–100 |
| *Rot. chart.* | *Rotuli chartarum in turri Londinensi asservati, 1199–1216*, ed. T.D. Hardy (RC, London, 1837) |
| *Rot. litt. claus., 1204–24* | *Rotuli litterarum clausarum in turri Londinensi asservati, 1204–24*, ed. T.D. Hardy, 2 vols (RC, London, 1833–44) |

| | |
|---|---|
| *Rot. litt. pat.* | *Rotuli litterarum patentium in turri Londinensi asservati*, ed. T.D. Hardy (RC, London, 1835) |
| *Rot. parl.* | *Rotuli parliamentorum*, ed. J. Strachey et al., 6 vols (London, 1783) |
| *Rot. pipae Clonensis* | *Rotulus pipae Clonensis*, ed. R. Caulfield (Cork, 1859) |
| RS | *The chronicles and memorials of Great Britain and Ireland during the Middle Ages, published under the direction of the Master of the Rolls* ('Rolls Series'), 99 vols (London, 1858–96) |
| RSAI | Royal Society of Antiquaries of Ireland |
| *SHR* | *Scottish Historical Review* (1903–28; 1947–) |
| *Song of Dermot* | *The song of Dermot and the earl* [...], ed. G.H. Orpen (Oxford, 1892) |
| *SP Hen. VIII* | *State papers, Henry VIII*, 11 vols (London, 1830–52) |
| stat. | statute |
| *Stat. at large* | *Statutes at large passed in the parliaments held in Ireland, 1310–1800*, 20 vols (Dublin, 1786–1800) |
| *Stat. Edw. IV, pt 1* | *Statute rolls of the parliament of Ireland, first to the twelfth years of the reign of King Edward the fourth*, ed. H.F. Berry (Dublin, 1914) |
| *Stat. Edw. IV, pt 2* | *Statute rolls of the parliament of Ireland, twelfth and thirteenth to the twenty-first and twenty-second years of the reign of King Edward the fourth*, ed. J.F. Morrissey (Dublin, 1939) |
| *Stat. Hen. VI* | *Statute rolls of the parliament of Ireland, reign of King Henry the sixth*, ed. H.F. Berry (Dublin, 1910) |
| *Stat. John–Hen V* | *Statutes and ordinances and acts of the parliament of Ireland, King John to Henry V*, ed. H.F. Berry (Dublin, 1907) |
| *Stat. of the realm* | *Statutes of the realm*, ed. A. Luders et al., 11 vols in 12 (RC, London, 1810–28) |
| *Stat. Ric. III–Hen. VIII* | *Statute rolls of the Irish parliament, Richard III–Henry VIII*, ed. P. Connolly (Dublin, 2002) |
| Steele, *Secreta* | R. Steele (ed.), *Three prose versions of the* Secreta secretorum (EETS, London, 1898) |
| *Studies* | *Studies: An Irish Quarterly Review* (1912–) |
| TCD | Trinity College, Dublin |
| TNA | The National Archives of the United Kingdom [including former PRO], Kew |
| Tout, *Chapters* | T.F. Tout, *Chapters in the administrative history of mediaeval England*, 6 vols (Manchester, 1920–33) |
| *Trans. Hon. Soc. Cymmrod.* | *Transactions of the Honourable Society of Cymmrodorion* (1892–) |
| *TRHS* | *Transactions of the Royal Historical Society* (1872–) |
| *VCH* | *The Victoria county history of the counties of England* (London, 1900–) |
| *WHR* | *Welsh History Review; Cylchgrawn Hanes Cymru* (1960–) |
| Wood, 'Office of chief governor' | H. Wood, 'The office of chief governor of Ireland, 1172–1509', *PRIA*, 36:C12 (1923), 206–38 |

# Manuscripts and records cited

## IRELAND

*National Archives of Ireland, Dublin*

| | |
|---|---|
| 7/1 | Transcript of parliament roll, 2–3 Richard III |
| EX 2/1 | Calendar of memoranda rolls |
| Ferguson collection | Ferguson's collection of extracts and notes from Irish administrative documents, Edward I to Henry VII |
| RC 8 | Record Commission of Ireland, calendar of memoranda rolls |

*National Library of Ireland, Dublin*

| | |
|---|---|
| D | Ormond deeds |
| MS 1, 2 | *Collectanea de rebus Hibernicis*, compiled by Walter Harris (vols 1–2) |
| MS 760, 761 | Betham's extracts from the pipe rolls |

*Royal Irish Academy, Dublin*

| | |
|---|---|
| MS 12 D 10 | Ferguson's extracts from the pipe and memoranda rolls |

*Trinity College Library, Dublin*

| | |
|---|---|
| MS 557/7 | Reeves' transcript of the register of Primate John Mey (vol. 1 of 2) |
| MS 569 | Index to inquisitions and rolls of services in the remembrancer's office, court of the exchequer, Ireland, 20 Richard II to 19 Elizabeth I |
| MS 671 | Notes from records in Bermingham tower (17th century) |
| MS 2429 | Curtis papers: calendar in preparation of BL, Add. MS 6041 |
| MS 2452 | Curtis correspondence |
| MS 3486 | Curtis papers (miscellaneous papers presented by C.F. Synge [uncatalogued]) |
| MS 4717/147–50 | Otway-Ruthven papers |
| MS 7962 | Curtis correspondence (with Charles McNeill) |

*Public Library, Armagh*
MS G.II.13
MS H.II.16

UNITED KINGDOM

*British Library, London*
Additional MS 4790
Additional MS 6041
Additional MS 7966A
Additional MS 8835
Cotton Charter II
Cotton Titus B XI
Egerton MS 165
Harleian MS 3756
Lansdowne MS 482
Royal MS 18 C XIV

*Cambridge University Library*
Additional MS 3104

*Corpus Christi College Library, Cambridge*
MS 37

*The National Archives of the United Kingdom, Kew*

Chancery

| | |
|---|---|
| C 47 | Chancery miscellanea |
| C 135 | Inquisitions *post mortem*: series 1, Edward III |

Exchequer

| | |
|---|---|
| E 101 | King's remembrancer, accounts various |
| E 159 | King's remembrancer, memoranda rolls |
| E 364 | Foreign accounts rolls |
| E 372 | Pipe rolls |
| E 401 | Receipt rolls |

Special collections

| | |
|---|---|
| SC 1 | Ancient correspondence |
| SC 8 | Ancient petitions |

INTRODUCTION TO SECOND EDITION

# On bumper crops and stiffening winds: a bibliographical essay

*Peter Crooks*

The first edition of *Government, war and society*, published in 2008, opened with a dark Shakespearean declamation about the state of medieval Irish history. Ten years on, there is little room for complacency. As a discipline we have weathered the storm, but in comparative terms we remain under-resourced and under-staffed. Among students and the public at large, however, we are by no means under-valued. On the contrary, the appetite for medieval Irish history has never been stronger. The efflorescence of scholarship during the past decade provides its own justification for continued and expanded investment at the level of Ireland's political and cultural institutions, including our universities. The present conspectus of published works (2008–18) supplements the 'Guide to further reading' from the first edition. As there, the focus is the English Lordship of Ireland, 1171–1541, specifically works that address the themes into which I corralled the wide-ranging essays of Curtis, Otway-Ruthven and Lydon.

Two scholarly trends are worth emphasizing. First, the arrival of the monograph. Late-medieval Ireland is no sleepy corner in the wider discipline of Irish history. In many respects, given the small number of practitioners, we are at the vanguard. A greater number of single-author, book-length studies on later medieval Ireland appeared in the ten years since 2008 than were published in the previous half century. This is tremendously exciting. The new monographs are tightly themed, argumentative and analytical. My top ten (here ordered chronologically across the half millennium they cover) is: M.T. Flanagan, *The transformation of the Irish church in the twelfth century* (Woodbridge, 2013); D. Ó Corráin, *The Irish church, its reform and the English invasion* (Trinity Medieval Ireland Series 2, Dublin, 2017); C. Veach, *Lordship in four realms: the Lacy family, 1166–1241* (Manchester, 2014); D. Brown, *Hugh de Lacy, first earl of Ulster: rising and falling in Angevin Ireland* (Woodbridge, 2016); K. Busby, *French in medieval Ireland, Ireland in medieval French: the paradox of two worlds* (Turnhout, 2017); C. Ó Clabaigh, *The friars in Ireland, 1224–1540* (Dublin, 2012); A. Foley, *The royal manors of medieval Co. Dublin: crown and community* (Dublin, 2013); B. Smith, *Crisis and survival in late medieval Ireland: the English *of Louth and their neighbours, 1330–1450* (Oxford, 2013); S. Booker, *Cultural exchange and identity in late medieval Ireland: the English and Irish of the four obedient shires* (Cambridge, 2018); S.G. Ellis, *Defending English ground: war and peace in Meath and Northumberland, 1460–1542* (Oxford, 2015). K. Simms, *Gaelic Ulster in the Middle Ages: history, culture and society* (forthcoming, Trinity Medieval Ireland Series), will add immeasurably to our understanding of the interaction between the Gaelic lordships and the earldom of Ulster.

Beyond the richness of the evidence these books deploy and the significance of the individual arguments they advance, the mere fact of their existence *as* monographs marks a definitive structural shift in publication trends. Curtis, Otway-Ruthven and Lydon were celebrated above all for their single-volume histories of medieval Ireland. To be sure, these works incorporated coal-face research on the primary sources. In that sense, they were analytical and not merely synthetic. But they were unmistakably *general* histories, narrating and surveying with an eye, predominantly, on political and institutional developments. The shorter writings of those Lecky Professors were essays in the proper – dare I say, forgotten? – sense: well-crafted, sometimes stylish, experiments in argument and interpretation, probing new evidence, testing new approaches, floating novel ideas. The essays in turn nourished their work as generalists. For those pioneers, cultivating in virgin soil, the relative paucity of secondary literature was an advantage. Today scholars toil in an entirely different landscape, teaming with research articles. With the arrival of the monograph, the later medieval Lordship of Ireland enters a new stage in its historiographical life-cycle.

A second trend of note is the continued effort to set the Irish experience in broader contexts. Wider worlds and the world beyond are the loose connecting themes of several recent *Festschriften*: J. Bradley, A.J. Fletcher and A. Simms (eds), *Dublin in the medieval world: studies in honour of Howard B. Clarke* (Dublin, 2009); B. Smith (ed.), *Ireland and the English world in the late Middle Ages: essays in honour of Robin Frame* (Basingstoke, 2009); C. Maginn and G. Power (eds), *Frontiers, states and identity in early modern Ireland and beyond: essays in honour of Steven G. Ellis* (Dublin, 2016); T.R. Baker (ed.), *Law and society in medieval England and Ireland: essays in honour of Paul Brand* (London, 2017). For historiographical comment, see P. Crooks, 'Medieval Ireland and the wider world', *Studia Hibernica*, 35 (2009). B. Smith offers a fresh perspective on this historiographical development in his editor's introduction to *The Cambridge history of Ireland*, i: *600–1550* [hereafter, *CHI*, i] (Cambridge, 2018), where he considers 'how Ireland has featured in the historiography of medieval Europe' (p. 2). Once historiographically peripheralized, the geographical peripheries of Europe, including Ireland, are now increasingly integrated within the mainstream story of Europe's 'Europeanization' in the Middle Ages. So it is, too, with medieval English historiography. Three door-stoppers in the Yale English

Monarchs series (New Haven and London) have appeared since 2008, each of which weaves the Lordship of Ireland into royal biography: J.R.S. Phillips, *Edward II* (2010); W.M. Ormrod, *Edward III* (2012); C. Given-Wilson, *Henry IV* (2016). In structuring the contents of *CHI*, i, Smith commissioned scholars from outside the Irish academy to set the Irish experience in wider contexts (N. Vincent, 'Angevin Ireland'; M. Bennett, 'Late medieval Ireland and the wider world'). And indeed almost all of the contributors to *CHI* raise their eyes above the horizon.

This can only be welcomed. As Frame remarks: 'Viewing Ireland in broader contexts does not threaten the integrity of "Irish history". When well done, it enriches the analysis by opening up comparisons and contrasts, and by encouraging careful consideration of what is or is not distinctive about the Irish past' ('Contexts, divisions and unities: perspectives from the later Middle Ages' in *CHI*, i, 523). Quite so – when well done. Any consensus risks becoming cosy. And a mulch of context, like horticultural compost, can both stifle and enrich. 'We are all revisionists now' was the limp conclusion from the last significant historical controversy to engulf late-medieval Ireland.[1] The present generation of historians, comfortable in the knowledge that the old Hibernocentrism has been left far behind, can cry, 'We are all contextualists now!'

A problem, or so it seems to me, lies with the poverty of conceptualization. The publication bumper crops of the past decade have drawn upon an expanding pool of primary sources, available in a dizzying array of formats: digitized images of medieval manuscripts, digitized images of printed editions, keyed-in text from previously published editions, print versions of digital publications, born-digital critical editions, stand-alone print editions. The proliferation of evidence has, by any objective measurement, enhanced access to records from Ireland's Middle Ages. But a digital revolution will be led by conservative revolutionaries if we merely provide swiftly-delivered answers to age-old questions. We also require a new set of expectations about what can be done with the evidence. The sheer scale of the material – and a great deal more is coming – ought to provide its own liberation. It is frankly impossible to *do* empiricism any longer in the old sense of forensically analyzing *all* the available primary evidence. Or rather, it may be possible, but it involves grinding the evidence down into minute fragments that yield unambitious questions and disaggregated interpretations. Nor is the solution for the humanities to be found in that blunt analytical instrument of the social sciences – the 'research question' – which funding agencies force unfortunate students to wield even before their immersion in evidence has begun.

1 Roy Foster, '"We are all revisionists now"', *The Irish Review*, 1 (1986); and see below, Crooks, 'The Lecky Professors', p. 33 n. 62, for the related views of Edmund Curtis and James Lydon.

Instead, I would urge that we control the evidence by becoming active problematizers and conceptualizers. *Problématique* need not be problematical. Problematization is not about finding problems where there were none. It is rather about disrupting our collective assumptions and, in doing so, making plain the central interpretative issues – the problematics – at stake in our research. This opens the door to constructive disagreement and to historiographical progress. To achieve this, we must learn to be critically reflexive about the terms of analysis we employ and the baggage they carry. We need to be attentive to the vocabulary of our sources and, crucially, to how this language relates to our own analytical categories. And we must be sensitive to the complexity of ideas and the range of meanings that our sources reveal. Conceptualization, in this sense, serves as an interpretative bridge between 'theory' (so-called) and evidence. Even the mildest effort to conceptualize gives a comparison analytical bite. This is when the wider contexts in which we set the Irish evidence become meaningful and enriching. It is also when the particularity of the Irish experience will become significant to practitioners further afield.

Jeremy Catto once gently chided his avowedly empiricist colleagues in later medieval English history that their discipline would benefit from the 'the stiffening wind of controversial general ideas, developed at length'. Irish medievalists are not *avowed* in their empiricism. We may simply, as a group, have been too busy getting on with empirical research to stand back and take stock. What is needed next is not so much a new synthesis – or, at least, not quite yet – but a searching debate about what it all means and why it matters. Having weathered one kind of storm, we should welcome some 'sharp and invigorating controversy' by summoning up stiffening winds of another kind.[2]

## BIBLIOGRAPHIES AND GUIDES TO THE SOURCES

A decade ago, I was able to recommend the bibliography compiled by P.W.A. Asplin as a useful starting point for secondary reading (P.W.A. Asplin, *Medieval Ireland,* c.*1170–1485: a bibliography of secondary works* [1971]). Asplin is now a curiosity. The pace at which secondary publications appear shows no sign of slackening. 'Irish History Online', maintained through the Royal Irish Academy, is now the indispensable, up-to-the-minute bibliographical tool, and a growing monument to a democratic tradition of collective historical endeavour. Other jurisdictions have relocated their national bibliographies behind paywalls. 'Irish

2 J. Catto, review of *The church and learning in later medieval society: essays in honour of R.B. Dobson*, *Reviews in History* no. 349: https://www.history.ac.uk/reviews/review/349 (accessed 7 Oct. 2018).

History Online' remains free at the point of online access: see B. Cunningham, 'Multiple histories: historical bibliography in a divided Ireland' in K. Rexová, B. Cunningham, V. Horécákova and V. Hanelová (eds), *Historical bibliography as an essential source for historiography* (Newcastle upon Tyne, 2015). The Friends of Medieval Dublin study group has also produced a thematic bibliography ranging from pre-Viking Dublin to the Reformation city. Such was the importance of Dublin in the history of English Ireland that the bibliography is useful for the study of the Lordship of Ireland at large.[3]

For qualitative assessment of selected secondary works, R. Frame's masterly survey, first published in the Helicon History of Ireland series in 1981 and republished by Four Courts Press in an expanded second edition, includes a guide to further reading: Frame, *Colonial Ireland, 1169–1369*, 2nd ed. (2012). For reasons outlined by its editor, *CHI*, i, is weighted towards the later Middle Ages: 14 of its 19 chapters examine the political and cultural development of Ireland in the half millennium after 1000. These chapters, together with their accompanying bibliographies, make *CHI*, i, a resource of the first importance for research on government, war and society in the Lordship of Ireland. Gaelic Ireland in the later Middle Ages receives more intermittent attention. Simms appositely notes Eoin MacNeill's lament about the 'peculiar obsession of mind that makes Ireland appear a sort of hotel, in which the important people are always distinguished visitors, and the permanent residents, when they are not under orders, are occupied with quarrelling children and other household worries in the garret or the basement'. In *CHI*, i, the 'permanent residents' receive attention in chapters on religious life and material culture by C. Ó Clabaigh and R. Moss, while K. Simms offers two beautifully written overviews of 'The political recovery of Gaelic Ireland' and 'Gaelic culture and society'.[4]

For guidance on administrative sources, P. Connolly, *Medieval record sources* (Dublin, 2002), remains indispensable, but it largely predates the digital age. A new edition is required to take account of the latest online resources and platforms, including the publication of a number of seams of evidence from the National Archives UK that have a direct bearing on medieval Irish history because of the intimate relationship that existed between the colonial administration based (mostly) at Dublin and its 'mother' administration at Westminster. Two resources especially rich in Irish material are the edition and translation of the rolls of the English parliament,[5] and the Henry III Fine Rolls

3 Irish History Online: https://www.ria.ie/research-projects/irish-history-online; Friends of Medieval Dublin Bibliography: http://fmd.ie/bibliography-2/(both accessed 7 Oct. 2018). 4 MacNeill, *Phases*, p. 349, quoted in K. Simms, 'The political recovery of Gaelic Ireland', *CHI*, i, 272. 5 C. Given-Wilson (gen. ed.), *The parliament rolls of medieval England, 1272–1504*, 16 vols (Woodbridge, 2005).

project.[6] Otway-Ruthven would, I hope, have been glad to see the Irish Chancery Project, which she established in 1978, bear fruit in 2012 with the launch of CIRCLE: A Calendar of Irish Chancery Letters, 1244–1509 (https://chancery.tcd.ie/). On this historical enterprise, see P. Crooks, 'Reconstructing the past: the case of the medieval Irish chancery rolls' in N.M. Dawson and F. Larkin (eds), *Lawyers, the law and history: Irish Legal History Society discourses and other papers, 2005–2011* (Dublin, 2013); R. Frame, 'Rediscovering medieval Ireland: Irish chancery rolls and the historian', *PRIA*, 113:C (2013). The next several years will see the listing, digitization and online release of a host of materials of the kind Philomena Connolly classed as 'Substitute Sources' – that is, post-medieval transcripts and calendars that can be used to compensate for the destruction of the Public Record Office of Ireland in 1922. The Beyond 2022 website (www.beyond2022.ie) will be the portal for resources of this kind. An early example of a recently discovered source from the College of Arms is provided by Randolph Jones, 'Lost and found: a missing exchequer issue roll of 1414 rediscovered', *Archive Fever*, no. 5 (May 2018).[7]

For Irish narrative sources and other non-administrative texts, including the Latin annals produced within the English Lordship, D. Ó Corráin (ed.), *Clavis litterarum Hibernensium: medieval Irish books and texts,* c.*400*–c.*1600* (Turnhout, 2017), is a work of astonishing range and erudition. The section most relevant to the English Lordship is 'Later medieval (mainly Anglo-Irish) annals and chronicles', *Clavis*, ii, nos. 731–59 (pp 970–88). On the Gaelic annalistic compilations, see D.P. McCarthy, *The Irish annals: their genesis, evolution and history* (Dublin, 2008); and K. Simms, *Medieval Gaelic sources* (Dublin, 2009), ch. 1. Bernadette Williams continues her work on the Anglo-Irish annalistic tradition. Complementing her edition and translation of *The annals of Ireland by Friar John Clyn* (Dublin, 2007), Williams has edited *The 'Annals of Multyfarnham': Roscommon and Connacht provenance* (Dublin, 2012), and has nearly completed her edition of the Dominican annals of Pembridge. For the emerging tradition of chronicle writing in Dublin, see A.J. Fletcher, 'The annals and chronicles of medieval Dublin: an overview' and R. Gillespie, 'Dubliners view themselves: the Dublin City chronicles', both in Duffy (ed.), *Medieval Dublin VIII* (Dublin, 2008); and A.J. Fletcher, 'The earliest extant recension of the Dublin chronicle: an edition with commentary' in Bradley et al. (eds), *Dublin in the medieval world.*

One distinctive trend in source-based analysis has been the turn away from texts towards manuscripts. On the complex manuscript tradition of Gerald of

6 *Calendar of the Fine Rolls of Henry III*, ed. P. Dryburgh and B. Hartland (Woodbridge, 2007–). 7 Featured within the 'Archive Fever Articles' section of the project website for Beyond 2022: Ireland's Virtual Record Treasury (https://beyond2022.ie/archive-fever/).

Wales (Giraldus Cambrensis), see N. Ní Bheaglaoi, 'Exploring the relationship between text, image and artefact in manuscripts of Gerald of Wales' *Topography of Ireland*', *The Imbas Journal*, 2 (2012); Ní Bheaglaoi, 'Two topographies of Gerald of Wales? A study of the manuscript tradition', *Scriptorium*, 67:2 (2013). On the translation of Giraldian writings into the vernaculars of late fifteenth-century Ireland, see A. Byrne, 'Family, locality and nationality: vernacular adaptations of the *Expugnatio Hibernica* in late medieval Ireland', *Medium Aevum*, 82:1 (2013); and C. Whelan, 'New readers, old history: Gerald of Wales and the Anglo-Norman invasion of Ireland' in L. Cleaver and A. Worm (eds), *Writing history in the Anglo-Norman world: manuscripts, makers and readers, c.1066–1250* (York, 2018). Other than the *Expugnatio Hibernica*, the main source for the invasion is the versified narrative published by Orpen as *The Song of Dermot and the Earl*. This is subjected to close analysis in a book that has proved instantly indispensable: Busby, *French in medieval Ireland, Ireland in medieval French*. Busby also provides a path-breaking study of the representation of Ireland as wilderness and wonderland in romance. On the literature in English emanating from or consumed within the colony, see now the authoritative edition of the 'Kildare manuscript', famous for its Middle Hiberno-English verse: T. Turville-Petre (ed.), *Poems from BL MS Harley 913, 'the Kildare manuscript'* (Oxford, 2015). The poems themselves are interpreted in D.L. Moore, *Medieval Anglo-Irish troubles: a cultural study of B.L. MS Harley 913* (Turnhout, 2016); and more briefly, but in several respects more persuasively, in J. Scattergood, 'London, British Library, MS Harley 913 and colonial Ireland in the early fourteenth century' in B. Besamusca, M. Meyer, K. Pratt and A. Putter (eds), *The dynamics of the medieval manuscript: text collections from a European perspective* (Göttingen, 2017).

On the role of professional scribes and notaries in the creation of texts and manuscripts, see T. O'Byrne, 'Manuscript creation in Dublin: the scribe of Bodleian e. Museo MS 232 and Longleat MS 29' and H.E. Fox, 'Langlandian economics in James Yonge's *Gouernaunce*: translation and ethics in fifteenth-century Dublin', both in J.J. Thompson, K. Kerby-Fulton and S. Baechle (eds), *New directions in medieval manuscript studies and reading practices: essays in honor of Derek Pearsall* (Notre Dame, 2014); C. Whelan, 'James Yonge and the writing of history in late medieval Dublin' in S. Duffy (ed.), *Medieval Dublin XIII* (Dublin, 2013); T. O'Byrne, 'Notarial signs and scribal training in the fifteenth century: the case of James Yonge and Thomas Baghill', *Journal of the Early Book Society for the Study of Manuscripts and Printing History*, 15 (2012).

## PART I: GOVERNMENT

*Ireland and the English Crown*

The theme of Lydon's 1995 presidential address to the Irish Historical Society on 'Ireland and the English crown' is taken up in P. Crooks, 'The structure of politics in theory and practice, 1210–1541' in *CHI*, i, where I survey the framework of ideas that structured the political life of the English Lordship. The essay concerns structures of *governance*, rather than the institutions of government that so interested Otway-Ruthven. For the period before 1210, the contemporary understanding of the title *dominus Hibernie* ('lord of Ireland') is explored in S. Church, 'Political discourse at the court of Henry II and the making of the new kingdom of Ireland: the evidence of John's title *dominus Hibernie*', *History*, 102:353 (2017). For early Angevin engagement with imperial ideas, see J. Gillingham, 'Expectations of empire: some twelfth- and early thirteenth-century English views of what their kings could do' in S. Duffy and S. Foran (eds), *The English isles: cultural transmission and political conflict in Britain and Ireland, 1100–1500* (Dublin, 2013); and N. Vincent, 'Angevin Ireland' in *CHI*, i. The complex, sometimes cross-cutting, representations of Ireland in clerical and secular texts from the era of the invasion are analyzed in C. Veach, 'Henry II and the ideological foundations of Angevin rule in Ireland', *IHS*, 42:161 (2018). M. Staunton likewise moves beyond Giraldus Cambrensis to reveal that a range of attitudes to the conquest – from apologetics to ambivalence to outright distrust – were expressed by contemporary chroniclers: M. Staunton, *The historians of Angevin England* (Oxford, 2017). The interrelation of image and text in constructing history is a theme illuminated in L. Cleaver, *Illuminated history books in the Anglo-Norman world, 1066–1272* (Oxford, 2018), which includes Ireland in its analysis of maps and other imagery in the Giraldian manuscript tradition. On the role of Ireland in escalating the general crisis of John's reign, see C. Veach, 'King John and royal control in Ireland: why William de Briouze had to be destroyed', *EHR*, 129:540 (2014) – an interpretation that has already proved influential, e.g., D. Carpenter, *Magna Carta* (London, 2015).

For the theme of Ireland and the English crown at the cusp of the early modern era, perhaps the most important addition to the literature is C. Maginn and S.G. Ellis, *The Tudor discovery of Ireland* (Dublin, 2015), which includes new editions from the 'Hatfield compendium' of several of the best-known Tudor treatises on Ireland, including the widely-read *Breviat* of Patrick Finglas – for which see, additionally, the listing in D. Heffernan, 'Patrick Finglas's *A Breviat of the Conquest of Ireland and the Decay of the Same*, *c.*1535, and the Tudor conquest of Ireland', *The Sixteenth Century Journal* (2017). The *Tudor discovery of Ireland* is a work of the first importance, but the interpretative weight placed on the idea of a Tudor 'discovery' perhaps underestimates the extent to which earlier Plantagenet and Lancastrian kings engaged with Irish affairs. Evidence of such engagement, and of continuity in the elaboration of ideas, is provided in M.J. Bennett, 'The *Libelle of English Policy*: the matter of Ireland' in L. Clarke (ed.), *The Fifteenth Century XV* (Woodbridge, 2017), which speculates on the Irish connections and interests of the author of the *Libelle* (*c.*1436) and, still more importantly, demonstrates a connection between the *Libelle* and the mysterious fifteenth-century political tract on Ireland, the *Salus Populi*, which underlay the famous treatise 'State of Ireland and its Reformation' (1515). See also M. Bennett, 'The Plantagenet Empire as "enterprise zone": war and business networks, *c.*1400–50' in P. Crooks, D. Green and W.M. Ormrod (eds), *The Plantagenet Empire, 1259–1453* (Donington, 2016). On the change to political structures effected by the 1541 elevation of Henry VIII to be 'king of Ireland', see C. Maginn, 'The Gaelic peers, the Tudor sovereigns, and English multiple monarchy', *Journal of British Studies*, 50:3 (2011); and D. Heffernan, 'The reduction of Leinster and the origins of the Tudor conquest of Ireland, *c.*1534–1546', *IHS*, 40:157 (2016). Early modern historians have laboured under the assumption that the 1541 Act for the Kingly Title sought to remedy some perceived insufficiency in the title 'Lord of Ireland' – in other words that the king of England was somehow less than fully sovereign in Ireland before 1541. Perhaps this is how things came to be remembered, especially in the context of the break with Rome, but I am unconvinced that late-medieval conceptions of *dominium* in the temporal sphere were in any way trammelled: see Crooks, 'Structure of politics' in *CHI*, i. The astonishing quantity of later sixteenth-century 'reform' treatises, and the complexity of their interpretation, emerge from twin works by D. Heffernan: *Debating Tudor policy in sixteenth-century Ireland: 'reform' treatises and political discourse* (Manchester, 2018); and Heffernan's IMC edition of several of the most important, and neglected, examples from this rich vein of material: *'Reform' treatises on Tudor Ireland, 1537–1599* (2016).

The wider context that has attracted Irish historians of late has caused Ireland to be integrated into works that explore successive dynastic 'empires' – Norman, Angevin, Plantagenet. For the period before 1224, see D. Bates, *The Normans and empire: the Ford Lectures delivered in the University of Oxford during Hilary Term 2010* (Oxford, 2013); C. Veach, 'The Angevin Empire in the British Isles' in S. Church (ed.), *The Angevin Empire: new interpretations* (forthcoming). For the 'empire' of the Plantagenets in the later Middle Ages, see P. Crooks, 'State of the union: perspectives on English imperialism in the late Middle Ages', *P&P*, 212 (2011); and P. Crooks, D. Green and W.M. Ormrod, 'The Plantagenets and empire in the later Middle Ages' in Crooks et al. (eds), *Plantagenet Empire*. All these works place the English ruling dynasty at, or near, the centre of their analyses. In this respect, they represent a different enterprise from the 'new British history' of old. Recent works of 'British history' integrate

Ireland into the wider scene. For the period before 1300, the best works of this kind are J. Gillingham, *Conquests, catastrophe and recovery: Britain and Ireland, 1066–1485* (London, 2014); and D. Crouch, *Medieval Britain,* c.*1000–1500* (Cambridge, 2017). N. Vincent, *A brief history of Britain, 1066–1485* (London, 2011), is a sparkling read but, as its author would be first to confess, it surveys English, not British, history. For the later Middle Ages, M. Brown, *Disunited kingdoms: peoples and politics in the British Isles, 1280–1460* (London, 2013), is especially impressive for its attention to Gaelic Ireland as well as the travails of the English Lordship.[8] Building on this approach, but offering a more expansive comparison of aristocratic power in these two zones, see M. Brown, 'The Plantagenet Empire and the insular world: retrospect and prospect' in Crooks et al. (eds), *Plantagenet Empire*; and M. Brown, 'Realms, regions and lords: Ireland and Scotland in the later Middle Ages', *Anales de la Universidad de Alicante: Historia Medieval*, 19 (2015–16).

*Institutions of Central and Local Government*

Two rich collections of comparative essays on governmental life in late-medieval England are open to the criticism that they say next-to nothing about English Ireland. Their approaches are, nonetheless, highly suggestive for historians of the Lordship. See C. Fletcher, J.-P. Genêt and J. Watts (eds), *Government and political life in England and France,* c.*1300*–c.*1500* (Cambridge, 2015); and B. Thompson and J. Watts (eds), *Political society in later medieval England: a* Festschrift *for Christine Carpenter* (Woodbridge, 2015). By contrast, J.R.S. Phillips, 'Royal authority and its limits: the dominions of the English crown in the early fourteenth century' in J. Ní Ghrádaigh and E. O'Byrne, *The march in the islands of the medieval west* (Biggleswade, 2012), places royal authority in Ireland within the wider ambit of Plantagenet overlordship.

The governmental institutions of the medieval lordship are examined in B. Smith, 'Before reform and revival: English government in late medieval Ireland' in Maginn and Power (eds), *Frontiers, states and identities*. The power and limitations of English royal bureaucracy are set in comparative contexts in P. Crooks, 'Before Humpty Dumpty: the first English empire and the brittleness of bureaucracy, 1259–1453' in P. Crooks and T.H. Parsons (eds), *Empire and bureaucracy in world history: from Late Antiquity to the twentieth century* (Cambridge, 2016). For the literate mentality, see K. Kerby-Fulton, 'Competing archives, competing histories: French and its cultural locations in late-medieval England: 4. Competing archives, competing languages: office vernaculars, civil servant raconteurs, and the porous nature of French during Ireland's rise of English', *Speculum*, 90:3 (2015).

8 See also P. Crooks, 'Review: *Disunited kingdoms*', *The Mediaeval Journal*, 5:1 (2015).

On the chief governors of fourteenth-century Ireland, see P. Dryburgh, 'Roger Mortimer and the governance of Ireland, 1317–1320' and B. Hartland, 'Policies, priorities and principles: the king, the Anglo-Irish and English justiciars in the fourteenth century', both in Smith (ed.), *Ireland and the English world*. The policies of the Black Prince in Aquitaine and his brother Lionel of Antwerp in Ireland are compared in D. Green, 'Lordship and principality: colonial policy in Ireland and Aquitaine in the 1360s', *Journal of British Studies*, 47:1 (2008). Tensions between chief governors and the wider community of the Lordship are examined in P. Crooks, 'Representation and dissent: "parliamentarianism" and the structure of politics in colonial Ireland, *c.*1370–1420', *EHR*, 125:512 (2010). The sophistication of the Lordship's political culture is also apparent in E. Matthew, 'Henry V and the proposal for an Irish crusade' in Smith (ed.), *Ireland and the English world*, which examines the background to the Irish parliament's request (1421) to Henry V to lead a crusade to Ireland. The Irish parliament features strongly in Gwilym Dodd's recent study of the legislative power of the Westminster parliament in the context of the 'Plantagenet Empire': Dodd, 'Law, legislation, and consent in the Plantagenet Empire: Wales and Ireland, 1272–1461', *Journal of British Studies*, 56:2 (2017). See also, on the topic of 'counsel', the important collection of essays: J. Rose (ed.), *The politics of counsel in England and Scotland, 1286–1707* (PBA 204, Oxford, 2016).

Through the 'Medieval Petitions' project (University of York) more than 17,000 documents in The National Archives UK series of 'Ancient Petitions' have been catalogued and made accessible online.[9] Petitions relating to Ireland were previously surveyed in P. Connolly, 'Irish material in the class of ancient petitions (SC 8) in the Public Record Office, London', *AH*, 34 (1987), while the petitions from Edward I's reign received analysis in B. Hartland, 'Edward I and petitions relating to Ireland', *Thirteenth Century England*, 9 (Woodbridge, 2003). However, the Ancient Petitions project has greatly advanced our methodological sophistication in handling this class of records. The procedure of petitioning is illuminated in W.M. Ormrod, G. Dodd and A. Musson (eds), *Medieval petitions: grace and grievance* (York, 2009). The evidence of Irish petitions is usefully placed in wider contexts by G. Dodd in 'Petitions from the King's dominions: Wales, Ireland and Gascony, *c.*1290–1350' in Crooks et al. (eds), *Plantagenet Empire*.

Biographical miniatures put flesh and blood back on the boiled skeletons left by Otway-Ruthven's austere approach to institutional history. For notable essays that trace the transnational careers of members of the Lordship's legal establishment, see P. Brand, 'A versatile legal administrator and more: the career of John of Fressingfield in England, Ireland and beyond' in Smith (ed.), *Ireland*

9 Accessible through the website of the National Archives of the United Kingdom.

*and the English world*; R. Frame, 'Profits and perils of judicial office in Ireland: Sir Elias Ashbourne (d. 1356), chief justice and marcher lord' in Baker (ed.), *Law and society in medieval England*. Professor Lydon himself published a final essay: Lydon, 'The case against Alexander Bicknor, archbishop and peculator' in Smith (ed.), *Ireland and the English world*. The office of sheriff, which I noted in 2008 was yet to receive close attention, has been examined by several authors. Particularly useful as a basis for further investigation are lists of local officials. Indeed, all existing lists of local officials could profitably be brought together in a standard format and presented within a single publication. At present the sheriffs of Dublin may be found listed in A. Foley, 'The sheriff of Dublin in the fourteenth century' in S. Duffy (ed.), *Medieval Dublin XII* (Dublin, 2012); while the sheriffs of Louth (together with the keepers of the peace) are listed in Smith, *Crisis and survival*, table 1. The same authors offer perspectives on the role of violence in shaping the character of local office-holding in Ireland. B. Smith's case study of 'The murder of John Dowdall, sheriff of Louth, 1402' in S. Duffy (ed.), *Princes, prelates and poets in medieval Ireland: essays in honour of Katharine Simms* (Dublin, 2013), serves as the gruesome sequel to his early essay: Smith, 'The murder of Richard Gernon, sheriff of Louth, 1311', *JLAHS*, 21:4 (1988). The theme of violence and local authority is explored across a broader canvas in A. Foley, 'Violence and authority: the sheriff and seneschal in late medieval Ireland', *PRIA*, 117:C (2017). On this theme, see also A. Foley, 'Violent crime in medieval county Dublin: a symptom of degeneracy?' in S. Duffy (ed.), *Medieval Dublin X* (Dublin, 2010); A. Foley, 'High-status execution in fourteenth-century Ireland' in J. Bothwell and G. Dodd (eds), *Fourteenth Century England IX* (Woodbridge, 2016).

The depth of office-holding and its role in the structuring of 'gentry' society in fifteenth-century Meath and Dublin are the primary themes of the important study by B. Coleman, 'County office and county society in Dublin and Meath, *c*.1399–*c*.1513' (PhD, University of Dublin, 2016). The thesis includes tables of the local officials for these shires from the sheriffs and keepers of the peace down to the under-sheriff, sub-serjeant, assessors and collectors. Entirely different in approach is J. Sabapathy, *Officers and accountability in medieval England, 1170–1300* (Oxford, 2014), who uses Irish evidence to illustrate his thesis about the development by the late thirteenth century of sophisticated mechanisms for effectively holding local officers accountable. The case study of John de Valle (pp 29–37), bailiff in Ireland of Agnes de Valance (d. 1310), demonstrates just how much a properly developed problematic can wring from seemingly-unpromising record evidence concerning Ireland.

On the question of the application of English law to Ireland, one stimulus to further research was the joint 800th anniversaries of Magna Carta in England in (1215/2015) and of its transmission to Ireland (1216/2016). The Magna Carta Project, launched online for the 800th Anniversary in 2015, not only provides access to a new critical edition, translation and commentary on a document with a direct bearing on the development of the common law and institutional structure of the medieval Lordship of Ireland; the site has also published a number of special features highlighting the Irish evidence. Particularly notable are N. Vincent and M.T. Flanagan, 'Irish fines and obligations to King John' (Feb. 2015); and D.A. Carpenter, 'The copies of Magna Carta 1216 in the *Archives Nationales* in Paris and the 1216 Irish Magna Carta' (May 2015).[10] Ireland's early place in the global dissemination of Magna Carta is sketched in P. Crooks, 'Exporting Magna Carta: exclusionary liberties in Ireland and the world', *History Ireland*, 23:4 (2015). The passage of the 1216 Magna Carta to Ireland was marked by an Irish Legal Society Conference in November 2016, whose proceedings will be published as P. Crooks and T. Mohr (eds), *Law and the idea of liberty in Ireland: from Magna Carta to the present* (forthcoming).

While the octocentennial of Magna Carta was duly marked in Ireland, barely a whimper was raised about the 650th anniversary of the Statute of Kilkenny (1366) earlier the same year. Fifty years previously, in 1966, on the occasion of the sixth centenary, the late Geoffrey Hand (d. 2016) published in the *Irish Jurist* a paper on the 'forgotten Statutes of Kilkenny' (*Ir. Jurist*, n.s. 1:2 [1966]) – a reference to the provisions of the statute which were of procedural and legal interest. Fifty years on, it is the notorious statutes of Kilkenny that appear to have been forgotten – the provisions that sought to inhibit social contact and cultural exchange between the Irish and the English. The most recent study is D. Green, 'The statute of Kilkenny (1366): legislation and the state', *Journal of Historical Sociology*, 27:2 (2014), which places the acts passed at Kilkenny in the context of the burgeoning Englishness of England and the intrusiveness of the Plantagenet state in the decades after the Black Death. This is a valuable study. The risk is that over-contextualization explains away what is most significant about the legislation of 1366 in its Irish setting, namely the undeniable politics of intolerance. There is, moreover, a certain amount of basic textual work still needing to be done on the Statute of Kilkenny. One of the many tragedies associated with the curtailed career and early death of Dr Philomena Connolly in 2002 was that a lecture she prepared on the manuscripts of the Statute of Kilkenny was never published.[11] Among her acute observations is the fact that the manuscript evidence for the Statute of Kilkenny is problematic and our existing editions are deficient. There are no surviving fourteenth-century manuscripts, so we are reliant mostly on transcripts from the Carew manuscripts at Lambeth. A new edition of the Statute, currently in preparation by K. Busby, will be very welcome indeed. On the growing exclusiveness of English law, see R. Frame, 'Ireland after 1169: barriers to acculturation on an "English" edge' in

**10** The Magna Carta Project: http://magnacarta.cmp.uea.ac.uk/ **11** TCD, MS 1181/2/4/6 (Philomena Connolly Papers).

A. Jotischky and K.J. Stringer (eds), *Norman expansion: connections, continuities and contrasts* (Farnham, 2013). Fresh research by S.G. Hewer explores the extent to which persons of Irish descent were accessing the English royal courts in the late-thirteenth century: Hewer, 'Free Gaelic people in English Ireland, *c.*1250–*c.*1327', *History Ireland*, 23:6 (2015); Hewer, 'The myth of the "five bloods": from fiction to legal custom in the English royal courts in fourteenth-century Ireland', *PRIA*, 118:C (2018).

The centrality of the institution of 'lordship' to the governance of the polities of the medieval British Isles is a key theme of R.R. Davies, *Lords and lordship in the British Isles in the late Middle Ages*, ed. B. Smith (Oxford, 2009). The interplay of regional lordship and court politics in the making and breaking of a magnate's career is brought out in R. Frame's study of the Geraldine leader, Maurice fitz Thomas (d.1356): Frame, 'Rebellion and rehabilitation: the first earl of Desmond and the English scene' in P. Crooks and S. Duffy (eds), *The Geraldines and medieval Ireland: the making of a myth* (Trinity Medieval Ireland Series 1, Dublin, 2016). Perhaps the most important case study of transregional lordship from late-medieval Ireland is the Mortimer family, earls of March and Ulster, on whom see now B. Smith, 'Dressing the part in the Plantagenet empire: the death of Roger Mortimer, earl of March and Ulster, in 1398' in Crooks et al. (eds), *Plantagenet Empire*; and B. Smith, 'Transnational lordship and the Plantagenet Empire: the Mortimer lords of Wigmore, 1247–1425', *WHR*, 29:1 (2018).

## PART II: WAR

Research on the composition of English armies sent to Ireland in the later Middle Ages has been greatly facilitated by the Soldier in Late Medieval England project led by Adrian Bell and Anne Curry.[12] The database contains the names of soldiers who fought for the English crown between 1369 and 1453, mostly in France but also in Ireland and other theatres of warfare. The materials have yet to be properly exploited for Ireland, but their potential is apparent from A.R. Bell, A. Curry, A. King and D. Simpkin, *The soldier in later medieval England* (Oxford, 2013).

On the expansion of the English lordship by dint of aristocratic conquest and royal intervention, see C. Veach, 'Conquest and conquerors' in *CHI*, i; Veach, 'The Geraldines and the conquest of Ireland' in Crooks and Duffy (eds), *Geraldines*. The origins of many of these *conquistadores* are reconsidered in S. Duffy, 'The Welsh conquest of Ireland' in E. Purcell, P. MacCotter, J. Nyhan & J. Sheehan (eds), *Clerics, kings and Vikings: essays on medieval Ireland in honour of Donnchadh Ó Corráin* (Dublin, 2015); and Duffy, 'Gerald of Windsor and the

12 The Soldier in Late Medieval England https://www.medievalsoldier.org/

origins of the Geraldines' in Crooks and Duffy (eds), *Geraldines*. For the quickening pace of military resistance to English overlordship in the later thirteenth century, see S. Duffy, 'Irish and Welsh responses to the Plantagenet Empire in the reign of Edward I' in Crooks et al. (eds), *Plantagenet Empire*; and James Lydon, 'Dublin and the Scottish threat, 1315–18' in S. Duffy (ed.), *Medieval Dublin XV* (Dublin, 2016). The 700th Anniversary of the Bruce invasion of Ireland in 1315 was marked by the Trinity Medieval Ireland Symposium 2015, which took as its subject 'The Irish–Scottish World in the Middle Ages'. The proceedings, which will be published in the Trinity Medieval Ireland Series, placed the Bruce invasion in the context of the long history of interconnection between Ireland and Scotland in the Middle Ages. Several of the chapters have a direct bearing on issues explored by Lydon in the essays included within Part II of the present volume. Robert Bruce himself is the subject of a new biography: M. Penman, *Robert the Bruce: king of the Scots* (New Haven, 2014). More generally, Dauvit Broun (Glasgow) has transformed the evidence base for the study of the Scottish wars of independence by developing a remarkable suite of online prosopographical and textual resources, culminating in 'People of medieval Scotland, 1093–1371' (https:// www.poms.ac.uk/); and see now an associated project, 'The community of the realm in Scotland, 1249–1424', led by Alice Taylor (King's College London). On the place of Ireland within England's military enterprises in the era of the Hundred Years War, see D. Green, 'The Hundred Years War, colonial policy and the English lordships' in D.J. Kagay and L.J.A. Villalon (eds), *The Hundred Years War, part III: further considerations* (History of Warfare 85: Leiden, 2013); D. Green, 'Imperial policy and military practice in the Plantagenet dominions, *c.*1337–*c.*1453' in J. France (ed.), *Journal of Medieval Military History*, 10 (2016).

On King Richard II and Ireland, the book-length overview by D. McGettigan (*Richard II and the Irish kings* [Dublin, 2016]) is accessible and has the virtue of paying close attention to the capable Gaelic kings who confronted Richard II in Ireland: Art Mac Murchadha, king of Leinster, and Niall Mór and Niall Óg Ó Néill of Tír Eoghain. But perhaps the most substantial and enriching recent interpretation is S. Egan, 'Richard II and the wider Gaelic world: a reassessment', *Journal of British Studies*, 57:2 (2018). Egan identifies the deepening connections between the Gaelic Irish and Scottish nobilities as a factor that helps explain Richard II's decision to intervene in Ireland. The essay serves as an illustration of a wider programmatic point: that historians should pay more attention to the 'Gaelic west as a force within "British" politics'. An earlier study by Douglas Biggs, *Three armies in Britain: the Irish campaign of Richard II and the usurpation of Henry IV, 1397–1399* (Leiden, 2006), rather overplays the idea of Richard II as a successful strategist.[13] S. Duffy is closer to

13 See Crooks, 'Medieval Ireland and the wider world', *Studia Hibernica*, 35 (2009).

the mark in apostrophizing Richard II as 'that vainglorious nincompoop' (*History Ireland*, 26:5 [2018]). For Richard's itinerary in Ireland, especially during his Leinster campaign of 1394, see S. Kinirons, 'In the footsteps of a king: tracing the route taken by Richard II during his campaign against Art MacMurrough in 1394', *History Ireland*, 24:1 (2016); and Kinirons, 'Richard II and Art MacMurrough: conflict in Carlow in 1394', *Carloviana* (2017). On the self-conscious anachronisms adopted by Gaelic kings in the era of their military and cultural resurgence against English power, see K. Simms, 'The barefoot kings: literary image and reality in later medieval Ireland', *Proceedings of the Harvard Celtic Colloquium*, 30 (2010). Artistic patronage is examined in R. Moss, 'Substantiating sovereignties: regal insignias in Ireland, *c.*1370–1410' in Crooks et al. (eds), *Plantagenet Empire*, notably the shrine of the Book of Moling, with its inscription styling Art Mac Murchadha as king of Leinster. In addition to the famous submissions, the massive second tome of Thomas Walsingham's *Chronica Maiora* has appeared in the Oxford Medieval Texts series: *The St Albans Chronicle: the* Chronica Maiora *of Thomas Walsingham*, ii: *1394–1422*, ed. J. Taylor, W.R. Childs and L. Watkiss (Oxford, 2011). The account is important for its description, from a hostile English commentator, of Richard II's Irish expedition of 1394–5. On the aftermath of the Lancastrian usurpation in 1399 – until recently perhaps the most obscure decade in the history of the medieval Lordship – see K. Simms, 'The Ulster revolt of 1404: an anti-Lancastrian dimension?' in Smith (ed.), *Ireland and the English world*; Smith, 'The murder of John Dowdall' in Duffy (ed.), *Princes, prelates and poets*; and the online 'Soldier Profile' by Randolph Jones on the 'right valiant knight' Walter Bitterley, seneschal of Ulster, whose death is recorded in the Chronicle of Henry Marlborough for 1403.[14]

For factional conflicts in the Lancastrian and Yorkist eras, see P. Crooks, 'James the Usurper and the origins of the Talbot–Ormond feud' in S. Duffy (ed.), *Princes, prelates and poets*; P. Crooks, 'The ascent and descent of Desmond under Lancaster and York' in Crooks and Duffy (eds), *Geraldines*. Randolph Jones's indefatigable investigation of obscure manuscript sources has led to revelations about a series of key episodes, including the granting of civic swords to Dublin and Drogheda: 'Mayor John Drake and his victory near Bray in 1402', *Dublin Historical Record*, 60:1 (2007); 'The battle of Ballymacaw and its aftermath: fresh perspectives on Waterford's role during the Lancaster–York struggle in Ireland', *Decies*, 72 (2016); 'James Dokeray, mayor of Drogheda and constable of Carrickfergus Castle (*fl.*1444–82)', *The Ricardian*, 27 (2017); 'How Drogheda won its civic sword in the 1460s: the battle of Corbollis by Mapastown

14 R. Jones, 'Sir Walter Bitterley, seneschal of Ulster, k. 1403' in The Soldier in Late Medieval England soldier profiles: https://www.medievalsoldier.org/about/soldier-profiles/sir-walter-bitterley/.

Bridge and its aftermath', *Journal of the Old Drogheda Society*, 23 (2017); '"Hys worthy seruice done in that vpror": Sir John Whyte and the defence of Dublin during Silken Thomas' rebellion, 1534' in S. Duffy (ed.), *Medieval Dublin XI* (Dublin, 2011). On the remarkable events of Lambert Simnel's coronation as 'king of Ireland' in 1487 in Dublin, the most recent treatment is J. Ashdown-Hill, *The Dublin king: the true story of Lambert Simnel and the princes in the tower* (Stroud, 2015). I am suspicious of any book whose title claims to offer 'truth'. M. Bennett, *Lambert Simnel and the battle of Stoke* (Gloucester, 1987), remains indispensable, but new evidence concerning the correct date of the coronation is presented in R. Jones, 'New evidence for "Edward VI's" reign in Ireland', *The Ricardian Bulletin* (2014); R. Jones, 'Janico Markys, Dublin, and the coronation of "Edward VI" in 1487' in S. Duffy (ed.), *Medieval Dublin XIV* (Dublin, 2014).

## PART III: SOCIETY

*Settlement, Agriculture, Economy*

Towns in Ireland formed the subject of one of the last pieces of original historical research completed by Otway-Ruthven, which remained unpublished until its rediscovery in 2008. In the autumn of 1975, Otway-Ruthven delivered a lecture entitled 'The medieval Irish town' to the Historical Society in University College Cork, and she made further revisions to her text *c.*1977–8 with the intention of bringing it to publication. I identified the essay among Otway-Ruthven's unsorted papers in 2008 and prepared it for publication, together with a bibliographical note: Otway-Ruthven, 'The medieval Irish town' in S. Duffy (ed.), *Medieval Dublin X* (2010). Towns as an 'instrument of colonization' was one of Otway-Ruthven's most influential ideas from her seminal essay of 1965 on the 'Character of Norman settlement in Ireland'. The most detailed examination of the 'law of Breteuil' in Ireland is now C. Buldorini, 'Drogheda as a case study of Anglo-Norman town foundation in Ireland, 1194–1412' (PhD, University of Dublin, 2009), ch. 3, which bears out Otway-Ruthven's distinction between the larger, established urban settlements for which the 'law of Bristol' was sufficient, and inchoate 'towns' that required the incentive of the 'law of Breteuil' to become viable. Some three decades ago, Gearóid Mac Niocaill set out an agenda for 'getting behind the somewhat constitutionalist bias which studies of Irish urban history have laboured under, at the same time as they have profited by it' ('Socio-economic problems of the late medieval Irish town' in D. Harkness and M. O'Dowd (eds), *The town in Ireland: Historical Studies XIII* (Belfast, 1981), p. 21). See now K. Hoare, 'The evolution of urban oligarchies in Irish towns, 1350–1534' in L. Klusáková and L. Teulières (eds), *Frontiers and identities: cities in regions and nations* (Pisa, 2008).

Of works that follow Otway-Ruthven in using record sources 'retrogressively' to identify pre-and post-invasion territorial divisions, none is more important than P. MacCotter, *Medieval Ireland: territorial, political and economic divisions* (2008) – an astonishingly learned investigation of its subject. The study of Irish historic settlement remains vibrant. A representative sample of recent work drawing on the disciplines of history, geography and archaeology is collected in V. McAlister and T. Barry (eds), *Space and settlement in medieval Ireland* (Dublin, 2015). The most important, in-depth interdisciplinary study is undoubtedly M. Murphy and M. Potterton, *The Dublin region in the Middle Ages: settlement, land-use and economy* (Dublin, 2010). On agriculture more generally, see M. Stout and M. Murphy (eds), *Agriculture and settlement in Ireland* (Dublin, 2015), especially two essays on the later Middle Ages: G. Stout, 'The Cistercian grange: a medieval farming system' and M. Murphy, 'Manor centres, settlement and agricultural systems in medieval Ireland, 1250–1350'. See also G. Stout, 'St Mary's Abbey, Dublin, and its medieval farm suppliers' in S. Duffy (ed.), *Medieval Dublin XIV* (2015); M. Murphy, 'From swords to ploughshares: evidence for Templar agriculture in medieval Ireland' in C. Ó Clabaigh and M. Browne (eds), *Soldiers of Christ: the Knights Hospitaller and the Knights Templar in medieval Ireland* (Dublin, 2015); Á. Foley, 'Chieftains, betaghs and burghers: the Irish on the royal manors of medieval Dublin' in S. Duffy (ed.), *Medieval Dublin XI* (Dublin, 2011). For Ireland's economy, see B.M.S. Campbell, 'Benchmarking medieval economic development: England, Wales, Scotland, and Ireland, *c.*1290', *Economic History Review*, 61:4 (2008); K. Hoare, 'The economy of the English Pale, 1377–1534' in Maginn and Power (eds), *Frontiers, states and identity.*

*Frontiers, Language and Identity*

Among the papers of Professor Lydon, accessioned by the Library of Trinity College after his death in 2013, is an unpublished lecture which he delivered in 1993: 'The problem of the frontier: new thoughts'. Here Lydon lamented that his now-famous 'frontier' paper had made 'almost no impact on Irish historical studies' since it was first published in 1967. He specifically noted that the contributors to R. Bartlett and A. Mackay (eds), *Medieval frontier societies* (Oxford, 1989), made only glancing reference to his article. 'I have had to accept the fact', he wrote, 'that I might as well never have published it, at least not in an obscure American journal'!

The situation today could hardly be more different. Two collections I neglected to cite in 2008 – both of which pay more attention to definitional and conceptual problems than Bartlett and Mackay, *Medieval frontier societies* – are D. Power and N. Standen (eds), *Frontiers in question: Eurasian borderlands, 700–1700* (New York, 1999); D. Abulafia and N. Berend (eds), *Medieval frontiers:*

*concepts and practices* (Abingdon, 2002). For both European history at large, and Irish history specifically, the frontier has lost none of its fascination in the past ten years: see S.G. Ellis and R. Esser (eds), *Frontiers and the writing of history, 1500–1850* (Hannover-Laatzen, 2006); S.G. Ellis, R. Esser, J.-F. Berdah and M. Řezník (eds), *Frontiers, regions and identities in Europe* (Pisa, 2009). Lydon's former pupil, Brendan Smith – who has himself published extensively on the medieval Irish march, most recently in *Crisis and survival*, ch. 7 ('The Marches') – identified 'the frontier' as an important concept for integrating Ireland into the general European experience (*CHI*, i, pp 3–4). The concept appeals to historians and archaeologists in equal measure. Indeed, there is a serious risk that the term is so widespread that it has lost all analytical purchase. For works that emphasize frontiers of settlement, see L. Shine, 'Frontier settlement in Cavan in the high medieval period (1169–1550)' in J. Cherry and B. Scott (eds), *Cavan history and society: interdisciplinary essays on the history of an Irish county* (Dublin, 2014); and two chapters in Ní Ghrádaigh and O'Byrne (eds), *The march in the islands of the medieval west*, namely L.M. Doran, 'New Ross: from European archetype to town "situated in the Marches"'; M. Murphy, '"The key of the county": Saggart and the manorial economy of the Dublin march, *c.*1200–1540'. For frontiers as a discursive category within the imaginative geography of the Middle Ages, see S.V. Torres, 'Journeying to the world's end? Imagining the Anglo-Irish frontier in Ramon de Perellos's *Pilgrimage to St Patrick's Purgatory*' in K.D. Lilley (ed.), *Mapping medieval geographies: geographical encounters in the Latin West and beyond* (Cambridge, 2013).

The study of frontiers is bound up with acculturation and hybrid identities. Several contributors to Crooks and Duffy (eds), *Geraldines*, address the theme of mixed Geraldine identity. On social exchange and its limits, see Booker, 'The Geraldines and the Irish: intermarriage, ecclesiastical patronage and status'; and on the Geraldines' cultural engagement, see the complementary studies by K. Simms, 'The Geraldines and Gaelic culture', and A. Byrne, 'The Geraldines and the culture of the wider world'. The latter chapter, in turn, builds upon Byrne's detailed analysis of Kildare's private library: Byrne, 'The earls of Kildare and their books at the end of the Middle Ages', *The Library*, 14:2 (2013). The most substantive contribution to our understanding of acculturation in the heart of the English colony is now S. Booker, *Cultural exchange and identity in late medieval Ireland*. See also Booker, 'Irish clergy and the diocesan church in the "four obedient shires of Ireland", *c.*1400–*c.*1540', *IHS*, 39:154 (2014); Booker, 'Intermarriage in fifteenth-century Ireland: the English and Irish in the "four obedient shires"', *PRIA*, 113C (2013); Booker, 'An English city? Gaelicization and cultural exchange in late medieval Dublin' in S. Duffy (ed.), *Medieval Dublin X* (Dublin, 2010). Whereas Booker emphasizes the degree of

Irishness within 'the Pale', Frame has warned about exaggerating the decline of English institutions in southern Ireland: R. Frame, 'Lordship beyond the Pale: Munster in the later Middle Ages' in R. Stalley (ed.), *Medieval art and architecture in Limerick and south-west Ireland* (Leeds, 2011). For acculturation in the other direction, see F. Verstraten Veach, 'Anglicization in medieval Ireland: was there a Gaelic Irish "middle nation"?' in Duffy and Foran (eds), *The English Isles*. Perspectives from historians of art and architecture are offered in D. O'Donovan, 'Callan and Ormond: architecture of the "Middle Nation"?' in Ní Ghrádaigh and O'Byrne (eds), *The march in the islands of the medieval West*; K. Ralph, 'Medieval antiquarianism: the Butlers and artistic patronage in fifteenth-century Ireland', *Eolas* (2014). For the end of the Middle Ages, see G. Power, 'English-born men in Ireland, *c.*1450–1530' in Maginn and Power (eds), *Frontiers, states and identity*; G. Power, *A European frontier elite: the nobility of the English Pale in Tudor Ireland, 1496–1566* (Hannover, 2012); Ellis, *Defending English ground*.

* * *

## BREXIT VELOCITY

Where, then, will frontier research in late-medieval Irish history take us across the next decade? Precise predictions are bound to be proven wrong, but I cannot conclude without remarking on a historic coincidence. 2019 marks both the 850th anniversary of the Anglo-Norman Invasion (1169) and Year Zero of that other great caesura in Anglo-Irish relations – Britain's exit from the European Union, taking with it Northern Ireland. That Brexit will have its aftershocks is beyond doubt. Less certain is how they will be felt historiographically.

The 'new British history' as an experiment took its initial impetus from a now-famous lecture delivered by J.G.A. Pocock in 1973, the year the UK and Ireland together entered Europe against the backdrop of British decolonization in the 1960s. 'The British cultural star cluster is at present in a highly dispersed condition', Pocock then observed, 'various parts of it feeling the attraction of adjacent galaxies; the central giant has cooled, shrunk, and moved away, and the inhabitants of its crust seem more than ever disposed to deny that the rest of us ever existed.'[15] Pocock's plea for British history as a 'new subject' served as an argument against a curdled mode of historical investigation that was on the point of collapsing into nationalistic introspection. That phrase *more than ever disposed to deny that the rest of us ever existed* reads today like a haunting

15 J.G.A. Pocock, 'British history: a plea for a new subject', *Journal of Modern History*, 47:4 (1975), 621.

premonition. As Irish historians, what we must hope – what we must work to ensure – is that Britain's exit velocity will be harnessed to propel some serious collaborative scholarship on the deep history of cultural interconnection, in both insular and continental contexts.[16]

16 The era of the Anglo-Norman invasion of Ireland is, for instance, urgently in need of systematic textual and prosopographical study of the kind that Scottish historians can now take for granted. See N. Vincent, 'Angevin Ireland', *CHI*, i, 185: 'Rather than gather the charter evidence into coherent sequence, or complete the work of prosopography and manorial descent begun by Orpen and Eric St John Brooks, modern historians have preferred to scratch the itch that is Gerald [of Wales].'

INTRODUCTION

# The Lecky Professors

*Peter Crooks*

A future generation of historiographers will surely note with interest that, in the roaring years of the early twenty-first century, there seemed to be something rotten in the state of medieval Irish studies. In a letter to the *Irish Times* of May 2003, Donnchadh Ó Corráin, the eminent historian of early medieval Ireland, stepped into the role of Marcellus. With devastating eloquence, Ó Corráin exposed the 'alarming philistinism' and 'appalling neglect' that had been visited upon Irish medievalism in the recent past.[1] A key symptom of this was the failure of Ireland's premier universities to make appointments to professorships in Irish studies. Illustrious chairs lay vacant, some falling into complete dereliction. Other academics were soon found – whether in print or university corridors – condemning the conjunction of affluence and philistinism that characterized the Ireland of the third millennium. Before too long, the *Irish Times* had published its own jeremiad under the banner, 'What future for the medieval?'[2]

One professorship was particularly prominent in the flurry of correspondence generated by Ó Corráin's letter. This was the Lecky chair at Trinity College, Dublin, which had been established in 1913 from a substantial endowment made by the widow of the great historian of eighteenth-century Ireland, William Edward Hartpole Lecky.[3] A series of correspondents referred to Trinity's 'chair of medieval history', which by 2003 had been vacant for a decade.[4] These references to the 'Lecky' as a medieval chair are revealing in a way that was quite unintentional. Mrs Lecky's endowment was for a chair of modern history – albeit modern construed in the broadest sense of history since Constantine – which was to be called 'the Lecky chair of history'.[5] The 'Lecky'

1 *Irish Times*, 3 May 2003. 2 Ibid., 7 June 2003. See also ibid., 13 May 2003, 15 May 2003, 17 May 2003, 21 May 2003. 3 See McDowell and Webb, *TCD*, pp 412–13. The first Lecky professor was elected on 25 June 1914 (*DUC 1914–5, pt 1*, p. 41). 4 *Irish Times*, 3 May 2003, 7 June 2003, 30 Oct. 2003, 5 Nov. 2003. The chair has since been filled: on 1 October 2006, I.S. Robinson – a specialist on the history of the reform papacy and Germany in the high Middle Ages – became the sixth Lecky professor, arising from the award of a personal chair in history (*DUC 2007–8, pt 1*, p. B18). 5 The will of Mrs Catharina E.B. Lecky stipulates that the grant shall be 'applied to the endowment of a chair of Modern History to be called the Lecky chair of History'. The will is dated 6 Apr. 1911 and probate was granted on 22 June 1912. I am grateful to Dr Seán Duffy for supplying me with a copy of this document.

is described in the Dublin University calendar as a chair of 'modern history' from 1914 until 1964. In that year, T.W. Moody – Erasmus Smith's professor of modern history and chairman of the history school committee at Trinity – was on sabbatical leave. In his absence, the then incumbent of the Lecky chair, A.J. Otway-Ruthven, spearheaded the creation of an autonomous department of medieval history.[6] In the following academic year, the university calendar reverts to the language of Mrs Lecky's original endowment and describes Otway-Ruthven simply as the Lecky professor of history.[7] In the course of Otway-Ruthven's palace revolution, the redundant qualifier 'modern' had been silently dropped.

It is precisely that all this is of such marginal interest that is – in the context of the present volume – significant; for it brings home the extent to which Trinity's Lecky chair has become indelibly, indeed emotionally, identified with medievalism. Just as in the Middle Ages, innovations, unless soon suppressed, become custom immemorial.[8] That this should be so is undoubtedly a testament to the scholarly contribution not just of Otway-Ruthven, but also two other occupants of the chair she held: her predecessor but one, Edmund Curtis (d.1943); and her successor, James Lydon.[9] All three were specialists in the field of later medieval Irish history. Between them, they held the Lecky chair across five decades, between 1939 and 1993. The social backgrounds, historical concerns and scholarly styles of Curtis, Otway-Ruthven and Lydon are, of course, highly individual; but there is a unity to their work on medieval Ireland. The present collection of twenty-one of their essays includes several of the most influential studies ever undertaken on the social, institutional and political character of the English colony in Ireland between the invasion of the late twelfth century and the act for kingly title in 1541. To read them is to trace a distinctive tradition in Irish historiography from inception to maturity.

6 Salters Sterling, 'Professor Otway-Ruthven, FTCD: Lecky professor of history, 1951–81 [*sic*]' in Susan M. Parkes (ed.), *A danger to the men? A history of women in Trinity College, Dublin, 1904–2004* (Dublin, 2004), p. 266. 7 *DUC 1964–5*, p. 32; *DUC 1965–6*, p. 33; cf. the terms of Mrs Lecky's will, cited above, n. 5. 'Lecky professor of history' was also the title held by James Lydon (*DUC 1980–1*, p. 42). 8 M.T. Clanchy, 'Remembering the past and the good old law', *History*, 45 (1970), 165–76, esp. p. 172. 9 The dates of their tenures of the Lecky chair are as follows: Edmund Curtis (1939–43); A.J. Otway-Ruthven (1951–80); James Lydon (1980–93). For convenience, when I refer to the 'Lecky professors' collectively, it will be in reference to these three scholars. Two holders of the Lecky chair were modernists in the 'narrow' sense. The first Lecky professor, Walter Alison Phillips, held the chair from 1914 to 1939 (T.G. Otte, 'Phillips, Walter Alison (1864–1950), historian' in *ODNB*, xliv, 154–5). Phillips was succeeded by Edmund Curtis, who died in 1943. Following his death, Constantia Maxwell – famous as the author of *Dublin under the Georges, 1714–1830* (London, 1936) – was elected as Lecky professor on 6 June 1945 and held the chair until 1951 (*DUC 1945–6*, p. 29; *DUC 1951–2*, p. 27). She was first appointed to a lectureship at Trinity in 1911 and, in 1939, six years before ascending to 'the Lecky', she was granted a personal chair (McDowell and Webb, *TCD*, p. 352).

## 'E.C.'

At the risk of being overly schematic, the work of the Lecky professors can be viewed together as a project in three phases. As such, one of its notable features is how little it owed to the 'revolution' in Irish historiography that took place in the wake of the foundation of *Irish Historical Studies* in 1938.[10] Long before the 'impatient young men' of the 1930s began setting agendas,[11] Edmund Curtis had pioneered what he understood to be a 'scientific' approach to the history of medieval Ireland.[12] Indeed, it is a mark of Curtis' success that, at the time of the foundation of *IHS*, it was the historiography of modern Ireland that was most in need of professionalization.[13] The appreciations that followed Curtis' death in 1943 make it abundantly clear that his work won him fame and affection from a remarkably broad constituency of readers.[14]

Little of that affection remains. Above all, the nationalist sentiment with which his work is infused has tarnished his reputation. There have been some valiant attempts at rehabilitation;[15] and still more might be made of the point that Curtis used the language of 'home rule' in a conscious effort to make the late medieval period – which was still virgin historiographical soil in 1923 – accessible to a general audience. Nonetheless, sound bites such as the 'Anglo-Irish patriot party', 'aristocratic home rule' and the 'all-but kingship' of Kildare have proved all too easy to pillory.[16] As Robin Frame has recently observed:

10 For which, see Ciaran Brady, '"Constructive and instrumental": the dilemma of Ireland's first "new historians"' in idem (ed.), *Revisionism*, pp 3–31; Evi Gkotzaridis, *Trials of Irish history: genesis and evolution of a reappraisal, 1938–2000* (Abingdon, 2006). 11 The phrase is that of Brendan Bradshaw, 'Nationalism and historical scholarship in modern Ireland' in Brady, *Revisionism*, p. 215; 1st pr. *IHS*, 26:104 (1989), 1–18. 12 See Curtis, 'Irish history and its popular versions', *Irish Rosary*, 29:5 (1925), 321–9; repr. below, 'Prologue'. Otway-Ruthven also received her training in the days before *IHS*, while the professional rivalry she enjoyed with T.W. Moody is well known. Lydon's remarks about Moody's alleged obsession with footnotes are entertaining: see his interview with Seán Duffy, '"A real Irish historian"', *HI*, 3:1 (1995), 11–14, at p. 13. 13 J.J. Lee, *Ireland, 1912–1985* (Cambridge, 1989), p. 588. It is interesting to note the comment of McDowell and Webb that 'Curtis ... brought to the school [of history] – albeit at the cost of a certain dryness – a severe professionalism which it had hitherto lacked' (McDowell and Webb, *TCD*, p. 412). 14 See, e.g., 'Edmund Curtis: an appreciation', *Irish Times*, 14 Apr. 1943; James Hogan, 'Edmund Curtis', *AH*, 16 (1946), 387–9. 15 James Lydon critiques the critics in an important reassessment: 'Historical revisit: Edmund Curtis, *A history of medieval Ireland* (1923, 1938)', *IHS*, 31:124 (1999), esp 536–9. See also J.A. Watt, 'Approaches to the history of fourteenth-century Ireland' in *NHI*, ii, 303–6; and Bradshaw, 'Nationalism and historical scholarship in modern Ireland' in Brady, *Revisionism*, p. 216. 16 See, e.g., Curtis, *Med. Ire.* (2nd ed.), pp 215–7, 288–9, 295–6, 309, 322; idem, *A history of Ireland from the earliest times to 1922: with a new introduction by Seán Duffy* (new ed., London, 2002), pp 95–6, 114, 122–3, 127–37; idem, 'Richard, duke of York, as viceroy of Ireland 1447–1460' (repr. below ch. 14); idem in Conway, *Hen. VII & Ire.*, pp 132–3. For criticism, see G.O. Sayles, 'The rebellious first earl of Desmond' in J.A. Watt, J.B.

'Curtis might be said to have become a victim of his gift for encapsulating in vivid phrases views with contemporary resonance: these have proved more memorable than the qualifications that often accompany them.'[17]

Curtis was born in Bury, Lancashire, in 1881, to parents of 'good Donegal planter stock'.[18] The tale of how the talented boy-poet was saved from labouring in a London rubber factory and given an education is familiar and does not need to be rehearsed here.[19] In 1900, Curtis went up to Oxford with a scholarship, where he was drilled in Stubbsian constitutional history, a subject he later taught at Trinity.[20] He graduated from Keble in 1904 with a first class degree. After a year engaged in journalism, Curtis was appointed to a lectureship at the University of Sheffield.[21] There he pursued a topic that first attracted his notice at Oxford: the Norman colonization of southern Italy and Sicily. In *Roger of Sicily* (1912),[22] many of the skills that mark out Curtis as an engaging historian are already on display, primarily his uncanny ability to find a neglected topic and popularize it – a recurring feature of his work on Irish history.

Even before completing *Roger of Sicily*, Curtis' interests were turning westward to the land of his forebears. After graduating, he paid several visits to relatives in Ireland and took courses in old Irish. In 1908, at the time of the foundation of the National University, Curtis applied for a post at University College, Dublin, but his application was unsuccessful.[23] His appointment as Erasmus Smith's professor of history in Trinity was something of a spiritual homecoming and a watershed in his professional life. He dedicated his next

Morrall and F.X. Martin (eds), *Medieval studies presented to Aubrey Gwynn, S.J.* (Dublin, 1961), pp 225–7; Steven Ellis, 'Historiographical debate. Representations of the past in Ireland: whose past and whose present?', *IHS*, 27:108 (1991), 301. **17** See Robin Frame, 'Historians, aristocrats and Plantagenet Ireland, 1200–1360' in C. Given-Wilson, A. Kettle and L. Scales (eds), *War, government and aristocracy in the British Isles, c.1150–1500* (Woodbridge, 2008), p. 132. I am grateful to Prof. Frame for providing me with a copy of his article before publication. **18** T.W. Moody, 'Edmund Curtis (1881–1943)', *Hermathena*, 63 (1944), 69–78, at p. 69. **19** Moody, 'Edmund Curtis', pp 69–72; Robert Walsh (ed.), *The Oxford companion to Irish literature* (Oxford, 1996), pp 129–30; Lydon, 'Historical revisit: Edmund Curtis, *A history of medieval Ireland*', pp 539–40; ; Seán Duffy, 'Introduction' in Curtis, *A history of Ireland from the earliest times to 1922* (new ed.), pp ix–x; T.W. Moody, rev. R.F. Frame, 'Curtis, Edmund (1881–1943), historian' in *ODNB*, xiv, 765–6. Curtis also merits a brief entry by Robin Frame in S.J. Connolly (ed.), *The Oxford companion to Irish history* (2nd ed., Oxford, 2002), p. 139. **20** James Campbell, 'Stubbs, Maitland, and constitutional history' in Benedikt Stuchtey and Peter Wende (eds), *British and German historiography, 1750–1950: traditions, perceptions, and transfers* (Oxford, 2000), pp 99–122. **21** A relic of Curtis' time at Sheffield is a pamphlet prepared for the Historical Association, which is initialed 'E.C.': *Short bibliography of the history of Sheffield*, The Historical Association, leaflet no. 25 (June, 1911). **22** Edmund Curtis, *Roger of Sicily and the Normans in lower Italy, 1016–1154* (London, 1912). **23** Moody, 'Edmund Curtis', p. 74, n. 10; Donal McCartney, *UCD – a national idea: the history of University College, Dublin* (Dublin, 1999), p. 29. In 1912, Curtis applied for lectureships in the Universities of London and Newcastle, again without success (TCD, MS 3486 [uncatalogued: 'Memoirs of former years derived from diaries']).

1. Edmund Curtis, TCD, MS 3184a/1, no. 4, courtesy of the Board of Trinity College, Dublin.

three decades to the study of medieval Irish history.[24] In 1914, this was still an uncharted subject. The neglect was remedied to some extent when the final two volumes of *Ireland under the Normans* by Goddard Henry Orpen (d.1932) were published in 1920, a work that remains indispensable for the period before 1333.[25] For the period thereafter, Curtis claimed 'the merits, as I admit the shortcomings, of a pioneer in a stretch of our history where sources are little known, legends many, and guides almost non-existent'.[26] Unlike many pioneers, who jealously protect their discoveries, Curtis was not reluctant to go into print. Indeed, he published prolifically both scholarly and popular articles.[27] No modern research assessment exercise could hope to frighten so much out of a single scholar, and given that Curtis operated in an academic environment in which many published little or nothing at all, his output is especially remarkable. Mary Hayden (d.1942), who was appointed to the lectureship at UCD in 1909 for which Curtis was an unsuccessful candidate, published just eight articles between 1913 and 1943 (the last posthumously); in the same period, Curtis published thirty-six.[28]

This effusion of work began some years before Curtis landed in Trinity. In 1907, while still at Sheffield, he began a correspondence with Orpen. In the decades that followed, the two men – despite their different politics – developed a deep mutual understanding and respect.[29] It was Reginald Lane Poole (d.1939), the Oxford don and founding editor of the *English Historical Review*,[30]

24 His fragmentary memoirs record that he began his residency in Trinity College on 9 September 1914: TCD, MS 3486. 25 Orpen, *Normans*. On Orpen's contribution to medieval Irish history, see Seán Duffy, 'Historical revisit: Goddard Henry Orpen, *Ireland under the Normans, 1169–1333* (1911–20)', *IHS*, 32:126 (2000), 246–59; repr. Orpen, *Normans*, new ed., 4 vols in 1 (Dublin, 2005), pp xi–xxiii. 26 Curtis, *Med. Ire.* (1st ed.), p. v. He quotes these words again in Curtis, *Med. Ire.* (2nd ed.), p. vi. 27 See T.W. Moody, 'The writings of Edmund Curtis', *IHS*, 3:12 (1943), 393–400. 28 David Dickson, 'Historical journals in Ireland: the last hundred years' in Barbara Hayley and Enda McKay (eds), *Three hundred years of Irish periodicals* (Mullingar, 1987), pp 89–92; Lee, *Ireland, 1912–1985*, p. 588. A brief necrological note on Hayden in *IHS* politely states that, after her appointment by UCD, 'she [Hayden] concentrated mainly on the teaching of her subect during the following thirty years' (*IHS*, 3:12 (1943), 401–2). A more positive assessment of Hayden's historiographical contribution – which takes into account the popular success of her *Short history of the Irish people from the earliest times to 1920* (Dublin, 1921) – is provided in Mary O'Dowd, 'From Morgan to MacCurtain: women historians in Ireland from the 1790s to the 1990s' in Maryann Gialanella Valiulis and Mary O'Dowd (eds), *Women and Irish history: essays in honour of Margaret MacCurtain* (Dublin, 1997), pp 51–2. On other aspects of Hayden's career, particularly her role as a founder-member of the Irish Association of Women Graduates and Candidate Graduates, see McCartney, *UCD – a national idea*, esp. pp 79–80. 29 Their growing friendship can be traced in Orpen's letters to Curtis, which are preserved in TCD, MS 2452. The earliest, from 1907 (ibid., no. 1), begins 'Dear Mr Curtis'; by 1921, this had become 'My dear Curtis' (ibid., no. 4). 30 On Poole's career and his involvement with the *English Historical Review*, see G.N. Clark, 'Reginald Lane Poole', *EHR*, 55:217 (1940), 1–7; Doris S. Goldstein, 'The origins and early years of the *English Historical*

who first suggested that Curtis should write to Orpen for advice about a piece on the Hiberno-Norse community in post-invasion Ireland that he was hoping to have accepted by the *Review*.[31] A number of daring articles by Orpen exploring the history of motes in Ireland had recently appeared in the pages of *EHR*,[32] and Poole gave Curtis the impression that Orpen was now at work on the Ostmen. Orpen assured the young lecturer from Sheffield that Poole was mistaken,[33] and, after answering some trivial queries about the Ostmen, he closed the letter with a generous offer of assistance: 'If I can be of any further use to you please let me know. You have an interesting field of investigation almost to yourself (since Haliday)[34] so far as I know.'

Curtis was to take up that offer many times. Indeed, it was rare for him to commit any major piece of work to print without consulting Orpen, whose responses were invariably courteous and exhaustively detailed.[35] In 1923, Orpen provided support of a different kind when he wrote a reference for Curtis testifying to the value of the latter's *History of Mediaeval Ireland*, which was nearing completion.[36] In his testimonial, Orpen felt bound to admit of their considerable differences of interpretation.[37] This caused the well-meaning senior historian some little anxiety: 'I trust you will not mind my saving clause that, "the facts sometimes make a different appeal to me" … I think I have expressed the difference in our outlook as gently as possible.'[38] A few days later,

*Review*', *EHR*, 101:398. (1986), 6–19. 31 It appeared as Curtis, 'The English and Ostmen in Ireland', *EHR*, 23:90 (1908), 209–19; repr. below, ch. 17. 32 Goddard H. Orpen, 'Mote and bretesche building in Ireland', *EHR*, 21:83 (1906), 417–44; idem, 'Motes and Norman castles in Ireland', *EHR*, 22:86 (1907), 228–54; ibid., 22:87 (1907), 440–67. In his letter to Curtis, Orpen mentions these articles and remarks that their conclusions are 'deemed in Ireland at least, rank heresy!' He further comments wryly that 'there are signs however that the … old gods are about to be renounced': TCD, MS 2452, no. 1 (Goddard H. Orpen [G.H.O.], Monksgrange, Enniscorthy, to Edmund Curtis [E.C.], 12 Aug. 1907). 33 Poole may have been thinking of Orpen's masterpiece, the first two volumes of which were then in gestation (Orpen, *Normans*). 34 A reference to Charles Haliday (d.1866), author of *The Scandinavian kingdom of Dublin* (Dublin, 1881; 2nd ed., 1884). 35 In addition to works by Curtis discussed in the text, Orpen's comments on the following articles by Curtis are extant: 'The viceroyalty of Lionel, duke of Clarence, in Ireland, 1361–1367 [*sic*]', *JRSAI*, 47 (1917), 165–81; ibid., 48 (1918), 65–73; 'The FitzRerys, Welsh lords of Cloghran, Co. Dublin', *JLAHS*, 5:1 (1921), 13–17; 'Murchertach O'Brien, high king of Ireland, and his Norman son-in-law, Arnulf de Montgomery, *circa* 1100', *JRSAI*, 51 (1921), 116–24; 'Unpublished letters from Richard II in Ireland, 1394–5', *PRIA*, 37:C (1927), 276–303. 36 By *c.*1919, Curtis was already well advanced in his work on the volume, as he wrote to T.F. Tout about the possibility of publishing it with Manchester University Press. Tout's reply survives. It states that 'we would normally be glad to consider such a book, but at present … we are congested with material': TCD, MS 2452, no. 3 (T.F. Tout, 1 Oak Drive, Fallowfield, Manchester, to E.C., 27 Jan. 1920). Ultimately, Curtis published with Methuen. 37 TCD, MS 2452, no. 9 (G.H.O., Monksgrange, Enniscorthy, to whom it may concern, 16 Mar. 1923). 38 TCD, MS 2452, no. 8 (G.H.O., Monksgrange, Enniscorthy, to E.C., 16 Mar. 1923).

Orpen had finished reading Curtis' proofs and he wrote to Curtis again. This time he was more forthright:[39]

> To be quite frank, I do not think you are always fair to the Normans, or give them due credit for the vast improvement produced in the state of Ireland, wherever and so long as their rule was effective. Perhaps I erred, on the other hand, by not displaying more sympathy with the Gaelic element, but I was writing mainly about Norman rule and trying to correct the travesties of history that had too often appeared before I wrote. On the other hand you pass lightly over the dynastic and other conflicts that incessantly broke out among the Irish themselves, and gloss over their raids of plunder and destruction by such terms as the 'Irish Resurgence' – a risorgimento that led not to national unity, but to the chaos and retrogression of the 15th century. Well they have got their 'Great Deliverance' now, and all I can say is Heaven help Ireland!

In letting this southern unionist cat out of the bag, Orpen exposed the political chasm that could separate two firm friends and colleagues, both of whom were – to use the term that Curtis came to prefer – 'Irish Protestants'.[40] For Orpen, the course of events since 1916 had been demoralizing.[41] As well as the barbarity (as he saw it) of the war of independence, his own published work had been subjected to public vilification by Eoin MacNeill (d.1945).[42] Orpen's barbed reference to a Gaelic 'risorgimento' was a private – and, one hopes, satisfying – confutation of MacNeill's proposal that the Norman advance in the thirteenth century was greeted by an 'Irish rally',[43] an idea taken up by Curtis in his new history.[44] The mixture of despondency and indignation evinced by Orpen lies in strong contrast to the mood of Curtis, who was at his most optimistic during these tumultuous years. He was the paragon of what Roy Foster has called that 'odd and little-noted Irish subculture: Trinity College nationalism'.[45] In 1919, his article on the spoken languages of medieval Ireland appeared. In its way, it is a work of pioneering scholarship, but Gaelic revivalism is a strong subtext in

39 TCD, MS 2452, no. 10 (G.H.O., Monksgrange, Enniscorthy, to E.C., 19 Mar. 1923). 40 '"Anglo-Irish": what does the word mean? Views of Professor Curtis', *Irish Times*, 21 Feb. 1933. 41 Goddard Henry Orpen, *The Orpen family, being an account of the life and writings of Richard Orpen of Killowen, Co. Kerry, together with some researches into his forbears in England and brief notices of the various branches of the Orpen family descended from him* (London [private circulation], 1930), pp 189–91. 42 Eoin MacNeill, *Phases of Irish history* (Dublin, 1919), esp. chs 11 and 12. MacNeill's comments are analyzed in Duffy, 'Historical revisit: Goddard Henry Orpen, *Ireland under the Normans*'. 43 MacNeill, *Phases of Irish history*, ch. 12. 44 Curtis, *Med. Ire.* (1st ed.), ch. 6, 'Expansion of the colony, and the first Irish resurgence, 1216–1272'; ch. 9, 'The second Irish resurgence'. 45 R.F. Foster, '"Colliding cultures": Leland Lyons and the reinterpretation of Irish history', in idem, *The Irish story: telling tales and making it up in Ireland* (London, 2001), p. 48.

the piece and Curtis' picture of a titanic struggle between the Irish and English languages (Irish naturally emerges triumphant) leads to a certain amount of teleological distortion.[46] The year after producing this essay, Curtis published an anthology of contemporary Gaelic verse.[47] It was in these heady days that the first edition of his *History of mediaeval Ireland* appeared, prefaced with a mournful quatrain on Ireland as absentee lordship by the eighteenth-century poet, Aodhagán Ó Rathaile.[48]

It is significant that, in the second edition of his *History*, this poem was cut.[49] The years since 1923 had been ones of disillusionment and distress: disillusionment with what Curtis saw as the manipulation of history in the new Free State; distress in his personal life. Curtis' marriage broke down during 1924–5 when his wife eloped with the novelist, Liam O'Flaherty (d.1984),[50] and then caused a sensation by publishing a sexually-charged short story under her maiden name in *To-morrow*, a radical new journal supported by W.B. Yeats.[51] The scandal that ensued was deeply embarrassing for Curtis and pushed him to the fringes of college life.[52] It was in the midst of this distressing episode, on 17 February 1925, that Curtis delivered a memorable lecture to the Dublin Literary Society in which he complained of the 'lack of historical perspective' in the history curriculum of the fledgling Irish Free State.[53]

> Will Irish history be, as it was mainly in the past, a fictitious version of the nation's story, one-sided in putting all the blame on the English and other foreigners, unreal in expecting us to believe in a pious, noble, and patriotic race led by gallant, brilliant, and wise soldiers and statesmen, who, strange to say, lost every time? … Or shall we have what other nations consider 'scientific history', founded on fact and judicial research, putting us in our place as members of the European family …?[54]

46 Curtis, 'The spoken languages of medieval Ireland', *Studies*, 8 (1919), 234–54; repr. below, ch. 19. Curtis returned to this theme in 'The decay of English in Ireland', *Irish Statesman*, 14 Sept. 1929 – a review article of St John D. Seymour, *Anglo-Irish literature, 1200–1582* (Cambridge, 1929), and Jeremiah J. Hogan, *The English language in Ireland* (1927). 47 Éamonn Cuirtéis, *Cuisle na hÉigse* (Dublin, 1920). 48 Curtis, *Med. Ire.* (1st ed.). 49 Noted in Lydon, 'Historical revisit: Edmund Curtis, *A history of medieval Ireland*', p. 535, n. 1. 50 On whom, see John Cronin, 'O'Flaherty, Liam (1896–1984), novelist and short-story writer' in *ODNB*, xli, 552–4. 51 Margaret Barrington, 'Colour', *To-morrow*, 1:1 (Aug. 1924). 52 For brief discussion, see R.F. Foster, 'The normal and the national' in idem, *The Irish story*, p. 106; R.F. Foster, *W.B. Yeats: a life*, ii: *the arch-poet, 1915–1939* (Oxford, 2003), pp 271–2. 53 On the teaching of history in Ireland at this time, see Francis T. Holohan, 'History teaching in the Irish Free State, 1922–35', *HI*, 2:4 (1994), 53–5; David Fitzpatrick, 'The futility of history: a failed experiment in Irish education' in Ciaran Brady (ed.), *Ideology and the historians. Historical Studies XVII: papers read before the Irish Conference of Historians held at Trinity College, Dublin, 8–10 June 1989* (Dublin, 1991), pp 168–83. 54 Curtis, 'Irish history and its popular versions', *Irish Rosary*, 29:5 (1925), 321–9; repr. below, 'Prologue'.

There was nothing original about Curtis' call for 'scientific' history, especially for a historian who received his training before the devastation of the Great War.[55] His scientific pretensions recall those of John Bagnell Bury (d. 1927) – after Lecky, perhaps Trinity's greatest historian – who enjoined the audience at his Cambridge inaugural in 1903 to remember that 'though [history] may supply material for literary art or philosophical speculation, she is herself simply a science, no less and no more'.[56] In the Ireland of 1925, however, Curtis' proposition was explosive, and he followed it with a rapid review of the pantheon of Irish heroes and an unceremonious debunking of their associated myths. From his closing remarks, it is clear that Curtis anticipated controversy: 'That this paper will offend many good people, and provoke some bitter people to attack my views and me, is inevitable.' Still, he can hardly have foretold the 'cat-calls' and 'parrot-cries' with which his address was greeted, nor the extent to which the animosity was predicated solely on the fact that Curtis was a professor in that bastion of Irish Protestantism, Trinity College. The editors of the *Irish Rosary* were moved to mount a robust defence. They described Curtis as one of 'that group of scholarly and liberal-minded Irish Protestants', including Osborn Bergin and Douglas Hyde, 'whose talents and accomplishments would shed lustre upon any country'.[57] As for Curtis' detractors, the editors stated that:

> There can be no excuse for the unjust and scurrilous attacks that have been made upon Prof. Curtis on the score of his lecture. His anonymous assailants seemed to be incapable of understanding any part of the lecture from start to finish … The chief libeller, whose knowledge was on a level with his manners, admitted that he knew nothing about Prof. Curtis except that he was a professor in Trinity College.

In light of this episode, it is difficult to accept without significant qualification the assertion recently made by Steven Ellis that Curtis was 'appropriating the

55 Peter H. Slee, *Learning and a liberal education: the study of modern history in the universities of Oxford, Cambridge and Manchester, 1800–1914* (Manchester, 1986), pp 122–52; John Kenyon, *The history men: the historical profession in England since the Renaissance* (2nd ed., London, 1993), pp 181–2. For the impact of the Great War, see Christopher Parker, *The English historical tradition since 1850* (Edinburgh, 1990), ch. 5. 56 J.B. Bury, 'The science of history', *An inaugural lecture delivered in the Divinity School, Cambridge, on January 26, 1903* (Cambridge, 1903), p. 42. At the time of Curtis' appointment to the Lecky chair in 1939, the *Irish Times* noted that Curtis' editorial projects were 'part of the remarkable advance in the scientific writing of Irish history within the past forty years' (*Irish Times*, 17 July 1939). Similar opinions were expressed at the publication of the first volume of *Ormond deeds* (*Irish Times*, 8 Apr. 1933). 57 'Professor Curtis and his critics', *Irish Rosary*, 29: 5 (1925), 388–9. For Protestant involvement in the Gaelic cultural revival, see esp. David Greene, 'The Irish language movement' in Michael Hurley (ed.), *Irish Anglicanism, 1869–1969: essays on the role*

past for the Irish Free State'.[58] By the same token, Brendan Bradshaw does Curtis a cruel disservice by associating him with Herbert Butterfield's argument for 'purposeful unhistoricity'.[59] The idea of propagating a 'received version of Irish history ... its wrongness notwithstanding'[60] would have been anathema to Curtis – 'green' as he was. During the 1920s, Æ's journal, the *Irish Statesman*, provided him with a soap-box from which to explode historical myths wherever he saw them.[61] In doing so, he was decades ahead of more famous warriors against national pieties and historical mythology.[62]

The mid-1920s, then, saw Curtis intellectually isolated – embraced neither by the Trinity establishment nor by nationalist Ireland. By the 1930s, his situation seems to have become happier. Two things are likely to have made this so. One was the death in 1927 of Provost John Henry Bernard, who had made strenous objections to the 'indecent' literary endeavours of Mrs Curtis. The new provost was Edward John Gwynn (d.1941),[63] a distinguished Celticist and brother of Curtis' friend and walking-companion, Brian Gwynn.[64] Although no radical, Gwynn may have eased Curtis' path within college. Curtis never became a fellow – F.S.L. Lyons describes him drifting 'helplessly in the cross-currents of Trinity academic life'[65] – but he was awarded the degree of doctor in letters in 1931 in recognition of his published work.[66] Curtis' rehabilitation may also have been aided by his embarkation on a new project in 1930. This was a monumental calendar of the medieval deeds pertaining to the Butler lordship in Ireland, then in private possession and stored in the muniment room of

*of Anglicanism in Irish life presented to the Church of Ireland on the occasion of the centenary of its disestablishment by a group of Methodist, Presbyterian, Quaker and Roman Catholic scholars* (Dublin, 1970), pp 110–9. **58** Steven G. Ellis, 'The empire strikes back: the historiographies of Britain and Ireland' in idem (ed.), *Empires and states in European perspective* (Pisa, 2002), p. 108. This is the most recent and most explicit statement of a familiar refrain, dating back to an important article: Steven Ellis, 'Nationalist historiography and the English and Gaelic worlds in the late Middle Ages' in Brady, *Revisionism*, pp 162–80; 1st pr. *IHS*, 25:97 (1986), 1–18. **59** Bradshaw, 'Nationalism and historical scholarship in modern Ireland' in Brady, *Revisionism*, pp 213, 216. See also Bradshaw's interview with Tommy Graham, 'A man with a mission', *HI*, 1:1 (1993), 52–3. **60** Bradshaw, 'Nationalism and historical scholarship' in Brady, *Revisionism*, p. 212. **61** His interests as critic were wide-ranging. See, for instance, his sending up of a 'new kind of hero-worship, that of the plain man of humble origin, whose path to greatness lies between the Log Cabin and the White House' (Curtis, 'Abraham Lincoln and the cult of the log cabin', *Irish Statesman*, 16 Jan. 1926). **62** See, e.g., T.W. Moody, 'Irish history and Irish mythology' in Brady, *Revisionism*, pp 71–86 (1st pr. *Hermathena*, 124 (1978), 7–24); Roy Foster, 'We are all revionists now', *Irish Review*, 1 (1986), 1–5. Foster's closing remarks (at p. 5) are close to Curtis': 'In a country that has come of age, history need no longer be a matter of guarding sacred mysteries. And to say "revisionist" should just be another way of saying "historian"'. Cf. Lydon's comment that 'history is by its nature revisionist' in Duffy, '"A real Irish historian"', *HI*, 3:1 (1995), 13. **63** McDowell and Webb, *TCD*, pp 439–40. **64** Katharine Simms, pers. comm. (2008). **65** F.S.L. Lyons, 'T.W.M.' in idem and R.A.J. Hawkins (eds), *Ireland under the union: varieties of tension: essays in honour of T.W. Moody* (Oxford, 1980), p. 8. **66** *DUC 1932–3*, p. 567.

Kilkenny castle. After the Four Courts blaze of 1922, this was, as Curtis put it, 'the largest single collection of mediaeval deeds and records now extant in Ireland'.[67] From the moment the first volume appeared in 1932, it was clear that the calendar of Ormond deeds – which eventually extended to six volumes plus ancillary publications – would win Curtis and Trinity a good deal of fame.[68] The reception in the British press is particularly noteworthy. The *Times Literary Supplement* still apparently conceived of Ireland as circling in an imperial orbit:[69]

> Macauley might think it strange that every schoolboy should know of Montezuma and Atahualpa, while so little interest should be taken in the events that led up to the conquest of India. But it is probable that the average Englishman (and Irishman for that matter) at this date knows more of the beginnings of the English association with India that he does of the mutual history of the two sister islands, of the beginnings of that uneasy partnership that has lasted nearly 800 years to our own day. And it is well to be reminded of those far-off events by the publication of this first Calendar of Ormond Deeds, which takes us back to the very first years of that pregnant adventure.

For the readers of the *TLS*, as for the fellows of Trinity College, the calendaring of the Ormond deeds was a thoroughly respectable enterprise. Specialists in Ireland were more prickly.[70] Charles McNeill (d.1958), the distinguished antiquarian and elder brother of Eoin MacNeill,[71] was particularly quick to tax Curtis privately for his editorial blunders. In reply to his critic, Curtis was restrained and self-effacing:[72]

> I need hardly repeat how gladly I welcome any corrections, suggestions or criticisms of my work especially from a fellow worker like yourself. This is all a question of scholarship and the true scholar tho' he may be saddened by his slips and mistakes must not take criticism in a personal

67 *COD*, i, p. v. 68 See, e.g., favourable reviews by Maude V. Clarke of *COD*, i, in *EHR*, 49:194 (1934), 329–32; and *COD*, ii, in *EHR*, 51:203 (1936), 518–20. 69 'Strongow's Ireland', *Times Literary Supplement*, 21 Sept. 1933. 70 The most insightful review is that of D.B. Quinn in *IHS*, 1:1 (1938), 81–5. One comment therein (at p. 83) has a distinctly 'modern' ring to it: 'The vigorous and elaborate development of feudal organisation on a particularist basis can now be treated by historians of the later medieval period in sufficient detail to balance the older over-emphasis on the decay of English rule and on the phenomenon of the Anglo-Normans becoming "more Irish than the Irish themselves".' 71 For a biographical sketch of his life and work, see Aubrey Gwynn, 'Obituary: Dr Charles McNeill', *JRSAI*, 88 (1958), 185–7. See also *Irish Times*, 15 Feb. 1946. 72 TCD, MS 7962 (E.C. to Charles McNeill, 10 May 1933). Curtis included Charles McNeill's comments in his introduction to the second volume of *COD* (pp viii–x).

> way ... I do not claim to be anything but an amateur in this business doing it entirely in the spirit of 'noblesse oblige' ... I shall be only too glad if you will in any review you write of my book point out all those errors slips or misreadings (in your view) so that scholars may the less be led astray. I am completely without vanity in this matter for I am but an amateur & a man with other work to do & in a properly constituted country would not be serving my days at work which a Record Office should be doing.

Such lack of vanity is extraordinary, but of little avail to scholars today who must pick their way gingerly through the gaps and gaffes in Curtis' calendar.[73] The time has certainly come for the Irish Manuscripts Commission to set in train a new diplomatic edition of the deeds, although even with the benefit of Curtis' spadework it will require a small batallion of editors and a large pot of research-funding simply to match the existing English calendar, which Curtis completed with the utmost economy and expedition. How then should we assess the work of Curtis as editor? A line is suggested by David Knowles, who chose as the theme of his presidential lectures to the Royal Historical Society, 'great historical enterprises'. When it came to the deeply-flawed 'Rolls Series',[74] Knowles challenged his audience: 'Who, among English medievalists of the past seventy years, could have done without it or would have wished it away?'[75] Substitute 'Irish' for 'English' and Knowles' judgment could stand as an honest appraisal of Curtis' calendar – undoubtedly one of the great historical enterprises of twentieth-century Irish medievalism – and the use to which Irish historians have put the Ormond deeds in the seven decades since the first of the six volumes was published.

Curtis' most substantial piece of historical writing – the second edition of his *History of medieval Ireland* – was published in 1938, which was coincidentally also the centenary of Lecky's birth. The anniversary was marked by a lecture delivered by the incumbent Lecky professor, Walter Alison Phillips.[76] Phillips retired at the end of the same academic year, returning home to England, where he died in Surrey just over a decade later.[77] A game of musical chairs ensued, as Curtis vacated the Erasmus Smith's chair and became Lecky professor of modern history on 1 October 1939.[78] The same summer, a young T.W. Moody

73 For some comments and information supplementary to *COD*, especially on the post-medieval deeds, see C.A. Empey, 'Ormond deeds in National Library of Ireland', *Journal of the Butler Society*, 7 (1977), 519–21; Kenneth Nicholls, 'Further notes on Ormond material in National Library', ibid., 7 (1977), 522–6. 74 *The chronicles and memorials of Great Britain and Ireland during the Middle Ages, published under the direction of the Master of the Rolls* ('Rolls Series'), 99 vols (London, 1858–96). 75 M.D. Knowles, 'Presidential address. Great historical enterprises, IV: the Rolls Series', *TRHS*, 5th ser., 11 (1961), 159. 76 W. Alison Phillips, *Lecky: a lecture in celebration of the centenary of Lecky's birth, delivered in the Graduates' Memorial Hall, Trinity College, Dublin, on 29 November, 1938* (Dublin, 1939). See also, *Irish Times*, 30 Nov. 1938. 77 Otte, 'Phillips, Walter Alison' in *ODNB*, xliv, 155.

arrived in Trinity from Queen's and was soon installed as Erasmus Smith's professor of history. More than one scholar has asserted that Curtis was by now 'past his prime' and 'if not a dying man, at any rate a spent force'.[79] A similar sentiment was expressed some decades later by Otway-Ruthven, who described the appearance of the second edition of Curtis' *Medieval Ireland* in 1938 as the end of an era: 'Curtis had been the principal figure among Irish medievalists since the second decade of the [twentieth] century, and … his work was almost done.'[80] In retrospect, it doubtless seemed that way. But, in fact, Curtis' working life did not draw to a natural close. It was cut short tragically in 1943. In no sense did Curtis make way for Moody, nor, in accepting the Lecky chair, was the older scholar being put out to grass.[81] On the contrary, the perception in 1939 was that Curtis' election to the Lecky professorship was a promotion,[82] made in recognition of his tireless work on the calendar of Ormond deeds, as well as the enormous popular success of his general *History of Ireland* (1936) and the second edition of *Medieval Ireland* (1938).[83] The pace of Curtis' work continued unabated until his final six months when his health deteriorated with terrible swiftness. In the autumn of 1942, he was overtaken by pernicious anaemia and entered a nursing home. Although he still gave lectures in Hilary term, 1943, his health was now beyond recovery and he died on his sixty-second birthday – 25 March 1943. Fortunately, by the time Curtis died, his most brilliant student, Jocelyn Otway-Ruthven, had joined the staff at Trinity.[84]

78 *DUC 1939–40*, p. 28. 79 The quotations are taken respectively from Helen F. Mulvey, 'Theodore William Moody (1907–84): an appreciation', *IHS*, 24:94 (1984), 125; and Lyons, 'T.W.M.' in idem and Hawkins (eds), *Ire. under the union*, p. 9. Lyons arrived at Trinity 1941, so he would have witnessed first-hand Curtis' deterioration in the winter 1942–3. I suspect this coloured his view of Curtis' position three years before. For Lyons' student career at Trinity, see R.F. Foster, 'Francis Stewart Leland Lyons, 1923–1983', *PBA*, 70 (1984), 464–5. 80 A.J. Otway-Ruthven, 'Thirty years' work in Irish history (I): medieval Ireland (1169–1485)', *IHS*, 15:60 (1967), 359. 81 Indeed, in 1951, Moody applied for the Lecky professorship, but was beaten to the post by Jocelyn Otway-Ruthven (Sterling, 'Professor Otway-Ruthven, FTCD' in *A danger to the men?*, p. 265). 82 See, for instance, *Irish Times*, 17 Jul. 1939. The annual salary attached to the Erasmus Smith's professorship in 1939 was only £100 (Lyons, 'T.W.M.' in idem and Hawkins (eds), *Ire. under the union*, p. 8, n. 1). 83 Curtis, *A history of Ireland from the earliest times to 1922*; Curtis, *Med. Ire.* (2nd ed.). 84 *DUC 1938–9*, p. 28. After Otway-Ruthven's arrival at TCD, she and Curtis began to work together. The fruits of their collaboration survive. See, e.g., TCD, MS 2429: a calendar in preparation entitled, 'Mortimer charters of the earldom of Ulster and lordship of Connacht' (BL, Add. MS 6041). Curtis prepared a typed introduction to the calendar describing the manuscript and its contents, as well as providing an outline history of the earldom of Ulster. There follow two appendices in manuscript booklets written in the hand of Otway-Ruthven, whom Curtis thanks in his introduction for her 'valuable assistance' and 'careful work'. Otway-Ruthven's work on place-names remains of great value. Curtis published the French epitomes of the 'Connacia' portion in his 'Feudal charters of the de Burgo lordship of

## 'THE OT'

If Curtis' greatest attribute was his ability to reach out to more than one Irish tradition, Otway-Ruthven's contribution was her unparalleled scholarly rigour. Rigour was the 'first and lasting impression' that the formidable Otway-Ruthven made on F.S.L. Lyons when he and his fellow freshmen 'tremblingly presented [themselves] in her lecture-room'.[85] Today's freshmen encounter 'the Ot' – as the 'Boadicea of the History School' is still affectionately known[86] – through her equally formidable *History of medieval Ireland* (1968). Their first and lasting impression is often one of *rigor mortis*. But anyone conducting research on Irish history between 1171 and 1496 will turn, at some point, to Otway-Ruthven for guidance. Curtis had called for a 'scientific' approach to Irish history. It was Otway-Ruthven who did most to make of it a 'science'. As has been remarked of the prose of another 'scientific' historian: 'The biscuit is certainly exceedingly dry; but at any rate there are no weevils in it.'[87]

Annette Jocelyn Otway-Ruthven was born in Dublin in 1909 to Robert Mervyn Otway-Ruthven of Castle Otway, Co. Tipperary, and Margaret, daughter of Julius Casement of Co. Wicklow.[88] Her career in history arose – in the most literal way – from the ashes of Civil War. On the morning of 3 August 1922, Castle Otway was burned to the ground.[89] Jocelyn's father had died in 1919 from injuries sustained during the Great War and, with the family now in straitened circumstances, Jocelyn's mother married for a second time and moved with her family to Dublin.[90] Academia provided the young Jocelyn with a means of advancement and escape, as well as satiating the 'sheer damned curiosity' that was the motor behind her historical research.[91] In 1927, Jocelyn

Connacht, 1237–1325' in John Ryan (ed.), *Féil-sgríbhinn Eóin Mhic Néill: essays and studies presented to Professor Eoin MacNeill* (Dublin, 1940; repr. 1995), pp 286–95; a note on the 'Ultonia' section appears in the *Report of the deputy keeper of the records, Northern Ireland* (1928), pp 15–16. **85** F.S.L. Lyons, 'Foreword' in Lydon, *Eng. & Ire.*, p. xi. **86** The phrase is that of William Trevor, 'Alma Mater' in idem, *Excursions in the real world* (London, 1993), p. 66. The passage is popularly supposed to refer to Otway-Ruthven, although it is possible that the author intended Constantia Maxwell. In either case, the description captures the Ot very well. **87** Lytton Strachey, *Biographical essays* (London, 1948), p. 274, quoted in Robert Brentano, 'The sound of Stubbs', *Journal of British Studies*, 6:2 (1967), 1. **88** *Burke's Irish family records* (London, 1976), pp 217, 998. The Dublin census of 1911 includes a record for the young Jocelyn, in which her punctilious father gives her age as 1 5/12 and records that she cannot read or write. The family was then living in Donnybrook, Co. Dublin (see http://www.census.nationalarchives.ie/search/, s.n. 'Otway-Ruthven' [accessed, 23 Apr. 2008]). My thanks to Prof. Robin Frame for bringing this to my attention. **89** *Irish Times*, 5 Aug. 1922. **90** The foregoing details are drawn from Salters Sterling, 'In retrospect: Annette Jocelyn Otway-Ruthven', *Search*, 24:1 (2001), p. 61. **91** This was her reply to a foreign student at Cambridge who asked Miss Otway-Ruthven why she studied history and was surprised not to receive a philosophical answer: Robin Frame, pers. comm. (2008).

won an entrance exhibition to Trinity College where she read history and political science. From the moment she entered Trinity, her gifts as a researcher were apparent. She was elected as a non-foundation scholar in 1929 and graduated in 1931 with first class honours and a large gold medal.[92] By the time she retired as Trinity's Lecky professor half a century later, it was apparent that the over-arching theme of that research was her tireless reconstruction of the record sources for medieval Ireland that had been destroyed by the catastrophic fire in the Four Courts of June 1922.[93]

As an undergraduate at Trinity, Jocelyn encountered Edmund Curtis in his prime. His teaching had a profound impact on her. Years later she dedicated her *magnum opus* to his 'honoured memory' and expresed the hope that her own pupils would remember her 'with as much gratitude and affection as I do him'.[94] After a glittering undergraduate career, she engaged in a brief stint of research with Alison Phillips before winning a Gardiner scholarship to Girton College, Cambridge, in 1932. The Cambridge phase of Jocelyn's student career brought her into proximity with Helen Maud Cam (d.1968), one of the most redoubtable minds of her generation of English medievalists.[95] Cam had a powerful personality and, aside from her historical investigations, she was an active socialist and a champion of women's rights. Jocelyn flourished under her supervision: she was awarded her doctorate in 1936 along with the Thirlwall prize, which, for the first time, went to a woman. 'What luck you are having', wrote Cam from faraway Rangoon on hearing of this run of success,[96] before pithily setting out what she hoped would be the future trajectory of Jocelyn's career: '(a) PhD; (b) Prize Essay; (c) job?'[97]

The new Dr Otway-Ruthven remained in contact with Cam after graduation,[98] and the pair became lifelong friends and correspondents.[99] When

92 *DUC 1934–5*, p. 584. 93 In her interview with the *Irish Times*, 8 Feb. 1968, Otway-Ruthven notes that her *Med. Ire.* is compiled mostly from records from the seventeenth to the nineteenth centuries, as most of the original documentation was lost in 1922. 94 Otway-Ruthven, *Med. Ire.* (1st ed.), 'Foreword', p. v. 95 Kathleen Major (rev.), 'Cam, Helen Maud (1885–1968), historian' in *ODNB*, ix, 595–7. 96 In 1936–7, Cam was on leave of absence from Girton and toured India, Burma and the Middle East: see Euan Taylor and Gina Weaver, 'Helen Cam (1885–1968): charting the evolution of medieval institutions' in Jane Chance (ed.), *Women medievalists and the academy* (Madison, WN, 2005), pp 255–72, esp. p. 266. 97 Helen Cam to Jocelyn Otway-Ruthven, c/o Mrs Casement, Clonagh House, Ashford, Co. Wicklow, 15 Oct. 1936. The letter survives among Otway-Ruthven's uncatalogued correspondence in the library of the Medieval History Research Centre, TCD (box labelled, 'Letters to the Ot'). The core of this invaluable research library is made up of Otway-Ruthven's personal collection. The letters have been retrieved from between the pages of the books. 98 Helen Cam's 'Dear Jocelyn' of 1936 becomes 'My dear Jossie, You are an angel' within a few short years (Medieval History Research Centre, TCD, 'Letters to the Ot'). 99 Otway-Ruthven expresses her thanks to Cam in the foreword to A.J. Otway-Ruthven, *The king's secretary and the signet office in the XVth century* (Cambridge, 1939). Helen Cam acknowledges academic debts to Otway-Ruthven in Cam, 'The evolution of the medieval

2. A.J. Otway-Ruthven, pictured in her rooms in Trinity College, 1968. Photograph © *Irish Times*, 8 February 1968.

Cam died in 1968, Otway-Ruthven published a concise memoir of her former supervisor. It is largely a bland recital of Cam's career and achievements, but it closes with an uncharacteristically emotional salute, albeit one executed with customary precision:

> She [Cam] was a convinced Socialist, much interested in local government in the present as in the past. She was at all times a lively and stimulating companion and a devoted friend; as a teacher she was superb, instilling her own exacting standards of scholarship and her own passion for enquiry, and she was always ready to help the humblest scholar. Her work on English constitutional history will long hold an unchallenged place, and at her death she was unquestionably the greatest of living English medievalists.[1]

Many of these attributes Otway-Ruthven shared with Cam – first among them her remorseless precision of mind, but also her passion for gardening and especially Alpine plants;[2] her advocacy of 'parity of esteem' for women academics; and surprisingly (at first glance, at least) her ardent trade unionism.[3]

With Cam, too, Otway-Ruthven shared an abiding interest in administrative history, specifically the history of local government and franchisal institutions. In pursuing these subjects in an Irish context, she was filling a major gap in Curtis' treatment of Anglo-Ireland. In 1938, Henry Gerald Richardson (d.1974) devoted a typically searching review article to the question of English institutions in medieval Ireland, a subject that Richardson considered to be glaringly absent from the second edition of Curtis' *Medieval Ireland*:[4]

English franchise' in eadem, *Law-finders and law-makers in medieval England: collected studies in legal and constitutional history* (London, 1962), p. 22, note 1; eadem, 'The quality of English feudalism' in eadem, *Law-finders & law-makers*, p. 54. 1 Helen M. Cam, *Historical novels*, Historical Association, general ser., no. 48 (London, 1961; repr. with memoir by A.J. Otway-Ruthven, 1968), p. 4. Among Otway-Ruthven's papers in the Medieval History Research Centre, TCD, there is a memorial photograph of Cam from her funeral service in Girton College chapel. 2 Her writings on the subject of Alpine plants are noted in P.W.A. Asplin, 'The writings of Professor A.J. Otway-Ruthven to 1980' in Lydon, *Eng. & Ire.*, p. 255. Her correspondence ('Letters to the Ot', Medieval History Research Centre, TCD) includes a letter thanking her for her subscription to 'The Cyclamen Society' (Gay Nightingale, 'The Cyclamen Society', Lavendar house, 47 Lechmere Ave., Chigwell, Essex, 3 Jan. 1978). In the course of the letter, the secretary apologizes for 'a number of printing slips [in the society's newsletter], such as capital letters for species names. I do hope we shall have no more of these in future'. Clearly, the Ot's ability to inspire punctiliousness extended beyond the walls of Trinity! 3 Sterling, 'In retrospect: Annette Jocelyn Otway-Ruthven'; idem, 'Professor Otway-Ruthven, FTCD' in *A danger to the men?* 4 H.G. Richardson, 'English institutions in medieval Ireland', *IHS*, 1:4 (1939), 382–92. Curtis and Richardson, however, still respected each other greatly. In the early 1940s, they were in correspondence on the matter of a compendium of Irish constitutional documents: TCD, MS 2452, no. 36 (H.G.

> I cannot but feel that Dr. Curtis would have learnt much, and his readers would have learnt more, if he had collected such material as is readily accessible on the central and local institutions of government in the area under the control of the English king, and had told a story of each.[5]

In a single sentence, Richardson presented Irish medievalists with a research agenda that would dominate the following decades. Much of the work was done by Richardson himself with his collaborator, George Osborne Sayles (d.1994);[6] but among Irish medievalists, it was Otway-Ruthven who answered the call.[7] Investigation of medieval civil institutions in Ireland was gravely hampered by the destruction of the records of central government during the Civil War; but it was precisely this calamity that made Otway-Ruthven so superbly equipped to tackle the subject.[8] Her doctoral thesis at Girton took as its subject the office of the king's secretary in the fifteenth century.[9] Hitherto, research on this topic had faced the seemingly insuperable obstacle that the records of the department over which the king's secretary presided – the signet office – were not extant. Indeed, the general consensus was that the signet records did not survive because they had never existed. Otway-Ruthven provided ample evidence that this was so much nonsense. As she noted in her address to the Royal Historical Society in January 1936, the absence of a class of signet records could 'be

Richardson, High Barn, 14, Sheridan Road, Merton, SW19, to E.C., 28 Aug. 1941). The volume (*IHD*), which Curtis edited jointly with R.B. McDowell, appeared in 1943. 5 Richardson, 'English institutions in medieval Ireland', p. 383. The 'agenda setting' is more explicit in H.G. Richardson, 'Agenda for Irish history, I: Norman Ireland', *IHS*, 4:15 (1945), 254–8. 6 The key works are Richardson and Sayles, *Ir. parl.*; idem, *Admin. Ire.*; and idem, 'Ir. revenue'. Their contribution is noted in Otway-Ruthven, 'Thirty years' work in Irish history (I): medieval Ireland (1169–1485)', p. 363. A stimulating discussion of Sayles is David N. Dumville, *The mediaeval foundations of England?*, The G.O. Sayles Memorial Lecture, 2005 (Aberdeen, 2006). I am grateful to Prof. Robin Frame who sent me his unpublished lecture, 'G.O. Sayles and Ireland', delivered at a symposium on Sayles held at Aberdeen in 2005. 7 See, e.g., Otway-Ruthven, 'The native Irish and English law in medieval Ireland', *IHS*, 7:25 (1950), 1–16 (repr. below, ch. 6), which expands upon arguments presented by Richardson in 'English institutions'. Richardson was already acquainted with Otway-Ruthven from her Cambridge days (Cam to Otway-Ruthven, 15 Oct. 1936). Before 1941, Otway-Ruthven had been recruited by Richardson to work on a volume of documents illustrative of the history of the Irish parliament in the fifteenth century (TCD, MS 2452, no. 36), which was to serve as the counterpart to Richardson and Sayles, *Parls & councils*, the title page of which reads 'volume 1'. The second volume never appeared. 8 See Herbert Wood, 'The public records of Ireland before and after 1922', *TRHS*, 4th ser., 13 (1930), 17–49; Philomena Connolly, 'The destruction of the Public Record Office of Ireland in 1922: disaster and recovery', *Archivum*, 43 (1996), 135–46. For a highly romanticized account of the PROI fire – one that would doubtless have enraged Otway-Ruthven – see Ernie O'Malley, *The singing flame* (Dublin, 1978), esp. pp. 114–5. 9 A.J. Otway-Ruthven, 'The king's secretary in the fifteenth century', *TRHS*, 4th ser., 19 (1936), 81–100; Otway-Ruthven, *King's secretary and the signet office*.

explained without supposing that they never existed, for a letter of 15 January, 1618/19 states that "the banqueting house at Whitehall was on Tuesday night set on fire ... All the records of the signet and privy seal offices are burnt"'.[10] To compensate for this disaster, Otway-Ruthven undertook an exhaustive trawl of the PRO and other archives for substitute materials from which the records of the signet office might be reconstructed.[11] Historical inquiry of this sort requires, in Flaubert's indecorous formula, 'drinking an ocean and pissing a cupful'.[12] The cupful proved that Otway-Ruthven was peerless in her terrier-like pursuit of record evidence. It was this that gave her a reputation as a second Tout.[13] As one reviewer mischievously put it: 'Miss Otway-Ruthven's book rivals the reconstruction of the Java man. From imperfect fragments she has re-created that masterful Tudor exemplification of *homo sapiens*, the king's secretary.'[14]

No training could have better prepared Otway-Ruthven for a second career working on medieval Irish institutional history mostly using substitute source material. There is thus a gratifying symmetry in the fact that her contribution to a *Festschrift* for Helen Cam dealt with the royal chancery of medieval Ireland.[15] Despite the arduousness of the work, her publication rate was impressive, culminating with her magisterial synthesis, *A history of medieval Ireland*, which appeared in 1968, precisely three decades after Curtis' work of the same title. 'Thirty years', was the Ot's dry response to the correspondent who dared ask how long she had laboured over it.[16] Little wonder, then, that as the work entered its final stages, the Ot began to safeguard against fresh calamities. In the academic year of 1965–6, she was crossing the threshold of the fifteenth century. When spring came, boxes containing thousands of index cards on which she compiled her meticulous notes were taken carefully from her college rooms and deposited in her home in Brighton Road lest something bad happened to Trinity at Easter 1966. Her students found this highly amusing – until Nelson's Pillar was blown up![17]

10 Otway-Ruthven, 'King's secretary', *TRHS*, 4th ser., 19 (1936), 83. 11 Otway-Ruthven's notes are extant and in the possession of the Medieval History Research Centre, TCD. The range of substitute material can be assessed from J.L. Kirby (ed.), *Calendar of signet letters of Henry IV and Henry V (1399–1422)* (London, 1978). 12 John Pemble, *Venice rediscovered* (Oxford, 1995), p. 82, quoted in Richard J. Evans, *In defence of history* (London, 1997), p. 23. The quotation is attributed to Flaubert and occurs in Pemble's discussion of the great Ranke, who seemed to be 'doing the opposite'. 13 Dr Salters Sterling, pers. comm (2008). The reference is, of course, to T.F. Tout (d.1929), author of *Chapters in the administrative history of mediaeval England*, 6 vols (Manchester, 1920–33). 14 H.L. Gray, review of Otway-Ruthven, *King's secretary and the signet office in the XV century*, *AHR*, 45:3 (1940), 621. Gray notes the similarity between Otway-Ruthven and Tout (ibid., p. 622). 15 A.J. Otway-Ruthven, 'The mediaeval Irish chancery' in *Album Helen Maud Cam*, 2 vols (Studies presented to the International Commission for the History of Representative and Parliamentary Institutions, nos. 23–4: Louvain-Paris, 1960–1), ii, 119–38; repr. below, ch. 4. 16 *Irish Times*, 8 Feb. 1968. 17 Robin Frame, pers. comm. (2008), who took Otway-

That Otway-Ruthven's approach to medieval institutions owes much to Helen Cam and the school of English administrative history founded by Tout is a conspicuous fact. Less obvious, perhaps, are differences in the character and texture of their histories. Helen Cam was an engaging and imaginative historian. Her medieval institutions are alive and dynamic. A neat illustration of her human orientation on a potentially dry-as-dust subject comes from her discussion of the development of England's legal personality: 'who made the rule of the road?', she asked rhetorically.[18] Tout, too, occasionally took vacations from the king's wardrobe to explore the cultural by-products of medieval administrators and what he described as the 'human side' of medieval records.[19] By contrast, Otway-Ruthven's institutions are rarefied and austere, even static. This may explain why so few of her students became devotees of institutional history.[20] Her research interests were not, however, restricted to what she termed the 'government of the Norman-Irish state'.[21] She was also deeply interested in topography, maps and historical geography.[22] From early in her career, she was employing onomastic evidence in a compelling way.[23] Likewise, her use of field patterns was extremely original, reminiscent of the 'retrogressive' methods of the *Annalistes*,[24] although her exemplar was almost certainly not Marc Bloch, but F.W. Maitland – an iconic figure in the Cambridge of her day,[25]

Ruthven's special subject in 1965–6. **18** Helen M. Cam, 'Introduction: the rule of law in English history' in eadem, *Law-finders and law-makers*, p. 21. **19** T.F. Tout, 'The English civil service in the fourteenth century', *BJRL*, 3 (1917), 185–214; idem, 'The human side of medieval records', *TRHS*, 4th ser., 11 (1928), 1–16; idem, 'Literature and learning in the medieval civil service', *Speculum*, 4:4 (1929), 365–89. **20** As noted by Provost Lyons: 'Medieval constitutional history is perhaps too much of an acquired taste ever to attract a large following in this age of declining Latinity, and Miss Otway-Ruthven had less opportunity to found a school than did her own teacher, Edmund Curtis' (F.S.L. Lyons, 'Foreword' in Lydon, *Eng. & Ire.*, p. x). Likewise, K.W. Nicholls commented of her *Festschrift* that there was 'little to cavil at, unless it be the absence ... of any essay on a theme which Professor Otway-Ruthven particularly concerned herself with, institutional history' (review of Lydon, *Eng. & Ire.*, in *Peritia*, 3 (1984), 579). **21**Otway-Ruthven, *Med. Ire.*, ch. 5. **22** For samples of Otway-Ruthven's cartographical work, see the maps that accompany the following works: 'The medieval county of Kildare', *IHS*, 11:43 (1959), 181–99; *Dowdall deeds*; 'Knights' fees in Kildare, Leix and Offaly', *JRSAI*, 91 (1961), 163–81; 'The mediaeval church lands of Co. Dublin' in J.A. Watt, J.B. Morrall and F.X. Martin (eds), *Medieval studies presented to Aubrey Gwynn, S.J.* (Dublin, 1961), pp 54–73; eadem, 'Parochial development in the rural deanery of Skreen', *JRSAI*, 94 (1963), 111–22; eadem, 'The partition of the de Verdon lands in 1332', *PRIA*, 66:C5 (1968), 401–55. **23** Otway-Ruthven, 'Place-names in Ireland', *Irish Geography*, 2:2 (1950), 45–51. For a discussion of the study of Irish place-names in the past two centuries, see Nollaig Ó Muraíle, 'Some thoughts on matters onomastic', *JGAHS*, 53 (2001), 23–46. **24** Peter Burke, *The French historical revolution: the* Annales *school, 1929–89* (Oxford, 1990), pp 23–4. **25** G. Kitson Clark, 'A hundred years of the teaching of history at Cambridge, 1873–1973', *Historical Journal*, 16:3 (1973), 535–53, esp. p. 546. Helen Cam states that she loves Maitland 'this side [of] idolatry' in Cam, 'Stubbs seventy years after', *Cambridge Historical Journal*, 9:2 (1948), 129.

who espoused working 'from the modern to the ancient, from the clear to the vague, from the known to the unknown'.[26] These studies proved seminal and her approach has been embraced not just by records-historians, but also by archaeologists and historical geographers. Consequently, if Otway-Ruthven may be said to have founded a 'school', it is a school for the study of medieval settlement in Ireland.[27]

Otway-Ruthven's *History of medieval Ireland* was published in 1968 to favourable notices in Irish learned journals, although she was occasionally chided for her neglect of Gaelic Ireland.[28] An incisive comment of a different kind came from a young Joseph J. Lee. He saw Otway-Ruthven's monolithic digest as marking the 'end rather than the beginning of an era' – an era that had been characterized by the 'tyranny of the diplomatic method'.[29] After two centuries of Irish historical scholarship in which evidence lagged behind interpretation, now for the first time, Lee claimed, 'interpretation lags behind evidence'.[30] Similar, but more carping, was the criticism of Brendan Bradshaw, who, in 1989, described Otway-Ruthven's *Medieval Ireland* as 'an extreme example of "extrusion [of national sentiment] by stealth" for the medieval period'.[31] The comment is misdirected. There was nothing stealthy about Otway-Ruthven's approach: 'to any historian surveying the writing of the last thirty years', she asseverated in 1967, 'there could be no more hopeful sign than the gradual disappearance of the old crude nationalism.'[32] This could hardly be more unequivocal. Nor is her overt extrusion to be understood as anti-nationalist. It is merely a manifestation of the no-nonsense attitude that prevailed among adminstrative historians of her generation who had rubbished Stubbsian whiggery (though not Stubbs' scholarship)[33] – an attitude that Tout's

26 G.R. Elton, *F.W. Maitland* (London, 1985), p. 22 (quotation). See F.W. Maitland, *Domesday book and beyond: three essays in the early history of England* (Cambridge, 1897), cited in Otway-Ruthven, 'Character of Norman settlement in Ireland', below, ch. 17, n. 21. 27 Robin Frame, *Colonial Ireland, 1169–1369* (Dublin, 1981), ch. 4, summarizes research on settlement at the time of Otway-Ruthven's retirement. John Gillingham assesses her contribution in the wider context of Europe-wide colonization in 'A second tidal wave? The historiography of English colonization of Ireland, Scotland and Wales in the twelfth and thirteenth centuries' in Jan M. Piskorski (ed.), *Historiographical approaches to medieval colonization of east central Europe: a comparative analysis against the background of other European inter-ethnic colonization processes in the Middle Ages* (New York, 2002), pp 303–27, esp. pp 306–7. 28 F.X. Martin, review of Otway-Ruthven, *Med. Ire.*, *Studia Hibernica*, 14 (1974), 143–60; J.F. Lydon, *IHS*, 17:65 (1970), 123–8. Other reviews are listed in Asplin, 'Writings of Professor A.J. Otway-Ruthven to 1980' in Lydon, *Eng. & Ire.*, p. 261. 29 Joseph Lee, 'Some aspects of modern Irish historiography' in Ernst Schulin (ed.), *Gedenkschrift Martin Göhring: Studien zur Europäischen Geschichte mit einem Geleitwort von Jacques Droz* (Wiesbaden, 1968), p. 440. 30 Ibid., p. 441. 31 Bradshaw, 'Nationalism and historical scholarship in modern Ireland' in Brady, *Revisionism*, p. 208 32 Otway-Ruthven, 'Thirty years' work in Irish history (I): medieval Ireland (1169–1485)', *IHS*, 15:60 (1967), 360. 33 Helen Cam is laudatory in 'Stubbs seventy years after', pp 129–47. H.G. Richardson and

disciples shared with the alternative band of medievalists that followed Bruce McFarlane down the garden path of Namierism.[34] It is only relatively recently that 'political culture' has returned to the agenda of the new constitutional historians in England.[35] In Ireland, a remedy for the deficit of interpretation identified by Lee and Bradshaw was provided long before in the person of James F. Lydon, who had joined the staff at Trinity in 1959.[36]

## 'J.F.L.'

James Francis Michael Lydon was born in 1928 into a Catholic family from Galway, the tenth of eleven children.[37] His father was a baker who hailed ultimately from Connemara; his mother was a native Irish speaker. The family held a firm conviction in the value of education and all the children were sent

G.O. Sayles are decidedly critical in *The governance of mediaeval England from the Conquest to Magna Carta* (Edinburgh, 1963), esp. pp v–vii, 1–21, though they praise Stubbs' work as an editor for the 'rolls series'. 34 On McFarlane, see Karl Leyser, 'Kenneth Bruce McFarlane, 1903–1966', *Proceedings of the British Academy*, 62 (1976), 485–506. For Sir Lewis Namier's influence, see K.B. McFarlane, 'Parliament and "bastard feudalism"' in idem, *England in the fifteenth century: collected essays with an introduction by G.L. Harriss* (London, 1981), p. 19; Steven Gunn, 'The structures of politics in early Tudor England', *TRHS*, 5th ser., 5 (1995), 62–3. 35 C. Carpenter, 'Introduction: political culture, politics and cultural history' in L. Clarke and C. Carpenter (ed.), *The fifteenth century IV: political culture in late medieval Britain* (Woodbridge, 2004), pp 1–20. See also E. Powell, 'After "After McFarlane": the poverty of patronage and the case for constitutional history' in D.J. Clayton, R.G. Davies and P. McNiven (eds), *Trade, devotion and governance: papers in later medieval history* (Stroud, 1994), pp 1–16; G.L. Harriss, 'The dimensions of politics' and C. Carpenter, 'Political and constitutional history: before and after McFarlane', both in R.H. Britnell and A.J. Pollard (eds), *The McFarlane legacy: studies in late medieval politics and society* (Stroud, 1995), pp 1–20, 175–206. 36 It is interesting, and important, to note that Lydon's own review of Otway-Ruthven, *Med. Ire.*, is not a world away from Bradshaw in its comment that: '[I]f it is true, as the author [Otway-Ruthven] suggests, that we must be careful not to read the attitudes of ninteenth and twentieth-century nationalism back into the medieval Irish church, it is equally true, I think, that we must be careful not therefore to underestimate the pernicious influence of such racial feelings as did undoubtedly exist and which manifested themselves regularly, on every level, to the end of the middle ages. Racialism and national feeling were sometimes real forces, and not just among the Gaelic Irish' (*IHS*, 17:65 (1970), p. 126). 37 With James Lydon, we move from the recorded past towards a period of 'living history'. Consequently, some of the biographical details in what follows are drawn from personal knowledge and the recollections of students of Prof. Lydon. For sketches of his career, see Sheelagh Harbison, 'James Lydon: an appreciation' in *Colony and frontier*, pp xi–xiii; *Irish Times*, 15 June 1965; *Irish Times*, 24 Sept. 1998. I am grateful to Seán Duffy who gave me access to a tape recording of an interview he conducted with Lydon in 1994. The text was published in part as '"A real Irish historian"', *HI*, 3:1 (1995), 11–14, but the full interview contains much valuable information that remains unpublished. It will be cited hereafter as 'Lydon–Duffy interview (1994)'.

to secondary school and on to third level. Lydon took his first degree at University College, Galway, where he studied English and history. English (specifically Anglo-Saxon) at first took precedence and he claims to have 'damn-near failed history in the Leaving Certificate'.[38] The leading light in the history department at UCG was Mary Donovan O'Sullivan (d.1966), a respected economic historian who published a fine book on *Old Galway* in 1942, shortly before Lydon entered UCG.[39] O'Sullivan left a deep imprint on the young Lydon. She placed a premium on research, even at undergraduate level, and emphasized the importance of style and literary expression. After Lydon graduated with first class honours in 1950, he stayed on to undertake research for a master's degree. It was Mrs O'Sullivan who suggested that Ireland's contribution to the military activities of the English crown in the thirteenth century might be a subject that would repay investigation – a topic recommended by her work on Italian merchant bankers in thirteenth-century Ireland.[40]

Lydon's master's took him overseas to London, where his research was funded partly by a Travelling Fellowship in the National University of Ireland and partly 'self-financed' with night work as a railway porter in St Pancras. During the daylight hours, he toiled in Chancery Lane and London's other libraries, including the Institute of Historical Research. It was in the convivial atmosphere of the IHR, where students and professors mingle freely away from the dusty tomes, that a memorable encounter took place. When the secretary of the IHR discovered that Lydon was from Ireland, he arranged for him to meet the director, the great Welsh historian, John Goronwy Edwards (d.1976).[41] Lydon and Edwards got on 'like a bomb' and their meeting led directly to the next phase in Lydon's career. After returning to Galway to finish his master's in 1952, Lydon was astonished to receive a letter from the IHR inviting him to apply for a research fellowship.[42] In the subsequent competition, a senior Tudor specialist asked the young Irish student the subject he proposed to research for his doctorate. When Lydon replied that he wanted to continue his work on Irish

38 Lydon–Duffy interview (1994). 39 M.D. O'Sullivan, *Old Galway: the history of a Norman colony in Ireland* (Cambridge, 1942). For a sketch of O'Sullivan's career, see the facsimile reprint of *Old Galway* with an introduction by William J. Hogan (Galway, 1983). Her role among women historians in Ireland is contextualized in O'Dowd, 'From Morgan to MacCurtain: women historians in Ireland from the 1790s to the 1990s' in Valiulis and O'Dowd (eds), *Women and Irish history*, p. 53. 40 O'Sullivan, *Old Galway*, pp 27–9; eadem, 'Italian merchant bankers and the collection of papal revenues in Ireland in the thirteenth century', *JGAHS*, 22 (1947), 132–63; eadem, 'Some Italian merchant bankers in Ireland in the later thirteenth century', *JRSAI*, 79 (1949), 10–19. Her work on this subject later grew into a short but well-crafted monograph: M.D. O'Sullivan, *Italian merchant bankers in Ireland in the thirteenth century: a study in the social and economic history of medieval Ireland* (Dublin, 1962). The preface to this volume makes special reference to Lydon. 41 J.F.A. Mason, 'Edwards, Sir (John) Goronwy (1891–1976), historian' in *ODNB*, xvii, 927–8. 42 Duffy–Lydon interview (1994).

3. James F. Lydon, pictured in March 1993 at the launch of the journal *History Ireland* in the Tailor's Hall, Dublin. Photograph © Brigid Fitzgerald.

participation in the king's enterprises in the Middle Ages, he was informed that he would be wasting his time. J.G. Edwards was also on the interview panel. Ever courteous, but not one to suffer fools gladly, the director asked his colleague to stop talking nonsense and awarded the research fellowship to Lydon.[43] The episode brings out rather nicely the sea-change that has overtaken the historiography since the early 1950s. Such insularity is now scarcely imaginable. A large measure of the credit for opening up medieval Ireland to the academic world outside must go to Lydon and his students.

Lydon used his three years at the IHR to extend his research to the closing years of the reign of Edward II (1307–27). His doctorate was an exercise in military history, though not the history of battles and tactics but rather that specialized branch of the discipline, military logistics – the organization of war, the problems of transport and supply, finance and purveyance, and the repercussions of the war effort on domestic law and order.[44] His research on these topics was facilitated by the 'belly-full' of training in administrative history, along with advanced palaeography and diplomatics, that he received at the Institute. 'J.G.' supervised Lydon's doctorate, but valuable mentoring of a different kind came from the eminent Oxford historian, Sir Maurice Powicke (d.1963).[45] When Lydon completed his thesis in 1955, he still had a year left to run on a Travelling Fellowship in the National University of Ireland that he had won after the expiry of his research fellowship from the Institute. Powicke advised Lydon to use the residue of the funding to travel on the continent, issuing him with strict instructions to stay clear of archives. Instead, he was to read, visit galleries, listen to music, meet people and generally lift his eyes beyond the confines of the Record Office in Chancery Lane. So the young Lydon was packed off to Rome in the autumn of 1955, with Powicke promising to write letters to the National University testifying that he was working hard and his research was progressing well. Lydon found his 'grand tour' invigorating and it added something extra to his impressive array of gifts. From his boyhood proximity to rural Ireland, he had gained an enduring love of the countryside and the Irish language; the intensive seminar regimen of the IHR made him an authority on English record sources; now the Italian experience had given him an appreciation of European 'culture' in its broadest sense.[46] It

43 J.F.L., pers. comm. (2008). 44 James Lydon, 'Ireland's participation in the military activities of English kings in the thirteenth and fourteenth centuries' (PhD, University of London, 1955). See below, chapters 9–12. 45 R.W. Southern, rev. Alan Harding, 'Powicke, Sir (Frederick) Maurice (1879–1963), historian' in *ODNB*, xlv, 148–50. For a more anecdotal account, see Norman Cantor, *Inventing the Middle Ages: the lives, works, and ideas of the great medievalists of the twentieth century* (New York, 1991), pp 233–44. 46 Duffy–Lydon interview (1994). Sometimes this cultural appreciation is clearly in evidence: note how Lydon – a great lover of opera – says of the Perkin Warbeck conspiracy that 'in retrospect it might assume the guise of a comic opera escapade' (Lydon, 'Ireland and the English crown, 1171–

was this unique blend of the best of Curtis and Otway-Ruthven that was to enable Lydon to bring the historiography of late medieval Ireland to maturity.

With Powicke's encouragement, Lydon returned to UCG in 1956 where he taught in the history department through both English and Irish. Three years later, a lectureship opened up in Trinity. The decision to uproot himself from Galway and move to Dublin was made at the urging of Mrs O'Sullivan, who considered that the facilities and prospects for academic advancement in Trinity were more favourable than in Galway. In fact, staff facilities in the Trinity of 1959 were less than salubrious: Lydon's junior lectureship entitled him to a peg for his gown on the lower level of the 1937 reading room. Soon, however, he was running up the academic ladder: he was made a full lecturer in 1962, elected to fellowship in 1965, became an associate professor in 1967, and eventually succeeded Otway-Ruthven as Lecky professor of history in October 1980.[47]

During these decades, Otway-Ruthven was at the height of her powers as a records-historian. Nonetheless, Lydon's contribution on that level was, if not greater, certainly as important. As a student at Galway, he had travelled to the record office in the Four Courts only to be told by Margaret C. Griffith – then deputy keeper of the public records – that there was nothing there to interest a medieval historian. This view still prevailed in the 1960s, despite earlier advertisements by Richardson and Sayles to the contrary.[48] In 1966, Lydon unveiled the riches of the PROI and other archival repositories in Ireland when he published a painstaking survey of the surviving materials for the memoranda rolls of the Irish exchequer.[49] In parallel with this work in Dublin, Lydon's research in the PRO, London, brought another seam of records to notice – this time not substitute materials but original enrolments of audited Irish exchequer accounts. When Lydon first worked on these records, sand fell onto his desk in Chancery Lane: the accounts had never been unrolled – except partially for cataloguing purposes – since the anonymous exchequer clerk filed them away centuries before. They have since become the staple of all histories of the period.[50]

Lydon's background in administrative history inevitably led to a centralist conception of English political society in Ireland. In that sense, his interpretation is of a kind with Otway-Ruthven.[51] Where Lydon departs from

1541', *IHS*, 29:115 (1995), 284; repr. below, ch. 1). 47 Harbison, 'James Lydon: an appreciation' in *Colony and frontier*, p. xi–xii; *DUC 1962–3*, p. 32; *DUC 1968–9*, p. 33; *DUC 1965–6*, p. 521; *DUC 1980–1*, p. 42. 48 Richardson, 'Agenda for Irish history, I: Norman Ireland', pp 254–8; *Parls & councils*, pt 1, passim. 49 James F. Lydon, 'Survey of the memoranda rolls of the Irish exchequer, 1294–1509', *AH*, 23 (1966), 49–134. For the range of archives consulted, see ibid., pp 71–3. On the memoranda rolls, see Philomena Connolly, *Medieval record sources* (Dublin, 2002), p. 22. 50 Duffy–Lydon interview (1994). Much of this material has since been calendared by the late Philomena Connolly in *IExP*. 51 The influence of English institutional history on Irish historiography is discussed in Peter Crooks, 'Factions, feuds and noble power in the lordship of Ireland, *c.*1356–1496', *IHS*, 35:140 (2007), 431–7.

Otway-Ruthven is in his great imaginative power. In this, he is more akin to his idol, Maurice Powicke, who had reacted against the administrative strictures of Tout and declared himself interested in 'the interplay of experience and ideas in the formation of medieval political societies'.[52] Lydon's effervescence as a teacher is well attested. His acting experiences as a student in Galway gave him a taste for the dramatic and an enviable ability to capture an audience. Those who heard Lydon lecture recall how he held them spell-bound with abstruse details of medieval administrative procedure and how he sent them from the lecture hall with the impression that they somehow knew the barons and chamberlains who staffed the medieval Irish exchequer.[53] That same enthusiasm is communicated in his compelling prose. Administrative and political history dominate in his work; but Lydon is no arid records-historian and he was combining administrative sources with literary texts – notably bardic poetry (a subject later opened up by his pupil, Katharine Simms)[54] – at a time when the latter were thought to lack gravitas by 'serious' historians.[55]

Lydon was also active in opening up Trinity to new influences even before demands for liberalization had become commonplace.[56] Soon after joining the staff in 1959, he became involved in Catholic politics within the college and campaigned to secure the provision of chaplaincy facilities for Catholics on the staff and within the student body.[57] The reiteration of the 'ban' by Archbishop McQuaid in 1967 resulted in Lydon's appearance on the *Late Late Show*, which brought the issue to public attention. To some extent, this broadening of horizons is reflected in the historiography of the period. Historical scholarship in Ireland since 1922 had operated, to a remarkable extent, in noble isolation.[58] Lydon was instrumental in increasing scholarly engagement across the Irish Sea. A case in point is the joint meeting of the British Academy and Royal Irish

52 F.M. Powicke, *Ways of medieval life and thought: thoughts and addresses* (London, 1949), p. 5, quoted in *ODNB*, xlv, 149. For discussion of Powicke's reaction against Tout, see M.T. Clanchy, 'Inventing thirteenth-century England: Stubbs, Tout, Powicke – now what?' in P.R. Coss and S.D. Lloyd (eds), *Thirteenth Century England V* (Woodbridge, 1995), pp 1–20, esp. p. 5. 53 I am reminded of Fredric Cheyette's comment upon re-reading Georges Duby's *La société aux XIe et XIIe siècles dans la région mâconnaise* (Paris, 1953): 'Duby's book gave you the uncanny feeling that families you had never heard of, and would never hear of again ... were familiar figures, something like distant cousins that people told stories about at family holiday gatherings' (F.L. Cheyette, 'Georges Duby's *Mâconnais* after fifty years: reading it then and now', *Journal of Medieval* History, 28 (2002), 293). 54 Katharine Simms, 'Bardic poetry as historical source' in T. Dunne (ed.), *The writer as witness: literature as historical evidence. Historical Studies XIV* (Cork, 1987), pp 58–75. 55 See esp. Lydon, 'The problem of the frontier in medieval Ireland', *Topic*, 13 (1967), 5–22; repr. below, ch. 20. 56 For Trinity in this period, see J.V. Luce, *Trinity College Dublin: the first 400 years* (Dublin, 1992), ch. 15. 57 James Lydon, 'The silent sister: Trinity College and Catholic Ireland' in C.H. Holland (ed.), *Trinity College Dublin and the idea of a university* (Dublin, 1991), esp. p. 48. See also *Irish Times*, 15 Apr. 1967. 58 Robin Frame, 'The "failure" of the first English conquest of Ireland' in idem, *Ire. & Brit.*, pp 4–7.

Academy held at Dublin in 1982.[59] This colloquium was the occasion for Lydon's 'Middle nation' lecture – perhaps the finest illustration of his craftsmanship as an essayist – which has been enormously influential both in Ireland and further afield.[60] Although a contribution to a self-consciously 'British history' followed,[61] the credit for bringing Ireland into this wider framework must go to Lydon's pupils – Robin Frame, above all.[62] Yet the medieval branch of the 'British history' industry would scarcely have been so successful had not Lydon's early research and teaching (albeit unwittingly) laid the groundwork. His doctoral dissertation on Ireland's participation in England's wars of domination knitted Irish and English history together in surprising ways. Later work was comparative as well as integrative. The 'frontier' is now so ingrained in medieval Irish historiography that it is is difficult to remember how novel it was in 1967 to invoke Frederick Jackson Turner and toy with a 'frontier thesis' for medieval Ireland.[63] Such a conceptual leap was a world away from Otway-Ruthven, who always refused to move an inch beyond the evidence. It was also novel by comparison with other historians of his day. In 1967, J.G.A. Pocock's much-vaunted 'plea for British history' was some years off,[64] while the great exponent of the 'British' approach among medievalists, Rees Davies,[65] had only recently submitted his doctorate and was still firmly entrenched in the March of Wales.[66] It is only relatively recently that

59 James Lydon (ed.), *The English in medieval Ireland: proceedings of the first joint meeting of the Royal Irish Academy and the British Academy, Dublin, 1982* (RIA, Dublin, 1984). **60** See, e.g., R.R. Davies, *The age of conquest: Wales, 1063–1415* (Oxford, 1991), p. 103; 1st pr. *Conquest, coexistence and change: Wales, 1063–1415* (Oxford, 1987). James Muldoon, *Identity on the medieval Irish frontier: degenerate Englishmen, wild Irishmen, middle nations* (Gainesville, 2003), is less successful in its attempt to translate the concept overseas. The book's significance for this discussion lies in its demonstration of the extent to which Lydon's ideas have been internalized. Lydon's 'middle nation' essay does not appear in the bibliography! **61** James Lydon, 'Lordship and crown: Llywelyn of Wales and O'Connor of Connacht' in R.R. Davies (ed.), *The British Isles, 1100–1500: comparisons, contrasts, connections* (Edinburgh, 1988), pp 48–63. **62** See, esp., Robin Frame, *The political development of the British Isles, 1100–1400* (Oxford, 1990); idem, *Ire. & Brit.* **63** Lydon, 'Problem of the frontier', *Topic*, 13 (1967), 5–22; repr. below, ch. 20. An early treatment of the subject was Archibald R. Lewis, 'The closing of the mediaeval frontier, 1250–1350', *Speculum*, 33:4 (1958), 475–83, whose work on medieval Europe may have suggested some of Lydon's terminology. **64** J.G.A. Pocock, 'British history: a plea for a new subject', *Journal of Modern History*, 47:4 (1975), 601–21; idem, 'The limits and divisions of British history: in search of the unknown subject', *AHR*, 87:2 (1982), 311–36. **65** R.R. Davies, 'In praise of British history' in idem (ed.), *British Isles*, pp 1–26. **66** R.R. Davies, 'The Bohun and Lancaster lordships in Wales in the fourteenth and early fifteenth centuries' (DPhil, University of Oxford, 1965). Davies' superb monograph on lordship in the Welsh march appeared in 1978: idem, *Lordship and society in the march of Wales, 1282–1400* (Oxford, 1978). The same year a change of direction was in evidence with his move to Aberystwyth: R.R. Davies, *Historical perceptions: Celts and Saxons. An inaugural lecture delivered at the University of Wales, Aberystwyth on 22nd November 1978* (Cardiff, 1979). Earlier work hinted strongly at the broader approach that was to come,

exponents of 'British' history for the early modern period – finding the archipelago somewhat crowded – have begun to seek out new comparative frameworks and have invented (or rather re-invented) 'Greater Britain' and the 'Atlantic World'.[67] Lydon had reached the New World long before. To this day, the potential for cross-fertilization between medieval and modern historiographies has yet to be fully realized.

All is not idolatry (nor should it be). Lydon's portrait of the English colonists of the fifteenth century as 'separatists'[68] – a reincarnation of the 'patriot party' of Edmund Curtis – has been criticized by Steven Ellis in his consideration of the nationalist tradition in twentieth-century Irish historiography.[69] Lydon does not, however, consider nationalism to be incompatible with good history, and, if anything, his nationalist sentiment has become more apparent in recent years.[70] For other tastes, Lydon's 'refreshing downrightness' can take him a step too far. 'Now and then his very enthusiasm ... leads him to use exaggerated language ... In the end our responses are dulled; we suspect him of crying wolf; and would welcome a splash of cool analysis.'[71] So cavilled Robin Frame in 1974 with some justice and, one suspects, some trepidation too, since he had only recently completed his apprenticeship with the master.[72] And, indeed, the stripling ended on an appreciative note with which few could disagree: 'If at times Professor

e.g., R.R. Davies, 'Marc Bloch', *History*, 52 (1967), 265–82. **67** From an ocean of historiography, see esp. David Armitage, 'Greater Britain: a useful category of historical analysis?', *AHR*, 104:2 (1999), 427–45; Jane Ohlmeyer, 'Seventeenth-century Ireland and the new British and Atlantic histories', ibid., 446–62; J.G.A. Pocock, 'The new British history in Atlantic perspective: an antipodean commentary', ibid., 490–500. See also David Armitage and Michael J. Braddick (eds), *The British Atlantic World, 1500–1800* (Basingstoke, 2002); David Armitage, *Greater Britain, 1516–1776: essays in Atlantic history* (Aldershot, 2004). The earlier phase of 'Atlantic' historiography is best approached through the *Festschrift* for D.B. Quinn: K.R. Andrews, N.P. Canny and P.E.H. Hair (eds), *The westward enterprise: English activities in Ireland, the Atlantic and America, 1480–1650* (Liverpool, 1978). For dissatisfaction with the inclusion of early modern Ireland within an Atlantic framework, see esp. Hiram Morgan, 'Mid-Atlantic blues', *Irish Review*, 11 (1991/2), 50–55; and the response by Andrew Hadfield, 'Rocking the boat: a response to Hiram Morgan', *Irish Review*, 14 (1993), 15–19. **68** Lydon, *Lordship* (1st ed.), pp 262–6; ibid. (2nd ed.), pp 202–6; idem, *Ireland in the later Middle Ages* (Dublin, 1973), ch. 5. **69** Ellis, 'Nationalist historiography and the English and Gaelic worlds in the late Middle Ages' in Brady, *Revisionism*, pp 172–3; idem, 'Representations of the past in Ireland: whose past and whose present?', p. 301. **70** See Lydon interview with Seán Duffy, '"A real Irish historian"', *HI*, 3:1 (1995), 13–14. Lydon reaffirms his 'separatist' interpretation in 'Ireland and the English crown', *IHS*, 29:115 (1995), esp. 289–91; repr. below, ch. 1. Noticeably whig is James Lydon, *The making of Ireland: from ancient times to the present* (London, 1999), a book Lydon was commissioned to write to replace Curtis, *A history of Ireland from the earliest times to 1922*. **71** Robin Frame, review of James Lydon, *Ireland in the later Middle Ages* (Dublin, 1973) in *Studia Hibernica*, 14 (1974), 162–6, quotation at p. 163. **72** R.F. Frame, 'The Dublin government and Gaelic Ireland, 1272–1361: the making of war and the making of peace in the Irish lordship' (PhD, University of Dublin, 1971).

Lydon is provocative rather than measured, that may be no bad thing. In a sense it is the price we willingly pay for the sheer vigour of his thought and writing.'[73]

* * *

When James Lydon retired in 1993, a former pupil observed that 'it is difficult not to sense the end of an era'.[74] Mrs Harbison was echoing sentiments expressed earlier about both Lydon's predecessors. The extended vacancy of the Lecky chair after 1993 was, however, a constant reminder that the Lydon era had ended without due provision for the future.[75] The furore over the 'Lecky' in 2003 was not without its heartening aspects. It was revealing not of a general intellectual malaise, so much as a gulf between national and institutional policy-making on the one hand and popular and academic interest on the other. Historiographers of a future generation will note, one hopes, that public concern for Ireland's heritage has rarely been greater, nor have there ever been so many labourers tilling the field of medieval Irish history. A great many of these scholars are the academic progeny – children, grandchildren, great-grandchildren, great-great-grandchildren – of Curtis, Otway-Ruthven and Lydon. In that sense, the legacy of the Lecky professors is assured. 'This book can be no more than an interim report', declaimed the Ot of her *magnum opus* four decades ago: 'on almost every aspect of the Middle Ages in Ireland there is still an infinity of work to be done.'[76] In the 'postmodern' world which we apparently inhabit, her statement will always hold true. History *is* an interim report. The present collection of essays by the Lecky professors is offered not with the grand hope that forty more years' hard labour will bring their work near to completion, but rather with the still grander hope that, in another forty years, students of Irish history will be more curious and inquiring than ever.

73 Frame, review of Lydon, *Ire. in the later Middle Ages*, p. 166. 74 Harbison, 'James Lydon: an appreciation' in *Colony and frontier*, p. xi. 75 Lydon's own letter to the *Irish Times*, 5 Nov. 2003, is particularly poignant. 76 Otway-Ruthven, *Med. Ire.*, 'Foreword', p. v.

PROLOGUE

# Irish history and its popular versions*

*Edmund Curtis*

The following remarks are the fruit of a good deal of experience as an examiner for the intermediate and other boards in the subject of Irish history. Like the native language, native history is being made compulsory for many posts and educational distinctions, and unfortunately, just as there is a lack of good reading matter in Irish, so there is a lack of good histories of Ireland, as a whole or in periods.

But as books must and will be produced to meet the demand, it is now both timely and fair to ask what kind of 'Irish history' are we going to have? As a race, we have an extraordinary habit of make-believe. Thus the kilt is spoken of in the papers as the 'national garb' though only a few school-children and one or two grown-up enthusiasts wear it. The 'national language', in spite of the way we talk about it in English, is only the language of about one Irishman in twenty. Are we to have a similar established and solemn sham called 'national history', which no one must criticize?

Will Irish history be, as it was mainly in the past, a fictitious version of the nation's story, one-sided in putting all the blame on the English and other foreigners, unreal in expecting us to believe in a pious, noble and patriotic race led by gallant, brilliant and wise soldiers and statesmen, who, strange to say, lost every time, and conceited in wanting us to believe in some extraordinary virtue and intellect in the Irish people, marking them off from all others. Or shall we have what other nations consider 'scientific history', founded on fact and judicial research, putting us in our place as members of the European family and as having the ordinary defects and virtues of ordinary human beings acting under certain extraneous circumstances of climate, religion, geography etc.? The old type of history we have in abundance; and up till lately it was treason to question it. The new type, as written by John MacNeill and a few others, will no doubt make its way among the thoughtful; the question is, how long it will be till Ireland as a whole accepts it, and learns that truth is infinitely more interesting than fiction, and that what Irish men and women have performed, labouring under the drawbacks of their human nature and the imperfections of

* A lecture delivered before the Dublin Literary Society, 17 February 1925, and first published in the *Irish Rosary*, 29:5 (1925), 321–9.

external things, is more remarkable, credible and creditable than the things they are supposed to have done as immaculate saints, invincible heroes, and ponderously perfect scholars.

Irish history has always been the favourite field of the legend-maker and it must be admitted that as a race we have generally preferred a good story about a thing rather than the facts about the thing. Hence it comes as a shock to many to hear from our modern scholars, such as MacNeill and Bergin, that the 'history of Ireland' from the time of the flood to the first century or two of the Christian era, as told in the Four Masters and Keating, was most of it just manufactured by scholars and poets after Ireland became Christian, when the need of a written chronicle which could be fitted in with the Bible story and world history was felt. Hence the occurrence of names such as Heber, Solamh, Partholan in our early annals, which are simply the Jewish Heber, Solomon, Bartholomew. But, disappointing though it may be to many to have to give up this legendary history, do we not gain by having our ancestors presented in true historical setting as Mediterranean dark-whites, Alpine or Celtic red blonds, Nordic fair blonds, who came from the continent at various times and have their kinsmen there still?

Far be it from me to disparage the value of tradition, folklore, legend. The discoveries of Sir Arthur Evans and others have shown that the minotaur, the labyrinth, the brazen bull etc., which used to be thought fictions of the Greeks, were actual and historic facts in the remarkable civilization of Knossos in Crete. So, in our early records, legends conceal much historic verity; thus the Firbolg would seem to be the early inhabitants of neolithic or Mediterranean race; the story that Labhraidh Loingsech, having been exiled to Gaul, came back with 2,200 Gaulish men, from whose broad spears (Ir. *laigin*) the province of Leinster got its name, points to some early Gaulish settlement in the south-east of our country, which perhaps was spread over many years.

But legend and tradition must be carefully used by trained scholars, who can discern what is true and what is false in them, and often make discoveries from them more wonderful than the legends themselves. Thus Dr John MacNeill, noting the tribe-names and personal names in our earliest records, has proved from them how the first ancestors of the Eugenian and Dalcassian dynasties of Munster were Gauls and worshippers of Gaulish gods, and how there were German tribes in early Ireland, such as the Menapii, from whom, with the customary change of 'P' to the Gaelic 'Ch', the name Fermanagh comes. Here surely is a case where scientific history is more fascinating in its interpretations than unverified tradition or invented history.

It must be admitted that a good deal of what passes for 'Irish history' with Irish people consists of mere fireside stories, or impressions derived from sermons, political speeches, or trashy articles in newspapers. As far as written history is known, it is generally derived from popular works of the D'Arcy

M'Gee and John Mitchel type of historian. This type makes the history of Ireland that of a virtuous, noble, intensely patriotic and deeply religious race, whose troubles have come entirely from foreigners. As a nationalist of the old home rule type said to me once: 'I believe that the virtues of the Irish are all their own, their defects have been put into them by their conquerors!' I believe that this brand of national history, which served its turn in keeping up the self-esteem of the people in dark days, has now rather curdled on the national stomach. It is only too evident and must now be admitted by all that, though the Irish cause in general was a good one, it was badly fought; most of our leaders were of inferior calibre, and even when great men like Hugh O'Neill or Owen Roe O'Neill came along, their genius and strivings came to nothing because of the treachery or folly or faint-heart of those who, having once joined the cause, should have followed them to the death.

What we have to learn in Ireland now is that history is a science, that it is concerned with cause and effect, and that it must serve the truth at all costs. It is not a branch of rhetoric or religious conviction, or politics or racial pride. It may be natural and right hold that our father, mother, brothers and sisters can do no wrong, but we must not treat the whole of the Irish people, some millions strong, as if it were our family, and get personally annoyed if our past is critically examined. Up to this, Irish history, and perhaps history in general, has been very badly taught in our country, and very few seem to regard it as a serious subject, even in our universities. My experience has been that when an examination question is set on certain people and subjects in our past, there almost inevitably follows a gush of legend, rhetoric, passion or panegyric, which may be very natural, but is not 'history'.

One is almost afraid to set a question on St Patrick, Brian Boru, the early Irish church, Owen Roe O'Neill, Cromwell, the penal laws, Sarsfield or Daniel O'Connell. Seldom, for instance, does one get an historical answer about our national apostle; what one generally gets is blurred memories of the customary panegyric which the child has heard every St Patrick's day since he can remember in his parish church. Nearly always we are told of the meeting with the Ard Rí Laeri at Tara and such late legends of the saint, the answer often ending with the sweeping statement that Patrick put an end to paganism, and in his lifetime 'turned us into a nation of saints and scholars'.

How much more interesting and human is the Patrick whose life and achievements have been the subject of great European historians such as Zimmer, Todd, Bury and that great living Benedictine scholar Gougaud. His achievements both in bringing in the Christian faith and European civilization into our country are the natural pride of all Irishmen, but we detract from the glory of these achievements if we attribute too much to him. It is certain that he did not christianize all Ireland in his lifetime. For over a century, the high kings refused to touch the new religion which, with its gospel of meekness and emancipation of slaves, made little appeal to the warlike Gaelic aristocracy; and King Diarmaid, who died in 565, held the pagan *feis* of Tara in 557.

Now if we had not got such a Christian conceit into our blood, and had more historical sense, we would find it quite natural and even admirable that Gaelic paganism made a bit of a fight against the new faith. The proud and sincere man who stands by his opinions is a far finer asset, when you do win him over, than the man who comes over at once. Irish druidism was not anything we need to be ashamed of, but an organized faith full of natural poetry and philosophy, with a great learned class of *file*s or sages behind it. The historical mind knows that such great changes as the conversion of a whole people is a slow process; it has to work through human agencies and human minds, and even has to compromise with the thing it displaces. It seems clear that there was a good deal of compromise in Ireland, the druids accepted baptism, but kept up their pagan lore and became the Gaelic poets of Ireland, and Celtic paganism left up till very recent times a very strong imprint upon the Irish mind.

On all this history of the early church in Ireland in the dark ages which were a golden age for Irish Christianity, the picture drawn is generally too impossibly perfect. It is the fashion to paint monastic Ireland of that time as perfectly learned, artistic and sinless. We must give our children a more manly and actual conception of this and other aspects of Irish history; we must impart to them something of the stern joy that monks, missionaries and heroes had in grappling with the defects and passions of other people's human nature and their own, and teach them that historical achievements are relative, not absolute, and God works through very imperfect men and women. Colmcille, who was so human, and Patrick, who was so self-diffident, hearing the kind of panegyrics that are pronounced upon them year in and year out, as if they never were assailed by the passions that battle in the restless heart of man, must reflect that little of their spiritual modesty has descended upon us.

To turn to Brian Boru. A picture derived from many popular histories comes at once to us of an aged king with a crown and a terrible lot of white hair and beard, riding between the ranks before the battle of Clontarf, lifting up a crucifix and adjuring the Irish to fight for the faith against the pagan Norse. I don't know where this picture comes from. It is not found in the life of Brian given in the *Wars of the Gael and Gall*, written soon after his time. From that and other sources, Irish and Norse, we know that half the army which faced Brian were Christian Leinstermen in revolt against Brian. The Danish king of Dublin, Sitric, was a Christian and had married Brian's daughter. Earl Sigurd was apparently not a pagan, nor do the Norse sagas make it to be a pure fight between Odin and the White Christ; they mention Brodir, the Viking who slew Brian, as one who had forsaken the faith, 'turned God's dastard and worshipped fiends', as though this was exceptional. The Norse at Clontarf were, we might say, pagans tinctured with Christianity. It is equally certain the Irish were

Christians tinctured with paganism. This is shown in the Irish account of how, when Brian was in his tent waiting for the issue of the battle and constantly repeating prayers, psalms and pater-nosters, he pauses to tell his attendant that the banshee of the Dalcais, Aoibhill of Cragliath, had come to him the night before and told him he would be slain that day. Another pagan passage relates how, as the lines were forming for battle, one Dunlaing O'Hartigan appeared, fresh from the fairy mounds, to his bosom friend, Murchadh, son of Brian, and says that he has abandoned great delights – namely, life without death, without cold, without thirst, without hunger, without decay, beyond all delights of the earth until the Judgment – to be with Murchadh and the Dal-cais that day, and moreover it is fated that both Murchadh and himself shall fall that day. 'That is not good encouragement for the battle', answered Murchadh, 'but often was I myself offered in fairy hills and mansions that world and those gifts you speak of, but I never abandoned for one night my country or my inheritance for theirs.'

So far, then, from being a crusading battle between Norse pagans and Irish Christians, Clontarf was a grim out-and-out fight between the army which Brian had drawn from the southern half of Ireland, and a confederacy of rebel Leinstermen and Dublin Danes, to whose help Earl Sigurd of Orkney had brought a great Viking army. It was the supreme moment of Brian's fifty years of empire-making, and he took up the challenge like a man, to end the last revolt and put a final crown on Dalcassian supremacy. No other interpretation of his last battle need be given.

Brian, though in many ways he was more humane than others of his time, and though he grew milder as he grew old, was, we must remember, essentially a warrior and statesman, not a saint. Let us note the account given in the *Wars of the Gael and Gall* of what happened after Mahon and Brian defeated the Norsemen at Limerick in 968. The Irish, we are told, followed their foes into the fort, and slaughtered them in the streets and houses, twenty hundred in all.

> Then they [the Irish] carried off their jewels and their best property, their saddles beautiful and foreign, their gold and silver, their beautifully woven cloth of all colours and of all kinds, their satin and silk cloth pleasing and variegated, both scarlet and green and all sorts of cloth in like manner. They carried away their soft, youthful, bright, matchless girls, their blooming silk-clad young women, and their active well-formed boys. The fort and the good town they reduced to a cloud of smoke and red fire afterwards. The whole of the captives were collected on the hill of Saingel, and every one that was fit for war was killed, and every one of them that was fit to be a slave was enslaved.

We pass from Brian, who was a great realist and constructive statesman, to Silken Thomas, Lord Offaly, who was the very opposite. Yet both are reckoned

Irish heroes. Actually I can see nothing romantic about Silken Thomas but his name; he owes his reputation mainly to Thomas Davis' absurd ballad on the Geraldines; and the fact is that Thomas was about the most idiotic and futile young hothead that ever smashed up all the crockery. His family had ruled Ireland for sixty years and, had he obeyed his father's sage advice and the counsel of wiser men, he might have ruled it too, and, who knows, might have kept it for Catholicism and Irish ways against all the designs of Henry VIII. But on hearing a false rumour of the death of his father in the Tower, which he does not try to verify, out he bursts, allows an archbishop to be foully murdered, fails to take Dublin Castle, blunders round, does not even fight a good battle, though he had most of Ireland at his beck and call, and at last, when he should have died sword in hand, miserably surrenders and is miserably hanged at Tyburn. The ruin of the Geraldine supremacy was a heavy price to pay for the romantic rashness of this mere boy, who is much to be pitied, but when he is treated as an Irish hero, I have no patience with him.

Owen Roe O'Neill is a true hero and with reluctance would one criticize the generous emotions that the name of this noble and good man evokes. But when I am told, as I nearly always am told, or when I see in print as I sometimes do, that Owen Roe stood for the Old Irish cause of complete separation and national independence, while Preston and the Catholics of the Pale asked only for religious tolerance and home rule from the English crown, I find myself again in the presence of a legend which passes for history.

The evidence is conclusive that O'Neill was ready at all times to accept Charles I as his king, though of course on terms securing the national pride, the right to freedom of religion, and the government of the kingdom of Ireland under the Stuart crown by native Irishmen. Owen's last letter, written five days before his death, to the earl of Ormond, protested that he had always been loyal to the crown: 'my resolution from first to last in these unhappy wars tended … truly and sincerely to the preservation of my religion, the advancement of his majesty's service, and the just liberties of this nation.'

Moreover, Owen Roe found it as hard as any one else to be consistent in that kaleidoscopic time. After the execution of Charles I, Owen's old enemies, the Scots in Ulster, declared for Charles II, while a Cromwellian army held out in Derry for the English commonwealth. One of Owen's last acts was to send supplies to Coote and so enable him to break the siege of Derry, while his last act of all was to accept Ormond as head of the royalist forces in Ireland and to march in the king's name against Cromwell, when as we know he died on the way.

Instead of holding up Owen Roe and other leaders as models of consistent and uncompromising patriots, how much more humanly true and interesting it would be to teach them to watch with admiration and understanding the spectacle of brave men struggling with crushing difficulties and making the best of them.

I pass from heroes to subjects. On certain subjects, examinees, whether children or adults, go off in a breathless whirl of words. Take the penal laws: ask a question about them, and you evoke at once a perfect shower-bath of 'facts' and assertions without discrimination, order or restraint, in which the comparatively unimportant law that the Roman Catholic could not possess a horse worth more than five pounds is put alongside of the deprival of the franchise and such weighty matters, and no attempt is made to compare the penal laws in Ireland with those in European countries or in England itself, as if ours was the only country where religious persecution prevailed. Teachers and textbooks should be able to tell our children that Protestants were persecuted out of existence in France, Spain and Italy, and that Bohemia in the Thirty Years War was converted by armed force from Calvinism back to Catholicism. They should know that few, and these not the great churches, believed in religious toleration till within a hundred years ago. It is generally known that many good Protestants disapproved of the penal laws when they were passed, just as all Protestants regret them now, and our generous-minded people give them credit for this. No one will grudge our Catholic fellow-countrymen the glory and honour of having stood so true to their faith and endured so much for it, yet that glory will not be diminished by being set beside a parallel picture of what other nations and minorities have suffered for their creed in other countries.

This comparative picture we must have if we are to have history in the true sense, for the essence of an understanding of history is to put things and men in their time and place and judge them by such circumstances. But, of all the things a teacher or examiner looks for in 'history candidates' in Ireland, that which is most lacking of all is 'historical perspective' and 'historical atmosphere'; candidates nearly always write as if St Patrick was a modern archbishop, and talk as if in seventeenth- and eighteenth-century Ireland there should have been the democratic and tolerant sentiments that we all share today.

Goodness knows we do not want to create young cynics in Ireland; hero-worship is a fine and natural thing, and all right-minded children and adults feel it. But we are so undiscriminating in our heroes, and so many of them are presented out of all human proportion, that we wonder if that kind of hero-worship can be of any use in filling the young mind with noble images and exemplars. So general is what I may call 'the panegyric mind', that really when a youth does present you with some unexpected unconventional or 'minority' view, you cannot but welcome it, even if it strikes on you as cynical; for porridge is impossible without some salt, and seldom do examinees on Irish history put in the salt.

An example occurs to me of a child in the senior grade who, in his answer to a question about the Irish brigade in France, declared that Louis XIV used Irish soldiers for hunting down the French Huguenots, that the Irish exiles took to the work with enthusiasm as a way of avenging the wrongs they themselves had suffered, and that so general was the terror inspired by them that when in a

Huguenot village the cry of 'voilà les Irlandais' was raised, a general panic set in and all the villagers fled. Now I do not know where the boy got the story, and I know many of my readers will be indignant at it; yet, was it not a welcome sign of the passing away of a lot of our old national self-righteousness? The Irish never persecuted, it is true, but then they never got the chance to persecute. We know, however, that it is human to wish for revenge, the Irish are human, and certainly eighteenth-century Gaelic poetry is full of what the 'Clanna Gaedheal' would do to the 'Lutherans' and 'Calvinists' if once the Stuart king came home.

This boy, I say, had 'historical perspective' and something of the 'historical method'. But someone may say, he was probably from the North. Very well, let me finish by saying that the heroes who are worshipped in the North, and such subjects as the rise and progress of the Orange Order, are every bit as distorted and out of proportion as much of our national history here in the south, and probably with less saving grace of humour and toleration. Certainly, no historical person could be more unlike the legendary representation of him than the tolerant and honourable William III, who has become the hero and symbol of Protestant intolerance and self-righteousness among a large section of our countrymen in the north-east. Too many of us err in talking as if always: 'On our side is virtue and Erin; on theirs is the Saxon and guilt.' They err in taking as exaggerated a view on the other side.

I have said enough, I hope, to drive home my points that we want a complete re-presentation of Irish history. That this paper will offend many good people, and provoke some bitter people to attack my views and me, is inevitable. As regards the latter type, cannot we now, in the name of all that is reasonable, get out of the stage and attitude in which we were always looking for 'another insult to Ireland'? Imagine a man who, when it is pointed out to him that he is very much like other people and that while he has many good points he has many faults, flames up at once and asserts that any such criticism is an intolerable insult. What would we think of him except that he has neither humour nor manliness, and that he must be singularly lacking in true self-esteem and modest dignity? Of course, if such people hold in their hearts or say with tongue or pen that unless you belong to the faith and politics of the majority here and accept legendary views, you have no right to speak or write on such things as Irish history, language etc., there is no reply to them except that those who dare to hold what they consider salutary if untraditional views do not intend to let themselves be silenced.

Many of the religious minority here have in the past shared all the enthusiasm of the majority about Irish subjects, even when they thought that enthusiasm uncritical and over-impassioned; but now that Irishmen have charge of their own destinies, they think it time to do what every honest European nation has to do, namely, to look itself in the face and recognize the facts, the faults and merits of its past and its present, a task in which the historian can give invaluable aid.

# PART I

# *Government*

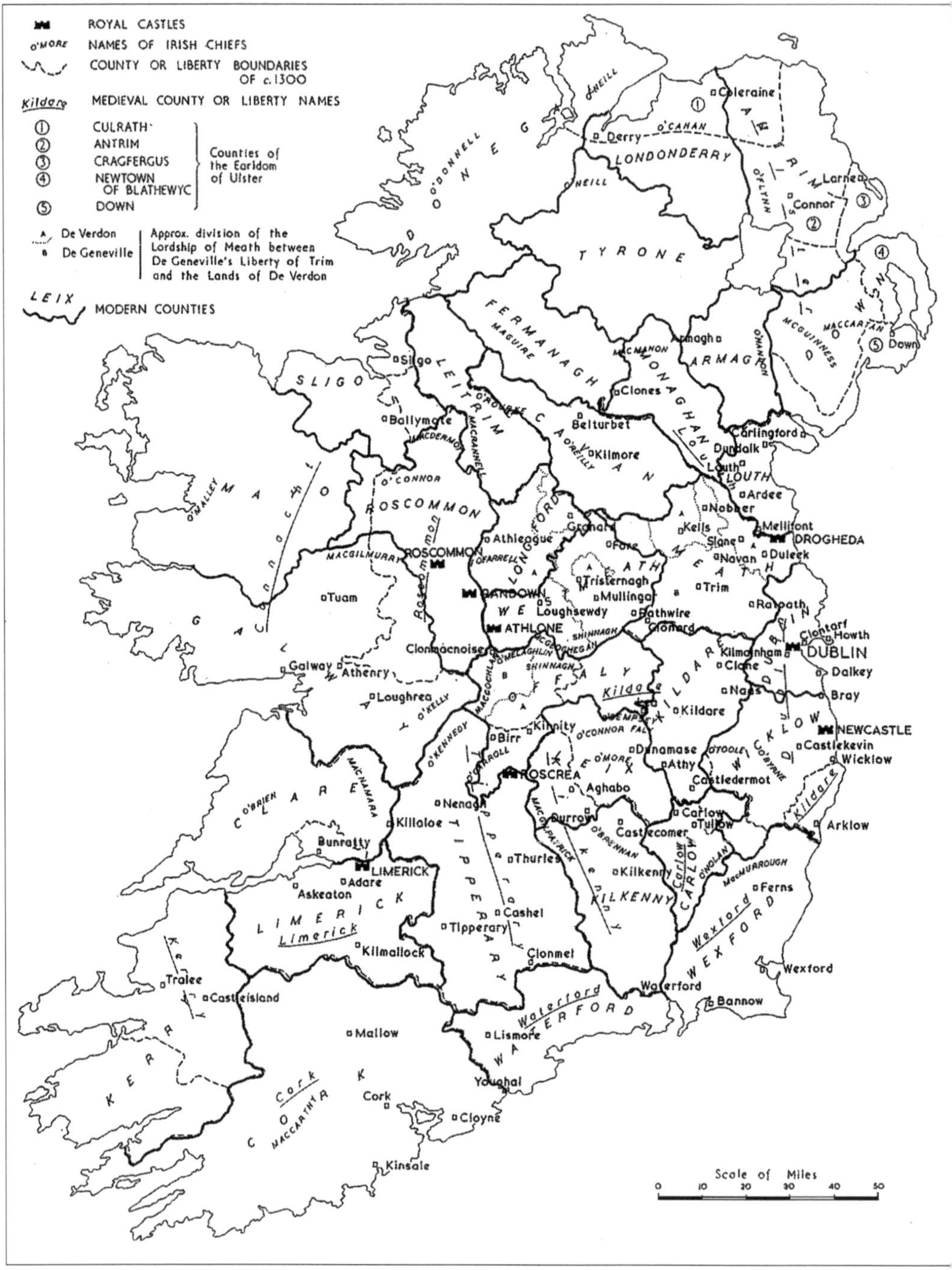


Map 1. Ireland in 1300

CHAPTER I

# Ireland and the English crown, 1171–1541*

*James Lydon*

When the earl of Pembroke met Henry II at Newnham in Gloucestershire in 1171, in the words of Gerald of Wales he surrendered Dublin (significantly called *regni caput*), the adjacent cantreds, the maritime towns and castles to the king. 'As for the rest of the land he had conquered, he and his heirs were to acknowledge that it was held of the king and his heirs.'[1] Already Mac Murchada had given King Henry 'the bond of submission and oath of fealty'.[2] Later Mac Carthaig did homage as well as fealty, gave hostages and an annual tribute and 'voluntarily submitted to the authority of the king of England', while other Irish submitted and swore fealty. Most significantly, according to Gerald, Ó Conchobair of Connacht 'obtained the king's peace, became dependent for the tenure of his kingdom on the king as overlord, and bound himself in alliance with the king by the strongest ties of fealty and submission'.[3] All in Ireland became the king's subjects, and Henry's lordship was accepted by all. It was later confirmed by the pope and publicly proclaimed by his legate, Cardinal Vivian, at a synod in Dublin.[4] From 1171, then, until 1541, when an Irish parliament declared Henry VIII to be king of Ireland, Anglo-Irish relations were governed by one simple fact: the king of England was *ipso facto* lord of Ireland. Throughout that period, the royal style never changed.[5] In all charters and formal letters issuing from his chancery, he was *Rex Anglie, Dominus Hibernie* etc.

It was Gerald of Wales too who first voiced the new reality which faced Ireland after 1171. When he composed a dedication to King John of a new edition of his *Expugnatio Hibernica*, sometime around 1209, he reminded him that he should not neglect Ireland and wrote that 'the Irish kingdom was made subject to the English crown, as if through a perpetual indenture and an indissoluble chain'.[6] We might note in passing that Gerald refers to Ireland as a

* Presidential lecture read to the Irish Historical Society in December 1993; first published in *IHS*, 29:115 (1995), 281–94. 1 Giraldus, *Expug. Hib.*, pp 88–9. 2 Ibid., p. 27. 3 Ibid., pp 92–5. 4 Ibid., p. 183. Alexander III wrote letters to the bishops of Ireland, to the king and to the 'kings and princes of Ireland' in which he accepted the fact of the conquest and referred to the oaths of fealty sworn by the Irish (M.P. Sheehy (ed.), *Pontificia Hibernica: medieval papal chancery documents concerning Ireland, 640–1261*, 2 vols (Dublin, 1962–5), i, 19–23). 5 There was, of course, one very significant change which had nothing to do with Ireland: from being *rex Anglorum* he became *rex Anglie*. 6 Giraldus, *Expug. Hib.*, p. 264.

'kingdom' and he is fairly consistent in that usage throughout that work. Official records of the first quarter of the thirteenth century also contain many references to the 'kingdom of Ireland'.[7] This raises great problems.[8] How could Ireland be termed a 'kingdom' if it had no king until 1541 and if it was, to use a later term, a 'parcel' of the English crown? The formal style of the king of England as ruler of Ireland was *dominus Hibernie*, and what he exercised in Ireland was *dominium* or lordship. Historians commonly refer to the 'lordship of Ireland' in Middle Ages. But the proper term, the one used in all official records during the Middle Ages was *terra Hibernie*, the land of Ireland. Ireland was a land, just like Aquitaine or any other land under the dominion of the king of England. It was the 'land of Ireland', with certain reservations, which was granted to the young Edward in 1254.[9] But lordship was not included. The king, Henry III, remained lord of Ireland and retained that title in his royal style until the day he died. His son Edward never styled himself *dominus Hibernie*, but always simply *primogenitus* or 'first-born son'.[10] So that 1254 charter neatly made the distinction between land and lordship and points to the fact that the two were not necessarily inclusive of each other. He who held the land of Ireland did not necessarily possess the lordship of Ireland. Lordship was vested in the English crown and could not be alienated. This had not always been the case, as the 1177 arrangements at the council of Oxford made plain. As Gerald of Wales put it, when writing of the Lord John's expedition to Ireland in 1185, 'the lordship of the kingdom of Ireland [had] previously [been] transferred into his hands'.[11] But, by the mid-thirteenth century, the doctrine of inalienability had been clearly defined. The lordship of Ireland could no longer be separated from the English crown.

This remained true, right to the end of the Middle Ages. In 1388, Ireland was called a 'parcel' of the English crown. Later still, in 1474, when an Irish parliament sent Gilbert Debenham to the king with what it called 'enstruccyons youen and opened … to be presented and shewed for the hasty socour and relief of the said land to the kinges highnes in England', the messenger was given particular orders that he was to remind the king that 'his land of Irland … ys oon of the membres of his moost noble corone and eldest membre therof'. An Irish parliament in 1536 enacted a statute that 'the land of Ireland is parcell of the crown of England, governed by one prince and lord'. Finally, in 1541, an Irish parliament 'enacted, ordained and established by authority of the present parliament that the king's highness, his heirs and successors, kings of England,

7 When King John surrendered Ireland to the pope in 1213, it was as the *totum regnum Hibernie* (*Rot. chart.*, p. 195). In 1200 and again in 1205, Ireland was called a *regnum* (ibid., p. 71; *Rot. litt. claus., 1204–24*, p. 40). 8 As late as 1329, a memorandum of business to be discussed by the king's council in England contained an item that because 'our lord the king is named lord of Ireland and not king [Fr. *seigneur Dirlaunde et nient roy*] the prerogative ought to be held there just as in England' (*Affairs Ire.*, no. 164). 9 *Foedera*, i, 270. 10 See J.R. Studd, 'The Lord Edward and King Henry III', *BIHR*, 50 (1977), 4–19. 11 Giraldus, *Expug. Hib.*, p. 227.

be always kings of this land of Ireland'. Their kingship was to be forever 'as united and knit to the imperial crown of the realm of England'.[12]

That, then, was the constitutional or legal basis for Anglo-Irish relations throughout the Middle Ages. The lordship of Ireland was vested in the English crown and not in any one king or dynasty. This, of course, had all sorts of implications for the people of Ireland, some of which I examine later in this paper. But first I want to stress one consequence which had far-reaching effects. As lord of Ireland, the king of England at any given time had a duty to protect his subjects there, and it was to the crown that the liege people of Ireland looked. The king was the ultimate source of justice, patronage, reward and, where appropriate, retribution. It was to him, and only to him, that liege homage was due, just as it was to him that each man in Ireland owed loyalty, no matter who that man's immediate lord might be. If his subjects in Ireland had a responsibility to protect his lands, defeat his enemies, support him in his time of necessity, he in turn was bound to guard their rights and above all protect them in their property. When, in 1308, Edward II belatedly sent the statute of Winchester to Ireland, to help in maintaining the peace there, he said that he was all the more anxious about it 'because we are hereto bound by the bond of an oath'.[13] This reference to his recent coronation oath, which made him the protector of the realm, showed an awareness that Ireland was now inseparable from the English crown and that therefore he as king was bound to protect the land of Ireland. Protection normally included the defence of the liege people from enemies, who were nearly always, and by definition, the Irish. In 1357, when Edward III sent an important set of ordinances 'made for the state of the land of Ireland', he explained why in the past he did not 'provide defences and other remedies, as behoves us'[14] – thereby admitting the obligation on the crown to provide defence. Three years later, in 1360, a great council meeting in Kilkenny sent messengers to the king and his council in England informing them of 'the mischief, perils and state of your said land and your lieges of those parts', saying that they 'were on the point or being lost' unless they received what they called 'succour and remedy' from the king. This letter is often quoted because in listing the principal causes of their distress they included the Black

12 *Rot. parl.*, iii, 231; Bryan, *Great earl*, p. 22; Quinn, 'Bills and statutes', p. 142; *IHD*, p. 77. 13 *Stat. John–Hen. V*, p. 245. 14 Ibid., p. 412. In 1359, when he was about to set out for France, the king wrote to Ireland making provision for 'the government of Ireland … that it may remain safe during the king's absence from England' and explaining that he could not 'send men or money to Ireland at present, although it is said that they are needed there' (*CCR 1354–60*, pp 599–600). Good government was to be provided for the common good. In 1335, the Irish chancery issued a writ of *liberate* for the payment of £40 to Robert Poer for his expenses in keeping the peace *pro utilitate reipublice* (*RCH*, p. 41, no. 28). Interestingly, the Kilkenny chronicler Clyn used the same term when he described the earl of Ulster in 1333 as *reipublice et pacis amator* (*AClyn*, p. 25).

Death – 'the pestilence which is so great and so hideous among the English lieges and not among the Irish' – but for us the important part of the message is the conclusion. They asked for what they called 'a good and sufficient captain, stuffed and enforced by men and treasure' to save them and the land of Ireland, which was to be provided by the king 'as a noble and gracious prince is bound to do to his lieges [Fr. *come noble et graciouse prince est tenuz de faire a ses lieges*]'.[15] Similarly, the 1474 message reminded the king that he 'is bound to the defense of his land of Irland by resoun that it ys oon of the membres of his moost noble corone'.[16]

The defence of Ireland, then, was an obligation which the king of England could not shirk, and it was an obligation of which he was reminded from time to time. Perhaps the most famous of these reminders is contained in a political poem, *The libelle of Englyshe polycye* (*c.*1436). Its author was the first to emphasize the importance of sea power in English foreign policy. Control of the sea, and in particular of the English Channel, was vital to England's political as well as commercial interest. In this context, he stressed the importance of Ireland to England. Even the fact (as he thought) that Ireland was full of gold and silver, so that it could provide a solution to England's shortage of bullion, demanded that the king should provide there

pese and gode wylle
To myne and fyne and metall for to pure.

But it was the strategic importance of Ireland which demanded that the island be protected. Therefore the king was admonished

To kepen Yreland that it be not loste,
For it is a boterasse and a poste
Undre England ...[17]

Ireland was beginning to emerge as 'the back door to England', and the Yorkist plots later in the century were to demonstrate to all this dangerous fact. When Lambert Simnel, not long after he had been crowned Edward VI in Christ Church cathedral in Dublin, invaded England with a large army from Ireland, including the brother of the earl of Kildare and 2,000 German mercenaries under their captain Martin Schwarz, the new Tudor dynasty faced disaster.[18] The Perkin Warbeck plot shortly afterwards, though in retrospect it might assume the guise of a comic opera escapade, gave added emphasis to the potential danger of Ireland when used by foreign enemies of the ruler of

15 *Parls & councils*, no. 16. 16 Bryan, *Great earl*, p. 22. 17 *Libelle Eng. polycye*, lines 689–91, 700–2. 18 F.X. Martin, 'The crowning of a king at Dublin', *Hermathena*, 144 (1988), 20–4.

England. When O Domhnaill plotted with the king of Scotland, and the earl of Desmond with the emperor, it was time for the king of England to take seriously his responsibilities in Ireland.[19] The Tudor monarchy was subsequently forced to attempt a radical solution to the problem of the defence of the land of Ireland. Military conquest and plantation, however, proved to be an expensive solution, and one which was certainly beyond the resources of medieval governments.

For most of the Middle Ages, however, it was the enemy within which preoccupied successive governments. The author of the *Libelle of Englyshe polycye* argued that if some of the money wasted on a useless war in France were to be diverted to the war in Ireland, then the English could finally conquer Ireland in one short year. A final conquest was a hopeless proposition, however, beyond the capacity of any medieval king. But protection of subjects and their property against an enemy which was always there was certainly a duty which every English king had to accept. There were frequent reminders of this from Ireland, from individuals, from local communities, but most important of all from the *communitas Hibernie* (the community of Ireland) itself. Sometimes it was even suggested that Ireland would be lost if the king did not fulfil his duty to his subjects there, as in 1474 when he was told that 'thextreme subduyng and destrucyon of the sayd land as well by the Kynges Iryssh ennemys and Englysh rebelx, as by the meanes of Scottes which … proposen and dayly conspiren to subdue al thys land to the obeysaunce of the Kyng of Scottes'.[20] From time to time the king responded, sometimes in a spectacular way, by mounting large and expensive military expeditions to Ireland, as when Edward III sent his own son Lionel in 1361.[21] Budgets prepared in England to plan expenditure for the year ahead sometimes show how high a priority was given to what was always called simply 'the war in Ireland'.[22] In one short period, 1361–76, over £91,000 was spent on wages alone for the armies sent from England to Ireland.[23] To put this sum in perspective, we should remember that the total revenue of the Irish exchequer each year rarely came to more than £2,000.[24] So in the Irish context we are talking about astronomical sums – something like the total revenue of the Dublin government for over forty years.

The climax came with the two expeditions of Richard II, the only king (apart from King John in 1210) to discharge personally the obligations of the crown in Ireland. He brought the largest army to invade Ireland in the Middle Ages.[25] This is not the place to examine in detail the effect of his intervention. He had

**19** Conway, *Hen. VII & Ire.* **20** Bryan, *Great earl*, pp 18–19. **21** Philomena Connolly, 'Lionel of Clarence and Ireland, 1361–1366' (PhD, University of Dublin, 1977). **22** See, for example, Dorothy Broome and T.F. Tout, 'A national balance sheet for 1362–3, with documents subsidiary thereto', *EHR*, 39:155 (1924), 114–19. **23** Philomena Connolly, 'The financing of English expeditions to Ireland, 1371–76' in Lydon, *Eng. & Ire.*, p. 117. Of this, over £16,000 came from Irish resources. **24** Richardson and Sayles, 'Ir. revenue', p. 100. **25** See Lydon, 'Richard II's expeditions to Ireland' (below, ch. 13).

a vision of a new Ireland, in which all the inhabitants would be joined, where the lordship of the English crown would be established over the whole island and a new unity created in which the entire community, Irish as well as Anglo-Irish, would share as the king's lieges. All would become the subjects of the king of England, sharing his law and receiving his protection. Of course, he failed in this high ideal and, indeed, lost his crown in the attempt.[26] From that time on, English intervention was intermittent and half-hearted, except on occasions when the interests of the English crown were being seriously challenged in Ireland or when the lordship was posing a danger to the security of the king on a shaky throne in England itself. But at no time did a king ever relinquish lordship in Ireland, or consider relinquishing it, or contemplate reneging on his primary obligation of protecting his subjects there. That obligation to protect remained a permanent feature of Anglo-Irish relations to the end of the Middle Ages. If ever there was a danger of the king forgetting, or even diluting, the duty of a good lord to protect his subjects, then the community of the land of Ireland was quick to remind him.

Here we may ask what may seem a simple question, hardly worth asking. Who were the king's subjects? We now know that for English kings this was a complex question.[27] How did aliens living in England become denizens and acquire the rights of subjects? How did English living abroad, even members of the royal family, retain their status as subjects of the king of England? In Ireland the position was, if anything, more complex. By the time Henry II came to Ireland in 1171, the law of England seemed to be quite clear on the matter. To be born in territory within the dominion of the king made one a subject – and that vast territory henceforth included Ireland. So all were subjects, Irish as well as English, and it is true that from time to time we find the king addressing Irishmen as if indeed they were subjects. In July 1244, for example, twenty-one of the leading Irishmen (with the notable exception of Ó Conchobhair of Connacht) were summoned to join the king on his forthcoming expedition against the Scots.[28] Yet, from about the middle of the thirteenth century, the Irish as a race were excluded from the common law, the very badge of being a subject and the means by which a subject got from the king the protection to which he was entitled.[29] Apart from the so-called 'five bloods', the Irish had to purchase a charter of denizenship which would entitle them to avail of English law. Without it, they were aliens. So, although such charters were very expensive, many Irish who could afford to do so purchased them and so enjoyed

26 See, in general, Dorothy Johnston, 'The interim years: Richard II and Ireland, 1395–1399' in Lydon, *Eng. & Ire.*, 175–95; eadem, 'Richard II and the submissions of Gaelic Ireland', *IHS*, 22:85 (1980), 1–20. 27 Ralph A. Griffiths, 'The English realm and dominions and the king's subjects in the later Middle Ages' in idem, *King and country: England and Wales in the fifteenth century* (London and Rio Grande, 1991), pp 33–54. 28 *CR 1242–7*, pp 254–5. 29 K.W. Nicholls, 'Anglo-French Ireland and after', *Peritia*, 1 (1982), 372–7.

the benefit of the king's protection.[30] But the vast majority could not afford to do so and therefore suffered severe disability. In 1331, an English parliament enacted that that there should be one and the same law (L. *una et eadem lex*) for English and Irish in Ireland.[31] But that too seems to have been ineffective, and charters of denizenship continued to be purchased by Irishmen, especially in the fifteenth century.[32]

When, in 1360, the Kilkenny great council, consisting (as they said) 'of your lieges, your justiciar, council, prelates, peers and commons of your said land', referred to themselves as 'your liege subjects', they clearly excluded the Irish from that category. It was against those same Irish that they demanded protection, since they were the agents of that 'loss and destruction' which threatened.[33] The fact is that the protection which the king was obliged to extend to his English subjects in Ireland was normally against the Irish, who by the mid-fourteenth century were increasingly identified as enemies, so that to be *Hibernicus* (Irish) was tantamount to being *inimicus* (an enemy). The concept of natural enmity – that is, that every Irishman was by nature an enemy of the king's subjects in Ireland – was being well established long before the end of the Middle Ages. The identification of the Irish as 'wild' – an epithet which in contemporary European usage had come to mean 'uncivilized', 'not reasonable', 'savage' (the term that was normally used in French) – meant that they were not amenable to law and therefore could never be trusted.[34] In the sixteenth century, would-be social engineers who wished to transform Ireland through plantation or colonization adopted this as a self-evident truth, so that teaching the Irish civility (a polite way of civilizing them) became a basic principle governing all plans for 'reforming the state of Ireland'.[35] It was the necessary preamble for making the Irish equal before the law, something that the Anglo-Irish, and in particular the gentry of the Pale, believed to be next to impossible. The 1541 act, making Henry VIII king of Ireland, had the effect of making all the Irish subjects of the king. Sir Thomas Cusack made this clear to the English privy council. 'Wherefore before they were taken as Irish enemies', he said, they are now 'accepted as subjects' and in this way 'by good wisdom' they will continue 'in peace and obedience'.[36] But most of the Anglo-Irish knew better. The long tradition of regarding the Irish not only as 'enemies', but 'wild' as well, governed their attitude and explains their horrified reaction to the effect of the 1541 act. Without 'civility' no Irishman could ever be a true subject.

30 Hand, *Eng. law*, ch. 10. 31 *Stat. John–Hen. V*, p. 324. 32 Bryan Murphy, 'The status of the native Irish after 1331', *Ir. Jurist*, 2 (1967), 116–28. 33 *Parls & councils*, no. 16. 34 Lydon, 'The middle nation' (below, ch. 21). A petition of 1317–19 from the 'mean people of Ireland', asking the king to remedy the state of Ireland, refers to *les sauvages et les udives gents* who kill the loyal people (*Affairs Ire.*, p. 101). 35 Henry VIII laid great stress on civility: see Steven G. Ellis, *Tudor Ireland: crown, community and the conflict of cultures, 1470–1603* (London, 1985), p. 112. 36 Brendan Bradshaw, *The Irish constitutional revolution of the*

That, then, was another important strand in Anglo-Irish relations. In all their dealings with the English crown, the Anglo-Irish community consistently referred to themselves as 'the community of the land of Ireland' and took it for granted that their superior position to the Irish in law would be safeguarded. They had shown the strength of that conviction as early as the 1270s, at a time when Edward I was negotiating with the agents of the Irish, led by the archbishop of Cashel, for the purchase of a general grant of English law to the whole of Gaelic Ireland.[37] The king referred the whole matter to the Anglo-Irish. Writing on 10 June 1280 to the 'archbishops, bishops, abbots, priors, earls, barons, knights and all other English in Ireland', he said that he did not wish to make such a concession to the Irish without their consent, and he ordered that they should meet to debate whether or not such a grant could be made 'without prejudice to themselves, their liberties and customs'.[38] The grant was never made, and we can only conclude that a meeting of Anglo-Irish – a parliament or great council – objected on the ground that a grant would prejudice their status in the community of Ireland by making all Irishmen their equals before the law. So the Irish were left outside the law, with the status of aliens, and thus suffering the same kind of disabilities before the law which aliens in England had to endure. Because of that, they could never be true subjects of the crown, a fact which Richard II seemed to recognize when he tried to bring the heads of lineages back into the king's peace as liege subjects sworn to obedience. After arriving in Ireland, he wrote his famous letter to his council in England, in which he carefully distinguished between the 'wild Irish, our enemies' and a group which he called 'Irish rebels'. The latter can only have been 'rebels' because they were subjects who had betrayed their loyalty to the crown, and the king himself recognized that they had a legitimate grievance because they had never received justice. They were the ones he could turn into liege subjects.[39]

We have seen that the land of Ireland was a member of the English crown; that this imposed an obligation on the king as lord of Ireland to protect his subjects there; that the Anglo-Irish regularly reminded him of that obligation; and that, for all practical purposes, such protection was against the threat posed by the 'wild Irish', natural enemies of the Anglo-Irish, who were not fit to be subjects of the king. Yet, in 1488, when the king's ambassador Sir Richard Edgecombe was trying to impose unacceptable terms on Kildare and others who had been involved in the Simnel treason, they not only refused to accept those terms but uttered the ultimate threat – they would rather become Irish, they said, every one of them.[40] This was worse than crowning an imposter. It was a

*sixteenth century* (Cambridge, 1979), p. 234. As a result of this 1541 act making Henry king of Ireland, the term 'Irish enemy' ceased to be used subsequently in statutes (ibid., pp 265–6). 37 A.J. Otway-Ruthven, 'The request of the Irish for English law, 1277–80', *IHS*, 6:24 (1949), 261–70. 38 *CDI 1252–84*, no. 1681. 39 Johnston, 'Richard II and the submissions of Gaelic Ireland', pp 6–7. 40 Walter Harris, *Hibernica, or some ancient pieces relating to*

denial of the crown itself, a renunciation of their status as subjects, a repudiation of the constitutional links which bound the lordship of Ireland to the English crown – that very 'perpetual indenture and indissoluble chain' which Gerald of Wales had written about nearly three hundred years earlier.

Without getting involved in the origins and implications of that famous threat, it is clear enough that the Anglo-Irish did not mean it. They had no real intention of ever repudiating the crown. There is no evidence that the Anglo-Irish community, or even a substantial part of it, ever seriously considered breaking that link with the crown in the Middle Ages. Even when they refused to accept the first of the Tudors and crowned Lambert Simnel as 'Edward VI', they were preserving that link by maintaining what they considered to be the legitimate Yorkist line of succession in England. Yet they could utter that threat to Edgecombe in 1488 – and this was by no means the first occasion on which they had so acted. In October 1341, the Anglo-Irish meeting in parliament denounced the ham-fisted attempts at reform by the 'new men' sent over from England by Edward III.[41] A crisis was reached in July 1341, with the resumption of all grants made since 8 July 1307.[42] This horrendous proposal threatened the foundations of many a noble family in Ireland, and it is no wonder that, as the Dublin chronicler put it, there was 'a notable and manifest division between the English of England and the English of the land of Ireland' because of the crisis. But the same chronicler reflected a much more serious development in the Anglo-Irish position when he added that 'a great dispute arose in the land, and the land of Ireland was on the point of being utterly lost from the hands of the king of England'.[43] This certainly called in question the constitutional link which bound the lordship to the English crown. It can hardly represent the considered view of the majority of the Anglo-Irish. But the chronicler reported what may have been the kind of idle gossip on the streets of Dublin, or more likely what he heard around the corridors of St Mary's abbey, where many of the parliamentary representatives were staying. It certainly indicates that some people at least were so frightened or frustrated that they could adopt such a radical position.

Commenting on all of this, one writer has remarked that 'the outlook of the magnates was not "separatist" but "loyalist" – with all the ambiguity that epithet implied'.[44] Whatever about their loyalty to the crown – and as was stated earlier, there is no substantial evidence that the Anglo-Irish ever seriously considered repudiating the lordship exercised by the king in Ireland – it can certainly be argued strongly that the Anglo-Irish community which had found its political voice in 1341 was, or certainly became, separatist. They wished to assert that

*Ireland* (Dublin, 1770), pt 1, p. 32. **41** Robin Frame, 'English policies and Anglo-Irish attitudes in the crisis of 1341–1342' in Lydon, *Eng. & Ire.*, pp 86–103. **42** *CFR 1337–47*, p. 234. For comment, see Frame, *Eng. lordship*, pp 248–9. **43** *CStM*, ii, 383. **44** Frame, *Eng. lordship*, p. 331.

they were separate from the land of England, but not from the crown. That is why in 1487 Lambert Simnel was crowned not just king of England, but king of Ireland as well.[45] In 1487, the Anglo-Irish were anticipating what happened in 1541: there would be one king, but two kingdoms separate from each other.

The most famous occasion on which this high doctrine was clearly enunciated was, of course, in 1460: 'That whereas the land of Ireland is and at all times has been corporate of itself, by the ancient laws and customs used in the same.' The application of the radical theory of corporations to Ireland is startling and is a clear and unambiguous declaration of separateness. One symbol of that is that it had its own 'ancient laws and customs' – the very same 'liberties and customs' which Edward I had wanted to protect in 1280. The statute elaborated further: the land of Ireland was 'freed of the burthen of any special law of the realm of England, save only such laws as by the lords spiritual and temporal and the commons of the said land [Ireland] had been in great council or parliament there held, admitted, accepted, affirmed and proclaimed according to sundry ancient statutes thereof made'.[46] One interesting feature of this statute is that it is not declaring for the first time the independence of the Irish parliament, or that Ireland is not bound by the statutes of an English parliament. It is taking these things for granted as accepted facts, so that the independence of the great seal of Ireland might be established, and, more important, so that nobody in Ireland should be answerable to writs under the great seal of England.

> It has not been seen or heard that any person or persons inhabiting or resident in any other Christian land so corporate of itself, ought to obey any mandate within the same land given or made under any other seal than the proper seal of the same, by which any person should be had or compelled to go by any such mandate out of the same land.

What this famous statute enacted was not the independence of the Irish parliament, or freedom from statutes other than those enacted in an Irish parliament, or even that Ireland was a corporation – that was all accepted as self-evident truth. What the legislation enacted, by the authority of parliament, was that 'no person or persons being in the said land of Ireland, by any command given or made under any other seal than the said seal of the same land, [be] compelled to answer to any appeal or any other matter out of the said land'.[47]

45 *COD*, iii, no. 272: 'Edwardus dei gratia Rex Anglie et Francie et Hibernie'. Kildare is also called *locum nostrum tenente* in the same letter. 46 *Stat. Hen. VI*, p. 645. 47 Ibid., p. 647. This was the famous 'pretensed prescription' which was subsequently annulled by Poynings' parliament (Conway, *Hen. VII & Ire.*, p. 120). One of the 'articles' sworn to by Kildare in 1496 before the king and council in England was a promise to see to it that writs from England would be obeyed 'notwithstanding any Acte statute or custume had or made within the said land of Ireland' (ibid., p. 231). A great council that met at Naas in 1441 told the king

And also that 'any appeal of treason taken in this land be determined ... within the said land, and in no other place'.

The aim of the legislation may well have been to protect the person of the duke of York, already attainted by the Coventry parliament; but the effect was to state clearly that Ireland was separate from England, and therefore not subject to any laws enacted in an English parliament or writs issuing under the English great seal. A later statute enacted by the same parliament is equally explicit. This statute set up an Irish currency of lesser value than the English one, in itself good evidence of the separatist position of the Anglo-Irish community in 1460.[48] But if we examine the wording of the statute we find the same emphasis on Ireland's freedom from English laws, and a telling comparison is made with the duchy of Normandy and the duchy of Guienne, when they too were (as the statute puts it) 'under the same obedience of the realm of England'. Like them

> the said land of Ireland, although it be under the obedience of the said realm, is nevertheless separate therefrom and from all laws and statutes thereof, except such as are there by the lords spiritual, temporal and commons, of their own liberty, and freely admitted and accepted in parliament or great council.[49]

Note carefully the term used in the statute: *separate* from England. There is no ambiguity here.

Interestingly too, this parliament proceeded to order that two new coins should be minted, both with significant names. The first was to be engraved with the name *Ireland*, with a lion on one side and a crown on the other; and the other coin was to have the name *Patrick* engraved on it, with a half crown on one side and a cross on the other.[50] It can hardly be doubted that these new coins were to symbolize the land of Ireland, separate from the land of England, but under obedience to the crown. That, of course, posed another problem. If Ireland were under obedience to the crown, then the king could exercise his royal prerogative in Ireland no less than in England. We can see in the actions of both Edward IV and Richard III in their dealings with Ireland in the years after 1460 that both monarchs were indeed anxious to assert the royal prerogative there. But, by the late fifteenth century, it was difficult, if not impossible, to assert the superiority of royal authority over the authority of parliament, and certainly in the case of Ireland the king was unable to do that. Edward IV had to use the Irish parliament to enact legislation which would decide between contradictory

that the custom was that no one was summoned out of Ireland by English writs save in cases of treason against the person of the king, or a writ of error in parliament (Otway-Ruthven, *Med. Ire.*, p. 370). 48 See J. Moore McDowell, 'The devaluation of 1460 and the origins of the Irish pound', *IHS* 25:97 (1986), 19–28. 49 *Stat. Ire. Hen. VI*, pp 663–5. 50 Ibid., pp 665–7.

statutes by rival parliaments summoned by Kildare and the king's deputy Lord Grey.[51] The king might arbitrate, as indeed he did; but only an Irish parliament could overturn the legislation of another Irish parliament.

Here we are entering the murky waters of constitutional law, difficult enough in our own day, but much more complex in the fifteenth century, as evidenced by the contrary opinions voiced by eminent jurists like Fortescue.[52] The historian will perceive that, for whatever reason and whatever the implications, it was self-evident in 1460 that Ireland was separate from the land of England. A long tradition of Anglo-Irish separatism had found a remarkable expression in the legislation of that parliament.

How this tradition of separatism came into being is beyond telling here.[53] It is the story of the middle nation (as they called themselves), which discovered its own identity early on, became conscious of its history and tradition, its laws, customs and liberties, its own culture, which, while remaining English, was very different to that of England. It is too easy to dismiss the occasions on which that middle nation articulated its distinction as aberrations which have no bearing on the realities of political life in Ireland. Then as now, ambition, self-seeking and greed were the most powerful forces determining political action. But not always. Men who studied at the Inns of Court in London or at the great universities of England and Europe were not entirely ignorant of, or wholly uninterested in, the nature of authority in their contemporary world. They could and they did articulate that interest. The Dublin notary, James Young, who provided not just a translation but almost a new version suitable for Ireland of the pseudo-Aristotelian *Secreta secretorum*, cannot be dismissed too easily.[54] His patron, the fourth or 'white' earl of Ormond, for whom that book was written, was certainly ambitious and used politics for his own profit. But what was he doing with such a book? Why did he persuade Young to compose it? If he wished merely to adorn his library, he could have stocked much more suitable and less dangerous texts, as did the earl of Kildare later.[55] I would even go so far as to suggest that in late medieval Ireland there was a tradition of political speculation among the Anglo-Irish community which was to leave more tangible traces in the writings of the sixteenth century.

51 Gilbert, *Viceroys*, pp 592–9, for 'King Edward's directions concerning two parliaments held in Ireland'. It should be noted that Kildare subsequently caused to be enacted only those parts of the king's instructions which suited him; in particular, he ignored the command that the 1460 act 'restreyning that noo man within that land shuld be called out of the said land by any precept or commaundment made under the Kyng's grete seall, prive seall, or signett in England be utterly revoked and adnulled': see his legislation in *Stat. Edw. IV, pt 2*, pp 683–831. 52 In Tiptoft's parliament of 1467–8, it was acknowledged that 'the learned people of this land are of different opinions whether the said statute [of rapes] should be of force in this land without a confirmation had upon the said statute in this land', and the parliament agreed that it 'be ratified and confirmed and adjudged, by authority of this said parliament' (*Stat. Edw. IV, pt 1*, p. 619). 53 See Lydon, 'Middle nation'. 54 Steele, *Secreta*. 55 Bryan, *Great earl*,

There is one final strand in Anglo-Irish relations which played its part in shaping the political consciousness of the Anglo-Irish community. The crisis of 1341 brought into the open anti-English feelings which had been dormant for years. The Anglo-Irish strongly identified with Ireland, which they regarded as their *patria* or homeland. Anyone from England was regarded almost as a foreigner. Indeed, that was the very word used by Arnold Power on a famous occasion in the Dublin parliament of 1324 when he was trying to rouse hostility against the English bishop of Ossory, Richard Ledred. He reminded his audience that Ireland 'was wont to be called the island of saints' and never entertained heretics. But 'now if you please this foreigner comes from England and says that we are all heretics ... and because the defamation of this land touches the persons of all of us, it is the duty of all of you to take part against him'.[56] The foreigner out of England was the bishop of Ossory! Notice too the identification with Ireland and the pride in her history – the same pride which Richard Stanihurst was to manifest three hundred years later.[57] For that is the paradox of the Anglo-Irish. They paraded their Englishness, right to the very end. Indeed, that is how they were known in official terminology – they were always 'the English of the land of Ireland'. Yet, at the same time, they identified with Ireland and resented interference by foreigners from England.

In one sense, then, the nadir of Anglo-Irish relations was reached when the Anglo-Irish were formally classed as aliens in England. In 1441, the Irish council bitterly protested about this, saying that Englishmen born in Ireland should have the same rights in England as Englishmen born in England.[58] The Anglo-Irish naturally resented being classed as foreigners. But that was the way they were commonly perceived in England, at a time when contempt for all foreigners was rife.[59]

This naturally helped to stiffen among the Anglo-Irish a sense of their own separate identity. Over the years, that sense began to find expression in a pride in their own history, mainly through the work of Gerald of Wales. His *Expugnatio Hibernica* was translated into English, and abbreviated versions appeared to satisfy those who wanted the substance of the glorious achievements of their ancestors.[60] It is plain too that while stressing their Englishness and continuing to regard the Irish as 'wild' and lacking in 'civility', the Anglo-Irish assimilated part of the

pp 268–70. **56** Thomas Wright (ed.), *A contemporary narrative of the proceedings against Alice Kyteler* (Camden Soc., 1st ser., 24, 1843), p. 17. An early fourteenth-century petition from Ireland seeking remedies of problems reminded the king that when St Patrick came he 'found that there were no heretics in the land' (*Affairs Ire.*, p. 99) **57** Colm Lennon, *Richard Stanihurst the Dubliner, 1547–1618* (Dublin, 1981); Bradshaw, *Irish constitutional revolution*, pp 282–4. **58** Art Cosgrove, 'England and Ireland, 1399–1447', *NHI*, ii, 530 **59** Ralph Griffiths, *The reign of Henry VI* (London, 1981), ch. 8, 'Frontiers and foreigners'. **60** F.J. Furnivall (ed.), *The English conquest of Ireland, A.D. 1166–1185* (EETS, London, 1896). Even in a formal legal agreement of 1410, such pride could be reflected in a reference to when 'Sir William Rosselle was a conqueror of Ireland' (*Reg. Gormanston*, p. 17).

rich cultural heritage of Gaelic Ireland and even took pride in it. What one modern historian has called 'patriotic sentiment' characterized some of their later writings.[61] Identification with Ireland as their *patria* produced what one treatise in the early sixteenth century claimed to be a 'natural affection' for Ireland, which the Anglo-Irish called their 'native country'. Another wrote of them calling Ireland their 'own mother'.[62] National sentiment could hardly go much further. Such expressions of national identity in the sixteenth century were the result of generations of self-consciousness as a 'middle nation' and were the most important single result of Anglo-Irish relations during that time. That middle nation had managed to preserve its own identity and independence, while asserting a traditional loyalty to the English crown. It was when religious change forced the Anglo-Irish to face the terrible problem of a dual loyalty to two crowns – that of the papacy and that of England – that their real test as liege subjects of the king of England came. But in the Middle Ages, between 1171 and 1541, the Anglo-Irish (and for that matter most of the Irish as well) had no real crisis of loyalty. Ireland remained a 'parcel' of the English crown – indeed the 'oldest member thereof', as the Anglo-Irish community of the land of Ireland proudly reminded Edward IV in 1474.

61 Bradshaw, *Irish constitutional revolution*, p. 276. 62 *SP Hen. VIII*, ii, 167, cited in Bradshaw, *Irish constitutional revolution*, p. 276; *Salisbury MSS*, 24 vols (HMC, London, 1883–1976), i, no. 498, cited Bradshaw, *Irish constitutional revolution*, p. 281.

CHAPTER 2

# The chief governors of medieval Ireland*

*A.J. Otway-Ruthven*

Governmental institutions in Norman Ireland were inevitably modelled on those of England, developing on the same lines as the Middle Ages progressed with an increasing complication of organization. In twelfth-century England, central government was still the affair of the king and his unspecialized *curia*, dealing with a range of business within the competence of any man of normal ability and average experience of affairs. Certain specialized departments were indeed beginning to appear, but at the time of the Norman conquest of Ireland all this was still in its infancy, and the central government of the new colony was to begin with organized very much as that of England had been in the early twelfth century, developing the newer institutions as they developed in England, though usually rather later.

There was, of course, one major difference between the two governments: the king was almost never in Ireland, and never for more than a few months. But the twelfth century had seen in England the development of an office to meet a very similar position: that of the justiciar, who was the permanent head of the administration and governed for the king during his frequent absences on the continent. The office was ready made to be imported into Ireland, and after some initial vacillation the chief governor of Ireland normally had the title of chief justiciar or justiciar of Ireland till the later fourteenth century. The justiciar was an omnicompetent official in an age when specialization of governmental function was only beginning: he was at one and the same time the military chief of the colony, the head of its civil administration and its supreme judge, subject always, of course, to the over-riding power of the king, whose deputy he was. In the later fourteenth century, we begin to find the appointment of the king's lieutenants,[1] and, in the later fifteenth century, this becomes the normal title. Many of these lieutenants were absentees, who governed through deputies. We also find from time to time in the later thirteenth and fourteenth centuries keepers, whose appointment seems to have been of an emergency nature.[2]

* First published in *JRSAI*, 95 (1965), 227–36. 1 Up to 1377, there are detailed lists of chief governors in *Admin. Ire.*, 73–91. Lists for the whole period will be found in *HBC* [EN. See also *NHI*, ix, 469–85]. Gavaston was appointed as lieutenant in 1308, Mortimer in 1317 and the earl of Ulster in 1331, but no further lieutenant was appointed till 1361. 2 Wood, 'Office of chief governor', pp 210–12.

The chief governor, whatever his title, was normally appointed by the king, but there was a long-established and obviously necessary tradition, supposed in the fifteenth century to have been established by Henry II (the 'statute of fitz Empress'), by which should a justiciar die, leave the country without appointing a deputy, or be suddenly removed from office, the Irish council should appoint a successor until the king made other arrangements. This was probably done in December 1264, when the fitz Geralds took the justiciar prisoner and Geoffrey de Geneville acted as justiciar for some time, but the first definite record of it is in 1288, and further cases occur throughout the Middle Ages. In 1357, John de Bolton, the treasurer, was elected as justiciar on the death of Thomas de Rokeby 'by the council of those parts, with the consent of the community of that land'; in 1404, on the sudden departure of Stephen Lescrope, deputy of the lieutenant, without making any provision for the government of the country, a great council at Castledermot appointed the earl of Ormond as justiciar; and finally, in 1479, 'as there has been great ambiguity and doubt among the judges' as to the manner of election, it was decided that it should be done by the whole council, together with the archbishops of Dublin and Armagh, the bishops of Meath and Kildare, the mayors of Dublin and Drogheda, and the lords of parliament of the Pale.[3]

The powers of the justiciar are not detailed in early appointments, but are implicit in the oath prescribed for Maurice fitz Gerald in 1232: he was to swear to be faithful to the king; to render justice to everyone according to his lawful power, legal knowledge and the custom of the kingdom; faithfully to preserve the rights, liberties and dignities of the king. By the fifteenth century, lieutenants were taking an oath almost identical with the English coronation oath.[4] But in the thirteenth century, the powers necessary to fulfil these implicit duties were left largely unexpressed, and though in the fourteenth century they began to be listed in the commissions of chief governors, it was not till the fifteenth century that many powers which had certainly been exercised from the earliest times were formally conveyed by their commissions. Thus, as early as 1220, the king ordered the justiciar to redress complaints of his abuse of prisage; in 1342, it was expressly laid down that the chief justiciar or his lieutenant had power to take victuals and carriage for payment, according to the king's prisage and the usages reasonably accustomed. But the right of the chief governor to purveyance is not mentioned in any appointment till that of Thomas of Lancaster as lieutenant in 1401.[5]

3 *CCR 1354–60*, p. 375; *PKCI*, p. 269; *Stat. Edw. IV, pt 2*, pp 660–2; *Ir. parl.*, 330–1. See also *RCH*, p. 106, no. 26: the appointment of the bishop of Ossory by the council, as the earl of Ormond was released from office and his successor had not yet arrived (1379). 4 *CDI 1171–1251*, no. 1977; Gilbert, *Viceroys*, p. 485. 5 *CDI 1171–1251*, nos. 968, 971; *Stat. John–Hen. V*, pp 358–9; *CCR 1341–3*, p. 515; *CPR 1399–1401*, p. 507. Prisage and purveyance were the right to take goods whether the seller were willing or not. The existence of the associated

Though the title of king's lieutenant was clearly intended to convey a status higher than that of justiciar, it is hard to see that their powers differed very greatly in the fourteenth century. It is with the appointment of William of Windsor as lieutenant in 1369 that the commission begins to develop its completed form, but all the powers expressly granted to him had, in fact, been exercised by earlier justiciars. He was given power to admit into the king's fealty and peace English and Irish rebels, and to make them letters of pardon (subsequently explained as not extending to cases where a prelate, earl or baron had committed laity was loss of life or limb, or forfeiture of goods served for the king); to receive fines and ransoms made by them; to grant leases of lands recovered from the king's enemies, confiscated, or wasted by war and derelict; to supervise the king's ministers and remove the useless from office, appointing others (this power did not extend to the offices of the chancellor and treasurer); to do justice for all according to the laws and customs of Ireland; to order all things for the good rule and safety of the land and the recovery of the king's rights. The third and fourth of these powers were to be exercised in conjunction with the chancellor and treasurer.[6]

All these powers had, in fact, been exercised by earlier justiciars, whether by grant or not. The last two were implicit in the whole character of the office and were indeed expressed in the oath of 1232; of the others, the first and second were expressly granted to John de Charleton in 1337 and became a regular feature of appointments after this, though, in fact, charters of pardon seem to have been freely issued by earlier justiciars, except for a short period in the 1320s when, as a result of petitions to the king complaining that the power had been abused, it was temporarily withdrawn. The third power was expressly granted to John Darcy in 1329; while the fourth first appears in the grant to Geoffrey de Genville of the power to remove sheriffs and bailiffs in 1274, and then to Roger Mortimer in 1319 of the power to remove all officials except the chancellor, treasurer, the justice appointed to hold pleas following the justiciar (the later chief justice of the king's bench), and the chief justice of the bench. This very important power, usually excepting officers appointed by patent under great seal of England, was a normal feature of the powers of justiciars throughout the fourteenth century.[7]

There was thus nothing in the powers granted in 1369 which was not a normal feature of the justiciar's commission. Other powers were later added. In 1385, Philip de Courtenay was empowered to remove the common bench and

right to compel carriage, or transport, is clearly implied in an inquisition taken *c.*1260 (*Reg. Alen*, p. 103; and cf. *CJRI 1305–7*, p. 266). 6 *CPR 1367–70*, pp 221–2, 225. 7 *CCR 1323–7*, p. 10; *CCR 1337–9*, p. 155; *CPR 1317–21*, pp 317, 551; *CPR 1321–4*, pp 354–5, 363–4; *CPR 1327–30*, p. 373; *CDI 1252–84*, nos. 1021, 1025–7, 1032. We should note that in 1377 the Irish council, noting that the king's commission to Ormond as justiciar made no mention of charters of pardon, agreed that he should have this power (*RCH*, p. 103, no. 21).

exchequer from time to time, in conjunction with the council; in 1399, Thomas duke of Surrey might respite homages; while, in 1403, Thomas of Lancaster was empowered to receive fealties of archbishops and bishops and the homage of lay tenants.[8] In 1401, as we have seen, Thomas of Lancaster was expressly granted rights of purveyance. In 1413, John de Stanley was empowered to grant licences for the acquisition of lands in mortmain. In 1420, the earl of Ormond was given express power to summon parliaments and councils and to make statutes and ordinances in them, and to proclaim that the service due to the king (that is, military service or scutage) should be rendered; but in 1342, it had been expressly declared that 'it appertains to the justiciar to make summons to the king's service, whenever he sees that there be necessity to ride to war, in land which is at war'. In 1396, we find the power to make war on the king's enemies and rebels (which justiciars had certainly exercised from the beginning) first expressly mentioned, and it does not become a regular part of the commission till 1428.[9] As these clauses were added to the commissions of successive lieutenants they became permanent features, and while many, indeed most, of them had certainly existed in practice earlier, there was equally certainly a slackening of direct royal control in the fifteenth century which needs discussion at greater length than can be attempted here.

The justiciar's salary first appears in 1226, when Geoffrey de Marisco was granted £580 a year for the custody of Ireland. Two years later, it was fixed at £500 a year for Richard de Burgh, and this became the standard sum for the rest of the Middle Ages. But it was, of course, totally inadequate for the expenses of government, or even for those military expenses for which it was primarily intended (the theory seems to have been that it should provide for the custody of castles and for the justiciar's bodyguard, while other military expenses should be provided for by the royal service due to the king). For the year from Michaelmas 1277, the justiciar was paid £3,758 0*s*. 23½ *d*. 'for the maintenance of Ireland', besides a further £480 for unspecified purposes – a sum which had been steadily rising since the beginning of the reign, when it had been only £563 8*s*. 2½ *d*. for the year beginning at Michaelmas 1274. The grant of £500 a year to Stephen, bishop of Waterford, as justiciar, in 1285 recognized the facts and provided that, 'if disturbance arise in Ireland whereby it becomes necessary to fortify the king's castles and incur expense for the defence of the land', money shall be paid out of the exchequer for these purposes to a clerk appointed by the treasurer and barons – an official who later became a

8 Homage, which was much more solemn than fealty, might normally be done only to the king himself, but fealty, a simple oath to be faithful, might be done to an official. In 1299, Richard Tyrel, heir to Castleknock, did fealty to the king before the justiciar and in presence of the council (*CJRI 1295–1303*, p. 246). 9 *CPR 1381–5*, p. 540; *CPR 1396–9*, p. 29; *CPR 1401–5*, p. 212; *CPR 1413–16*, pp 53–4; *CPR 1416–22*, p. 256; *CPR 1422–9*, p. 475; *Stat. John–Hen. V*, pp 358–61.

permanent feature of the administration as the clerk for the wages of war. In 1295, this arrangement was repeated in the appointment of John Wogan, and his military obligation in return for the £500 was defined as the maintenance of 20 men-at-arms and as many armoured horses, presumably representing the knights of the king's household for whom robes and saddles had earlier been provided by the Irish exchequer, while some of them had had annual fees. It was first expressly stated that the justiciar was himself to be the twentieth man of the men at arms in the appointment of Edmund le Botiller in 1315, and this remained the fixed form throughout the Middle Ages.[10]

By the middle of the fourteenth century, justiciars and lieutenants alike were entering on their office by way of indenture with the king. These indentures, though they might contain other provisions, were primarily concerned with the military forces they were to maintain beyond the men provided by their fee, and the payments which they were to receive for them. In 1349, Thomas de Rokeby was to bring with him from England at the king's wages twenty additional men-at-arms, four of whom were to be knights, and forty mounted archers, whom he was to have for three months, 'the better to establish the peace of the land on his going thither'. After that he might have extra forces only by the advice of the council, and only 'for the time of an expedition to bridle the enemies'.[11] But with the increasing disorder of the second half of the century, such measures became too blatently inadequate to be continue; and in 1369, William of Windsor was to have the enormous sum of £20,000 for military purposes, and in 1373 the very considerable sum of £11,213 6*s.* 8*d.* for wages and reward for himself and a retinue of 200 men-at-arms and 400 archers for one whole year from the day of their landing in Ireland, as well as 500 marks a year for himself.[12] In 1372, Robert de Assheton as justiciar was by indenture to have 80 hobblers (light-armed footmen) and 200 kernes on foot, to be recruited locally and paid out of the Irish revenues (the Irish council decided to change these for certain English men-at-arms and archers, who threatened to return to England unless their pay was raised).[13] In 1385, Philip de Courtenay, lieutenant, was to have all the issues and profits of the land, including any subsidies granted for its government, and in 1413 John de Stanley was to have all the issues and profits of Ireland without accounting for them (by this time they were not very great), and in addition £2,000 a year from England without being bound to retain any specified number of men.[14]

By the later fourteenth century, it was becoming usual to appoint a chief governor for a term of years, no longer during pleasure. In practice, however,

10 *CDI 1171–1251*, nos. 268, 1413, 1577; *CDI 1252–84*, nos. 891, 1038, 1496; *CDI 1285–92*, nos. 122, 136; *CDI 1293–1301*, no. 267; *CPR 1313–17*, p. 207. 11 *CCR 1349–54*, p. 52. In 1344, Ralph de Ufford was to have 40 men-at-arms and 200 archers at the king's wages for his period of office (*CCR 1343–6*, p. 304). 12 *CCR 1370–4*, p. 345. 13 *CCR 1374–7*, pp 170–1. 14 *RCH*, p. 128, no. 15; *PPC*, ii, 130–1.

this did not secure as much continuity as might be thought, for all the chief governors, whether lieutenants or justiciars, had power to appoint deputies in their absence, and where the justiciars of the thirteenth and fourteenth centuries had normally remained in Ireland unless specially summoned to the king in England,[15] many fifteenth-century lieutenants remained in England, acting almost entirely by deputy, while even these deputies might themselves act by deputy. Thus, in 1405, Sir Stephen Lescrope, deputy of the lieutenant, Thomas of Lancaster, appointed the third earl of Ormond as his deputy, and again, in 1407, the fourth earl.[16] If the chief governor were in Ireland, these appointments were normally made by Irish letters patent warranted by him, but if he were not they were made by his own letters, which might or might not be entered on the chancery rolls. In 1423, the Irish council had grave doubts about the sufficiency of Edmund Mortimer's appointment of the bishop of Meath as his deputy, because it was under his own seal – the Irish chancellor had refused to admit the bishop to office without consultation with the council – but he was eventually admitted, and the point seems to have been settled by this. As with other offices in Ireland, if a deputy died during his term of office, his chief's appointment automatically came to an end. Thus, in 1454, the appointment of the duke of York had to be ratified because his deputy, Sir Edward FitzEustace, had died.[17]

From time to time, a chief governor, even though present in Ireland, might appoint a deputy to deal with a specific matter: in 1299, to hear a plea which 'cannot without difficulty be duly decided elsewhere than in the parts of Ros'; in 1389 and 1403, to hold local councils. In 1477, the deputy was even empowered to appoint 'any honest person' to hold parliaments if he were unable to do so himself. In the later fourteenth century, however, there appeared a tendency, even though the chief governor were present in the country, to appoint a deputy not for one specific occasion, but to govern a specific district. This was undoubtedly due to the growing pressure of war and breakdown and dislocation of government, and must often have meant only the handing over of areas such as Connacht to the locally dominant powers in the faint hope of preventing completely independent action. Thus when, in 1376, the earl of Kildare was appointed as justiciar, Stephen, bishop of Meath, was appointed as his subordinate to govern Meath and Munster. In 1384, deputies were appointed for Munster with power to do everything in the manner and form which the

15 Thus, in 1300, all the chief officials of the Irish administration seem to have been with the king at York (*CDI 1293–1301*, no. 710; *CChR 1300–26*, p. 27); and, in 1314, Theobald de Verdun and, in 1347, Walter de Bermingham were summoned to English parliaments as justiciars (*CCR 1313–18*, p. 199; *CCR 1346–9*, p. 413). 16 *RCH*, p. 179, no. 29; *COD*, ii, no. 391. In 1428, the Irish parliament complained of the frequent changes of governor (*RCH*, p. 247, no. 9). 17 *RCH*, p. 232, no. 1; *RCH*, p. 233b; *CPR 1452–61*, p. 202; and cf. Otway-Ruthven, 'The medieval Irish chancery' (below, p. 114).

lieutenant would use if he were present, and to issue writs which should have the same force as if they had been issued under the great seal. In the next few years, we find deputies appointed at different times for Connacht, Louth and Kilkenny; and in 1396, when Roger Mortimer was appointed as lieutenant, he was to act in Ulster, Connacht, and Meath – these were, of course, the lands of his inheritance – while William Lescrope was appointed justiciar in Leinster, Munster and Louth, though all writs were to be under Mortimer's sole testimony.[18] Under Henry IV, we find local deputies in Connacht, Ulster, Kildare and Carlow, though no later appointments seem to survive.

Like other officials, deputies were of course sworn in on taking office. Their powers are seldom detailed, but in 1407 when Ormond was appointed as deputy of Lescrope, himself the deputy of the lieutenant, he was given

> authority to keep our peace and the laws and customs of that our land, and to chastise and repress all, both English and Irish enemies, who rise against us and our peace and the laws and customs of the same for the purpose of preying and devastating of that land, and to repress and punish them by all means that seem best for the good governance of our land, lieges and subjects, according to the discretion of the said Earl, if necessary with the royal power and according to their demerits as abovesaid; or to make peace with them and reform them. Also that he may do all and singular that pertains to the office of deputy.

What this may have been is unhappily not stated, but was presumably substantially what the lieutenant might do, subject to any limitations as to the gift of offices and so on, which may have been stated in the indentures entered into when the deputy was appointed. We possess one such indenture, made in 1444 between Ormond as lieutenant and Sir Richard Nugent, baron of Delvin, appointed as deputy. Nugent is to receive 210 marks (£140) a quarter, half in cash and half in kind; £80 for the wages of his retinue and the balance for the expenses of his household. Elaborate assignments are made to secure the payment of this for the first quarter. Vacancies in offices which belong to the gift of the deputy by virtue of his office are, if they exceed the annual value of ten marks, to be filled by the advice of the deputy of the chancellor, the chief justice of the common place, the chief baron, and four other named persons, presumably all councillors; the same is to be done with benefices. The profits from the grant of offices are to go half to the lieutenant and half to the deputy. If any profit come to the deputy by making of peace or war with MacMahon, he is to divide it equally with the lieutenant. If any prisoner is taken during his term of office

18 *CJRI 1295–1303*, p. 260; *RCH*, p. 121, no. 77; *RCH*, p. 146, no. 190; *RCH*, p. 178, no. 78; *Stat. Edw. IV, pt 2*, pp 464–6; *CPR 1374–7*, pp 244–5; *CPR 1391–6*, pp 710–11; *CPR 1396–9*, pp 23, 29, 58, 62.

whose ransom exceeds 100 marks, he is to divide it equally with the lieutenant. He is to give no charter (of pardon) to certain named persons. The lieutenant is bound to find the deputy sixty archers in Co. Kildare and sixty in Co. Louth, with competent captains, to do him service at all places and times as long as there is no war in their own counties.[19]

This indenture vividly suggests the financial possibilities open to the chief governors, but we have not much other evidence as to the ways in which they might legitimately enrich themselves. The ordinance of 1323 provided that no justiciar or other minister in Ireland might purchase lands within the bounds of his bailiwick without special licence, and that for every bill of grace 4*d.* only might be paid for the justiciar's seal, and 2*d.* for the writing.[20] That their illegitimate rewards might be very considerable is suggested by the accusations made against Stephen de Fulbourne in 1284 and 1285: that he had abused his official position in every conceivable way for his own financial advantage, and 'his bishopric is by extent of the escheator not worth more than £46, and the bishop before he became treasurer and justiciar had no lands or property; as he can now spend, as he himself says, £1,000, it is plain that this increase was derived from the issues of the offices'.[21] There is, at any rate, only one known case of refusal to accept the office: that of Sir Richard de Pembridge, who in 1372, having been appointed as lieutenant and ordered to go to Ireland and there abide upon the keeping and defence of the land, utterly refused to take his journey according to the king's command, to the king's great displeasure for his ingratitude and disobedience.[22]

Who were these chief governors? From the beginning many were Norman-Irish magnates, though from time to time English administrators, such as Alan de la Zouche under Henry III, or John Darcy under Edward III, were sent over. From the appointment of Lionel of Clarence as lieutenant in 1361, there was an increasing tendency, becoming almost the rule in the fifteenth century, to appoint English magnates, who governed largely through deputies who were usually Anglo-Irish magnates. It is only occasionally that we can see them through the eyes of contemporaries, but the citizens of Dublin, writing to Edward II in October 1320, say that Mortimer, who had just returned to England, 'thought much of saving and keeping the peace of your land'; Thomas de Rokeby, who died as justiciar in 1357, is said by the annalist to have 'well fought the Irish, and well paid for his provisions, saying, "I will eat and drink from wooden vessels, and pay gold and silver for food and clothing and wages"'; and Thomas Cranley, archbishop of Dublin, justiciar in 1414, was praised by the Irish parliament as having governed justly and benevolently.[23] But

19 *COD*, ii, no. 391; *COD*, iii, no. 161. A statement of the way in which the office of deputy was to be exercised was entered on Ir. close roll, 19 Edw. IV (*RCH*, p. 270, no. 11; Gilbert, *Viceroys*, pp 598–9). **20** *CPR 1321–4*, pp 363–4. **21** *CDI 1252–84*, no. 2332; *CDI 1285–92*, no. 2. **22** *CCR 1369–74*, p. 420. **23** Gilbert, *Hist. & mun. docs*, pp 391–2 (the letter is

denunciations are much more frequent. Reference has already been made to the accusations made against Stephen de Fulbourne in 1285; Philip de Courtenay, lieutenant 1384–6, was removed from office on account of the complaints of his oppressions; John Talbot left Ireland in 1419 'carrying along with him the curses of many, because hee, being runne much in debt for victuall and divers other things, would pay little or nothing at all', and both he and John Stanley, who died as lieutenant in 1414, were accused more generally of extortions and oppressions, while Ormond was hotly denounced in 1444.[24]

But we cannot, of course, be sure that these views are impartial, and perhaps the most striking denunciation of all – that of Ralph de Ufford, appointed as justiciar in 1344, who died in office on 9 April 1346 – is highly suspect. The Dublin annalist tells us that on his arrival in July 1344, fine weather immediately changed to tempests and rain, which continued throughout his life. None of his predecessors had been comparable to him: he robbed rich and poor, clergy and laity, and neither observed the rights of the church nor kept the law of the kingdom. On his death, fine weather immediately returned, the people rejoiced, and the clergy celebrated Easter with especial joy.[25] But an examination of the facts suggests that the annalist was actuated mainly by strongly partisan feeling. Ufford's principal action had been to repress the rebellion of Maurice fitz Thomas, earl of Desmond, who – according to the sworn statements of a number of juries in the south and west – hoped to make himself king (as had been alleged fifteen years earlier), and who had certainly been in arms against the king's banner and had been outlawed when he refused to appear to answer the charges brought against him. The annalist cannot be supposed to have been entirely ignorant of the facts, some of which at least must have been the common gossip of Dublin, both in 1345–6 and earlier, in 1331–3; and, since he shows a marked partiality for Desmond and his associates in his account of both occasions, and represents Desmond, when he finally surrendered to a new justiciar in 1346 and was sent to the king in England, as going to seek justice for the injuries done to him by Ralph de Ufford, we may perhaps see his charges against Ufford as the reckless statements of a partisan. Certainly the Irish council, writing to the king shortly after Ufford's death, spoke warmly of him.[26]

undated, but since it mentions Kildare as Mortimer's deputy can only belong to 1320); *CStM*, ii, 392–3. **24** *RCH*, p. 128, no. 9; *RCH*, p. 126, nos. 205–6; *RCH*, p. 221, no. 111; *RCH*, p. 248, no. 19; Marlborough, *Chronicle*, p. 28; *Stat. Hen. VI*, pp 50–3. **25** *CStM*, ii, 385–9. **26** For the whole career of Desmond in the light of new evidence, see G.O. Sayles, 'The rebellious first earl of Desmond' in J.A. Watt, J.B. Morrall and F.X. Martin (eds), *Medieval studies presented to Aubrey Gwynn, S.J.* (Dublin, 1961), pp 203–2 [EN. The evidence concerning the career of Desmond has since been the subject of considerable revision. See Robin Frame, 'Power and society in the lordship of Ireland, 1272–1377', *Ire. & Brit.*, pp 215–18; Frame, *Eng. lordship*, pp 207–14, 262–74, 296–7; A.F. O'Brien, 'The territorial ambitions of Maurice fitz Thomas, first earl of Desmond, with particular reference to the barony and manor of Inchiquin, Co. Cork', *PRIA*, 82:C3 (1982), 59–88; Keith Alan Waters, 'The earls

Finally, we may note that in the performance of his varied functions the chief governor was from the beginning assisted by a council, which at first was inevitably of baronial composition. But as, in the course of the thirteenth century, the governmental structure of Ireland developed the specialized officials who had already appeared in England, the justiciar's council, or rather the king's council in Ireland, became, as in England, a primarily official body, afforced from time to time by the presence of certain magnates. But the continual council, which, with the chief governor as its president, supervised all the day to day business of government, was necessarily dominated by the officials who had to carry out that business; and, by the later fourteenth century, it seems that not only the chief justices and the chief baron of the exchequer, the chancellor and the treasurer, but also all the other judges, the keeper of the rolls of chancery, and sometimes other officials of less importance, were members of the council by right of office. It does not seem that anyone had a right to attend council meetings unless summoned, though obviously the chancellor and treasurer, with whom the justiciar was constantly directed to act, could not well be excluded. But otherwise, it seems to have been a matter for the chief governor's discretion who should be summoned to any particular meeting, or to deal with any particular matter. It was only very occasionally that he was ordered not to act without the assent of the whole council, though this was required in 1327 for the grant of pardons for felonies and for the release of prisoners or hostages taken in the time of the late justiciar.[27] From time to time, the official council was afforced by magnates, but there is no evidence that they concerned themselves with normal routine business.

Thus constituted, the council itinerated endlessly with the justiciar, just as the English council itinerated with the king, and had thus no fixed centre. In conjunction with the chief governor, it exercised all the powers of government: no detail was too small for it; nothing not expressly reserved to the king was too great.[28] But in everything they did, the chief governor and council in Ireland were of course subject to the over-riding control of the king. It is clear that close contact was kept, the normal method being for the justiciar, or the justiciar and council, to send messengers to the king, usually with detailed reports in writing setting forth the state of the country, while the king in turn sent emissaries 'to survey the state of Ireland' or to deal with specific matters. From time to time, justiciars were summoned to England 'to certify regarding the state of Ireland', and, particularly in the thirteenth century, a constant stream of directions on specific points was sent to them under the English great seal. This appears to slacken in the fourteenth century and later, but it is reasonably certain that, in

of Desmond in the fourteenth century' (PhD, University of Durham, 2004), pp 19–97].
27 *CCR 1327–30*, p. 134. 28 For the composition and functions of the council, see *Ir. parl.*, chs 3 and 12.

fact, the directions continued, though now under the privy seal and later the signet, the records of which have not survived. There was no doubt a slackening of direct royal control in the later Middle Ages, but we need not suppose that it was as great as the surviving records would suggest.[29] But given the slowness and uncertainty of communications between England and Ireland at any period of the Middle Ages, royal control was necessarily remote, and the importance of the part played by justiciars or lieutenants in our history can hardly be overstated.

29 *CDI 1171–1251*, nos. 379, 815; *Stat. John–Hen. V*, p. 3; *RCH*, p. 8, no. 75; *RCH*, p. 66, nos. 14, 22; *RCH*, p. 89, nos. 114–15, *RCH*, p. 102, no. 75; *RCH*, p. 103, no. 91; *RCH*, p. 216, no. 43; *RCH*, p. 240, no. 59; *RCH*, p. 243, no. 29; *RCH*, p. 245, no. 12; *RCH*, p. 252, nos. 37–9; *RCH*, p. 263, no. 21; *54th rep. DKPRI*, pp 30–1, 38, 39, 42; *CCR 1360–4*, p. 157; *PKCI*, pp 255–7, 261.

CHAPTER 3

# William of Windsor and the Irish parliament*

*James Lydon*

William of Windsor, lieutenant from 1369 to 1372, and governor and keeper between 1373 and 1376, was one of the most controversial English officials to govern Ireland during the Middle Ages.[1] An Irish chronicler summed up the contemporary Irish opinion of Windsor when he described him as *nimis cupidus*,[2] a phrase which has found a modern echo in Miss Clarke's portrait of Windsor as a grasping colonial official who was determined to wring as much money as he could out of unwilling and overburdened colonists.[3] Whatever the truth of this, there can be no doubt that his career in Ireland was a stormy one. He antagonized the commons of the Irish parliament to such a degree that they mounted a vigorous, and even vicious, attack on him and his administration, accusing him of bribery, extortion and peculation while he was in office.[4] The result of these charges, and of the detailed investigations of them in Ireland, is that Windsor's career is better documented than that of any other chief governor in the Middle Ages. In particular, his relations with the Irish parliament, and more especially the commons, were closely investigated, so that a mass of evidence is now available on the history of that parliament during a critical stage in its evolution.[5] In recent years, this evidence has been subjected to careful scrutiny by three scholars, first by the late Maude Clarke, and more recently by Mr Richardson and Professor Sayles. They reached widely different conclusions. Miss Clarke, in her pioneer study, thought that under Windsor's influence 'the

* This paper was read to a meeting of the International Commission for the History of Representative and Parliamentary Institutions, held in Dublin in Aug. 1963. The theme discussed at the meeting was 'Representatives and their powers'. The essay was first published in *EHR*, 80:315 (1965), 252–67. 1 For Windsor's career in Ireland, see Clarke, 'Windsor'; *Ir. parl.*, pp 80–5. The accounts in Curtis, *Med. Ire.*, and M. McKisack, *The fourteenth century, 1307–1399* (Oxford, 1959), pp 386–7, are based on Clarke and need to be corrected. 2 *CStM*, ii, 282. 3 'The detailed evidence of the enquiry into his administration shows him to have been a vigorous and greedy representative of the Crown' (Clarke, 'Windsor', p. 71). 4 Much of the relevant documentation has been printed by Miss Clarke in the article cited above, but a substantial addition was made by Richardson and Sayles (*Parls & councils*, pp 26–86, esp. no. 28). In the introduction to this volume (at p. xxiv), the editors draw attention to other important sources in print [EN. To which list, add *Affairs Ire.*, nos. 234, 241–2]. 5 Many of the financial records of Windsor's administration survive in TNA (PRO).

Irish parliament acquired the shape, coherence, and functions which it retained until the Reformation', so that Windsor is almost entitled 'to be styled the true founder of the Irish parliament'. She regarded the charges brought against him as substantially true and she saw him as the focal point in the English movement of resistance against the dominant court party at whose centre was Alice Perrers, the mistress of Edward III and the wife of Windsor.[6] Mr Richardson and Professor Sayles are loath to believe the charges against Windsor. They see him as the victim not of his own avariciousness and will to power, but of the preoccupation of Edward III with his continental wars, which prevented him from adequately financing an Irish war. They point out that it was impossible to sustain adequately a war in Ireland 'unless there was peace with France, the condition under which Richard II was to undertake his expedition to Ireland'.[7] Windsor is, therefore, not to be blamed for what he did in Ireland. Nor do they agree with Miss Clarke's suggestion that changes of far-reaching importance are to be associated with Windsor's career in Ireland.

To my mind, Richardson and Sayles offer the more convincing argument. But it is not my purpose here to investigate the truth of the charges brought against Windsor, because I intend to use only that part of the evidence which was never denied by Windsor and his supporters, and which can, therefore, be accepted as the truth. However, it is important to know something of Windsor's career in Ireland, which brought about these charges, and to try to understand what Windsor was trying to do. Only in this way can we understand his relations with the Irish commons, an understanding which is vital if we are to appreciate the crux of the quarrel between them. For I hope to show that the issue was a simple one which, interpreted rightly, can throw light on the whole question of representatives and their powers in Ireland at that time.

His career can be briefly outlined. He first came to Ireland in the company of Edward III's son, Lionel, earl of Ulster and later duke of Clarence.[8] Windsor was one of the people who supplied large contingents for Lionel's army, and he seems to have remained in Ireland for a number of years, with one break, possibly until 1366, when Lionel returned to England.[9] He had, therefore, first-

6 Clarke, 'Windsor', pp 56–7, 77. 7 *Ir. parl.*, p. 85. They also point out (ibid., p. 81) the very important fact that Windsor's financial support from England was inadequate. 8 No adequate study of Clarence in Ireland has yet been made, despite the profusion of material in TNA (PRO) [EN. This lacuna has since been filled by Philomena Connolly's doctoral dissertation, 'Lionel of Clarence and Ireland, 1361–1366' (PhD, University of Dublin, 1977)]. Professor Sayles has suggested to me that the continuity between the expeditions of Clarence and the later ones of Windsor is important, that they are all part of the same effort at reconquest. This, I think, is true. They failed for want of adequate support from England. 9 Windsor contracted with the king on 10 June 1362 to supply a force of sixty men-at-arms and sixty archers for one year from 24 June (E 101/68/4, no. 82 [original indenture]; copy in E 101/28/27, r. 5). In fact, he served for nearly a month longer than the stipulated year (E 101/28/22, fos. 8*v*–9 [book of particulars of Walter Dalby, clerk of the wages]). He also

hand knowledge of Ireland, particularly as a soldier, before he was appointed lieutenant of the king in 1369. That appointment lasted until early in 1372. As lieutenant, he had charge of the king's government in Ireland. He waged war on a lavish scale, as is witnessed by the cost of his military enterprises.[10] But he was also responsible for some notable reforms in the administration of Ireland, in the exchequer – an aspect of his career which has so far been overlooked.[11] In the course of trying to procure additional revenue, he ran foul of the commons in parliament and, from 1371 onwards, complaints against him began to reach the king in England. Eventually, these reached such a volume that Edward III recalled Windsor and ordered an inquiry into his administration in Ireland. Despite the evidence produced against Windsor by this investigation, however, the king was satisfied that the charges brought against him were without foundation and, late in 1373, he was reappointed to office in Ireland. This time he was given the new title of governor and keeper; his powers were increased so that, when he returned to Dublin early in 1374, he was able to carry out his financial policy with greater vigour than before. But again, the commons refused to cooperate and an impossible situation developed, with both parties at loggerheads with each other. The king sent a special agent to Ireland in an effort to break the deadlock, but to no avail. So once again, in February 1376, Windsor was ordered to England, together with the principal officers in his administration and representatives of the Irish commons. New charges were formulated against him, more extravagant than the previous ones. These were presented to the English council and some of the more important Irish officials were brought to trial. By now, Irish affairs were entangled with developments in England during the period of the Good parliament; and although Windsor surrendered himself to stand his trial, late in 1376 all proceedings against him were dropped. The chief officers of the crown in Ireland were dismissed, a new justiciar was appointed and Windsor's connection with the country was severed for good. No further action was taken against him. As Miss Clarke has said: 'Like so many other attacks on the medieval administration, the whole agitation ended in a confused compromise.'[12]

brought an additional six archers (E 101/28/27, r. 5). A roll of the names of his retinue has survived (E 101/28/13), together with a list of his horses and their value (E 101/28/11, m. 2). He came back to Ireland with another retinue in Feb. 1364 (E 101/28/22, fos. 16*v*–17*v*; E 364/3, r. 7*d*), but I have no information on how long he stayed. It is probable that he contracted for one year's service. **10** There is a great deal of information available on the size and composition of the retinues of Windsor in Ireland, but it is far too complex to be analyzed here. The most important sources are (enrolled accounts) E 364/7, m. 7; E 364/12, m. 1; E 364/13, m. 6; E. 364/17, m. 7; (particular accounts) E 101/29/33, 30/1–2, 31/25, 33/3, 33/35–8 (these last four are retinue rolls). **11** For example, he instituted a new system for compiling the memoranda rolls, based on the English system. See his letter of 11 July 1369 to the treasurer and barons of the Irish exchequer (NAI, RC 8/30, pp 98–100 [Ir. memo. roll, 47–8 Edw. III]). **12** Clarke, 'Windsor', pp 65–6.

Windsor was typical in one respect of many of the governors who came to Ireland in the fourteenth century. He came as a soldier, with an army – a *miles strenuus in armis et animosus*, as the chronicler calls him[13] – and his primary task was to restore law and order in Ireland by means of that army and the armed forces he could raise in the colony. This meant a war policy – war on the Gaelic princes who were recovering so much of the land of Ireland, and on the degenerate or rebel English who, for one reason or another, were defying the authority of the king's government in Ireland. It is impossible to regard him, as Miss Clarke saw him, as a fourteenth-century Wentworth, coming to Ireland with a policy of 'thorough', determined not only to make Ireland pay her way, but to supply a surplus of cash which he would make available to the English king. Such a view cannot be harmonized with the facts, as we know them, of the contemporary situation in Ireland. It is necessary to know these facts if we are to understand what Windsor tried to do and, more important, understand the violence of the reaction which met his efforts. The first fact which we must keep in mind is that Gaelic Ireland had begun a remarkable recovery. Such was the strength of the Gaelic position that the Dublin government, and even Windsor himself, had to fall back on the desperate expedient of buying off the chieftains (or captains of their nations, as the English called them) as dubious allies; or more frequently paying a sort of blackmail (black rent, as it was called) to the more powerful chieftains in order to secure, at best, an unfavourable neutrality in the never-ending wars.[14] As the area controlled by the government declined, so did the state revenues. There is a definite connection between these two factors, though there were other, less important, reasons for the falling off in exchequer receipts throughout the fourteenth century.[15] This financial decline had been made vividly clear, to the embarrassment of the government, during the crisis of the Bruce invasion early in the century.[16] During the interval between then and the arrival of Windsor in 1369, the situation had shown no signs of improving; if anything, it worsened. That is the second fact which is important. A consequence of that was that the Irish government became financially dependent on England. Hitherto, it had been a source of profit; now, during the fourteenth century, it gradually became a liability.[17] The Irish

13 *CStM*, ii, 282. 14 Many such payments figure on the Irish issue rolls. See, for example, those on the roll for 1365–6 (E 101/244/10) under *Dona et concessiones regis* and *Vadia Hibernicorum*. 15 For the decline in exchequer receipts, see Richardson and Sayles, 'Ir. revenue', pp 87–100. 16 J.F. Lydon, 'The Bruce invasion of Ireland' in G.A. Hayes-McCoy (ed.), *Historical studies IV: papers read before the fifth Irish Conference of Historians* (London, 1963), pp 119–20 [EN. Repr. as 'The Bruce invasion of Ireland: an examination of some problems' in Seán Duffy (ed.), *Robert the Bruce's Irish wars: the Scottish invasions of Ireland, 1306–1328* (Stroud, 2002), pp 71–88]. 17 For details, see Richardson and Sayles, 'Ir. revenue', pp 89–90, 91; and James Lydon, 'Edward II and the revenues of Ireland in 1311–12', *IHS*, 14:53 (1964), 39–57.

government found that its meagre income was inadequate to cope with the resurgent Irish and the rising tide of lawlessness and disorder. And so most of the large-scale military enterprises against the insurgents had to be financed by England.[18] This financial drain on England is the third important fact to be remembered.

Another result of the Gaelic revival and the decline in the ordinary revenue of the government was an increase in taxation. The burden of waging war in the localities fell upon the local communities and could be met only by local taxation. The development of this system of levying subsidies for local purposes in Ireland, a system which has no real parallel in England, cannot be discussed here. But it seems to have been well established even as early as the reign of King John, from which time it became a permanent feature of medieval Ireland.[19] At any rate, the incidence of local taxation seems to increase during the fourteenth century.[20] This is a most important factor which has, I think, been sometimes given a wrong emphasis.[21]

It does not mean that parliamentary taxation, as distinct from taxation on a local basis through individual negotiation with each local community, was slow to develop in Ireland. Local taxation of this kind was necessary in Ireland because of the peculiar conditions which were present throughout the Middle Ages. The prevalence of local wars, and the adoption of the principle that the local community must bear the main burden of that war, meant that local taxation persisted as long as these two conditions prevailed. But side by side went the steady growth of parliamentary taxation, not, indeed, as an alternative to local taxation, but as an adjunct to it in time of crisis. In fact, I would suggest that the principle of parliamentary taxation was already well established in Ireland long before the advent of William of Windsor, and perhaps even as early as the reign of Edward I. It is true that local particularism always remained strong in Ireland and may even have made the development of parliamentary taxation especially difficult; but the evidence provided by writs of summons to parliament, which is discussed below, seems to show the principle of parliamentary taxation developing from the end of the thirteenth century. The prevalence of local taxation, then, which was a burden on the commons of Ireland, is another fact to keep in mind. Some others might have been added – such as the high incidence of absenteeism, which left lands defenceless, increased the dangers the liege people of Ireland had to face, and added to the burden they already carried. But the main facts of the situation are the ones already outlined: a successful Gaelic resurgence; declining state revenues; financial dependence on

**18** The most outstanding example is the expedition of Clarence, which up to Aug. 1364 cost more than £22,000 (E 101/28/22, fo. 16*v*). **19** *Ir. parl.*, p. 51. **20** Ibid., pp 115–16. **21** Clarke, 'Windsor', 66–71; D.B. Quinn, 'The Irish parliamentary subsidy in the fifteenth and sixteenth centuries', *PRIA*, 42:C11 (1935), 219–22; Joseph R. Strayer and George Rudissil, 'Taxation and community in Wales and Ireland, 1272–1327', *Speculum*, 29:2 (1954), 414.

England; and an increase in taxation. How then is it possible to suggest that William of Windsor was charged with the task of making the English colony in Ireland a source of profit to the king, such as it had been in the thirteenth century? Quite obviously, his administration had no such purpose. His main function was to recoup losses by waging war, to restore peace if possible and, finally, to make Ireland pay her own way. This could only be achieved at a heavy price, to be met in the first instance by England. When Windsor entered the king's service, his indenture, which laid down the conditions of service, specified that he was to be paid the sum of £20,000 for the maintenance of himself and his retinue in Ireland.[22] And, during his second period of service, he contracted with the king for the payment of more than £11,000 for the service of himself and his men during the first year in Ireland.[23] The cost to England, therefore, was heavy. But Ireland too was expected to share this burden. In one of his letters, Edward III recounts how he had

> incurred great costs and expenses upon the upkeep of the war in Ireland without taking any revenues or profits therefrom, and neither the king nor his subjects of England can comfortably bear these expenses in the same way as they bore those formerly occasioned by the wars with France and Spain.[24]

And, in another letter, he says that he 'cannot support such expenses any more, especially as he has divers wars elsewhere'.[25] Where could an impecunious Irish government find money to help to pay for the costs of these wars? Obviously, the only answer was in an Irish parliament, which would grant subsidies and new customs on a national scale. Windsor had no alternative, therefore, but to have recourse to taxation. And it was this which brought him into contact with the Irish commons, for on them the main burden of this new taxation would fall.

During his first period in office, Windsor summoned four parliaments and four councils; and, on his second visit, three parliaments and one great council.[26] In every one of these twelve assemblies, held in the short space of less than five years, he requested a subsidy of some kind. It is quite clear, in fact, that the main, if not the only reason for summoning these parliaments and councils was financial. Hence, representatives of the commons and eventually proctors for the lower clergy were summoned to most of them.[27] But it was these same

**22** E 101/68/4, no. 82. **23** E 101/33/3; E 364/13, m. 6; *CPR 1370–4*, p. 345. **24** *CPR 1374–7*, p. 117. **25** Ibid., p. 120. **26** These are listed in *Ir. parl.*, pp 341–3. **27** The one meeting to which we know for certain that representatives of the commons were not summoned was that at Cashel in 1371. From Windsor's own account of what happened there, it is clear that this was an afforced council, to which only magnates from the district were summoned. To Windsor's request for advice about a subsidy the magnates replied 'quod absque parliamento in quo omnes prelati, magnates et communitates dicte terre Hibernie essent congregata ipsi de materia predicta consilium dare noluerunt' (*Parls & councils*, p. 44).

representatives who resisted the request for subsidies, when the prelates and magnates seemed willing to comply. According to complaints sent to the king, they refused assent to the new taxation because of their losses in the Irish wars and the heavy burden of taxation.[28] When Windsor, despite their protests, went ahead with the levying of the disputed subsidies, the king was forced to order a halt. He did so because he was convinced, temporarily at least, that they had been 'unlawfully laid' upon the people.[29] And, when he finally ordered the assessment and levy to go ahead, it was because he was now convinced that the subsidies had been 'granted of their own free will by the lords, nobles and commons of Ireland' in parliament, and were therefore lawful.[30] One thing, therefore, is patently clear. The principle of parliamentary consent to taxation was accepted by the king and Windsor on the one hand, and by the Irish commons on the other. Without the free consent of the commons in parliament, the subsidies were not lawful.

This was something Windsor never disputed. On the contrary, he consistently maintained, and succeeded in convincing the king of the truth of his claim, that consent had been sought of, and freely given by, the commons. The argument put forward by the commons was not that they had withheld consent in parliament, but that their consent was not voluntary. They complained of the pressures brought to bear on their representatives by Windsor in order to procure their consent. The commons of Co. Meath, for example, said that on 8 June 1371 a parliament was held at Ballyduagh, a waste place where there were no suitable buildings to house their representatives and where no provision had been made for feeding them. At the parliament, Windsor asked for a subsidy, but the representatives refused their consent. After three days' resistance, however, worn out by their stay in that place and by the tedium of their argument, they capitulated and gave their consent. But it was not, they said, freely given.[31] At another parliament, it was claimed, the representatives of Co. Louth were thrown into prison by an angry Windsor when they refused to agree to his request for a subsidy.[32] These are typical of the complaints made by the commons of other shires and towns. They gave their consent, 'per cohortionem locum tenentis', and the subsidies are being levied 'contra voluntatem communitatis comitatus', or 'encountre lour volunte par extorsion'.[33] Indeed the commons of Co. Meath accused Windsor of coercing one of their representatives at the parliament at Kilkenny in January 1372 to seal a letter to the king stating that the subsidies had been granted by him 'de mera et spontanea voluntate'.[34]

Subsidies are a matter for a full parliament, to which representatives of the commons must be summoned. **28** Clarke, 'Windsor', pp 114, 117; *Foedera*, iii, pt 2, p. 977. **29** *CCR 1369–74*, pp 246, 257, 265, 380. **30** Ibid., p. 529. **31** *Foedera*, iii, pt 2, p. 978 [EN. The correct location of this parliament is Ballydoyle, par. St Patrick's Rock, bar. Middlethird, Co. Tipperary]. **32** *Foedera*, iii, pt 2, p. 977. **33** Clarke, 'Windsor', pp 114, 87; *Foedera*, iii, pt 2, p. 977. **34** Clarke, 'Windsor', p. 115.

The truth of these accusations does not concern us. But they do establish the elementary principle which both sides in the quarrel accepted. One of the powers exercised by the commons in parliament was the granting or withholding of subsidies.[35] There can be no question about that. Indeed, so firmly is this accepted that we are forced to conclude that the principle of parliamentary taxation was well established before this in Ireland. If we look again at the complaints made by the commons of Co. Meath about the subsidies granted in parliament, we see that they admitted that the subsidies were assented to by their representatives, 'nomine dicte communitatis'.[36] Clearly, then, the assent of the representatives would bind the communities they represented: they were, in fact, the attorneys of those communities. Windsor appreciated this fact and, once he had procured consent in parliament, he acted in the belief that this consent was binding on the communities. Why, then, did the commons of Co. Meath, to take one example, refuse to accept the legality of these subsidies? They said that they had tried to bind their elected representatives before they went up to parliament not to agree to a subsidy – thus implying that they accepted the principle that they would be bound by whatever these representatives agreed to in parliament. But this was not the basis for their objection to the levying of the subsidies. Their representatives had given their consent in parliament, but, because it was not freely given, it was not legally binding. This was their argument. Had such consent been voluntary, then the community would be bound by it. In order to develop this argument, it is necessary to look more closely at the credentials of the representatives elected by the shires, liberties and boroughs in Ireland. It must be admitted at once that the almost complete dearth of information on this subject makes it impossible to examine it in any detail. Hardly any writs of parliamentary summons have survived, practically no returns to such writs, and almost no information on elections, expenses paid, and matters of that kind. But enough has survived to make an investigation worthwhile and to enable us to arrive at definite conclusions of a general nature. The surprising thing is that, so far as I am aware, no investigation of this kind has been made before. And yet, without such an inquiry, we cannot discuss the question of representatives and their powers. The writs summoning representatives of the commons to parliaments and councils convened by William of Windsor preserved a more or less common form. The

35 During the discussion which followed the reading of this paper in Dublin, the question was raised whether the commons could, in fact, refuse to grant a subsidy. Whatever the practice in England, in Ireland the commons quite clearly believed that they had the right to refuse outright a request for a subsidy. The charges against Windsor show this; but even clearer evidence is an example, to be discussed below, of an outright refusal to the request of the king, made through his special agent Nicholas Dagworth, in the Kilkenny parliament on 9 Oct. 1375.
36 *Foedera*, iii, pt 2, p. 977. The king, in ordering the suspension of the collection of disputed subsidies, stated that under duress the representatives of Dublin and Drogheda had granted sums to Windsor 'for themselves and the commonalty' (*CCR 1369–74*, pp 246, 265).

sheriff of the county or cross (church land in a liberty, which was under royal administration), the seneschal of the liberty, the mayor and bailiffs of the town are ordered to cause two of the best and most sufficient men of the community to be elected to attend the parliament. They are to be elected 'de communi assensu et voluntate' of the community. It was understood that they were to be paid their reasonable expenses.[37] And finally, and most important of all as far as we are concerned here, they are to have full power to treat and advise, to do and to consent to what must be done in parliament.[38] It is the inclusion of such a *plena potestas* clause to which I wish to draw particular attention. It is now generally accepted that the evolution of such a clause in English writs of summons had important consequences. Sir Goronwy Edwards showed that in England the development of a formula in the writs, by which it was required that the representatives should be given *plena potestas* to bind their communities, was almost completed by 1295; and that this marked an important transition from the belief 'that consent to taxation should be a personal, individual consent' to the idea of parliamentary taxation binding on all.[39] If this is true, then surely the appearance of a similar *plena potestas* formula in Irish writs must also have had important consequences. Now, it is interesting to discover that such a formula appears in Ireland almost as soon as in England. The first Irish parliament for which we have proof of this is the Dublin parliament of 1297. No writs of summons are extant, but the account of the parliament in the Black Book of Christ Church describes the summonses.[40] We learn that the sheriffs of Dublin, Louth and the other counties, and the seneschals of the liberties, were ordered to assemble the full county or liberty court, and there to cause two knights to be elected by the community, the knights having 'plenam potestatem de tota communitate comitatus et libertatis etc. ad faciendum et recipiendam etc.' Unfortunately, the formula is not quoted in full, but there can hardly be any doubt that it approximated to the formula then in use in England. For all we know, such a formula went through much the same process of development in Ireland as in England. At any rate, it is in use by 1297. The next parliament for which we have knowledge of the summonses sent to the counties is the Dublin parliament of 1300. And again the formula is included, this time in more specific terms. The counties and boroughs are to elect two, three or four to represent them, 'specialem potestatem habentes ac si omnes fuissent presentes'.[41] It could hardly

37 While this is not stated in the writs of summons, it is shown by other evidence. See, for example, *CCR 1374–7*, pp 373, 374. 38 Lynch, *Legal institutions*, pp 319–20. 39 J.G. Edwards, 'The *plena potestas* of English parliamentary representatives', *Oxford essays in medieval history presented to Herbert Edward Salter* (Oxford, 1934), pp 141–54. 40 *Stat. John–Hen. V*, pp 194–212 [EN. For a new edition and translation of this text, see Philomena Connolly, 'The enactments of the 1297 parliament' in Lydon, *Law & disorder*, pp 139–61]. 41 *Stat. John–Hen. V*, p. 230. The use of the adjective *specialem* suggests that particular importance was attached to this parliament, from which Edward I hoped to procure a large

be any clearer. The representatives were to be, in the fullest sense, the attorneys of those who elected them. From then on, the formula is always present in the writs. Its form might change from parliament to parliament, but its purpose is always the same. For example, for the Kilkenny parliament of 1310, the representatives of the commons were to have

> plenam potestatem ex parte communitatum predictorum comitatum, civitatum et burgorum ad parliamentandum, tractandum et ordinandum cum predicto justiciario et consilio nostro et cum ceteris proceribus terre predicte super eisdem negotiis et ad faciendum et consenciendum ordinacionibus ibidem per ipsos ordinandis.[42]

For a parliament in 1360, the formula is much the same:

> qui plenam potestatem habent pro communitate dicte civitatis ... ad tractandum ibidem super premissis cum justiciario nostro Hibernie et aliis de consilio nostro una cum prelatis, magnatibus et proceribus predictis ad consensiendis hiis que tunc ibidem pro nostris honore et commode favente Domino contigerit ordinari.[43]

Unless this were an empty formula, and as we shall see there is good evidence to the contrary, then obviously the king expected the representatives of the Irish commons to come to parliament with power to bind their communities. When Windsor included the formula in the writs of summons to the parliaments he convened, he too expected the elected representatives to have this power. And the Irish commons themselves accepted this principle, which is why they tried to bind their elected representatives not to agree to the subsidies the lieutenant was seeking. I might add here that what I have said about the commons holds equally true for the proctors elected by the lower clergy. For the Kilkenny parliament of 1371, for example, the archbishop of Armagh was ordered to attend personally and to have two proctors elected to represent the clergy of the diocese. The writs of summons specified that the proctors were to have 'potestatem sufficientem', and the return made by the archbishop shows that they were in fact given power 'ad tractandum et concordandum'.[44] The bishop of Cork was ordered to have proctors elected for the council of 1372 at Ballyhea, the proctors to have sufficient power to represent the clergy of the diocese and 'ad tractandum et consenciendum'.[45] Other examples might be quoted, but these are sufficient to show that the proctors, like the representatives of the shires and other local communities, were expected to have power to bind those who elected them.

subsidy for the Scottish war. 42 Ibid., p. 62. 43 Lynch, *Legal institutions*, p. 318. 44 *Parls & councils*, pp 36–7. 45 Ibid., pp 49–50.

That the *plena potestas* formula was not an empty one, but was intended to be implemented in parliament, can be demonstrated from an important series of enrolments concerning a special meeting of the English council in 1376. A special royal agent, Nicholas Dagworth, had been sent to Ireland in an attempt to persuade the Irish commons to grant further subsidies.[46] It was obviously anticipated that Dagworth would fail, because, when parliament refused the request for a subsidy, Dagworth showed an order from the king commanding that two proctors from each diocese, two knights from each county, and two citizens or burgesses from each city or borough should come to England to consult with the king and council about the government of Ireland and an aid for the king. He also delivered to Windsor a letter from the king, saying that, in the event of a refusal by parliament to support the cost of the war in Ireland, the governor was to see to it that representatives, as stated above, were to come to England. It seems that the English government, in bypassing the Irish parliament in this unprecedented way, was hoping that what Dagworth failed to achieve in Ireland could be accomplished in England under its own immediate influence. Subsidies which were refused in an Irish parliament might be more difficult to refuse in the presence of the king himself. But it was essential, of course, that the representatives who were sent to this special meeting in England should have full power to bind their communities to whatever was agreed upon. Hence, the question of *plena potestas* became an open issue when the summonses were issued in Ireland and when the recipients of writs of summons made their returns to the Irish chancery. And, because of this, the writs and returns were separately enrolled and sent to the king in England. There they fortunately survived, and they enable us to gain an insight into the election of representatives and the powers delegated to them which otherwise we might never possess.[47]

One of the first things which emerges from a study of these records is the claim of the commons, which is nowhere denied, that they are under no obligation to answer the summonses and send representatives to England. In the past, of course, Irish magnates had been present at meetings of parliament and council in England, and had even assented to taxation there, as in 1275, when they granted new customs.[48] And petitions from Ireland had been heard in the English parliament, and grievances had been redressed there.[49] But now, in the winter of 1375–6, the commons dispute the right of the king to summon them to England. The archbishop of Armagh, for example, in his return to the

46 For this and what follows see Thomas Leland, *The history of Ireland from the invasion of Henry II, with a preliminary discourse on the ancient state of that kingdom*, 3 vols (London, 1773), i, 263–5. Leland printed in the second appendix to his book the enrolment of writs and returns which was sent to England, from Sir Joseph Ayloff (ed.), *Calendar of the ancient charters* (London, 1772). As he himself said: 'I have taken the liberty of annexing it to this volume'! 47 In addition to the long record printed by Leland, see also Gilbert, *Facsimiles*, iii, pl. 19 and text, and Clarke, 'Windsor', pp 127–30. 48 *Ir. parl.*, pp 66–7. 49 Ibid., p. 247.

chancery states that by common counsel and assent of the clergy of the diocese he has to reply that 'according to the liberties, privileges, rights, laws and customs of the church and of the land of Ireland' proctors cannot be obliged to attend parliaments or councils in England.[50] Similar returns were made by the other bishops, even by the bishop of Meath, who had been a keen supporter of Windsor and was himself under attack by the commons. The counties and towns make the same sort of answer: according to the liberties, customs, etc., of Ireland since the conquest, they cannot be obliged to send representatives to an assembly in England – Louth adding for good measure, 'according to the customs etc. of Ireland since the conquest *and before*'![51] But, because of the state of Ireland and the gravity of the situation there, and out of reverence for the king, they are willing on this occasion, of their own free will and saving their liberties, to accede to the request of the king.

This claim, nowhere denied by the king, might very well be true, just as it was true that Irish tenants-in-chief, who held by knight service, were not obliged to render that service outside Ireland. That principle had been accepted by the king long before, in the thirteenth century, at a time when he refused to accept the same principle in England.[52] If it is true that representatives of the Irish commons were not obliged to attend parliament in England, then a number of interesting questions follow, some of which were to be important in the future. For example, was Ireland bound by statutes and ordinances promulgated in England by parliaments and councils in which the commons were not represented and which they did not have to attend? The simple answer, of course, is yes – because such legislation could be extended to Ireland by the authority of the king, which at that time was superior to the authority of parliament, an authority which as yet had scarcely even been defined. But, not long after this, in 1381, and again on a more famous occasion in 1460, this very question was raised.[53] In 1381, the Irish clergy objected that they were not bound by any statute made by a parliament in which they were not represented, and though this objection was overruled by the king subsequently, it might have been strengthened by the claim that they were not bound to attend any parliament in England. It may well be that a study of this Irish claim might teach us something of the development of the doctrine of the authority of parliament.

The writs of summons to this meeting in England in 1375–6 contained a *plena potestas* clause which was phrased in more explicit terms than was customary. The elected representatives were to have 'potestatem sufficientem …

50 Leland, *History of Ireland*, i, 368: 'quod non tenemur juxta libertates, privilegia, jura, leges, et consuetudines ecclesie nec terre Hibernie aliquos de clero nostro eligere nec mittere ad partes Anglie ad parliamenta seu consilia in Anglia tenenda'. 51 Leland, *History of Ireland*, i, 378. 52 For example, see the letter of Henry III, June 1244, on the occasion of the proposed expedition to Scotland (Gilbert, *Hist. & mun. docs*, p. 102). 53 *Parls & councils*, pp 205–6; *Stat. Hen. VI*, p. 644.

ad tractandum, consulendum et concordandum nobiscum, tam super gubernatione dicte terre, quam pro auxilio et sustentatione guerre nostre ibidem'.[54] Keeping in mind the refusal of the commons to listen to Dagworth's appeal and grant a subsidy, we can understand the government's anxiety now to ensure that the representatives sent to England should have full power to grant financial aid for the war in Ireland. Three archbishops and ten bishops received orders to have proctors elected in their dioceses. The returns they made show a determination to resist taxation which must have astonished Windsor in Dublin. Leighlin and Emly refused to elect any proctors because of the poverty of the diocese, though Emly allowed the proctors of Lismore to speak and act on its behalf. And Cashel elected only one proctor, because it had not the means to support two. All the proctors were given power 'ad tractandum, informandum, consulendum et concordandum ... super statu, salvatione et gubernatione terre Hibernie'; but, in the case of those from Armagh, Kildare and Waterford–Lismore, power to assent to subsidies was specifically withheld. In the case of Waterford–Lismore, the return of the bishop said that this power was not given to the proctors, 'lest by the granting of such power the liberties of the church and of the land of Ireland should be infringed'. In the returns from Cashel, Meath, Ossory and Ferns, a reservation was made in granting power in the case of 'the liberties of the church and the free customs of the land of Ireland', which, on the basis of what was said by the bishop of Waterford–Lismore, should probably be interpreted to exclude power to assent to subsidies. And, in the returns from Limerick, Cork, Cloyne and Kerry, no *plena potestas* formula was included (despite specific instructions about this in the writs); consequently, the returns were defective. The only diocese to comply fully with the writ of summons and grant full power to its proctors was Dublin – and this can probably be explained by the fact that a vacancy existed there at the time. Apart from Dublin, then, all the returns were defective because they did not contain a *plena potestas* formula of the kind specified in the writs of summons.

Turning to the shires, liberties and boroughs, we find that much the same thing happened. Eight counties received summonses. Of these, three (Dublin, Louth and Kildare) refused power to grant subsidies; one (Waterford) made a reservation about the liberties and free customs of the land of Ireland; one (Carlow) refused to elect representatives because of poverty; and three (Wexford, Limerick and Cork) said nothing at all about the power delegated to their representatives. All the returns, therefore, were defective. Much the same is true of the liberties and crosses. Meath and Kilkenny withheld power to grant subsidies; Tipperary made a reservation about liberties and free customs; Kerry complied with the writ. Of the towns, three (Dublin, Drogheda and Waterford) withheld power to assent to subsidies; three others included no *plena potestas*

54 Leland, *History of Ireland*, i, 366–7.

formula in their returns; and three (Limerick, Wexford and Youghal) returned representatives with power 'prout breve requirit'.

These returns need a greater degree of analysis than I can give them here. But it seems to me that there was some sort of collusion between those communities which refused full power to their representatives. They were mounting a united opposition. The same phrases, almost word for word, are used in their returns. They are, they say, safeguarding the liberties and free customs of the land of Ireland. Their poverty and the heavy expenditure they have incurred in the defence of their lands are the reasons they all put forward for refusing to incur the burden of new taxation. Their representatives will explain this more fully to the king when they meet him. And, finally, they all use a phrase – 'aliter ad presens respondere non possumus' – which seems to imply that normally they would have complied with the writs of summons and returned representatives with full power.

Here, then, was an open refusal by the commons to grant their representatives full power to bind them. What was Windsor's reply to this defiance? Unfortunately, we do not possess sufficient information to answer this question, except in the case of the liberty of Kilkenny and the county of Dublin. One of the two representatives elected in the liberty of Kilkenny was the bishop of Ossory. But this was contrary to the writ of summons, in which it was clearly stated that only laymen should be elected. So the election was suppressed and a new one ordered. But in ordering the new election, Windsor was careful to point out that his first reason for doing this was that the commons of the liberty had not given their representatives 'potestatem concordandi prout breve domini regis requirebat'.[55]

In the case of Dublin, we have fuller information and it is worth examining in some detail.[56] In answer to the original writ of summons, two knights – Nicholas Houth and Richard White – were returned as elected by the county. They had full power to do all things except to agree to a subsidy. Apparently, a petition was addressed to Windsor, the chancellor and other members of the council by 'many sufficient persons of the county', protesting against the election on the ground that Houth and White were cousins. We cannot be sure of the date of this petition, of the people who sealed it, or of when it was received by the council. But on 29 November, Windsor ordered a new election. Two reasons were put forward by him: Houth and White were elected without sufficient power, as specified in the return – 'which return', he says, 'without the power of consent we regard as less than sufficient'; and secondly, a majority of the electors of the county did not agree to the choice of Houth and White. To

55 Leland, *History of Ireland*, i, 382. It should be noted that when a new election was held the bishop was replaced by a layman, but again power to consent to subsidies was withheld.
56 Gilbert, *Facsimiles*, iii, pl. 19 and text; Clarke, 'Windsor', pp 127–30.

avoid further complications, Windsor ordered the treasurer and chief justice of the bench to supervise the new election. They were to see to it that full power was given to the newly elected representatives. If the electors refused to do this, then they were to be 'distrained by all their lands and chattels' to give their consent. In due course, the new election was held, presided over by the two royal officials. But despite their presence and threats of penalties, the county, according to the return made by the sheriff, re-elected Houth and White, and again refused to give them full power. The treasurer and chief justice in their return, however, said that a new man, William FitzWilliam, had been elected in place of Houth (by 24 votes to 20). But they also had to say that the county had again refused full power and added that 'in no other way would the said commons agree to make election'. Because of this, the returns, and the returns from the other communities, were nearly all defective. They were, therefore, enrolled with the writs of summons in the chancery, and the roll was sent to England.

It seems clear, then, from the evidence provided by the records of these elections, that the *plena potestas* formula in the writs of summons was intended to be taken seriously. Indeed, there can hardly be any doubt that Windsor tried to influence the Dublin elections in an attempt to force the county to give full power to its representatives, first by sending two royal officials (both of whom were supporters of his policy) to supervise the elections, and secondly by threatening penalties if full power was refused. This surely is sufficient proof of the importance attached by the government to the *plena potestas* formula. And on the other hand, the commons too realized the importance of the formula and on this occasion, because of the special circumstances surrounding the elections, refused to incorporate it in the returns they made to the chancery. As I indicated earlier, these were abnormal circumstances. Under more normal circumstances, full power would be given to their representatives, who could thus bind their communities to contribute to whatever subsidies were granted to the king in parliament.

In the history of William of Windsor's relations with the Irish commons, therefore, we can see that there are two stages. In the first, the commons complain that their representatives in parliament have been coerced into granting subsidies; the subsidies are therefore illegal and they resist any attempt to levy them. In the second stage, they are more cautious. They expressly refuse to give their elected representatives the power to grant subsidies so that, even if the representatives are again coerced into making a grant (as was quite likely to happen in England), the commons can later refuse to be bound by that grant. It was this refusal to grant *plena potestas* which finally became the open issue between them and the governor. The attention focused on the *plena potestas* formula, and the importance attached to it, had the effect of bringing into the open the question of representatives and their powers. But it must not be thought that because this subject became a matter for debate in the 1370s that it was only then, and because of that debate, that the powers of representatives became defined in Ireland. As far as taxation is concerned, the evidence suggests that at least one of the powers delegated to representatives by the communities in Ireland was the power to grant or withhold subsidies in parliament, and to bind the communities by their decision. The debate with Windsor may have clarified this power, but it certainly did not initiate it.

CHAPTER 4

# The medieval Irish chancery*

*A.J. Otway-Ruthven*

Little published work exists on the institutions of medieval Ireland, and it seems worth making an attempt to outline the development of the chancery, which, though based on the English model, was necessarily on a smaller and less elaborate scale. The repeated losses of records, which have so complicated the task of the Irish historian, make it impossible to hope that we can ever reconstruct it in full detail – in particular, no single roll of the Irish chancery survived the destruction of 1922 – but it remains possible to recover a fair amount of information, and this paper is offered as a first sketch, which may later be filled in.

The Irish exchequer, which had certainly been organized before 1200,[1] appears to have been the first administrative department of the Anglo-Irish government, though no doubt the justiciars who administered the country had their own clerks. But the English chancery was still in the twelfth century so intimately connected with the royal household that we need not be surprised that it does not seem to have been copied in Ireland till 1232, when the English chancellor, Ralph Neville, bishop of Chichester, was granted the chancery of Ireland to hold for life, with all the liberties and free customs thereto belonging.[2] The writ speaks as if the chancery already existed, but probably there was in fact only some sort of writing office, possibly, as Richardson and Sayles suggest, in connection with the exchequer.[3] Neville nominated a deputy to execute the office in his place: having taken oath, he was to have free administration of the office of chancery and the seal with which the affairs of the king and of the land of Ireland are transacted;[4] he was to be present at the councils of the justiciar and the management of the king's affairs; he was to have a clerk at the exchequer of Dublin to keep a counter-roll, and a clerk at the assizes before the justiciar to keep a roll *de banco* and writs of pleas, as the chancellor had in England.[5] After 1244, when, on the death of Neville, his deputy, Robert Luttrell, was continued as chancellor, the Irish chancery had a continuous existence, independent of the

* First published in *Album Helen Maud Cam*, 2 vols (Studies presented to the International Commission for the History of Representative and Parliamentary Institutions, nos. 23–4: Louvain-Paris, 1960–1), ii, 119–38. 1 *Rot. chart.*, p. 61b. 2 *CR 1231–4*, pp 112–13. 3 *Ir. parl.*, pp 23–4. 4 *CR 1231–4*, pp 112–3. 5 This strongly suggests, though it does not prove, that a royal seal, distinct from that of the exchequer, already existed in Ireland.

English chancery.[6] It should, however, be observed that this did not mean that the English great seal ceased to have validity in Ireland: as a seal in direct contact with the king it had exactly the same validity in Ireland as in England. Thus, in 1339, the king addressed letters close to the escheator of Kilkenny ordering him to deliver to the bishop of Ossory the temporalities of his bishopric: the sheriff had been ordered to do so by writ under the great seal used in England, and had refused to receive or execute the writ, 'asserting that he will not execute it unless it comes from the chancery of Ireland under the seal used there, at which the king is much angered, chiefly because all his subjects are bound by their allegiance to obey his orders under the great seal of England'.[7] It was, however, felt to be proper that at any rate writs of course in Irish affairs should issue from the Irish chancery: when, in 1305, Nigel le Brun, as executor of a will, petitioned for a writ of the English chancery against the testator's bailiff, the answer was, 'Quod sequatur versus eum per breve de cancellaria Hiberniae si sibi viderit expedire'.[8]

The organization of the Irish chancery during the thirteenth century is very obscure. The custody of the rolls seems to have been irregular,[9] and in 1300 all the records of the time of the then chancellor up to that year were accidentally burnt in a great fire at St Mary's abbey, Dublin. What remained was delivered to Walter de Thornbury, the new chancellor, in 1309, by the late chancellor's executors: it included only one roll earlier than 1300, and it would appear that, whatever had happened to the bulk of the thirteenth-century chancery records, they had not been in the chancellor's custody.[10] By the early nineteenth century, when the remaining chancery rolls were calendared for the Record Commissioners, further substantial losses had occurred; and the destruction of our public records in 1922 has left this brief Latin calendar of a mere fragment of the records of the medieval chancery, all later than 1300, as our main guide to the manner in which it conducted its business.

6 Lists of chancellors and keepers of the rolls are given in F. Elrington Ball, *The judges in Ireland*, 2 vols (New York, 1927), and more detailed lists of all Irish officials for the period 1272–1377 by H.G. Richardson and G.O. Sayles will be published shortly by IMC [EN. This projected volume was published in 1963 (*Admin. Ire.*). For an accessible list of Irish chancellors to the end of the Middle Ages, see *NHI*, ix, 500–8. There are detailed lists of chancery officials and other officers in the Dublin administration during the reigns of Henry V and Henry VI in E.A.E. Matthew, 'The governing of the Lancastrian lordship of Ireland in the time of James Butler, fourth earl of Ormond, *c.*1420–52' (PhD, University of Durham, 1994), app. 1]. 7 *CCR 1339–41*, p. 259. 8 F.W. Maitland, *Records of the parliament holden at Westminster on the twenty-eighth day of February, in the thirty-third year of the reign of King Edward the First, A.D. 1305* (RS, London, 1893), p. 239. Cf. *CCR 1374–7*, pp 481–2, and *CJRI 1305–7*, pp 74–8. 9 It was alleged *c.*1285 that, 'as to the rolls of the justiciar and chancellor … it is found that the justiciar has retained those rolls in his chamber for two years at his will … of the rolls of Fromund le Brun, the chancellor' (*CDI 1285–92*, p. 5). 10 *RCH*, p. 12, no. 416. There are certainly some inaccuracies in this. Thus the Ir. close roll

We know, therefore, almost nothing of the development of the Irish chancery in its early days. It is clear that there was a good deal of exchequer influence, and that a clerk could easily pass from one department to the other.[11] Even as late as 1392, Richard Wals, parson of Carlow, says in a petition that 'il ad travaille en le service nostre seigneur le roy en son chancellerie et eschequer Dirland par ces xl. anns et plus'.[12] But our first positive statement comes from *c.*1285, when it was alleged that

> in the chancery there is now only one clerk, John Esturmy, who knows little of the chancery. Writs issuing are reproved in the common pleas and elsewhere as wanting in matter and form; there is a very great want there of clerks knowing the form of chancery; and therefore the justices of the common pleas have supplicated the king to provide better in these matters.[13]

Although the register of writs had been transmitted to Ireland in 1227,[14] in 1254 the king sent his justices of Ireland a transcript of a writ out of the Irish chancery which did not accord with the course of the English chancery, ordering them not to proceed on this writ, but to cause one to issue according to English form.[15] It was perhaps as a result of such complaints that an English chancery clerk, Robert de Haliwell, was sent to Ireland under Edward I: in 1304, the king ordered that, as he had served him well in the chancery of England and of Ireland and elsewhere, he was to be replaced and retained in as good estate in the chancery of England, in table and court, as he had in the time when John de Langton was chancellor.[16] At least one other English clerk, Henry de Thrapston, served in the Irish chancery in this period.[17] But again, *c.*1333, the Irish council represented to the king that:

> en votre chauncellerie Dirlaunde il ny ad forsqe un clerc et un clerionnet, mes nul de eux sciet riens qui appent al office du roule, ne nule busoigne apoy que soit hors de cours exploiter en la place, ne brief duement faire, dont votre corone ad sentu trop grantz desheritesons et damages; et votre chaunceller, qad porte uncore la charge des tieux briefs faire, ne pust cele

calendared as that of 10 Edw. II (1316–17) seems to be that of 10 Edw. III (1336–7), while the Ir. close roll calendared as that of 9 Hen. VI (1430–1) belongs to 8–9 Hen. V (1420–2) [EN. In addition, Ir. close rolls, 3 Edw. II (1309–10), 8 Edw. III (1334–5) and 5 Ric. II, pt 2 (1381–2), are erroneously identified in *RCH* as patent rolls; while the patent roll calendared as that of 7 Hen. IV, pt 1 (1405–6), belongs to 10 Hen. V (1422)]. 11 Many of the early chancellors had had previous connections with the exchequer. See Ball, *Judges in Ireland*. 12 *PKCI*, pp 11–12. 13 *CDI 1285–92*, no. 2. 14 Pollock and Maitland, *Hist. of Eng. law* (1923 ed.), pp 170–1. 15 *CR 1231–4*, p. 114. 16 *Calendar of chancery warrants, 1244–1326* (London, 1927), p. 233. Haliwell was described as the Irish chancellor's clerk in 1298 (*CDI 1293–1301*, no. 508). 17 *CDI 1293–1301*, no. 720. Cf. *CPR 1292–1301*, p. 241.

charge ovesqe les auters charges qil ad entour voz grosses busoignes endurer, par qoi il busoigne que ascun sachant clerc del office des roules, et de faire briefs de fourme a luy commaundez, soit hastivement envoiez en Irlaunde.[18]

But still, in 1356, we hear that Walter de Wygan, 'per multos annos propter clericorum cancellarie paucitatem graviter laborasset'.[19]

By this time, however, it is clear that the organization of the chancery had been considerably developed. The office of keeper of the rolls existed in Ireland at the time of the Bruce invasion (1315–18), for in 1323 the Irish treasurer and chamberlains were ordered to deliver to the Irish chancellor 'all rolls, writs, inquisitions and memoranda of the chancery of Ireland of the king's time and of the time of his progenitors, to wit those that Walter de Kynefare, late keeper of the rolls of said chancery, delivered to the treasurer and chamberlains when the king's Scotch enemies were in that land, to be kept by the chancellor to make execution and other things pertaining to the office of chancellor'.[20] This sounds as if the office had been allowed to lapse; but in 1324, William de Bardelby was keeper of the rolls and held the office till 1333, when Edmund de Grymmesby – the first of a series of English chancery clerks who appeared in Ireland as keepers of the rolls during the century – was appointed.[21] It is not clear whether Grymmesby ever took up office: Bardelby was still described as keeper in August 1334 and was still working in the chancery in 1335;[22] but Robert de Hemmyngburgh – another English chancery clerk, appointed in 1337 – certainly did act, and we may take it that the office was effectively organized after this date. Hemmyngburgh brought with him another chancery clerk – William de Drayton, who continued to appear in the Irish chancery till 1359 – to serve under him; while Henry Gilofre of Leicester (probably the Henry de Leycestre who became keeper of the rolls in 1364) came over with Thomas de Cotyngham in 1356.[23]

The office of keeper of the hanaper does not appear in the surviving records till considerably later, though of course this cannot be taken to prove that it did not exist. But the first clerk of the hanaper to be named is Nicholas Hotot, who petitioned for remuneration for his service as clerk of the hanaper and had a writ of *allocate* on 6 March 1382, by which time he had been superseded.[24]

18 *PKCI*, p. 320. The editor dated this document to *c.*1345 because of the reference to the mainpernors of the earl of Desmond, whose recognisances were estreated in that year, but the recognisances had been executed in 1333, and the passage on the chancery can hardly belong to any later date (ibid., pp liii–iv). **19** *RCH*, p. 67, no. 145. **20** *CCR 1323–7*, pp 10–11. **21** *RCH*, p. 31, no. 51; *CPR 1330–4*, p. 470; *CCR 1333–7*, p. 158. **22** *RCH*, p. 38, no. 12; *RCH*, p. 41, no. 24. **23** *CPR 1334–8*, pp 515, 517; *CPR 1354–8*, p. 433. **24** *RCH*, p. 111, nos. 5–57; *RCH*, p. 112, no. 95; *RCH*, p. 117, no. 45. He was to be allowed £4 19*s*. 4*d*., which suggests that he had been in the office for at least a year, for in 1425 the annual fee was £5 (*RCH*, p. 239, no. 10).

Several of the fourteenth-century clerks of the hanaper later became keepers of the rolls.[25] The clerk of the crown in chancery does not seem to be mentioned till 1382;[26] in 1481, he was described as 'clerk of the crown of our sovereign lord the king of his chancery and of his parliament of his land of Ireland'.[27]

Beyond these named officials, it is very difficult to discern anything of the organization of the chancery staff. We cannot tell whether or not there was anything corresponding to the ordered hierarchy of the first and second grade clerks of the English chancery. No more than two, or at the most three, clerks of chancery ever occur by name at any one time, and though there must have been others who are not named it is clear that the whole structure must have been smaller and less elaborate than that of the English chancery. The name which appears on a chancery writ up to the middle of the fifteenth century is, as often as not, that of the keeper of the rolls or of a clerk who will shortly become keeper of the rolls; but other names occur, including, between 1427 and 1443, that of Thomas Broun, clerk of the crown under Henry IV, Henry V and Henry VI.[28] The names of the clerks who appear from time to time as being granted rewards for their 'tres grandes travalx en escrivant diverses briefs combien des parlements come des conseiles as diverses seignours Dirland', or 'for their expenses in following the justiciar and chancellor and writing commissions and writs touching the king and the business of Ireland', do not appear on the writs: they were clearly persons of inferior status, receiving no regular salary.[29]

The regular salary of the chancellor himself throughout the period was forty pounds.[30] In addition, however, he had in the thirteenth and fourteenth centuries the issues of the seal: this is stated *c.*1285, and when John Larcher was appointed in 1346 the patent expressly stated that he was to have the issues of the seal 'as other chancellors there have used to have'.[31] The issues of the seal continued to be specified in patents till the end of the century; but when, in 1395, the bishop of Meath was appointed, the king reserved to himself 'all issues and profits of the great seal, there usually received heretofore by the chancellors', granting the chancellor instead an annual sum of eighty pounds for the expenses of his establishment.[32] In 1399, he was granted instead the accustomed fee and 10*s*. daily at the exchequer of Ireland, and subsequent grants of wages 'for the

25 See below, table 1. 26 *RCH*, p. 111, no. 57. 27 *Stat. Edw. IV, pt 2*, p. 886. 28 A few original writs have survived among the Ormond deeds (*COD*), the Dowdall deeds (*Dowdall deeds*), and in more scattered sources, while a number are fully transcribed in the registers of the archbishops of Armagh. 29 *PKCI*, pp 89–90; *RCH*, p. 45, no. 68; *RCH*, p. 58, no. 1; *RCH*, p. 150, no. 7; *RCH*, p. 240, no. 50; *RCH*, p. 245, nos. 20–1; *RCH*, p. 247, no. 43; *RCH*, p. 263, no. 12. The only exception seems to be Hugh Wogan, whose name appears on a good many writs between 1443 and 1451, when he was clerk of the crown, and who had a reward for his labour in the chancery in writing *necessaria regem tangencia* in 1440 (*RCH*, p. 263, no. 5). 30 *CDI*, ii–iv (1252–1301), passim; *RCH*, p. 12, no. 25; *RCH*, p. 38, no. 39; *RCH*, p. 243, no. 11, and passim. 31 *CDI 1285–92*, no. 2; *CPR 1345–8*, pp 211–12. 32 *CPR*

support of the clerks of the chancery, servants and horses' vary from 5*s*. a day to 10*s*., though in 1461 John Dynham was granted only £53 6*s*. 8*d*. a year, 'for the maintenance of the clerks of the chancery of Ireland'.[33] What this involved is stated, in 1395, to be that the chancellor 'is now required by ordinance of the king and council to find a keeper of the rolls of chancery and other clerks for the said chancery, and to have them at his table, and whilst they are on eyre to find the cost of their horses, one clerk being assigned by the chancellor as keeper of the hanaper'.[34] This obligation cannot have been entirely new: the assumption made when William de Whithurst was appointed as keeper of the rolls in 1346 was apparently that the chancellor was bound to maintain him.[35]

In addition to the normal fees and wages of his office, the chancellor – since, like every other official in Ireland, he not infrequently found himself engaged in warlike operations – might be in receipt of wages for the maintenance of men-at-arms, light horsemen (hobelars) and archers. Thus, in 1364, the appointment of Robert de Assheton as chancellor provides that, 'because he must often ride at war with the king's son, Lionel duke of Clarence, lieutenant in that land, in his progresses, and at other times by himself, he may retain six men-at-arms and twelve mounted archers at the king's wages usual in that land', to be paid by the treasurer.[36] In 1370, John de Botheby, then chancellor, had a similar grant 'for as long as he shall be in that office and the war there shall last'.[37] In 1368, the chancellor was actually taken prisoner by rebels in the marshes of Carbury, Co. Kildare, though the great seal seems to have been saved.[38] These military considerations no doubt explain why the prior of the Hospitallers was so often appointed as chancellor. And finally, the chancellor could, of course, rely on presents of all kinds – from the five marks for wine given by the prior and convent of Christ Church cathedral, Dublin, in 1339, to the ten marks of annual fee for life granted to Sir Roland Fitz Eustace when he was chancellor by Octavian, archbishop of Armagh, 'pur la liberte du dit Octavian et pur le bone counseill du dit Roulande empense et de estre empense al dit primate'.[39]

The fee of the keeper of the rolls seems to have been at first a matter of considerable uncertainty. When Edmund de Grymmesby was appointed in 1333, the king, 'wishing to ascertain what yearly fee such a keeper ought and was wont to receive, and if the fee ought reasonably to suffice for the said keeper', ordered the justiciar, chancellor and treasurer to inform him on this.[40] But in 1346, when William de Whithurst was appointed, the king was still 'not fully informed how much others have used to receive for this custody' and ordered that

*1391–6*, p. 602. 33 *CPR 1399–1401*, p. 112; *CPR 1408–13*, p. 282; *CPR 1452–61*, p. 641; *RCH*, p. 185, no. 68(d); *RCH*, p. 198, no. 16; *RCH*, p. 224, nos. 15–16; *RCH*, p. 225, no. 28; *RCH*, p. 239, no. 5; *RCH*, p. 243, no. 10; *RCH*, p. 245, no. 6; *RCH*, p. 251, no. 5. 34 *CPR 1391–6*, p. 602. 35 *CPR 1345–8*, pp 158–9. 36 *CPR 1364–7*, p. 25. 37 *CPR 1367–70*, pp 450–1. 38 *Jacobi Grace, Kilkenniensis, Annales Hiberniae*, ed. R. Butler (IAS, Dublin, 1942), p. 154. 39 *Account roll Holy Trinity*, p. 18; *Stat. Edw. IV, pt 2*, p. 844. 40 *CCR 1333–7*, p. 158.

> if the chancellor of Ireland be not willing to receive him with as many men and horses at the charges of the chancellor as others who have stood in the office before these times have had at such charges, the said William shall have twenty pounds at the exchequer of Ireland, half at Michaelmas and half at Easter, out of the yearly fee which the chancellor receives at that exchequer by reason of his office.

In either case, William was to have 'the fee pertaining to him by reason of the enrolment of charters and other memoranda relating to his office'.[41] This seems to have fixed the fee (which does not seem to have been deducted from the chancellor's fee in practice): Thomas de Cotyngham was granted only 20 marks in 1356,[42] but all subsequent grants are of a fee of £20; the additional 10 marks granted to Robert de Faryngtoun in 1395 does not seem to have been continued for his successors.[43] In addition to fees, the keepers of the rolls were also normally granted benefices. When appointed keeper of the great seal in the chancellor's absence, as he often was, his fee was appropriately increased.

The usual fees of the clerk of the hanaper are mentioned from 1398 on, but it is not till 1425 that we find a definite statement that they are 100*s.* a year,[44] and they do not seem to have varied during the century, though no doubt there were unspecified perquisites. The fee of the clerk of the crown was 10 marks a year in 1402, and this too seems to have remained unchanged during the century.[45] As to the lesser clerks, they seem to have depended on rewards granted from time to time, though no doubt they too had perquisites, might be granted benefices, and they could count on gifts from time to time. Thus, in 1345, William de Drayton, clerk of the chancery, had 3*s.* 4*d.* of the gift of the prior of Christchurch, 'pro consilio suo et auxilia pro quodam brevi perquirendo habendis'.[46]

How far the chancery had any fixed headquarters during this period it is difficult to say. Certainly, it was more often than not in Dublin, and a petition, which should probably be assigned to *c.*1320, complains that the citizens of Dublin 'par lour hastiuesse demeysne' to resist the Scots

> fesoyent arder le maner le roi pres du chastel de Dyuelyn dehors les murs ou les playdes de tote la terre soleynt tout temps estre tenuz auxi bien les playdes la chef justice et du baunk come del escheker et du meisme la counte et la place de la chauncellerie, par quoy les playdes de cheskune place de la dite terre sont tenuz en diuers luyes en la dite ville de Diuelyn, issint qe nul ministre poet venir ne conseiler od autre en diuers caas cant busoygne le demaunde sicome il soleyent et deuereynt faire par reison.[47]

41 *CPR 1345–8*, pp 158–9. 42 *CPR 1354–8*, pp 432–3. 43 *RCH*, p. 80, no. 1; *RCH*, p. 83, no. 12; *RCH*, p. 85, no. 13; *RCH*, p. 122, no. 3; *RCH*, p.151, no. 3; *CPR 1461–7*, p. 26; *Stat. Edw. IV, pt 2*, p. 60. 44 *RCH*, p. 239, no. 10. 45 Ibid., p. 202, no. 22. 46 *Account roll Holy Trinity*, p. 93. For Drayton, see above, p. 109. 47 SC 8/118/5881.

But in practice the chancery was endlessly itinerant, as is shown not only by the places at which writs are dated, but also by entries showing that, for instance, the seneschal of Christchurch rode to Drogheda in 1345, 'pro uno brevi de super modo et causa ad cancellarium tunc ibidem petendo'; that John Wytecod, bishop of Cloyne (1351–61), 'fuit apud Cork cum Justiciario domini Regis, et intravit cancellarium, ubi invenit clericos scribentes processum de Dromor'; that, in 1377, John Walshe of the Island exhibited an instrument in the chancery at Cork to be enrolled; and that, in 1393, a case was pleaded in the chancery at Kilmallock.[48] But there was perhaps a certain tendency to settle down in the fifteenth century, and in any case in the fifteenth century the area effectively controlled by the Dublin government was reduced to the counties in the immediate neighbourhood of Dublin.

The itinerant nature of the chancery produced in Ireland, as in England, its own difficulties. In Ireland, however, there was no such development of other seals as took place in England, for the English small seals originated in the royal household, and the constantly changing chief governors of Ireland could obviously produce nothing of the kind. It is true that, in 1405, we find a reference in English letters close to the great or petty seal of Ireland,[49] but there seems to be no evidence that such a seal ever really existed. When we find notes of warranty on surviving chancery instruments, they are 'per billam Johannis de Bermyngham comitis Loueth justiciarii Hibernie' (1322–3);[50] by bill of privy seal of the deputy (1464);[51] the justiciar's privy seal attached to a petition (1446).[52] In 1343, Christchurch paid 2*s*. 'privato clerico domini justiciarii pro j billa, clericis cancellarii directa, de supersedeas'.[53] As for the courts of law, the problem of judicial writs was met, at least from 1375, not by providing them with their own seals as in England, but by authorizing the judges to issue them without seals, reserving the fee for the seal to the chancellor or the hanaper.[54] Earlier, it would seem that some writs had been issued under the exchequer seal, for, in 1351, the treasurer and chancellor of the Dublin exchequer were ordered

> not to seal any judicial writs of any of the king's pleas in Ireland, except those which touch the pleas of the said exchequer, with the exchequer seal, while the great seal of the chancery there is within twenty miles of the exchequer, but to permit the chancellor to have the sealing of such writs, as is customary in the chancery of England.[55]

48 *Account roll Holy Trinity*, p. 93; *Rot. pipae Clonensis*, p. 35; *RCH*, p. 102, no. 83; *PKCI*, pp 202–4. 49 *CCR 1402–5*, pp 419–20. 50 *RCH*, p. 36, no. 84. 51 *Stat. Edw. IV, pt 2*, p. 448. 52 Ibid., p. 558. 53 *Account roll Holy Trinity*, p. 44. 54 *RCH*, p. 94, no. 154; *RCH*, p. 137, no. 230; *RCH*, p. 141, nos. 208–9; *RCH*, p. 176, no. 160; *RCH*, p. 203, no. 38. 55 *CCR 1349–55*, p. 293.

In 1395, it was ordered that the chancellor should remain in Dublin, except in case of emergency: if he should be obliged to leave Dublin to attend on the lieutenant or justiciar, he might, if prevented from doing so by infirmity or other cause, send the great seal to them 'by some sufficient person for whom he will answer for doing and executing what he himself would do if personally present'.[56] In practice, the chancellor seems, however, to have continued to itinerate as before,[57] and was, moreover, not infrequently absent from Ireland, having been sent as a messenger to the king in England, or for some other reason. On such occasions, he appointed a deputy – often the keeper of the rolls – and the custom of Ireland, accepted by the king, was that, if the appointment lapsed for any reason, the office of chancellor automatically became vacant. Master Thomas Chace had to be reappointed in November 1436 because his deputy had died while he was in attendance on the king and council in England.[58] Deputies were also appointed when the chancellor, though in Ireland, was for any reason unable to attend to his duties.[59]

Since all the records of the Irish chancery have been destroyed, there is little that can be said of them with certainty. It is, however, clear that there was never the elaborate subdivision of rolls that developed in England. When the surviving records of the chancery were listed in 1309, we hear of only two classes of rolls, patent and close, and the calendar printed in 1828 makes it clear that these remained the only rolls throughout the Middle Ages.[60] The close rolls contain a very large number of writs of *liberate* throughout the period; that of 1343–4 has almost the character of a plea roll.[61] The patent rolls are more normal, but that of 1407–8 was, if the calendar is to be trusted, in great part a fine roll.[62] Besides the rolls, there were files of the justiciar's bills and of escheator's inquisitions and other miscellaneous matter.[63] In 1372, the keeper of the rolls had a grant 'pro quadam arca precii 5 marcarum rotulos et alia memoranda cancellarii nuper deferente, et pro cariagio eorum'.[64]

The development of the jurisdictional powers of the Irish chancellor seems to have begun before the end of the thirteenth century. In 1299, in a case in which three men were charged with fraudulent assay

> because the last two are foreigners, and the justice cannot at present have leisure to take inquisition, it is agreed that the chancellor, at a certain day and place when he shall have leisure for it, shall take inquisition in

56 *CPR 1391–6*, p. 607. 57 *RCH*, p. 158, no. 112; Hore, *Wexford*, vi, 212, citing Ir. memo. roll of Trinity term, 2 Hen. IV; the bishop of Ferns has gone into Munster in his capacity as chancellor, taking the great seal with him. 58 *CPR 1436–41*, p. 28; *RCH*, p. 219, no. 49. 59 *RCH*, p. 155, nos. 62–3; *RCH*, p. 172, no. 14; *RCH*, p. 180, no. 1. 60 *RCH*, p. 12, no. 146. 61 *RCH*, pp 43–5, passim. This roll is for two regnal years. 62 *RCH*, p. 188. 63 *RCH*, p. 12, no. 416. 64 *RCH*, p. 83, no. 97.

> presence of the parties, and do justice in the matter; and shall certify to the justiciar as quickly as he can.[65]

In 1327, Matthew Rynger came into the chancery at Kilkenny seeking to replevy certain lands taken into the king's hand, though the case then seems to have been referred to the common bench.[66] But later in the century such cases were finally decided in the chancery, and no doubt formed the main part of its judicial business at this period.[67] Petitions to the lieutenant and council were, as in England, sometimes referred to the chancery, and might, as in England, be heard there before the common law judges.[68] There does not seem to be any sign of the development of a strictly equitable jurisdiction during the Middle Ages, but the surviving records are far too scanty to enable us to speak with any certainty on this point.

It is possible that a more thorough search of unprinted materials than has been possible for the purposes of this paper may enable us to fill up some of the obvious gaps in this account of the Irish chancery, but the loss of records has been so great that many questions will always remain unanswered. But at least this paper may serve as a starting point for further work.

TABLE I

OFFICERS OF THE IRISH CHANCERY, 1377–1485

*1.1 Chancellors of Ireland*[1]

| | |
|---|---|
| 20 Aug. 1377 | Alexander de Balscote, bishop of Ossory[2] |
| 26 Sept. 1377 | Robert de Wikeford, archbishop of Dublin[3] |
| *15 Dec. 1378* | *Robert de Sutton, keeper of the rolls, keeper*[4] |
| 8 Apr. 1380 | John Gilbert, bishop of Hereford[5] |
| 8 May 1380 | John de Colton, dean of Dublin[6] |
| 26 Nov. 1381 | William Tany, prior of the hospital[7] |
| 27 June 1383 | Ralph Cheyny, kt[8] |
| 10 Sept. 1384 | Robert de Wikeford, archbishop of Dublin[9] |

65 *CJRI 1295–1303*, p. 268. 66 *RCH*, p. 35, no. 66. 67 *RCH*, pp 43–5, passim; *CCR 1354–60*, pp 459–60. 68 *COD*, iii, 361–2. 1 Keepers of the great seal, appointed when no chancellor existed, are shown in italics. The dates given are those of appointment; the date of taking up office (given when ascertainable) might be some months later. The list of deputies is certainly very incomplete, but it seems worth naming them where possible. Brief biographies of most of the chancellors and keepers of the rolls are given in F. Elrington Ball, *The judges in Ireland*, 2 vols (New York, 1927). 2 *CPR 1377–81*, p. 18. 3 Ibid., p. 27. 4 *CCR 1377–81*, p. 168. 5 *CPR 1377–81*, p. 459. 6 Ibid., p. 463. 7 *CPR 1381–5*, p. 56. He took oath on 15 Feb. 1382 and received the seal on 19 Feb. (*RCH*, p. 111, nos. 83–5; *RCH*, p. 117, no. 39). 8 *CPR 1381–5*, p. 292. 9 Ibid., p. 455. He received the seal on 8 Nov. 1384

| | |
|---|---|
| 8 Mar. 1385 | Alexander de Balscote, bishop of Ossory[10] |
| | Deputy: Thomas de Everdoun[11] |
| *26 Apr. 1388* | *Robert de Preston, kt, keeper*[12] |
| | Deputies: Christopher de Preston and Robert Sutton, clerk[13] |
| 27 Aug. 1389 | Alexander de Balscote, bishop of Meath[14] |
| *11 Sept. 1391* | *Robert de Preston, kt, keeper*[15] |
| 28 Feb. 1392 | Robert Waldby, archbishop of Dublin[16] |
| | Deputy: Robert Sutton, keeper of the rolls[17] |
| 29 May 1393 | Richard Northalis, bishop of Ossory[18] |
| *1 July 1394* | *Robert Sutton, keeper of the rolls, keeper*[19] |
| 1395 | Robert Waldby, archbishop of Dublin |
| | Deputy: Robert de Faryngtoun, keeper of the rolls[20] |
| 10 June 1395 | Alexander de Balscote, bishop of Meath[21] |
| *19 June 1395* | *Thomas Everdoun and John de Kirkeby, keepers*[22] |
| 1397 | Robert Braybrooke, bishop of London[23] |
| *17 Oct. 1397* | *Robert de Sutton, king's clerk, keeper*[23] |
| 24 Apr. 1398 | Thomas Cranley, archbishop of Dublin[24] |
| | Deputy: Thomas Bache, archdeacon of Meath[25] |
| 18 Nov. 1399 | Alexander de Balscote, bishop of Meath[26] |
| | Deputy: John Kyrkeby, keeper of the rolls[27] |
| 4 July 1401 | Thomas Cranley, archbishop of Dublin[28] |
| | Deputies: Thomas de Everdon, keeper of the rolls (in 1402); Robert Sutton, keeper of the rolls (in 1406)[29] |
| 14 July 1406 | Laurence Merbury, kt[30] |
| *28 June 1407* | *Robert Sutton, keeper of the rolls, keeper*[31] |
| 18 Mar. 1410 | Patrick Barrett, bishop of Ferns[32] |
| | Deputy: Robert Sutton, keeper of the rolls[33] |

(*RCH*, p. 120, nos. 41–4). **10** *CPR 1381–5*, p. 532. He received the seal on 12 Apr. 1385 (*RCH*, p. 129, no. 21). **11** Appointed on 12 Jan. 1386 to keep the seal in the absence of the chancellor, who left for England on 20 Jan. 1386. Robert Sutton was first appointed (*RCH*, p. 124, nos. 78–9; *RCH*, p. 125, no. 136). **12** *CPR 1385–9*, p. 438. **13** Described as Preston's deputies in May 1389 (*RCH*, p. 142, no. 252). **14** *CPR 1388–92*, p. 109. He was sworn on 25 Oct. 1389 (*RCH*, p. 144, no. 79). **15** *CPR 1388–92*, p. 474. He was sworn on 3 Oct. 1391 (*RCH*, p. 148, nos. 46–7). **16** *CPR 1391–6*, pp 51, 115. **17** *PKCI*, pp 46, 226. **18** *CPR 1391–6*, p. 276. **19** Ibid., p. 449 **20** There is no patent, but Faryngtoun was appointed deputy during his absence, 11–18 Apr. 1395 (*RCH*, p. 153, no. 24; *RCH*, p. 155, nos. 62–3). **21** *CPR 1391–6*, p. 582. He received the seal on 1 Aug. 1395 (*RCH*, p. 152, nos. 46–8). **22** *RCH*, p. 152, no. 42. Balscote's appointment cannot have been known in Ireland at this date. **23** Braybrooke's patent does not seem to have survived, but Sutton was appointed to keep the seal till he could go to Ireland (*CPR 1396–9*, p. 246). **24** Ibid., p. 344. He remained in office till 4 Jan. 1400 (*CPR 1399–1401*, p. 479). **25** *CPR 1396–9*, p. 346. **26** *CPR 1399–1401*, p. 112. He died on 10 Nov. 1400. **27** *RCH*, p. 158, no. 112. **28** *CPR 1399–1401*, p. 512. **29** *RCH*, p. 172, no. 14; *RCH*, p. 180, no. 1; *RCH*, p. 184, no. 126. **30** *CPR 1405–8*, p. 203. He received the seal on 5 Sept. 1406 (*RCH*, p. 184, no. 126). **31** *CPR 1405–8*, p. 342. **32** *CPR 1408–13*, p. 282. **33** He appears as deputy in Trinity term, 1410, and in May 1412 (Hore, *Wexford*, vi, 210, n. 4; ibid., p. 212; *RCH*, p. 199, no. 99).

| | |
|---|---|
| 20 Apr. 1413 | Thomas Cranley, archbishop of Dublin[34] |
| 2 Mar. 1414 | Laurence Merbury, kt[35] |
| | Deputy: Hugh Banent (or Bavent)[36] |
| 21 Aug. 1421 | William fitz Thomas, prior of the hospital[37] |
| 1422 | William Yonge, archdeacon of Meath[38] |
| 4 Oct. 1422 | Laurence Merbury, kt[39] |
| | Deputy: Richard Sydgreve[40] |
| 19 May 1423 | Richard Talbot, archbishop of Dublin[41] |
| 1424–5 | William fitz Thomas, prior of the hospital[42] |
| Sept. 1426 | Richard fitz Eustace, kt[43] |
| 23 Oct. 1426 | Richard Talbot, archbishop of Dublin[44] |
| 26 Feb. 1430 | Master Thomas Chace[45] |
| | Deputies: Thomas Straunge, kt (in 1435); James Cornewalsh (in 1440)[46] |
| 7 Aug. 1422 | Richard Talbot, archbishop of Dublin[47] |
| 4 Mar. 1443 | Richard Wogan, chaplain[48] |
| | Deputies: Robert Dyke, archdeacon of Dublin; William Chevir[49] |
| 12 Aug. 1446 | John Talbot, kt[50] |
| | Deputies: Robert Dyke, archdeacon of Dublin (Jan. 1447);[51] Thomas Talbot, kt, prior of the hospital (10 Nov. 1451);[52] William Welles, kt (29 Aug. 1454);[53] Michael Tregury, archbishop of Dublin (5 Apr. 1458)[54] |
| 24 Feb. 1460 | Edmund, earl of Rutland[55] |
| 5 Nov. 1460 | John Dynham, esq.[56] |
| | Deputy: Robert Preston, kt[57] |
| 18 Jul. 1461 | William Welles, kt[58] |

**34** *CPR 1413–16*, p. 90. **35** Ibid., p. 163. He was sworn and received the seal on 18 Sept. 1414 (*RCH*, p. 205, nos. 61–3). **36** He was appointed on 21 Mar. as deputy during Merbury's absence in England till 1 Aug. (*RCH*, p. 218, no. 27). **37** Appointed by the lieutenant and council on the grounds that, as Merbury was still absent and the appointment of his deputy had lapsed, the office was vacant. Merbury was reappointed by English letters patent on the same day, but this does not seem to have taken effect. Fitz Thomas was sworn on 25 Aug. and received the seal on 28 Aug. (*RCH*, p. 219, no. 49; *CPR 1416–22*, p. 394). **38** He appears as chancellor in 1 Hen. VI (*RCH*, p. 224, no. 15). **39** *CPR 1422–9*, p. 3. **40** *RCH*, p. 225, no. 27; *RCH*, p. 228, no. 74. **41** *CPR 1422–9*, p. 103. **42** He appears as chancellor in 1424 or 1425, and seems to have held office till 10 Sept. 1426 (*RCH*, p. 239, no. 5; *RCH*, p. 224, no. 35). **43** *RCH*, p. 243, no. 9. **44** *CPR 1422–9*, p. 379. He was sworn on 12 Jan. 1427 (*RCH*, p. 245, no. 5). **45** *CPR 1429–36*, p. 49. He received the seal in Oct. (*RCH*, p. 253, no. 18). He was reappointed in 1436 and 1438 (*CPR 1436–41*, pp 28, 151). **46** *RCH*, p. 257, no. 57; *COD*, iii, 119. **47** *CPR 1441–6*, p. 91. **48** Ibid., p. 126. **49** In 1444, Dyke was said to have been deputy chancellor on various occasions; this may have been for Archbishop Talbot. Chevir was deputy in Aug. 1444 (*COD*, iii, 143, 158). **50** *CPR 1441–6*, p. 91. He succeeded his father as earl of Shrewsbury, and died 10 July 1460. He was granted the office for life; on 5 Apr. 1448, Thomas Fitz Gerald, prior of the hospital, had a grant of it in reversion, but this never took effect (*CPR 1446–52*, p. 167). **51** *Stat. Hen. VI*, p. 59. **52** *CPR 1446–52*, p. 560. **53** *CPR 1452–61*, p. 179. **54** *CCR 1454–61*, p. 289. **55** *Stat. Hen. VI*, p. 747–9. **56** *CPR 1452–61*, p. 640. This was ratified by Irish letters patent of 2 May 1461 (*RCH*, p. 268, no. 43). **57** *RCH*, p. 268, nos. 45–6. **58** *CPR 1461–7*, p. 21.

| | |
|---|---|
| 25 Jan. 1464 | Thomas Fitz Maurice, earl of Kildare[59] |
| 31 Jan. 1464 | John Tiptoft, earl of Worcester[60] |
| Apr. 1472 | Roland fitz Eustace, kt[61] |
| 5 Aug. 1474 | Gilbert Debenham, kt[62] |
| 1476 | Roland fitz Eustace, kt[63] |
| 15 Feb. 1478 | Master Richard Martyn[64] |
| 5 Oct. 1479 | William Sherwood, bishop of Meath[65] |
| *1482* | *Walter Champfleur, abbot of St Mary's, keeper*[66] |
| 11 Jan. 1483 | Robert de St Lawrence, lord of Howth[67] |
| 1483 | Thomas Fitz Gerald, kt[68] |

### *1.2 Keepers of the rolls of chancery*

| | |
|---|---|
| 5 Oct. 1377 | Robert Sutton[69] |
| 15 Jan. 1386 | Thomas de Everdoun[70] |
| 19 Sept. 1386 | Robert Sutton[71] |
| 15 Jan. 1395 | Robert de Faryngtoun[72] |
| 18 June 1395 | John de Kirkeby[73] |
| 10 July 1395 | Robert Sutton[74] |
| 26 Sept. 1398 | John Kirkeby[75] |
| 10 Jan. 1402 | Thomas Everdon[76] |
| 6 May 1404 | Robert de Sutton[77] |
| | Deputies: John Passavaunt and William Sutton (2 June 1423)[78] |
| 13 July 1437 | Robert Dyke[79] |
| 1 Jan. 1438 | John Forthey[80] |
| 17 Nov. 1448 | Robert Dyke[81] |
| 14 Aug. 1450 | John Chevir[82] |
| 1460 | Thomas Colt[83] |
| 15 Jan. 1461 | Amaury de St Lawrence[84] |

He died late in 1463. **59** *Stat. Edw. IV, pt 1*, p. 167. This was an Irish grant for life: he certainly acted for a time. **60** *CPR 1461–7*, p. 294. **61** *Stat. Edw. IV, pt 2*, pp 22–4. This was an Irish grant in survivorship with John Tapton, clerk. **62** *CPR 1467–77*, p. 461. **63** This is the date given in Ball, *Judges*: the patent seems to be lost, but he was certainly in office for the next few years (*Stat. Edw. IV, pt 2*, passim). **64** *CPR 1476–85*, p. 65. It is not clear that this grant ever took effect. **65** Ibid., p. 164. He died on 3 Dec. 1482. **66** This date is given in Ball, *Judges*, without a reference: Ware's note on him says simply that, while abbot, 'factus interim ad tempus magni sigilli Hiberniae custos' (*CStM*, i, 379; ibid., ii, 38–9). **67** *CPR 1476–85*, p. 335. The grant was repeated on 20 May and 12 July (ibid., pp 348, 363). **68** The patent seems to be lost, but he was certainly chancellor under Richard III (Bryan, *Great earl*, pp 85–7, quoting unpublished transcripts of Ir. stat. rolls). **69** *CPR 1377–81*, p. 27. This was a reappointment. **70** *RCH*, p. 124, nos. 80–2. He was sworn on 20 Jan. 1386. **71** *RCH*, p. 131, no. 33. **72** *RCH*, p. 151, no. 3. **73** *RCH*, p. 152, no. 41. **74** *CPR 1391–6*, p. 599. **75** *CPR 1396–9*, p. 414. He was reappointed on 20 Oct. 1399 (*CPR 1399–1401*, p. 113). **76** *RCH*, p. 162, no. 73. **77** *CPR 1401–5*, p. 389. He was reappointed in 1422 and 1423 (*CPR 1422–9*, pp 62, 79). **78** *RCH*, p. 226, no. 18. **79** *CPR 1436–41*, p. 70. **80** Ibid., p. 143. **81** *CPR 1446–52*, p. 205. **82** Ibid., p. 404. The original grant was under the Irish seal. **83** He was in office in this year (*Stat. Hen. VI*, p. 725). **84** *CPR 1452–*

| | |
|---|---|
| 2 May 1461 | Patrick Cogley[85] |
| 4 Aug. 1461 | Peter Trevers[86] |
| 10 Sept. 1464 | Thomas Colt[87] |
| 7 Sept. 1467 | William Norys, kt[88] |
| 10 Sept. 1471 | Thomas Douedall[89] |

### *1.3 Clerks of the hanaper*

| | |
|---|---|
| 1381 (?) | Nicholas Hotot[90] |
| 11 Jan. 1382 | Richard Carran[91] |
| 28 Jan. 1382 | Thomas Talbot[92] |
| 8 Mar. 1382 | John de Newport[93] |
| (12 Feb. 1386) | John Bykeley[94] |
| 21 Oct. 1386 | Robert Sutton[95] |
| 8 Jul. 1388 | Robert de Huntyngdon[96] |
| 8 Feb. 1390 | Robert Sutton[97] |
| (26 Jan. 1393) | Thomas Everdoun[98] |
| (12 Apr. 1395) | Robert Claydoun[99] |
| 20 Sept. 1398 | John Maufeld[100] |
| 20 Oct. 1399 | Hugh Bavent[101] |
| 4 June 1410 | John Passavaunt[102] |
| 16 July 1425 | Stephen Roche[103] |
| 8 Feb. 1435 | William Sutton[104] |
| 29 July 1439 | Thomas Beltoft |
| | John Bolt[105] |
| (28 June 1441) | Adam Veldon[106] |
| 22 Nov. 1454 | James Prendregaste, alias Collyn[107] |
| 1 Mar. 1459 | Patrick Cogly[108] |
| (1468) | James Predregast, alias Collyn[109] |
| (1479) | Richard Nangle[110] |

*61*, p. 639. **85** *RCH*, p. 268, nos. 35–6. He was sworn on 19 May. **86** *CPR 1461–7*, p. 26. He was sworn on 20 Sept. (*RCH*, p. 268, no. 13). **87** *CPR 1461–7*, p. 329. **88** *CPR 1467–77*, p. 34. **89** *Stat. Edw. IV, pt 1*, pp 735–7. **90** On 6 Mar. 1382, Hotot was granted a sum, which suggests that he had held the office for about a year (*RCH*, p. 117, no. 45). **91** *RCH*, p. 111, no. 55. **92** *RCH*, p. 111, no. 57. **93** *RCH*, p. 112, no. 95. **94** He was in office at this date (*CPR 1385–9*, p. 443). **95** *RCH*, p. 131, no. 41. **96** *RCH*, p. 138, no. 27. **97** *RCH*, p. 144, no. 107. **98** He was in office at this date (*PKCI*, p. 112). **99** He was in office at this date (*RCH*, p. 155, nos. 60–1). **100** *CPR 1396–9*, p. 411. **101** *CPR 1399–1401*, p. 113. **102** Appointed on the resignation of Bavent (*RCH*, p. 195, no. 23; *RCH*, p. 196, no. 59). This was confirmed on 26 Jan. 1414, and again by English letters patent 'in consideration of his great labours in the Irish chancery since the coronation of Henry IV' (*CPR 1422–9*, p. 67). **103** Appointed on the death of Passavaunt. Repeated 7 Sept. 1425 (*RCH*, p. 237, no. 86; *RCH*, p. 239, no. 10; *RCH*, p. 243, no. 13). **104** He was sworn on 4 Apr. (*RCH*, p. 256, nos. 27–8). **105** *CPR 1436–41*, pp 301, 414. Bolt seems to have been at work in July 1444 (*Reg. Swayne*, p. 191). **106** He was in office on this date (*RCH*, p. 264, no. 53). **107** *Stat. Hen. VI*, pp 325–7. This was a grant for life. **108** *CPR 1452–61*, p. 482. **109** He was in office in this year (*Stat. Edw. IV, pt 1*, p. 540). **110** He was in office in this year (*Stat. Edw.*

*1.4 Clerks of the crown in chancery*

| | |
|---|---|
| 12 Jan. 1382 | Thomas Talbot[111] |
| 12 Jan. 1402 | Thomas Browne[112] |
| 20 June 1443 | Hugh Wogan[113] |
| (20 June 1461) | Patrick Cogly[114] |

*IV, pt 2*, p. 688). **111** *RCH*, p. 111, no. 57. **112** He was appointed for life and was still in office in May 1428 (*RCH*, p. 162, no. 69; *RCH*, p. 202, no. 22; *RCH*, p. 245, no. 7). **113** *Stat. Hen. VI*, pp 71–3. This was a grant for life. He was still in office in 1460 (ibid., p. 727). **114** He was in office on this date, but the Irish patent granting him the office for life is dated 7 Sept. 1461 (*RCH*, p. 268, no. 42; *Stat. Edw. IV, pt 1*, p. 277). He still held the office in 1481 (*Stat. Edw. IV, pt 2*, p. 886).

CHAPTER 5

# Anglo-Irish shire government in the thirteenth century*

*A.J. Otway-Ruthven*

The organization of the medieval Anglo-Irish lordship was designed to reproduce as exactly as possible the administrative system of England, but it was not introduced suddenly or all at once. Of the eleven shires which were governed by royal sheriffs at the end of the thirteenth century, Dublin is the only one which can be traced back to the twelfth century, and even then does not appear in the records till the 1190s.[1] It seems probable that at this date no other shire yet existed in Ireland, though it is possible that Waterford, with Cork, was already organized as a shire.[2] But though the older school of historians, relying on the statement of Roger of Wendover that during his visit in 1210 John established in Ireland 'the laws and customs of England, appointing sheriffs and other officers', believed that the shiring of Ireland was completed at that time,[3] yet in 1211–12, when the organization of Ireland under John is first revealed to us in detail by the recently-published pipe roll of the fourteenth year of the reign, there were still only three shires: Dublin, Waterford with Cork, and Munster (that is, Limerick, Tipperary and Thomond). Waterford had clearly existed as a shire at least as early as 1208,[4] but it possible that the shire of Munster had been established 1210, which would provide a basis of fact for Wendover's statement,[5] while in that year Ulster with Uriel, and Meath had

* First published in *IHS*, 5:17 (1946), 1–28. 1 *CDI 1171–1251*, no. 272; H.G. Richardson, 'Norman Ireland in 1212', *IHS*, 3:10 (1942), 149. 2 The city of Waterford with 'all the surrounding province' had been granted in custody to Robert le Poer in 1177, and the original grantees of the kingdom of Cork died in 1182 and 1185 (see Orpen, *Normans*, i, 371; ibid., iii, 39–50). It is possible that Waterford and Cork were organized as a single custody soon after this, and that, as Mr Richardson remarks in the article cited above, 'John's visit in 1185 may have been more effective than has been supposed'. It should be observed that Thomas Bloet, sheriff of Waterford in 1211–12, had apparently married the heiress of Miles de Cogan, one of the first grantees of Cork (see Orpen, *Normans*, ii, 49, n. 3, and *Pipe roll 14 John*, p. 48). 3 The falsity of this belief was exposed by Orpen (*Normans*, ii, 270–7). 4 See *Pipe roll 14 John*, p. 49, where the sheriff accounts for various sums 'as contained in the roll of the eleventh year', while he seems to have been responsible for Cork as early as 1207, since he accounts for arrears of the eleventh and twelfth years, and of the preceding year. 5 The occasion of the establishment of Munster as a shire may well have been the final forfeiture of

been entrusted to royal officers, who are not, however, described in the pipe roll as sheriffs, but as seneschals or stewards.

It is not till 1228–9 that we again get the general survey of the administrative framework which is provided by a pipe roll,[6] but we have a good deal of information as to Waterford and Cork in the interval. In 1215, the custody of the county of Waterford, with the castles of Waterford and Dungarvan, and the king's demesnes in that county, excepting the city of Waterford, and the custody of the county of Desmond with the city of Cork and the king's demesnes there, were granted to Thomas fitz Anthony and his heirs for an annual payment of 250 marks, the only instance of the creation of an hereditary sheriffdom in Ireland. In 1222, these custodies were given to the justiciar, and in 1223 to John Marshal, but Thomas had recovered them by 1225. In December 1226, however, they were granted to Richard de Burgh, and in 1232 to Peter of Rivaux.[7] It is not clear whether or not they continued to be administered by a single sheriff after this date, but in 1259 John fitz Thomas, who had married one of Thomas fitz Anthony's daughters and co-heiresses, succeeded in obtaining from the future Edward I a grant of all the lands of 'Desya and Desmond' with their bailiwicks, which had belonged to Thomas fitz Anthony, to hold in fee for an annual payment of 500 marks and the service of one tenth of a knight's fee. The justiciar refused him seisin, alleging that the charter had been obtained by deceit, but John forcibly took possession, and according to the verdict of a jury in 1282 was at his death in July 1261 seised as of fee and not in serjeanty of the shrievalties of Waterford, Cork and Kerry.[8] Kerry had appeared as a separate shire as early as 1232–3,[9] though it was evidently included in the grant of Desmond. Since John's son and heir was killed with his father, the inheritance passed to Thomas fitz Maurice, John's grandson, who did not come of age till 1282. During this time, it was, of course, in the king's hands as a wardship: when Thomas came of age the shrievalties, which he seems to have exercised for a short period, were recovered from him by legal process.[10] In 1292, however, he was regranted the lands of Decies and Desmond with all 'bedelries' belonging to that land. This did not, apparently, include the shrievalties, but only the serjeanties, since it is distinctly stated that the bedels whom Thomas and his heirs appoint are to be subordinate to the sheriffs for the time being of those counties, and on the same date the royal grant to Thomas de la Roche of

William de Braose, for which see Orpen, *Normans*, ii, 236ff. 6 The earliest pipe roll which survived in the PROI in 1922 was that for 13 Hen. III (1228–9), and it, with the six others of that reign which then remained, is calendared in *35th rep. DKPRI*. 7 *CDI 1171–1251*, nos. 576, 580, 584, 1060, 1107, 1108, 1292, 1462, 1502, 1969. 8 *CDI 1252–84*, nos. 629, 1474, 1912, 2215, 2217. 9 *35th rep. DKPRI*, p. 37. 10 *CDI 1285–92*, nos. 16, 17, 18, 1051. Thomas did not get seisin of his inheritance till 1284 (*CDI 1252–84*, nos. 2215, 2217). He exercised the sheriff's function of collecting the king's debts in Waterford and Kerry, and presumably also in Cork, for a short time after this (*CDI 1285–92*, nos. 45, 251). For the

the custody of the county of Cork was renewed.[11] During the period after 1284, Cork and Waterford were often administered by a single sheriff, but Kerry, from its first appearance as a separate county in 1232, seems always to have had a sheriff of its own.[12]

Having thus traced the development of the shires along the south coast, we must return to the reign of Henry III. Uriel (or Louth), which was administered together with Ulster by a steward in 1212, was still in this position in 1215; by 1233, it had become a shire with its own sheriff.[13] In the midlands, the sheriff of Munster continues to appear in the records till shortly before 1254, when Limerick and Tipperary became completely separate administrative units.[14] Further west, Connacht was a shire by 1247,[15] but the sheriff of Roscommon does not appear till 1292, though the shire had probably been formed some ten years earlier, after the rebuilding of the castle by Robert d'Ufford.[16]

In 1297, there were thus nine shires – Dublin, Waterford, Cork, Kerry, Louth, Limerick, Tipperary, Connacht and Roscommon – and two more were added to the list by an act passed in the parliament of that year. The immediate occasion was the return of the liberty of Kildare to the crown, but opportunity was taken to reorganize the shire of Dublin, which then included not only the modern county of that name, but also much of the modern county of Wicklow and the de Verdun half of the former liberty of Meath.[17] In addition, the sheriff of Dublin exercised direct jurisdiction over the crosslands[18] of the four liberties of Leinster and of the liberties of Trim and Ulster; and, should the seneschals of any of these liberties fail to execute a royal writ, the sheriff of Dublin was the person directed to enter the liberty and put the writ into execution.[19] It is true

serjeanties, see below, pp 135–6. 11 *CDI 1285–92*, nos. 1048, 1050, 1051. 12 *35th–47th rep. DKPRI*, passim. The medieval county lay north of Desmond proper, but was evidently included in the grant. 13 Above p. 121; *CDI 1171–1251*, no. 611; *35th rep. DKPRI*, p. 36. 14 A serjeant of Munster was appointed as late as Jan. 1251 (*CDI 1171–1251*, no. 3106), and the sheriff of Limerick is referred to in Feb. 1254 as having been in existence some time earlier (*CDI 1252–84*, no. 318). Limerick had been regarded as a separate shire within Munster as early as 1235 (*35th rep. DKPRI*, p. 35), when it presumably had its own county court, presided over by the sheriff of Munster 15 *CDI 1171–1251*, no. 2909. It may have been formed much earlier, as a mandate of 1236 is addressed to 'constables, sheriffs, farmers, castellans, and all the king's other bailiffs in Connaught, Thomond, and elsewhere in Ireland' (ibid., no. 2339). 16 *CDI 1285–92*, no. 1148, and see Orpen, *Normans*, iv, 109–11. 17 After Walter de Lacy's death in 1241, his liberty of Meath was partitioned between his two granddaughters, who married respectively Geoffrey de Geynville and John de Verdun. De Geynville succeeded in obtaining a grant of the liberties enjoyed by de Lacy in 1252 (*CDI 1252–84*, nos. 69, 78; *Reg. Gormanston*, p. 178), and his liberty of Trim was on the whole successfully maintained throughout the century. The same liberties were claimed by the de Verduns, but, though they apparently obtained them for a time, they were recovered for the crown in 1280 by legal process, and it must have been then that the de Verdun lands became part of Co. Dublin (*CDI 1252–84*, nos. 740, 810, 1645, 1666, 1670, 1673; *35th and 36th rep. DKPRI*, passim). 18 The crosslands were the lands held by the church directly from the crown, and were exempt from liberty jurisdiction (see below, pp 125–6). 19 For examples, that a considerable area in Dublin and the Wicklow mountains was comprised in the liberty of St Sepulchre (the lands of the archbishop of Dublin, which formed an extensive secular immunity, largely excluding the activities of the officers of the crown),[20] while the city of Dublin was also an immunity. But this did little to mitigate the difficulties of the sheriff of Dublin in administering so extensive and so scattered an area; and the first act of the parliament of 1297 – declaring that the dispersion of the various parts of the shire resulted in inefficiency from the point of view of both the government and the governed – established a sheriff in the crosses of Ulster to administer them and to execute writs in the liberty of Ulster when necessary, to the exclusion of the sheriff of Dublin; made Meath and its crosslands a separate shire, with its own sheriff and county court; and declared that Kildare and its crosslands should in future be a separate shire, entirely absolved from the jurisdiction of the sheriff of Dublin, with its own sheriff, 'as it has now'.[21] It will surprise no one familiar with medieval legislation to learn that the only part of this act which was completely effective was the last. In Ulster, the position seems to have remained completely unchanged.[22] Meath did indeed become a separate shire in name, and the new county court at Kells was no doubt more convenient to the suitors and litigants of Meath than the county court of Dublin had been. But as the new shire normally shared a sheriff with Dublin, the act made little other difference in practice, except to provide an occasional welcome point of error for a hard-pressed litigant, who could allege that a writ had been directed to the sheriff of Dublin when the sheriff of Meath should have been named.[23] But Kildare was already a shire (its sheriff was one of those who were directed to have knights elected in their county courts for this parliament and to come to it themselves),[24] and, like the other liberties, had been organized on the lines of a shire even while it was a liberty, so that its organization needed change only in detail in the eyre, which the justiciar himself held at Kildare from 21 July 1297 until April 1298.[25] In short, as far as Kildare was concerned, the act only registered existing fact, and was so far effective. A second Leinster liberty, that of Carlow, also reverted to the crown, and was treated as a shire, after the death without issue of Roger Bygod in December 1306.[26]

see *CJRI*, passim. Writs intended for the liberties of Leinster were directed to the sheriff of Dublin, who forwarded them to the seneschal concerned. In the liberty of Trim, the lord of the liberty was entitled to have royal writs directed immediately to him or to his seneschal, though this right was not always respected by the authorities in Dublin (see, e.g., *CDI 1252–84*, no. 1666). **20** The baronies of Upper and Nether Cross later represented that part of the liberty which lay in the modern Co. Dublin (see *The civil survey A.D. 1654–56*, ed. R.C. Simington, 10 vols (IMC, Dublin, 1931–61), vii, pp xxiii–xxvi). **21** *Stat. John–Hen. V*, pp 196–8. **22** See, e.g., *CJRI 1295–1303*, pp 216–17, 249. **23** Ibid., p. 438. For sheriffs of Dublin and Meath, see *38th rep. DKPRI*, pp 60–2. **24** *Stat. John–Hen. V*, p. 194. **25** *CJRI 1295–1303*, pp 167–208. **26** *CDI 1302–7*, nos. 367, 617; *CJRI 1305–7*, pp 251, 356,

At the death of Edward I, the area directly governed by royal officials was thus greater than at any other period of the Middle Ages. In south-eastern Ireland, only Wexford, Kilkenny and Trim were still liberties; in the south-west the great liberties of the second period of Anglo-Irish rule had not yet come into existence. Moreover, the existence of a liberty did not exclude the king's writ, only the king's sheriffs, and the seneschal of a liberty took oath to the king as well as to his lord.[27] Ulster was perhaps too far distant to be very easily controlled by the Dublin government, but though it appears comparatively seldom in the records, the liberty of Ulster was in the king's hand and governed by his officials for considerable periods during the thirteenth century.[28] Only the north-western corner of Ireland was altogether outside the sphere of shire or liberty, though there were, of course, enclaves of territory still held by the Irish wherever wild or mountainous country provided a sufficient protection.[29] Moreover, though Ulster might be left to itself, the central government still exercised a vigorous supervision elsewhere. Wogan, as justiciar, visited even the most distant shires, holding his court and correcting the misdeeds of local officials,[30] while the system of itinerant justices was still in regular operation at the end of Edward's reign.[31] Not only this, but *quo warranto* inquiries resulted in the surrender of many claims to minor immunities,[32] and the great liberties seem to have been undergoing a gradual internal erosion by the extension of the area of church lands exempt from their jurisdiction.

As has been said, the crosslands were church lands exempt from liberty jurisdiction and attached to the nearest shire for administrative purposes.[33] But it is clear that not all church lands were crosslands in this sense. The royal grants of liberties in Ireland all expressly reserved the crosses to the king, and this seems to have meant that lands held by the church at the time of the grant were to be held immediately from the crown, and were therefore exempt from the jurisdiction of the liberty, forming enclaves of land in which the royal administration had full force, limited only by such private jurisdiction as existed everywhere in a feudal state. But land subsequently granted to the church might or might not be crossland in this sense: that depended on the terms of the grant, and on the person by whom it was made. A grant by a subtenant clearly could not obliterate the superior rights of the lord of the liberty in the land unless the lord consented to this.[34] In the very interesting dispute between William de Vescy, lord of the liberty of Kildare, and the abbot of St Thomas about the

358, 392–3, 395. 27 *CJRI 1295–1303*, p. 242. 28 See Orpen, *Normans*, iii, ch. 21; ibid., iv, ch. 36. 29 Ibid., iv, 259–61; Curtis, *Med. Ire.*, ch. 9. 30 *CJRI*, passim. 31 Ibid., and *CDI*, passim. 32 See, e.g., *CJRI 1295–1303*, pp 102–3. 33 See above, p. 123, n. 18. Under Edward III, separate sheriffs appear for the crosses of each liberty, perhaps because the growth in the number of liberties had made the old arrangement impracticable. 34 For the parallel case of frankalmoign tenure, in which the rights of an overlord remained unless by his express grant, see Elisabeth G. Kimball, 'Tenure in frank almoign and secular services', *EHR*, 43:171

abbey's lands in Kildare, the case really turns on the question of whether or not charters of the Marshals – granting the monks the free and peaceful enjoyment, so far as belongs to the lord, of all the possessions which they had acquired in his land of Ireland – were to be interpreted as exempting the lands and benefices concerned from the jurisdiction of the liberty. The abbot said that, by these deeds, William de Vescy and his parceners could claim no right in the lands in dispute and that, from the time of the making of those deeds, they had always been intentive to the king. De Vescy maintained that the deeds, which made no reference to cognizance of causes, did not grant anything of the kind, and that cases arising in those lands, with the exception of the four reserved pleas of the crown, had continued to be pleaded in the court of the liberty till recently. The jury confirmed him in this statement, but, unfortunately for his claim, during a vacancy of the abbey, while it was in the king's hand, the royal officers had seen to it that these cases were brought before the king's courts; and the English court *coram rege,* to which the dispute eventually went, was not disposed to relinquish this addition to the royal rights, asserting that the lord of the liberty had no jurisdiction over the abbot or his possessions, but that the abbey held of the king in chief.[35] In exactly the same way, the sheriff of Dublin, while the bishopric of Meath was vacant, asserted that the lands of the church of St Patrick of Trim, which had formerly been part of the liberty of Trim, were crosslands, exempt from the jurisdiction of the liberty court.[36] It seems as if, towards the end of Edward's reign, the church, encouraged by the royal courts, was successfully extricating its lands from the secular liberties and making them shireland.

We know very little of the subdivisions of the shires. The English hundred in its territorial sense was not introduced: the references to hundreds in the records, and they are many, all refer to the courts of towns.[37] The subdivision of the Irish shire was the cantred, which owes its name to the equation made by the Anglo-Normans of the twelfth century between the Gaelic *tricha cét*, a territorial unit which seems already to have been obsolescent in the greater part of Ireland, and the Welsh *cantref*, a unit similar to both the *tricha cét* and the hundred. Some few of the Norman cantreds can be shown to have been identical with earlier *tricha cét*s, but over the greater part of the country they

(1928), 341–53. 35 *CDI 1293–1301*, nos. 22, 101, 145, 146, and the parallel dispute about an advowson (ibid., nos. 26, 42, 141, 146). See also the series of complaints against de Vescy (ibid., no. 106). There was clearly a personal enmity between de Vescy and the abbot. 36 *CJRI 1305–7*, p. 391. See also *CDI 1285–92*, nos. 452, 1075. 37 This is, of course, a well-known secondary use of the term hundred (see Mary Bateson, *Borough customs*, 2 vols (Seldon Soc., London, 1904–6), passim). There were a great many small boroughs associated with manors in Ireland, which never really became towns. Territorial hundreds are mentioned in a few early grants, but these do not seem to correspond to any administrative reality (*CStM*, i, 80, 274; ibid., ii, 162; C.M. Butler and J.H. Bernard, 'The charters of the Cistercian abbey of Duiske in the county of Kilkenny', *PRIA*, 25:C1 (1918), p. 18; *Ir. mon. deeds, 1200–1600*, p. 100; *CDI 1171– 1251*, no. 2282), and are probably to be accounted for by seem to have been formed as settlement proceeded.[38] No doubt, like the English hundred, each cantred had its court, where presumably the sheriff held his tourn,[39] but the records have nothing to say of them.[40] Of the existence of shire courts there is, however, abundant evidence: that of Dublin appears in the 1190s,[41] and as the thirteenth century progresses references to them are frequent. Like the English shire courts, they were held monthly on a fixed day of the week, normally in the principal town of the shire, and the duty of attendance was territorialized, if not from the beginning at least early in the reign of Henry III.[42] The principal royal officer in these shires was, of course, the sheriff. During the greater part of the thirteenth century, sheriffs were appointed by a variety of methods: sometimes under the English great seal,[43] sometimes by the Irish treasurer or justiciar, who often drove a hard bargain with them. Such an appointment might be subsequently confirmed by a grant under the English great seal.[44] Sometimes the justiciar was expressly given power

the automatic use of English formulae. 38 James Hogan, 'The *tricha cét* and related land-measures', *PRIA*, 38:C7 (1928–9), 148–235. The Welsh land connections of many of the Norman settlers in Ireland are sufficiently well-known, and it is interesting to observe that, in the thirteenth century, analogies based on conditions in the marches of Wales were being applied to the conditions of border warfare in Ireland (*Reg. Gormanston*, p. 181). It should be observed that the cantred was not quite universal: the liberties of Trim and Wexford had honors and baronies respectively in the late thirteenth century, and in Dublin we hear of serjeanties which sound as if they might have been organized around the royal manors of that county – the serjeanties of the vale of Dublin on the side of Leinster in the regions of Taxagard and Newcastle of Lyouns, Bree and Newcastle M'Kynegan, Fynegal on one side of the water of Gouere and Fynegal on the other side of the water of Gouere (*temp.* Edw. II and Edw. III: *39th rep. DKPRI*, pp 53, 69; *42nd rep. DKPRI*, pp 29, 52; *43rd rep. DKPRI*, p. 32; *44th rep. DKPRI*, p. 18). Cf. Helen M. Cam, '*Manerium cum hundredo*: the hundred and the hundred manor', *EHR*, 47:187 (1932), 353–76; repr. eadem, *Liberties and communities in medieval England: collected studies in local administration and topography* (Cambridge, 1944). A document of *c.*1514 (pr. Hogan, 'Tricha cét', p. 233) equates cantred with hundred or barony. 39 See below, p. 132. 40 The existence of a court for each cantred is implied not only by the existence of the sheriff's tourn, but also by the communal responsibility of the cantreds for amercements (*38th rep. DKPRI*, p. 29; *CDI 1293–1301*, pp 249, 294; *CJRI 1305–7*, pp 410, 412) and its separate representation in the eyre (*CJRI 1295–1303*, pp 167, 170, 173, 176). 41 *CDI 1171–1251*, no. 272. 42 *CDI 1171–1251*, no. 2282; *CDI 1285–92*, p. 312; *CDI 1293–1301*, no. 605; NLI, MS 1 [Harris], fo. 288 (a petition from the archbishop of Armagh asking that he may be freed from the burden of suit to the county court for a manor which he has recently acquired); *CJRI 1295–1301*, pp 246, 402; *CJRI 1305–7*, p. 112. 43 *CDI 1171–1251*, no. 2909; *CDI 1252–84*, nos. 631, 1125, 1185, 1414; *CDI 1285–92*, nos. 123, 602, 654, 734, 1048, 1050. The exchequer ordinance of 1293 states that sheriffs and other bailiffs have often been appointed under the English great seal (*Stat. John–Hen. V*, p. 190). 44 It was stated, *c.*1285, that 'almost no one can be in any office in the exchequer, nor in any shrievalty or custody of a castle, unless he gives or sells land to the justiciar, or bestows on him a moiety of his fee ... This is so in respect to Walter Uncle and the profits of the county of Tipperary, who every year gives more in horses than he answers to the king for the profits of the county' (*CDI 1285–92*, pp 3–4). Uncle had a grant of the custody of the county to dispose of the custody of a shire or shires;[45] sometimes persons were sent as sheriffs from England.[46] In 1293, however, it was laid down that, in order that they should be more obedient to the exchequer, sheriffs and other bailiffs who answered at the exchequer should be appointed by the treasurer and barons of the exchequer and removed by them and not by others, and should be responsible before them for what pertained to their office.[47] On the whole, this arrangement seems to have been adhered to, though in the last few years of the reign of Edward I a number of grants of Irish shrievalties were made under the English great seal as a reward for good service during the war in Scotland,[48] and on one occasion a new sheriff was appointed for Co. Waterford in the justiciar's court.[49] Grants under the English seal were frequently made for periods as long as ten years, but many of the sheriffs appointed by the exchequer held office only for short periods, though the same sheriff was frequently reappointed after an interval. Acceptance of the office was, as in England, compulsory, and could be avoided only by the holder of a royal charter exempting him from service, but grants of such exemptions were rare during this period.[50] But in fact the office was evidently extremely popular. Grants under the great seal were eagerly petitioned for; prospective sheriffs were believed to be ready to bribe the justiciar heavily to secure office. Occasionally, the candidate designated by the exchequer refused to take office in spite of all that could be done by way of distraint,[51] but it seems clear that such cases were unusual. Certainly, there were great opportunities for extortion, but the financial responsibilities of a sheriff were very heavy, and most sheriffs seem to have bequeathed to their heirs debts to the crown which took years to pay off.

Serious misconduct by the sheriffs was naturally most common in the shires furthest from the centre of government. When the justiciar visited Limerick and Kerry in 1295, his court had to deal with long lists of charges of violence and oppression of all kinds brought against sheriffs and ex-sheriffs.[52] The degree of disorder which existed in these two shires was quite exceptional, and

under the English great seal in 1282 (*CDI 1252–84*, no. 1979). See also *CDI 1252–84*, no. 2194; *CDI 1284–92*, nos. 16, 17, 18, 19, 120. The county of Tipperary was let to Roger de Penbrok 'in full exchequer' at £100 a year (*CDI 1285–92*, no. 999). **45** *CDI 1252–84*, nos. 1021, 1025. **46** In 1281, the treasurer wrote to the king that, 'as for the sheriffs sent to Ireland, as Thomas de Mynimes, Henry Picot and others, who have nothing, they are injurious to the king and more to the people, because they receive the king's money and then go away, having nothing to be distrained by. And because their malice cannot be borne with they embroil the Irish settlers with their friends of England, calumniating the former' (*CDI 1252–84*, nos. 1881, 1882). Thomas de Mynimes or Mymmys was sheriff of Louth in 1276–7 (*36th rep. DKPRI*, p. 38). In 1280, having 'laudably and long served the king in Ireland', he was granted an annuity of 6*d*. a day for life, payable at the exchequer, Dublin (*CDI 1252–84*, no. 1719). **47** *Stat. John–Hen. V*, p. 190. **48** *CDI 1302–7*, nos. 10, 24, 274. **49** *CJRI 1305–7*, p. 119. **50** *CDI 1252–84*, nos. 1730, 1733, 2297. **51** Gilbert, *Hist. & mun. docs*, pp 528–9. **52** *CJRI 1295–1303*, passim.

even they revealed nothing at all comparable in later visitations; but a whole series of petitions alleging extortions by the sheriff of Waterford had been presented to the king in the Easter parliament of 1290,[53] and there can be no doubt that there was always a good deal of bribery of the kind revealed to the justiciar in 1306, when it emerged from a dispute about the office of coroner in the cross of Meath that two persons elected to that office had paid the sheriff 20*s*. and one mark respectively to release them. Afterwards, however, the sheriff had found it expedient to bribe them in turn, lest they should denounce him to the exchequer officials then in Drogheda;[54] and, in general, it may be doubted whether the amounts which could be made in this way were altogether worth the risks involved when the machinery of central government was functioning efficiently. Walter Uncle, sheriff of Tipperary, took a bribe of four marks to harbour a man mistakenly indicted for harbouring a thief; when detected by the itinerant justices, he was amerced in the sum of £100.[55] Moreover, the sheriff was exposed to a constant risk of amercement for the undue return of writs, for the default of his subordinates, whom he could not always easily control, and in general for any slip in the performance of a very exacting set of duties.[56] The attractiveness of the office was perhaps as much a matter of prestige as anything else, for its legitimate rewards do not seem to have been large. The sheriff was entitled to a fee, or allowance for maintenance, and to a fee for each of his tourns, but, while it is not clear how much all this amounted to, the total cannot have been very great: in 1299, the justiciar and council fixed the fee of the sheriff of Kildare at £10 a year, besides the fee which he took for his tourns, and it must be remembered that a sheriff had to provide himself with a considerable staff.[57] He was, of course, also entitled to certain customary fees from those on whose behalf he performed such functions as giving seisin of land in execution of a decision of the courts or a royal charter, but it is quite impossible to calculate how much these fees amounted to.[58] When the pleas and perquisites of the county were farmed, the sheriff could no doubt make a legitimate profit, but not a large one. But even if the office involved much responsibility and little profit, it was often an important stage in the career of the professional class of administrators, who might begin as sub-escheators, continue as sheriffs, and end as justices of the bench.[59]

53 *CDI 1285–92*, no. 622. 54 *CJRI 1305–7*, p. 175. 55 *CDI 1293–1301*, nos. 107, 212, 213. He was granted a respite of this amercement in 1295, in return for his service in the Welsh war. 56 *CJRI*, passim; *CDI 1302–7*, nos. 4, 30, 344; TCD, MS 671, 31 Edw. I (a seventeenth-century collection of notes from the Irish pipe rolls and plea rolls). 57 *Stat. John–Hen. V*, p. 219; *CJRI, 1295–1303*, pp 13–14, 51, 233; *38th rep. DKPRI*, p. 91; *CDI 1252–84*, no. 2257; *CDI 1285–92*, p. 316. 58 'Ralph de Trubleville represents that the sheriff of Dublin exacts from him 100*s*. for livery of seisin of the land of Balimadan. As it is the custom of England that no sheriff shall exact anything for giving seisin, save an ox, which Ralph has rendered, he is to have peace concerning the 100*s*.' (*CDI 1171–1251*, no. 1536). 59 See, e.g., the career of Hugh Canoun.

The duties of the Anglo-Irish sheriff were, as far as can be seen, identical with those of his English counterpart. He might or might not hold his shire at farm, but the pleas and perquisites of the county, which were included in his farm, were the least part of the revenue which he had to collect, varying from £3 8*s*. 8*d*. for two and a quarter years (Sept. 1299–Jan. 1302) in Roscommon, to £27 4*s*. 2*d*. for one year (1297–8) in Tipperary, 'and no more because there was war there'. For the same periods, these sheriffs accounted for other sums amounting to £128 7*s*. 3*d*. and £195 6*s*. 10*d*. respectively.[60] Tipperary was the shire whose profits were largest: in 1281–2, they amounted to £100, and the shire was subsequently farmed at £100; but, in 1290, the farm was reduced to £40 after some of the customary revenues had been abolished by the justiciar.[61] None of the other shires came near this imposing total, but this customary revenue – estimated in 1284 to amount to no more than £265 7*s*. 6*d*. at the best for the whole of Ireland[62] – was of comparatively little importance. Most of the revenue which the sheriffs had to collect, and which was never farmed, was the product of the activities of the central government. The sheriff, under the orders of the exchequer, was responsible for the collection of amercements imposed by the royal courts, fines for having the king's grace, fees for chancery writs, the arrears of former sheriffs' accounts, and all the other items which made up the ordinary revenue of the crown, as well as the scutages of the lesser tenants-in-chief 'when royal service ran', and sometimes a local subsidy.[63] In the eyes of the crown, this was their most important function, and no doubt the oath which they took on appointment was largely concerned with their accountability at the exchequer.[64]

Besides collecting revenue, the sheriff might have to expend considerable sums in the course of his administrative duties. Thus he might have to provide for the repair of gaols or of the king's castles; he might have to provide for the expenses of the emissaries of the central government, paying out sums varying from £9 delivered by the sheriff of Limerick to Thomas Cantok, chancellor, going to Munster to establish the king's peace, to 12*d*. paid by the sheriff of Louth towards the expenses of a man carrying a summons direct to the

60 *38th rep. DKPRI*, pp 29, 54. 61 *CDI 1252–84*, nos. 1979, 2329; *CDI 1285–92*, nos. 734, 999. 62 *CDI 1252–84*, no. 2329. 63 Generally speaking, the sheriff collected all revenue except that from those towns which had the right of farming themselves and were to a great extent exempt from his jurisdiction (at the end of the thirteenth century, these were Dublin, Waterford, Cork, Limerick and the two Droghedas); from those magnates who had the right to answer themselves at the exchequer for the liberties; from the new custom, and from general subsidies, which were separately administered; and from lands which were in the king's hand as wardships, escheats, or the property of vacant bishoprics and religious houses, for which the escheator was responsible. 64 *Stat. John–Hen. V*, p. 190; Gilbert, *Hist. & mun. docs*, pp 528–9. They were to swear to appoint only bailiffs for whom they were willing to answer, as in England. For instances of the enforcement of this responsibility, see *38th rep. DKPRI*, p. 91; *CJRI 1305–7*, pp 220, 509.

seneschal of Ulster; he might be required to spend very large sums on the purchase of provisions for the king's French, Welsh or Scottish wars; and, towards the end of Edward I's reign and afterwards, it became a regular practice to have the fees of exchequer officials paid direct by the sheriffs.[65] Most of the sheriffs made regular payments into the treasury in each of the principal exchequer terms; but their final accounts, when all the allowances duly warranted by writs were made up, occur at irregular intervals – the pipe roll account for any particular county generally covering several years, sometimes as many as six.[66]

But the sheriff was not only concerned with the revenue; he had many other functions. He was an essential officer of the royal courts, wherever they were held. When the justiciar made his circuit the sheriff was ordered to

> have here at that day all assises of mort d'ancestor and novel disseisin, before whatever justices assigned in this county, with the original writs and all other things concerning the assizes, and to notify the parties to be here to do and receive what shall be just. And to make come all prisoners of this county, and all persons mainprised to pleas of the king's crown by precept of the justiciar, with the indictments and all other things touching the delivery of the prisoners; and to make public proclamation that all who would complain of the king's ministers or others be here to prosecute their plaints, and to do and receive what the king's court shall adjudge. And to make come 24 of the best and most discreet, as well knights as others, of this county, to certify the justiciar here on articles touching the tranquillity of the peace to be required of them. And that the sheriff be here to certify what he shall have done in the premises.[67]

When the justices in eyre made their visitation, he had, as in England, to summon his whole shire before them, to bring all pleas before them, to ensure the presence of all who had been sheriffs or coroners since the last eyre, to summon all claiming liberties to appear with their bailiffs, and to proclaim that all who wished to complain of the king's ministers or others might do so before the justices.[68] One of the most onerous of his duties was to get defendants and jurors into court; another, which must have been no less burdensome, was that of levying debts recovered by judgment of the court. Indignant creditors regularly complained that the sheriff had corruptly failed to levy debts which could well have been recovered, and the sheriff was amerced. But in fact, when

65 *35th–47th rep. DKPRI*, passim. 66 For sheriffs' payments, see the receipt rolls (*CDI 1285–92*; *CDI 1293–1301*; and *CDI 1302–7*, passim). 67 See, e.g., *CJRI 1305–7*, pp 167–8. 68 A set of writs relating to the Meath eyre of 1322 was printed in Herbert Wood, 'The muniments of Edmund de Mortimer, third earl of March, concerning his liberty of Trim', *PRIA*, 40:C7 (1932), 338–41.

the money could only be recovered by the process of seizing goods and selling them, it was often impossible to do anything in face of the refusal of the countryside, whether from fear or favour, to buy. Another difficulty was that goods seized were often violently taken from the sheriff's officers, but this was an offence dealt with energetically by the courts.[69] Finally, the sheriff was responsible for the custody of prisoners, whether before their trial or after it, till they had found pledges for the payment of their amercements. In most cases, persons accused were released on mainprise till the arrival of justices, and in that case the sheriff was responsible for accepting the security.[70]

The sheriff, in Ireland as in England, had judicial functions of his own. In the county court he was of course only a president, but he was responsible for the conduct of its business. The administrative functions of the county courts were indeed becoming more important than their judicial ones by the end of the thirteenth century: it was in them that proclamations of all kinds were made and private charters published; knights of the shire and coroners were elected in them; and they must have provided the framework for those local assemblies in which subsidies were sometimes granted.[71] Outlawries could be pronounced only by the county courts, or by their equivalents in the liberties, and though outlawry was by the late thirteenth century mainly procedural, it was of importance as a means of procuring the appearance of defendants before the justices. The judicial functions of the county courts, though curtailed by the legislation of Edward I, remained not unimportant; appeals of felony were brought in them,[72] and they still dealt with a variety of civil cases.

The court in which the sheriff exercised real judicial power was his tourn, in which he took inquisitions and dealt with minor offences himself, reserving the pleas of the crown for the judgment of the royal justices. Most of our evidence as to the working of this court in Ireland comes from the liberties, but, as they were organized in much the same way as the ordinary shires, it is safe to assume that their tourns did not differ from those of the shires, and we are fortunate in having a detailed list of the articles of the tourn in the liberty of Trim preserved in the register of Tristernagh.[73] They present the usual combination of judicial and administrative inquiries: the sheriff was to enquire whether cases belonging to the liberty court had been held elsewhere, whether cases not concerning wills

69 *CJRI*, passim. 70 See *CJRI*, passim, and *RCH*, p. 4: 'as there is now no prison in Co. Connacht where prisoners can be safely kept, the sheriff is given power to release them on sufficient security, provided that those accused of arson or malicious homicide shall make fine for this grace.' 71 *Stat. John–Hen. V*, p. 194; *CDI 1285–92*, p. 312; *CJRI 1295–1303*, pp 71, 303–4, 411. For these local subsidies, see Clarke, *Med. representation*, pp 44–54. 72 E.g., the appeal brought by John Harold, sheriff of Limerick, in his county court against the earl of Ulster and others of the death of his son and robbery of his goods (*CJRI 1295–1303*, pp 120–1). 73 Some fifteenth-century records of the sheriff's tourn in the liberty of Tipperary are calendared in *COD*, iii. The articles of the tourn, apparently of the late thirteenth century, are pr. *Reg. Tristernagh*, pp 32–3.

or matrimony had been brought into the church courts, and as to arson, treasure-trove, rape, forestalling and the minor pleas of the crown.[74] He was to ask whether dove-cots, parks, fisheries or warrens had been robbed, whether there had been any offences in connection with weights and measures, whether thieves had been taken with stolen goods and allowed to redeem themselves without judgment, and whether anyone had harboured thieves. Wardships, marriages and escheats belonging to the lord's liberty were to be enquired into, and the sheriff was to ask whether watch and ward had been kept, whether hue and cry had been unjustly raised, whether serjeants had taken money for remitting complaints, whether roads had been obstructed, or waters impeded or turned from their right course. He was to enquire about those who had been accused of felony and outlawed in the lord's court: who had proclaimed them, and who could have attached them and had not done so. Finally, he enquired as to burglaries and homicides, as to the slaying of Englishmen and their burial without view of the coroner, and as to the forgers of writings and seals. The list differs very little from those commonly found in England, and may reasonably be taken as representative of those in use throughout Ireland at the end of the thirteenth century. It will be observed that there is no mention of view of frankpledge, one of the few English institutions which does not appear to have been successfully established in Ireland, though it is occasionally referred to, and may have existed in some places.[75]

In the shires, our chief evidence as to the existence of the sheriff's tourn comes from the complaints made to the justiciar, or even to the king in parliament, as to the fees levied by the sheriff in connection with it. Thus, in 1290, the people of the county of Tipperary complained that whereas formerly only half a mark from each barony had been taken at each tourn, the sheriff was now exacting the same sum from each knight's fee.[76] In 1302, the archbishop of Tuam complained to the king that the sheriffs of Connacht levied fees from his tenants for their tourns in the lands of the archbishopric, which, he maintained, they were not entitled to do, but it is doubtful whether such an exemption really existed. The complaint made against the sheriff of Limerick in 1295 that he took his tourn in some places three and in some places four times a year, though not substantiated, was obviously connected with the same question of fees. As in England, the tourn was supposed to be held twice a year.[77]

74 Arson, rape, treasure-trove and forestalling were reserved to the crown in all the Irish liberties; the minor pleas of the crown belonged to the lord of the liberty. 75 *CDI 1293–1301*, no. 801. 76 Barony is apparently here the feudal, not the later territorial, barony. The territorial unit in Tipperary at the time was certainly the cantred, and the tourn was probably held in each cantred (see above, pp 126–7). 77 *CDI 1285–92*, p. 316; *CJRI 1295–1303*, pp 52, 377. Geoffrey de Geneville's charter to the magnates of Meath, *c.*1262–70, provides that the sheriff of Trim shall hold his tourn in the lordship of the magnates twice a year, or oftener if necessary (*Reg. Gormanston*, p. 176).

The military functions of the sheriff were naturally more prominent in Ireland than in England, since none of the Irish shires was free from border warfare. In the earlier part of the thirteenth century, he was often the keeper of one of the royal castles within his shire, though this seems to have become less usual as Edward I's reign progressed.[78] He might be ordered to keep an armed guard in the marches of his county,[79] and it was his duty to see that those persons who had been obliged by local ordinances to keep such guards should do so.[80]

These military duties shaded imperceptibly into his police duties. The attempt to attach persons indicted in his inquisitions was frequently resisted by force necessitating the calling out of the *posse comitatus*, which might also be required to levy a debt from lands in the marches, or a subsidy granted for local defence.[81] On his own initiative, or by the special command of the justiciar, he might intervene to prevent a threatened breach of the peace,[82] and he might exceptionally be commissioned to negotiate with 'felons and disturbers of the peace', whom he had, of course, no authority to pardon in the ordinary course of his duties.[83]

His other administrative duties were very varied. He was frequently directed to take inquisitions *ad quod damnum* or *post mortem*, to explain, usually in conjunction with the coroner, why lands had been taken into the king's hand, to value property, or to establish boundaries.[84] When in the course of border war a horse had been killed, it was the sheriff's duty to ascertain its value and the circumstances in which it had been lost, and to levy the compensation payable.[85] The sheriff saw to it that coroners were elected in the county court and forced them to undertake the office.[86] He was responsible for the election of knights of the shire when they were summoned to parliament.[87] He proclaimed statutes in his county courts and in market towns and fairs, and where necessary had persons chosen to carry them out and administered the prescribed oaths.[88] It was he who obliged those whose tenure required them to repair bridges or causeways to do so.[89] If weirs or mills had been erected in a river so as to impede navigation or damage fisheries, it was the sheriff who was instructed to have them removed.[90] Though writs were normally served by his serjeants, he might in special cases have to deliver them himself, perhaps undertaking a considerable journey for the purpose,[91] and he might be required to conduct prisoners from

78 *35th rep. DKPRI*, pp 30, 35; *36th rep. DKPRI*, p. 38; *CDI 1171–1251*, no. 2792; *CDI 1252–84*, nos. 631, 1038, 1125, 1242, 1258, 1698, 1907; *CDI 1285–92*, no. 169. 79 *CJRI 1305–7*, pp 242–3. 80 *38th rep. DKPRI*, p. 88. 81 *CJRI 1295–1303*, pp 7, 60, 74, 147; *CJRI 1303–5*, pp 13, 479. 82 *CJRI 1295–1303*, pp 74, 350; *CJRI 1305–7*, p. 2. 83 *CJRI 1295–1303*, p. 72. 84 *CDI 1293–1301*, nos. 16, 481; *CDI 1302–7*, no. 411; *CJRI*, passim. 85 *CJRI 1305–7*, pp 85, 325–6. 86 *CJRI 1295–1305*, pp 60, 71, 411; *CJRI 1305–7*, p. 174. 87 *Stat. John–Hen. V*, p. 194. On this occasion (the parliament of 1297), the sheriffs were required not only to have knights elected in their county courts, but also to attend parliament themselves, but this does not seem to have been repeated. 88 E.g., the statute of false money (*CJRI 1295–1303*, p. 265). 89 Ibid., p. 175; *CJRI 1305–7*, p. 192. 90 *CJRI 1305–7*, p. 259. 91 *CJRI 1295–1303*, pp 131–

Ireland to appear before the king, wherever he might be.[92] From time to time, he was commanded to take with him four discreet men of his shire and go to the court of some immunity to make a record of a plea held there.[93] He had powers of purveyance, and was, finally, responsible for the construction of all kinds of public works – from the erection of a bar in the house where pleas which follow the justiciar are held in Dublin, to the building of a new hall in the king's castle of Randown;[94] and, in general, any duty which no other official was at leisure to perform might be thrust upon him.

The sheriff obviously required a considerable staff to assist him in the performance of this array of duties. He seems normally to have had a sub-sheriff, appointed by himself, who could take his place in his absence, and who found sureties in the exchequer for the performance of his duties;[95] one or more clerks, who took charge of the writs addressed to him (and sometimes lost them), and who must also have been responsible for the rolls of the county;[96] and sometimes, perhaps always, a receiver, who took charge of the moneys collected and issued receipts in the form of tallies.[97] Besides this office staff, there was a body of serjeants – the equivalents of the English hundred bailiffs – who were in theory, but apparently in theory only, controlled by the sheriff. The justiciar's court refuses angrily to accept certain returns made by the sheriff of Tipperary, saying that he cannot be excused because his serjeants did nothing, and that he returned certain frivolous and false excuses, which he says were returned to him by the chief serjeant of the county, which the court does not admit.[98] Again, it supports the contention of the attorneys of Agnes de Valence when they say that the sheriff of Limerick ought not to be excused for the default of any serjeant, unless the serjeant be a bailiff of fee, having return of writs, such as the seneschals of liberties from which the sheriff is excluded unless specially authorized to enter by the king's writ.[99] But it is clear that the sheriff had at least a reasonable defence when he maintained that he did no trespass, because the execution and answers were made by Walter Maunsel, the chief serjeant in the county, to whom the sheriff by custom sends the writs directed to him to be executed, without whom the sheriff can do nothing concerning them. In most, if not all, of the counties of Ireland, there was an hereditary chief serjeant – the chief serjeant of fee – who held his office as a fief from the king, and was not apparently in practice subject to any control by the sheriff, though he could be removed for misconduct by the justiciar or the

2; *CJRI 1305–7*, p. 132. 92 *CDI 1252–84*, no. 2310; *CDI 1285–92*, no. 169. 93 *CJRI 1295–1303*, pp 84, 112, 328. 94 *CDI 1252–84*, no. 1577; *38th rep. DKPRI*, p. 54; *CJRI 1305–7*, pp 250, 414–15. 95 *CJRI 1295–1303*, pp 22, 26, 49, 202, 375, 424; *CJRI 1305–7*, pp 160, 209, 250, 509; TCD, MS 671, 29 Edw. I. 96 *CJRI 1295–1303*, pp 1, 25, 48, 49, 82, 426; *CJRI 1305–7*, pp 119–21; *CDI 1252–84*, no. 2108. 97 A receiver appears in Kerry (*CJRI 1295–1303*, p. 53), and Tipperary (*CJRI 1295–1303*, p. 349; *CJRI 1305–7*, pp 54, 115, 460). 98 *CJRI 1305–7*, pp 193–4, 269, 319. 99 Ibid., pp 207–8.

justices in eyre, only to recover his office by making fine with the king.[100] The serjeanty of Munster, held by Walter de Abbetot till his forfeiture, was granted to Walter Maunsell 'for ever' in 1251.[101] When Munster was divided into the counties of Tipperary and Limerick, the serjeanty became the two chief serjeanties of Tipperary and Limerick, but there was only one chief serjeant for the two counties. At the end of the century, the office was held by Robert Maunsel, who was succeeded on his death in 1299 by his son Walter; and, in the fourteenth and fifteenth centuries, the office of chief serjeant of the liberty of Tipperary continued to be held by this family.[102] In Meath, there was the family of Bacun;[103] in Louth, that of de Crus, which also held the chief serjeanty of Dublin or Leinster. In 1610, the chief serjeanty of Co. Dublin was still held by this family.[104] In Waterford, Cork and Kerry, the chief serjeanties were finally granted to Thomas fitz Maurice and his heirs in 1292 after many vicissitudes,[105] but this did not become immediately effective, for the serjeanties of Cork and Kerry had been let to farm.[106] When Thomas died in 1298, his heir (later created earl of Desmond) was a minor, and these lands and offices were granted to his widow, who gave the chief serjeanty of Waterford to her second husband, Reginald Russel.[107] Inquisitions taken in 1421 on the lands of John, earl of Desmond, at his death in 1398 state that he held in fee the office of chief serjeant of counties Waterford and Cork; Kerry was then a liberty, but the earl held in fee the office of the cross of that county.[108]

The chief serjeant, who frequently exercised his office by a deputy,[109] was generally responsible for the whole county. Under him, there were serjeants of cantreds whom he appointed,[110] and who, in turn, had their own sub-serjeants.[111] The organization of the serjeanties of Kildare seems to have differed to some extent from that of the other counties: here we find the serjeant of each cantred described as a chief serjeant of fee, though that of Offolan seems to have been the most important. Its serjeant is more frequently mentioned than that of any

**100** *CDI 1293–1301*, no. 363; *CJRI 1295–1303*, pp 17, 81, 318; *CJRI 1305–7*, p. 337; *38th rep. DKPRI*, p. 91. **101** *CDI 1171–1251*, nos. 318, 570, 3106. **102** *CJRI*, passim; *Reg. Gormanston*, p. 118; *COD*, ii, 131; *COD*, iii, 95. **103** *CJRI*, passim; *Calendar of chancery warrants, 1244–1326* (London, 1927), p. 513. I owe this reference to the kindness of Mr H.G. Richardson. **104** Lynch, *Legal institutions*, pp 105–6, where it is stated that the office was held under a grant from John. See also *CDI 1252–84*, no. 2310; *CDI 1285–92*, no. 149; *CDI 1293–1301*, nos. 21, 363; *CJRI*, passim. In 1297, Richard de Crus, while remaining chief serjeant of Leinster, got leave to enfeoff his brother, Nicholas, of the serjeanty of Louth, to hold of the king in chief (*CJRI 1295–1303*, p. 81). **105** See above, pp 122–3. **106** *CDI 1252–84*, nos. 2194, 2329; *CDI 1293–1301*, nos. 21, 329, 391, 550, 587, 658, 825; *CJRI 1302–7*, nos. 58, 72. **107** *CJRI 1295–1301*, p. 295; *CJRI 1305–7*, pp 71, 120–1, 162, 211. **108** *COD*, iii, 32–6. **109** *CJRI*, passim. **110** See, e.g., *CJRI 1295–1303*, pp 16–18. When, exceptionally, a serjeant in Co. Waterford was appointed by the sheriff, not by the chief serjeant, it was because Thomas fitz Maurice's widow had granted him her life-interest in that serjeanty (*CJRI 1295–1301*, p. 424; *CJRI 1305–7*, pp 120–1). **111** See, e.g., *CJRI*

other cantred, and it rendered 100*s*. a year to the king, while each of the other four serjeanties rendered only 2*s*. a year.[112] This organization had existed when Kildare was a liberty, and the only modification made when the liberty was shired seems to have been that, whereas the chief serjeants had previously acted as coroners in their cantreds, separate coroners were now appointed; while the crosslands, which had formerly been organized as a separate serjeanty, were now merged in the cantreds in which they were situated.[113] The organization of Co. Dublin also presented certain peculiarities, since it included the crosslands of the whole of Leinster and of Ulster, for which there were serjeants.

The office of serjeant in all its grades was a profitable one, for which relatively considerable sums might be paid. Under Edward I, the chief serjeanty of Cork was farmed for £10,[114] and, in 1298, after the death of Thomas fitz Maurice, the escheator paid £11 into the treasury for the issues of the serjeanty of Cork over a period which can have covered only a few months.[115] When the chief serjeanty of Limerick was taken into the king's hand in 1295, Robert Maunsel undertook to pay a fine of £10 to recover it, and later his son Walter was willing to pay 40 marks to recover the serjeanty of Tipperary.[116] The valuation of Thomas fitz Maurice's lands made in 1299 estimated the annual value of the serjeanty of Waterford at £10 0*s*. 4*d*., and that of Kerry at 66*s*. 8*d*.[117] The annual payment due at the exchequer for the chief serjeanty of Waterford in 1302 was 12 marks, which was recoverable from the serjeants of cantreds.[118] The annual revenue of the serjeanty of Meath at the beginning of the fourteenth century seems to have amounted to 10 marks.[119] As for inferior serjeanties, the chief serjeant of Limerick took 28*s*. for the serjeanty of one cantred for a term of five years, while we find sub-serjeants themselves dealing in their offices in what was evidently a perfectly legal manner.[120]

Of the legal rewards of a serjeanty we know little, but since all the routine duties of the sheriff were in fact performed by the serjeants of the county, the office was one which lent itself to bribery and extortion of every kind. They might put poor men on juries, sparing the rich for reward, or summon partisan juries; they released those whom they had attached, allowed fugitives to escape from sanctuary, failed to make distraints, retained goods taken for debts to their own use, revealed the names of jurors to those indicted, suppressed indictments, suppressed writs which endangered their own interests, had their enemies indicted, levied more than was due for the sheriff's fee and kept the balance. In 1295, no fewer than nine serjeants in Co. Kerry were found guilty of such offences.[121] But while the rewards, legal or illegal, of a serjeanty were evidently considerable, the

*1295–1303*, pp 280, 300. 112 *CJRI 1295–1303*, p. 167; *CDI 1293–1301*, no. 481. 113 *CJRI 1295–1303*, p. 167. 114 *CDI 1252–84*, no. 2329. 115 *CDI 1293–1301*, no. 550. 116 *CJRI 1295–1303*, p. 17; *38th rep. DKPRI*, p. 91. 117 *CDI 1293–1301*, no. 551. 118 *CJRI 1295–1303*, p. 424. 119 *CJRI 1305–7*, p. 23. 120 *CJRI 1295–1303*, pp 18, 133; *CJRI 1305–7*, pp 286–7. 121 *CJRI 1295–1303*, pp 19, 20, 32, 34, 35, 45, 64, 107, 234, 280, 281, 296, 298, 342, office was not without risks, both financial and physical, and must always have been strenuous. The serjeant was financially responsible for those whom he had placed in office: should they fail to exercise their office properly, he was liable for the payment of any amercements which they were unable to pay themselves;[122] he might incur heavy amercements if prisoners escaped from his custody; and he ran the risk of amercement and even of the forfeiture of his office if he failed to perform its duties to the satisfaction of the justiciar.[123] The serjeants of Dublin might find themselves obliged to journey through half Ireland;[124] and as for the physical risks involved, it will be sufficient to quote the case of the serjeant who, having taken a sickle as distraint to secure the appearance of a defendant at the county court, was set upon by the neighbours, armed with axes, and threatened with death unless he gave it up.[125]

The chief serjeant was normally a man of some position, a fairly substantial landowner. The sub-serjeants were naturally men of much lower social standing who risked less by misconduct, and it is against them that the majority of the more serious charges are made. The main offence of most chief serjeants seems to have been systematic neglect of their duties, carried to a particularly high degree by Walter Maunsel, who, having repeatedly failed to execute writs, was deprived of his office of chief serjeant of Tipperary by the justices itinerant at Cashel early in 1306.[126] Serjeants, like other officials, were sworn on taking office,[127] but the terms of their oath do not seem to have survived. Chief serjeants, as we have seen, usually inherited their office, but on the occasions when it was in the king's hand, a chief serjeant might be appointed by the itinerant justices, or might be elected in the county court in the same way as a coroner.[128] The chief serjeant appointed his immediate subordinates, but the royal courts might disqualify anyone found guilty of serious misconduct from ever holding the office again, and the chief serjeant of Limerick was removed from his office in 1295 because he had recommitted serjeanties to such men.[129]

The sheriff and serjeants were not the only royal officials in the shires, though they are the most prominent in the records. In many shires, the escheator had permanent deputies, and coroners of course existed everywhere. In Ireland, there seems to have been a coroner for each cantred, but it is not possible to compile a complete list.[130] As in England, the coroner was elected by the oath of twelve men in the county court (or by the community of the cross

394; *CJRI 1305–7*, pp 55, 117, 238, 267, 288, 414–15; *38th rep. DKPRI*, pp 52, 75–6, 91–2. **122** *CJRI 1295–1303*, pp 172, 280. **123** *CJRI*, passim. **124** *CDI 1285–92*, nos. 598, 830: the chief serjeant of Co. Dublin was sent with an open letter under the seal of the exchequer to Ross, Waterford, Youghal, Cork and Limerick. **125** *CJRI 1305–7*, p. 482. **126** Ibid., pp 193, 337, 341. **127** *CJRI 1295–1303*, pp 1, 17, 55; *CJRI 1305–7*, p. 46. **128** *CJRI 1295–1303*, p. 17; *CJRI 1305–7*, pp 337, 341. **129** *CJRI 1295–1303*, pp 16–17. **130** Ibid., p. 167 and passim. The earliest reference to coroners in Ireland that I have found occurs in the inquisitions taken as to the liberties of the archbishops of Dublin, *c.*1264, which imply

concerned) and, as in England, the office was an unpopular one, which could sometimes be avoided by bribing the sheriff, whose duty it was to see that the election took place and to distrain the person elected to take oath and accept the office.[131] The duties of the coroner were those of his English counterpart: he was concerned with the pleas of the crown, and in particular with violent deaths; and when the claim of the bishop of Down to have pleas of the crown and ransom of felonies was disputed in the justiciar's court in 1297, it was a sufficient definition of the duties of a former coroner in the crosses of Ulster to say that he made inquisitions and views of slain.[132] It was before the coroner that felons who had taken sanctuary abjured the realm.[133] He was responsible for taking into the king's hand deodands and the goods of persons indicted in his inquisitions, but when arrests were made he was obliged to rely on the sheriff, who ordered the serjeants to act.[134] When for any reason the sheriff was disqualified from acting – he might, for instance, be a party to the case – the coroner was directed to act instead. Thus, in 1297 when the earl of Ulster alleged that John Harold, sheriff of Limerick, had maliciously appealed him of the death of his son in his county court, the coroners of the county were directed to cause the appeal to be recorded in full county court in presence of the justiciar. As it appeared to the justiciar's court that the county had erred in outlawing the earl and others involved, the coroners and whole community were amerced in £10 for false judgment and appeal.[135] On other occasions, the sheriff and coroners might be directed to act together in taking inquisitions for the information of the justiciar, but the coroner's actions might not be questioned before the sheriff in the county court.[136]

Besides the sheriffs and coroners, there were also the keepers of the peace, of whose office very little appears at this period, but who seem to have had a much more military character than their counterparts in England. Towards the end of the reign of Edward I, we find several in each cantred of Waterford – the whole body was amerced 'for default in keeping the peace' and their names have thus been preserved – and they existed also in Tipperary, Limerick, Kerry, Kildare, the vale of Dublin and no doubt elsewhere. The Waterford list contains no fewer than forty-three names, but elsewhere we find only a few persons

that there were coroners in the time of Archbishop John Comyn (1182–1212), and there is no reason to doubt this, though the surviving records do not mention them till towards the end of the reign of Henry III (Charles McNeill, 'The secular jurisdiction of the early archbishops of Dublin', *JRSAI*, 45, (1915), 81–108, esp. p. 103). **131** *CJRI 1295–1303*, pp 60, 71, 411; *CJRI 1305–7*, pp 174–5; *CDI 1293–1301*, no. 72. **132** *CJRI 1295–1303*, p. 103. **133** *CJRI 1295–1303*, pp 34, 174, 405–6; *CJRI 1305–7*, p. 513. **134** *CJRI 1305–7*, p. 437. **135** *CJRI 1295–1303*, pp 120–1; *38th rep. DKPRI*, p. 75. See also *CJRI 1295–1303*, p. 387; *CJRI 1305–7*, p. 92. When the sheriff himself was appealed in the county court, it was the coroner who took charge of the proceedings (*CJRI 1295–1303*, p. 348). **136** *CJRI 1295–1303*, pp 24, 106, 255; *CJRI 1305–7*, pp 271, 513; *CDI 1302–7*, no. 411.

mentioned. Where the reason for their appointment is given, it is 'to repress the malice of felons invading from day to day divers parts of this country'.[137]

Besides these purely local officials, there were from time to time all sorts of emissaries of the central government: exchequer officials might be sent to hasten the collection of the king's debts; clerks of the markets investigated weights and measures; the escheator visited the lands which he administered; the justiciar and his court were regularly itinerant; the justices in eyre held prolonged and heavy-handed sessions. In nearly every respect, the local government of the lordship of Ireland during the thirteenth century was a copy, as exact as possible, though no doubt less efficient, of that of England. There were already some interesting divergences from the pattern, but during our period they were relatively unimportant.

137 *CJRI 1305–7*, pp 116, 518; *38th rep. DKPRI*, pp 64, 99; *RCH*, p. 5; *CDI 1252–84*, nos. 2241, 2310; *CDI 1285–92*, no. 169; *CDI 1302–7*, no. 58. The sums levied by the sheriff of Limerick for keeping the country in 1295 and paid to those assigned to keep the country were presumably for the keepers of the peace (*CJRI 1295–1303*, p. 40). The earliest reference I have been able to find is to a conservator of the king's peace in the vale of Dublin in 1283 (*CDI 1252–84*, no. 2241; *CDI 1285–92*, no. 169).

CHAPTER 6

# The native Irish and English law in medieval Ireland*

*A.J. Otway-Ruthven*

The problems set by the Norman conquest of Ireland which began under Henry II cannot be properly appreciated if they are viewed in isolation. Similar problems had been set by the Norman conquest of England only a hundred years earlier; similar problems existed in Wales. In England, however, the conquest had been both rapid and complete, and problems which were to last throughout the Middle Ages in Ireland were solved in England by the merging of the two peoples in a relatively short time. Moreover, in England, no such clash of laws as was to come about in Ireland had followed the conquest: the Anglo-Saxons had possessed a well-developed system of local administration which was taken over with little or no modification by the Norman kings. Since all law was then customary – 'found' by those who used it – and the Norman kings were desirous of preserving the 'law of the Confessor', which, except in the matter of land held by feudal tenure (a concept unknown to Anglo-Saxon law), harmonized well enough with their own customs, the two systems of law merged without great difficulty. But a century later, a distinctive legal system – the common law – centrally directed and administered by royal judges, was already emerging in England, and the infinite variety of local custom which had survived the conquest, and had even been added to by it, was being very slowly eradicated. The law of the king's court, the 'tremendous empire of kingly majesty', was already showing its power of indefinite development and would tolerate no competitors: it was, moreover, already far from the primitive simplicity of the law of the eleventh century.[1] Thus, such an amalgamation of customs as had occurred in England was impossible for the common law of the late twelfth century and Irish law, even had the conquest of Ireland been complete.

In Wales, on the other hand, though at first sight there may seem to be a closer parallel to conditions in Ireland, the whole course of Norman conquest was very different. The marcher lords, whose power covered a great part of Wales, had been able to build up a distinctive system of march law at an early date, and the common law was excluded from this area till the sixteenth century.

* First published in *IHS*, 7:25 (1950), 1–16. 1 Pollock and Maitland, *Hist. of Eng. law*.

Elsewhere in Wales, for the greater part of the thirteenth century, both marcher lords and Welsh princes endeavoured to have applied to their disputes whichever system they thought most favourable to their claims, while, within the Welsh principalities, Welsh law was of course applicable. Finally, in the statute of Wales of 1284, a system of law was laid down for Wales outside the marcher lordships, which though based on the common law included parts of the Welsh customary law, which it seems clear had been developing along lines which brought it closer to English law than has sometimes been supposed.[2]

In Ireland, the crown had intervened in the conquest at a much earlier stage than in Wales. Clearly, no complete conquest of Ireland was envisaged by Henry II: the treaty of Windsor, an agreement between Henry and Rory O'Connor, the high king, concluded in a great council held at Windsor in October 1175, provides that only the area already occupied by the Normans – Leinster and Meath, with the whole coastline from Dublin to Dungarvan – was to be removed from the jurisdiction of the high king. Elsewhere, Rory was confirmed in his kingdom of Connaught and the high kingship, and the feudal relationship was established between him and Henry. Rory was to be responsible for the collection of the English tribute (one hide for each ten animals slain) from the province kings, but his jurisdiction within this area was in no way affected by the treaty.[3] In May 1177, at the council of Oxford, the kingdoms of Cork and Limerick – that is, the whole province of Munster – were given to de Cogan and Fitzstephen, and at some time shortly after this a formal grant of Ulster must have been made to de Courcy, for it is impossible to believe that Henry would, for instance, have allowed him to be employed as justiciar in the absence of a regularization of his position in Ulster. These events have usually been regarded as the final abrogation of the treaty of Windsor, but Dr O'Doherty has shown reason to suppose that O'Connor acquiesced in the grant of Munster for his own reasons, and I think it is probable that he may also have done so in the case of Ulster. Certainly, the treaty seems to have been still regarded as operative in 1181.[4]

It is unnecessary for our purposes to trace further the expansion of the area controlled by the government at Dublin. From the first, the principle of two distinct administrative and legal systems had been adopted, and though when, in the reign of Edward I, English power in Ireland was at the highest point it ever reached during the Middle Ages, something like three quarters of the country was at least nominally subject to the control of the Dublin government,[5] those areas still governed by Irish chiefs were not even in theory within the scope of the

2 See F.M. Powicke, *King Henry III and the lord Edward: the community of the realm in the thirteenth century* (Oxford, 1947), ch. 15. 3 J.F. O'Doherty, 'St Laurence O'Toole and the Anglo-Norman invasion', *IER*, 5th ser., 50 (1937), 623–4; R. Dudley-Edwards, 'Anglo-Norman relations with Connacht, 1169–1224', *IHS*, 1:2 (1938), 137, n. 2. 4 See O'Doherty, 'St Laurence O'Toole and the Anglo-Norman invasion', *IER*, 5th ser., 51 (1938), 136–8. 5 See Otway-Ruthven, 'Anglo-Irish shire government in the thirteenth century' (above, ch. 5).

common law. The best and clearest examples of this come from the earldom of Ulster, where, even in Antrim and Down as late as 1333, three Irish chiefs held considerable territories by the service of maintaining 'satellites' for the earl's wars and, apparently, a rent of cattle. There is nothing whatever to suggest that as far as their internal affairs were concerned these territories were not autonomous, and they lay outside the administrative framework of shires within which the earl's officials exercised their functions.[6] These Irish rulers, with the exception of O'Donnell and his sub-chiefs, were all involved in some sort of feudal relationship either directly to the crown or to the lord of the liberty within whose area their territories lay. During the first half of the thirteenth century, hostages were obtained from a number of them on various occasions,[7] and they paid rents which seem usually to have been heavily in arrears. On a number of occasions during the century, Irish rulers were asked to join in expeditions against Scotland, and O'Neill and others of the Irish of Ulster were liable to the characteristically feudal obligation of money aids for the king's wars.[8] It is clear that chiefs were nominated (though not always successfully) by the agents of the crown or of the lord of the liberty, and the individual chief seems to have been regarded, and indeed to have regarded himself, as a tenant at will.[9] With the Irish resurgence of the fourteenth century, this position was of course to change, and Irish rulers were to recover a far greater degree of independence than they had enjoyed during the first 150 years of the colony's existence, but the position during the later Middle Ages has not yet been worked out in detail, and accepted views may need modification. The areas thus left to the undisputed supremacy of Irish law were, however, in the thirteenth century, a comparatively small part of the country, and over the rest of Ireland the existence of English administrative machinery, whether in shire or liberty, ensured the dominance of the English common law, though it must be remembered that everywhere there were pockets of difficult country where the Irish were able to maintain a large degree of independence disturbed only by occasional punitive expeditions, as for instance in the Wicklow mountains.

So far, we have a position somewhat similar to that which existed in Wales before 1284, though it does not appear that Irish law was ever pleaded in the

6 C 135/36, no. 25 (summarized by Goddard H. Orpen, 'The earldom of Ulster', *JRSAI*, 43 (1913) 30–46, 133–43; ibid., 44 (1914), 51–66; ibid., 45 (1915), 123–42) and C 47/10/20, no. 14. 7 See, e.g., *ALC*, s.a. 1238, 1248; *AU*, s.a. 1242, 1252. The hostages of Cenél-Conaill were obtained in 1238 and 1242, but there is nothing to suggest that O'Donnell was ever regarded as being in the same position as O'Neill, and though an inquistion in the PRO, London [TNA], represents him as having been obliged to maintain eighty 'satellites' for the earl of Ulster (C 47/10/20, no. 14), this statement does not occur in the inquisitions taken after the murder of William de Burgo in 1333, and may have been made in error. 8 Gilbert, *Facsimiles*, ii, pl. 73; Davies, *Discovery* (1787 ed.), p. 13; *CDI 1171–51*, no. 2716; *Foedera*. 9 *CDI 1252–84*, no. 929; *AU*, s.a. 1286, 1291; BL, Add. MS 4790, fo. 144*d*.

king's court as Welsh law was, and nothing comparable to the immunities of the Welsh marcher lordships existed in the Irish liberties.[10] But whereas, in dealing with Wales, the English administration thought of law as territorial, in Ireland it seems from the first to have been thought of as personal. It was, indeed, reported by Matthew Paris, writing in the thirteenth century, that at Lismore Henry II had held a council where the laws of England were by all freely received and confirmed with all solemnity, and some have seen in this the origin of the celebrated privilege of the 'five bloods'.[11] But though there is no doubt some genuine tradition behind this story, it is certainly misleading in the form in which we have it, and it is to John that the records attribute the establishment of English laws and customs in Ireland.[12] But though John would appear to have granted a charter concerning English law to Ireland, it was certainly a charter to the settlers only, for from the first it is clear that the right to use English law in Ireland was something which the individual Irishman must obtain from the king, and frequently did obtain by a charter to himself and his heirs. Records of many of these charters have survived, and one granted by Henry II to the Ostmen of Waterford was pleaded in the Anglo-Irish courts in the early fourteenth century.[13] It should be observed that though at first the lords of liberties granted English law to their Irishmen,[14] later only the king himself could grant such charters: the justiciar was not empowered to do so unless specially authorized.[15] There is reason to believe that many such charters of which no record has survived were granted by Henry II, by John when lord of Ireland, and by Edward I before he became king, a period of which our knowledge is particularly deficient, since the prince's letters were not, of course, enrolled in his father's chancery.

The most famous of these charters is that supposed to have been granted by Henry III to five septs. In one of the Cottonian MSS, there is a statement, said to be taken from the archives in Dublin castle, that 'Rex H[enricus] 3 in anno regni sui 3 by especial graunt enfranchised and enobled 5 principal bloods or septs of the Irishrie, to take the benefit of the lawes of England vz. Oneale de Vltonia, Omalaghlin de Midia, Oconnoghor de Connachia, Obrien de Tothmonia, et McMourgho de Lagenia'.[16] This statement presents serious difficulties: it is a mere note, not a transcript, and we have no means of checking its accuracy,

**10** See Powicke, *Henry III and the lord Edward*. **11** See below, pp 144–5. **12** *Stat. John–Hen. V*, pp 21, 23. **13** Gilbert, *Facsimiles*, iii, pl. 7. **14** In 1299, a charter of English law granted by William Marshal, lord of Leinster, in 1208–9, was pleaded in the justiciar's court (*CJRI 1295–1303*, p. 271). **15** See, e.g., *CPR 1313–17*, pp 563–4; SC 8/119/5944 and SC 8/177/8820, cited by H.G. Richardson, 'English institutions in medieval Ireland', *IHS*, 1:4 (1939), 390–1. It was always, however, possible for any lord to give a charter to an Irishman making him of 'as free condition as any Englishman among his tenants' as far as the lord himself was concerned, and he could then apparently sue against the lord in the king's court (*CJRI 1305–7*, pp 321–3). **16** BL, Cotton Titus B XI, pt 1, fo. 70.

while the list of names would appear to be much more appropriate to the reign of Henry II than to that of his grandson. But that some such grant was made, though not necessarily in 1218–19, appears certain, for in 1354 it was pleaded in the king's court at Dublin that, by the grant of the king's ancestors, five bloods, of whom the O'Neills of Ulster were one, ought to enjoy and use English liberties, and this was not disputed, though the defendant unsuccessfully tried to prove that the plaintiff was not in fact an O'Neill of Ulster.[17] It may be observed that, by 1222, O'Neill was certainly in some sort of contact with the Dublin government.[18]

It is clear, then, that numbers, probably very large numbers, of the free Irish in the areas of English settlement obtained grants of English law, and became assimilated to the colonists. This process is difficult to trace, for in the thirteenth century it is quite clear that many Irishmen living among the English went by English names, though it is only exceptionally that one can prove this in any particular case.[19] The juries of law-worthy Irishmen to which the episcopal records of Limerick and Cloyne refer were presumably to be drawn from men who had been thus enfranchized.[20]

But while many individual Irishmen were thus granted the use of English law (the right to plead in the English courts in Ireland), many more were not, and here we must distinguish between the two main legal classes, the free and the unfree or semi-free classes, which existed in every country of Europe and had existed in Ireland before the Norman conquest. The Norman settlers were all personally free and had no need to introduce servile tenants from England: just as had happened in England a hundred years earlier, the servile tenants of the new Norman manors were provided by the existing inhabitants, many of whom had been in exactly the same position before the conquest. The treaty of Windsor contains a clause which seems to be designed to secure the return of fugitive unfree tenants to the lands of their new Norman lords.

These unfree tenants are to be found all over the country, most often under the name of betaghs (from the Irish *biatach*),[21] occasionally as *nativi* (a term also applied to the same class in England), and sometimes as *hibernici,* the use of which leads to the utmost confusion, since it is often not possible to determine from the context whether in any particular case it means a servile tenant or a free Irishman who has not been granted English law.

**17** BL, Add. MS 4790, fos. 67*d*–68; Davies, *Discovery* (1787 ed.), pp 83–4. BL, Cotton Titus B XI, appears to have been used by Davies in writing the *Discovery*. **18** *CDI 1171–1251*, no. 1001. **19** The cases in which we have definite evidence are nearly all cases in which unenfranchized Irishmen have sought to merge themselves with the colonists by taking English names – see, e.g., *CJRI 1295–1303*, p. 342; *CJRI 1305–7*, p. 520; *Liber primus Kilkenniensis*, pp 6–9; Davies, *Discovery* (1787 ed.), p. 90; Cambridge University Library, Add. MS 3104, p. 49*d*. **20** *Black bk Limerick*, p. 27; *Rot. pipae Clonensis*, pp 34–5. **21** The earliest document in which I have found the term betagh used is *Pipe roll 14 John* (1212);

The Irish betagh was in much the same position as the English villein. In some cases, he was in theory completely at the disposal of his lord, as for instance were the men of the betaghs of the bishop of Cloyne, who are clearly of pre-conquest origin. Their position in the middle of the fourteenth century is described in some detail in the survey of the episcopal property which we still possess, and this description would no doubt apply equally to a much earlier date, since the church, being in the position of a trustee, was necessarily more conservative than lay lords. We are told of a number of named septs that all their members are 'pure men of St Colman and belong to the church'; that the bishop may take them and their children, wherever they are, and place them on his lands wherever he wishes; that he may seize their goods and sell them; and that, on their death, all their property is at his disposal, while they may not make a will without his leave. Elsewhere, we hear that the men of St Colman may not move from the land of the church without the bishop's leave, and that all the goods and lands of one of them belong to the bishop because all of the race of Okarny are Irishmen of the church of St Colman and *nativi*. Their labour services seem to be on the whole very little mitigated by customary limitations, though in some parts of the see lands betaghs, who do not seem to have been 'men of St Colman', were by now paying money rents. Nevertheless, one of these men of St Colman was found to be enjoying a considerable prosperity, owning house property in Cloyne which brought him in the comfortable sum of 45*s*. a year.[22] Perhaps the most curious part of the decidedly archaic social structure of the episcopal lands of Cloyne was the position of some of the burgesses of the bishop's town of Kylmaclenyn, who were betaghs and might not leave the town except to pasture on the bishop's demesne lands surrounding the burgage lands – a statement which might not be quite so surprising if it applied to the early twelfth century, but is the negation of everything normally implied by the name of burgess at any later date.[23] All these burgesses had English names and it is likely that, in Ireland as elsewhere by this time, unfree status was coming – apart from such exceptional cases as the 'men of St Colman' – to depend less on descent than on the possession of land held by unfree tenure. Even in Cloyne, there are men who are said to hold in betaghry, but are not described as betaghs, probably representing a transitional stage.[24] Earlier in the fourteenth century in some other parts of Ireland, we

earlier documents speak of *nativi*. The only instances I have found of the use of the word villein in an explicitly Irish context are in 1341 and 1393 (BL, Lansd. MS 482, fo. 140; *PKCI*, pp 138–40). Occasionally, we get *hibernicus* used with precision: in 1305, we hear of a man who is an *hibernicus* of the king and his *nativus* (*CJRI 1305–7*, p. 150); and, in 1273, the countess of Ulster distinguishes between certain *hybernienses liberos* and certain others who are called *betagii seu nativi* of the said countess (SC 1/8/149; I am indebted to Mr H.G. Richardson for my knowledge of this document). **22** *Rot. pipae Clonensis*, pp 8–9, 26, 38–9. **23** Ibid., pp 15, 18, 20–1. **24** Ibid., pp 6, 7, 30–2.

occasionally find betagh lands occupied by tenants who are clearly not betaghs, but it is impossible to trace the further development of this.[25]

It is probable that in most of the Irish dioceses, there were betagh septs in the position of the men of St Colman, but it is only for Cloyne that we possess a detailed rental. Outside the church lands, there is no reason to suppose that this extreme degree of subordination existed, at any rate by the late thirteenth and early fourteenth centuries when we begin to get fairly full information. In 1225, we find the justiciar directed to remove the Irishmen living on land granted to the bishop of Down and settle them elsewhere on the king's land,[26] but this is the only instance of the kind I have been able to find. Betaghs were, of course, bound to the soil and might be recovered in the sheriff's tourn if they fled;[27] but, as their property consisted of cattle,[28] it must have been easy, particularly for those living near the marches, to leave their lords. In the rare instances where extents or rentals give the names of unfree tenants, we find betagh septs in occupation of the land,[29] and before the end of the thirteenth century, labour services and renders in kind had very commonly been commuted for a money rent.[30] Though the unfree tenant might theoretically be a tenant at will, in eastern Ireland, where few septs seem to have remained, he was commonly succeeded by his son, as in England;[31] where the land was occupied by betagh septs, succession was probably regulated in the manor court according to the rules of Irish customary law. It is clear from the enumeration of the betagh's obligations given by the rentals that he was in fact protected by fixed custom.[32] And when labour services had been generally commuted for a money rent, the emancipation of betagh or villein was well in sight. In 1403, a betagh tenant of the earl of Ormond had his own seal.[33] We continue to hear of betaghs till the end of the Middle Ages, and *nativi* still existed on the lands of the archbishop of Dublin in 1531;[34] but when the lands of the Irish monastic houses were surveyed after the dissolution, though everywhere there are small tenants owing labour services and rents in kind, all valued in money, the only reference to unfree tenants is the statement on several manors, 'here there are no *nativi*'.[35]

In Ireland, as elsewhere, unfree tenants were excluded from the king's courts. Their tenures were a matter for their lords' courts, for the common law took no cognizance of lands held in villeinage or equivalent tenures.[36] They could have

25 *CDI 1302–7*, no. 167. 26 *CDI 1171–1251*, no. 1264. 27 Ibid., no. 120; *CDI 1252–84*, no. 52; *CDI 1285–92*, no. 622, at p. 309; *39th rep. DKPRI*, pp 53, 69; *CJRI 1305–7*, p. 379. A bull of Pope Urban IV speaks of laymen bound to the soil who are vulgarly called *betagii* (*Reg. All Hallows*, pp 129–31). 28 *CJRI 1305–7*, pp 326–7. 29 *CDI 1285–92*, no. 459. 30 See, e.g., *CDI 1293–1301*, no. 551; *Red bk Ormond*, passim. The king's betaghs were paying money rents in the reign of John (*Pipe roll 14 John*, pp 7, 10, 12, 20, 30, 44). The whole question of this transition to a money economy deserves separate treatment. 31 Hore, *Wexford*, i, 15, 26. 32 For a full description of typical labour services, see *Lisronagh rental*. 33 *COD*, ii, no. 374. 34 *Reg. All Hallows*, pp 131–2. 35 *Extents Ir. mon. possessions*, passim. 36 See W.S.

no civil actions in the king's courts, for their property was held to belong to their lords, and it was the lord, therefore, who must sue for any wrong done to them. They themselves being the lord's property, it was also he who must sue for any personal injury done to them, though if a breach of the peace were involved the offence would be presented by a jury in the royal courts in the ordinary way. Felonies and misdemeanours committed by betaghs were normally justiciable in their lords' courts, though much would depend on the kind of jurisdiction possessed by the particular lord. It would appear, for instance, that every lord who had a court had the right of trying his own betaghs on charges of theft. If, however, the thief escaped, the lord lost his jurisdiction: fugitives could only be outlawed by the shire court (or by the liberty court which was its equivalent) and were then justiciable only by the royal courts or by the courts of the lord of the liberty. The chattels of the convicted *hibernicus*, however, belonged to his immediate lord, wherever he had been judged.[37] But though every lord with a court had the right to deal with thefts committed by his *hibernici*, by no means every lord had the right to deal with the charge of the 'death of an Englishman' – an offence regarded as of particular gravity, exactly as the 'death of a Norman' had been in England after the conquest, and no doubt for exactly the same reasons.[38]

The really peculiar feature about the situation in Ireland is that the free Irishman who had not been admitted to English law was, as far as the royal courts were concerned, in much the same position as the betagh. Technically, he was excluded from the royal courts, though in fact there are instances of persons with Irish names, who may or may not have had charters of English law, successfully bringing actions in the justiciar's court.[39] It might, however, always be objected that the defendant was not bound to answer because the plaintiff was an Irishman, and if this were proved by the verdict of a jury the action would be dismissed because the court had no jurisdiction. The plaintiff was not, however, without a remedy: his proper course was to induce his lord to bring an action, and since it was the lord's interest to secure the prosperity of his tenants there are many instances of this kind. Sometimes we find the Irishman joined with his lord as a plaintiff; if he can show that the rights of the crown are involved, he may sue himself as attorney for the king, even against his own lord.[40]

Holdsworth, *History of English law*, 17 vols (London, 1903–72), iii, 198–209. It should be observed that the king's betaghs do not seem to have been excluded from the royal courts – see Richardson, 'English institutions in medieval Ireland', p. 389. **37** *CDI 1285–92*, no. 591; *CJRI 1295–1303*, pp 34, 95, 133, 162, 254–5, 333–4; *CJRI 1305–7*, pp 67, 405; H.G. Richardson and G.O. Sayles, 'The Irish parliaments of Edward I', *PRIA*, 38:C6 (1929), 143; Richardson, 'English institutions in medieval Ireland', 387–8; *Reg. Gormanston*, p. 176. **38** *CJRI 1295–1303*, pp 68, 175, 204. **39** *CJRI 1295–1303*, pp 53, 209, 342. See also *CDI 1252–84*, no. 360, and *43rd rep. DKPRI*, p. 16. **40** Richardson, 'English institutions in medieval Ireland', pp 390–1. See this paper and the references given there for the whole

Moreover, if a breach of the king's peace were involved, the offence would eventually be presented by a jury before the justices in eyre.[41] The most serious civil grievance was that Irishmen not admitted to English law were apparently not held capable of holding land in fee and inheritance, and on their death their heirs might be denied admission on the grounds that they had used Irish law,[42] while Irishwomen married to Englishmen were not entitled to dower. Closely connected with this is the complaint made by the archbishop of Tuam and other clergy to the king and the pope in 1255 that, among other grievances, the barons prevented Irishmen faithful to the king from bequeathing their chattels. The king commanded his son to call a council of magnates and provide a remedy, but we do not know what was done.[43] Another grievance reported to the pope was that Englishmen were admitted to back their claims by oath helpers and Irishmen were not; but, in fact, the wager of law was much blown upon in the royal courts by this time and does not seem to have survived, outside the towns at any rate, by the end of the thirteenth century, though of course it may have continued in the private courts, of whose procedure we know practically nothing. It should be observed that an Irishman made a burgess was, by the custom of all the towns of Ireland, entitled to English law as far as the towns were concerned, though it seems to have been thought prudent to have a royal charter of English law as well.[44]

The great problem facing the English administration in Ireland was, of course, that common to the whole of medieval Europe: how to secure that offenders should appear to stand their trial in the courts. In England, the frankpledge system, which does not seem to have been developed till after the Norman conquest, had been the solution adopted at least as early as the beginning of the twelfth century. But in Ireland, though almost every other device of Anglo-Norman government was introduced, there seems to have been no view of frankpledge. Instead of this device of securing the collective responsibility of neighbours, the Anglo-Irish administration seems to have relied on two older principles: the responsibility of the kin and of the lord.[45] We have little or no evidence as to how the responsibility of the kin worked in practice: we have occasional entries of collective fines made with the king for pardon of suit of the peace for all felonies, but no evidence as to the workings of the responsibility of

subject. See also *CJRI 1295–1303*, p. 133. 41 *CJRI*, passim. 42 *CJRI 1295–1303*, pp 121–3, and cf. ibid., p. 336; *CDI 1285–92*, no. 558. A royal letter of 1253 directs that two Irishmen whose petition alleges that they and their ancestors were always faithful to the king's fealty and service shall be allowed to sell their lands as if they were Englishmen if this be so (*CDI 1252–84*, no. 164). 43 *CDI 1252–84*, no. 460; *CPL 1198–1304*, pp 73–5, 283. See also *Reg. All Hallows*, pp 129–31. 44 *CJRI 1305–7*, p. 352, and cf. the cases of Hugh Kent in Galway and Robert of Bray in Dublin (references in H.G. Richardson, review of M.D. O'Sullivan, *Old Galway: the history of a Norman colony in Ireland* (Cambridge, 1942), in *IHS*, 4:16 (1945), p. 363). 45 Richardson and Sayles, 'Irish parliaments of Edward I', p. 142.

the kin for the offences of individuals. But there are numbers of instances of Anglo-Irish lords making fine with the king for all their offences and those of their Irishmen, and we must suppose that they were held responsible for them.[46] We find also Irishmen who are not, apparently, tenants paying 'head money' to lords to be in their 'advowson'.[47]

In criminal law, the influence of Irish custom on English law seems to have been felt early. The Irish thief, though if convicted in the justiciar's court he will usually be hanged like an Englishman, is often allowed to pay a fine and go free by private lords,[48] and this eventually extends to Englishmen too. Homicides presented a difficult problem: here the principle seems at first to have been adopted that the penalty should be that prescribed by the law appropriate to the victim. When in 1228, Henry III ordered that John's charter as to the observance of the law and custom of England and Ireland should be proclaimed and kept in Ireland, he added that 'of the death or of the chattels of Irishmen slain, nothing be decided on our behalf before the quinzaine of Michaelmas in the twelfth year of our reign, upon which point we have given respite to our magnates of Ireland until the said term'.[49] The outcome of this does not appear, but in 1297 it was stated in the Irish parliament that 'the killing of Englishmen and of Irishmen require different modes of punishment',[50] and there is ample evidence that the killing of an Irishman was normally punished by the exaction of a fine, which by the end of the thirteenth century seems to have been standardized at 5½ marks (£3 10*s*.).[51] But though the culpable killing of an Englishman was punishable by death according to the common law, in fact the influence of Irish law seems to have extended to this too at a comparatively early date. In the middle of the thirteenth century, we find both the archbishop of Dublin and the bishop of Down taking ransoms for the death of Englishmen, though it was said in 1297 that the bishop of Down had no warrant to do so.[52] By the early fourteenth century, however, it was being complained that royal justices admitted manslayers to ransom, and attempts were made to repress the practice.[53]

Though, as we have seen, the Irishman not admitted to English law was neither rightless nor deprived of legal protection, the position for those resident among the English must have had many practical inconveniences; and though it is clear that individual charters of English law could readily be obtained, the

46 See calendars of the pipe rolls in *Rep. DKPRI*, passim; *CJRI 1305–7*, p. 186. 47 *Red bk Ormond*, pp 40–1. The payment was 4*d*. a year. 48 *CJRI 1295–1303*, p. 95, and passim. 49 *Stat. John–Hen. V*, pp 23–4. 50 Ibid., p. 210. 51 It was, of course, his lord who was entitled to the payment. See the writ printed in Richardson, 'English institutions in medieval Ireland', p. 387, and *CJRI 1295–1303*, p. 283 and passim. 52 Charles McNeill, 'The secular jurisdiction of the early archbishops of Dublin', *JRSAI*, 45 (1915), pp 93–4, 96, 99, 101–2; *CJRI 1295–1303*, pp 102–3; William Prynn, *An exact chronological vindication of our kings' supreme ecclesiastical jurisdiction over all religious affairs*, 3 vols in 6 (London, 1665–8), iii, 775–6. 53 *CCR 1313–18*, pp 358–9.

necessity of applying to the king himself put difficulties in the way, while the assumption that an Irishman did not enjoy English law unless it was specifically proved that he did must have been a constant irritant. Accordingly, we find, early in the reign of Edward I, a movement, led by the archbishop of Cashel, to obtain the general extension of English law to the Irish as a whole. The negotiations – by the end of which, the archbishop and his supporters, the bishops of Emly and Killaloe, were undertaking to induce five other bishops of the province of Cashel to join them in guaranteeing the payment of a sum of 10,000 marks in return for such a grant of English laws – lasted from 1277 or late in 1276 till 1280, when they seem to have broken down, and were not, so far as we know, renewed.[54] The opportunity thus lost of extending English law to the whole of Ireland, with the exception of the northwest, which was excluded from the proposals, at any rate in their original form, was never to occur again during the Middle Ages.[55] But there does not seem to have been any general opposition to individual grants of English liberties. In the reign of Edward II, both magnates and the 'middling people of Ireland' were petitioning that the justiciar should have power to admit to English law all Irishmen who desired it, saving the rights of lords over their betaghs.[56] This was, of course, a perfectly proper exception: only the lord himself could free his servile tenants. Moreover, by this time there seems to have been a growing uneasiness as to the effect of the system of ransoming thieves and manslayers, which appears to have been extended even to the death of Englishmen; and, in 1316, the justiciar was ordered to ascertain the opinion of the whole community, or at least of the prelates and magnates, 'concerning the peace of the land, and by what law the people should be treated', and to inform the king of the result, so that the council might make an ordinance as to the grievances concerning the issue of charters of pardon and taking of ransoms, which had been reported in a petition which asked that such things should be done only in parliament and with the consent of the king's council and faithful subjects there.[57] We do not know the result of this, but in 1321 it was ordered that Irishmen admitted to English law should use the English law of life and limbs – that is, be subject to the penalties of the criminal law.[58] In 1328, a petition from John Darcy to the king and council asked that all the Irish

54 For a discussion of the whole episode in light of previously unpublished documents, see A.J. Otway-Ruthven, 'The request of the Irish for English law, 1277–80', *IHS*, 6:24 (1949), 261–70 [EN. See also now *Affairs Ire.*, nos. 18–19]. It was stated, *c.*1290, that the king in his great council at London had declared that all who demanded a grant of English laws should have it, and this may have been the final answer to the bishops in 1280 (*CDI 1285–92*, p. 525).
55 It should, however, be remembered that we do not know whether or not the scheme really had any support among the Irish outside the ecclesiastical province of Cashel. Certainly its promoters envisaged a certain amount of opposition to it among the Irish.
56 SC 8/119/5944 and SC 8/177/8820, cited in Richardson, 'English institutions in medieval Ireland', pp 390–1.
57 *CCR 1313–18*, pp 358–9.
58 *Stat. John–Hen. V*, p. 292.

of Ireland should have English law by a statute to be made in the Irish parliament, and the justiciar was ordered to ascertain if the magnates would assent to this.[59] In the next year, the justiciar was given power to grant English law to the Irish. Finally, in 1331, it was ordered that 'one and the same law be made as well for the Irish as the English, except the service of betaghs in the power of their lords, in the same manner as is used in England concerning villeins'.[60] By this was presumably intended the full extension of English law to the free Irish living among the English, and it seems to have been immediately pleaded in the Anglo-Irish courts – a plaintiff replying to the exception that he was an Irishman that the king had established in his parliament that all Irishmen, being at the king's peace, should answer at the common law, and winning his case.[61]

Though it is impossible in the present state of our knowledge to be sure how far this ordinance was effective, a new chapter in the history of English law in Ireland had begun. But the development of the whole problem in the later Middle Ages requires to be worked out in detail before anything can be said with confidence. The abandonment of that principle of the personality of law which had so unfortunately been adopted in the early days of the Norman conquest of Ireland is not the least important of the many problems of our medieval history which still await discussion.[62]

**59** James F. Baldwin, *The king's council in England during the Middle Ages* (Oxford, 1913), p. 474; *CCR 1327–30*, p. 312; *Foedera*, ii, pt 2, p. 758. I am indebted to Mr H.G. Richardson for drawing my attention to these documents. **60** *Stat. John–Hen. V*, p. 325. **61** Betham, *Const. Eng. & early parl. Ire.*, p. 292. **62** I am greatly indebted to Mr H.G. Richardson, who very kindly read the draft of this paper and sent me a number of most helpful suggestions and criticisms.

# PART 2

# *War*

CHAPTER 7

# Knight service in Ireland*

*A.J. Otway-Ruthven*

The system of military feudalism imposed by the Normans on their conquests in Ireland inevitably followed the general pattern with which they had been familiar in England.[1] But though the circumstances of the first generation of conquerors in Ireland were in many respects similar to those of their ancestors in England a hundred years earlier, the whole structure of society was already in rapid change by the time the conquest of Ireland began, while, though Henry II intervened in Ireland at an early stage of the conquest, it was not initiated and carried out by the king in the way that the conquest of England had been organized by the duke of Normandy in 1066. There were, therefore, certain modifications. In the first place, nearly half of the military service owed to the crown in Ireland was due from four great tenants – 100 knights for Leinster, 50 from Meath, and 60 from the two grantees of Cork.[2] This represented a far greater concentration of power in the hands of individual subjects, holding compact blocks of land, than the Conqueror had allowed to occur in England. In the second place, whereas in England the Conqueror had imposed tenure by military service on all bishoprics and important abbeys (and his son had found reason to complain that their contingents were unsatisfactory), in Norman Ireland the lands of the church were held in frankalmoign, or sometimes in fee farm, with certain quite unimportant exceptions.[3] An enormous amount of land was thus at once removed from the scope of the system of military feudalism.

* First published in *JRSAI*, 89 (1959), 1–15. 1 For the structure of English feudalism at the time the conquest of Ireland began, see F.M. Stenton, *The first century of English feudalism, 1066–1166* (Oxford, 1932). 2 The total number of knights owed to the crown in Ireland was about 425 (see below, pp 158–9). By the middle of the thirteenth century, Leinster had of course been divided among a large number of Marshal heirs, and Meath between de Genville and de Verdun (see Orpen, *Normans*, iii, 79–107, 260–1). For Henry II's grant of Cork to Robert fitz Stephen and Miles de Cogan and its descent, see Orpen, *Normans*, ii, ch. 13, passim. 3 Among the chief exceptions were the grant of Coillacht to the see of Dublin, to be held by the service of one knight (*Crede mihi*, p. 33; *CDI 1171–1251*, no. 849; *CDI 1293–1301*, no. 104) and ⅔ of a service owed by the archbishop of Armagh for lands in Co. Louth (*38th rep. DKPRI*, p. 72). Though the grant of Coillacht speaks simply of the service of one knight, it was among the fees for which it was later claimed that service should be done in person at the gate of the castle of Dublin (see below, p. 161). Grants of subtenancies to the church might also involve it in obligations of military service (*Calendar of deeds in the Pembroke Estate Office* (Dublin, 1891), no. 4; *Crede mihi*, pp 50–1). It should be

Moreover, grants in fee farm – hereditary tenures liable not to military service but to a fixed rent – seem to have been more commonly used than in England, though for subtenants rather than for tenants-in-chief, while military subtenants quite commonly owed a fee farm rent in addition to military service or scutage.[4] Tenure by serjeanty[5] seems, on the other hand, to have been less used than in England, probably because it was already obsolescent in the late twelfth century. One curious serjeanty was created (or perhaps only continued) as late as 1207 by the grant to Richard le Latimer of lands as held by his father to hold of the king by the service of interpreting (L. *latimeriae faciendae*) in Co. Dublin.[6] But the chief example of this tenure that we know of in Ireland is the existence in almost every county of a chief serjeant – the sheriff's principal assistant – who held the office and the land attached to it in fee and inheritance either from the king or the lord of the liberty.[7]

observed that ecclesiastics sometimes had military tenants themselves (*Red bk Ormond*, pp 86–7; *Rot. pipae Clonensis*, passim). That they held in frankalmoign did not of itself exempt ecclesiastics from the general obligation of all free landholders to share in the burden of local defence, though some of the abbeys intermittently established such an exemption (*CCR 1339–41*, p. 244; *CStM*, i, 302–3; *RCH*, pp 45, 89, 92, 105). 4 See below, pp 159–60. Serjeanty tenures required homage and gave the lord reliefs and the rights of wardship, marriage and escheat as in the case of military tenures, with which they may be classed for many purposes. The position of the fee-farm tenures varied: the chief lords in Ireland claimed the same rights of wardship and marriage as if they had been military tenures, particularly if they required homage, but also apparently when they did not. In 1285, the English court *coram rege*, citing a case before the itinerant justices at Cashel in 1267, ruled that because the law ought to be one and the same in England and Ireland (see below, p. 168), and in England the chief lords have no rights in the custodies of tenements held of them, by reason of homage, unless the tenants are bound to render some military service, such wardships belonged not to the lord, but to the next heirs (*CDI 1285–92*, no. 58). The claim, however, continued to be made, and, in 1331, the order of 1285 was repeated (SC 8/262/13051; *CCR 1330–3*, pp 203–4). It seems, however, that by the fifteenth century such tenancies had been assimilated to military tenancies as far as wardship, marriage and reliefs were concerned, the local custom having prevailed over English law (H.J. Lawlor, 'A calendar of the *Liber Niger* and *Liber Albus* of Christ Church, Dublin', *PRIA*, 27:C1 (1908), 30–1). In the fourteenth-century extent of the lands of the bishop of Cloyne, wardship is specified for many fee-farm tenures (*Rot. pipae Clonensis*, passim). 5 Tenure by the performance of public services, often of a non-military or only quasi-military character. See E.G. Kimball, *Serjeanty tenures in medieval England* (New Haven and London, 1936), and A.L. Poole, *Obligations of society in the XII and XIII centuries* (Oxford, 1946), ch. 4. 6 *CDI 1171–1251*, no. 342. 7 In Dublin, the office (sometimes called the serjeanty of Leinster) was held with the ploughland of Mallahow by Henry Tyrel, to whom it was granted by John when count of Mortain, and later by the family of Crus (*CPR 1334–8*, pp 415–6). In Meath, it was held by the family of Bacun, to whom it must have been granted by the de Lacys, and who in the second half of the thirteenth century and later exercised it in both the liberty of Trim and the royal county of Meath. For these chief serjeants in general, see A.J. Otway-Ruthven, 'Anglo-Irish shire government in the thirteenth century' (above, ch. 5).

We are concerned, however, with the strictly military tenures, and these were constituted much on the English pattern. As we have seen,[8] nearly half the service owed to the crown was concentrated in large blocks in Leinster, Meath and Cork, and here the royal officials dealt directly either with the lord of a liberty, or with a relatively small number of parceners. Dublin,[9] on the other hand, apart from the very extensive lands of the church in this county – well over half the total area – and the royal demesne lands in Newcastle Lyons, Esker, Saggart, Crumlin and Newcastle (Co. Wicklow), was divided among some thirty-seven small tenants-in-chief, most of them holding by the service of half a knight, or less. Other counties varied between these two extremes. It should be observed that the holding of a fractional fee did not mean that personal service was impossible: Westpalstown, Co. Dublin, owed the service of one foot serjeant, which was equated with the service of ½ knight when a scutage was taken.[10] More awkward fractions might arise by division among heiresses, or might be deliberately created after the idea of personal service had been abandoned. There does not seem to be any trace in Ireland of small military tenants combining to furnish a knight, though it is not impossible that this occurred, as it certainly did in England. There must, in any case, have been customary rules in Leinster, Meath and all the greater holdings as to which of the subtenants should serve on any particular occasion when personal service was demanded, but no trace of what these rules may have been has survived.[11]

The original purpose of these tenures had, of course, been to put an army in the field whenever the crown required it.[12] But already by the time of the Norman conquest of Ireland, the feudal host was ceasing to be a satisfactory form of military organization, and scutage – the money commutation for personal service with the host – had appeared in England as early as 1100, to be finally fixed in the thirteenth century at 40*s*. for each knight's fee. It was entirely within the king's discretion whether money or service was taken on any particular occasion or from a particular tenant, and he had a theoretical right to levy it as often as he chose, provided that an army was actually put in the field, though the term of service had been limited by custom to forty days in any one year, and too frequent a levy would be greatly resented. Conditions in Ireland

8 Above, p. 155. **9** Till 1606, the northern part of the modern Co. Wicklow was included in Co. Dublin, but a great part of this area was church land. **10** BL, Royal MS 18 C XIV, fo. 159, and Cotton Titus B XI, pt 2, fo. 246*d*. Other Dublin holdings were in the same position. In the manor of Thurles, Co. Tipperary, each fee is said to answer for five armed men and one barded horse, but this was probably an assessment for purposes of local defence (*Red bk Ormond*, pp 71–3). **11** Cf. Poole, *Obligations of society*, pp 40, 45–6. **12** The intervention of Henry II ensured that this should be so in Ireland as in England: in the marches of Wales, from which so many of the conquerors of Ireland were drawn, and which had been conquered at the beginning of the twelfth century by the independent enterprise of their ancestors, uncontrolled by the crown, feudal organization was directed towards the military

meant, however, that the occasion for a levy arose more frequently than in England.[13] It was disputed in England whether personal service was due overseas; in Ireland the point seems never to have arisen, though in at least one case overseas service seems to have been performed in 1254.[14]

In Ireland, instances of actual personal service with the army occur throughout the thirteenth and fourteenth centuries. Sometimes individuals serve;[15] occasionally, a seneschal brings the forces of a liberty to serve under the king's banner.[16] When, in 1228, the justiciar led an expedition to Connaught, Nicholas de Verdun was directed by him to remain to guard the marches and so rendered his service to the king: he successfully claimed exemption from scutage.[17] As late as 1355, tenants by knight service seem to have come in person to Newcastle McKynegan (Newcastle, Co. Wicklow) to do their service there.[18] But, in general, military service in Ireland, particularly for the smaller tenants, seems to have been on a basis of scutage, if not quite from the first at any rate very early: as early as 1222, those holding of the king in Munster (that is, the later counties of Tipperary and Limerick), Des (Waterford), Desmond and the vale of Dublin were ordered that when the justiciar went with an armed force into Ulster and Keneleon, or other remote parts, to fortify castles etc., they were to render in money the service due to the king.[19] These were all areas containing a comparatively large number of small tenants-in-chief: nothing is said of the liberties of Leinster and Meath, of Cork, or of Louth, which was mainly divided between the de Verduns and the Pippards. No doubt a few relatively large contingents could more easily be absorbed in the royal army than could the many small military tenants of the other areas.

The amount of military service actually due to the crown in Ireland was not very great. By the end of the thirteenth century, a scutage at the rate of 40*s*. a fee brought in about £50 from Dublin, £73 16*s*. from Louth, £55 from Connaught,

needs of each separate lordship, and could not be used by the crown in this way. 13 Cf. *CDI 1252–84*, no. 1801. 14 In 38 Hen. III, Hugh Tyrel 'fecit servicium suum in exercitu domini Henrici regis ad guerram suam Vasconie sustinendum' (C 47/10/15, no. 5). 15 *Pipe roll 14 John*, p. 52; *35th rep. DKPRI*, p. 38; *36th rep. DKPRI*, p. 73; *38th rep. DKPRI*, p. 60; *44th rep. DKPRI*, p. 21. 16 *CDI 1171–1251*, no. 1581; *43rd rep. DKPRI*, p. 46. 17 *CDI 1171–1251*, no. 1581. The de Verduns had been granted Dundalk to hold by the service of 20 knights, increased at some date before 1238 to the service of 22½ (C 47/10/15, no. 3). In 1290, Geoffrey de Genville was directed by the justiciar and council to pay a third of the sum he owed for a scutage to Peter de Genville for the defence of the marches of Delven (C 47/10/17, no. 5; *CJRI 1305–7*, pp 72, 73, 74, 83). Cf. *37th rep. DKPRI*, p. 55; *CJRI 1305–7*, p. 242). 18 *RCH*, pp 57, 62. 19 *CDI 1171–1251*, no. 1048. The payment of scutage does not seem to have been recorded on the Irish pipe rolls before 1238 (C 47/10/15, no. 3). For the special position of some of the Dublin tenants-in-chief, see below, pp 161–2; but it should be noted that Hugh Tyrel of Castleknock served in person in the expedition to Maycove in 1253, for the Gascon war in 1254, and in the expedition to Greencastle in 1262, though he paid scutage for an expedition to Kymaleon in 1258 (C 47/10/15, no. 5).

£123 10*s*. from Cork, £19 10*s*. 4*d*. from Waterford, £117 1*s*. 8*d*. from Tipperary, £102 13*s*. 8*d*. from Limerick, £200 from Leinster, £100 from Meath and £6 from Ulster – a total of just under £850, representing not quite 425 fees.[20] But there were, of course, many more fees than this in the country, for all the greater tenants-in-chief had, as in England, created a much larger number of fees by subinfeudation than was needed to perform their bare quota of service, and the total received by the crown when a scutage was proclaimed was considerably increased if any of the great liberties were in the king's hand. Thus Meath, which owed the service of fifty knights to the crown, contained between 100 and 120 fees by the middle of the thirteenth century;[21] and Leinster, which owed a hundred, seems to have contained about 180;[22] while Ulster, assessed at only three, had 16⅞₀ in 1333.[23] This process, of course, went further down the scale: the more important subtenants themselves made a profit on each proclamation of a royal service. Thus, an extent of the Butler lands in Carlow in 1303 shows that, while the Butlers owed the lord of the liberty £8 for royal service, they took from their tenants £11 7*s*., and this at rates averaging about a third of the standard 40*s*. for a knight's fee.[24] In Tipperary, 180 acres in Balilothnan were held of Otho de Grandison by James, son of Richard, who owed Otho 2*s*. for royal service; James' tenant of this land, William de Naungle, owed James 12*s*. for royal service.[25] Also in Tipperary, the Butlers owed the crown 6*s*. 8*d*. for the royal service of the lands held in the manor of Thurles by their tenant, Grimbald de Samlesbury: Grimbald owed them 10*s*. But with Grimbald himself, who held only a single fee, we have reached the level at which the immediate lord no longer made a profit at each proclamation of royal service, for his tenants owed only 3s. 4*d*. towards it.[26] We should observe that, as in this

20 For the documents on which this list is based, see below, pp 164–6. The total varies slightly from time to time, and the sum due from Louth seems to have dropped to £57 15*s*. 4*d*. by the fifteenth century as the result of a considerable reduction in the service due from Ardee. A list of *c*.1282 gives a total of 418½ fees and 19*s*. 10*d*. (*CDI 1252–84*, no. 2329); a slightly later one, 427 fees and a fraction (Mary Bateson, 'Irish exchequer memoranda of the reign of Edward I', *EHR*, 18:71 (1903), 497–513). It seems probable that, in the 1280s, there was a general attempt to define and enforce all services due to the king (see below, p. 162). In 1372, the Irish exchequer was ordered not to enforce the payment of scutage for lands 'now by the Irish rebels wasted and occupied' (*CCR 1369–74*, pp 380–1). 21 Cf. *Reg. Gormanston*, pp 10–13. This is a list of the 59½ services and a fraction owed to de Genville; we have no list of the services owed to de Verdun, the other parcener of the de Lacy inheritance, but it is safe to assume that he had approximately the same number of fees in Meath. 22 There is no complete list of the knights' fees of Leinster, but the Marshal inheritance was divided into five shares and each of the three parceners whose share is fully known to us got thirty-six fees and a fraction in Leinster. I hope to reconstruct the remaining two shares elsewhere [EN. See A.J. Otway-Ruthven, 'Knights' fees in Kildare, Leix, and Offaly', *JRSAI*, 91 (1961), 163–81]. 23 *CIPM*, vii, 377–8. 24 *Red bk Ormond*, pp 2–3. It should be observed that in Ireland royal service is the term almost invariably used for scutage. 25 *CJRI 1308–14*, p. 130. 26 *Red bk Ormond*, pp 7, 59–60.

case, many subtenants who were said to hold one or more fees paid scutage at rates much lower than the standard 40*s*. for each fee. It seems likely that, where this occurred, it represented a recognition of the fact that these tenants were in a position exposed to constant attack by the Irish and thus needed greater resources to meet their scutage obligations than those in the 'land of peace'. Many of John's grants to tenants-in-chief also require the service of fewer knights than the number of fees granted, no doubt with this intention.[27] Elsewhere, as in Meath and, apparently, Louth, the same result was achieved by varying the size of the knight's fee, which was half as large again in the marches.[28] It should be observed that the subtenant paying scutage not uncommonly paid a fee-farm rent as well.

When it had been decided to take a scutage – by the fourteenth century, this was being done in parliaments,[29] and earlier was no doubt done in the great council of tenants-in-chief – the sheriffs and seneschals of the whole country were ordered to proclaim throughout their bailiwicks that all who owed service to the king should be before the justiciar at a specified day and place with horses and arms and suitable equipment to do their service.[30] The proclamation might be followed immediately by a writ ordering the sheriffs to take the service in money, but our sources are so imperfect that we cannot be certain whether this was usual and necessary or not, though it is reasonable to suppose that it was.[31] It is interesting to note that during the reign of Henry III, though not apparently later, half a service – that is, a scutage at the rate of 20*s*. a fee – was sometimes taken;[32] and it was established practice in the early part of the reign to grant to a subject the service due from a specified area, sometimes for the full period of forty days, sometimes for only twenty, to aid him in fortifying a castle, a practice which sometimes occurs under Edward I; while *c.*1319, the earl of Kildare petitioned the king to grant him, 'ses services en Irlande en eyde daler en Thochemound pur venger la mort Sire Richard de Clare, qi morust en service nostre seignur le rey'.[33]

Service in the army – the *expeditio* of feudal documents – though the most usual was not, of course, the only possible duty of a military tenant. Castle-guard, or garrison duty, had been of great importance in the early days of Norman feudalism in England, and was certainly a dominant feature in the subinfeudation of the marcher lordships of south Wales,[34] from which so many

27 *CDI 1171–1251*, passim. Cf. *CStM*, i, 65, 66. 28 See below, p. 164. 29 *Parls & councils*, pp 9–10. 30 Armagh Public Library, MS G.II.13, fo. 6*d*; *RCH*, p. 9; *CDI 1302–7*, nos. 62–4. 31 *RCH*, p. 11. 32 *35th rep. DKPRI*, p. 42; *Reg. Gormanston*, p. 13. 33 *CDI 1171–1251*, passim; *CJRI 1295–1303*, p. 230; *CDI 1302–7*, no. 48; SC 8/119/5946 [EN. pr. *Affairs Ire.*, no. 121]; *CCR 1318–24*, pp 80, 90. De Clare was killed in May 1318, but the petition seems to belong to the first half of 1319. 34 By the time we have clear evidence, the obligation had been very generally commuted for an annual payment known as 'wardsilver', but the system was clearly still in working order in south Wales in the second half of the twelfth century. See

of the Norman conquerors of Ireland were drawn. There is no clear evidence of the position in Ireland, but castleries – areas in which subinfeudation was organized primarily to provide a garrison for a castle – are mentioned in the first generation of the conquest in connection with Co. Louth;[35] and in 1335, it was stated that Walter Slymberge, who died shortly before 1332, had held five ploughlands and 100 acres of the earl of Ulster by the service of 6*d.* and suit at the earl's court of Carrickfergus, and finding an armed man for the tower called Pollardstoure in the castle of Carrickfergus in time of war, and another man with two barded horses in time of the earl's war.[36] This service is not mentioned in the inquisitions taken after the murder of the brown earl in 1333, and it is probable that there were other unrecorded tenures of the same type in this area.

A group of tenancies in Co. Dublin presents some curious features: their service was to be performed in guarding the city of Dublin, or at the gate of the castle of Dublin, and their genesis is most probably the charter of Henry II which granted Hugh de Lacy, 'omnia feoda que prebuit vel que prebebit circa Duueliniam dum ballivus meus est, ad faciendum mihi servicium apud civitatem meam Duuelinie'.[37] Some at least of these tenancies were created in the first instance by de Lacy, his charters specifying service at the city of Dublin, though this was not always mentioned in the royal charters which subsequently replaced de Lacy's. One of these tenancies (we know of ten, and no doubt some of the other tenants-in-chief of the county fell into the same group) was, however, deliberately created in 1207 in place of an existing fee-farm tenure.[38] In the 1280s, a violent dispute broke out as to their position, two successive treasurers – Stephen de Fulburne, bishop of Waterford, and Nicholas de Clere – claiming that these tenants should pay scutage 'according to the custom of England', while the tenants maintained that they and their

*A calendar of the public records relating to Pembrokeshire*, ed. H. Owen, 3 vols (Cymmrodorion Record Ser., 7, London, 1911–18), iii, passim; *Cartae et alia munimenta quae ad dominium de Glamorgancia pertinent*, ed. G.L. Clark, 6 vols (new ed., Cardiff, 1910), ii, 650–1; *Rot. litt. pat.*, p. 79; 'Appendix to "Notes on Huntingdon Manor"', *Archaeologia Cambrensis: The Journal of the Cambrian Archaeological Association*, 4th ser., 4 (Oct., 1870), ['Original Documents'], pp i, iii. 35 *Reg. St Thomas*, pp 9, 43, 44. 36 Armagh Public Library, MS G.II.13, fo. 9. 37 *Reg. Gormanston*, p. 177. I hope to discuss the problems involved in this charter at greater length elsewhere. 38 *RCH*, p. 4; *CDI 1171–1251*, nos. 345, 346; *CDI 1285–92*, p. 315; *Calendar of deeds in the Pembroke Estate Office*, no. 4; Bateson, 'Irish exchequer memoranda', p. 508; *Cal. Carew MSS*, v, 227; SC 8/258/12880; C 47/10/15, no. 5; Armagh Public Library, MS H.II.16, fo. 102. The tenancies involved were Coillacht (1 service), Bray (2 services), Rathdown (1½ service), Dundrum (1 service), Donnybrook (½ service), Castleknock (3 services), the Ward (½ service), Kilsallaghan (½ service), Howth (1 service), and an unidentified half fee in the honor of Lusk. It should be noted that the grants of Bray and Donnybrook were made not by de Lacy, but by Strongbow, acting on behalf of the king. The charters of Castleknock (C 47/10/15, no. 3) and Hugh Tyrel's petition (SC 8/258/12880) were printed with a commentary by E. St John Brooks, 'The grant of Castleknock to Hugh Tyrel', *JRSAI*, 63 (1933), 206–20.

ancestors had always done their service in person with horses and arms at the gate of the castle of Dublin. An undated exchequer memorandum states that eight of them were making this claim, though the pipe roll of 23 Henry III (1239) showed that they had paid scutage in that year; in 1286, Nicholas de Howth alleged that he and his ancestors had done their service in person at the gate of the castle of Dublin; about the same date, Hugh Tyrel was making the same claim for his barony of Castleknock in an angry petition to the king; and in 1290, Theobald le Botiller complained that, though he held Bray in chief by the service of finding an armoured horse at the gate of the castle of Dublin, and he and his predecessors had always performed the service in person, the justiciar had now arbitrarily converted it into a demand for money.[39] It seems very doubtful that these claims were in fact justified: in spite of their charters, and in spite of the verdict of a jury in the case of Castleknock that, 'predictus Hugo fecisset servicium predictum in toto tempore suo secundum tenorem cartarum predictarum cum equis et armis ad castrum Dublinie in tam debito sicut omnes antecessores sui a tempore primi feoffamenti sui fecerunt et facere consueverunt',[40] the exchequer officials had no difficulty in showing from the pipe rolls that they had either served in person in the army or paid on a number of occasions during the century, and after this date they were absorbed without further protest into the general scutage-paying community.[41] It seems likely that the whole incident was connected with a general policy of enquiring into and enforcing royal rights which seem to have been embarked on in the 1280s,[42] which would naturally provoke a reaction from the tenants concerned; and we may observe that, at the same period, Theobald de Verdun was complaining that though his charter only required the service of 20 knights for his land of Dundalk, the treasurer was exacting the service of 22½. The pipe rolls showed, however, that the service of 22½ knights had been continuously exacted from Dundalk since 1238, when scutage was first entered on them.[43]

The other incidents of feudal tenure in Ireland show no features of particular interest. The obligatory aids were the same in Ireland as in England, reliefs were on the same scale, and distraint of knighthood appears under Edward III.[44] The rights of wardship and marriage were also the same, but in the liberties of Leinster and Meath the king abandoned his right of prerogative wardship – the right to the custody during a minority of all the lands of a tenant-in-chief, no matter of whom they were held – in favour of the lord.[45] Thus, the lords of

39 Bateson, 'Irish exchequer memoranda', p. 508: *Cal. Carew MSS*, v, 227; SC 8/258/12880; *CDI 1285–92*, p. 315. 40 SC 8/258/12880. 41 Bateson, 'Irish exchequer memoranda', p. 508; C 47/10/15, no. 5. In the pipe roll of 30 Edw. I (1302), Hugh Tyrel's son accounted for £50 arrears of service for Castleknock before Michaelmas term, 1286 (*38th rep. DKPRI*, p. 60). 42 See below, pp 164–5. 43 C 47/10/15, no. 3. 44 *47th rep. DKPRI*, p. 28; *54th rep. DKPRI*, p. 53; *CPR 1345–6*, p. 547; *CCR 1346–9*, p. 565. 45 *Rot. chart.*, p. 178; *CDI 1252–84*, nos. 195, 264, 740. This was also the position in the palatinate of Durham, the lands

these liberties had the wardship of all the lands held of them within their liberties, even though many of their tenants also held in chief of the king elsewhere. It is not clear whether or not the lords of Leinster and Meath themselves enjoyed the right of prerogative wardship within the liberty, as the bishop of Durham did in Durham:[46] Edmund Mortimer asserted it in Meath in the later fourteenth century, but a jury alleged that it was then an innovation.[47]

The chief remaining point of interest is that of the size of the knight's fee. At the time of the Norman conquest of England and for some two generations after that, it is clear that Norman feudalism had as yet evolved no conception of a standard knight's fee: charters define a knight's service, but not his fee, which might be composed of separate parcels of land, lying many miles apart. But, by the middle of the twelfth century, we begin to get charters which suggest that the conception of a knight's fee of definite size or value is already developing, and it must have been this conception – or rather, conceptions, for there was never a single standard but rather standards, which varied widely as between one feudal honour and another – that the Normans brought with them to Ireland.[48] Certainly, the language of many of the early grants can only mean that, in the mind of the king or his officials, a knight's fee was equated with a definite area of land. There is, for instance, a grant of 1199 to Lambekin fitz William of named lands in the cantred of Huhene as a fee of five knights: if the lands contain less than five knights' fees, the king will supply the deficiency; if more, the surplus shall remain to the king.[49] Earlier, Earl Richard (Strongbow), acting for the king, had granted to Alfred Gulafre a carucate of land in Dochlon (near Rathland, Co. Dublin) to hold 'per liberum servicium militis quod pertinet une carucate terre Dublin' faciendum' – language which clearly implies that the number of ploughlands appropriate to a knight's fee in Co. Dublin was fixed and known.[50] Walter de Ridelesford was granted ten ploughlands for the fee of one knight at about the same date,[51] and the grant of Rathfarnham and neighbouring lands to Milo le Bret to hold by the service of one and a fifth knight's fees no doubt reflects a calculation of the same kind.[52] Calculations of value are rare but, at the end of the twelfth century, Coillacht was granted to the archbishop of Dublin as twenty librates of land for the service of one knight;

of the archbishop of Canterbury and the marcher lordships of Wales (*Stat. of the realm*, i, 22). **46** *Registrum palatinum Dunelmensis*, ed. T.D. Hardy, 4 vols (RS, London, 1873–8), iii, 62. **47** *COD*, iii, 350–5. **48** For this whole subject, see Stenton, *First century of English feudalism*, pp 151–68. **49** *CDI 1171–1251*, no. 96. **50** *Crede mihi*, pp 47–8 **51** *RCH*, p. 4. It should be noted that it is impossible to establish any exact equivalent to this in terms of acreage: the ploughland is generally thought to have contained about 120 acres of arable land, but an indefinite amount of waste or uncultivated land might be included, and the Irish acre was certainly larger than the statute acre. Mills thought that in Co. Dublin it was equivalent to about 2½ statute acres (James Mills, 'Notices of the manor of St Sepulchre, Dublin, in the fourteenth century', *JRSAI*, 19 (1889), 35–6). **52** *CDI 1171–1251*, no. 100.

and, under Edward I, John Walhope got five ploughlands for thirty librates of land to hold by the service of one knight.[53] Similar calculations may lie behind the grant to Adam de Hereford of four ploughlands in Aderrig and its neighbourhood to hold by the service of half a fee,[54] which was rather smaller than seems to have been usual in this neighbourhood; and that to Dermot Mac Gilmeholmoc of fifteen ploughlands held by his father in Rathdown to hold by the service of one knight and two otterskins yearly, which was certainly unusually large.[55] But while a knight's fee of ten ploughlands seems to have been a fair average in Co. Dublin, in Castleknock, the largest lay holding in the county, the Tyrels held sixty ploughlands of the crown by the service of three knights.[56] This exceptionally large area must be related to the position in Meath, for the original grant of Castleknock was made by Hugh de Lacy, and there is clear evidence that in the subinfeudation of Meath twenty ploughlands, as in Castleknock, were considered to be the equivalent of a knight's fee in the land of peace, while the figure rose to thirty ploughlands in the marches.[57] There are indications of the same structure in Co. Waterford;[58] and, in the original subinfeudation of Co. Louth, a thirty ploughland fee seems also to have been usual in the marches, at any rate in the neighbourhood of Ardee.[59]

Elsewhere, the evidence is nothing like so clear-cut. The large blocks of service imposed by Henry II on Leinster and Meath did not, of course, depend on any close calculations of area or value, and John's grant of Ulster to Hugh de Lacy speaks simply of a knight for every cantred.[60] As for subinfeudation, apart from the twenty and thirty ploughland fees of Meath and, possibly, Louth, we find fees of from ten to twenty ploughlands in Wexford.[61] In Kilkenny, ten seems to have been the average,[62] and there is some evidence for a ten ploughland fee in Tipperary in the Butler manor of Thurles.[63] But in many parts of the country, the evidence is greatly confused by the common practice of imposing on subtenants scutage liabilities considerably lower than the standard rate.[64]

That a record should be kept of the services due to the king was obviously desirable. In 1281, a memorandum highly critical of the conduct of the Irish treasurer says that 'all services, as scutage in England, ought to be entered for remembrance on the king's rolls, lest service should be withdrawn from the

53 *Crede mihi*, pp 33–4; *CDI 1293–1301*, no. 228. Cf. a grant of 30 librates in Connaught to be held by the service of half a knight's fee (*CDI 1293–1301*, no. 108). 54 *CDI 1171–1251*, no. 341. The four ploughlands of the manor of Gormanstown which lay in Co. Dublin were also counted as half a fee (*CIPM*, v, no. 272). 55 *CDI 1171–1251*, no. 356. By the end of the thirteenth century, this service had been changed to one knight and a foot serjeant, i.e. 1⅛ fees (BL, Royal MS 18 C XIV, fo. 159). 56 *CJRI 1295–1303*, p. 246. 57 *Reg. Gormanston*, pp 10–13; *Song of Dermot*, p. 310; *CIPM*, vii, no. 67. But cf. *CIPM*, v, no. 272. Balrothery was probably in the same position as Castleknock. 58 *RCH*, pp 58, 67. 59 *CIPM*, v, no. 583. 60 *Rot. chart.*, p. 151; *CDI 1171–1251*, no. 263. The grant of Ulster to Walter de Burgo in 1263 reduced this to a total service of three knights (BL, Add. MS 6041, fo. 100*d.*). 61 *CDI 1302–7*, nos. 306, 764. 62 *Red bk Ormond*, passim. 63 Ibid., pp 53, 71–3. 64 See above, pp

king, the more especially as the book called Domesday, touching those services and other rights of the king, has been burned'[65] – the earliest entry in the long and depressing history of the destruction of our public records. We are not told whether anything was done to follow this up,[66] but there are several surviving attempts to set forth the full list of the royal service of Ireland, of which the earliest must be assigned to the end of the thirteenth century. This survives in three separate but very closely related texts, which seem to go back to a common original: a MS of *c.*1345, preserved in the library of Corpus Christi college, Cambridge;[67] a very corrupt text preserved among the Carew MSS at Lambeth;[68] and another very badly written and corrupt sixteenth-century transcript, made by someone who did not know the places concerned, which is preserved in the British Library.[69] The original was not earlier than 1298, since it includes the service of one tenth of a knight's fee for Thorncastle from William le Deveneys, which was created in that year;[70] on the other hand, it is probably not much later, since it notes that Ballygodman used to owe one service, but is now quit by the lord's charter. Ballygodman had been granted to the nuns of Lismullen by Richard de la Cornere, bishop of Meath, *c.*1250, and the lord's charter, which is otherwise unrecorded, must have been a charter of Edward I while lord of Ireland during his father's lifetime.[71]

The second list is considerably later: it is contained in a volume of collections as to the king's revenue in Ireland made by a royal official at the end of the fifteenth century.[72] It is clear and well written, and the place-names are given in their normal form: it was no doubt made in the exchequer at Dublin, and though the sources are not given – they were almost certainly the lists of sums due for scutage in the pipe rolls – some of them were clearly of considerable antiquity, since Walter de Burgo (who died in 1271) is said to owe twenty services for Connaught, and Richard de Burgo (who died in 1326) three for Ulster. But there is a list of fees in Co. Wexford which appears to be about a generation later than the list assigned by Dr Brooks to 1425,[73] and was probably compiled for the purposes of a scutage taken while the liberty was in the king's hand.

The third of the lists, though the latest, is in many ways the most interesting. It is a 'Liber repertorium omnium inquisitionum et aliarum rerum in officio

159–60. **65** *CDI 1252–84*, no. 1879. **66** Ibid., no. 2329 (*c.*1284), though it lists the rents due to the king in detail, gives only the total number of services due from each county without saying by whom or for what lands they were due. It seems, however, that the 1280s were a period of general inquiry into, and enforcement of, the rights of the king, and it is probably significant that both the treasurers of this period aroused widespread hostility. See above, p. 161. **67** Corpus Christi, Cambridge, MS 37, ed. Mary Bateson in 'Irish exchequer memoranda of the reign of Edward I', pp 497–513. **68** *Cal. Carew MSS*, v, pp 230–4. Both this and the Corpus Christi MS add lists of rents due to the king and some exchequer memoranda, the Corpus Christi version being the more complete of the two. **69** BL, Cotton Titus B XI, pt 2, fos. 246*d*–247*d*. This list is incomplete, omitting Meath, Tipperary and Limerick. **70** *CDI 1302–7*, no. 422. **71** *CPR 1367–70*, p. 124. **72** BL, Royal MS 18 C XIV, fos. 159–65. **73** Brooks, capitalis rememoratoris scaccarie Hibernie factus per Walterum Harold deputatus rememoratoris ejusdem scaccarie', and is headed 1557, though in fact some of the entries go up to the twentieth year of Elizabeth.[74] It seems to have been intended as a record of royal rights, and it includes a long section on royal services, taken for the most part from the pipe rolls. First, however, comes a 'rotulus regalis servicii Comitis Marchie tempore Leonelli comitis Ultonie et Johanne uxoris sue', the source of which is not stated, but which must, I think, have been taken from the inquisitions *post mortem* taken after the death of Roger Mortimer, whose son later married Lionel's daughter and heiress, in 1360. The Irish part of these inquisitions has not survived except insofar as this may be an extract from them, but it should be observed that there is no other indication in the MS that in 1557 there remained in the Irish exchequer any inquisition earlier than the twentieth year of Richard II.

This is followed by the royal service of Dublin, taken from a pipe roll of the reign of Henry VII, that of Louth from a pipe roll of Edward IV, that of Meath from the pipe roll of 10 Henry VI, that of Kildare from the pipe roll of 13 Henry VI,[75] that of Tipperary from the pipe roll of 13 Henry IV, that of Wexford from a pipe roll of the reign of Henry V, and finally a detailed list of the royal service due to the lords of the manor of Castleknock in the early sixteenth century. While not as complete, in some respects, as the earlier lists, it gives us fuller information as to the subinfeudation of certain of the liberties than is available from any other source. But interesting as these lists are, their detailed consideration must be left for another occasion.

It is clear that Norman feudalism, which was introduced into Ireland at the point of time when its English variant had, after a century of development, assumed its classical form, underwent no significant changes in Ireland. Though it is, I think, certain that under Henry II, and even under Henry III, it was still contemplated that it would make an important contribution to every military expedition, its contribution became almost entirely financial long before the end of the thirteenth century. The whole organization thus became largely static, steadily declining in even its financial importance as new methods of taxation were applied.

In conclusion, we may profitably compare Irish feudalism with that of certain other European countries. It was, as we have seen, purely an offshoot of English feudalism, which was itself derived from Normandy. We can thus best compare it with that of other areas of Norman feudalism which, apart from England, spread to southern Italy and thence to the principality of Antioch.[76]

*Knights' fees.* 74 TCD, MS 569. 75 This is almost, though not quite, identical with that printed by H.F. Hore from BL, Harl. MS 3756 (H.F. Hore, 'The rental book of Gerald, ninth earl of Kildare, A.D. 1518', *Journal of the Kilkenny and South-east of Ireland Archaeological Society* [*JRSAI*], new ser., 5 (1864–6), 529–46), and both are certainly based on the inquisition *post mortem* of the second earl of Kildare, made in January 1329, which is preserved in the 'Red book of Kildare'. 76 Claude Cahen, *Le régime féodal de l'Italie normande* (Paris, 1940).

There are thus, outside Normandy, two main lines of development: England, Wales and Ireland on the one hand,[77] and south Italy and Antioch on the other. But it is remarkable that, in certain important respects, the feudalism of the marches of Wales resembles that of southern Italy, not that of England, from which it was immediately derived, while that of Ireland, in spite of the fact that a high proportion of the first conquerors were themselves Welsh marchers, was entirely English in pattern. There are two sets of circumstances which seem to explain this: in the first place, the Norman conquerors of south Wales at the end of the eleventh century and the beginning of the twelfth were only one generation removed from the parent stock in Normandy and thus far nearer not only in time, but also in tradition and outlook, to the men who had set up their petty states in Italy in the middle of the eleventh century than were the Anglo-Norman conquerors of Ireland in the second half of the twelfth century. In the second place, though Ireland was not, as England had been, conquered entirely by the initiative and under the direction of the king, nevertheless Henry II intervened at an early stage to make certain that his sovereign power and position should be effectively recognized and respected. In south Wales and in Italy apart from Sicily, on the other hand, the conquest was carried out by a number of petty leaders acting independently. It is true that the Welsh marchers always recognized the overlordship of the king of England, but in practice they were the almost independent rulers of petty principalities;[78] in southern Italy, the monarchy did not appear till after the initial conquests had taken place, and its authority was imposed on all the feudatories only gradually, and not without considerable difficulties.

The really striking parallel between the marcher lordships of south Wales and the Norman state in south Italy is in the matter of the personality of feudal law. In Norman England, law was from the first territorial, and by the reign of Henry II the common law – the practice of the king's court – was already rapidly beginning to obliterate the old variety of provincial custom. Though much Anglo-Saxon law was incorporated in this developing body of law and custom, it did not affect the law relating to military tenures, which were governed entirely by the ordinary rules of feudal law, even if, exceptionally, they were held by men of Anglo-Saxon descent. This principle was followed also in Ireland. The majority of the native Irish population were, indeed, excluded from the benefits of English law,[79] but if an Irishman held a knight's fee, as some did,[80] he held it by exactly the same rules of law as any Norman. But in

77 Scotland should really be included in the series, since the development of Scottish feudalism was largely influenced by England. 78 See A.J. Otway-Ruthven, 'The constitutional position of the great lordships of south Wales', *TRHS*, 5th ser., 8 (1958), 1–20. 79 See A.J. Otway-Ruthven, 'The native Irish and English law in medieval Ireland' (above, ch. 6). 80 See, e.g., *CDI 1171–1252*, no. 356. Cf. *Red bk Ormond*, p. 20 and passim, which shows a number of Irishmen holding fee-farm tenancies.

both the Welsh marches and southern Italy we find a different principle adopted. In the Welsh marches, we find, side by side with normal military tenancies, Welsh fees which descended according to the rules of Welsh customary law, which divided an inheritance among all the male heirs, taking no account of whether they were legitimate or not, and which gave the lord no right of either wardship or marriage.[81] The fragmentation in which this resulted – in 1325, eleven such fees in Pembrokeshire were said to be in the hands of 'innumerable tenants'[82] – must have made it impossible to ensure the performance of any services, and clearly the lord had very little control over them. In just the same way, we find in southern Italy that certain tenants held by Lombard law, which divided an inheritance among all the heirs, male and female, but regarded a woman as always juridically a minor, while others held by 'Frankish' law – this is, by the ordinary rules of Norman feudalism as they developed in this area.[83] Nothing of the kind was, however, possible in Ireland, for the guiding principle, constantly reiterated, was that the law of Ireland was, and ought to be, the same as that of England.[84] In northeast Ulster, a number of Irish rulers, who retained a semi-independent position outside the framework of Norman administration, and whose territories were clearly areas of Irish law, did indeed nominally hold of the earl by the service of providing 'satellites'[85] for his wars, but this service was completely outside any feudal category.[86]

Irish feudalism must be classed, then, simply as an almost unmodified extension of that branch of Norman feudalism which was established in England: in this, as in other respects, the comparison with the Welsh marches which the identity of the conquerors of Ireland inevitably suggests proves to have very little relevance. The development of the power of the monarchy and of the common law under Henry II was apparently an impassable barrier preventing any eccentric development.

81 *Calendar of the public records relating to Pembrokeshire*, iii, 97; 'Transcript of the register book of the barony of Kemeys, Pembrokeshire' in *Baronia de Kemeys from the original documents at Bronwydd, printed for the Cambrian Archaeological Association* [supplement to *Archaeologia Cambrensis: The Journal of the Cambrian Archaeological Association*, 3rd ser., 8] (London, 1862), pp 72–4. 82 'Transcript of the register book of the barony of Kemeys, Pembrokeshire', *Baronia de Kemeys*, pp 72–4. 83 Cahen, *Régime féodal*, pp 38–9, 82–9. In both Italy and Wales, the juridical status of the fee did not necessarily correspond to the racial origins of the tenant. 84 *Stat. John–Hen. V*, pp 20, 21, 23–4, 30, 31–2, 33, 35; *CDI 1171–1251*, nos. 1430, 1458, 1481, 1679; *CDI 1285–92*, no. 318. See Pollock & Maitland, *Hist. of Eng. law*, i, 221; *The collected papers of Frederic William Maitland*, ed. H.A.L. Fisher, 3 vols (Cambridge, 1911), ii, 81–3; H.G. Richardson and G.O. Sayles, 'The early statutes', *Law Quarterly Review*, 50 (1934), p. 548. See above, p. 156, n. 4. 85 Identified as kern in 1329: 'satellites domini Johannis de Bermyngham comitis Loueth qui vocantur ketherne' (C 47/10/19, no. 18). 86 See Edmund Curtis, 'The "bonnaght" of Ulster', *Hermathena*, 46 (1931), 87–105.

CHAPTER 8

# Royal service in Ireland*

*A.J. Otway-Ruthven*

In the later twelfth century, the feudal army – the assembly under arms of the tenants-in-chief, each with the quota of knights which his enfeoffment required – was already past its prime as a form of military organization. There is clear evidence that, as early as 1100, scutage – a money payment instead of personal service in the host – was known in England, and it does not seem that it was then an innovation.[1] But it was not till the thirteenth century that personal service can really be said to have become unimportant, and in such a border district as Cheshire, where there was constant war against the Welsh, scutage seems to have been unknown till 1277.[2]

When the Normans came to Ireland, the idea of an army composed of the king's tenants by knight service, bringing with them their own military subtenants to make up their quotas, was thus still a known and normal one, though already decaying, and the conditions of life in the Norman colony were certainly such as to emphasize the importance of personal service. The payment of scutage as an alternative, if the king chose to require it, was also a known and normal possibility; but on the first occasion on which we know that the feudal service was summoned in Ireland (there must of course have been earlier ones, but the evidence is lacking)[3] – the army led to Clones by John de Grey in 1212 – we hear nothing of any scutage, but only of three knights who performed more service than was due for their fiefs and were paid accordingly.[4] The first mention of scutage in connection with Ireland is in 1222, when those holding of the king in Munster (Tipperary and Limerick), Des (Waterford), Desmond and the vale of Dublin were ordered to render in money the service due to the king when the justiciar went with an armed force into Ulster and Keneleon or other remote parts.[5] This in itself implies that these tenants had been serving in

* First published in *JRSAI*, 98 (1968), 37–46. 1 The most recent discussion is C. Warren Hollister, *The military organization of Norman England* (Oxford, 1965), pp 195–200. 2 James Tait, 'Knight service in Cheshire', *EHR*, 57:228 (1942), 453–4, 485. 3 The army of Ormond, which must have been after 1208, is mentioned in *Pipe roll 14 John*, p. 70, but there is no indication of its composition. 4 *Pipe roll 14 John*, p. 52. See also the case of Richard Dullard (below, n. 22). 5 *CDI 1171–1251*, no. 1048. Ulster is here being used for Antrim and Down only. The order is no doubt connected with the threat presented by Hugh

person, and that others would continue to do so. These were areas where there were many small tenants-in-chief, and the motive behind the order was probably the difficulty of absorbing them in the royal army; but the case of the tenants of the vale of Dublin may be different. Many of them, or rather their fathers, had been enfeoffed to hold by the service of serving with horses and arms at the city of Dublin, or at the gate of the castle of Dublin, and it seems possible that an attempt was being made to convert a service which was no longer of practical use into cash. Whether or not this succeeded in 1222 we cannot tell, but by the middle of the century these tenants were either serving in person in such expeditions as the army of Maincoue of 1253, or paying scutage. As far as we know, no protest was made till the 1280s, when the tenants complained bitterly that the treasurer was wrongfully forcing them to pay scutage 'according to the custom of England', instead of allowing them to perform the service required by their charters. These protests were, however, unavailing, and they are found regularly paying scutage after this time.[6] Their original service was, of course, a form of castle guard, and such services were certainly more widespread in the original infeudation of Ireland than the surviving sources show.[7]

Our next reference to scutage in Ireland is in 1228, when Nicholas de Verdon complained that the exchequer was attempting to extract it from him for the expedition of 1227 to Connacht, although he had been directed by the justiciar to stay behind to guard the marches, and so rendered his service to the king.[8] In 1234, the feudal tenants were called on to serve in person against Richard Marshal, for a number of them in Munster and Kerry were amerced because they had not come to join the king's army when summoned.[9] And that scutage cannot have been an important item of revenue at this period is strongly suggested by the statement made by the barons of the Irish exchequer in 1293 that the pipe roll of 22 Henry III (1237–8) was the first on which scutages were entered.[10] After this, however, it seems to have become a regular part of the revenue, although it is not unusual to find individual tenants serving in person even in the first half of the fourteenth century.

de Lacy. The services due to the king in Ireland are mentioned in 1205 (ibid., no. 268), but it is probable that personal service, not scutage, was intended. 6 Otway-Ruthven, 'Knight service in Ireland' (above, pp 161–2). They had apparently ceased to pay scutage for some time before this, for, in 1302, the heir of one of them was accounting for arrears of services before Michaelmas 1286, which seem to represent perhaps ten armies, so that he may have resisted payment since the end of the 1260s (see below, table 2). Even as late as 1341, the magnates were complaining that ministers levied money for services which should be rendered in person (*Stat. John–Hen. V*, pp 358–60). 7 Otway-Ruthven, 'Knight service in Ireland' (above, pp 160–1); eadem, 'The partition of the de Verdon lands in 1332', *PRIA*, 66:C5 (1968), 408. For castle guard in England, see Hollister, *Military organization of Norman England*, ch. 5. 8 *CDI 1171–1251*, no. 1581. 9 *35th rep. DKPRI*, p. 35. 10 Otway-Ruthven, 'Partition of the de Verdon lands', pp 443–4. Their statement is consistent with the fragmentary notes from the rolls of Henry III, which are all that remain

Stipendiary troops had, of course, been an important element in Norman armies from the beginning. The core of every Norman-Irish army was the justiciar's permanent bodyguard. This seems to have been first defined in 1295, when John Wogan's appointment as justiciar required him to maintain twenty men-at-arms and as many armoured horses;[11] but in 1224, the archbishop of Dublin, reporting the preparations against the arrival of Hugh de Lacy, wrote of the *familia* of the king's army and of the placing of a good *familia* of knights in the castles of Ulster.[12] Later in the century, we find the knights of the king's household being given robes, saddles and annual fees.[13] But this small group of permanently employed professionals was supplemented when necessary by bodies of hired horse and foot soldiers, many of whom were Irish, such as the troops from Munster and Desmond whom the bishop of Norwich brought to serve under John in 1210, and again the Irish contingents to be found serving under Thomas de Rokeby in the 1350s.[14] With the transition from personal service to the payment of scutage (invariably called royal service in Ireland), which seems to have taken place quite abruptly *c.*1238, the stipendiary element became all-important in almost every army.[15] The leaders were, of course, very often tenants-in-chief who both paid scutage and served for pay, but the troops they raised and led were foot-soldiers and hobelers (light cavalrymen), much more useful in the circumstances of Irish warfare than the heavily armoured knight of the strictly feudal army.

By the second half of the thirteenth century, scutage was thus a regular part of the Irish revenue, and since the conditions which justified it – the putting of an army in the field – arose very regularly, it was levied with much greater frequency than in England.[16] The lists below (table 2) – which are probably not complete, though they are as full as our sources allow – show that between 1253 and 1315 there was a proclamation of royal service approximately every second year, and sometimes in each of several successive years. After this, their frequency is considerably less, the Bruce invasion having apparently been a dividing line, but it must be remembered that we have no pipe roll evidence after 1348, so that our main source is lacking for the second half of the fourteenth century and the whole of the fifteenth. By this time, however, the importance of scutage as a source of revenue was declining, partly because of reductions in the quotas of

to us, and most of the rolls of the reign were still extant in the later seventeenth century (see *Pipe roll 14 John*, p. 75). It is probably significant that this is at the beginning of the period when military activity was mainly in Ulster. 11 *CDI 1293–1301*, no. 267. 12 SC 1/66/120. Earlier, we hear of the knights of the *familia* of John de Grey (*Pipe roll 14 John*, p. 34). 13 *CDI 1252–84*, pp 150, 178, 179, 180. 14 *CDI 1171–1251*, p. 61; NAI, RC 8/26, pp 349–53, 657–73. The pay of a man-at-arms in the 1350s was 12*d.* per day, an archer 4*d.*, a hobelar 2*d.* or 3*d.*, a foot soldier 1*d.* or 1½*d.* Men-at-arms and archers were elite troops, appearing in small numbers in the retinues of ministers. 15 The whole service of Leinster came in person against the Irish of Leix and Offaly in 1288 (*CDI 1285–92*, no. 559). 16 Cf.

service owed for certain areas,[17] but even more because of the progressive decline in the area controlled by the Dublin government, which, as early as 1372, necessitated an order that scutage should not be levied on lands 'now by the Irish rebels wasted and by them occupied'.[18]

In an earlier period, however, scutage had been a very substantial part of the Irish revenue. Though the total of knight service owed to the king in Ireland was not very great – at the end of the thirteenth century it was estimated at just over 427 fees[19] – this represented a sum which was by no means inconsiderable in relation to the total revenue, and might moreover be considerably increased if any of the great lordships were in the king's hand. All of them contained a considerably greater number of fees than the total at which they were assessed: Leinster, assessed at 100 fees, actually contained about 180; while Meath, assessed at 50, seems to have had just under 120.[20] In the ordinary way, the lord took the difference between the scutage which his subtenants paid to him and that which he himself paid to the king as his own profit,[21] but if the land were in the king's hand the whole went to the crown. Thus, at the rate of 40*s.* for each fee, which was standard at least by the second half of the thirteenth century,[22] a scutage should bring in just over £850, and might bring in very substantially more. When we consider that the average annual sum received by the treasurer between 1278 and 1299 amounted to no more than £6,300, falling between 1299 and 1315 to £4,190,[23] the importance of scutages in the Irish revenue will be immediately apparent. On the other hand, it should be remembered that scutage payments were usually slow to come in, and the pipe rolls show tenants-in-chief accounting for arrears of services over many years.

The lists of proclamations of royal service which follow are certainly extremely incomplete for the period up to 1252, for which very little evidence has survived. After that they are probably fairly complete, at least up to the later fourteenth century, though there may well have been others of which I have not

*CDI 1252–84*, no. 1801. **17** See, e.g., the case of Kildare, where the earls of Kildare claimed to owe only the five services specified by the charters of 1316 and 1317, while the exchequer demanded the 33⅓ services which had been owed by the Marshal heirs for this entire area (A.J. Otway-Ruthven, 'The medieval county of Kildare', *IHS*, 11:43 (1959), 198–9). **18** *CCR 1369–74*, pp 380–1. **19** Mary Bateson, 'Irish exchequer memoranda of the reign of Edward I', *EHR*, 18:71 (1903), 497–513. See Otway-Ruthven, 'Knight service in Ireland', pp 158–9. **20** See G.H. Orpen, 'The earldom of Ulster', *JRSAI*, 45 (1915), 139–40; A.J. Otway-Ruthven, 'Knights' fees in Kildare, Leix, and Offaly', *JRSAI*, 91 (1961), pp 153–4; Otway-Ruthven, 'Partition of the de Verdon lands', p. 415. **21** See above, Otway-Ruthven, 'Knight service in Ireland', p. 159. **22** Our only indication of what a service might have been assessed at earlier is the statement that the seneschal of Meath paid 13*s.* 4*d.* for the work of Richard Dullard at Clones because he was elsewhere in the king's service (*Pipe roll 14 John*, p. 22), but this does not necessarily, or even probably, refer to military service, and in any case we do not know what Dullard held. Under Henry III, a scutage was sometimes taken at half the standard rate (*Reg. Gormanston*, p. 13). **23** Richardson and Sayles, 'Ir. revenue', 87–100.

found evidence. But since some of them have left no evidence except in the list of arrears of services owed by a single tenant-in-chief, it is always possible that other similar lists may be found which will fill in gaps. Some of these services are not dated precisely in the records, which may give no date at all, or may refer only to a service in the time of a certain justiciar. Where they can be certainly identified with a known expedition, they have been dated without comment in the list; merely probable dates have been given a question mark. At any rate, however incomplete these lists may be, they are offered as a contribution towards the elucidation of some of the problems of the Irish revenue in the Middle Ages.

TABLE 2
PROCLAMATIONS OF ROYAL SERVICE IN IRELAND, 1212–1480

| | |
|---|---|
| 1212 | The army of Clones[1] |
| 1223 | Probably against Hugh de Lacy[2] |
| 1226 | Probably an expedition to Connacht[3] |
| 1227 | An expedition to Connacht[4] |
| 1234 | The army against Richard Marshal[5] |
| 1238 | An expedition to Ulster[6] |
| 1247 (?) | The army of the Bann[7] |
| 1248 (?) | The army of Kenelowen[8] |
| 1252 | The army of Maincoue[9] |
| 1254 | Perhaps an expedition to Ulster[10] |
| 1258 | The army of Kenelowen[11] |
| 1261 | The army of Desmond[12] |
| 1262 | The army of Roscommon[13] |
| 1262 | The army of Greencastle[14] |
| 1269 | The army of Roscommon[15] |

1 *Pipe roll 14 John*, p. 52. 2 *CDI 1171–1251*, no. 1030: a grant to William Marshal of the service which he owes for the seventh year of the reign. 3 *CDI 1171–1251*, nos. 1269, 1439: a similar grant of the service for the tenth year. We have no other evidence for these two services. 4 *CDI 1171–1251*, nos. 1030, 1048, 1581, and cf. no. 1269. 5 *35th rep. DKPRI*, p. 35. 6 A.J. Otway-Ruthven, 'The partition of the de Verdon lands in 1332', *PRIA*, 66:C5 (1968), 443–4. We know that there was an expedition to Ulster in this year, and the scutage entered on the rolls must have been for it. 7 Gerrard, 'Notes', pp 262–5. 8 Ibid., pp 262–5. 9 Ibid., pp 262–5; C 47/10/15, no. 5. Hugh Tyrel served in person in this army. 10 Ibid. Tyrel did his service in person with the king in Gascony in this year, and it would hardly have been noted on the pipe roll if there had not been a scutage in Ireland. 11 Ibid. Tyrel paid scutage on this occasion. 12 *35th rep. DKPRI*, pp 42, 45. The army of Desmond was an occasion on which only a half service was required. 13 Ibid. 14 Ibid., p. 43; TNA (PRO), C 47/10/15, no. 5; SC 1/17/185; NAI, RC 8/13, p. 493. I am indebted for this and other references to the Ir. memo. rolls to Mr R.F. Frame. It is odd to find two services in the same year: perhaps only some of the tenants-in-chief were summoned on each occasion. Tyrel served in person in this army. 15 RIA, MS 12 D 10, p. 41. I am indebted to Mr R.F.

| | |
|---|---|
| 1270 | The army of Dunmore[16] |
| 1271 | The army of Dunmore[17] |
| 1273 | The army of Athenry[18] |
| 1274 (?) | The army of Roscommon[19] |
| 1275 | The army of Castledermot[20] |
| 1277 (?) | The army of Castledermot[21] |
| 1278 (?) | The army of Athenry[22] |
| 1279 (?) | The army of 'Confy'[23] |
| By 1284 | The army of Castledermot[24] |
| By 1287 | The army of Cashel[25] |
| By 1287 | The army of the New Town of Leix[26] |
| 1288 (9 Sept.) | The army of Kildare[27] |
| 1289 (?) | The army of Roscrea[28] |
| By 1295 | The army of Alterie[29] |
| 1295 | The army of Castledermot[30] |
| 1297 | The army of Castlecomer[31] |
| 1299 (16 Aug.) | The army of Dundalk[32] |
| 1302 | The army of Newcastle McKynegan[33] |
| 1304 (7 Jan.) | The army of Kilkenny[34] |
| 1305 | The army of Kildare[35] |
| 1306 | The army of Ballymore[36] |
| 1307 | The army of Loughsewdy[37] |
| 1309 | The army of Castlekevin[38] |

Frame for this reference. **16** Ibid., p. 43; TNA (PRO), SC 1/17/185 [*temp.* R. de Ufford (1268–70)]. **17** *CDI 1252–84*, no. 889; RIA, MS 12 D 10, p. 43; TNA (PRO), SC 1/17/185 [*temp.* J. de Audeley (1270–2)]. **18** SC 1/17/185 [*temp.* M. fitz Gerald (1272–3)]. **19** SC 1/17/185; TCD, MS 671, fo. 7 [*temp.* G. de Geneville (1273–6)]. **20** *36th rep. DKPRI*, pp 26, 46. **21** TNA (PRO) SC 1/17/185; RIA, MS 12 D 10, p. 57; *36th rep. DKPRI*, p. 40. This and the next two services are dated only as *temp.* R. de Ufford (1276–81). **22** *36th rep. DKPRI*, p. 74. **23** Ibid., p. 46; *38th rep. DKPRI*, p. 75; *CDI 1252–84*, no. 1879. It is not clear where 'Confy' was. A roll of 1315–16 suggests that it may have been in west Wicklow (NAI, RC 8/10, pp 298–9). [EN. probably Quin (Ir. *Cuinche*), Co. Clare]. **24** *CDI 1285–92*, no. 149; *37th rep. DKPRI*, p. 43 [*temp.* S., bishop of Waterford (1281–6)]. **25** *37th rep. DKPRI*, pp 24, 27, 28, 38, 43; *CDI 1293–1301*, no. 86. This and the next service are dated only as *temp.* S., archbishop of Tuam (1286–8). **26** *CDI 1293–1301*, no. 86. **27** *CDI 1285–92*, no. 559. **28** *38th rep. DKPRI*, pp 87, 90, 101 [*temp.* J., archbishop of Dublin (1288–90)]. **29** *CJRI 1295–1303*, p. 43. **30** *CDI 1293–1301*, nos. 221, 259, 346, 389, 442, 509; *38th rep. DKPRI*, pp 75, 87, 90. **31** *CDI 1293–1301*, nos. 442, 473, 509. **32** *CJRI 1295–1303*, p. 362; NAI, EX 2/1, p. 150 [Ir. memo. roll, 31–5 Edw. I, m. 20*d*]. This service is dated 22 Edw. I (1294) in *CJRI 1305–7*, p. 296, but the internal evidence shows plainly that this is a mistake for 27 Edw. I. **33** NAI, EX 2/1, p. 150 [Ir. memo. roll, 31–5 Edw. I, m. 20*d*]; *38th rep. DKPRI*, pp 60, 70, 71. **34** NAI, EX 2/1, p. 67 [Ir. memo. roll, 31–5 Edw. I, m. 3*d*]; *CJRI 1305–7*, p. 296, puts this in 31 Edw. I (1302–3). **35** *CJRI 1305–7*, pp 215, 242, 296; NAI, EX 2/1, p. 150 [Ir. memo. roll, 31–5 Edw. I, m. 20*d*]. **36** NAI, EX 2/1, p. 180 [Ir. memo. roll, 31–5 Edw. I, m. 28*d*]; NAI, RC 8/4, pp 507–8. **37** *CJRI 1308–14*, pp 3–4; NAI, RC 8/5, pp 376, 794–5; RC 8/7, p. 357. **38** NAI, RC 8/4, pp 455, 507–8; *39th rep. DKPRI*, p. 49; *RCH*, p. 9, nos. 106–7; *RCH*, p. 11, nos. 410–12.

| | |
|---|---|
| 1311 (25 June) | The army of Carrickfergus[39] |
| 1312 (?) | The army of Cork[40] |
| 1315 | The army of Greencastle[41] |
| 1324 | The army of Tullow[42] |
| 1330 | The army of Athassel[43] |
| 1332 (5 Oct.) | The army of Limerick[44] |
| 1336 | The army of Kilkenny[45] |
| 1341 | The army of Castledermot[46] |
| 1345 | The army of Moydesshell[47] |
| 1348 (after Easter) | The army of Mallow[48] |
| 1350 | The army of Wicklow[49] |
| 1355 (May or June) | The army of Newcastle McKynegan[50] |
| 1359 | The army of Carlow[51] |
| 1368 | The army of Kilkenny[52] |
| 1372 (2 Jan.) | The army of Kilkenny[53] |
| 1372 (23 Apr.) | The army of Castledermot[54] |
| 1378 (20 May) | The army of Cashel[55] |
| 1381 (5 Oct.) | The army of Cashel[56] |
| 1384 (1 Mar.) | The army of Kilmallock[57] |
| 1388–9 | The army of Carlingford[58] |
| 1394 | The army of Kilmallock[59] |
| 1408 | The army of New Ross[60] |
| 1415 | The army of Carlingford[61] |
| 1418 | The army of Louth[62] |
| 1421 | The army of Louth[63] |
| 1423 | The army of Mullamast[64] |
| 1429–30 | The army of Mullamast[65] |
| 1434 (13 Dec.) | The army of Louth[66] |
| 1436–7 | The army of Mullingar[67] |

**39** *RCH*, p. 19, nos. 8, 27; NAI, RC 8/5, pp 531–2, 762. **40** NAI, RC 8/10, pp 214–5. **41** NAI, RC 8/10, pp 471, 524–5, 559; *39th rep. DKPRI*, p. 69. **42** *42nd rep. DKPRI*, pp 53, 68, 73. **43** *43rd rep. DKPRI*, p. 36; Gerrard, 'Notes', p. 284. **44** *Parls & councils*, pp 9–10. **45** *45th rep. DKPRI*, pp 36, 39; NAI, RC 8/21, pp 357–8, places this service in 11 Edw. III (1337). **46** *47th rep. DKPRI*, pp 52, 68; NAI, RC 8/23, pp 467–8: this service was in the time of John Morice, lieutenant of the justiciar, so it must have been after 16 May 1341. **47** *54th rep. DKPRI*, p. 23. **48** *COD*, iii, 342; *CCR 1346–9*, p. 580. Easter was 20 Apr. in this year. **49** *COD*, iii, 342. **50** Ibid.; *RCH*, p. 57, no. 134; *RCH*, p. 59, nos. 16–17; *RCH*, p. 62, no. 111. **51** *COD*, iii, 342. **52** NLI, MS 761, pp 297–8. **53** Ibid.; NAI, RC 8/30, p. 204. **54** *CCR 1369–74*, pp 380–1; *RCH*, p. 82, nos. 50, 72; *RCH*, p. 83, no. 102; *RCH*, p. 85, nos. 144–5, 150–1. The only other occasion on which there seem to have been two services in the same year was 1262. **55** NLI, MS 761, pp 297–8; *RCH*, p. 105, nos. 90–1; *RCH*, p. 106, no. 112. **56** *RCH*, p. 119, nos. 132–3. **57** Gerrard, 'Notes', pp 289–90; NLI, MS 761, pp 297–8. **58** NLI, MS 761, pp 297–8; *Llanthony Cart.*, p. 169. **59** NLI, MS 761, pp 297–8. **60** Ibid.; Marlborough, *Chronicle*, p. 22. **61** NLI, MS 761, pp 297–8. **62** Ibid.; Gerrard, 'Notes', p. 266. **63** *RCH*, p. 220, nos. 96–7; NLI, MS 761, pp 297–8. **64** NLI, MS 761, pp 297–8. **65** Ibid.; *RCH*, p. 252, no. 34. **66** NLI, MS 761, pp 297–8; Hore, *Wexford*, v, 131. **67** *RCH*, p. 264, no. 29.

| | |
|---|---|
| 1450 | The army of ?[68] |
| 1467 (26 June) | The army of Kildare[69] |
| 1473 (8 Feb.) | The army of Wexford[70] |
| 1480 (11 Sept.) | The army of Kildare[71] |

**68** *Stat. Hen. VI*, pp 187–9. **69** Gerrard, 'Notes', p. 284 **70** Hore, *Wexford*, v, 132; *Stat. Edw. IV, pt 2*, p. 766. **71** Gerrard, 'Notes', pp 266, 287–9.

CHAPTER 9

# The hobelar: an Irish contribution to medieval warfare*

*James Lydon*

The Irish soldier abroad is a familiar figure to all students of history and Ireland's contribution to the armies of England, France and Spain, to mention but a few, has been recognized for generations past. But it is not generally realized that long before the Wild Geese left their country, centuries before the formation of the famous Irish regiments in the French and Spanish service, soldiers from Ireland had already seen service on continental battlefields. As far back as the middle of the thirteenth century, Irish and Anglo-Irish soldiers had gone campaigning with the kings of England in Wales, Gascony, Flanders and Scotland. The story of these mercenaries remains yet to be told. In this article, an attempt will be made to outline the history of one particular type of Irish soldier who played a prominent part in the evolution of the most effective fighting man of the Middle Ages – the mounted archer.[1]

In the thirteenth century, the countries of western Europe, despite their experience during the crusades, still clung obstinately to the outmoded military tactics that had prevailed since the fall of the Roman empire. They were rigidly tied to the traditions of chivalry, and the charge of the mail-clad horseman upon an armoured horse was the sole concept of battle. A battle, in fact, was little more than a large-scale tourney, in which the combatants were still bound by the rigid code they embraced with knighthood. In such encounters, the foot soldier played a very minor part as 'an auxiliary arm of no very great efficiency'.[2] All this was changed, however, with the advent of Edward I in England. That monarch's campaigns in Wales soon taught him the value of infantry when properly used in combination with horse. They brought to light also the power of the longbow, which in the hands of English bowmen was to decide many a field.[3] From then on, foot soldiers occupied a prominent place in the composition of all English armies, and contributed in no small extent to their victories.

* First published in *Ir. Sword*, 2 (1954–6), 12–16. 1 For the evolution of the mounted archer, see J.E. Morris, 'Mounted infantry in mediaeval warfare', *TRHS*, 3rd ser., 8 (1914), 77–102. 2 Sir Charles Oman, *A history of the art of war*, 2 vols (2nd ed., London, 1924), ii, 57. 3 J.E. Morris, 'The archers at Crecy', *EHR*, 12:47 (1897), 427–36; T.F. Tout, 'The tactics of the battles of Boroughbridge and Morlaix', ibid., 19:76 (1904), 711–15; Oman, *Art of War*, ii, 57–61.

With the commencement of the wars in Scotland, however, a new problem was encountered. Wallace and Bruce both realized that they could never hope to defeat the English in pitched battles, so they adopted guerrilla tactics and a hit-and-run method of fighting. 'Bruce's great contribution to military history is that he mounted his men on ponies to avoid battle, to starve out the English, and to retaliate by devastating raids … Therefore more important than the combination of horse and foot in the Anglo-Scottish wars, was the discovery by the English, of some method to catch the Scots and bring them to battle.'[4] The solution of this problem was found, in the first instance, in the hobelar. At a later stage, infantry, and notably archers, were mounted on light ponies swift enough to pursue the Scots and bring them to battle. But between the fully armoured knight on the *equus coopertus* and the lightly armoured archer on the *equus discoopertus* there was an intermediate stage. This intermediary, this connecting link as it were, was provided by the hobelar.

The first reference to the hobelar is in 1296, when 260 of them were among a contingent of Irish troops led by John Wogan to the aid of Edward I of Scotland.[5] It was not until four years later that there was any reference to English hobelars. There can be little doubt therefore that the hobelar as a type of soldier originated in Ireland. The word comes from 'hobin', the name given to the type of small horse upon which they were mounted. This itself is indicative of their Irish origin, for this small animal, of twelve to fourteen hands, was the native Irish horse indigenous to the country.[6] There is some suggestion that 'hobin', which is a French word, may be derived from the Gaelic 'obann', meaning swift. Apart from the resemblance in sound, some support for this theory is to be found in the fact that Ware expressed the opinion that they derived the name by reason of their 'mollem gressum'.[7] The same writer is our authority for saying that these horses were well known abroad and valued highly by the Irish themselves. Edward I procured six of them from Decies for his own use.[8] But their small size rendered them quite unsuited for the role of *equus coopertus*, and men mounted upon them were incapable of mounted charge upon the field of battle. This disparity with the Norman destrier was further increased by the fact that Irish riders habitually rode without saddles, or stirrups, or bridles.[9] Nor did they wear mail. In consequence, there grew up in Ireland an entirely different type of mounted soldier. This man was highly mobile, and excelled in scouting, reconnaissance and patrols. Sir Anthony St Leger said of them later, 'for light scourers [scouts] there are no properer horsemen on Christian ground, nor more hardie'.[10] They were eminently suited

4 Morris, 'Mounted infantry', p. 79. 5 E 101/5/26, E 101/6/5; E 372/153 [Eng. pipe roll, 1 Edw. II], m. 39. 6 Robert Francis Scharff, 'The Irish horse and its early history', *PRIA*, 27:B6 (1909), 81–6. They are represented today by the Connemara pony. 7 Sir James Ware, *De Hibernia et antiquitatibus eius disquasitiones* (London, 1654), p. 34. 8 SC 1/17/192. 9 *Giraldi Cambrensis opera*, v, 150. 10 Richard Cox, *Hibernia Anglicana: or the history of*

to the terrain in which military operations had to be conducted in Ireland. However superior the Norman knight might be upon the field of battle, the bogs and woods of Ireland gave little opportunity for the mail-clad charge.

The Normans soon found this, to their cost. An enemy who refused to stand and fight, who could retire to the hills and the marshes where they could not be pursued by the heavy cavalry of chivalry, presented a new problem in war. It was, incidentally, the same problem that faced Edward I in Scotland. Gerald of Wales, though no military tactician, realized that the best way of combating the Irish was by the employment of light armed troops, and he advocated the use of Welsh bowmen in particular.[11] He even went so far as to advocate mounting the infantry with the cavalry. This, in fact, the Normans proceeded to do. 'None of the barons who won Ireland ever marched forth without a large provision of bowmen, and after a time they habitually mounted them.'[12] Thenceforth, the Anglo-Normans relied upon them extensively in all their military undertakings, and even in peacetime, for what amounted virtually to police duties. In 1297, for example, an Irish parliament declared that as felons frequently escaped with their booty, because the people had not horses to pursue them, thenceforth 'every tenant holding xx. librates of land, whether in the march or in land of peace', must have a horse suitably caparisoned, and all others have 'hobbies or other horses unarmed [unarmoured] according to their abilities'.[13]

Thus there evolved in Ireland, as an habitual part of every Anglo-Norman force, a type of light horsemen, which came to be known as the hobelar. It was only a matter of time until this phenomenon found its way across the Irish Sea, and into other Anglo-Norman armies. The opportunity was provided, as we have seen, when his campaign against the Scots in 1296 disclosed to Edward I the urgent necessity for light, highly mobile, troops. It took only twenty-one weeks to bring Balliol to his knees, and in consequence it would appear that the new arm got little opportunity to prove itself. But we are told that they pursued the enemy 'per montanes et loca secreta'.[14] This was a task for which they were eminently suited, and the nature of the Scots terrain was entirely familiar to them. Apparently they made a good impression, for when the Irish expeditionary force returned home, many of the hobelars remained in Scotland. Six of them were included in the garrison of Lochmaban castle, during its siege by the earl of Carrick.[15] The employment of small numbers of them, or even of a single individual, was quite a feature of their service in Scotland. They were apparently extensively used as scouts, or when more than one, for patrols. Thus, in July 1299, Robert de Clifford[16] requested that wages be paid without further

*Ireland from the conquest thereof by the English to this present time* (London, 1689–90), p. 34. 11 *Giraldi Cambrensis opera*, v, 396–7. 12 Oman, *Art of War*, i, 404, 409n. 13 *Stat. John–Hen. V*, p. 201. 14 H.R. Luard (ed.), *Annales monastici*, 5 vols (RS, London, 1864–9), iii, 404. 15 *CDS 1272–1307*, no. 1089; ibid., no. 1115 (at p. 283). 16 Ibid., no. 1084.

delay to Robert le Brut 'an Irish hobelur, retained to spy the passings and haunts of the enemy by night and day, and who has been on duty six weeks and three days, lest he take himself off for want of sustenance'. They seem also to have attracted the attention of King Edward himself. In organizing his next expedition against Scotland in January 1300, he bespoke three hundred hobelars from Ireland, 'the most able that can be found', to attend the muster at Carlisle in the following June.[17] If this were intended in the nature of an experiment with these new troops, Edward was doomed to disappointment upon this occasion. For, while an Irish contingent did attend this muster and took part in the siege of Carlaverock, they had only fourteen hobelars with them.[18] On the other hand, the very fact that it was thought worthwhile to bring even fourteen hobelars serves to emphasize the importance that was attached to their services.

In the following year, however, Edward was more successful, and included in the force of 2,300 men that came from Ireland were 390 hobelars.[19] In 1303, an Irish contingent of 3,400 men included 499 hobelars.[20] The steady increase in the number of hobelars employed is an indication that the first comers among them had justified their recruitment. Indeed, the adoption of the hobelar by the English king was confirmed when they began to be raised in England itself. It was not, in fact, until the reign of Edward II that they were called out in England in any great numbers,[21] and it is unlikely that the English hobelar had the very swift and sturdy mounts possessed by the Irish hobelars.

When England began to raise her own force of hobelars, she did not, for that reason, forego the assistance of the Irish hobelar. Both Edward I and his son continued, when they could get them, to enlist Irish hobelars. It cannot be said, however, that they attracted a great many recruits. During 1311–12, a small band of Irish hobelars, twenty-five in number, went to Berwick castle and garrisoned it.[22] Even on the eve of the Bruce invasion of Ireland, small troops of Irish hobelars were to be found on the English king's service in various parts of Scotland.[23] Irish hobelars comprised almost half the force with which Andrew de Harcla relieved Carlisle when it was besieged by Bruce after the rout of Bannockburn.[24]

Edward Bruce's invasion of Ireland stopped, for the time, any question of the Norman lords sending assistance to their liege lord in Britain. They had now enough to do to hold their own in this country. In 1332, however, when Edward II was preparing to lead his last expedition against the Scots, he sought to raise in Ireland a thousand hobelars.[25] But his negotiations with his Irish tenants-in-

**17** *CPR 1292–1301*, p. 408. **18** E 101/8/20; *Liber quotidianus contrarotulatoris garderobae, 28 Edward I, 1299–1300*, ed. J. Topham et al. (London, 1787), pp 242, 245, 248–9, 253. **19** TNA (PRO), E 101/6/5, E 101/10/1; BL, Add. MS 7966A, fos. 92*v*, 100–100*v*. **20** TNA (PRO), E 101/11/2; BL, Add. MS 8835, fos. 48*v*–9, 54. **21** Morris, 'Mounted infantry', pp 81–2. **22** *CDS 1307–57*, pp 395–6, 414–15. **23** E 101/14/32, fo. 6; E 101/14/34, E 101/376/7, fo. 2*v*. **24** J.E. Morris, 'Cumberland and Westmorland levies in the time of Edward I and Edward II', *Transactions of the Cumberland and Westmorland Antiquarian and Archaeological Society*, new ser., 3 (1903), 316–17. **25** *CCR 1318–23*, pp 529–30.

chief were unsuccessful, and eventually the earl of Louth led into Scotland, to the king's assistance, a small force, of which only 189 were hobelars.[26]

On two occasions in the reign of Edward III were Irish hobelars found in the English king's service overseas. In 1335, John d'Arcy led an expeditionary force into Scotland, which included 260 of them.[27] Twelve years later, fifty of them served under the earl of Kildare at the siege of Calais.[28] But the need for them was passing. In 1333, there had appeared the first mounted archer.[29] In him, the light horseman that was typified by the hobelar was combined with the longbowman. The result was to produce the most effective fighting man of the age, and one who combined fire and movement in a fashion hitherto unprecedented. The process of evolution had rendered the hobelar redundant.

It remains only to discuss the arms and equipment borne by the hobelar. Unfortunately, no contemporary description has survived of the Irish hobelar. We may presume that he was armed much in the manner of his English successor, concerning whom we have ample information. If this assumption be correct, then he may be presumed to have worn a haqueton (a leather jacket, or the like, worn under mail), a hauberk (a coat of ring or chain mail), and a basinet (a light steel helmet with a visor). In addition, he would have carried a sword, a long knife and, frequently, a lance. Above all else, however, his most distinguishing feature was the 'uncovered' (L. *discoopertus*) pony which he rode, and which had no protective covering of either armour or leather.

There is another side to the story of the Irish hobelar, however, and one which affected the fortunes of the Anglo-Norman settlement in Ireland. If we consider the military activities of these soldiers abroad as part of the large-scale withdrawal of troops from Ireland by Edward I to aid him in his relentless attacks upon Scotland, we shall quickly see that they also contributed to the virtual downfall of the Anglo-Norman colony in Ireland. For the absence of the great lords and their followers on campaigns overseas, and the over-extension of their military strength, weakened the uncompleted settlement considerably, and gave the Irish the opportunity which they sought. Encouraged by the successes of their fellow-Celts against the 'foreigner', and strengthened by the influx of Gallowglasses, they became conscious of a new, if short-lived, feeling, akin to nationalism. In consequence, they became inspired to a remarkable rally, which in time engulfed the greater part of the area where once the king's writ ran and feudal law was supreme. Thus, the Norman conquest of Ireland was never completed, and the unifying effect that their conquest had had upon England was lost to Ireland. The effect of this has been so profound upon our history as to be incalculable.

**26** E 101/16/16, m. 1. **27** E 101/19/16. **28** George Wrottesley, *Crécy and Calais* (London, 1898), p. 183. **29** A.E. Prince, 'The army and the navy' in J.F. Willard and W.A. Morris (eds), *The English government at work 1327–1336*, i: *central and prerogative administration* (Cambridge, MA, 1940), p. 341.

CHAPTER 10

# An Irish army in Scotland, 1296*

*James Lydon*

From early historic times, Ireland and Gaelic Scotland were linked by many ties, a connection which was particularly close between Ulster and the western isles. Scottish gallowglasses were an important element in the Gaelic revival in Ireland from the mid-thirteenth century onwards, a fact which is well known to students of Irish history. What is less familiar is the form which was given to this relationship at the end of the thirteenth century, when Ireland played an important part in the attempt of Edward I of England to extend his feudal suzerainty over Scotland. Threatened with the loss of their independence, the Scots found Irish mercenaries ranged against them on the side of England, and Irish ships, war supplies and money supporting the English in every campaign. Admittedly, the leaders of these mercenaries were for the most part of Anglo-Norman extraction and the expeditions were mounted and paid for by feudal Ireland; but Gaelic Ireland too, in the persons of minor chieftains and hundreds of foot-soldiers from Ulster, had a place in this onslaught on Scotland. Their participation was not without precedent, for in July 1244, Henry III had attempted to procure the assistance of twenty-one Irish chieftains, many of them from Ulster, for a campaign in Scotland;[1] in the following year, Felim O'Connor, at the head of three thousand native Irish, participated in the Gannoc campaign in Wales.[2] So when the earl of Ulster, Richard de Burgh, was asked to supply contingents of soldiers for Scotland, it was natural that he should call on the great Ulster chieftains, all of whom (with the exception of O'Donnell) owed him military service to the extent of 345 *satellites*.[3]

The reasons for Edward I's attack on Scotland need not detain us here: suffice it to say that the revolt of his vassal king, John Balliol, after signing a defensive treaty with France in 1295, was the immediate cause of the invasion.[4] Thwarted in his plans for a continental campaign, Edward was determined to

* First published in *Ir. Sword*, 5 (1961–2), 184–90. 1 *CR 1242–7*, pp 254–5. Even though the campaign was subsequently cancelled, there is evidence to suggest that some at least of the Irish had set out for the rendezvous at Carlingford (ibid., p. 255). 2 *CPR 1232–47*, p. 461. 3 G.H. Orpen, 'The earldom of Ulster', *JRSAI*, 45 (1915), 131–41. In 1329, *satellites* were identified as kern: see Otway-Ruthven, 'Knight service in Ireland' (above, p. 168, n. 185). 4 A good recent account of the events leading to the war will be found in F.M. Powicke, *The thirteenth century, 1216–1307* (1st ed., Oxford, 1953), ch. 12.

teach the Scots a lesson they would not quickly forget. The largest possible army must be assembled so that Scotland would be quickly and efficiently brought to heel, leaving Edward free to deal with the French. Aware of the full significance of the Franco-Scottish alliance, the king began his preparations for a campaign before the end of 1295.[5] On the first day of 1296, writs of military summons were addressed to Richard de Burgh and twenty-seven other *fideles* of Ireland, requesting them to be at Whitehaven by 1 March following.[6] The king's messenger who carried the writs to Ireland subsequently submitted a report to the king, describing his attempts to contact the leading Irish magnates and the reception he had from them.[7] This report, unique for Ireland, shows clearly what the attitude of these magnates was to service overseas. They proved evasive in their replies, hedging for time in an effort to secure the best terms possible of service from the king. Not from any sense of loyalty towards Edward or because of any obligation to render military service would they join the king in Scotland, but rather for what they could get out of it for themselves. And in this the earl of Ulster at least was successful, for during the campaign he received the highest rate of pay ever allowed to an earl in these wars. The others, though allowed pardon of debts at the Dublin exchequer, and the normal rates of pay on a privileged fortnightly basis, were otherwise not so lucky in their bargaining on this occasion. Later, on the occasion of the Flanders campaign, they were so successful that the king had to withdraw from the terms made on his behalf, considering them 'rather harsh'.[8]

Because of the delaying tactics employed by the magnates they did not leave themselves much time for their preparations for the campaign. Though asked to muster in Whitehaven by 1 March, we find Theobald Butler raising his contingent as late as 20 April, on which date he drew up an indenture for military service with a certain John de Neville.[9] This military indenture, the earliest Irish one now extant, is of great interest as showing that indentured service was practised in Ireland at this early date. It is similar in form to the typical military indenture of later times, specifying the period and place of service, the strength of the contingent to be provided (in this case three fully armed horse) and the amount to be paid for transportation and the journey to Scotland. The wages to be paid are not specified, the indenture merely stipulating that after they returned home Theobald would reward John 'secundum laboris sui et exigenciam ad utriusque honorem'.

Thomas de Snyterby, one of the king's justices of common pleas in Ireland, was appointed paymaster to the army, and from the accounts which he presented at the Irish exchequer we can form a clear picture of the size and

5 Ranald Nicholson, 'The Franco-Scottish and Franco-Norwegian treaties of 1295', *SHR*, 38:126 (1959), 116. 6 *Parl. writs*, i, 277, no. 9. 7 *Docs illus. Scot. hist.*, ii, 124–5. 8 *CCR 1296–1302*, p. 69. 9 *Red bk Ormond*, no. 53.

composition of the expedition to Scotland.[10] On 26 March, he began making arrangements for assembling the army and transporting it to Scotland, work which occupied him until 29 April. By then, most of the twenty-four contingents from different parts of the country had arrived at the ports of embarkation: Dublin, Drogheda and Carrickfergus. There the contingents were regrouped under nine leaders and were further grouped under two commands: those at Dublin under the justiciar, John Wogan; and those at the other two ports under the earl of Ulster. Altogether, a total of 3,157 men, the majority of them foot, were ready to sail for Scotland.[11]

The provision of a fleet large enough to carry this number, with their horses, equipment and military stores, was a mammoth job which taxed the efficiency of the paymaster and the king's administration to the utmost. Finding the ships and fitting them out for such specialized work was difficult enough, but inclement weather and adverse winds resulted in accidents which delayed operations on many occasions. For example, one of the ships allocated to the earl of Ulster was driven off course and, with nine of his horses on board, ran aground at Dalkey. Rescue operations failing to save the ship, the horses and all equipment had to be transferred to another vessel. But despite such delays, a fleet of well over 150 ships (many of them Irish) was finally assembled at a cost of £560. This was probably the largest fleet ever assembled in Ireland up to this time. Many of the ships were quite small, even by 1296 standards, some of them carrying as few as six horses; indeed, one could only manage four. Yet they proved adequate to the task in hand and eventually landed the Irish safely in England.

The date of their departure is far from certain, but it was probably shortly after 29 April, the day Snyterby finished his work in Ireland and the first *solutio* ('payment') to the different Irish contingents was completed.[12] Only one of the Irish annals is of any help here, and even it is vague in its statement that the Irish left around 6 May and met the king in Scotland at Roxburgh castle a week later, Pentecost Sunday.[13] From there, we lose sight of the Irish until they join the king again at Stirling in June.[14] Since Edward did not arrive at Stirling until 14 June,[15] a month had elapsed since the Irish first joined him. Where were they in the meantime? The simple answer is that we do not know. Possibly the bulk of them remained with Edward during the interval, though some at least did

10 The final audited account of the Irish pipe rolls has not survived; but that on the English pipe roll is in E 372/153 [Eng. pipe roll, 1 Edw. II], m. 39. Particulars of receipts and payments are in E 101/5/26; and E 101/6/5 gives a neat summary of the entire force. Unless otherwise indicated the information in this essay is taken from these sources. 11 For details, see table 3, 'Leaders and their contingents, 1296'. 12 The first *solutio* began on different dates for the different contingents, depending on when the local musters occurred before the journeys to the ports were begun. 13 *CStM*, ii, 326. 14 Harry Rothwell (ed.), *The chronicle of Walter of Guisborough, previously edited as the chronicle of Walter of Hemingford or Hemingburgh* (Camden Soc., 3rd ser., 89, 1957), p. 279; Nicholas Trivet, *Annales sex regum Angliae, 1135–1307*, ed. T. Hog (London, 1845), p. 347. 15 *Docs illus. Scot. hist.*, ii, 28.

not. The annalist of Dunstable – who says that the Irish came to the assistance of the English during the battle of Dunbar and were later used to pursue the Scots 'per montanas Scotie et loca secreta' – may offer a solution.[16] His statement, of course, is wrong on one major point, for the battle of Dunbar was fought before the army left Ireland. But this does not mean that his evidence is to be entirely dismissed, for while his chronology is wrong it may well be that he is right in suggesting that the Irish were used against the Scots at large in the mountains and 'secret places'. That the Irish, or at least one section of them, were ideally suited for this sort of skirmishing is beyond question. The hobelars, now seen for the first time outside Ireland, mounted on their fast ponies (L. *hobini*) and lightly armed, were faster and more mobile in every way than the heavy English cavalry, and were well suited for pursuit work in the mountainous districts between Roxburgh and Stirling. This fact must have been immediately apparent to Edward I, one of the greatest innovators in medieval warfare; indeed, so impressed was he by the speed and general mobility of the Irish hobelars that not only did he use them in all his subsequent campaigns in Scotland, but he developed this type of light cavalry in England also.[17] It would have been natural for him to exploit their usefulness in the different terrain he encountered after leaving Roxburgh. We know that, after Dunbar, no action was seen by the army in Scotland, and yet the Irish lost horses (presumably in action against the Scots) for which they had to be compensated later in accordance with the agreements signed with the king.[18]

Even if they did not play an active part in the little fighting which occurred, the arrival of this force of more than three thousand men from Ireland proved a welcome addition to the army with which Edward hoped to impress the Scots once and for all. His plan was to amass the largest army possible and overawe the Scots with a huge display of military strength. But because of his other commitments, he did not find it easy to put such an army into the field; indeed, his need for reinforcements had been so great that he was forced to issue an appeal from Berwick to criminals and vagrants asking them to join him in the campaign in return for pardon and immunity.[19] After the battle of Dunbar, Scottish resistance was broken and the rest of the campaign became, as Tout has said, but a military promenade. The presence of the Irish, then, made a considerable addition to the army with which he hoped to impress the Scots. They remained with the king during his procession through Scotland. On 7 August, they set out for the coast on their way home to Ireland – de Burgh, le Poer and Butler to Newcastle on Ayr; Wogan, Fitz Thomas and the rest to Furness. Some difficulty was experienced in providing them with transport,[20] with the result that the first group did not sail until 24 August and the latter until 6 September.

**16** H.R. Luard (ed.), *Annales monastici*, 5 vols (RS, London, 1864–9), iii, 404. **17** For the hobelar, see Lydon, 'The hobelar: an Irish contribution to medieval warfare' (above, ch. 9). **18** *CDI 1293–1301*, nos. 320, 369 etc. **19** *Docs illus. Scot. hist.*, ii, 38–9. **20** The earl of

The delay might be explained by the fact that some of the ships which had carried the army from Ireland had been used in an attack on Alexander of Argyle in the Scottish isles.[21] After the army had been put ashore at Furness, thirty of the ships had been retained there at the request of the king. On 4 June, they were dispatched northwards to attack Alexander and were in the king's pay for that purpose until at least 1 July. But it is not unlikely that they were retained in the king's service after that date for it was not until the autumn of 1296 and the spring of 1297 that Alexander became really active.[22] If this is what happened, then these ships at least would not be available that autumn for transporting the Irish home, and finding suitable replacements may have caused the delay. Whatever the reason, the Irish took a belated departure. John Wogan, the justiciar, did not sail with them. He returned to the king for a consultation, possibly about the campaign the king was planning for Flanders, and remained in Scotland for a further forty-seven days.[23]

The costs of this large-scale military expedition from Ireland, the first in Edward's reign, were a heavy drain on the resources of the Dublin exchequer. Altogether Snyterby, the paymaster, accounted for nearly £7,500, of which he received £2,500 from the keeper of the king's wardrobe while in Scotland.[24] Other smaller sums were contributed in Ireland which do not figure on Snyterby's accounts, such as the £5 15*s*. 3*d*. paid from the farm of Drogheda borough on the side of Uriel to Eustace le Poer for the journey to Scotland, or the unknown sum expended by the collectors of the new custom at Youghal in repairing five ships and paying the wages of sailors bringing them to Dublin to carry the army to Scotland.[25] There is no way of knowing how much money was contributed towards the expenses of the expedition in this way, so that the full cost cannot be ascertained. But probably it would amount to about £8,000. Small as this figure may appear when compared with the huge sums disbursed by the English wardrobe on the campaign, it must be considered in an Irish context if we are to appreciate its full significance. According to the audited accounts of the Irish treasurer for this year (24 Edward I), the total receipt of the exchequer amounted to rather less than £6,400.[26] So that, by Irish standards, the cost of mounting this expedition to Scotland was very high indeed. Taken in conjunction with the sums expended on provisions for this

Ulster and the others who were returned by way of Newcastle were delayed for 14 days, those at Furness for 21 days. **21** Payments at Drogheda in this year, recorded on Ir. pipe roll, 27 Edw. I, include £20 'paid to Peter de Paris in part payment of wages of himself and other seamen of 30 ships sent against Alexander de Argyle and the Scottish islands' (RIA, MS 12 D 10, p. 119). Three constables, 499 mariners and the masters of thirty ships constituted the entire force. **22** D. Macpherson, J. Caley, W. Illingworth and T.H. Horne (eds), *Rotuli Scotiae in turri Londiniensi et in domo capitulari Westmonasteriensi asservati (1291–1516)*, 2 vols (Edinburgh, 1814–19), i, 31, 40; *Docs illus. hist. Scot.*, ii, 187–90; *CDS 1272–1307*, p. 225. **23** E 159/84 (KR, memo. roll, 5 Edw. II), m. 17. **24** E 372/153 (Eng. pipe roll, 1 Edw. II), m. 39; *CDS 1272–1307*, p. 205. **25** *38th rep. DKPRI*, pp 31, 43. **26** *CDI 1293–1301*, no. 346.

campaign and for the Welsh and French wars, it placed an intolerable burden on the financial resources of Ireland.

On 12 September, or shortly after the last of the Irish had returned home, a general pardon 'pro homicidiis, latrociniis, roberiis et aliis transgressionibus quibusque contra pacem nostram in terra nostra Hibernie usque ad diem confectionis presentium factis' was issued by Edward to all who had served in the war.[27] At the same time, individual pardons were issued to many of these, de Burgh and Fitz Thomas being the most notable among them.[28] These pardons mean an additional loss of income to the Irish exchequer. But worse, they established a dangerous precedent which was followed by Edward I throughout the remainder of his reign. The facility with which such pardons were obtained from the king for service overseas must be held partly responsible for the great increase in lawlessness in Ireland from this time onwards. Great numbers of such pardons were issued not only by Edward I, but also by his son. Finally, in 1317 and again in 1323, Edward II was compelled to curtail the grant of such pardons because, as he said, 'others had been encouraged to commit crime on account of the facility of obtaining such pardons'.[29]

The participation of an Irish army in the war of 1296 is therefore an event of some importance and significance. For the first time in this reign, Irish soldiers had taken the field in large numbers in one of Edward's campaigns. The Irish hobelar, who was to help to revolutionize the art of war, now makes his first appearance outside Ireland. And the Irish administration had felt the first effects of a sustained effort to meet the demands of the king for help in maintaining a war. But it was only a beginning, for the war of 1296 marks but the start of Edward's long and fruitless effort to conquer Scotland. From now to the end of his reign, the northern kingdom remained a problem. Year after year, he sent or led armies to the north, never to meet with lasting success. In the process, he drained the English treasury and contracted crushing debts which he could not pay. The frustration of his plans had a disastrous effect on his Irish lordship also. As his needs became greater, his demands on Ireland increased and the Dublin government was forced into debt in its efforts to meet the numerous orders for assistance of one sort or another. Not the least important of these were the repeated requests for military aid, and although the Irish government managed to raise only two large armies in the years following 1296, smaller contingents of men and naval forces participated more frequently in the Scottish war.

In another way, too, 1296 was important. The Irish who went to Scotland did so after contracting for special terms of service with the king. They were not obliged to serve overseas, to render the military service due to the king for the

27 *Docs illus. Scot. hist.*, ii, 101–2. 28 *CPR 1292–1301*, pp 197–8, 210; *CDI 1292–1301*, nos. 315, 319, 324, 344, 354 etc. 29 *CCR 1313–18*, p. 405; *CPR 1321–4*, pp 354–5.

lands they held in Ireland ('servitium debitum regi') outside of this country. And so they were paid for their service. But more than that, they were able to bargain with the king for privileged rates, and though most of them failed to procure the terms of service they demanded they established a precedent which was followed in all subsequent engagements with the king. For this alone, their participation in the war of 1296 marks an important stage in the development of contract service in Ireland.

TABLE 3
LEADERS AND THEIR CONTINGENTS, 1296[1]

| *Name* | *Earls* | *Bannerets* | *Knights* | *Squires* | *Hobelars* | *Crossbowmen* | *Foot* |
|---|---|---|---|---|---|---|---|
| Richard de Burgh, earl of Ulster | 1 | – | 3 | 109 | 168 | – | 1,231 |
| Eustace le Poer (banneret) | – | 1 | 1 | 18 | 1 | – | 172 |
| Theobald Butler (banneret) | – | 1 | 1 | 42 | 21 | – | 235 |
| John fitz Thomas (banneret) | – | 2 | 8 | 31 | 25 | 3 | 239 |
| John Wogan (banneret) | – | 2 | 5 | 48 | 24 | 24 | 512 |
| Maurice de Rocheford (banneret) | – | 1 | 5 | 20 | 17 | – | 160 |
| Hugh Purcel (banneret) | – | 1 | 1 | 5 | 5 | – | – |
| Henry Cantoke (knight) | – | – | 2 | 3 | – | – | – |
| Richard Barry (squire) | – | – | – | 9 | – | – | – |
| **Subtotals** | 1 | 8 | 26 | 285 | 261 | 27 | 2,549 |

TOTAL: 3,157

1 E 101/5/26 and E 101/6/5. The latter has been calendared, with some errors, in *Docs illus. Scot. hist.*, ii, 124–6. J.E. Morris, 'Mounted infantry in medieval warfare', *TRHS*, 3rd ser., 8 (1914), 80, gives totals based on E 101/5/26, though these are incorrect. I have included the leaders in the figures opposite their names.

CHAPTER II

# Irish levies in the Scottish wars, 1296–1302*

*James Lydon*

In the autumn of 1296, while an Irish army was on its way home from Scotland, John Wogan, the justiciar, remained in the north for a conference with King Edward I.[1] It is probable that at the conference Irish affairs generally were discussed, but there can be little doubt that Edward's plans for a campaign in Flanders the following year and the part which Ireland might play in furthering those plans were also among the matters discussed. Certainly, on his return from Scotland, Wogan set about raising an army for Flanders, contracting with the leading magnates for their service overseas. In the event, the king withdrew from these contracts, considering them too expensive, so that only a small Irish force under John Fitz Thomas actually served in Flanders.[2]

Meanwhile in Scotland, the great triumph of 1296 was proved to be ephemeral. Hardly had the king recrossed the border on his way south when local risings broke out over a widespread area, and before long a new leader, William Wallace, was leading a general revolt against the English king. At Stirling Bridge, the English were utterly routed and, though new armies were sent against the Scots in 1298 and smashed the rebel army at Falkirk, they accomplished little of permanent value. A series of campaigns in the years following did little to solve the Scottish problem beyond the relief of a few castles under pressure from the Scots. Finally, a truce was signed after the failure of yet another campaign in 1301, to last until the end of 1302. By then, Edward hoped to come to terms with the French, leaving him free to concentrate all his energies on Scotland.[3]

In this series of campaigns, the Irish lordship had an important role to play, most notably in helping to feed the English armies and garrisons in the west. But Irish levies, too, participated in the war, though in 1297 the Flanders campaign and the failure of Edward's negotiations in Ireland meant that only a few Irish served in Scotland.[4] The dispute between the earl of Ulster and John

* First published in *Ir. Sword*, 5 (1961–2), 207–13. 1 See Lydon, 'An Irish army in Scotland, 1296' (above, ch. 10). 2 BL, Add. MS 7965 (wardrobe book, 25 Edw. I), fos. 68*v*, 86*v*; N.B. Lewis, 'The English forces in Flanders, August–November 1297' in R.W. Hunt, W.A. Pantin and R.W. Southern (eds), *Studies in medieval history presented to F.M. Powicke* (Oxford, 1948), pp 310–18. 3 For all this see F.M. Powicke, *The thirteenth century, 1216–1307* (1st ed., Oxford, 1953), p. 683ff. 4 *Docs illus. hist. Scot.*, ii, 232–3; *CDI 1293–1301*, nos. 416, 432, 537–8.

Fitz Thomas was another factor which made it impossible for the justiciar to raise an army in Ireland. Although the king wrote to the earl in March 1298, urging him to hold himself in readiness to go to Scotland and keep the peace ('pax et tranquillitas') in Ireland so that as many as possible might be able to go campaigning in Scotland,[5] the quarrel remained unsettled until October 1298, by which time it was too late to join the king.[6] No evidence whatever exists to substantiate Walter of Guisborough's statement that, of the foot soldiers sent into Scotland in that year, 'quasi omnes erant Hibernici et Wallenses'.[7] A naval expedition, under the command of Hugh Biset, lord of Glenarm, set sail late in the year 'to harass the king's Scotch enemies by sea', though what it accomplished beyond the occupation of the island of Arran remains a mystery.[8]

During the following year, 1299, no military writs were received in Ireland. There were, however, some small troops of Irish hobelars in the king's service in Scotland in that year, doing garrison duty and acting as scouts 'to spy the passings and haunts of the enemy by night and day'.[9] The king was obviously impressed with their performance for, in January 1300 when ordering military stores from Ireland, he enclosed a request that 300 hobelars, 'the most able that can be found', be selected by the justiciar to come to the muster at Carlisle the following June.[10] No other type of military assistance was sought for this campaign. But Edward's hopes for the arrival of a large body of hobelars from Ireland were not realized, however, for although a contingent of Irish troops participated in the campaign of 1300, there were very few hobelars in their ranks.[11] Varying in number from 315 to 377, when they were at their strongest, at most they included only eighteen hobelars (counting four mounted constables of foot); the rest were all archers on foot. They figure on the payrolls from 30 June until 24 August, were present at the storming of Carlaverock castle (the only notable incident in the whole sorry campaign), and afterwards joined the king in his aimless wanderings through Galloway.

The siege of Carlaverock castle has made this campaign famous and a contemporary poem celebrating this episode has survived to the present day. The author recounts the names and arms of the principal men who were present on that occasion. Among them was the Irish knight, Nicholas de Carew, in the company of the earl of Pembroke, 'a valient man of great fame, which had often been displayed both in cover and on the plains against the rebellious people of Ireland. He had a handsome yellow banner with three lions passant

5 *Foedera*, i, 888; *Parl. writs*, i, 312, no. 34. 6 Orpen, *Normans*, iv, 119. 7 Harry Rothwell (ed.), *The chronicle of Walter of Guisborough, previously edited as the chronicle of Walter of Hemingford or Hemingburgh* (Camden Soc., 3rd ser., 89, 1957), p. 324. The bulk of the foot were in fact Welsh. 8 E 372/144 (Eng. pipe roll, 27 Edw. I), m. 25*d*; *CDI 1293–1301*, no. 555; *CJRI 1295–1303*, p. 218; *Chronicle of Walter of Guisborough*, p. 329. 9 *CDS 1272–1307*, nos. 1084, 1089, 1115, p. 283. 10 *CPR 1292–1301*, p. 488; *CDI 1293–1301*, no. 716. 11 See table 4, 'Irish in Scotland, 1300'.

sable'.[12] The author also draws attention to the non-English troops who were there in force, but makes no mention of the Irish – another indication that their numbers were small and that no large troop of hobelars was present, as strange fighters such as these would surely have attracted the attention of the author.[13]

In 1301, after a short truce with the Scots, Edward made yet another attempt to win control of the northern kingdom. This time, however, he had evolved a new plan of campaign. Two approaches were to be used, the first through Berwick in the east under his own personal command, the second by way of Carlisle in the west under the command of his son. This two-pronged attack would, he hoped, prove successful where more orthodox tactics had failed. But it demanded an enormous number of men and a well organized commissariat, particularly since he intended to continue to war through the winter months if this were necessary. Accordingly, Ireland was called on to make a special effort in this war and this meant supplying the greatest possible number of men, in addition to military stores and as much money as could be raised. All of this Irish contribution to the war effort was to be concentrated on the western theatre of war, where the young prince of Wales was in charge of operations.

Early in February 1301, the king wrote to Wogan saying that, as he was 'preparing to totally repress the malice of the Scots' the following summer, he would need ten ships from Ireland.[14] A few days later, the justiciar was further instructed to survey the naval resources of Ireland so as to ascertain how many ships were available for the transportation of troops and how many men and horses each vessel could carry.[15] Wogan soon satisfied himself that Irish shipping would be inadequate for any large-scale military expedition, so in March twelve ships from the Cinque Ports were ordered to proceed to Dublin in June.[16] Immediately this problem was solved, the king began to treat, through Wogan, with the Irish tenants-in-chief for service in the coming campaign. On 28 March, he commissioned the justiciar and four others – among them Richard de Bereford, the treasurer – to come to terms with those vassals by proffering an opportunity to each of securing a pardon of all their debts at the Dublin exchequer.[17] At the same time, letters on the subject were addressed to de Burgh and thirty-five other Irish magnates.[18] The one to the earl of Ulster contained a remarkable message from the king begging his counsel and aid in the coming war. Now for the first time also the mayors of Dublin, Cork, Waterford, Drogheda and Limerick, and the bailiffs of Ross and Kilkenny were requested

12 N.H. Nicolas (ed.), *The siege of Caerlaverock* (London, 1828), p. 17. 13 Ibid., p. 69. 14 *Foedera*, i, 928. They were to be procured as follows: Youghal, 3; Cork and Ross, 2 each; Dublin, Drogheda and Waterford, one each. Compare with the total of 52 sought in England at the same time. 15 *CCR 1296–1302*, p. 576. 16 *CDI 1293–1301*, no. 787. Later the number was increased to seventeen (*CPR 1292–1301*, p. 584). 17 *CPR 1292–1301*, p. 583. The agents were ordered to 'make a fixed subvention in the king's name for those so coming'. 18 *Parl. writs*, i, 329–30, nos. 13–14.

to assist this all-out effort by raising levies locally. Eventually, a rather complicated arrangement was proposed to the magnates by the king's agents: in return for the service of one hundred days, the king offered to pardon two-thirds of all debts owing at the exchequer, the remaining third to be allowed as wages, compensation for horses lost on campaign, or other expenses incurred; in addition, he agreed to provide transport to and from Scotland at his own expense; and finally, if the remaining one-third of debts did not suffice to cover expenses, the king guaranteed 'reasonable wages' in addition to make good the deficit.[19] It was on this basis that contracts for service in Scotland were negotiated by Wogan and the other royal agents, among whom was Geoffrey de Genville, one of the leading magnates of the day.

Despite the king's message to de Burgh that he relied on him 'more than other men in the land for many reasons', the earl proved difficult. Whatever the reason, he would not come to terms, even after the other magnates had accepted the generous terms offered. The king, naturally enough, was afraid lest the others might follow the example of the earl, at that time the most powerful and influential man in Ireland, and thought that he 'should without bargain or covenant more quickly and willingly than any others in that country come to the king's service'.[20] It is unfortunate that we do not have the full story, but we can guess the rest. A few years earlier, as we have seen, Edward withdrew at the last minute from agreements made with the Irish for service in Flanders. But Fitz Thomas, the earl's greatest enemy, had somehow managed to procure these terms for himself, and it is not unreasonable to suppose that the memory of this still rankled with the earl. There is no doubt, too, that, as in the past, de Burgh was trying to drive a hard bargain with Edward, making the most of the king's difficulties and need. Two years later, he adopted the same policy, only this time with a greater measure of success. Nor did Edward make any secret of his anxiety to have de Burgh with him in Scotland:

> Let the earl understand that the king, who has always been regardful of him and his estate, will be ready from the time the earl comes to his service to grant him such pardon, such allowance and such grace as ought to induce him to hold himself well paid. Wherefore it is not meet that the earl should separate himself from the king in this or any other matter. It seems to the king that the earl ought to give good example to others to come to the king's service, and not to make demands and so bear himself that others may take example to withdraw from that service.

More than that, the king feared de Burgh in Ireland – in his instructions to his agents, he made it quite clear that in the event of de Burgh's refusal to come to

19 *CDI 1293–1301*, no. 849 (instructions from the king to his agents); *CPR 1292–1301*, p. 595.
20 For this and what follows, see *CDI 1293–1301*, no. 849.

Scotland the justiciar was to remain in Ireland also. But not until the last did Edward lose hope: ships were held in expectation of de Burgh's arrival until the day the fleet sailed.[21]

It was Edward's intention that the Irish should travel by way of Arran island and arrive there by 8 July 1301, ready to join the prince of Wales at Ayr.[22] They were thus to form part of the picked body of troops with which the young Edward of Carnarvon was to win his spurs in battle.[23] Moreover, the king hoped that by means of this campaign in Ayrshire and Galloway he would catch the Scots in the rear, while he himself led the main army from Berwick. So, on 21 May – the day the temporary truce with Scotland expired – Wogan was ordered to get the Irish troops under way as soon as possible.[24] It was over five weeks later, however, before the Irish figured on the king's payroll.[25] Meanwhile, the royal purveyors at Dublin, Cork, Waterford, Youghal and Drogheda were busy arranging transportation for the expedition. In each of these ports, ships were inspected by the royal purveyors. Those which were seaworthy were sent on to Dublin, where they were fitted out to carry troops and horses and, where necessary, repaired.[26] Then they were assigned to the leaders of the different contingents.[27] It is not now possible to list all the ships which were impressed in this way – but the number certainly exceeded fifty and entailed an expenditure of more than £860, one of the costliest items on the expense account.

John de Hothum was appointed paymaster by the Irish council and, as one of his duties, he compiled an inventory of all the horses which the knights, squires and hobelars were to bring with them to Scotland. Each horse was inspected and valued; it was on the basis of this valuation that compensation was later paid for any horse lost during the campaign.[28] Muster rolls of the various contingents and inventories of arms were probably compiled at the same time. But, in addition to all this and to looking after transportation, the paymaster was also responsible for what were called the 'minuta pro passagio' – the provision of supplies for the journey, parchment for his accounts, barrels to

21 BL, Add. MS 7966A (wardrobe book, 29 Edw. I), fo. 103. 22 *CDI 1293–1301*, no. 849. 23 Hilda Johnstone, *Edward of Carnarvon, 1284–1307* (Manchester, 1946), pp 72–3. 24 *CCR 1296–1302*, p. 492. 25 BL, Add. MS 7966A, fos. 102–3*v*. This wardrobe book contains an account of payments to the Irish from 1 July. The final account of John de Hothum, paymaster to the troops, is in E 101/10/1; E 101/10/2 is a view of his account taken in the king's wardrobe at Roxburgh in Feb. 1302; E 101/9/19 lists those who served for pardon of debts; E 101/6/5 contains a summary account of the leaders and their contingents. Unless otherwise indicated, the information presented in this paper is derived from these sources. 26 Part of the expenditure on repairs to twenty-four ships consisted of £9 0*s.* 1½*d.* for 957 large planks, 13*s.* 10*d.* for 943 small planks, £1 8*s.* 2¾ *d.* for 1,556 large nails, and £1 3*s.* 6¼ *d.* for 1,743 small nails. 27 See table 6, 'Allocation of shipping'. 28 For exaple £46 6*s.* 8*d.* to John Wogan, 'pro restauro 6 equorum ad arma appreciatorum in Hibernia' by de Hothum. Roger de Lees bought his horses in Scotland, some on 9 Sept. and the rest on 15 Sept., on which days they were valued by de Hothum.

carry money with which to pay the troops, carriage of the money to Scotland and baggage animals to carry it from place to place while on campaign.[29]

When all the necessary preparations were completed, the Irish sailed for Scotland. The paymaster's accounts give no indication of the date of their departure from Ireland, though they do tell us that they were in the king's pay from 1 July. The annals of Ulster say they were in Scotland from 15 July:[30] they certainly were not there any earlier, for as late as 8 July two of the justiciar's clerks were sent to Drogheda to procure additional ships for the troops waiting at Dublin. At any rate, the justiciar carried out the instructions he had received from the king and landed first on the island of Arran. Before proceeding any further, he sent some ships from the Cinque Ports ahead to Ayr to ascertain if the prince of Wales had yet arrived and shortly afterwards he and the remainder of the Irish joined the prince there. They remained with him during the months of August and September while he was active in Galloway and Ayrshire,[31] until on 8 October the Irish army split into two groups. By then, they had been in the king's service for one hundred days, the period of time stipulated by their contracts for qualification for pardon of debts at the Dublin exchequer. This was sufficient service for most of them and so, on 9 October, they left Carlisle for home. They travelled by way of Skinburness, the port which served Carlisle, where they were delayed for over two weeks waiting for ships. During their sojourn in the port, they attacked the storehouses of the king, forced their way in and made off with a considerable quantity of provisions.[32] On the face of it, such undisciplined behaviour is a discredit to the Irish; but they were not without excuse on this occasion, for we know from the accounts of the receiver of the king's stores in Carlisle that he issued no food to the Irish during that fortnight. Faced with starvation, as they were, it is difficult to condemn them for procuring food as best they could.

Altogether, 120 *homines ad arma*, 178 hobelars and nearly 1,200 foot left for Ireland on 9 October, leaving behind a much-depleted force to hasten to the king at Linlithgow. Although the official accounts say that these came to Edward 'ad mandatum ejus', they were not expected by the king's paymaster. At any rate, no allowance was made for them on a wage-schedule which was compiled the day before the Irish left Carlisle, that is on 8 October.[33] They spent the winter with the king and were with him at Roxburgh the following February before he returned to England.[34] It was only then that the remnants of the Irish army made their way home to Ireland.

29 For example, two barrels for part of the money de Hothum brought with him cost 1*s.* 6*d.* and an additional 8*d.* for new hoops; £2 12*s.* 8*d.* was expended at Ayr on five asses to carry the money in Scotland. 30 *AU*, ii, 397. The annals of Loch Cé say the Irish were in Scotland from 18 July until 1 Nov. (*ALC*, i, 525). 31 For the prince's activities, see Johnstone, *Edward of Carnarvon*, pp 77–9; E. McL. Barron, *The Scottish war of independence: a critical study* (2nd ed., Inverness, 1934), p. 144. 32 BL, Add. MS 7966A, fo. 67. 33 *CDS 1272–1307*, no. 1241. 34 *Calendar of chancery warrants, 1244–1326* (London, 1927), p. 159.

When at its fullest strength, that is up to 9 October 1301, the army numbered nearly 2,000 in all.[35] Most of these served for remission of debts: the rates allowed were 3*s.* per day for each squire, 1*s.* 6*d.* for each hobelar and 6*d.* for each foot soldier – rates which were three times the normal wages paid in these wars. Some of the squires were knighted during September in Galloway, a practice which was becoming more and more common during this period.[36] Their knighthood under the circumstances is a tribute to their valour and efficiency in battle.

In addition to this main force, a smaller one set out for Scotland under Eustace le Poer and Thomas le Mandeville, obviously at the instigation of the earl of Ulster, with whom both were intimately connected. Certainly de Burgh sent with them 42 *homines ad arma* at his own cost, which formed part of the force under the two northern bannerets and brought its numbers to 2 bannerets, 4 knights, 39 squires, 86 hobelars and 128 foot.[37] Like the other Irish contingent, they were in the king's pay from 1 July. But no information can be found as to when they left Ireland, how their transport was provided, what route they followed, or whether they fought under the prince of Wales or not. Doubtless they were intended, like the rest of the Irish, to form part of the prince's army; but it is unlikely that they actually fought with him, for they certainly participated in the siege of Turnberry castle during late August and early September, at a time when the prince was campaigning elsewhere in the south-west. It is probable that they remained in the vicinity of the castle, where a continuous struggle between Scots and English was in progress on the outcome of which the safety of the port of Ayr depended,[38] until they left, on 7 October, to join the king at Bothwell. Both were expected and were included in the wage-schedule to which we referred earlier, le Poer receiving 300 marks for his services until Easter 1302.[39]

Taking both of these troops together, we find that during this war 2,234 Irishmen served in Scotland, a fall of nearly 1,000 on the figure for 1296.[40] But it is of some importance that the number of hobelars who served shows an increase of 131, a further indication of the more important role they were henceforth to play in these wars.

If the numbers fell – and that must be attributed to the absence of de Burgh – expenses remained high. Despite the fact that most of the army served for pardon of debts in lieu of wages, the cost of the expedition came to more than £3,600. In addition, a schedule of wages owing to Irish troops, compiled in the king's wardrobe after the campaign had been concluded, shows that more than £3,200 was due to them for the cost of their passage home, compensation for lost horses and the residue of their wages.[41] Because money was not available,

35 See table 5, 'Irish in Scotland, 1301' (exclude contingents under le Poer and de Mandeville). 36 On 25 Sept., for example, four of the squires with Wogan were knighted. 37 See table 5, 'Irish in Scotland, 1301'. 38 *CDS 1272–1307*, no. 1236. 39 Ibid., p. 317. 40 For the 1296 figure, see above, table 3, 'Leaders and their contingents, 1296'. 41 C 47/3/52,

de Hothum was unable to pay these arrears of wages and the debt still stood in the books after the return to Ireland. The king had already instructed Wogan in Roxburgh that he was to use the proceeds of the ecclesiastical tenth then current, as well as the ordinary issues of the exchequer, to pay off the debt. When these proved insufficient for the purpose, the justiciar, again on the instructions of the king, seized the money of foreign merchants in Ireland, notably that of the Spini of Florence – but even this drastic measure yielded only £585.[42] Most of the arrears of wages, therefore, remained unpaid and were to be a baulk to the king's plans in the future.

One part of the bargain which the king made with those who served in Scotland was adequately fulfilled. Debts were pardoned in great numbers at the Irish exchequer, a fact to which the pipe rolls alone bear ample testimony.[43] But the fact that part of their wages remained unpaid rankled with the Irish,[44] and when the king sought their aid once more in 1303 for yet another campaign in Scotland, he was to find them hard and unyielding, demanding extravagant and almost impossible terms as a condition of service. The earl of Ulster's caution in dealing with Edward I in 1301, his refusal to serve unless the king was prepared to meet his hard terms as a guarantee that he would be adequately recompensed, was proved in the long run to be more than justified. Little wonder, then, that the other Irish magnates followed his example in their future dealings with the English king.

mm 12–13. See also E 101/10/2 for a view of this section of de Hothum's accounts, taken in the wardrobe at Roxburgh, 17 Feb. 1302. 42 *CJRI 1305–7*, p. 164; *CDI 1293–1301*, no. 812. 43 *38th rep. DKPRI*, pp 60–1, 65, 70, 75 etc. 44 The Irish were not the only ones to have this grievance. In Berwick in 1302, the garrison mutinied because of long-standing arrears of pay (*CDS 1272–1307*, no. 1223).

TABLE 4
IRISH IN SCOTLAND, 1300[1]

| *Date* | *Place* | *Foot Archers* | *Hobelars* | *Constables* |
|---|---|---|---|---|
| 1 July | Carlisle | 300 | 12 | 3 |
| 5 July | Carlisle | 300 | 12 | 4 |
| 10 July | Carlaverock | 361 | 12 | 4 |
| 16 July | Kircudbright | 350 | 14 | 4 |
| 23 July | Kircudbright | 350 | 14 | 4 |
| 28 July | Twynham (?Twynholm) | 344 | 14 | 4 |
| 6–25 Aug. | Carlaverock | 306 | 13 | 4 |

TABLE 5
IRISH IN SCOTLAND, 1301[2]

| *Name* | *Bannerets* | *Knights* | *Squires* | *Hobelars* | *Foot* |
|---|---|---|---|---|---|
| John Wogan (banneret) | 4 | 6[3] | 105[3] | 146 | 748[4] |
| John Fitz Thomas (banneret) | 1 | 2 | 49 | 61 | 360 |
| Peter de Bermingham (banneret) | 1 | 1 | 19 | 44 | 140 |
| Roger de Lees (knight) | – | 1 | 5 | 1 | – |
| Reginald Russel (squire) | – | – | 10 | 24 | 40 |
| Philip Christofre (squire) | – | – | 4[5] | 4 | 22 |
| John de Hothum (squire) | – | – | 4 | 3 | 20 |
| John Belinger (squire) | – | – | 7 | 22 | 159 |
| TOTAL | **6** | **10** | **203** | **305** | **1,489** |
| Eustace le Poer (banneret) | 1 | 3 | 19 | 30 | 56 |
| Thomas de Mandeville (banneret) | 1 | 1 | 20 | 56 | 72 |
| TOTAL | **2** | **4** | **39** | **86** | **128** |
| TOTAL OF THE TWO SECTIONS | **8** | **14** | **242** | **391** | **1,617** |

1 E 101/8/20, 'Solucio facta peditibus'; *Liber quotidianus contrarotulatoris garderobae, 28 Edward I, 1299–1300*, ed. J. Topham et al. (London, 1787), pp 242, 245, 248–9, 251, 253, 255. 2 E 101/10/1 and BL, Add. MS 7966A, fos. 92*v*–95, 100–2. These figures represent the contingents at their greatest strength, to 8 October. I have included the leaders in the totals opposite their names. 3 On 25 Sept., four of the squires were knighted, giving 10 knights and 101 squires in Wogan's troop from that date. 4 This includes six crossbowmen, the only ones in the force. The rest of the foot were archers, led in groups of twenty by *vintenarii*. 5 Christofre was knighted on 25 Sept.

TABLE 6

ALLOCATION OF SHIPPING[1]

| For | Name of Ship | Master | Tunnage | Rate[2] | Where impressed | Total Cost £ | s. | d |
|---|---|---|---|---|---|---|---|---|
| John Fitz Thomas | *Sancte Crucis* of Youghal | Richard Fitz Simon | 140 | 7/– | Youghal | 46 | 11 | 0 |
| " | *La Michele* of Cork | Robert atte Waters | 40 | 7/– | Cork | 13 | 0 | 6 |
| " | *La Goudyer* of Tynemouth | Adam Elyne | 40 | 7/– | Cork | 13 | 0 | 6 |
| " | *La Magdaleyne* of Tenby | David Fitz Geoffrey | 46 | 7/– | Cork | 15 | 18 | 0 |
| " | *La Blithe* of Tynemouth | Walter Goodwin | 64 | 7/– | Cork | 21 | 7 | 0 |
| " | *La Goudyere* of Exmouth | Halewyn Philipp | 29 | 7/– | Cork | 9 | 16 | 0 |
| " | *La Garlaunde* of Youghal | Walter Taillefere | 40 | 7/– | Cork | 13 | 6 | 0 |
| " | *La Goudyere* of Lyme | John Patrick | 45 | 7/– | Waterford | 15 | 12 | 0 |
| " | *La Goudyere* of Dublin | William de Somereye | 33 | 7/– | Waterford | 11 | 6 | 0 |
| " | *La Messager* of Bristol | Henry Hull | 21 | 7/– | Waterford | 7 | 7 | 0 |
| " | *La Mariote* of Carlingford | Robert Drok | 36 | 4/– | Dublin | 6 | 18 | 0 |
| " | *La Nicholas* of Ross | William of Dungarvan | 20 | 4/– | Dublin | 3 | 16 | 0 |
| " | *St Thomas* of Cork | William Elyne | 40 | 7/– | Cork | 13 | 6 | 0 |
| The men of Maurice de Rocheforde | *La Margarete* of Shoreham | Elias Spark | 195 | 7/– | Waterford | 64 | 18 | 6 |
| " | *La Leonarde* of Bridgewater | Stephen Crouchere | 40 | 7/– | Waterford | 13 | 6 | 0 |
| " | *Sancte Crucis* of Youghal | Adam David | 60 | 7/– | Youghal | 19 | 19 | 0 |
| " | *La Maricost* of Waterford | Walter Scalpyn | 92 | 7/– | Waterford | 30 | 12 | 6 |
| " | *La Goudyere* of Tynemouth | Richard Dollyng | 28 | 7/– | Waterford | 9 | 9 | 0 |
| " | *La Vile Pentoun* | Adam Ney | 45 | 7/– | Youghal | 15 | 12 | 0 |
| John Wogan | *La Grace Dieu* of Cork | Nicholas Veel | 141 | 7/– | Cork | 46 | 11 | 0 |
| " | *La Rose* of Colchester | Henry Fynch | 140 | 7/– | Waterford | 46 | 11 | 0 |
| " | *La Katerine* of Dublin | Henry of Tynemouth | 110 | 4/– | Dublin | 20 | 18 | 0 |
| " | *La Goudhale* of Youghal | Thomas Porpeys | 60 | 7/– | Youghal | 19 | 19 | 0 |
| " | *La Cogge* of Dartmouth | Edward of Dartmouth | 30 | 4/– | Dublin | 5 | 14 | 0 |
| " | *La Mariote* of Dublin | Elias le Rede | 70 | 4/– | Dublin | 13 | 6 | 0 |
| " | *La Trinite* of Tynemouth | Walter Eustace | 30 | 4/– | Dublin | 5 | 14 | 0 |
| " | *La Hilary* of Drogheda[3] | ? | – | – | – | 6 | 14 | 0 |
| " | *St Stephen* of Dartmouth[4] | Nicholas Gaylord | – | – | – | | 115 | 0 |

| | | | | | | | | |
|---|---|---|---|---|---|---|---|---|
| The men of John de Bonevile | *La Mari Cogge* of Youghal | William Hill | 40 | 7 / – | Youghal | 13 | 6 | 0 |
| | *La Mariote* of Youghal | David Griffin | 90 | 7 / – | Youghal | 29 | 18 | 6 |
| John de Hothum | *La Mariote* of Conway | Thomas of Ireland | 29 | 4 / – | Dublin | 6 | 10 | 0 |
| The men of Philip le Bret | *La Solke* of Dublin | Edmund le Webbe | 31 | 4 / – | Dublin | 5 | 18 | 0 |
| Philip Christofre & Reginald Russell | *La Marie* of Youghal | William Christofre | 112 | 7 / – | Youghal | 37 | 5 | 6 |
| | *St Marie* of Youghal | John Godard | 25 | 7 / – | Youghal | 8 | 8 | 0 |
| The men of Thomas St John | *La Nicholas* of Dublin | Philip le Carpenter | 32 | 4 / – | Dublin | 6 | 2 | 0 |
| John Belinger | *Seinte Crouce* of Haverford | John Thomas | 30 | 4 / – | Dublin | 5 | 14 | 0 |
| " | *St Benedict* of Dublin | Philip of Drogheda | 50 | 4 / – | Dublin | 9 | 10 | 0 |
| Peter Bermingham | *La Simenale* of Gosforth | Robert Ypre | 120 | 4 / – | Drogheda | 22 | 16 | 0 |
| " | *La Goudyere* of Tynemouth | Richard of Cornwall | 112 | 4 / – | Drogheda | 21 | 6 | 0 |
| " | *La Michele* of Tynemouth | Robert Lamb | 55 | 4 / – | Drogheda | 10 | 10 | 0 |
| " | *La Sowe* of Drogheda | Robert le Connefer | 30 | 4 / – | Drogheda | 6 | 13 | 4 |
| " | ?5 | Philip atte Stieghal | – | – | – | 3 | 3 | 0 |
| The men of David de Cauntone | *La Welifare* of Dartmouth | William Cotman | 100 | 4 / 6 | Drogheda | 19 | 0 | 0 |
| | *La Sancte Dieu* of Ross | Robert le Waleys | 70 | 7 / – | Cork | 23 | 5 | 6 |
| The men of John de Fresyngfeld | *La Gaynyste* of Limerick | Walter de Mareis | 100 | 4 / – | Drogheda | 19 | 0 | 0 |
| | The ship of Gerald fitz John of Drogheda | Selyman Knyst | 40 | 4 / – | Drogheda | 7 | 12 | 0 |
| The men of John de Balewyn | ? | Gervase Jugelberge of Drogheda | 50 | 4 / – | Drogheda | 9 | 10 | 0 |
| " | *La Mariote* of Milcombe (?) | Nicholas de Veel | 50 | 4 / – | Drogheda | 9 | 10 | 0 |

1 The table is based on the accounts in E 101/10/1 and BL, Add. MS 7966A, fos. 102–3. 2 The rate was per tun, each twenty-one counting as twenty. 3 For the carriage of 30 tuns of red wine and 17 cranocks of salt of the justiciar from Drogheda to Ayr. The sum listed represents par payment only of the cost. 4 For the carriage of 5 tuns of victuals likewise to Ayr. 5 This ship was freighted to carry the victuals of de Birmingham from Dalkey to Ayr. There were six other ships impressed for the earl of Ulster, at a cost of £36; as they were not used they are not named in the accounts. Other vessels, in addition to those listed, were subsequently used for the expedition but particulars relating to them have not survived. Nor are the ships used by le Poer and de Mandeville listed in any of the accounts which have survived.

CHAPTER 12

# Edward I, Ireland and the war in Scotland, 1303–1304*

*James Lydon*

When Edward I launched what he hoped would be his final onslaught on Scotland in the summer of 1303, he was confident of achieving what he himself called the 'final and happy expedition of the war in Scotland'. For the first time since 1298, he and his army penetrated northwards as far as Kinloss on the Moray. He spent the winter in the field and, after the surrender of Stirling castle in July 1304, it seemed that Scottish independence had at last been crushed. Edward could now proceed with what he conceived as the final settlement of the Scottish problem.[1]

This expedition is also recorded in Anglo-Irish and Gaelic literary sources, preserving a memory of an important event. But more significant is the emphasis, in both traditions, on the involvement of the earl of Ulster with a great army.[2] From the Irish perspective, the success of King Edward was the result, at least in part, of the help which he received from Richard de Burgh and the men he led to Scotland. It is true that the earl was at the centre of Ireland's involvement in this war. But a study of the events soon reveals that the lordship was much more heavily committed to the war effort and that it was John Wogan, the Irish justiciar, who controlled the organization which provided the substance of Ireland's contribution.

Even as early as the winter of 1301–2, Wogan was with the king planning Ireland's contribution to this grand design of a final conquest of Scotland. After leading an army to the campaign of 1301, he and a group of important Irish magnates joined the king at his winter quarters in Roxburgh to discuss the terms of magnate involvement.[3] There was obviously a deal of hard bargaining. On 17 February 1302, the king sent the keeper of his wardrobe, John Droxford, south from Roxburgh with a clutch of petitions of 'some of the people of Ireland who have served the king in the war in Scotland' and asked the

* First published in James Lydon (ed.), *England and Ireland in the later Middle Ages: essays in honour of Jocelyn Otway-Ruthven* (Irish Academic Press: Dublin, 1981), pp 43–61. 1 For the war, see G.W.S. Barrow, *Robert Bruce and the community of the realm of Scotland* (2nd ed., Edinburgh, 1976), pp 176–85; Ranald Nicholson, *Scotland: the later Middle Ages* (Edinburgh, 1974), pp 64–8; Michael Prestwich, *War, politics, and finance under Edward I* (London, 1972). 2 *AC*, p. 205; *CStM*, ii, 331. 3 Lydon, 'Irish levies in the Scottish wars, 1296–1302' (above, ch. 11).

chancellor to take appropriate action.[4] The result was a flood of favours to Irishmen who had been in Scotland, which are hardly unrelated to the discussions then in progress at Roxburgh.[5] These resulted in an agreement that an Irish army would be provided for the 1303 campaign. We know little of the terms of service, except that Eustace le Poer and Thomas de Mandeville promised on behalf of the earl of Ulster that he would lead fifty men-at-arms at his own cost.[6] We have no way of knowing why the earl should agree to this; but subsequent negotiations in Ireland revealed that pardon of debts was one of the inducements to service offered by the king, and the earl certainly had much to gain from such a pardon.[7]

By 23 February 1302, the day on which a series of important letters was dispatched to Ireland, the terms of Ireland's involvement must have been agreed in broad outline at least. Although no numbers appear to have been specified at the Roxburgh discussions, a privy seal warrant of 23 February makes it clear that Edward was hoping for a force of 500 men-at-arms, 1000 hobelars and at least 10,000 foot.[8] But whatever size the army might eventually reach (and the king's expectations were far too optimistic to be realistic, at least where the foot were concerned), it was obvious that the most urgent necessity in Dublin was a supply of ready cash to meet the cost of mounting the expedition and of contributing to the successful outcome of the campaign in other ways. The payment of wages, the cost of transportation to and from Scotland, and compensation for lost horses would all eat up the money available at the exchequer. On top of that, the expected demand for wine and food would be an extra financial burden. If the army were to be retained over the long winter months in Scotland, then even larger amounts of money would be needed to meet a rapidly mounting bill. One of the letters sent to Wogan, with instructions which he had already received 'more fully by word of mouth', required him to supervise an inspection of exchequer records and produce an estimate of the 'whole receipt' for the following Easter and Michaelmas terms, so that it might be calculated how much money would be available for the expedition to Scotland by March 1303.[9] An issue roll entry preserves a record that the exchequer was kept open 'for examination of the clear debts of the king, in order that money might be speedily raised for his use for the war of Scotland'.[10]

On the same day, 23 February 1302, an old friend of the king, Geoffrey de Geneville, lord of Meath, was empowered with Wogan to negotiate with the earl

4 *Calendar of chancery warrants, 1244–1326* (London, 1927), p. 159. 5 *CDI 1302–7*, nos. 6–25, 28–30, 33–8, 43, 45, 48, 50–1. Such favours were necessary since arrears of wages had mounted up. One wardrobe schedule of wages owing to Irish magnates came to more than £3,000 (C 47/3/52/12). Another one, presumably later in date, shows over £2,400 still owing (C 47/3/52/11; E 101/10/2; *CDI 1302–7*, nos. 22–3). 6 *CDI 1302–7*, no. 151. 7 See below, p. 203. 8 *CDS 1272–1307*, no. 1295. 9 *CCR 1296–1302*, pp 518, 576. 10 *CDI 1302–7*, no. 3 (quotation at p. 3).

of Ulster and the other magnates of Ireland, 'conjointly and severally', for service in Scotland. The involvement of de Geneville, a man of vast experience, is a clear indication that the haggling over details of service would be delicate and difficult. The king also promised to confirm the terms agreed. Wogan was to inspect the available shipping, estimate the number of men and horses it could carry and certify the king by the following 12 September. Finally, letters close were sent to the earl of Ulster, John fitz Thomas and 183 others, informing them of the planned campaign and urging them to listen well to what de Geneville and Wogan had to tell them.[11] It is a measure of the king's anxiety that this huge list of people (actually greatly exceeding the number of English recipients of writs of military summons in November) should include the leading Irishmen of the day: O Neill, O Brien, O Connor and MacCarthy. The letter to the earl of Ulster is particularly important. He had refused to participate in the expedition of 1301; but now that he was the father-in-law of Robert Bruce, the king was especially anxious to have him on this final assault on the Scots. As we shall see, he was offered command of the army (a high distinction since the justiciar was normally in command) and, when the king eventually sent special agents to do the actual recruiting in Ireland, they were ordered to do so 'by counsel of the earl of Ulster'.[12]

After these letters were dispatched, there was a long silence until new letters were sent on 5 August 1302. This time, the number of recipients were drastically reduced: only the earl and eighty-two other 'fideles' of Ireland were addressed.[13] It must have been apparent to the Dublin government, and thus to the king in England, that to withdraw all the leading men from Ireland would be to court disaster. It is significant that when Edmund Butler arrived in Dublin to join the army, just before the fleet was due to sail, he was left behind for security reasons.[14] Some of the magnates, like John fitz Thomas, were well aware of the dangers implicit in the withdrawal of too many armed men and tried to ensure some measure of defence in their lands during their absence in Scotland.

It was not until 7 November that the king took the next step in the negotiations with a further series of letters to the magnates.[15] For the first time, two key figures were mentioned – William de Pederton and Nicholas de Bois – both of whom were now associated with Wogan in the negotiations. It is significant too that when, on 10 November, they were formally empowered to act on behalf of the king in Ireland, they were additionally instructed to treat with the 'communitas' of Ireland about aiding those who were willing to go to Scotland.[16] Money was going to be short and it was perhaps for that reason that Edward had now reduced his expectations from Ireland to 300 men-at-arms, 400 hobelars and 2000 foot.[17] Pederton and du Bois were given precise instructions about

11 *Foedera*, ii, pt 1, p. 938; *Parl. writs*, p. 363. 12 *CDI 1302–7*, no. 151 (quotation at p. 60). 13 *Parl. writs*, p. 365. 14 *CCR 1302–7*, p. 122. 15 *Parl. writs*, p. 367. 16 Ibid., p. 368. 17 *CDI 1302–7*, no. 151. Unless otherwise noted, what follows is based on this important text.

consulting with the magnates, pardoning debts and providing shipping. The earl of Ulster was to find nearly half the entire force. But if he were unwilling to leave Ireland, then Wogan, too, must remain behind and the king would pay all the men from Ireland who were willing to join him. Why the presence in Ireland of de Burgh in the absence of Wogan should make the king nervous is not at all clear. But it is one more indication of the tensions which existed and which were to make the negotiations for service in Scotland protracted and difficult. Finally, it was planned that the Irish army should serve in the west of Scotland with the prince of Wales.

The two royal messengers received letters of protection on 16 November 1302. But they do not seem to have left for Ireland until around 13 December, the worst time for crossing the Irish sea and for travelling in Ireland.[18] One reason for the delay was because the king had taken the opportunity of entrusting them with completing the important transfer of Ralph Pipard's Irish lands into royal hands and this complicated business must have occupied a fair deal of time.[19] We know that they had a meeting with the earl of Ulster at Drogheda sometime during Lent and that they were back in England with the king by Easter.[20] But, if we cannot follow their progress through Ireland, we at least have the substance of how the actual negotiations proceeded.[21] De Burgh said that he was willing to provide fifty men-at-arms at his own cost, as agreed at Roxburgh; but he would require guaranteed pay for a further fifty men-at-arms, 100 hobelars and 600 foot. He also demanded passage for all to and from Scotland. But his major condition was that all his debts 'which run in demand against him and his ancestors' must be pardoned under the seal of England. Inquiry at the exchequer revealed that apart from the account of Ulster and Connacht which was in arrears since 1285, the earl's debts came to a staggering £11,654 5*s*. 6¾*d*. No wonder that when it came to the point of decision, Wogan, the treasurer and the two royal messengers 'would not dare to make so dear a bargain without knowing the king's mind'. Finally, the earl said that if his terms were accepted he would serve for 100 days and no more, beginning on 1 July.

The other magnates made similar bargains. Peter Bermingham, for example, looked for payment of 200 marks, cancellation of a debt of £460, passage to and from Scotland for 20 men-at-arms, 20 hobelars and 100 foot for 100 days; Walter de Lacy and Reginald Russel both asked for release of debts to treble the rates of pay; John fitz Thomas asked for £250, cancellation of a debt of £450 and, most interesting of all, £150 'out of the service of Ireland', for all of which he would bring 40 men-at-arms, 40 hobelars and 200 foot. The demand of fitz Thomas for part of a royal service is especially interesting since it reveals the concern which he had for the safety of his lands while he was away. When he

**18** E 101/8/4/3. **19** *CDI 1302–7*, nos. 149–50. On 31 Jan., Pederton delivered relevant charters and letters to the treasurer and chamberlains of the Dublin exchequer (E 101/619/52). **20** *CDI 1302–7*, pp 58, 60. **21** Ibid., no. 151.

went to serve the king in Flanders in 1298, he had received £40 to fortify his castle of Lea as one of the terms agreed by the justiciar.[22] On that occasion, his apprehension was justified: while he was abroad the Irish burned his manor of Rathangan and devastated the surrounding countryside. On his return, fitz Thomas sought and obtained a royal service 'in aid of building a new fortalice against the Irish of those parts'.[23] The service was duly proclaimed at Dundalk on 15 August 1299, to be rendered in money. But because fitz Thomas was unable to commence work on the castle, payment to him was postponed.[24] This was the same service which he was now again demanding and it is important to remember that it represents a payment which was primarily intended for the defence of a land of peace against the Irish of Offaly. It is a reminder that magnates such as fitz Thomas were facing the military and social problems occasioned by Irish aggression at this very time. To be diverted to a war in Scotland was the last thing most of them wanted and it was probably this which made them demand impossible terms of service during the discussions with the royal messengers.

In the end, much of the discussion seems to have been fruitless, for it seems that of the leading magnates consulted, neither fitz Thomas, Bermingham nor Butler went to Scotland with the earl of Ulster. Neither did Wogan go. All of this requires some explanation. But none is readily forthcoming. Both Bermingham and Butler were connected with fitz Thomas: the first had entered his service years before and was also bound by mutual interest in the marches of Kildare; the second had married a daughter of fitz Thomas in 1302.[25] That Wogan remained in Ireland suggests strongly that they presented some kind of threat to the peace, though there is nothing in the sources to suggest what this might have been. Perhaps the volatile fitz Thomas was embroiled in the kind of dangerous involvement with Irish enemies which had caused such problems for the government in the late 1290s. Or it may simply be that the death of his son and heir in 1303 was sufficient to keep him at home.[26]

There is no sign that anything was amiss in the record of the negotiations with the magnates. But this record is in no way complete. It does not, for example, include all the terms that were finally agreed. Compensation for lost horses was a valuable concession which must have been made since other records contain the evidence of payments on this score – two of Eustace le Poer's men, for example, were compensated for horses lost on 5 February 1304[27] – but this is not included in the record of the negotiations. The main purpose of that record was to report generally on the course of the discussions and on the preparations

22 *CDI 1293–1301*, no. 438. 23 *CJRI 1295–1303*, p. 230. 24 Ibid., p. 362–3. 25 *Red bk Kildare*, no. 11; *CStM*, ii, 331. 26 *CStM*, ii, 331. The continuing arrears of wages owing to leaders of retinues in the 1301 campaign must have been a severe problem for the royal agents, even though a great effort had been made in the summer of 1302 to clear the debts with the payment of sums totalling £2,337 (*Rep. RCI, 1811–15*, pp 172–3). 27 E 101/13/36.

which were being made in Ireland. With regard to the ships that would be required to carry the troops, horses and supplies to Scotland, it reported that what was available in Ireland would not even amount to one-fourth of what was needed. This, of course, meant that ships would have to be found outside Ireland and the fleet of the Cinque Ports was called on to help bring up the numbers. In Ireland itself, agents scoured the coast looking for suitable vessels. Chief among those was the man who was to be clerk of the wages for the expedition, Alexander Bicknor, later to be prominent in the Irish administration and in the tempestuous politics of Edward II's England. Together with a knight, Maurice Russel, who was familiar with the Munster ports (he was sheriff of Waterford) he worked his way through the ports of Leinster and Munster during May, arresting suitable ships. Two others went even further afield into Connacht and Ulster, the first time the administration tried to find shipping for an expedition in these remoter parts of the lordship. This is a good indication of the great effort being made to collect the largest fleet which had ever been assembled in Ireland for the largest army raised in Ireland during these wars. We cannot now trace in the surviving records the manner in which the ships and sailors were pressed into service in the different ports.[28] But that local agents were employed, probably working under the direction of Bicknor is clear: two, for example, were appointed to arrest ships in Wexford and the seneschal of the liberty was ordered to give them whatever help was necessary to ensure that the vessels were in Dalkey by the following Trinity Sunday (2 June).[29] The appointment of Peter de Paris as the first ever Irish admiral (L. *Admirallus flote Hibernie*) is an indication that some kind of naval administration had emerged in Ireland to meet the demands peculiar to assembling a large fleet. This one reached the impressive total of 173 ships, of various sizes, by the time the expedition sailed for Scotland. The cost came to just short of £1000, yet another indication of the extra effort demanded from the hard-pressed Irish administration.

Only approximately thirty-seven of the ships finally assembled were Irish, an even smaller number than had been anticipated by the royal agents in the previous November. One reason for this was that too many of the vessels available were unsuitable, either because they were too small or in bad repair. Even many of those finally selected required repairing and all had to be fitted out to make them suitable for carrying troops and horses. The most important single job which this involved was the provision of hurdles, made of pliable rods woven together, which could be used for making stalls to hold the animals, or indeed to protect the sides of the frail boats from possible damage by the huge horses. The fortunate survival of a unique

28 E 101/10/30 is a wardrobe account of Bicknor's relating to the 'provision, arrest and preparation of ships for the passage of the earl of Ulster and other Irish coming to Scotland'. Further details are in E 101/11/2, which is Bicknor's main account as clerk of the wages. Only one particular account seems to have survived, that of John de Bovere and William de Cathenham of eighteen Irish ships from Dublin, Cork and Youghal (E 101/10/29). 29 *RCH*, p. 6, nos. 54–5.

account of the provision of rods (L. *virge*) for making hurdles (L. *claie*) in Dublin, for use on the ships carrying troops and horses, is a vivid reminder of what even a simple operation such as that meant in man hours and effort.[30] The financial cost was little enough, being just short of £7. But it involved work forces of thirty-three men, plus two overseers, cutting rods for six days in the wood at 'Balikey', and others at woods in Carrickbrennan, Clonkeen, Kinsaley and Balgriffin, all of which produced 420 separate loads which had to be taken to the priory of All Hallows in Dublin where the hurdles were being made. There were even men cutting rods as far away as Newcastle McKynegan, which produced two shiploads for the work at All Hallows. There a William Dunning of Santry was in charge of his own gang of eight men and worked for eighteen days; a gang of four others from Rathgar were employed for one day only, probably to hasten the completion of the work. One clerk supervised and kept records, and a watchman kept guard over the rods and hurdles until they were taken out of the priory. The finished hurdles were probably quite large: later ones measured around seven feet by four.[31] The account, unfortunately, does not say how many hurdles were made, or how they were brought to the ships. The number required for each ship would obviously depend on the number of horses being carried and that, on this expedition, varied between ten and thirty.[32] There seems to have been a standard freight rate of half a mark per animal, though one large contingent was shipped out of Carrickfergus on small boats (L. *navicule*) at exactly half the standard rate. While this may have been because of the shorter journey, it is likely, too, that the cargo consisted of hobbies – the much smaller horses used by the hobelars.

Arresting and outfitting ships was thus a complicated business which took weeks to complete. As a result, many vessels were tied up in port for an unreasonable period, unable to engage in legitimate trade. There must have been complaints about this, because a meeting of the Irish council, attended by the admiral of the fleet of the Cinque Ports,[33] agreed that masters and crews of foreign (that is, non-Irish) ships which had been arrested for a month or more before 9 June 1303 should be paid at inflated rates – twelvepence per day for each master and sixpence for each sailor. In the event, thirty-seven crews had to be paid the extra wages, which means that the remainder of the non-Irish ships were got ready with commendable speed.

30 E 101/11/3, which contains particulars of the £6 18*s.* 5½*d.* allowed in E 101/11/2 for 'virgis et claiis' provided at Dublin. This has been printed in translation, not always correctly and with some uninformed comments, by Patrick O'Connor, 'Hurdle making in Dublin, 1302–3', *Dublin Historical Record*, 13 (1952–4), 18–22. Another £17 13*s.* 8*d.* was spent on hurdles and boards for repairs at Dublin and £12 18*s.* 8¾*d.* at Drogheda, for which no particulars have survived.
31 H.J. Hewitt, *The organization of war under Edward III* (Manchester, 1966), p. 79.
32 Prestwich, *War, politics and finance*, p. 147. Of the eighteen ships listed in E 101/10/29, one could carry 10 horses, two 12, two 14, two 16, four 18, two 20 and the remainder 23, 24, 30, 31 and 32 horses each.
33 The admiral received £5 from Bicknor 'for his good help with the ships of the Cinque Ports and leading other ships' (E 101/10/30).

Dublin was the main port of embarkation, though it was in fact Dalkey which seems to have been mostly used because of the impossibility of berthing larger vessels at Dublin quay – merchants had long since become accustomed to discharging part of their cargoes at Dalkey so that the lighter load could find a passage across the Liffey sandbanks. Drogheda was also used and, as we have already seen, some horses were shipped out of Carrickfergus. But most of the magnates, including the earl of Ulster, sailed out of Dublin Bay. When exactly they set sail is not clear. The account of the clerk of the wages shows that the Irish were in pay from 17 June, so presumably they had mustered by then. We lose sight of them then until early August in Scotland. Most of the sailors were being paid from 9 June into July, and others from 9 to 23 July. It is possible, therefore, that there was considerable delay before the army set out for Scotland. It was not until 25 June that letters of protection were issued from the Irish chancery, and some are dated as late as 8 July.[34] More important, the clerk of the wages was receiving large sums of money in late June and early July, which suggests that the army was being paid before setting sail: £1000 on 28 June; £1000 and £300 on 1 July; and 210 marks on 1 July.[35] On balance, then, I favour 9 July as the date on which the Dublin fleet weighed anchor. Before then, the earl of Ulster, in what must have been a memorable service in Dublin castle, raised thirty-three of his men to knighthood.[36]

According to the rhyming chronicler Peter Langtoft, the earl of Ulster was with the king when it was decided to split the army in two after Scotland had been invaded; de Burgh, 'with some of the barons', was sent to the west 'to despoil the land'.[37] This is impossible since de Burgh cannot have left Dublin so early. But it does reflect a memory of Irish activity in the west of Scotland. We know that between 7 and 11 August the Irish army was ferried from the island of 'Batel' (possibly Bate) to Largs on the mainland. In the same month, they saw action at Inverkip castle, further to the north, where some horses were lost. Inverkip was in the lordship of James the Steward, who at that time was one of the Scottish envoys in Paris. More important for us, he was married to Egidia de Burgh, sister of the earl of Ulster, and it was therefore appropriate that his brother-in-law should have been given the task of taking Inverkip castle. Across the water, on Bute, lay another Steward castle, Rothesay. It, too, was invested and taken by the Irish and the earl placed a large garrison there (6 squires, 6 hobelars and 28 archers under the command of John Byset) from 4 August until the following 22 November, when the king ordered the castle to be handed over to the earl of Lincoln.

34 *RCH*, p. 5, nos. 21–2. 35 E 101/233/22, nos. 18–21; the corresponding writs of *liberate* (nos. 22–5) are endorsed to show that cash was paid. 36 *CStM*, ii, 331. Details of the composition of the army and its movements are in E 101/11/2, and in the wardrobe book BL, Add. MS 8835, fos. 48*v*–9, 56*v*. 37 Thomas Wright (ed.), *The chronicle of Peter Langtoft from the earliest period to the death of King Edward I*, 2 vols (RS, London, 1866–8),

The Irish remained at Inverkip until September, where the army was reviewed before setting off for Linlithgow from which the bulk of the Irish left for home on the twenty-eighth. On the same day, Alexander Bicknor wrote a letter which graphically describes how the Scots had openly collected 'all their power' so that the Irish were remaining in the vicinity of Linlithgow, 'where they can have nothing on which to live without ready money unless they rob the people who have come into the king's allegiance'. Lack of money meant lack of food. The Irish, according to Bicknor, 'see plainly that no one cares for them or their lives, and so they have packed up to depart for their own country'.[38] They had, in fact, brought some victuals with them from Ireland, but they cannot have lasted very long.[39] No wonder the fear was expressed that they might steal what they needed. The fear seems to have been well founded: there is evidence in an escheator's account for 1302–4 of 'tenants destroyed by the Irish' on one manor in Lanarkshire, as well as in the burgh of Glasgow.[40]

In theory, the king was under no obligation to supply food to these soldiers, the argument being that the wages they were paid should be sufficient to purchase what they required. In practice, of course, Edward had to ensure that adequate food was available for his army through the elaborate commissariat arrangements which were made in advance. It must have irked the Irish that none was provided for them, especially since they were not paid their wages, even though (as Bicknor reported) they had heard that money had arrived from Berwick. They left for home, then, as soon as they could after their hundred days' service was completed, seemingly disillusioned with the king and desperate enough to take what they needed by force. Those who remained were left short of wages and, at least for a time, had to be fed by the king. A royal letter from St Andrews in March 1304, written before the army moved out to begin the siege of Stirling, makes clear the king's anxiety to have adequate provisions for the Irish as well as the English who were with him.[41] But even then it does not seem that what was available was adequate, for in the same month the earl of Ulster was permitted to send servants southwards into England in search of food.[42]

For some, the problem was solved by the prince of Wales, with whom the Irish served after leaving Dunfermline in November 1303, probably on the twenty-fourth when the prince himself left.[43] On Christmas day, the earl of Ulster and other Irish magnates were among those who were lavishly

ii, 348–9. **38** E 101/11/36/25, pr. *Docs illus. Scot. hist.*, no. 626. **39** Bicknor was allowed £19 8*d*. for the cost of ships carrying the victuals of the earl of Ulster, and another £2 for those of Thomas de Mandeville and Nigel le Brun (E 101/10/30); the sheriff of Uriel was similarly allowed £5 14*s*. for another ship carrying victuals (*38th rep. DKPRI*, p. 72 [Ir. pipe roll, 31 Edw. I]). **40** *CDS 1272–1307*, no. 1608. **41** *Docs. illus. Scot. hist.*, ii, 476. **42** *CDS 1272–1307*, no. 1486. **43** The were still in Dunfermline on 18 Nov., but by 4 Dec., they were with the prince in Perth.

entertained by the prince, and they were present at other feasts on 1 January, 2 and 23 February, 1 March and 14 April.[44] But periodical high living for the selected few did nothing to alleviate the hardship occasioned by lack of wages. It is remarkable, too, that so many horses were lost by the Irish at Perth during the course of the winter: on 6 and 12 February, as many as seven and five were lost in a single day. It is likely that the losses were the result of action against Scottish marauders who were still active under John Comyn, though lack of fodder may also have taken its toll.

While the Irish remained at Perth, the earl of Ulster was engaged in diplomatic activity on behalf of the king. On 30 December, a messenger – appropriately named Duncan Lightfoot – brought instructions to the earl on 'the answer to be made to the Scottish demands'.[45] By early February, the negotiations had reached a successful conclusion: on 6 February, a report on the outcome was sent to the king and, on 9 February, the earl was one of four on the English side who put their seals to the indenture which formally set out the terms agreed to with Comyn.[46] After that, there is no evidence to suggest that either de Burgh or the Irish were in action other than the fact that horses were lost in the second half of February and were recorded for compensation in Dunfermline, where the king was in winter quarters. This might indicate that the Irish had participated in the *chevauchée* which the king sent against William Wallace, especially since it was a servant of de Burgh's who brought to the king news of the defeat inflicted on Wallace and Fraser.[47] The deaths of Walter le Poer, a knight, on 20 February and a squire on 23 February may have resulted from just such a military engagement.[48]

After that, the Irish remained with the prince in Perth and moved on to St Andrews in early March, when a parliament met to discuss the final stages of the campaign.[49] The taking of Stirling castle was the most important task facing the English and when the prince of Wales returned to Perth to make his preparations for the siege, the Irish went with him. The famous siege began on 22 April and the Irish were present to take part in the assault.[50] The loss of horses again suggests that they were in action. But only a rump of the original army now remained, even though that consisted exclusively of mounted men who were most useful in the kind of warfare which had occupied the winter months. It was not until 31 July that they began the long journey home.

At its greatest strength the Irish army numbered 3,457 men.[51] This was certainly the largest army to leave Ireland in the course of the Scottish wars of

44 *CDS 1272–1307*, no. 1516. 45 Ibid., no. 1419. 46 Francis Palgrave (ed.), *Documents and records illustrating the history of Scotland, and the transactions between the crowns of Scotland and England (21 Hen. III–35 Edw. I)* (RC, London, 1837), pp 282–3; Hilda Johnstone, *Edward of Carnarvon* (Manchester, 1946), p. 92. 47 BL, Add. MS 8835, fo. 42. 48 Ibid., fo. 56*v*. 49 *Docs. illus. hist. Scot.*, ii, 476. 50 Palgrave, *Documents and records illustrating the history of Scotland*, pp 267–74. 51 See below, table 7.

independence. But it is difficult to assess its contribution to the Edwardian plan for the subjugation of the Scots, since it was active in an area which has been ignored by Scottish and English historians alike. Yet it may have been the Irish who prevented the west from offering a safe base from which the Scots could threaten the king. And after the bulk of the army returned home, the earl of Ulster and his retinue not only played a part in the decisive siege of Stirling castle, but seem to have been active in containing the remaining pockets of Scottish resistance during the winter months.

The cost was high, not least because of the large number of debts which were pardoned in a series of royal letters of munificence, most dated 15 August 1304.[52] But the real cost can only be measured when added to the other contributions which the Irish exchequer had to make to this campaign. In May and June 1302, the Irish government was ordered to forward large quantities of wheat, oats, malt and wine to Scotland.[53] A king's clerk, Richard de Wardington, was sent to supervise the purveyance in Ireland and he was working out of Dublin between 4 June and 24 August.[54] So far as we know, however, nothing was shipped to Scotland until the following spring, when purveyors working out of Dublin, Drogheda and New Ross between February and June 1303 sent at least nine ships loaded with wheat, oats, fish and wine to Scotland.[55] With the king, prince of Wales and the English army parading up and down the other side of Scotland, there does not seem to have been much need of food supplies in the west during the summer. Not until 23 September was another order sent to Dublin, when the king revealed that 'for the final and happy expedition of the war in Scotland' he intended to spend the winter there.[56] As the victuals were intended to supply the castles of Dumfries and Lochmaben, the amounts sought were modest. By January 1304, when further orders were sent to Dublin, the amounts were increased and the king sent his clerk, William de Wythington, to supervise the purveyance 'with all haste'.[57] With the country in the depth of winter, the king could hardly have expected much from Ireland and his clerk certainly encountered considerable difficulty in finding the supplies needed.

52 *CDI 1302–7*, nos. 337–49. 53 Ibid., nos. 69, 82. 54 He was paid £6 3*s.* and also £15 13*s.* 4*d.* which he was owed in the wardrobe (E 101/10/7; *Rep. RCI 1811–15*, p. 172). 55 *38th rep. DKPRI*, p. 85 (Ir. pipe roll, 31 Edw. I). Details of cargoes may be found in transcripts of the orignal pipe roll accounts in RIA, MS 12 D 10, pp 139–41; NLI, MS 760, pp 252, 265. Payments on the issue roll, amounting to more than £860, include purveyors at Waterford; but no enrolled account for that port survived in the pipe rolls (*Rep. RCI, 1811–15*, p. 173). In Scotland, the receiver of the king's victuals at Skinburness accounted for a total of 48 quarters of wheat, 563 quarters of oats, 313 quarters of malt of oats, 202 quarters of beans and peas, 62 tuns of wine and 2 tuns of honey (BL, Add. MS 8835, fo. 35; TNA (PRO), E 101/11/19). Some of his original indentures of receipt with masters of different ships from Ireland have survived in TNA (PRO), C 47/22/3, nos. 41, 45, 48–50; C 47/22/9, no. 51 (calendared in *CDS 1272–1307*, nos. 1353, 1369–72, 1377). 56 *CDI 1302–7*, nos. 251–3. 57 Gilbert, *Hist. & mun. docs*, pp 503–4; *CDI 1302–7*, nos. 284, 286. He landed on 15 Feb. 1304 and remained until 12 May (*CDI 1302–7*, no. 306, at p. 108).

Nevertheless, he was able to organize purveyors in Dublin and Drogheda, who between them managed to send quantities considerably in excess of what had been ordered.[58] Not all of the cargoes reached Skinburness safely: one ship, for example, was wrecked while approaching the port and thirty tuns of wine and one of oats floated onto the coast where they were carried away by 'certain malefactors of those parts'.[59]

By comparison with the large quantities of supplies which had been shipped from Ireland for previous campaigns, the amounts sent in 1303–4 show a marked decrease.[60] It is true that with Berwick the base from which the English army was being supplied and Carlisle (with its port of Skinburness) merely being used to distribute victuals to some important castles in the west, there was not the same need to draw on Ireland. But there is also evidence that in the lordship, as was happening in England, purveyance was now being resisted by force. In Dublin itself, for example, Wythington met with resistance when he tried to exercise his office. He found that 'certain men enormously disturbed the king's market and forestalled, seized and hid in houses corn found in and corn coming into the city, so that it could not be brought to market', with the result that purveyance could not be made, 'in manifest contempt of the king'. When he sought the assistance of the municipal authorities, he was met with evasion, so that not even the mayor acted to allow the purveyance to go ahead.[61] There are other signs elsewhere of similar resistance. The king's receiver at Carlisle had sent an agent to Ulster to purchase wine, but the seneschal of the liberty imprisoned him because he was 'of the land of Scotland'.[62] The 'war effort' was having an impact on Ireland. In New Ross, on 28 June 1304, a fight broke out between the men of the town and sailors from Winchelsea ships, which led to murder.[63] A contingent of men being led by Maurice de Carru was savagely attacked while lodged in the Coombe near Dublin.[64]

Had the king badly needed Irish supplies in the west of Scotland for this campaign, it would have been difficult to meet his needs. Apart from the fact that winter scarcity would have made purveyance difficult – and we should not forget that yields per acre were so low that even quite modest demands for

58 *38th rep. DKPRI*, p. 86 (Ir. pipe roll, 32 Edw. I). Details of Dublin cargoes are in RIA, MS 12 D 10, p. 141; NLI, MS 760, p. 264, at a cost of £345. In his enrolled account, the treasurer was allowed £300 and £318 paid to purveyors at Dublin and Drogheda (TNA (PRO), E 372/150, m. 40*d*). No account for Drogheda has survived, though there is evidence of purveyors at work there (NAI, EX 2/1 [Ir. memo. roll, 31–5 Edw. I], pp 73, 101, 103). 59 *CPR 1301–7*, p. 356. 60 The allowances of payment to purveyors on the enrolled account of the Irish treasurer, Richard of Barford, show this clearly: 1300 – £1,874; 1301 – £1,349; 1303 – £277; 1304 – £618 (E 372/150, m. 40*d*). 61 Gilbert, *Hist. & mun. docs*, pp 504–7. The mayor, Geoffrey Morton, had a grievance: he was claiming payment of victuals which had been sent to the army in Gascony, as well as compensation of £260 for other victuals sent to Scotland, which, through long delays, had been lost 'by putrefaction' (ibid., pp 291–4). 62 *CJRI 1305–7*, p. 234. 63 Ibid., p. 106. 64 Ibid., p. 198.

wheat and oats would have placed an intolerable burden on some peasants in the hinterlands of Dublin and Drogheda[65] – the precarious financial state of the Dublin exchequer would have made it difficult to meet the cost. Some idea of what the expedition was costing the Irish government is revealed by a startling entry on an English receipt roll for 30 July 1305, which records the receipt of £11,267 4*s*. 5*d*. 'of the issues of Ireland' paid into the king's wardrobe.[66] In fact, this enormous sum of money is made up of smaller sums recorded in the wardrobe in 1303–4 and includes money which was sent from Ireland to pay the wages of the earl of Ulster and his army.[67] Even so, it is a colossal sum by Irish standards, when recorded receipts in the Dublin exchequer in those years came to only £5,080 in 1302–3, £4,164 in 1303–4, and £4,562 in 1304–5.[68] There can be no doubt that the Dublin exchequer was putting future revenues in pawn in order to meet the costs of its involvement in the Scottish war. After the collapse of Edward's Scottish settlement with the murder of John Comyn by Robert Bruce in February 1306,[69] the king began looking for victuals from Ireland again in March.[70] A stream of writs followed: twice within one week the Irish government was asked to 'hasten' or 'accelerate with the utmost despatch' the purveyance of victuals.[71] The response in Ireland reflected something of the same haste. During March and April, purveyors were appointed to the chief ports. Writs of *liberate* for various sums to be paid to those agents were directed to the Dublin exchequer during the following weeks.[72] But the treasurer could find no money to meet the king's demands, informing Edward that he 'could not raise it unless the payments to R. de Burgo, earl of Ulster, and others of that land, who were with the king in the war of Scotland, which the king commanded to be assigned for arrears of their wages, be deferred'.[73] Apparently, the earl agreed, in response to the king's letter of 20 April which made it plain that without a postponement of the arrears of wages the necessary provisions could not be found.[74]

In attempting to assess the Irish contribution to Edward's attempted final solution of the Scottish problem in 1303–4, it is easy to devalue it by measuring it on the scale of the English war effort. Even so it was not negligible. A force of

65 A modern estimate is that each acre produced a net average of only eight bushels of mixed grain (J.Z. Titow, *English rural society, 1200–1300* (London, 1969), p. 81). 66 E 401/160. 67 E 101/365/6, fos. 19*d*, 21*d*, 32*d*. 68 E 372/150, m. 40–40*d*; E 372/153, m. 35. 69 Wogan and Irish magnates were informed of this as a matter of great urgency (E 101/369/11, fo. 146). 70 *CJRI 1305–7*, pp 247–8. The supplies were to be found 'in places where they can do … the least hurt to the men of those parts'. Two clerks were sent to supervise the purveyance (*CDI 1302–7*, no. 506). Further writs 'de victualibus festinandis' were sent in April, and in May more messengers were sent 'cum omni festinacione' (E 101/369/11, fos. 143, 145*v*). 71 *CPR 1301–7*, p. 428; *CDS 1302–7*, no. 1763. 72 NAI, EX 2/1, p. 162; *CDI 1302–7*, nos. 500, 514, 548, 550–2, 579–82. 73 *CJRI 1305–7*, pp 268–9. On 28 Apr., the king, in a letter ordering receipts from the wool custom in Ireland to be recovered from the Frescobaldi, said that he 'understands that the exchequer stands very much in want of money' (*CDI 1302–7*, no. 515). 74 *CCR 1302–7*, p. 436. Edward told de Burgh that, 'those provisions cannot be made without a great sum of money, as the earl knows, and the king knows that the earl has

more than 3,400 men was an important addition to the army which crushed the Scots; the effectiveness of the Irish military presence in the west needs to be stressed; and the value of supplies through Skinburness to important castles was of some account. Nor is the expenditure of a sum well in advance of £11,000 on the army a matter of little significance.[75] But the real assessment is to be made only in the context of the lordship itself. The cost was high. There can be no doubt that the financial burden which was placed on the Dublin exchequer helped the process which was to reduce by nearly half the revenues available to the Dublin government in the early years of the reign of Edward II.[76] The pressures were insidious and not always of major proportions. For example, when the king's receiver at Carlisle bought sixty-four tuns of wine from a Dundalk merchant at Whitehaven in 1303, it was the Irish exchequer which had to pay the bill.[77] The slow trickle of payments of arrears of wages to de Burgh, le Poer and the others, often by the expedient of assignment, is another indication of the financial pressures generated at the exchequer.[78] Somehow Wogan's government had found the ready cash which was required in the summer of 1303 to supply Bicknor, the clerk of the wages, just before the army sailed for Scotland.[79] But some, at least, of this had to be borrowed, like the £500 which Adam le Blund of Callan and his wife Alice lent in June 1303.[80] Significantly, Adam had to hire men to protect it while on its way to Dublin 'on account of the dangers of the road'. More important, he was still awaiting repayment in 1307.[81]

More difficult to evaluate is the impact which the expedition had in other ways. The protections which were issued in June 1303 to those setting out for Scotland were in some cases produced in court causing litigation to be abandoned.[82] Pardons which were issued in return for service in Scotland were also used in court to escape punishment for crimes committed.[83] At a time when lawlessness was on the increase in Ireland, the issuing of such pardons was a dangerous expedient and was subsequently roundly condemned by Edward II.[84]

at heart the profit and honour of him and his realm and that it is not the earl's wish that the expedition should be delayed in any way for lack of such provisions'. 75 The financing of the expedition and the total cost to the Irish exchequer are now impossible to estimate. Sums like £25, 100 marks and the much larger £2,440, which Bicknor as clerk of the wages received in Scotland in Oct. and Nov., while they came from the Irish treasurer 'de thesauro regis' in Dublin, are not in fact accounted for by Barford in his enrolled account (E 101/364/13, fos. 38, 54*d*). 76 J.F. Lydon, 'Edward II and the revenues of Ireland in 1311–12', *IHS*, 14:53 (1964), 43, n. 12. 77 E 101/11/19 and E 101/233/22, nos. 26–7. 78 For a file of thirty-five receipts, see E 101/619/62; others are scattered through E 101/233/22. Some related writs of *liberate* are calendared in *CDI 1302–7*, nos. 357, 362, 365, 371. 79 E 101/233/22, nos. 18–21. It is perhaps significant that the writ of *liberate* of 28 June for £1,000 (no. 25) could only be met by twelve sums. 80 *RCH*, p. 6, no. 58. 81 NAI, EX 2/1, p. 216. 82 See NAI, RC 8/1, pp 235, 249, 257, 258, 260, for some examples. 83 *CJRI 1308–14*, p. 26. 84 *CCR 1313–18*, p. 105; *CPR 1321–4*, pp 354–5.

It is only when the deterioration in the condition of the Irish lordship is remembered that we can see the effect of this involvement in the Scottish wars. The significance of a petition to the king from a man who had served in some of the most dangerous engagements in Scotland, requesting an exchange of thirty librates of land held in chief 'in the king's demesnes in Ireland, joining the castle of Dublin', for only twenty librates in Scotland, is readily apparent.[85] We know that, by now, the Irish of the Leinster mountains were menacing not only the rich manors adjacent to the foothills, but the environs of Dublin itself. At such a time, it seems folly to concentrate so much energy and so many resources on Scotland. There is no evidence, in fact, that the absence of de Burgh and other magnates resulted in any immediate worsening of the growing military problem presented by the Irish, though it should be stressed that meagre sources may mislead us. That there was cause for worry seems obvious. We have seen that not only was Butler ordered to remain in Ireland for the security of the land, but that the justiciar, John fitz Thomas and Peter Bermingham also stayed behind when the army sailed for Scotland. Fitz Thomas was certainly worried about the position in south Leinster and, on 18 July 1303, he took the unusual step of buying the services of one of the leading Irish families in the area, a Nigel O More, by granting him not only lands but a castle as well.[86] Unfortunately, there is no evidence to show what was happening in that politically sensitive area during the summer. But the fact that Wogan was compelled to adopt defensive measures in Kildare in the autumn and that a service was proclaimed at Kilkenny certainly suggests that there was trouble.[87] It reached a gruesome climax with the murder of the leading O Connors of Offaly by Peter Bermingham while entertaining them in his castle of Carbury in 1305, an event which threw the whole of south Leinster into war.[88] At the same time on the other side of Leinster, the military problem had obviously worsened. By 1305, we are told that the important castle of Newcastle McKynegan was 'in a strong march'; the archbishop's manor of Ballymore at the foot of the mountains was burned by Irish enemies; the men had to be pardoned for consorting with the O Tooles because it was accepted that they did so 'for fear of death'.[89] When the government was finally forced to intervene, first proclaiming a service at Ballymore in 1306, the clerk of the wages accounted for well over £2000 on wages to the men sent to fight in Leinster.[90] At the same time, the Irish treasurer was paying out a total of nearly £2,500 to the purveyors of supplies for Scotland.[91] This shows clearly what the scale of priorities was.

From the early fourteenth-century perspective, however, there was nothing amiss in squandering the hard-pressed resources of the government on a foreign

85 *CDS 1272–1307*, no. 1969. 86 *Red bk Kildare*, no. 76. 87 *CJRI 1305–7*, pp 242–3, 296; Otway-Ruthven, 'Royal service in Ireland' (above, p. 174). 88 *CJRI 1305–7*, p. 82; *AI*, pp 395–7; Orpen, *Normans*, iv, 35–6. 89 *CJRI 1305–7*, pp 28, 504; *CStM*, ii, 333. 90 Otway-Ruthven, 'Royal service in Ireland', p. 174; *39th rep. DKPRI*, p. 24. 91 E 101/234/17.

war. After all, the issues of Ireland belonged of right to the lord of Ireland, now Edward I of England, to be spent as he thought fit. Nowhere do we find Wogan or any other minister complaining. They conscientiously carried out the mandates of their royal master as best they could. And if war in Scotland offered the magnates little scope for the honour and profit which later campaigning in France was to provide, it did mean high wages and lucrative terms of service for those who led retinues. Even some glory might be won, as the annals record.

But even the fourteenth century could see the effect of all this on an already dangerous situation in Ireland, as the 1311 condemnation of Edward II so clearly shows.[92] When he blamed the lack of money in the contemporary Irish exchequer on the demands of the Scottish wars in particular, and said it was this which more than anything else made it impossible for the government to adequately maintain the peace, he made no specific mention of any particular campaign. It was the cumulative effect of all the campaigns which did the damage. In this, the campaign of 1303–4, with its high cost in men, money and administrative energy, must take pride of place.

TABLE 7
IRISH SERVING IN SCOTLAND IN 1303–4[1]

| *Dates* | *Earls* | *Bannerets* | *Knights* | *Squires* | *Hobelars* | *Foot* | *Total* |
|---|---|---|---|---|---|---|---|
| 17 June–18 Aug. | 1 | 11 | 28 | 281 | 503 | 2,633 | 3,457 |
| 19 Aug.–28 Sept. | 1 | 10 | 29 | 281 | 503 | 2,633 | 3,457 |
| 29 Sept.–19 Nov. | 1 | 7 | 20 | 152 | 150 | 151 | 481 |
| 20 Nov.–6 Jan. | 1 | 7 | 18 | 149 | 149 | 145 | 469 |
| 7 Jan.–1 Feb. | 1 | 6 | 17 | 138 | 138 | 117 | 417 |
| 2–11 Feb. | 1 | 5 | 16 | 130 | 138 | 117 | 407 |
| 11–20 Feb. | 1 | 5 | 16 | 125 | 138 | 117 | 402 |
| 21–3 Feb. | 1 | 5 | 15 | 114 | 34 | – | 169 |
| 24 Feb.–1 May | 1 | 5 | 15 | 113 | 34 | – | 168 |
| 2 May–27 June | 1 | 5 | 15 | 109 | 34 | – | 164 |
| 28 June–31 July | 1 | 4 | 13 | 85 | 15 | – | 118 |

92 Lydon, 'Edward II and the revenues of Ireland', pp 52–3. 1 The table is based on E 101/11/2 and BL, Add. MS 8835, fos. 45*v*–49, 56*v*. There is a possibility that the figures in the first line should be increased by 3 knights, 20 squires, 20 hobelars and 100 foot. This is the number which Peter Bermingham promised to bring in 1302, in return for the cancellation of a debt of £460 and the payment of 200 marks (*CDI 1302–7*, p. 61). In an account of £493 on Ir. pipe roll, 32 Edw. I, he was, in fact, in accordance with this bargain, allowed £440 (*38th rep. DKPRI*, p. 88). But there is no record of any payment to him of the 200 marks and no evidence that he did serve in Scotland.

CHAPTER 13

# Richard II's expeditions to Ireland*

*James Lydon*

While much has been written about Richard II and Ireland, the military aspect of the subject has so far not received any very serious attention.[1] It is, however, of considerable interest; the military side of Richard's dealings with Ireland now seems to be a most important element in the story, and one which should be properly investigated if we are ever to understand the Irish policy of that king. In the following account, I have adopted a general approach, omitting as much of the technical details of the two campaigns as possible; this has, however, necessitated a rather detailed preliminary examination of Richard's motives in coming to Ireland and of the preparations he made for his expeditions.

Richard's motives in undertaking his first Irish expedition have frequently been misunderstood or misrepresented in the past. According to some writers, he was so distraught by the death of his wife, Ann of Bohemia, that he looked for an escape in Ireland and in the solution of his problem there. It is no doubt true that he did seek such a release, but he had already begun to plan an expedition some time before the death of Ann. Another suggestion is that his visit was something of a crusade to combat the growth of Clementist sympathies in Ireland, particularly in the Gaelic areas where strong currents of anti-English feeling made the Great Schism a political issue. But it is impossible to see Richard in the role of crusader, for all that he had already begun the rapprochement which led to the concordat of 1398 with Boniface IX. He may indeed have intended his Irish expedition to be construed as an anti-Clementist crusade in Rome, making easier the path towards reconciliation with the papacy; but that he undertook such an expensive and even dangerous enterprise solely for this purpose goes beyond the bounds of credulity. A much more interesting suggestion is the one that Richard put his military strength to the test in Ireland as the final step in his programme of autocracy. Tout was the great exponent of this view and the weight of his authority (plus the attraction of the thesis itself) has made the idea a popular one. There is no doubt a great deal of truth in it;

* This was the subject of a lecture delivered by the author to the Military History Society of Ireland in 1962. It was first published in *JRSAI*, 93 (1963), 135–49. 1 [EN. The original version of this essay was published without footnotes, but with a bibliographical note appended to the text. Where substantial quotations from printed sources appear, I have taken the liberty of adding references.]

but there is no doubt either that it cannot have been Richard's sole, or even primary, reason for coming to Ireland. In fact, this theory rests upon little evidence other than a reading of history backwards.

The plain fact of the matter is that Richard had very little choice but to lead the armed might of England against Ireland if he wished to hold on to his lordship there. And, unless we understand that, we will never fully appreciate the proper extent of his achievement in Ireland. For that achievement was primarily a military one and not, as it is often depicted, a diplomatic or a political one. Hence the importance of motivation. To understand what Richard did we must first understand what he set out to do in Ireland. And this can only be done by approaching the question through Ireland, through a consideration of the problem which had arisen there in the course of the fourteenth century.

The problem itself can be expressed in very simple terms. A Gaelic revival and the inflated power and pretensions of the middle race (or the 'Irish rebels', to use Richard's own terminology) seriously threatened the very existence of the English colony in Ireland. The only answer to that threat was the presence of the king himself at the head of the largest army he could bring together. The Irish great council of 1385 had said no more than was true when it reported 'the mischiefs and very great perils which the land of Ireland, the seignory of the King, and his poor lieges have in these parts', and said that 'at this next season, as is likely, there will be made a conquest of the greater part of the land of Ireland [that is, by the Irish and the Irish rebels]'. 'Considering', the council continued in its report, 'the weakness and poverty of the English lieges ... they are not in any way able to help themselves ... [and] are not able nor know how to find or think of other remedy except the coming of the King, our lord, in his own person.'[2] That there was no great exaggeration here can be easily demonstrated from the council roll of a few years later, 1392.[3] Almost every page of this record of proceedings before the Irish council illustrates the great increase in the power, prestige and daring of the Gaelic 'captains of their nations'. The condition of Carlow, which had been made the virtual administrative capital of the colony long before this because of its strategic importance in the march land, is another pointer towards the process of decline on the one hand and of growth on the other – the decline of the area now administered by the government and the growth of the area under the control of the Gaelic leaders and the feudal baronage. Carlow was now abandoned as an administrative centre and with it all hope of recovery in the area.

The fact is that on every side the English had lost ground in Ireland. The attempt of the government to cut its losses (the phrase is Curtis') in the Statutes of Kilkenny had been a disastrous failure, and more drastic measures were called for if the situation were not to get hopelessly out of hand. The causes of

2 [EN. *Stat. John–Hen. V*, pp 484–7 (*RCH*, p. 128, no. 18).] 3 [EN. *PKCI*, pp 1–252.]

this collapse need not concern us here; but all previous attempts to deal with it had been feeble or short-lived. And so the situation worsened to the position of 1392.

The greatest single threat, however, was posed by the Leinster Irish and most immediately by Art MacMurrough Kavanagh. Even at the beginning of the fourteenth century, the Leinster Irish had been strong enough to threaten Dublin itself. Expeditions led against them had been, for the most part, a failure, and the expedient of buying them off by means of pensions or 'black rents' could never be completely successful, as the constant complaints of the English lieges amply demonstrated. The real answer was armed force, and this Richard was prepared to apply. In fact, as events were to show, he wished to go further and drive the Irish out of Leinster altogether, turning that area into an English land, loyal and safe, thus anticipating the creation of the Pale. But, in the first instance, force must be met with force if the flight of the colonists from Ireland was to be halted before depopulation of the English areas occurred. For this flight was one of the side effects produced by the growing menace of Gaelic and rebel Irish power and their increasing persecution of the loyal English elements in Ireland. Many fled to England, increasing to danger level the incidence of absenteeism and allowing large areas of land to fall back into waste. As a preliminary to his armed invasion, Richard II tackled this problem by the simple expedient of ordering all emigrants back to Ireland under pain of forfeiture and of severe financial penalties which would help to pay the cost of the war there. It might be thought that legislation of this order remained a dead letter as had so often been the case with similar legislation in the past; but, in fact, all the evidence we have goes to show that on this occasion at least it was strictly enforced – in itself, a sign of the serious view Richard took of the Irish situation. The English chancery rolls contain the names of those who were granted exemption from this legislation by the king; for the period 1391–9, only twenty-one exemptions were issued to owners of land or holders of benefices, a tiny number of little significance when compared with those who came to Ireland with the king to defend their lands there. The number of ordinary emigrants who received licences of exemption – clerks, craftsmen, labourers – was very much higher and during the same period came to 521. But even this number is probably a fraction only of the total in England.[4]

4 These lists of ordinary emigrants in England are extremely interesting, showing the type of work upon which they were engaged. A full analysis of them would be of great value. Many of them, as we might expect, were clerks: but a great number were artisans and labourers. Some of the reasons for exemption from the legislation are interesting: one man 'in consideration of his blindness and old age', another 'in consideration of his poverty and feebleness' [EN. This analysis is now provided in J.L. Bolton, 'Irish migration to England in the late Middle Ages: the evidence of 1394 and 1440', *IHS*, 32:125 (2000), 1–21. See also Wendy R. Childs, 'Irish merchants and seamen in late medieval England', *IHS*, 32:125

I have no doubt, then, that the first point in Richard's programme of reform was the application of military force. And I think that it is important that we should stress this point, because too often it has been played down, or under-emphasized, by previous writers, of whom Curtis is typical. There is a suggestion that, before he came to Ireland, Richard had evolved a completely new answer to the Irish question, which included a complete pardon of those Irish rebels willing to make their submissions, the confirmation of the Gaelic leaders in the lands they had held since the conquest, and the creation of a new English land in Leinster. If Richard had any such plan in mind before he came to Ireland – and the evidence of the letters he wrote from Dublin suggests that it was evolved only after he had fought in Leinster – he must have realized that it was an impracticable one which, if it were to have any hope of success, would involve him in war in Leinster and probably elsewhere in Ireland as well. The full realization of any such programme, then, depended in the final analysis upon a successful military campaign in Ireland. And, as I hope to show, it was only because his military plans were successful that the rest of the programme could be put into operation.

Richard's policy, therefore, was in the first place a repetition of what had by now become the traditional policy of English kings – armed intervention from England. Where it differed was in the scale of the operation and in the fact that the king himself led the expedition. The army which came with Richard was by far the largest ever to land in Ireland during the Middle Ages, and was intended to stay here until the work of reform had been brought to a satisfactory conclusion. This was a complete break away from the idea of small armies, led by a chief governor or member of the royal family, fighting for a short season against a particular enemy or group of enemies and achieving no lasting success.

I have laboured this point of Richard's motive in coming to Ireland and of what he hoped to achieve here because it is only through understanding this that we can properly measure his achievement. Any estimate of his success must always come back to this point: his only real success was in the military sphere; all his other achievements were dependent on this and were, in any case, ephemeral, particularly the famous submissions of the Gaelic leaders.

Richard's reliance on military power becomes immediately obvious when we consider the careful way in which he set about preparing for his expedition, and the scale on which these preparations were conducted. From the middle of June 1394, when a general survey of the available shipping was instituted, transport arrangements went ahead in a methodical fashion and on a grand scale. The survey covered all merchant ships from the Thames to Exeter, Somerset,

(2000), 22–43; Virginia Davis, 'Irish clergy in late medieval England', *IHS*, 32:126 (2000), 145–60; Paul Brand, 'Irish law students and lawyers in late medieval England', *IHS*, 32:126 (2000), 161–73].

Devon, Cornwall, Bristol and south Wales, north Wales and Lancashire. As the results from the survey came in, they were sorted and, in August, special agents were commissioned for the different coastal areas with powers to arrest suitable ships, impress crews, and outfit and equip the vessels, all under general direction of the king's admiral, Edward, earl of Rutland. The whole business was carried through on an impressive scale, all the more striking when we remember that at the same time another flotilla was being assembled to carry John of Gaunt's expeditionary force to Gascony. We can follow the work of these royal agents in considerable detail and the scale on which they conducted their operations was, even by English standards, imposing. One example will serve to illustrate this – John Orewell, a king's serjeant, who on 23 June was commissioned to

> search and in all ways inform himself … from Thamesmouth and thence as far as Exeter … how many and what sort of ships and other vessels with their equipment may be had there for the passage of the king and his army to Ireland; to enjoin on the owners and masters that they have them prepared and arrayed with all speed under penalty of forfeiture, the masters and crews to be paid the usual wages from the time they leave port, and security taken from the masters and owners not to withdraw them; and so to certify all his proceedings hereunder to the king and council, also the names of masters and mariners, the number of ships and of what burden they are.

Orewell began his survey on the same day at the mouth of the Thames and, between then and 1 August, he worked his way along the coast to Exeter, inspecting all the ships in every port and marking out those large enough and strong enough to be adapted as troop ships or supply ships, or to be converted into carriers of horses. This done, he compiled his list of all suitable shipping and returned with it to London. There the results of other surveys were brought together, and from the complete dossier a final list of ships to be requisitioned was compiled and Orewell was made responsible for those in his area. On 11 August, he set out on his tour again and, armed with the king's power of arrest, commissioned the ships listed – three on 14 August, four on the fifteenth, one on the sixteenth, and so on, thirty-six in all. Indentures were drawn up with the owners and masters of each ship, giving the name and tunnage of the vessel, its compliment of constables and mariners, and the amount to be paid for their service. Some of the ships were large (100 tuns with one constable and twenty mariners), most were 60–70 tuns, and one was as small as 40 tuns with only one constable and six mariners. This side of the operation was complicated and time-consuming, which accounts for the slow rate of progress made by Orewell. Each ship, too, had to be inspected again to see if it were seaworthy and arrangements made for any repairs which were necessary. The agent had to see that each mariner was sufficiently well armed, and finally any necessary alterations in the structure of the vessel had to be planned. For the carriage of the troops or most war-supplies no alterations of any consequence were generally required; in the case of this expedition to Ireland, the journey by sea was short and any discomfort could easily be borne by the troops. But with horses it was a different matter. They were the heart of the army and, for all their great size and strength, were delicate and expensive animals who could not be subjected to the risks of a sea voyage without every precaution being taken to ensure their safety and comfort. A sick, maimed or even irritable animal was virtually useless to the army. The construction of stalls and hurdles, the provision of fodder, the building of special gangways, the erection of enclosures to hold the horses before they were taken on board – these were some of the jobs which made the shipping of horses a tiresome business for those responsible. Major alterations were necessary in those ships which had to be adapted for offensive purposes, consisting mainly of the building of castles at the bow and stern of the ship to offer protection to archers and positions from which they could loose their arrows to greater advantage. The illustrations in the Harleian manuscript of Creton's chronicle show vessels of this type engaged in the expedition to Ireland.[5] Finally, in many cases mariners had to be pressed into service to complete crews and this, as can be imagined, was often a difficult, and sometimes even a dangerous, job.

Throughout the summer, then, large-scale operations led to the assembly at Milfordhaven of a fleet sufficiently large to carry troops, horses, heavy artillery and military supplies of all kinds to Waterford with the king. So far, I have not been able to compile a list of all the ships which took part in the expedition. Richard's first expedition is well documented, but many of the records are fragmentary or scattered in different collections and are, therefore, difficult to analyze. But from what lists I have managed to put together, and considering that one of the king's agents arrested 108 ships during August, it seems that the fleet must have been very large indeed, so that probably more than five hundred vessels were engaged.

Commissariat arrangements formed another preoccupation of the royal administration during the summer of 1394, and here again the scale of the preparations indicates the seriousness of Richard's purpose. Since the expedition was to be a household enterprise (an important aspect of the affair to which I shall be referring again), household officers looked after the work of feeding, housing and supplying the army in Ireland. For example, on 2 July,

5 [EN. Jean Creton, 'Translation of a French metrical history of the deposition of King Richard the second, written by a contemporary, and comprising the period from his last expedition into Ireland to his death [...]', ed. J. Webb, *Archaeologia*, 20 (1824), pl. 3.]

Baldwin Radyngton and John Stanley (both household officers) were appointed to 'find quarters for the entertainment of the king and the magnates coming with him in his army to Ireland, and to provide the necessary victuals therefor, at the king's charges, with power to imprison contrariants'. A week later, the same pair were empowered to 'make divers purveyances against the arrival of the king and the great persons with him in his army for Ireland; in respect of carriage for them, their men and their baggage'. The sheriffs of most English counties were required to provide quantities of food for the army, but it seems that this was intended to feed the army on its way to Milfordhaven, while the household officers looked after feeding it in Ireland. The latter was the most important part of the work and nothing was left to chance. For example, in August, Radyngton and Stanley were ordered to arrest in England 'as many fishermen with their vessels, boats, nets, instruments and other engines as will suffice for catching fish at sea for the use of the household during the present expedition to Ireland' – an interesting illustration that the fishing industry of fourteenth-century Ireland was no better than it is now. Other agents were charged with finding the necessary horses 'for the chariots, wagons and sumpters [(?) baggage trains], with harness, for the expedition to Ireland'. So that some at least of the supplies to be consumed or used on the expedition were to be provided by England. But since Ireland at that time was producing a surplus of corn and meat, it was expected that she would be able to supply all the food that the army needed. To arrange for this, Radyngton and Stanley, with the bishop of Meath (who had just been appointed treasurer of Ireland), were sent ahead of the main force to Ireland at the end of July. With them went another knight, 41 squires (of whom one was a clarioner), 190 mounted archers, 9 foot archers and 52 household grooms. All of these were attached to the household and their function (despite the large number of armed men in the group) was to provide food and shelter for the main army when it arrived. The presence of so many squires and archers is an indication of what a formidable task these household officers faced in Ireland. There, to a much greater extent than in England, the king's right of purveyance had been greatly abused by royal officials and had become a standing source of grievance to merchants, traders and farmers during the fourteenth century. Lacking protection from the forces of the law, these people were now always prepared to resist purveyance in any form by resorting to the use of armed force. The household obviously expected such resistance and came prepared to deal with it. The purveyance was carried through, therefore, but not on the scale planned; so that in September, *en route* to Milfordhaven, the king had to order supplies from the English counties – an order which was repeated when supplies ran short early in 1395.

Of particular interest is the arrangement made for the adequate provision of arms and artillery for the expedition. Here again we can see the household character of the enterprise. This was the job of the privy wardrobe, which in

England looked after arms, armour and artillery for the king's army. Before the summer was out, a clerk and a valet were sent ahead to Ireland with a quantity of arms from this wardrobe, to be stored in Dublin castle until the king should need them. Then later, with the king, came the privy wardrobe itself with much of the arms which were normally stored in the Tower of London. This, perhaps more than anything else, is an indication of the scale on which Richard intended conducting his operations in Ireland. Unfortunately, none of the records of that wardrobe have survived for this year, so it is not possible to discover what quantity of arms was shipped to Ireland; but it must have been great. As for artillery, though some was undoubtedly brought to Ireland, there is no record of its ever being used here.

Finally, we come to the composition and size of the army led by Richard in this first Irish expedition. Its most interesting general feature, which Tout many years ago emphasized (and this is the feature most commonly noted by English historians ever since), was its household character. It was, as Tout said, 'the household in arms, largely directed by household officers and financed by wardrobe clerks', a fact which led him on to speak of 'Richard's autocracy beginning to clothe itself in military garb'.[6] This army was, in fact, a throwback to the time of Edward I and an almost complete departure from the contract system which had developed during the Hundred Years War. The king had already begun to develop the wardrobe on its military side. He had built up a large bodyguard of Cheshire archers in addition to maintaining the customary small band of household troops. He had also, like so many of the magnates, organized a large number of retainers wearing his livery (the white hart) and accepting his wages. These were liable to be called up for service at any time, and they now provided him with the bulk of the archers he intended bringing with him to Ireland. In July, all 'yeomen and archers of the crown of whatsoever condition, being at the king's wages and fees' were ordered to 'draw with all speed to the king's presence ... ready every man according to his estate and means and arrayed to sail with the king to Ireland'. These would form the nucleus of an army which would be under Richard's personal control and under household direction. But magnates and their retinues were also invited to join this army for pay – again in the fashion of Edward I – and many of them did so. In addition, the local militias were called out for service in Ireland.

Wardrobe accounts for this year have fortunately survived,[7] and though they are not complete now we have sufficient to give us a general picture of the composition of the army and to arrive at a figure for the number of soldiers who sailed with the king from Milfordhaven. By my count – though I can make no great claims for the accuracy of this figure – just over 5,000 men-at-arms and archers were in the king's pay in Ireland from October onwards, that is, they

6 [EN. Tout, *Chapters*, iii, 487ff.] 7 [EN. E 101/402/20.]

figure on the accounts of the paymaster which were eventually presented for auditing in the wardrobe. But this figure by no means includes all the soldiers who were with the king, because neither the Cheshire archers nor other retainers who are known to have been with him are mentioned in the accounts. How numerous they were is beyond calculation, but to hazard a guess let us take between one and two thousand. This would bring the total to between six and seven thousand men. But even that is not a final figure, because it does not include the contingents supplied by the English colony in Ireland. Shortly before he left England, Richard ordered commissions of array to be held in Ireland: all men capable of defending the land were to be arrayed in arms and were to be kept in array until the king should deploy them. The Irish magnates were asked to supply contingents to serve for pay, and the Irish justiciar was also commissioned to raise men in Ireland for the war. What all this amounted to cannot be guessed. The Irish exchequer records, which would contain details of the payments to these soldiers, are for the most part non-existent now, and what remains (mostly in the form of transcripts) is so fragmentary that so far I have not succeeded in making sense of it. But for the sake of getting some sort of picture of the size of the army Richard used in Ireland, we will allow two thousand men or so raised in this way. So if we say that the king had at his disposal something between eight and ten thousand men in Ireland we will not, I think, be very far wrong in our estimate.

This was a huge army by the standards of the time and by far the largest ever seen in Ireland. It is no wonder that the chronicler Froissart gives 4,000 men-at-arms and 30,000 archers as the figures for Richard's army. These figures are, of course, ridiculous; but they do illustrate the impression this great army made upon Richard's contemporaries. Froissart reports that 'it is not in memory that ever any king of England made such apparel and provision for any journey to make war against the Irishmen, nor such a number of men of arms nor archers'.[8] And he was only speaking the truth here. To get some idea of the actual size of this army in fourteenth-century terms, we can compare it with some other great armies raised in England. The largest of them all was the one collected by Edward III in 1346 for the war in France – 32,000, raised through the contract system which facilitated the raising of huge numbers, but which left the king with much less control over these forces; about 15,000 fought at Crécy; the army of 1359 (another notably large one) was 12,000; the army with which Henry V in 1417 conquered Normandy was 10,000 – all these under the contract system. So that armies of 10,000 were rare events: that which fought at Poitiers was about 7,000. The army which Richard brought to Ireland was, therefore, a large one; it had the added value of being more under the control of the king than any of the armies mentioned above. Not only was its nucleus

8 [EN. *The chronicles of Froissart*, ed. John Bourcher, Lord Berners (London, 1895), p. 430.]

formed by those who were retainers of the king, but those magnates who brought contingents to Ireland were all, with the notable exception of the duke of Gloucester, supporters of Richard and were numbered among those who fought for him subsequently in England. They were, therefore, more than was usually the case, willing to accept the leadership and personal direction of the king during the course of the campaign – an important point which is worth stressing because it means that whatever was achieved in Ireland in the war there was the achievement of Richard himself. What this means is that we will have to reassess Richard's ability as a soldier and dismiss any idea that he was totally incompetent in that respect. The wider implications of that judgement have an important bearing on any assessment of Richard's character.

Many of the magnates who accompanied him to Ireland also had a vested interest in this country. They stood to gain much if the expedition were successful. One of the largest contingents was supplied by the earl of March, who was also earl of Ulster, lord of Trim and titular lord of Connaught and a great part of Leix. Another contingent came with the earl of Nottingham, who was titular lord of Carlow and also had great Irish properties. But these were only two of many heirs to great Irish estates who were present in the army. Their personal stake in the success of the campaign made them only too eager to cooperate fully with the king in bringing the enterprise to a successful conclusion.

Richard landed at Waterford on 2 October and, from there, we can follow his itinerary in Ireland with fair accuracy and thereby work out the course of the main campaign in considerable detail. The letters he or members of his entourage sent back to England contain, in some cases, details of the movements of the king and his army and accounts of his engagements with the Irish of Leinster; and the testing clauses of many chancery letters can also help us to plot the path followed by Richard. So far, to my knowledge, no one has done this. The difficulties are formidable, mainly because the task of identifying place-names is in some cases an impossible one; but it can be done and is certainly worth doing. So far I have not made the attempt myself, so I am not prepared to speak with any authority on the subject. What is far more interesting is Richard's plan of campaign. It is quite clear that he conceived this after discussion with members of his Irish council, who were familiar with the Leinster terrain and with the tactics most likely to be used by MacMurrough. The obvious fact, which must have been made apparent to Richard at this time, was that unless he could bring MacMurrough into the open where he could make him stand and fight, the heavy cavalry of the English – the bannerets, knights and squires, who numbered nearly 1,500 and formed an important element in the army – would be virtually useless. Much more serious, however, was the position of the archers who formed the bulk of the army. These had by now become the trump card in every English army, particularly those who were mounted on light, fast horses which gave them a mobility unequalled in the western world since the barbarian migrations. As they demonstrated on innumerable occasions in France and Scotland, they could keep an enemy at a safe distance, could open up great gaps in an opposing mass of cavalry, could follow up in quick pursuit of a fleeing enemy, and could always be employed as scouts whenever the need arose. Their longbows could loose arrows with considerable accuracy over incredible distances and could be used with great rapidity. Many years before this, during the period of the Anglo-Norman invasion of Ireland, Gerald of Wales had recommended the use of the Welsh longbow against the Irish. He said that this neutralized their best means of attack, which was their use of a fearsome axe which was deadly at close quarters. Gerald also suggested the advantage of using light cavalry in Ireland and commented on the ineffectiveness of heavy cavalry against the Irish mode of fighting and in the treacherous Irish terrain. In all this, he was perfectly right. The Irish of Leinster in Richard II's day still relied to a great degree upon their proficiency in using their axes, which gave them a great advantage in close-quarter fighting. The Leinster terrain neutralized the efficiency of the English cavalry, so that under those conditions the Irish would probably be at a considerable advantage in any engagement with the English if they chose their ground carefully. This was a lesson some of the English learnt the hard way at a later stage during this campaign, and more particularly during that of 1399, when small troops found themselves face to face with MacMurrough's forces and were cut to pieces. The Irish too were extraordinarily mobile so that, even if the heavy cavalry could be brought into action against them, they would normally be much too slow and cumbersome. Creton, describing the campaign of 1399, says: 'For the horses of the country scour the hills and valleys fleeter than a bounding deer; wherefore they did much damage to the army of the king';[9] and Froissart, in 1394, remarks that the Irish 'know the country and are light people: for a man of arms being never so well horsed and run as fast as he can, the Irishman will run afoot as fast as he and overtake him, yea, and leap upon his horse behind him and draw him from his horse'.[10] The only answer to this was to use mounted archers whenever possible. They could prevent the Irish from coming too close where their axes (and the peculiar knives they also used, according to Froissart) could be used; and they were speedy enough to outrun the Irish, even in much of the rough country in which engagements were fought. It was a simple decision to take, then, that they should be used as much as possible. But it was soon discovered that, even late as October, there was too much foliage on the trees and too heavy undergrowth underfoot to allow the archers to be really effective. It was probably a consideration of this factor which had prompted Richard to undertake a campaign so late in the year, outside

9 [EN. Creton, 'Metrical history', ed. Webb, p. 34.] 10 [EN. *Chronicles of Froissart*, p. 430.]

the usual season, which was a most unusual occurrence. He had probably anticipated this trouble with the archers but miscalculated slightly. So he had to wait in Ireland for some time until the woods became passable again before full-scale operations could begin.

Richard's plan of campaign when it was fully evolved was, therefore, a simple one, and he was able to put it into operation only because of the huge forces he had at his disposal. He would use his mounted archers as much as possible when the circumstances were favourable, but he would also use his heavy cavalry, at least in part, in an unaccustomed role because they could not be used with any great success against the Irish method of fighting. What he did then was to throw a ring of heavily armed positions around MacMurrough's land in Leinster so as to pin the Irishmen inside. The number of points which he fortified and garrisoned heavily cannot now be ascertained fully, but many of them are listed in the exchequer accounts which have survived – in Wicklow, Wexford, Carlow and Kilkenny. But for our purpose here, it does not really matter that all these places cannot be listed or identified; what is important is that the pattern of these 'wards' (as Richard called them) clearly shows that the king was trying to surround the Irish with a ring of steel which they would find impossible to penetrate. Many of his knights and archers were installed in these garrisons, and by means of them Richard was able to prevent MacMurrough from breaking out and rampaging far afield. The king could thus devote his full attention to the slow and, if necessary, piecemeal reduction of Leinster. Here again, he was imitating his ancestor, Edward I, who had applied a similar strategy on a much larger scale, and with great success, against the Welsh. Richard also instituted a blockade by sea against the Irish, which may perhaps account for the incastellated ships he brought with him for possible naval engagements since they served no other function. An embargo on all exports from the colony to Leinster was rigorously imposed in the hope that the loss of necessary supplies would hasten the surrender of the Irish. The king also followed a scorched earth policy in the early stages of the campaign at least, thus cutting down MacMurrough's supplies of food. All this is again reminiscent of Edward I in Wales, where a similar policy was pursued. The bulk of the archers in Ireland was split into small raiding parties and it was these which carried out most of the fighting. Some of the letters sent to England describe some of the engagements which occurred; for example, under the Marshal, who

> had several fine engagements with them [the Irish], in one of which he slew many people of the said MacMurrough, and burned around E. [(?) Edrone] nine villages, and preyed of his cattle up to the number of 8,000. And on another 'journey' he broke in upon him, and, if he had not been foreseen, he would have found the said MacMurrough and his wife in their beds. But they, being told of the affray, escaped with great difficulty

> and at such short warning that they were very nearly taken. And among other things was found a coffer belonging to the said MacMurrough's wife, in which were certain articles of feminine use, but of no great value. And among other things was found the seal of the said MacMurrough, with the inscription around it:
>
> SIGILLUM ARTHURII MACMURGH DEI GRACIA REGIS LAGENIE.
>
> And when the said Earl Marshal failed to take MacMurrough, he was sorely vexed thereat, and determined to punish him, and had his house burned, which was in the said wood of L. [Leverough], as also some fourteen villages round about the said wood, and had four hundred cattle driven away with him.[11]

That, then, was Richard's plan of campaign: a ring of garrisons to pin down the Irish; an embargo on imports; a naval blockade; and the use of a fairly large number of separate troops of light cavalry, with great mobility and great striking power. Now the important thing about that plan is that it worked. Richard was successful in his war and was able to compel MacMurrough to surrender to him. This justified the huge army he had with him in Ireland and it made possible the other points in the king's programme for the reform of Ireland. I am absolutely convinced that the submission of most of the Gaelic leaders was the result of Richard's successful war policy. Froissart in his chronicle asks: 'How [did] these four kings [MacMurrough, O'Neill, O'Connor and O'Brien] of Ireland come so soon to the king's obeisance?' And he answers it:

> It is seen nowadays that earthly princes get little except by power and strength … The great puissance that the king had over with him, and tarried there in their country nine months, and every man well paid, abashed the Irishmen: also the sea was closed from them on all parts, whereby their livenges [livelihood] and merchandises might not enter into their countries … But when the Irishmen saw the great number of men of war that King Richard had in Ireland this last journey, the Irishmen advised themselves and came to obeisance.[12]

This is what happened and all the Irish kings came into Richard's house and made their submissions. They did this mainly because of the result of the fighting in Leinster. That there was fighting there can easily be demonstrated from the letters written from Ireland, from the numbers of English killed and

11 [EN. Curtis, 'Letters from Ric. II', p. 293. The words in square brackets are annotations by Prof. Lydon.] 12 [EN. *Chronicles of Froissart*, pp 433–4. In the chronicle, the answer is supplied by 'Henry Chrystede', Froissart's informant on matters Irish.]

the numbers of horses lost. It is unjust to Richard to say, as Steel said in his biography of the king, that '[t]here was … little actual fighting'.[13]

The king's triumph in Ireland, then, was a military one. He was successful in the first place as a soldier and the diplomatic triumph came after. But that triumph was short-lived. While the new garrisons around Leinster remained in position, Leinster remained quiet. But, as so often happened at this stage in Irish history, financial expediency was allowed to dictate a retreat from a policy which had been found to work and, for lack of money, the garrisons were withdrawn. Immediately, MacMurrough broke loose again, only this time in a more dangerous fashion than ever before. He allied himself with the earl of Desmond to lay waste the south, where O'Brien was also becoming active again. In Ulster, too, O'Neill began to move. Worst of all there were rumours of a great alliance of Irish and Anglo-Irish against the government: they were to begin by attacking the earl of Ormond, as a report to the English council said:

> MacMurrough is now gone to Desmond to aid the earl of Desmond to destroy the power of the earl of Ormond if possible; and afterwards he is to return with all the power he can get from the parts of Munster to destroy the country … O'Neill has assembled a very great host of people without number to war upon and destroy the whole country.[14]

So soon did the Gaelic leaders renounce the submissions they had made, less than three years after Richard's departure from Ireland. Whatever the value of these submissions in the future – and some use was made of them subsequently to justify a claim that Ireland had been conquered – they had no value at all in the troubled years of the last decade of the fourteenth century. MacMurrough at least had every reason for renouncing any bargain he had made with the king, because the Dublin government had failed to fulfil its side of the bargain. He had been promised, for example, an annuity of eighty marks, but this the government, despite frequent requests, failed to pay; he had also been promised that his wife would receive her inheritance of Norragh, which had long been withheld from her because by marrying MacMurrough she had contravened the Statutes of Kilkenny (a point which rankled particularly with her husband) – but this too had not been honoured. Small wonder, then, that Art repudiated his bargain. He refused to vacate Leinster as he had promised, though it is unlikely that he would have done so in any event. The fact is that as soon as Richard and his army had left Ireland and the garrisons had been removed from the perimeter of Leinster, there was nothing to prevent the Irish from carrying on as if nothing had happened.

13 [EN. Anthony Steel, *Richard II* (Cambridge, 1941), p. 208.] 14 [EN. *IHD*, p. 68; the document appears in the original Norman-French in *PKCI*, pp 261–9.]

In one of the engagements which were fought between the government and this new rising of the Irish, Roger Mortimer, the heir to the throne of England and a special favourite of the king, was killed. It was this which led to Richard's second expedition to Ireland. This time he came in anger, burning for revenge, a different man from the Richard who had come in 1394. As is well known, he failed disastrously on this occasion and was decisively defeated by MacMurrough on every point. This reversal is easily explained. The circumstances under which Richard now came to Ireland had greatly altered since 1394. He found it difficult to raise the necessary money for the expedition and could only do so by making himself very unpopular at home. Because of this, the army which came with him was a much smaller one, and so he found it impossible to put into operation the strategy which had proved so successful during the first campaign. Instead, he tried to bulldoze his way through Leinster with the whole army, heavy cavalry and all, and presented the Irish with an easy target which they sniped at and harried all the way to Dublin. There is no doubt either that MacMurrough had learnt a valuable lesson in 1394 and now knew how to keep out of Richard's way while relying on ambushes, night attacks and picking off stragglers from the main body of the English army. It is also probable that he had much larger forces at his disposal now as a result of his new alliances, thus making even more serious the small size of the English army. Richard, too, had to deal with treachery in his own camp, where supporters of Bolingbroke did everything they could to embarrass the king. Finally, there is some evidence that Richard was not quite sane at this time, a theory which is popular with one school of English historians. Certainly, there is much in his conduct of this campaign to suggest mental instability or at least the loss of a sense of proportion: the fact that, though the army was much smaller now, it was accompanied by much more of the pomp and trappings of monarchy than it was in 1394; the large number of minstrels who followed the king and his embroiderer from whom, it was said, he could not bear to be separated. It may well be true, therefore, that the king's mental condition made him unfit to conduct a successful military campaign in Ireland. But the main reason for the failure of the expedition was undoubtedly the deficiency of money, coupled with the dangerous situation Richard faced at home and the greater strength of the Leinster Irish. Whatever the reason, MacMurrough enjoyed a remarkable victory over the English and, what was even more important, created the circumstances which allowed Richard to be overthrown in England. Curtis expressed this well in one of his typical passages: 'And so Art Kavanagh, having first wrought the death of Mortimer, now, by delaying Richard in the wilds of Leinster, let in usurping Bolingbroke and wrecked the unity of England for a hundred years.'[15]

15 [EN. Curtis, *Med. Ire.* (1st ed.), p. 318; ibid. (2nd ed.), p. 277.]

But we must not let this defeat detract from the merits of Richard's first victory in Ireland. He showed himself a good soldier with a remarkable grasp of the difficulties of fighting in Ireland and of how they could be overcome. More important, he demonstrated that the only way to solve the problem of Ireland was by the application of military force and by the maintenance of a large army there. Policies of conciliation and the like were more than a hundred years out of date. There was a time when the Gaelic leaders could have been won over by persuasion and fair dealing; but many years of outlawry, discrimination or bad faith had ruined that chance. The only effective answer now was withdrawal or conquest. Richard II showed that conquest was not an impractical suggestion; his successors preferred withdrawal and created the Pale.

### *Original bibliographical note*

The exchequer and wardrobe accounts in the PRO, London [TNA], were a primary source of information, in particular the following: E 101/41/26–34, 39; E 101/42/9, 12; E 101/402/20; E 101/403/21; E 101/ 531/31. In the PROI, Dublin [NAI], the few extracts from the memoranda rolls in the Ferguson collection were of small use. Of the printed record sources, *CPR* (1391–9) and *CCR* (1392–9) were particularly useful, as was *RCH*. Curtis prints the texts and translations of the submissions of the Gaelic leaders, together with a number of useful letters, in Curtis, *Ric. II in Ire.* Other letters edited by him appear in Curtis, 'Letters from Ric. II'. *PKCI* and *PPC*, vol. 1, also contain much important material. Of the chronicles, two were most useful: that of Jean Froissart – I used Lord Berners' translation, *The chronicles of Froissart*, (London, 1895) – and Jean Creton's account of the deposition of Richard II (Creton, 'Metrical history', ed. J. Webb, *Archaeologia*, 20 (1824), 1–423). The most valuable of the modern works were Tout, *Chapters*, vols 3 and 4; Anthony Steel, *Richard II* (Cambridge, 1941); and, of course, Curtis, *Med. Ire.* (2nd ed.). The figures for English armies of the fourteenth century are taken from K.B. McFarlane, 'England and the Hundred Years War', *P&P*, 22 (1962), 4.

CHAPTER 14

# Richard, duke of York, as viceroy of Ireland, 1447–1460: with unpublished materials for his relations with the native chiefs*

*Edmund Curtis*

Of the English viceroys who appeared in Ireland in medieval times, none gained such influence or left so great and lasting an impression as Richard Plantagenet, duke of York. 'This race, both English and Irish', wrote Sir John Davies, 'did ever love to be governed by great persons.' The saying was never more justified than in him.

Richard, only son of Richard, earl of Cambridge, and Anne Mortimer, was born on 21 September 1411, on both sides a prince of the blood and high in the succession.[1] By a remarkable series of deaths, he found himself at the age of fourteen the heir to two branches of the royal family, one of them nearer in succession than the reigning dynasty itself. Left without father and mother while still a growing boy, he was the cornerstone uniting the greatest names of the realm. Born to rich estates in England, he inherited later the claim to vast lands in Wales and Ireland. By the extinction of the Mortimers, he became in the eyes of a powerful party the rightful heir of the Plantagenets against the usurping house of Lancaster and, finally, was led into a dynastic struggle in which, though he fell, two of his sons became monarchs of England and himself ancestor of all subsequent kings.

When Richard was but three years old, the first shadow of the family tragedy fell across his path. A plot was formed by his father, Richard, earl of Cambridge, to place Edmund Mortimer on the throne in place of the new king, Henry V. It was in July 1415 – just when Henry was about to sail for France – that Mortimer himself, an unambitious man, revealed the plot and Cambridge was taken, tried and executed. On 25 October 1415, Agincourt was fought and won; and Richard's paternal uncle, Edward of Albemarle or Aumale, duke of York, was

* First published in *JRSAI*, 62 (1932), 158–86 [EN. Notes 11[a], 14[a]–14[c], 15[a]–15[b], 16[a]–16[g], and 39[a]–39[h] below are annotations made by Curtis on the 'unpublished materials' that appear in this essay. These notes were originally included parenthetically in the body of the text. I have placed them in footnotes for the reader's convenience. The numbering and sequence of the notes otherwise remain unchanged]. 1 See table 8, 'Descent of Richard, duke of York'.

TABLE 8
DESCENT OF RICHARD, DUKE OF YORK

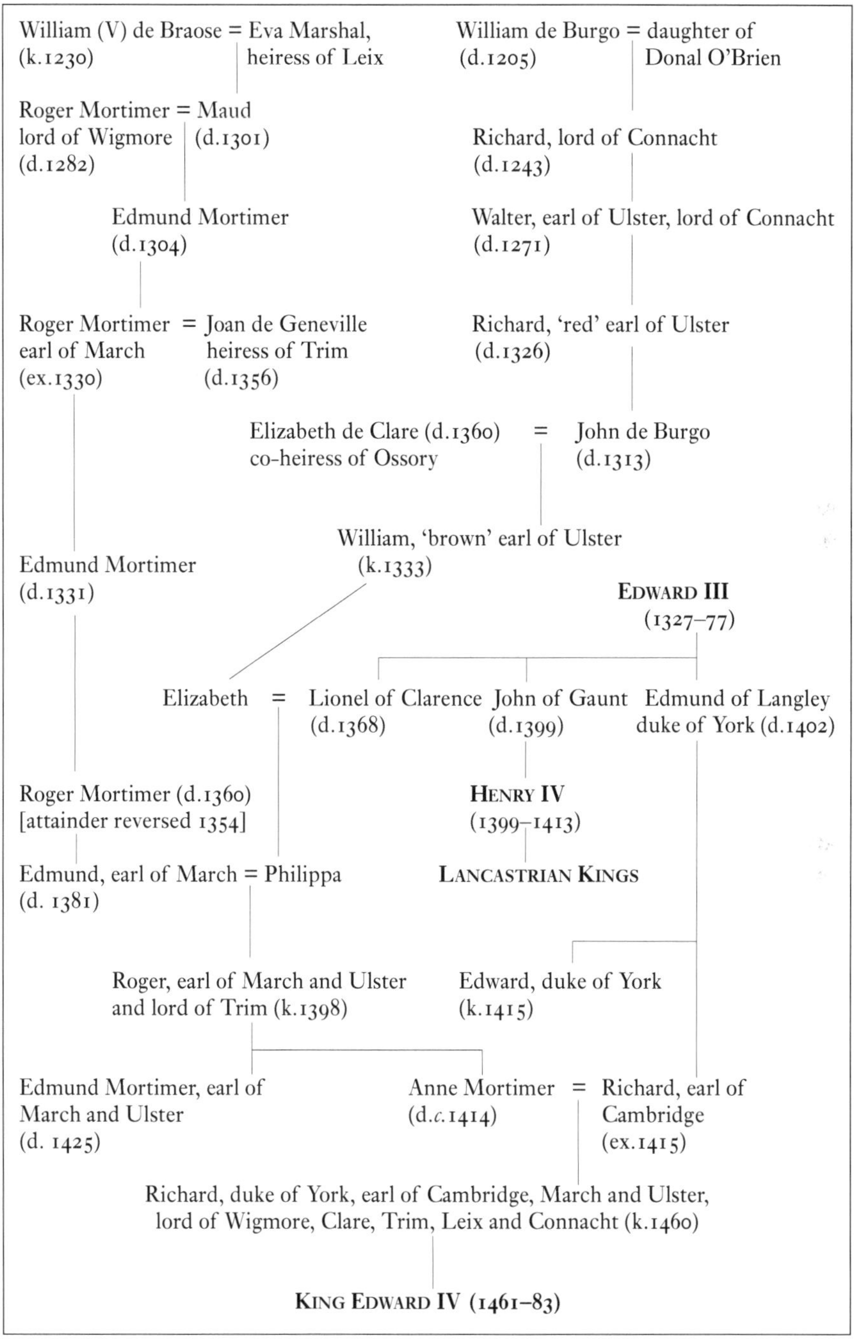

among the English dead. His titles, for he was childless, passed to the young Richard. They included the earldom of Rutland and an empty Irish title, the earldom of Cork, bestowed on this Albemarle by Richard II.

When he was about twelve, Richard was placed under the guardianship of Ralph Neville, earl of Westmoreland. Ralph was a Lancastrian and his first family of nine were the same; but marrying again, he had by Joan Beaufort a second family of fourteen. The latter, for whom there was little provision, not unnaturally fell out with the first brood and in the Wars of the Roses took the Yorkist side. It was with the second family that Richard grew up, and later he married the youngest of the daughters, Cecily, the beauteous 'rose of Raby'. Each of these Nevilles made a fortunate marriage and so Richard became the centre of a powerful family connection. Most important of these was his brother-in-law, Richard Neville, who acquired the earldom of Salisbury by marriage, and his son, again Richard, who in right of his wife became earl of Warwick and is known as the 'kingmaker'.

On 19 January 1425, Richard's only surviving uncle, Edmund Mortimer, died suddenly in Ireland where he was lord lieutenant. This was one of the momentous events of Richard's career. A childless man, Mortimer left to the young duke his great lordships in Ireland and Wales, the earldom of Ulster and the lordships of Trim and Leix in Ireland, the earldom of March, and the lordship of Clare in Wales. The death of Mortimer also made his nephew the cynosure of those who regarded the Lancastrians as usurpers. Edmund's father, Roger, had been by Richard II declared heir to the throne and the claim had passed to the son. More than once, Mortimer had been the occasion of dynastic plots; and now his place was taken by a young prince who was doubly a descendant of Edward III, and nearer to the throne – if descent by females was admitted – than Henry VI himself. As yet, however, the question did not arise. The government treated Richard well and, in 1426, he was fully admitted to the vast family estates, which included the duchy of York, the earldoms of Cambridge, March, Rutland and Ulster, and all the Irish lordships. As he was still a minor, the administration of them was granted to Humfrey, duke of Gloucester, youngest uncle of Henry VI. Gloucester took the young prince under his wing till he came of age in 1432, and York warmly embraced Gloucester's cause.

Richard was now in his full manhood. No personal description of him has come down to us, but there is little doubt that he was well favoured and handsome to a degree. His children, who inherited the good looks also of the 'rose of Raby', were a comely race; and Edward IV, 'the goodliest personage of his time', and after him his grandson, Henry VIII, were the handsomest princes in Europe. The good looks, the affability and the princely bearing of Richard of York were to win him many hearts, especially in this susceptible land.[2]

2 Dr Shaw in his sermon before the duke of Gloucester, afterwards Richard III, in June 1483, referred to York as 'that very Noble Prince, the speciall Patron of Knightly Prowesse, as well

In 1436, York was, through the influence of Gloucester, chosen to succeed the duke of Bedford as regent in France. Although a good soldier and in favour of a vigorous war policy, he could avail little to restore the falling cause of England there. Events were shaping in a menacing fashion for those who surrounded the throne of the young King Henry VI. Gloucester led a war faction in the Lancastrian circle; John Beaufort, duke of Somerset, and William de la Pole, earl of Suffolk, a peace-with-France party. York had a personal feud with Somerset and took Gloucester's side. John, first duke of Somerset, now died and his place was taken by his son Edward. In 1444, Suffolk, now supreme, procured a French wife for King Henry – Margaret of Anjou – at the cost of the cession of Maine. This ambitious and vigorous woman soon ruled the king, 'which was a gode, simple and innocent man'. Naturally, she joined the Beaufort party, which looked on Duke Humfrey as their chief opponent. They saw in the removal of Gloucester the only hope for their cause; but this solution would be disastrous to their side, for Gloucester was next in succession after the imbecile Henry and, if he went, then York would be the heir of the Plantagenets against the dynasty itself.

Finally, in February 1447, Gloucester died at Bury under mysterious circumstances which looked like murder. In the downfall of his party, York was naturally involved. But what could the Beaufort party do with so important a figure? He could not be murdered or attainted, for civil war had not yet begun. He was, therefore, appointed king's lieutenant in Ireland. The pretext was that Ireland was in rebellion and a vigorous governor was needed.[3] It was a feeble pretext, for the loss of France was the real fact in English politics and the decay of English rule in Ireland had continued so long that it had become almost an accepted situation. But York was a skilful politician. Somerset and Suffolk might seem to be getting rid of him by sending him into a virtual exile over the Irish channel; he, on the other hand, could utilize his powerful connections in Ireland to win the whole island over to his side in the impending struggle. He was well aware that his descent from de Lacys, de Burgos and Mortimers made him the greatest of Anglo-Irish magnates – 'lord of the foreigners of Ireland', as the Irish had called the Mortimers – and that on the native Irish he had also an ancestral claim, for he had in his veins the blood of Brian Boru, through the marriage of the first de Burgo with a daughter of Donal O'Brien, king of Thomond.

in all Princely behavior, as in the lineaments and favour of his visage' (Thomas More, *The historie of the pittiful life and unfortunate death of King Edward V and the then duke of York his brother; with the troublesome and tyrannical government of usurping Richard the third and his unfortunate end* (London, 1641), p. 145). 3 'A new rebellion began in Ireland to the great displeasure of the king and his council; for repressing whereof Richard duke of York with a convenient number of men was sent thither as the lieutenant to the King' (Edward Hall, *The union of the two noble and illustre families of Lancastre and York* [...] (London, 1548), the twenty-seventh year of 'the troublous season of Kyng Henry the sixte').

York's appointment as lord lieutenant of Ireland carries us back to Irish history. When his maternal grandfather, Roger Mortimer, was killed in battle with the Leinster Irish at Kellistown in 1398, leaving only an infant son and daughter, and when Richard II was deposed and murdered the year after, all hopes of recovering Ireland had to be suspended. Since the murder of the last de Burgo earl in 1333, the Ulster earldom had receded to the coasts of Antrim and Down, between Coleraine and Carlingford, where only a remnant of the English tenants – Mandevilles, Savages, Russells, Whites etc. – kept up the English tradition. The Gaelic chiefs, formerly vassals of the earls, had become independent and recovered large areas of the north. In the lordship of Connacht, Edmund and Ulick de Burgo had occupied the counties of Mayo and Galway and founded the semi-Gaelic lordships of Mac William Iochtar and Mac William Uachtar. Though their titles were never recognized by English law – for the Mortimers were the legal lords of Connacht – these Burkes could not be dislodged. Of the Mortimer inheritance, the liberty of Trim remained the most English and the richest portion. Leix had gone back almost entirely to the native race, for Laoiseach O'More had in 1342 recovered almost all this patrimony of his race and expelled the Englishry.

The minority of Edmund Mortimer completed the ruin of his Irish heritage. Treated as a dangerous subject and kept under restraint by Henry IV, he was not restored to the earldom of March and his Irish estates till 1413. Irish and Scots ravaged his lands in Ulster and the earl of Orkney did particular damage to this earldom while it was in the king's hands in 1407.[4] Finally, on 9 May 1423, Mortimer was appointed lord lieutenant of Ireland with the object of placating the English and Irish who looked upon him as the greatest of all their magnates.[5] He arrived in February 1424 and, in the winter, held court at Trim where the leading Gaelic princes of Ulster came to him. But on 19 January 1425, he died suddenly of the plague, and thus was extinguished the almost-royal name of Mortimer, three heirs of which had successively since 1380 been cut off in early manhood in this country. James, earl of Ormond, acting as justiciar, arrived on the scene and succeeded in making with Eoghan O'Neill – tanist to Donal, the reigning chief – a treaty in which he recognized the young Richard, earl of Ulster, as his lord and pledged himself to restore to him the 'bonnaght' or military service owed by the O'Neills and their vassals to the earls of Ulster.[6]

To return to the heir of Mortimer. On 9 December 1447, Richard, duke of York, was commissioned to act as king's lieutenant in Ireland for ten years on terms arranged between him and the government, but he did not arrive for eighteen months.

4 *Chronicon Adae de Usk, 1377–1404*, ed. E.M. Thompson (2nd ed., London, 1904), p. 62. 5 For the terms of his appointment, see *Lib. mun. pub. Hib.*, i, pt 4, pp 94–5. 6 See the treaty of 23 June 1425 at Dundalk in Edmund Curtis, 'The "bonnaght" of Ulster', *Hermathena*, 46 (1931), 95–8.

Of all the titles by which the chief governorship of Ireland was held, that of king's lieutenant was the highest.[7] Besides being invested with almost sovereign powers, the lord lieutenant was paid a substantial sum set forth in indentures between himself and the crown. In York's case, he was to receive the entire royal revenue of Ireland, without rendering account, and also from the English exchequer 4,000 marks for the first year and £2,000 yearly for the remainder. He could let the king's land to farm, appoint and replace all save the highest officers, levy and maintain as many armed men as he thought fit, appoint a deputy, and return home when he pleased. His duties were to keep and cause to be kept the king's peace and laws, to punish all lieges, whether English or Irish, offending against the same, to summon and convoke, prorogue and dissolve parliaments and councils, and make statutes and ordinances according to custom. Where necessary, he must cause proclamation to be made for all those having salaries or fees of the king's gift to be ready to set out with the lieutenant to resist the king's enemies and rebels in Ireland. For a reasonable fine, he might admit to the king's peace Englishmen and Irishmen who had rebelled. He might use the royal power if necessary against all English rebels and Irish enemies, and make provisions for the setting out and defending of land recovered from the enemy or confiscated from rebels.

Ireland, as a result of neglect and misgovernment, had by now fallen into that threefold division of race and law which it retained till 1603. Only in the 'land of peace' or 'obedient shires' were English speech and common law secure. At present, this still included most of Leinster and Meath, but it was steadily dwindling until it became the tiny 'Pale' of 1500. Another large part of Ireland was held on feudal terms by the Anglo-Normans, who had come over as Frenchmen rather than Englishmen. Their liberties, lordships and 'marcher lands' covered a third of Ireland. In a sense, they might still be reckoned English, for they never repudiated English loyalty or their tenures under the crown. Their leading magnates – the earls of Desmond, Ormond and Kildare – were barons of the king, spoke English, kept the English order and married wives of their own race. But the Burkes, Poers, Roches etc. of the south and west were more and more embracing the Gaelic order. Surrounded as they were by the fertile Gaelic stock, they were destined to succumb to the language and tradition of the majority. As early as 1366, the Statutes of Kilkenny had denounced them as 'degenerate English', but in defiance of these statutes they refused their homages and rents to the crown, abandoned common law for brehon law and 'march' law, married Irish wives, practised private war and

7 Wood, 'Office of chief governor', pp 207–8. *Cal. Carew MSS*, v, 477–8, gives a summary of the covenant between Henry VI and Richard for the government of Ireland, dated 29 Sept. 1449. Gilbert, *Viceroys*, p. 585, gives the duke's compact with the king on a later date. In *PPC*, vi, 92, the date of the indentures is given as 29 Sept. 1447.

imposed on their tenants, English as well as Irish, those exactions based on native custom which were known as 'coign and livery, bonnaght, sorren' etc.

A third element was the native Irish living under their own law. Since the Statutes of Kilkenny, they had been deemed 'Irish enemies' or 'mere Irish', outside the protection and duties of English law. Their position was very different from that of their Norman neighbours, for they had never been in any true sense 'liege subjects', nor had their countries ever been properly subjected to English government. Only a general conquest could now have brought them under that government. Only constant warfare could drive them back from the borders of the Pale. To make individual terms with them was now the policy, or to extend 'English law and liberty' to one chief or another by act of parliament or royal patent. Seldom did these treaties have any real success. To pass a general act of emancipation had formerly been tried and failed. Not till Henry VIII's reign was a single Gaelic prince made a tenant-in-chief under the crown, and not till James I's reign was the native population admitted to the benefits of the common law.

The Anglo-Irish had their parliament of prelates, peers, knights of the shires, burgesses and proctors for the lesser clergy, while above parliament, and forming the most important part of it, was the Dublin government, the standing council headed by the lieutenant or deputy, the chancellor, treasurer and chief justices. At one time, the council had controlled parliament in the English interest. Now a home rule party had grown up among the English of the Pale led by the great earls. They had many grievances in the neglect and misgovernment of Ireland, the loss of large areas to the Irish, the discrimination against Irishmen in England, the rapacity of English officials and their contempt for the Anglo-Irish, and the continued absence of the king and of many of the greatest proprietors. To govern Ireland by the Irish-born became their objective; the 'English by birth' were held enemies of the 'English by blood'; and a handful of nobles aimed at controlling the government in the name of a limited Anglo-Irish patriotism.

It was by no means certain that this class would welcome Richard of York if he attempted to restore the English lordship of Ireland. There was, however, a considerable party, drawn from the church, the towns and the lesser Englishry, which looked to England for support and thought English-born viceroys would keep order and justice better than the feudal magnates. This might be called a 'unionist' party. From 1419 to 1447, it was led by John Talbot, earl of Shrewsbury, several times viceroy, and his brother, Richard, archbishop of Dublin and chancellor till 1449, both strong Lancastrians. On the other hand, the patriot party rallied round James, fourth earl of Ormond, called the 'white earl,' who was several times viceroy from 1420 to 1446.

England had its factions; so had Ireland. As England was on the verge of a civil war inspired by feudal ambitions, so was Ireland.[8] Finally, the Anglo-Irish

8 See *PKCI*, where the introduction gives an account of the Talbot–Ormond struggle (pp

party was put into the saddle by the action of Richard of York, and not for fifty years did the unionist party lift up its head again.

In 1447, the earl of Shrewsbury abandoned his Irish office for good, and the appointment of York ended the Talbot and Lancastrian regime. Richard from England appointed as his deputy Richard Nugent, baron of Delvin, with commission to hold a parliament in his name in Dublin in March 1449. It was shown in this assembly how 'over-mighty subjects' and family factions were over-riding popular rights. The citizens of Limerick had been granted the privilege of assembling yearly to elect a mayor and two bailiffs to govern the city for the year. They now complained that for many years this privilege had been misused by the mayor and bailiffs who

> for that purpose, as well to take maintenances of false actions and quarrels of men of their nation, friends and allies, against others of their neighbours, as to have rule and government of the said city in their hands, continually to oppress and disseise their said neighbours, do assemble the day before the election and by covin amongst themselves, with the names of all the citizens who are of their party and of others who are against their intentions, they write only so many as they please, that they may have their purpose and prevail in the same election.

Only those written down would be summoned; many honest citizens not summoned dare not come. These circumstances resulted in oppressive injuries and false actions. It was therefore enacted that the intent of the charter should be put into effect.[9]

In April 1449, the English council gave orders for ships to be collected at Beaumaris for the conveyance of Richard and his suite, and finally, on 6 July, the duke of York landed at Howth 'with great pomp and glory', accompanied by his wife and a number of troops. The annals of the Four Masters say that he was 'received with great honour, and the earls of Ireland went into his house, as did also the Irish adjacent to Meath, and gave him as many beeves for the use of his kitchen as it pleased him to demand'. Such was the charm that Richard from the first displayed that, says Hall, 'he not only appeased the fury of the wild savage people there but also got him such love and favour of the country and the inhabitants, that their sincere, lovely and friendly affection could never be separated from him and his lineage'.

The first great act of Richard was to summon both English and Irish to his standard and recall them to the royal allegiance. Within ten days, he had called

xxxiii–li). See also J.H. Bernard, 'Richard Talbot, archbishop and chancellor, 1418–1449', *PRIA*, 35:C5 (1919), 218–29. 9 For the proceedings of this parliament, see *Stat. Hen. VI*, pp 129, 163.

out the 'royal service' of Ireland. After a short delay at Dublin, he took his way to Trim, stayed some while there in de Lacy's great castle, and then marched into Ulster, displaying the 'black dragon' banner of the earldom, in order to spare Irish feelings any exhibition of English pride and to show the men of Ulster that their hereditary lord had come.[10]

Some contemporary documents attest how willing the Gaels were to submit to so great a prince.[11] I quote them in the original:

> This bill makyth mencioun of the Yrisshmen that beth comen yn to my Lord of Yorke in so short a space, that is to say byfor the assumpcion of our Ladi A° Dom. MCCCCXLIX regni Henrici sexti XXVII° [15 August 1449].
>
> Fyrst Macgenos is come yn with VI^C men on hors and fote and 2 men harneysed and a nakyd[11a] man betwyxt them. Also Makemawn is come yn with VIII^C men well harnyssed on hors and fot. Also bothe theye Reyles with VII^C men on hors and fote in ye same way as is beforsaid. Also Makoelyn is come yn with VIII^C bassenettes on hors and fote with many oon other that beth the Kynges legemen. For these other Yrysshmen beth come yn by grace to do ye Kynges service so that the nombre of these people comyth to XXXM^l.

Accompanied by these forces[12] and the hosting of Meath and the Pale, Richard turned south and from Dublin invaded Wicklow to suppress O'Byrne (probably

**10** Gilbert, *Viceroys*, pp 352, 353; Hall, *Houses of Lancastre and Yorke*. **11** BL, Cotton Titus B XI, pt 1 – a collection of manuscript materials relative to Ireland, mostly transcripts of originals which have perished – contains the quoted documents, at pp 38, 38*d* and 40. Only a portion of these has been printed, namely in Gilbert, *Facsimiles*; otherwise, they have never been published. **11a** 'unarmoured'. **12** This number ('XXXM^l'), if meant for 30,050, is incredible and must be a mistake. It is more likely that 3,050 is meant, a substantial aid from the chiefs named. These are: Magennis of Iveagh (600 men), MacMahon of Oriel (800 men), the two O'Reillys of Cavan (700 men) and MacQuillan (800 men). Note the distinction drawn between the Irish *who come in by grace* (not being natural subjects) and MacQuillan and other English of Ulster that are the king's liegemen. MacQuillan was rightly a de Mandeville and his family, lords of the Route in north Antrim, were Norman in origin. This is also attested by the superior equipment of his troops who wore 'basnets', i.e. helmets, unlike the Irish. This portion of BL, Cotton Titus B XI, is printed in Gilbert, *Facsimiles*, iii, pl. 40 [EN. Curtis further elaborated his argument for identifying the Mandevilles with the MacQuillans in his articles, 'The medieval earldom of Ulster, 1333–1603', *Proceedings and Reports of the Belfast Natural History and Philosophy Society* (1932 for 1930–1), 67–80; and 'The MacQuillan or Mandeville lords of the route', *PRIA*, 44:C4 (1938), 99–113. The identification is undoubtedly erroneous. See Kenneth Nicholls, 'Anglo-French Ireland and after', *Peritia*, 1 (1982), 384; idem, 'Scottish mercenary kindreds in Ireland, 1250–1600' in Seán Duffy (ed.), *The world of the galloglass: kings, warlords and warriors in Ireland and Scotland, 1200–1600* (Dublin, 2007), pp 88–9].

Brian or Bernard, but his name is not given here), the chief enemy of the Dublin colony. After some skirmishing, O'Byrne submitted and was sworn to be the king's true servant. This is recorded in the document we are quoting thus:

> And so my lord went with that meyny [as above] into O'Bryns contre and there destroyed muche of his londes to the tyme that he came yn to my lord. And he is sworn to be ye Kyngs trewe servant and to bear the tribute to y[d] Kyng, that is II for every acre. And if any wrakke be, that is to say shippe or bote, y Kyngs Exchetour shall eschete it in y[e] Kynges name. Hymself, likewise his children and the best of his meyny shall weer English array and lern English.[13]
>
> All this my lord hath done in this short space.
>
> *per General' Receptorem.*

After this triumph, Richard knighted some of the English lords of the Pale who had served under him. There followed a great and general flocking in of Irish chiefs with presents for the victorious prince and also of Anglo-Norman lords to renew their homage to the state. It is recorded thus in the documents we are quoting:[14]

> These beth ye knyghtes that were made at Symondeswode in O Bryns contre. First y lordis of the Parlement. Robert Preston, lord of Gormanston and Christopher Plonket, lord of Kylene. Of Develyn Nicholas Woder, Mayr of Develyn, Robert Burnell, Shiref of Develyn. Of Meth William Welles, Richard Maureward, baron of Skrene, Robert Bernuall, John de la Hyde, John Kerdiffe, Richard Twete.[14a] Uryell John Gernon. These beth y[e] Yryshmen that beth come to my lord and hath present[14b] him. Ferall O Riall CCCLX kyne, Donald O Ferall CCC kyne, Arte McGynes CCC kyne, Bernard O Bryn CCCC kyne and II hobys[14c] to my lady, Toles O Farcele XL kyne, Felemen McMathan CCLXXX kyne, Faghten O More CCCXX kyne, Kayre O Dymsy CLXXX kyne, O Morough CXX kyne, Felemen O Nolan CXX kyne, Ferall McGoyoghan MCC kyne.

13 The provision regarding wrecks shows that O'Byrne could then command the Wicklow coast between Bray and Arklow. This part of the documents is signed by the Receiver General. Mr Liam Price informs me that 'Symondeswode' is Kiltimon (Ir. *Coill tSíomóin*), par. Killisky, bar. Newcastle, a few miles south of Newtownmountkennedy, Co. Wicklow. In Henry VIII's reign, the O'Byrne's had a castle there from which they ravaged the Pale. This castle was perhaps built by the Lawless family at the time of the original Anglo-Norman settlement of Wicklow. **14** BL, Cotton Titus B XI, pt 1, p. 38*d*. **14a** Tuite. **14b** 'made presents to'. **14c** 'light horses'.

These gifts of kine amount to 3,620, a handsome tribute. We must assume that they came in after the submission of O'Byrne, as he gives 400 cows and two hobbies. We note that McGeoghegan of Meath gives 1,200, three times more than any other chief, a great evidence of his wealth and of the fertility of his country.

Later on we have a general and final list of the great men, Irish and Anglo-Normans, who came in to the duke of York,[15] namely:

> Ferall O Riall, Donald O Ferall, Artor McGynes, Bernard O Bryn, Toles O Fercole, Felem McMathan, Faughten O'More, Kaire O Dymsy, O Morowgh, Felem O Hanlon, Ferall McGoyoghan, Donald McMorogh, Colo O Hanlon, Henry O Neel, Odo McMahan, Magonius Balow O Hanlan, Byrmyngham,[15a] Karolus O'Hanlan, Donald son of Donald O Hanlan, Mauricius son of Karol O Hanlan, Felem O Hanlan,[15b] Terencius sone of Patrick O Hanlan, Bernard sone of Patrick O Hanlan, Dewet McCan O Hanlan, the Erle of Desmound, the Lord Cogane, the Lord Dalabert, the Lord Roch, the Whight Knyght, the Lord Howeth.
>
> All these beth kynges, dukes, erlys and barones that beth come in to my lord of Yorke byfor Mighelmes A.D. 1449 anno regni Henrici sexti XXVIII° and beth sworn trew legemen to y^e Kyng of England and his heyrs male, and to my lord of York and to his heyrs male and leid hostages and beth ibound by endenture, and with the myght of Jesus or twelmonth come to an end y^e wildest Yrishman in Yrland shall be swore English.
>
> *per Philippum Wode.*

This is a very curious set of documents. It displays a pronounced intention to extol the duke to make out that this remarkable series of homagings and tributes was as much to him as earl of Ulster and lord of Meath as it was to him in his capacity of lord lieutenant for Henry VI. In short, while it would read well in England as a remarkable bringing to heel of 'rebel English' and 'Irish enemies', it was in reality a clever enlisting on the Yorkist side of all the enthusiasm and loyalty felt in Ireland by both races for the duke, who not only could assert hereditary claims to their loyalty, but affirmed them by his personal majesty and charm. Not only had he the lords of the Pale in his following, but the most powerful of the Old English of Munster had come in under the earl of Desmond, and an even greater number of Irish chieftains had sought his court with rich gifts. It is worthwhile examining the list of these dynasts to see what septs they represented.

**15** BL, Cotton Titus B XI, pt 1, p. 40. **15a** Bermingham of Carbury, Co. Kildare. **15b** Probably a repetition.

The Ulster chiefs are in order of importance: Henry O'Neill, son and heir of Eoghan the reigning dynast; Art Magennis of Iveagh; Felim and Odo[16] McMahon of Oriel; Ferghal and another O'Reilly of Cavan; and no less than nine O'Hanlons of Orior, anxious to show their loyalty, namely Colow,[16a] Karolus,[16b] Magonius Balow,[16c] Donal son of Donal, Maurice,[16d] son of 'Karol', Bernard[16e] son of Brian, Felim, Terence son of Patrick, Dewet[16f] McCan O'Hanlon. Their ancestors had several times affirmed their vassalage to the earls of Ulster. But there was no word of O'Cahan, O'Donnell, Maguire, McCartan, O'Neill of Clandeboy. From Meath and Leinster, the submitting chiefs were Mageoghegan, O'Dempsey of Clanmalier, O'More of Leix, Donal MacMurrough, O'Morrough of Co. Wexford, O'Farrell of Longford, O'Nolan of Forth in Co. Carlow and O'Toole of Fercullen.[16g] Among these the name of greatest repute was that of Donal Reagh Kavanagh MacMurrough, the Irish king of Leinster. His influence would bring in his nominal vassals, O'Morrough, O'More, O'Dempsey, O'Nolan, O'Byrne and O'Toole. The duke was indeed titular lord of Leix and hence had a claim to the allegiance of O'More, as he had to that of Mageoghegan as heir to the earls of Meath. But the motive of most of these chiefs must have been to stand in well with so great a prince with such Irish connections.

But too much must not be made of these pleasant interchanges. Events were soon to show of the duke, as of the unfortunate King Richard II, how 'the Irish mocked him with their light submission'. Bernard O'Byrne soon ceased to pay the annuities he had undertaken to pay to the king of England, and his other promises went the same way.

The naive and enthusiastic forecast that within a year, by God's help, 'the wildest Irishman in Ireland would become English' can but evoke a smile. Such hopes were often founded on the all too facile promises of our race, which never meant anything serious by them. Indeed, we may take it that the Irish chiefs were only buying off by gifts and facile submission a conquest which had menaced O'Byrne and might assail them all. When Duke Richard called out the royal service of Ireland, he had it in mind, while not despising the services of such chiefs as might come to his side, to march a great colonial force against the more dangerous of the Irish dynasts, especially the Leinster ones, and to end the scandal of the continuous recovery of Ireland and the bullying of the unfortunate settlers by the Gael. The enfeebled colony, however, was not capable of a response which might have led to a reconquest, and Richard had to be content with showy but useless homagings on the part of Gaelic chiefs,

16 Aedh. **16a** Cu-Uladh. **16b** (?) Cathaoir. **16c** (?) Mahon *Balbh*, 'the deaf'. **16d** Murchadh or Muircherbach. **16e** Brian. **16f** (?) Duach. **16g** So I read the curious 'Toles Ofarcele', which coming after Bernard O Bryn would seem to indicate the neighbouring sept of O'Tooles of Fercullen (present Powerscourt demesne).

which read well in England but meant little or nothing in Ireland. When the duke, on 16 June 1449, sent out the usual form of summons to John Mey, archbishop of Armagh, 'to send to him all the defensible men he might gather, and to have of archers and others purveyed with victuals for six days to go on a hosting with him, and to meet him at the Bree [Bray] on Lammas day now next coming at ten at the bell by fore none', the archbishop regretted his inability to attend 'his mighty and most worthy prince, his trusty and full gracious lord', because of his pending visitation of his diocese, and went on to give an account of the state of affairs in the north.

O'Neill, his sons and subjects, would not allow him to make his visitation of the north and had practised letting and undue occupation of the church lands and injuries and excesses to the archbishop and his people; therefore, he had found it necessary to impose upon him and his peers and subjects a general interdict 'of which we openly and with all solemnity did execution in the market of Dundalk on Monday now passed'.[17]

Since 1432, Eoghan O'Neill had ruled over Tyrone. He it was who had made the treaty of 1425, referred to above.[18] In that treaty, Eoghan had admitted himself liegeman of King Henry and vassal of Duke Richard. He had renounced all usurpations made by him or his ancestors against the duke, the archbishop of Armagh and the English tenantry of Ulster. But the treaty thus made Eoghan did little to observe. During his kingship, which lasted from 1432 to 1455, he proved himself an able and vigorous statesman, warrior and conqueror, who made the O'Neills dominant over all Ulster. One of his many conquests was that of the Fews, an extensive mountain country in south Armagh, which for long was the gate of the north. This he gave to his son Aedh, who founded the line of O'Neill of the Fews.

The time had now, however, come to renew this *entente* between the house of York and the O'Neill dynasty. Archbishop Mey, who ruled Armagh from 1444 to 1456, in this as in other matters laboured to make smooth the way of the great duke. But his own way in his northern diocese had not been too smooth among the wild fighting chieftains. More than once, they bound themselves to obey him spiritually and respect his temporal rights; but the impression is that they did little of either, for though an archbishop he was of the English, and they were the old race.[19] He had to begin his episcopate with an affectionate invocation to 'his dear sons, Eugene O'Neill, captain of his nation, and all and singular his spiritual sons and subjects, as well ecclesiastics as lay, who are held to our church of Armagh in fruits, rights, offerings, customs and services'; for O'Neill was the greatest temporal prince in the archdiocese. Later, Eugenius

17 Gilbert, *Viceroys*, p. 582. 18 See Curtis, 'The "bonnaght" of Ulster', pp 95–8. 19 See transcript of Mey's register, TCD, MS 557/7, pp 20, 106, 287, 475 [EN. Cf. *Reg. Mey*, nos. 2, 35, 138, 222].

O'Reilly of Cavan, 'captain of his nation', took an oath of obedience to his lordship, and bound thereto himself, his sons, brothers, kinsmen, successors and subjects forever.

The archbishops of Armagh, however, as English or Anglo-Irish, had since 1333 exercised little authority and received few rents from the northern part of their archdiocese, situated as it was 'inter hibernicos', that is among the O'Neills, McMahons and other chiefs who preserved in the north their Celtic independence. The archbishops generally resided at Termonfeckin in Co. Louth and got their revenues mainly from their Anglo-Irish subjects. Visits to the primatial city of Armagh were rare; so were visitations of the northern parts of the province, and could only be achieved by cooperation of O'Neill and the native chiefs of Derry and Armagh. So inveterate was the opposition of these chiefs, even to Mey – whom as a good man they honoured, though as a 'saxon' they kept him at bay – that Archbishop Mey had finally to launch the major excommunication at Eoghan O'Neill and Henry, his first-born.[20]

At least on this occasion, the good archbishop was able to bring the Great O'Neill to an imposing act of submission and, on 27 August 1449, at Drogheda, seven weeks after the duke's arrival, Henry O'Neill, eldest son of Eoghan, acting for his father who was now growing old, made by indenture terms with the duke similar to those of 1425.[21]

O'Neill bound himself, his father, brothers etc., to be the men of the duke as earl of Ulster and to restore to him all such manors, castles and lordships of the duke as were formerly possessed by the earls of Ulster and which Eoghan, Henry, their sons etc., have occupied; as also the ancient 'bonnaght' or military service due from the Irish chiefs of Ulster to the de Burgo earls. If the duke or his heirs or their deputies shall be at war with any Englishman or Irishman in his country of Ulster, Henry and his heirs will support them with a force of 500 horsemen well-armed and 500 foot with lances, axes and bows. He and they will surrender all lands usurped from the Englishry, especially the Fews, the heritage of the 'Pedelewes'. Also they will render all temporalities, rents and tithes due to the archbishop and other bishops and ecclesiastics. Finally, Henry undertakes for the homage and fealty of himself, his father, sons and brothers to pay 600 fat beeves to the duke.

Of this solemn treaty, we may remark that few of the positive clauses were carried out. Doubtless, the duke got his beeves, or the 300 for which he stipulated, condoning the rest. He seems to have received some military aid in Ireland from Henry O'Neill, for this 'loyal service' was publicly recognized later in an Irish act of parliament in 1481. The archbishop, for the time at least,

**20** For the excommunication of O'Neill, see transcript of Mey's register, TCD, MS 557/7, p. 475 [EN. Cf. *Reg. Mey*, no. 222]. **21** For the Latin text, see Curtis, 'The "bonnaght" of Ulster', pp 87–91.

seems to have recovered some authority among the Irish of his diocese and in his city of Armagh. But there is no evidence that English tenants received the lands which had passed again into native hands. Indeed, an enactment of the Irish parliament held before the duke himself in October 1449, less than two months after the signing the treaty, directed the removing of O'Neill and his power 'from certain lande of Bedlowes of the Rocke called "the fues" into which he forcibly entered'.

Nevertheless, the treaty had some enduring results. When Henry O'Neill succeeded his father, Eoghan, in 1455 as 'captain and principal of his nation', Archbishop Mey confirmed his election publicly in the monastery of SS Peter and Paul at Armagh, 'as a good man and likely to be of good to the church and people of Ulster'. Other pleasing interchanges followed between the archbishop and O'Neill; and later, in 1463, York's son, now king of England, sent Henry, as greatest of the Ulster chiefs who owed him traditional allegiance as earl of Ulster, a present of scarlet cloth and a collar of gold of the king's livery.[22]

It was with great apparent glory and triumph that Richard returned to Dublin, as it were the hero and hope of a united Ireland. We like to think that his beautiful wife, 'the rose of Raby', had made an impression on the Irish heart, as when O'Byrne presented her with two hobbys. At least there can be no doubt that it was a highly popular event when, on 21 October 1449, the viceroy's third son was born in Dublin – George, the future 'false, fleeting, perjured Clarence'. The bond already formed between the house of York and Ireland was doubly strengthened by this event. The young prince was looked upon as 'one of ourselves', an Irishman by birth as well as descent, and the devotion to his name was shown years later when Lambert Simnel was crowned king in Dublin in the belief that he was Clarence's son, Edward of Warwick. The earls of Ormond and Desmond stood sponsors at the font.

On 'the Friday next before the feast of St Luke the Evangelist' (18 October 1449), the duke opened his first parliament in Dublin.[23] At this, it was enacted that none should keep more horsemen or footmen than they could maintain, and it was declared felony to exact coigne, pledges or 'cuddies' for this purpose. In the preamble to this act were set forth the grievances suffered by the 'poor husbandmen and tenants' of Ireland. The marchers kept horsemen and footmen both English and Irish in far greater numbers than they could afford to maintain, and they solved this problem by descending on the unfortunate colonists, oppressing and destroying them by exaction of coigne; and, in the time of harvest, came upon their 'corn and meadows with horses both day and night, paying nothing therefor, but many times rob, spoil, and kill the husbandmen and tenants'.

**22** Curtis, *Med. Ire.* (1st ed.), p. 359. **23** For the acts of this parliament, see *Stat. Hen. VI*, pp 166–77.

> The captains of the said marchers, their wives and their pages, certain times of the year gather and bring with them the king's Irish enemies, both men and women, and English rebels, as well in times of war as of peace, to night suppers called cuddies upon the said tenants and husbandmen.

They lodged on one man as many as a hundred of their following for the night. The Irish profited too by spying out the secrecy of the land and were able to guide Irish enemies and their thieves into the English country to the utter destruction and undoing of the land. Another act was directed against robbers and evildoers who were increasing and destroying the commons with thievings, burnings, and manslaughterings. It was made lawful for any liege man to kill all manner of notorious and known thieves found robbing and spoiling or breaking houses by night or day.

This was virtually a confession on the part of the government that it could no longer govern. About this time, the English of the city and county of Cork addressed a memorial to York's young son, Edmund, earl of Rutland, who bore the title of earl of Cork, and to the viceroy and lords of the council in Dublin to the effect that ruin was impending in Munster on account of the dissensions of the English lords, the Carews, Barnewalls, de Courcys, Arundels etc.[24] These had fallen

> at variance amongst themselves; the weakest took Irishmen to their aid and so vanquished the enemies; but at last the Irish were stronger than they and drove them all away and have now the whole country, but that the lords Roche, Barry and Courcy do remain with the best part of their ancestors' possessions.

Wherefore, the townsmen of Cork, Kinsale and Youghal prayed that, after parliament, the duke and council would come to Cork and bind the English lords on pain of loss of lands, life and goods not to make war upon each other; that two good justices should be sent to set the general lawlessness in order, as also

> some captain with twenty Englishmen, that may be captains over us all; and we will rise with him when need is to redress these enormities all at our cost, and if you do not we are all cast away, and then farewell Munster for ever.

The duke of York took up his abode for the winter at Trim, and held his court in his ancestral castle there, which he restored. Before he left, his visit was marked by benefactions to St Mary's abbey, to which he gave a place called

24 Gilbert, *Viceroys*, pp 356–7. The petition was probably made in 1460 when the young Edmund, earl of Rutland and Cork (b.1443), was nominally chancellor of Ireland under his father, the duke. But it may have been addressed to him earlier as earl of Cork.

Porch-field. Perhaps the Yellow Tower, the only part of the abbey now remaining was built by him, for the abbey church had been built in 1368 and was restored at about this time; while the steeple of the parish church bears evidence of being his handiwork, for the arms of York and Mortimer, cut in stone, were built into it.[25]

In the late spring of 1450, Richard held his second parliament at Drogheda.[26] He was evidently disenchanted with the Irish in spite of their recent show of submission, and had he been properly supported from England might have again rallied the whole colony for a defensive war against them. For parliament granted that the royal service be proclaimed and a levy made, in spite of a previous statute prohibiting such proclamation for ten years, because the lieutenant

> has had no payment from our said lord the king for the protection of this his said land, and he is likely to bear great charges and costs in resistance of the Irish who, according to appearances, mean to go to war.

But even his stipulated salary did not reach the viceroy. As he became more and more straitened he wrote to his brother-in-law, the earl of Salisbury, recounting the damages he had suffered at the hands of MacGeoghegan who, 'with three or four Irish captains associated with a great fellowship of English rebels', had burned his town of Rathmore and several villages adjacent in his liberty of Meath, and begging that his payment might be hastened that he might 'wage men in sufficient number, for to resist the malice of the same enemies and punish them in such wise that others which would do the same for the lack of resistance in time may take example'. He insisted on his dire need; if the money should not be sent

> my power cannot stretch to keep this land in obeisance. And very necessity will compel me to come unto England to live there upon my poor livelihood, for I had lever be dead than any inconvenience should fall thereunto in my default; for it shall never be chronicled nor remain in scripture, by the grace of God, that Ireland was lost by my negligence.[27]

**25** Richard Butler, *Some notices of the castle and of the ecclesiastical buildings of Trim, compiled from various authorities* (Trim, 1854), p. 76. **26** *Stat. Hen. VI*, p. 181. **27** John O'Donovan (ed.), 'Covenant between Mageoghegan and the Fox, with brief historical notices of the two families' in *The miscellany of the Irish Archaeological Society* (IAS, Dublin, 1846), p. 181. See also *Cal. Carew MSS*, v, p. 288; Edmund Campion, 'A historie of Ireland written in the yeare 1571' in Sir James Ware (ed.), *The historie of Ireland, collected by three learned authors, viz. Meredith Hanmer, doctor in divinitie: Edmund Campion, sometime fellow of St Johns Colledge in Oxford: and Edmund Spenser* (Dublin, 1633), p. 98; Gilbert, *Viceroys*, pp 361–2.

MacGeoghegan was one of the chieftains who had come into his house the previous autumn bringing gifts of kine, but he was now in arms again. He committed 'great depredations upon the English', plundering and burning villages and towns in Meath to such an extent that 'it would be impossible to enumerate all that was destroyed by him during that war'. The duke advanced with the English of Meath, displaying the royal standard. He was met at Mullingar by MacGeoghegan's son 'with a great many horsemen well mounted and armed', an opposition so formidable that 'the English made peace with him, forgiving him all the spoyles he had done for graunting to them that peace'.[28]

Meanwhile in England, the duke of Suffolk – chief bulwark of the Lancastrian cause and peace with France – was impeached in February 1450, and done to death in trying to escape overseas by an English mob. Duke Humfrey was avenged, and 'thus began sorrow upon sorrow and death upon death'. Jack Cade's rebellion soon followed, and lasted from May to July. Its leader was a man of respectable position though of doubtful origin. He called himself John Mortimer and claimed to be a cousin of the duke of York, but this has never been substantiated.

York was, in truth, merely biding his time in Ireland; his ambitions were centered in England, where he was at last resolved to stand forward as the true Plantagenet and the saviour of the realm against the usurping Lancastrian house and the misgovernment of Somerset, Suffolk and Queen Margaret. He now thought the time had come, for he suddenly left Ireland in September 1450 and landed in Wales to the great alarm of his political opponents, who made vain but strenuous efforts to prevent his reaching the king. The false accusations of these enemies behind his back were sufficient cause of his return without royal permission. In a letter to the king on his arrival, York opens thus:

> Please your highness to conceive that since my departing out of this your realm by your commandment, and being in your service in your land of Ireland, I have been informed that divers language hath been said of me to your most excellent estate that would sound to my dishonour and reproach and charge of my person.

And further on he says, 'certain persons laboured to indict me of treason'.[29] The bickerings at court continued, but hostility was still veiled and, on 11 February 1451, the duke was confirmed in his office as lord lieutenant of Ireland.

During the ups and downs of the contest that finally, in 1455, became an open civil war, York had few thoughts to spare for Ireland; and so, for nine years

28 *AMacFirbis*, p. 226. 29 York was at Trim on 26 Aug. 1450 (Butler, *Notes on Trim*, p. 79). For the letter to Henry VI, see James Gairdner (ed.). *The Paston letters, A.D. 1422-1509*, 6 vols (London, 1904), i, 80.

of his absence, the land was governed by Anglo-Irish magnates, who put into effect their home rule policy. To let Ireland have constant parliaments was York's policy, for in England he posed as a constitutional champion.

James, fourth earl of Ormond, called the 'white earl', was an old and practised hand at the reins of government. He seems to have been a supporter of York, but his son James was a partisan of Lancaster, for he had married the sister and co-heir of the duke of Somerset and was created earl of Wiltshire in 1449. The old earl, whom Duke Richard created his deputy, held a great council in November 1450 at Drogheda, which was afterwards adjourned to Dublin.[30] This council provided that the next parliament should be held before Easter, in spite of the fact that

> the custom of the land of Ireland is, and has been for time whereof memory runs not, that it shall not be lawful for any lieutenant, deputy, justice, or any other governor to ordain, summon or hold any parliament in the said land except once a year.

Whether the proposed parliament of 1451 was held we cannot tell, as none of its records survive. The old earl of Ormond himself died in August 1452; he is styled in Irish annals, 'the best captaine of the English nation that was in Irland and England in those ages'.[31] He was succeeded as deputy by Sir Edward FitzEustace, who was probably appointed by the Irish council, since it was customary under the so-called 'statute of FitzEmpress' for this body to elect a governor in case of a sudden vacancy and until the king's pleasure should be made known.[32] FitzEustace was confirmed in office and held a parliament in Dublin in 1453, but died in October 1454.

Meanwhile, as a result of the Somerset–York feud in England, the authority of the duke as lieutenant of Ireland was being disputed. In May 1453, the new earl of Ormond and Wiltshire obtained a grant of this office from the English council in spite of the already existing commission of York which had still over four years to run.[33] Such conflicting grants of office were a feature of the political confusion of the time. Ormond was much too involved in English

30 William Dugdale, *The baronage of England, or an historical account of the lives and most memorable actions of our English nobility, in the Saxons' time, to the Norman Conquest; and from thence of those who had their rise before King Henry the third's reign*, 3 vols (London, 1675–6), under 28 Hen. VI (at p. 159), says that York, by indenture of covenants, retained James, earl of Ormond, to be his deputy. Herbert Wood dismisses the possibility that the deputy was the younger James, earl of Wiltshire (Wood, 'Office of chief governor', p. 236). *Stat. Hen. VI*, pp 250–91. 31 *AMacFirbis*, p. 232. 32 Wood, 'Office of chief governor', p. 236. The so-called 'statute of FitzEmpress' is recited in Ir. stat. roll, 2–3 Ric. III, c. 8 [EN. *Stat. Ric. III–Hen. VIII*, pp 60–3]. 33 On 11 Feb. 1451, the appointment of York as king's lieutenant from 9 Dec. 1447 for ten years had been confirmed (*CPR 1446–52*, p. 465).

politics to come over to Ireland and, in June, appointed a deputy – John Mey, archbishop of Armagh. The latter does not appear to have been very successful, for 'mysrule and mysgouvernaunce' were bitterly complained of during his year of office in a memorial despatched on 23 June 1454 from the county of Kildare to the 'myghty prince and oure right gracious lorde Richard, duke of Yorke'.[34] This asserted that

> this lande of Irland was nevir at the poynt fynaly tobe distrued sethen the Conquest of this lande, as it is now, for the trew liege people in this parties dar ne may not appier to the Kyngs oure said soverayn lordes Courtes in the said lande, ne noon other of the trew liege people ther, to go ne ride to market Tounes, ne other places, for dred to be slayne, take, other spouled of thar godes.

It spoke of

> a variance had betwix therle of Wiltesshire lieutenant of this said lande and Thomas fitz Morice of the Geraldynes for the title of the maners of Maynoth and Rathmore in the Counte of Kildare [which] hath caused more destruccionne in the said Counte of Kildare and liberte of Mith within shorte tyme now late passed, and dayly doth, then was done by Irish ennemys and English rebelles of long tyme befor.

It also related how English rebels and Irish enemies came into the said county of Kildare and burnt many towns and parish churches and took prisoners and spoil, and how William Butler, cousin to the earl, remained and did great oppression till the 'dayly sustenaunce' of the city of Dublin was destroyed; and how the mayor and commons of the city wrote several times to John, archbishop of Armagh, deputy of the earl of Wiltshire, relating these grievances, but 'he remedyed them not'.

On 10 October 1453 occurred the great event that hurried on the Wars of the Roses. Queen Margaret bore a son to the semi-imbecile king and a large part of England believed or affected to believe it was not the king's son at all. York was thus knocked out of the succession to which so far he had been the best heir. But he dissembled and, in February 1454, on the king's imbecility being pronounced, was made protector of England at the request of parliament and held this office till Henry recovered in January 1455. He was then dismissed and his party turned out of office by the queen and Somerset; among those installed in their places was James, earl of Ormond and Wiltshire, made treasurer. Arms now became the final resort and on 22 May 1455 took place the first pitched

34 Gilbert, *Facsimiles*, iii, pl. 41; Ellis, *Original letters*, i, no. 39.

battle of the Wars of the Roses at St Albans. Somerset was slain and, in November, York was made protector again. He turned the Lancastrians out of office and, among other appointments, had his nephew Richard, earl of Warwick, given the captaincy of Calais. For two years, a sham peace was observed.

While York was for the first time protector, the question as to who was legally lieutenant of Ireland was raised in the English council on 15 April 1454. The decision was in favour of York and, on 1 December of the same year, the letters patent of 11 February 1451, appointing him to the office for ten years from December 1447, were ratified. He was to hold the office from the death of Edward FitzEustace, knight, his deputy in office, to wit from 25 October last till the end of the said term, the king being unwilling that he should be prejudiced by the said death while he was in England as protector of the realm. This looks as though the grant to Wiltshire was to be ignored. York later received a re-grant of the lieutenancy on the same terms as before for ten years from 8 December 1457, that is, the date when the first grant was due to expire.[35]

Thomas, earl of Kildare, had been made justiciar by the Irish council on the death of FitzEustace and, in January 1455, York confirmed this choice by making Kildare his deputy. For the next four and a half years, Kildare directed the Irish government and held four parliaments in his name.[36] These were mainly concerned with measures of defence against French, Breton, Scottish and Spanish pirates at sea, and English and Irish enemies on land. The Irish kept the colony in a state of siege, and the parliament of 1455 sent urgent messages to the king telling of the imminent danger to his lordship of Ireland, which was 'like to be finally destroyed' if a remedy were not immediately forthcoming. The old English were as bad as the Irish. To the same parliament came a letter from the seneschal of the liberty of Wexford and the sovereign of Wexford town telling how Edmund Butler and seven others of his nation with Donal Reagh McMurrough and other Irish enemies had 'with banners displayed, ridden, burnt and destroyed the county of Wexford by time and space of four days and four nights, continually'.[37]

A similar petition and from the same county is found among the muniments of the marquess of Ormonde at Kilkenny Castle.[38] It runs thus:

35 *PPC*, vi, 172; *CPR 1452–61*, pp 202, 341; Gilbert, *Viceroys*, p. 585. 36 *Stat. Hen. VI*, 300–46, 352–437, 438–95, 496–575, 576–637. Parliaments were held at Dublin and Naas in Oct. 1453, Nov. 1456, 1458, and Feb. 1459. Gilbert, *Viceroys*, p. 585, gives the covenant of 7 Apr. 1457 between the king and York. 37 *Stat. Hen. VI*, p. 361. This petition, dated 18 Oct., 1455, was dealt with later in the parliament which met the same month. This outlawed the Butlers concerned, if they would not appear by a certain date to answer. 38 These I am editing for IMC; this document has never been published before. It is undated [EN. Curtis later published an English abstract of the document in *COD*, iii, no. 190; but for the original text he referred readers to the edition that appears here].

Ryght reverend and wyrshypfull lort[39] y recomaunde me onto yow certiffiyng yow that y ham hard sete on and put in grete case, that ys to say by Thomas of Dessemond, Omazyr[39a] M^c^agylffatryk Downyl Rehag' and wyte[39b] sarteyne gentil of Cownte of Weys, and that ys to say the Justise Deueros, the weche hat causyt and sete upone me Thomas of Dessemond and sarteyne gentil of Cownte of Weys, the wyche bene Downyl Rehag' ys mene; asse the beirer of this can informe yow. Werfor we pray yow that ye examine hyme, werfor we lete yow wyt that ye have no mor trewe men wyt in the cownte of Weys but only the Brennys and ther alyys; morhowr sayde Justice Deueras had labert[39c] Thomas of Dessemond so that he hat be at the syte of Dowylyng[39d] at a consayle hold ther befor Thomas fitz Moryse, Debite lyeutenaunt, etc., and ther the say de lyeutenaunt at graunt[39e] onto Thomas of Dessemond ffowrty pownde of the Kyng ys fee fferme of Lemryc and Corke and [is] at poynyt to send to howere souereyne lort the Kyng the sayd Deuerosse to have a confermacioun of the Kyng of the forsayd ffowrty pownd and to sue to have the sayd Thomas of Dessemond lyeutenaunt, etc., and also that ye dyde comaunde me to helpe and sucower the cownte of Weys y have do grete coste upon yt, the wyche y have be yhnd comay note cū bytt [*sic*]. Werfor y lete yow wyt that Deveros and oder mor at ys instansse they do thake fee of Downyl Rehag' and they hatt y bound a parcell of the Cownte of Weys to Thomas of Dessemound and to Downyl Rehag' and they had graunt to the said Thomas of Dessemound xx marke to do wers upone me and to the confucion of the trewe pepyle of the sayde town of Weys, werfor y pray yow to consider thys matyr aforsayd and see ye that a remedye be had in yower partyse, and by Godes lowe y challe defend theme in my partyse,

39 It is not clear who wrote this letter or what person is addressed in it. The 'right reverend and worshipful lord' might be John Mey, archbishop of Armagh, deputy lieutenant for the earl of Ormond from June 1453 to the end of June 1454. But the style could be given to a nobleman, and there is no indication that the person addressed was lord lieutenant. Possibly it is an original letter which, according to the instructions, is to be copied by some clerk and despatched to three noble persons who were particularly concerned with Co. Wexford and the Butlers. Of these, James Butler, fifth earl of Ormond (1452–61), had been created earl of Wiltshire in England on 8 July 1449. John Talbot, second earl of Shrewsbury (1453–60), was son of the famous John Talbot of the French wars. He took as his second wife Elizabeth, daughter of James, fourth earl of Ormond (d. 23 August 1452), and had by her five sons and two daughters. The title earl of Waterford came to the second earl of Shrewsbury from his father, who was so created on 17 July 1446. The latter had also a claim to the lordship of Wexford through his de Valence descent but this was contested with Lord Grey. Thomas, son of 'fitz Morice Fitzgerald, earl of Kildare' is referred to in the letter as deputy lieutenant. We must date it as 1455 and associate it with the above-mentioned appeal to the parliament. **39a** (?) O'Meagher. **39b** (?) 'with him'. **39c** 'laboured with'. **39d** 'city of Dublin'. **39e** 'has granted'.

> and send ye wrytyng by the beirer of thys asse it plese yow, etc., to wome y pray yowe to yowe feythe and credens y write, etc.
>
> [*Dorso*]
>
> Ye most make iii letres on to the Erle of Willeshyre the other to John Erle of Shrewysbury and Weys and another to my lady [...][39f] and upon every of thys yowr Selle of armys, etc. And asse to the Erle of Wylleshyr ye moste write in ys wrytyng as [...][39g] of Waterfforde and Lymeryc y praye yow to send [...][39h] content yow watever ye saylle comaund me, etc.

Here we see the evils of the time exemplified. The 'over-mighty subject' and his retainers, the feuds of the nobles, the corruption of justice, a chief justice Devereux accused of bringing in Irish enemies and English rebels into a loyal shire, the deputy charged with using parliament only to secure favours for another magnate, Thomas of Desmond. Why Co. Wexford should have been a special victim of these troubles is not evident; but we see a clear picture of a loyal county over-ridden by Butlers, the grandsons of an earl of Ormond, Donal Reagh MacMurrough, the Irish 'king of Leinster', Thomas, son of the earl of Desmond, his Irish allies O'Meagher and Macgillapatrick; and cannot tell which side was which or what the quarrel was about. The same conditions prevailed in England where 'lack of governance' was the great evil, but England was luckier in the fact that she had a native monarchy. In Ireland, unbridled feudalism prevailed, and the petty parliament and the Anglo-Irish aristocracy that ran it could or would do nothing effective to restore the royal power and save the Pale from destruction. They were lords in their own counties and, as for parliament, they dominated it in order that it should serve their interests and secure them the offices of state.

In England, the Yorkist party issued various manifestos against the Lancastrian regime and added that things would not be well till the old Plantagenet stock was restored. There was a sham 'love day' staged in London when parliament met on Lady Day in 1458, and the duke of York and the queen walked in procession hand-in-hand. But the lords who were there 'never came together again after that time to parliament or council, unless it were in field, with spear and shield'.

Finally, the gage was thrown down. But fortune favoured the crown, and by the 'rout of Ludlow' (12 October 1459) the Yorkist forces were scattered. York made for Ireland; his son Edward, earl of March, and his nephew, Richard of Warwick, made for Calais. These were at once the two refuges and jumping-off places reserved by the Yorkists for their cause in England. Especially did the duke see in Ireland a safe stronghold, and to keep it he was ready to rule according to Irish ideas.

**39f** The MS is faded: (?) 'Elizabeth'. **39g** The MS is faded: (?) 'earl'. **39h** The MS is faded.

The English parliament meeting at Coventry on 20 November attainted him, Salisbury, Warwick, his sons and their chief adherents, so that legally all his offices including that of lord lieutenant of Ireland ceased. On 27 January 1460, a mandate was sent to the treasurer of Ireland and the barons of the exchequer to take all his Irish properties into the king's hands. But all this was nothing to the Irish magnates and the home rule party. They now had a 'king of their own' and meant to make use of him. When Richard landed in Dublin on a November day in 1459, he was welcomed like a king and the enthusiasm of Dublin can only be imagined. He summoned parliament to Drogheda on 7 February 1460, and the Irish estates gave almost sovereign power to this superseded viceroy.[40] They ratified his appointment as lieutenant for the term indicated in the letters patent of March 1457, and gave his person as much honour and safeguard as if he were king himself, for to him as the royal deputy 'such reverence, obedience and fear ought to be given as to our sovereign lord, whose estate is thereby honoured, feared and obeyed'. To plot against the lieutenant was, therefore, as if to plot against the king. 'If any person imagine, compass, excite or provoke his destruction or death or to that intent confederate or assent with Irish enemies he shall be and stand attainted of high treason.' An opportunity soon occurred for putting these enactments into practice. One William Overey, a squire of the earl of Ormond and Wiltshire, ignorant of the danger he was running, arrived in Ireland with the writs for the arrest of York and his following according to the findings of the Coventry parliament. He was seized, tried before the duke, and found guilty of having introduced 'many writs and letters of privy seal contrary to the liberties and privileges' of Ireland, and of having 'imagined, compassed, and incited rebellion and disobedience' to the lieutenant. For this, he was convicted of high treason and executed.

The 'English nation in Ireland' now proceeded to assert its legislative independence. 'The land of Ireland,' it declared

> is and at all times has been corporate of itself by the ancient lords and customs used in the same, freed of the burden of any special law of the realm of England, save only such laws as by the lords spiritual and temporal and the commons of the said land had been in great council or Parliament there held admitted, accepted, affirmed and proclaimed.

Ireland had also her own great seal, 'of ancient custom, privilege and franchise', wherefore it was enacted that no person or persons in Ireland were to be 'by any command given or made under any other seal than the said seal of the same land compelled to answer to any appeal or any other matter out of the said land', and any officer putting such a command into execution, or 'any other

40 *Stat. Hen. VI*, pp 638–47.

thing prejudicial to ancient custom, privilege and franchise', was to forfeit land and goods and pay a fine of 1000 marks.

It was further enacted that appeals of treason were to be determined in Ireland before the constable and marshal of Ireland. Thus, not only were writs under the great seal of England excluded, but the practice of having Irish subjects called into England to answer appeals of treason, often done 'of great malice', was to be stopped as derogatory of Irish liberty. For 'it has not been seen or heard that any person or persons inhabiting or resident in any other Christian land so corporate of itself ought to obey any mandate within the said land given or made under any other than the proper seal of the same'.

Thus did Ireland assert a complete separateness from England except for the personal link of the crown. Richard accepted those measures for, whatever misgivings he may have had as an Englishman and possible English king, they certainly suited his purpose for the moment. He had enlisted on his side the Irish magnates and made Ireland a stronghold for the Yorkist faction.

This parliament passed sixty-three acts in all. After the opening ones, the rest fail away into personal petitions, administrative details and provisions for defence, such as were the main work of these assemblies. But three are noteworthy. One enjoins that each subject having twenty pounds yearly shall keep in his house

> one archer mounted and arrayed defensively with bow and arrows got for war according to the English fashion, to be ready at all times upon warning, for the defence of the said land in manner and form as heretofore or has been accustomed, so long as the most high, puissant prince, the duke of York, remain in the said land … [for] the defence of the English nation of this land from the danger and malice of the Irish enemies rests and depends on English bows, which to the said enemies give the greatest resistance and terror of any weapon of war used in the said land, now very nearly destitute of any great number of the said bows which are not in these days employed in exercise of the occupation of archery.

Another act was one of resumption, found necessary because the royal revenues from Ireland had so dwindled on account of multifarious grants that it was no longer sufficient to finance the government.

Another, that Ireland ought to have her own coinage, was declared to be an appropriate circumstance of independence. A shortage of coin was being severely felt at the time and was said to be due to two facts, namely, that the king had ceased to pay his officials in Ireland any salaries from the English treasury, and that merchants had ceased to come to Ireland to buy goods and bring money as before. Mints were therefore to be set up at the castles of Dublin and Trim, and three varieties of coin struck. A silver 'Ireland', valued at a penny sterling, with a lion on one side and a crown on the other, and the name Ireland written round the lion; a 'Patrick', valued at one-eighth of the 'Ireland', having a demi-crown with the name on one side and a cross on the reverse; and a groat, valued at four pence, bearing a cross and a crown and the name of the place where struck.[41]

Richard made his young son, Edmund, earl of Rutland, chancellor of Ireland and showed every sign of putting the Yorkists into power there. The English government could not hope to dislodge him with attainders and writs, and they had not the resources to proceed against him with force. While he was thus entrenched in Ireland, Warwick was as happily exiled in Calais, whence he sailed with a fleet of twenty-six ships in the spring of 1460 to confer with York in Waterford.[42] The Yorkist leaders resolved on an invasion of England. Warwick returned to Calais and from thence landed in Kent. Marching north, he defeated the Lancastrians and took the king prisoner at Northampton on 10 July 1460.[43] No sooner did the news of this victory reach York than he appointed the earl of Kildare his deputy and left for England accompanied by numbers of devoted followers from Ireland. He made a triumphal entry into London, with trumpeters and clarions, his duchess by his side, his sword borne before him and on his banners the whole arms of England displayed, as if he meant to assume the royal estate and power.[43] The throne of England was now almost within his grasp. Parliament by force of circumstance admitted his claim, but it was stipulated that Henry should continue to reign for the rest of his life with York as his chief minister, heir and successor.

The duke however did not live long to enjoy his triumph. On 31 December 1460, he was killed outside his own castle of Wakefield, having rashly offered battle with his small forces to many thousands of Lancastrian partisans, for he scorned 'to be held within walls by a scolding woman'. It is probable that many Irish retainers were with him in his last fight.

After the barbarous fashion of these wars, his young son Edmund, earl of Rutland and earl of Cork, was murdered after the battle. The heads of both were placed over the gate of York and Richard's was in derision crowned with a paper crown.

York's eldest son Edward, earl of March, however, soon avenged father and brother. Although Warwick was beaten at St Albans by the queen's forces and fell back on London, March – a gallant soldier and a handsome youth of nineteen years – marched from the west, entered London, was crowned by his party as Edward IV, and with lightning vigour hurried north and secured his kingdom at Towton (29 March 1461). After the battle, James, earl of Ormond

41 See James Simon, *An essay towards an historical acccount of Irish coins, and of the currency of foregin [sic] monies in Ireland* (Dublin, 1749), p. 20. 42 *Cal. Carew MSS*, v, 471. The date is given as 16 Mar. 1459, but the year should be (new style) 1460. 43 'Gregory's chronicle, 1189–1469' in *Historical collections of a citizen of London in the fifteenth century*, ed. James Gairdner (Camden Soc., new ser., 17, 1876), p. 208.

and Wiltshire, was taken and finally beheaded on 1 May. He had been one of the most determined opponents of York in England and Ireland, and had met him and his son in more than one encounter.

In the new king, the handsomest and tallest of his line, England welcomed a legitimist restoration. For Ireland, the event was a dazzling success, because through his descent and connections with Ireland Edward was almost an Irishman. The earl of Ulster, lord of Trim, Leix and Connacht was now the king, and the vast de Lacy, de Burgo and Mortimer estates merged in the crown. The hero-son of the beloved Richard of York governed both realms and the home rule aristocracy was put firmly in the saddle.

When Richard, duke of York, fell at Wakefield, he had not yet attained his fiftieth year. No personal description of him has come down to us, but the tradition was that he was a well-favoured and stately person. It was no small part of York's success in Ireland that he appeared as all that a prince ought to be – comely, tall, affable, gracious and commanding. To a race accustomed to lords, which 'desired always to be ruled by great persons', no finer union of ancestral and personal claims could be found than in him who was viceroy of Ireland for thirteen years.

So much for the showy side of Duke Richard's career in Ireland. In fact, his patriotism, thought and talents were reserved for England's service. Of his thirteen years as viceroy, he did not rule for two here in person. He was peculiarly fitted by descent to accomplish in his person a union of a much-divided land, to check the evils of rampant feudalism and ensure good government and prosperity to the people. But though he was a statesman who could reconcile men in his cause, who endeared himself and his cause to the greater part of Ireland by his popular gifts, he wrought no lasting service to her. His appointment as viceroy was an honourable banishment, an expedient to get him out of the way; he looked on his sojourn here as an exile, and cultivated Irish influence with one eye ever on his English aims. The true interests of Ireland he never had at heart, and did not scruple to drain her of her best men in the Yorkist cause to such an extent that, in the words of the chronicler, 'the English domination was dissolved and spoiled'.[44]

The results of the duke's fatal attraction on Ulster in particular may be gleaned from a record of a later time:

> [H]e so gained the hearts of the Irish nobility that divers of them, especially those of Ulster, Clandeboy, the Glines, and the Ardes, which at

44 'Hibernici in absentia Anglorum assumentes vires et opportunitatem insurrexerunt in Hibernia, et obsiderunt ubique castra et fortalicia, que tenuerunt usque tempora Henrici 7 et 8. [1449] Dux Eboracensis venit in Hiberniam cum magno scutto et exercitu ad pacificandos Hibernicos et rebelles, qui nihil estimabile potuit agere, nec [pacem] concludere, nec Hibernicos vincere' (*ADowling*, pp 29–30).

> that time was better inhabited with English nobility than any part of Munster or Connaught, came over with him against Henry VI, to divers famous battles, lastly to Wakefield, where they not only lost their lives with him but also left their country so naked of defence that the Irish, in the meantime, finding the enterprise so easy, cast up their old Cap[tain], O'Neale, relyed themselves with their ancient neighbours the Scots, and repossessed themselves of the whole country, which was the utter decay of Ulster.[45]

Richard of York might have seriously attempted to win over the native race by some great measure which would have admitted them to equal laws with the Englishry and made their chiefs tenants under the crown, a hard task no doubt and one probably beyond his powers. Or he might have come out on the unionist and pro-English side, made the Dublin government effective and powerful, and made war on the Irish with the aim of expanding the English area once more to what it had been a century before. Both these aims were entrenched in difficulties. What he did do was take the easy path of enlisting in the Yorkist cause the majority of the Anglo-Irish magnates by favouring the home rule cause and handing Ireland over to the native feudal interest. It was an *entente* advantageous to both sides. For forty years and even longer, Anglo-Ireland, under the leadership of Desmond and then of Kildare, embraced enthusiastically the Yorkist cause. Ireland enjoyed a period of home rule of an oligarchic nature, in which her parliament and law courts were internally supreme. This was York's real and lasting achievement.

When Henry VII triumphed at Bosworth, he saw in Ireland the most dangerous stronghold left to the beaten faction and, as a restorer of the Lancastrian regime, he regarded all that had been done since Richard of York was appointed as viceroy as pure usurpation. Hence, when he sent Sir Edward Poynings over in 1494, it was with the avowed object of ending forty years of home rule, restoring royal control to its original height, and ending the domination of Ireland by Kildare's Yorkist faction, the support of all pretenders.[46]

In the parliament of Drogheda, 1494–5, Poynings had the 'home rule' declaration of 1460 annulled as made in an unauthorized parliament, with other 'pretensed prescriptions', and brought Irish legislation under imperial control. Nevertheless, the supremacy of the house of Kildare remained intact for another forty years and, until its fall in 1534, the shadow and the name of the great duke of York did indeed hang visibly over Ireland.[47]

45 *Cal. Carew MSS*, v, 478. 46 Conway, *Hen. VII & Ire.*, ch. 7. 47 I desire to acknowledge with gratitude the assistance of my former pupil, Miss Helen Fitzgerald-Lombard, in preparing this paper.

# PART 3

# *Society*

CHAPTER 15

# The character of Norman settlement in Ireland*

*A.J. Otway-Ruthven*

The initial Norman conquest of Ireland was reasonably rapid, though its extension continued throughout the thirteenth century and did not reach its maximum till shortly before that decline of English power traditionally attributed to the invasion of Edward Bruce. But, by the end of the twelfth century, the whole of Leinster, the ancient kingdom of Meath (including not only Meath and Westmeath, but also south Longford and the north-western part of the modern Co. Offaly), Ulster east of the Bann and a great part of Munster were all effectively dominated by the new power.

The problems of organization presented by these conquests were immense. In England a hundred years earlier, the Normans had been confronted by somewhat similar problems and had dealt with them by a largely military occupation, retaining much of Anglo-Saxon law, custom and institutions, and superimposing their own developed system of feudalism. But the position in Ireland was very different: the structure of Celtic society differed far more widely from the general continental pattern than had that of Anglo-Saxon England; and, moreover, the new Anglo-Norman society was already setting on lines which precluded that ready adoption of alien custom which had been so marked a feature of Norman conquest in both Wales and Italy. Accordingly, the institutions which developed in Norman Ireland were of purely Anglo-Norman type, and there was, theoretically at least, no divergence between the law of England and that of the Norman colony in Ireland.[1]

The initial step was the granting out of the land to tenants-in-chief, holding directly of the king, in units ranging from the grant of Leinster to Strongbow to hold by the service of one hundred knights to the half and quarter fees of Co. Dublin,[2] and this was accompanied by the establishment of an elementary central government at Dublin, though the Irish exchequer does not seem to have been developed till the reign of John, and the chancery not till that of Henry III.[3] The

* First published in J.L. McCracken (ed.), *Historical studies V: papers read before the sixth conference of Irish historians* (Bowes and Bowes, London, 1965), pp 75–84. 1 See Otway-Ruthven, 'Knight service in Ireland' (above, ch. 7), and eadem, 'The native Irish and English law in medieval Ireland' (above, ch. 6). 2 Otway-Ruthven, 'Knight service in Ireland'. 3 *Ir. parl.*, pp 21–2; Otway-Ruthven, 'The medieval Irish chancery' (above, ch. 3).

development of local institutions is less easy to trace, but the Dublin county court was in existence by the 1190s and, by 1211–12, Waterford with Cork, and Munster (Tipperary, Limerick and Thomond) had been added.[4] But this introduction of English local institutions into Ireland depended on the way in which the tenants-in-chief organized their lands, and it is to this that we must now turn.

The extent to which the Norman conquest of Ireland was effective depended ultimately on the effective occupation of their lards by the great tenants. It was, of course, impossible for Strongbow, de Lacy or de Courcy to occupy the whole of Leinster, Meath or Ulster: they resorted to a process of subinfeudation. The greater part at least of the subinfeudation of Leinster was clearly completed by the end of the twelfth century, and has been worked out in detail.[5] That of Meath is less well known, since we have much less evidence for the early period; but, already in the time of Hugh de Lacy, lands in Longford were being granted to his followers and it is clear that, by the middle of the thirteenth century, the whole of the lordship of Meath, with of course the exception of the lands of the church, had been parcelled out into knight's fees.[6]

This, however, was only the first stage in the occupation of a lordship. Leinster, Meath and Ulster had almost palatine rights, excluding the king's officers almost entirely, and it was necessary, therefore, to erect in them replicas of the royal government. We have not very much early evidence as to the process but, by the end of the thirteenth century, the separate liberties which had been created by the Marshal partition of 1247, together with Trim and Ulster, all had their own chanceries and exchequers, which had clearly been in existence for a considerable time. The new royal system of assizes and juries had been adopted in Leinster by 1224; in Meath, the formulary writ system was only introduced by royal charter in 1257.[7] Each, moreover, had its system of shires: Leinster, probably beginning with a single county based on Wexford under Strongbow, had the four counties of Wexford, Carlow, Kilkenny and Kildare by the time the last Marshal died in 1245;[8] Ulster was divided into bailiwicks which later became shires by 1226.[9] Meath alone remained undivided, though after its partition between the granddaughters of Walter de Lacy, Geoffrey de Genville had his county court at Trim and the de Verdon half, after an obscure period as

4 *CDI 1171–1251*, no. 116; *Pipe roll 14 John*. For the development of further shires during the thirteenth century, see Otway-Ruthven, 'Anglo-Irish shire government in the thirteenth century' (above, ch. 5). 5 Orpen, *Normans*, i, 367–96; Brooks, *Knights' fees*; A.J. Otway-Ruthven, 'Knights' fees in Kildare, Leix and Offaly', *JRSAI*, 91 (1961), 163–81. 6 *Song of Dermot*, pp 309–10; Orpen, *Normans*, ii, 75–90; *Reg. Gormanston*, pp 10–13; BL, Cotton Charter II, 24. 7 *Reg. Gormanston*, pp 179, 201–2. 'Suis brevibus' on p. 179 should read 'sine brevibus'. 8 Orpen, *Normans*, iii, ch. 26. No further county could then be created since this would have infringed the rights of the persons to whom the profits of the county courts had been assigned. 9 *CDI 1171–1251*, no. 1468.

a separate liberty, was first attached to the royal county of Dublin and was then made into the separate royal county of Meath.[10]

Underneath all this was the organization of the lord's demesne manors and the lands of the subtenants. The first stage was the erection of some sort of strong point, often, but by no means always, a mote castle. Great lords threw up motes at the centres of their principal demesne manors, and might replace them when time and means allowed by stone castles, as at Trim; but the erection of a mote seems to have demanded greater resources than the lord of a single manor could normally command, and, for instance, at Moycarkey in Tipperary the de Samlisburys, who must have come with the Butlers from their Lancashire lands, had only a house and courtyard.[11] Even a much greater lord might content himself with a stone house and a courtyard, as the Butlers did at Bray.[12] But many motes were erected, and their distribution is a good index to the extent of Norman settlement.[13]

The manor and the parish are normally coincident.[14] It seems clear that the compact territorial parish with its system of tithes, which once it was established made it impossible to detach any part of it, had been unknown in Ireland at the beginning of the twelfth century.[15] The reform of the Irish church, as far as the creation of the new territorial dioceses was concerned, had been practically completed before the Norman conquest; only comparatively minor readjustments were made afterwards.[16] But it is, I think, certain that only a start had been made in the organization of the territorial parish, which in many districts does not seem to have existed at all. We find, therefore, that the new Norman lords grant both to the older monastic foundations, such as St Mary's, Dublin, and to the new foundations, such as Tristernagh in west Meath, 'the ecclesiastical benefices [that is, the tithes] of all my men and tenants', and in rare and fortunate cases we can trace over several generations the development of a series of parishes corresponding to the holdings of the principal subtenants.[17] But the area of a parish, normally several thousand acres, would alone suggest that even the lord of a single manor would not cultivate his whole holding as a home farm. Who were his tenants, what was their standing, where did they come from?

We have, unfortunately, very little evidence for the first period of the Norman colony; but from the reign of Edward I, records become relatively

10 *Stat. John–Hen. V*, pp 196–8. 11 *Red bk Ormond*, p. 56. 12 Ibid., p. 24. 13 Their importance was first pointed out by Orpen, and there is a map of their distribution (though many more exist than he has shown) in Orpen, *Normans*, ii. 14 That is, the civil parish, which is the ecclesiastical parish of medieval and early modern times. 15 Otherwise Gilbert of Limerick would not have thought it necessary to expound the system ('De Statu Ecclesie' in *The whole works of … James Ussher*, ed. C.R. Elrington, 17 vols (Dublin, 1847–64), iv, 501–10). 16 The best connected account of the reform of the church in the twelfth century is that given by the Rev. Aubrey Gwynn in the introductory chapters of Dermot F. Gleeson, *A history of the diocese of Killaloe* (Dublin, 1962). 17 See A.J. Otway-Ruthven, 'Parochial

abundant and they make it plain that, seen in its proper perspective, the Norman settlement of Ireland was no mere military occupation, supported by the settlement of English and French burgesses in a few large towns, but a part of that great movement of peasant colonization which dominates so much of the economic development of Europe from the eleventh to the fourteenth centuries, arising out of what can only have been a spontaneous growth of population and slackening as that growth slackens with the troubles of the fourteenth century.[18] The failure to recover from the disturbances of the Bruce invasion – the statement to be found in so many extents of the 1320s and 1330s that, in outlying districts, lands 'lie waste and uncultivated for lack of tenants'[19] – may well be explained in terms of the general European experience. And it is quite clear that, by the reign of Edward I, there had been settled over a great part of Leinster, in Meath and Westmeath, in Tipperary and Limerick, in parts of Cork and Kerry, in Waterford, in Louth and in eastern Ulster, an occupying, cultivating population of small free tenants of English, or occasionally Welsh, origin, who in some districts probably considerably outnumbered the native Irish. It was these men who provided the Dublin government with the necessary backing and bodied out the institutions of local government which, as we have seen, developed everywhere on the English model; it must have been they who introduced the strip holdings of the openfield system.[20] It is not necessary to suppose that any very great displacement of population was everywhere involved: the population of England at the time of Domesday Book has been estimated as perhaps 1,375,000,[21] and it is reasonable to suppose that two or three generations later the population of Ireland was of much the same order.

That there was a lack of men rather than a lack of lands is strongly suggested by the provision of the treaty of Windsor for the return of fugitives, and by charters of the first half of the thirteenth century providing for the return of *nativi* or betaghs belonging to the lands granted, unless indeed they had settled on the king's demesne, while a grant of demesne lands to the bishop of Down in 1225 provides that the Irishmen dwelling on that land shall be retained in the king's hand and settled elsewhere on his land.[22] Clearly the small tenant, whether free or unfree, could readily enough find land elsewhere, and the same impression is conveyed by the grant of leave in 1200 for Hamo de Valoignes to lead his men 'ad terram suam hospitandum', saving the demesne lands of the king, and the assize of the barons of Ireland touching their villeins.[23]

development in the rural deanery of Skreen', *JRSAI*, 94 (1964), 111–22. 18 See J.H. Clapham, John Harold and Eileen Power (eds), *The Cambridge economic history of Europe from the decline of the Roman empire*, i: *the agrarian life of the Middle Ages* (Cambridge, 1941). 19 See, e.g., TNA (PRO), C 47/10/18, no. 17; BL, Cotton Charter II, 24; *Reg. Alen*, pp 170ff. 20 See Otway-Ruthven, 'The organization of Anglo-Irish agriculture' (below, ch. 16). 21 Frederic W. Maitland, *Domesday Book and beyond: three essays in the early history of England* (Cambridge, 1897), p. 437. 22 *Foedera*, i, 31; *Crede mihi*, p. 71; *CStM*, i, 90; *CDI 1171–1251*, nos. 506, 1264; *CDI 1252–84*, no. 52; *CDI 1285–92*, p. 309. 23 *CDI 1171–1251*,

The conclusions to be drawn from the records as to the racial origins of the settlers depend, of course, on the assumption that an English surname can be equated with English descent, and it must be admitted that this was not always so: long before the legislation which required the Irish resident among the English to take English surnames,[24] anglicized Celts who wished to use English law without the trouble and expense of obtaining the royal grant which would entitle them to do so[25] passed under English names. Thus, in 1313, the jury in a case of felonious slaying confirmed the statement of the defendant, Philip le Waleys, that the dead man, Simon le Waleys, was his *hibernicus*.[26] Obviously, Simon had adopted his lord's surname. In 1300, a jury found that Walter de Capella was an Irishman of the name of the Offyns; in 1297, Simon de la Chaumbre was 'a very poor betagh of the king' and, therefore, presumably an Irishman; in 1307, that John Stakepol was an *hibernicus*, Oglassewan by surname.[27] On the other hand, in 1297, the jury said that Philip Beneyt, who it had been alleged was Irish, 'of the surname of M'Kenabbyth and born in the mountains of the Othothles', was in fact an Englishman; and, most confusingly, in 1311, that Adam Rauf was an Englishman on the day when he was slain, but he was commonly held among the commons of the town (of Drogheda) to be an Irishman from the first time when he came to town.[28] Presumably this means that Rauf was, in fact, of Irish descent and had obtained the right to use English law. It is clear, then, that an English surname is not infallible evidence of descent; but it is, I think, reasonable to assume that the overwhelming majority of those who had English surnames were, in fact, of English descent, and certainly in most of the comparatively few recorded cases the jury found that this was so.

It is not till the reign of Edward I that we begin to get any considerable number of detailed extents of manors which make it possible to arrive at estimates of their population and its composition, and even then the evidence is scattered and incomplete, for most of these extents occur in the inquisitions *post mortem* of tenants-in-chief, and while these may deal with the demesne manors in detail they tell us nothing of the position in the manors of the subtenants. We are, however, fortunate in having in the 'Red book of Ormond' some detailed extents of subtenancies at the beginning of the fourteenth century, and from this and other sources it is possible to form a reasonably clear picture of the population structure of a number of manors scattered over a wide area in the south and south-west. Before we embark on an analysis of the evidence, it will, however, be as well to consider the problem of how these populations were recruited, and from where they came.

no. 120. **24** *Stat. Edw. IV, pt 1*, p. 290. **25** See Otway-Ruthven, 'The native Irish and English law in medieval Ireland' (above, ch. 6). **26** *CJRI 1308–14*, p. 291. **27** *CJRI 1295–1303*, pp 119, 342; *CJRI 1305–7*, p. 520. See also *CJRI 1295–1303*, pp 14, 59; *CJRI, 1308–14*, p. 203; *Lib. prim. Kilkenniensis*, pp 6–9; Davies, *Discovery*, p. 90. **28** *CJRI 1295–1303*, pp 121–3; *CJRI 1308–14*, p. 167, 168. See also *CJRI 1295–1303*, pp 158, 454; *CJRI*

It is generally stated that Strongbow brought his followers from Pembrokeshire. In fact, however, he seems to have enlisted men from all the lordships along the coast of south Wales, and it must be remembered that he was not only earl of Pembroke, but also lord of Strigoil (Chepstow) in Monmouthshire, while such names as Lawless, still commonly found in parts of Leinster, are characteristic of medieval Glamorgan.[29] It was long ago pointed out that the place-names of parts of eastern Kildare would almost suggest that one was looking at a map of Wales rather than of Ireland;[30] and Welsh, as distinct from Welsh marcher, influence was particularly strong along the Kildare–Wicklow border, where, *c.*1282, Henry FitzRys, son of Henry, lord of Penkoyte, confirmed the grants of his ancestors to Christchurch of the advowson of the chapel 'anciently called Kylengly, but, after the arrival of the English and Welsh in Ireland, Penkoyte'. The family of Rys were also the original grantees of Imaal under Walter de Ridelesford.[31] Throughout Ireland, le Waleys was a usual name, and we also find such names as Breghenok, Gower, Cadigan, Howel. The surname Ewyas suggests an ancestor who came with Hugh de Lacy, lord of Ewyas Lacy, and many of de Lacy's tenants no doubt came from Shropshire, where he had his principal holdings.[32] At least one tenant of the Butlers in Tipperary, represented in 1303 by Grimbald de Samlesbury, must have come from their Lancashire lands. Names such as Deuenisshe, le Cornwaleys, de Exeter, are clear evidence of origin. But the great majority of lesser men (and even some greater ones) have unrevealing names of the type which start as nicknames or trade names – Black, Blund (or White), le Gros, Belejaumbe, Milward – and give us no indication of where they came from. As far as our evidence goes, a majority came from western England and Wales, but we cannot trace them at all closely. Clearly, however, a lord would do his recruiting in the first instance in the district from which he himself came, and there is room for systematic work on the places of origin of both tenants-in-chief and the greater subtenants, most of whom can be traced easily enough.

How the recruiting was done is another matter, and one on which I know of no direct evidence. A nucleus must have been provided by mercenary soldiers, many of whom no doubt settled down on the land, but their numbers were not really very great. But, as I have suggested elsewhere,[33] the very large number of small boroughs which were set up throughout the areas of Norman settlement –

*1308–14*, 102–3, 203; Davies, *Discovery*, pp 85, 91; *Dowdall deeds*, no. 290. **29** See, e.g., *Cartae et alia munimenta quae ad dominium de Glamorgancia pertinent*, ed. G.L. Clark, 6 vols (new ed., Cardiff, 1910). **30** Canon Sherlock, 'The original Anglo-Norman settlers of county Kildare', *Journal of the County Kildare Archaeological Society*, 3 (1899–1902), 293–4. **31** *20th rep. DKPRI*, no. 130; *COD*, i, no. 8. Penkoyte was Johnstown Penkoyte, still known as Johnstown pignot at the time of the civil survey, and now part of the townland of Killinane, par. Kilcullen. **32** Robert W. Eyton, *Antiquities of Shropshire*, 12 vols (London, 1853–60). **33** Otway-Ruthven, 'Organization of Anglo-Irish agriculture'.

places which can never have been more than large villages, but which were given the elements of an urban constitution, with burgage holdings, their own hundred courts and, usually, the law of Breteuil – strongly suggests that, as on the continent, burgess standing was widely used as a bait to draw settlers. Of course, not every manor had its burgesses, but a great many did, and some, like Moyaliff in Tipperary, seem to have had practically no other tenants.[34] There were certainly more of these settlements than we know of, for some are recorded only in chance survivals, but those of which we know are very widely scattered, and places such as Drumconrath or Sidan in Meath, Ardscull or Dunfert in Kildare, Moyaliff in Tipperary, Glenogra in Limerick, can never have had any real urban character. And though, by the fifteenth century, it was thought necessary to obtain authority from the crown to create a borough,[35] earlier not only the greatest lords with semi-regal powers – the Marshals in Leinster or the de Lacys in Meath and Ulster – but even the subtenants of their subtenants freely created boroughs. Thus Philip Teling, a subtenant of the Flemings of Slane, who were themselves subtenants of de Lacy, gave a charter to Sydan, *c.*1250 (?).[36] And that Irish lords too felt the need to attract men to their lands and made use of this device is strongly suggested by the fact that Bishop David O'Kelly of Cloyne established a borough at Kilmaclennan, probably in 1238, which was confirmed by a charter of Bishop Daniel in 1251, giving them the law of Breteuil. We have no means of knowing who Bishop David's burgesses were, but a rental of the middle of the fourteenth century names some twenty-seven persons, out of whom only four or five are Irish, the rest bearing names like Malefaunt, White, Barry, Gower, Eywas. It was clearly a purely agricultural settlement:

> omnes burgenses qui carucatam habeant arabunt domino per annum iiij dies, videlicet ij dies ad semen yemale, et ij dies ad semen quadragesimale, et sarculabunt bladum domini in estate, et autumpno, et quilibet habens domum inveniet unum hominem ad metendum bladum domini, et cariabunt per ij dies bladum domini in autumpno, quando summoniti fuerit per ballivum, et cariabunt domino ferrum, vinum, et salem.

But the oddest feature of this borough is the statement, 'quiquidem burgenses sint betagii, quare non possunt ire ex villa nisi facere pasturam super terras dominicas domini'.[37]

We may now turn to an examination of the composition of the population in particular areas. We have a detailed extent of the manor of Cloncurry, Co. Kildare, in 1304.[38] Cloncurry comprised the western part of the modern barony

34 *Red bk Ormond*, pp 64–7. 35 *Stat. Hen. VI*, pp 214–20. 36 *Stat. Edw. IV, pt 2*, pp 362–4. 37 *Rot. pipae Clonensis*, pp 15–18, 19–21. David O'Kelly was elected before September 1237 and translated to Cashel before January 1239. 38 *Red bk Ormond*, pp 27–34.

of Ikeathy and Oughterany: the parishes of Cloncurry, Scullogestown, Dunmurraghill and Donadea, with some unidentified lands in Meath. There were four knight's fees held of the manor, which can be equated with the parishes of Scullogestown, Dunmurraghill and Donadea, and with the lands in Meath. These can be excluded from our calculations, since we know nothing of their subinfeudation. Of the remaining free tenants, thirty-five in all, five held one ploughland or more, a total area of 7½ ploughlands and 30 acres. All these had no doubt subtenants, but we know nothing of them. One more had 96 acres; then come six, one of whom was Irish, each of whom held half a ploughland and each of whom probably had some cottiers on his land. Five more had each a quarter, which probably here means a quarter of a ploughland; one had 40 acres; four, of whom two were Irish, 20; one 15 acres; one 12; one 10; one 8; one 6; seven had only 5 apiece; and one had the site of a mill. There were thus seventeen free tenants, of whom all but two seem from their names to have been of English origin, holding 20 acres or less. There were in addition forty-eight farmers – that is, men holding on lease for a term of years – eight of whom also held as free tenants. Of the remaining forty, four have Irish names. The holdings of most were small, and there is a marked tendency for a number to hold in common – nine jointly hold 40 acres, and twelve 94. There were sixty-four betaghs, all presumably Irish, holding 341½ acres; eleven gavillers – tenants at will – two of whom were Irish; and forty-two cottiers, thirty-nine of whom were Irish. Finally, there were the burgesses, most or all of whom will have been of English origin, whose numbers are not stated, but who held 2 ploughlands in burgage for a rent of 112*s*. If we take it that the burgage rent was the usual one of 1*s*., this gives us 112 burgages and presumably approximately that number of burgesses, some of whom may of course also have been farmers or even free tenants. Nevertheless, we can reasonably take the number of persons of English descent as approximately 191 – 112 burgesses and 79 other tenants – and the Irish as 111, almost all betaghs and cottagers. As they were presumably all heads of households, we may estimate the total minimum population at 945 persons of English descent and 555 of Irish descent, but there must also have been cottiers and other small tenants, probably mostly of Irish descent, on the lands of the larger subtenants.[39]

The manor of Bray, Co. Wicklow, though much smaller, was not dissimilar. There were three free tenants, all apparently English, holding a ploughland, half a ploughland and one acre respectively; one Irish farmer holding 20 acres; two gavillers, both apparently English, holding 23 acres each; three betaghs, holding

39 The total acreage given by the extent is 2,900. If we accept Mill's equation of the medieval acre in the Dublin area with 2½ statute acres (James Mills, 'Tenants and agriculture near Dublin in the fourteenth century', *JRSAI*, 20 (1890), 54–6), this is not so far below the 8,390 acres of the modern parish that it cannot be explained by bog, scrub and other waste land, and mere inaccuracy of measurement.

22 acres between them; and seven cottiers, all probably Irish. There were also some thirty-two burgesses, holding half a ploughland, all probably English: a total of thirty-seven English and ten Irish.[40] Brun, the district behind Delgany, presents a very different picture: there were again three English free tenants, holding respectively 53 acres, 40 acres, and *quadam pecia terra* – perhaps about 40 acres – and 12 acres. The rest of the population consisted of twenty-two betaghs holding 134 acres between them, and nine cottiers. Clearly, in this area, the English settlers were completely outnumbered.[41]

Evidence for Co. Dublin is disappointingly lacking in precision. We have, however, detailed figures for the manor of Corduff: nine free tenants, all apparently English, with holdings ranging from 23 acres (the holder of this also had 22 acres at farm) to 3; eight farmers, of whom five were Irish; twenty-seven cottagers, who are not named, but some of whom, in this area, were probably English.[42] Again in Co. Dublin, we have apparently detailed extents of the lands of the archbishop in 1326, but it is impossible to extract statistics from them: the most that can be said is that the general picture is much the same as for Cloncurry, with a number of small English freeholders, a good many farmers, both English and Irish, a number of betaghs, and everywhere burgesses, not only in New Street, St Patrick's Street and St Kevin's Street in the suburbs of Dublin, but also 122 burgages at Swords doing labour services, as did the 36 burgages of Lusk, and the fifteen burgesses of Tallaght; sixty-six burgesses at Rathcoole; 32 burgages at Clondalkan with labour services; the burgagers of Dunlavan, who held 4 ploughlands; the 84 burgages of Donahymelagh (Burgage, Co. Wicklow); the 160 burgages of Ballymore; 17 burgages at Shankill with labour services; 39 at Dalkey; and 18½ at Kilmacberne ([?] Monastery, Co. Wicklow).[43]

In Munster, we have some very detailed extents of individual manors in Tipperary. At Moycarkey in 1304, there were thirty-nine free tenants, four of whom were probably Irish. One held 2 ploughlands, one a ploughland and a half, and one 1 ploughland. Three had half a ploughland apiece, one 40 acres, one (who may have been Irish) 28, three 20 acres each. All the rest of the holdings, except one of 16 acres, are of 10 acres or less, and seven hold only a messuage and courtyard: clearly these must have been wage-earners or craftsmen. Three of them seem to be Irish; the rest have English names. There are six farmers, three English and three Irish; the largest holding is 10 acres. Lastly, there are four cottiers, one of whom is not named, while one is English and two Irish. No betaghs seem to have existed on this manor and its population

40 *Red bk Ormond*, pp 24–5. The total area given in the extent is 561 acres, probably equivalent to about 1,402 statute acres. The area of the parish is 2,985 acres, much of which is mountain. 41 Ibid., p. 23. 42 Ibid., pp 25–7. The total acreage given in the extent is 404. Corduff has always been part of the manor of Lusk. 43 *Reg. Alen*, pp 170–96.

was clearly overwhelmingly English: thirty-nine English tenants as against nine Irish. This was a manor where the immediate lord was actually resident (it was, apparently, his only holding) and this may very probably explain its rather unusual structure.[44]

Moyaliff, also in Tipperary, was almost entirely a burgess settlement. *Circa* 1305, sixty-two burgesses, who owed carrying services, are named: all but three have English names. There is one English farmer; one free tenant holding a ploughland and one holding 16 acres; and three military tenants, two of whose holdings seem to be outside the parish. There are no other tenants at all, and here again the population is overwhelmingly English: sixty-two English names to three Irish.[45] But Moyaliff lies under the mountains and must always have been exposed to Irish pressure: in 1338, we hear that the demesne lands

> solebant esse sub carucis domini ... modo ad nullum precium extendunt pro eo quod predictus Jacobus concessit dictam terram Hibernicis ibidem per cartam suam ad pacem tenendam sibi et hominibus suis ibidem et ideo nulli Anglici ausi sunt dictam terram tenere nec allocare ibidem, ideo nichil inde percepi potest ... Placita et perquisita hundredorum ibidem ad nullum precium extendunt quia non ausi sint tenere placita ibidem pro Hibernicis.

The burgesses still remained, as did the two large military tenants and one free tenant, but clearly their position was becoming precarious.[46]

Of course, English settlement in Tipperary, even in the south of the county, was not everywhere as dense as in these manors. In 1333, Lisronagh, one of the manors held in dower by Elizabeth de Burgo, had not only one English free tenant holding a ploughland and two holding each half a knight's fee; an unspecified number of burgesses (probably about forty-eight since their burgage rent was 48*s.* 1*d.*, and probably all English); twelve cottiers, of whom ten have English names; and an unspecified number of gavillers; but also forty-three betaghs, of whom four have Welsh names, Rys and Walshe. It seems clear that more than half the population of the manor was of English descent, but that there was a very substantial Irish minority.[47]

In north Tipperary, the position was very different. In Dunkerrin, there were a number of tenants of English descent holding knight's fees and eighteen with

44 *Red bk Ormond*, pp 56–60. The total acreage given in the extent is 1,308. The parish contains 3,835 statute acres. 45 Ibid., pp 64–7. The inquisition is undated, but must belong to the same period as those of the other Tipperary manors. The total acreage, apart from the two large military tenants, is 1,395. The parish contains 8,021 acres, much of it mountain. Ardmail seems to have been a manor of precisely the same type, but the burgesses are not listed (ibid., pp 62–4). 46 C 135/55/5; *COD*, iii, 375. *CIPM*, viii, no. 184, omits the passage quoted. 47 *Lisronagh rental*.

substantial holdings of half a ploughland and upwards; but it is only round Roscrea, where there were of course burgesses, that there is any evidence of English smallholders: eight or nine holding from 1 to 22 acres. Seirkieran was held by twenty-three small tenants, only two or three of whom were English, with fifteen more very small farmers and cottiers, all of whom were Irish. There are betaghs in several places, as well as Irishmen holding in free tenure. Clearly, though there had been some English settlement in this area, it had not been at all dense.[48] Again, north of Nenagh, there had been relatively little English settlement: the inquisition *post mortem* of 1338 shows the Irish predominant in this area.[49]

For Co. Limerick, there is again a fair amount of evidence, though it does not lend itself to close statistical analysis. At Caherconlish in 1300, there were six tenants of English descent holding knight's fees, which must all have been outside the manor proper, and five more holding lands ranging from a ploughland to 'quadam placea communi in Rubia Mora'. The number of burgesses is not given, but they held 20 ploughlands in their burgages. There was one named Irish farmer, holding 10½ acres, and three English, holding 12, 9, and 7 acres; but there were also divers tenants unnamed, who held 78 acres between them, and others holding a ploughland. The cottiers again are not enumerated, nor are the betaghs, who held a ploughland. Clearly, there had been a substantial English settlement in the borough, but we have no indication of actual numbers.[50]

The partition of Atherlow, Athneasy and Lickadoon between the three sisters and heiresses of John de Multon of Egremond, in 1341, gave Walter and Elizabeth de Bermingham three English military tenants of Aherlow; four small English free tenants, holding from 18 to 8 acres; thirty-eight burgesses, of whom only one has a certainly Irish name; and ten cottiers, of whom nine seem to be English. In Athneasy, they got two betaghs; nineteen English free tenants, of whom one held 2 ploughlands, two 1½ each, two had each 1, three half a ploughland each, two had half a ploughland and a quarter between them, four had each a quarter, four held a quarter between them, and one had 6 acres. There were also nine cottiers, of whom probably six were Irish. In Lickadoon, they had three English free tenants holding 2 acres, 1 acre and half an acre; and four betaghs.[51] While it is impossible to base any exact statistics on this, since we know nothing of the other purparties, the picture is again one of a substantial settlement of small English tenants still persisting in this area in spite of the disturbances of the century.

At Glenogra, there were, in 1298, six ploughlands in burgages, for which the burgesses rendered 119*s.* 6*d.*: this probably means something like 120 burgages.

48 *Red bk Ormond*, pp 147–54. 49 *CIPM*, viii, no. 184. We may note that there were burgesses at Weyperous (Ballinacloch) who are not mentioned in the calendar (cf. C 135/55/5). 50 *Red bk Ormond*, pp 154–8. 51 *Reg. Gormanston*, pp 111–14.

There was one English free tenant holding four ploughlands and four holding a ploughland and a half between them; betaghs held three ploughlands.[52] At Newcastle in the same year, there was one large military tenant and twelve other English free tenants with holdings ranging from 3½ ploughlands to 10 acres; but here betaghs held a good deal of land, and the English settlers must have been in a small minority. At Shanid, there is a separate section dealing with the lands of the Irish, that is apparently the betaghs, who held a good deal, and though there are eighteen English free tenants there is only one really small holding: 12 acres held by two tenants. There are then 5 holdings each of half a ploughland, 3 of one ploughland, one of 3 ploughlands, and the rest are in the range of knight's fees. Clearly, an occupying English tenantry hardly existed here.[53] At the other side of the county, however, eleven named tenants of the vill of Any (Hospital) in 1339 are all English.[54]

More illustrations might be produced, but they would not alter the general picture. Clearly, in many parts of the country, there was a high proportion of English tenants holding either freely – that is, in fee and inheritance – or by burgage tenure, or on lease for a term of years holdings small enough to make it a practical certainty that they were cultivating them themselves. A peasant occupation of this character could only have been produced by a substantial immigration in the first couple of generations of the conquest, and its distribution must be closely related to the varying fortunes of the colony in the fourteenth century.

52 *CDI 1293–1301*, pp 254–5. 53 Ibid., pp 256–7, 258–9. 54 *Reg. Kilmainham*, p. 119.

CHAPTER 16

# The organization of Anglo-Irish agriculture in the Middle Ages*

*A.J. Otway-Ruthven*

The Anglo-Norman colony established in Ireland in the late twelfth century was necessarily of a largely rural character and it is clear that, as it developed, very considerable bodies of English settlers were established not only in the towns, but also in the countryside, all over south-eastern Ireland from Louth to Cork and Kerry along the coast, and inland wherever conditions were favourable. Manors were set up and were organized very largely on the English pattern, but with interesting differences. The most striking of these is, perhaps, the enormous number of places which were never more than villages which were, nevertheless, given the elements of a town constitution by their lords in the thirteenth century. The usual pattern was the customs of Breteuil, and the burgesses held their burgages at a low fixed rent and could deal in them freely, while they had their own court or hundred, quite distinct from that of the manor. They were, however, essentially agricultural settlements, and while there is, as far as I know, no evidence whatever as to how the communities of English farmers which were scattered all over the south-east, and indeed in many other parts of Ireland, were formed, I think there can be little or no doubt that the problem was approached very much as similar problems were approached on the continent, and that settlers were attracted by offers of easier tenures than they enjoyed at home and special advantages such as were given by the charters of the dozens of abortive towns of which we have evidence, while it is tempting to think that, as on the continent, professional 'locators' may have been employed to collect and organize groups of settlers and lay out the new villages.[1]

Everyone who has written on the history of medieval Ireland has assumed that the openfield system with its scattered holdings in a rigid structure of fixed and permanent strips of land arranged in a gridiron pattern, as opposed to the Celtic system of impermanent strips, was employed by the Anglo-Norman settlers, but so far as I am aware no attempt has yet been made to marshal the evidence for it. Unfortunately, no detailed terrier or survey seems to have

* First published in *JRSAI*, 81 (1951), 1–13. 1 See J.H. Clapham, John Harold and Eileen Power (eds), *The Cambridge economic history of Europe from the decline of the Roman empire*, i: *the agrarian life of the Middle Ages* (Cambridge, 1941), pp 83ff, 373ff.

survived from the Middle Ages, so that we can never hope to discover exactly how the lands of any Anglo-Irish village were originally laid out. But any collection of medieval Anglo-Irish charters will show on examination clear traces of a system of cultivation exactly similar to that which existed in the greater part of England and, indeed, in northwestern Europe as a whole.[2] Most of our surviving charters, of course, are concerned with grants of large areas to great men, but every collection also contains records of the holdings of humbler folk and these show quite clearly the existence of scattered holdings consisting of many small strips in a number of different fields, which are to be found all over south-eastern Ireland. Wherever such holdings existed, we may assume with confidence that the village lands were laid out in open fields. They were to be found all over Louth;[3] in Meath;[4] probably in Westmeath, though the evidence here is not conclusive;[5] all over Dublin;[6] in all the remaining counties of Leinster;[7] and the system seems to have extended at least as far as the borders of Tipperary and Limerick.[8] But we should observe that the charters also give the impression that a good deal of land was held in comparatively large blocks, and it is impossible to say how far this had been so from the time when the holdings were first laid out, and how far it was the result of the process of consolidation which was undoubtedly going on in many districts throughout the thirteenth century and later. Thus, a grant of an acre in Kyllannovyr, *c.*1250, to John, son of Stephen, describes it as in length from the land of the lord, E., to that of John, son of Stephen, W., and in breadth between the land of said John, S., and the land of the lord, N.[9] About 1305, Richard de Fraxineto granted to William, son of Philip Brun of Kilram, a stang[10] of land in the tenement of Gilbert de Kilram in Kilram, lying in length and breadth between the land of Philip Brun on both sides, in exchange for another stang of land in the tenement of Kilram in Tilathglasse.[11] About 1350, a grant of nine and a half acres in four parcels in Shortalstown, Co. Kilkenny, describes all of them as lying next the grantee's land; one parcel of three acres is in the field called the long land between grantee's land on each side.[12] Clearly, in all these instances and many more, scattered strips were being made into compact holdings. On the other hand, some of the larger blocks may be due to individual enterprise in clearing land for cultivation. For instance, *c.*1220, the archbishop of Dublin granted to William Gascoing, in exchange for property beside the archbishop's house in Dublin, sixteen acres which Robert Blund the smith held and which he cleared

2 Ibid., passim. 3 For Louth, see the Dowdall deeds in the National Library, a calendar of which will shortly be published by IMC [EN. *Dowdall deeds* appeared in 1960. The volume began under the editorship of Charles McNeill, but the finished product is mostly the work of Prof. Otway-Ruthven]. 4 *Reg. Gormanston*, passim. 5 *Reg. Tristernagh*, passim. 6 See, among many others, the deeds cited below. 7 See, in particular, *COD*, passim. 8 Ibid. 9 *COD*, i, no. 107. 10 A rood. 11 *COD*, i, no. 383. Kilram was in the manor of Gowran, Co. Kilkenny (cf. *Red bk Ormond*, p. 35). 12 *COD*, i, no. 841.

from the wood, lying between the archbishop's land and the land of Reginald de Bernevale.[13] We cannot tell which process lies behind such a charter as the late thirteenth-century one from Corbali (where it is quite clear that strip holdings existed), which mentions eleven and a half acres lying between the land of Thomas de Lega, the grantee, and the land of Sir Hamund le Gras in breadth; in length from the way leading to Tirschet to Thomas' wood called Hymegan.[14] But one thing is fairly clear: in most, though not in all, cases the demesne lands of the lord lay quite separate from the lands of the tenants.[15] Moreover, the lands of the unfree tenants, the betaghs, who existed on most, but not apparently on all manors, seem to have been entirely separate from the lands of other classes of the agricultural community; where they exist in any numbers, they are generally recorded as holding definite townlands.[16] Their holdings were, presumably, cultivated on the native system. Thus we must picture the area of strip cultivation not as continuous, but as divided not only by the commons, but also by compact areas of the lord's demesne lands and those larger individual holdings which we have seen in process of formation, as well as by the holdings of the betaghs.

All deductions made, however, it is clear that scattered strip holdings were of fundamental importance in the rural economy of medieval Anglo-Ireland. It may be as well to observe, before reviewing the evidence, that there is at least one document which strongly suggests that the word acre was sometimes used in Ireland, as in England, to mean merely the individual strip, the unit of cultivation, which might be very much smaller than the statute acre. It is a rental of the early fifteenth century, which seems to belong to Co. Kilkenny, and refers in several places simply to 'acres cultivated'.[17] We should note too that, where the acre is used as a measurement of area in medieval Ireland, it seems to be very much larger than either the statute acre or the Irish plantation acre. It probably varied from district to district, but Mills thought that round Dublin it was about 2¼ statute acres.[18]

We may begin a survey of the evidence, of which I have taken only a small sample from a great number of charters, with two late documents which give a full account of single holdings. The first dates from the middle of the sixteenth century and is headed, 'the tylling landis longing to oure Lady Church of Callane [Co. Kilkenny] as hit appereth her after euery parcell by hitself'. It is much too long to quote in full: it enumerates 52 distinct parcels of land, containing only 68¼ acres, and lying in seventeen distinctly named places. The

13 *Reg. St John the Baptist*, no. 338. 14 *COD*, i, no. 208. For Corbali, see below, p. 279. 15 See, e.g., *Lisronagh rental*. Some exceptions will be noted below. 16 James Mills, 'Tenants and agriculture near Dublin', *JRSAI*, 20 (1890), 54–6; *Lisronagh rental*, pp 45–7; *Rot. pipae Clonensis*, passim; *CDI*, passim. 17 *COD*, ii, no. 421, pp 313–4. 18 James Mills, 'Notices of the manor of St Sepulchre, Dublin, in the fourteenth century', *JRSAI*, 4th ser., 9 (1889), 35–6.

largest parcel of land is four acres and a stang, but the typical parcel consists of an acre or less.[19] The second relates to Rathcoole, Co. Dublin, and is included in a list of the property of Richard Stanyhurst, a Dublin merchant, in 1477. He owned twenty-six acres of arable and an acre of meadow, the arable held in twenty parcels, and the meadow in four: the whole was let in two separate farms.[20]

These are the only documents of the kind of which I know, but they clearly show the existence of an openfield agricultural system, for we cannot suppose that these strips, many of them less than an acre in size, were fenced. We may now take the single charters of which the bulk of the evidence consists, of which the most usual tvpe deals only with a single acre, as in a deed of 1404 preserved among the papers of Lord Talbot de Malahide, by which Nicholas White grants to Nicholas White, merchant, an acre of arable land in the field of Lite Nardaghes in Scryne, between the land formerly belonging to Henry Topp, butcher, E., and the land formerly Robert Topp's, W., with a stang of meadow between the meadow formerly Thomas White's, W., and Peter Coke's meadow, E.[21] But a large number of charters reveal the existence of widely scattered holdings in many parts of the country. Among the Dowdall deeds, there is one of the late thirteenth century by which William, son of Richard the deacon of Rath, grants to Richard de Graftoun two acres of land in Rathmakneue. Two separate half acres lie in the field called Morefurlong;[22] a stang lies *in curvo campo* with the land of Richard de Graftoun as its western boundary – an example of the tendency to consolidate holdings to which reference has already been made; a half stang lies in the place called Hokys; and one half acre and half stang lie in the common pasture of the vill of Rath. About 1332, another grant of land in the same village concerns a half acre and a half stang of which the half acre lies in the field which is called le litefeld in two parts and the half stang lies in the field called Tibbirsawan.[23] At Slane, Co. Meath, a deed of 1334 refers to 69 acres, with half an acre of meadow and pasture, of which 30 acres of land and meadow are of the land of William Wright, 13 acres are at Loghill, 5 at Cnokmark, 6 at Baretescarrig, 3 at Waritrehill, and the remaining 12 acres lie in twelve separate parcels, of which the largest is 2¼ acres and the smallest a stang, between the lands of other men east and west.[24] This deed is of particular interest as one of the few Irish instances in which the land of the lord appears

**19** *Ir. mon. deeds, 1200–1600*, pp 186–90. **20** J.G. Smyly (ed.), 'Old deeds in the library of Trinity College – part 5', *Hermathena*, 71 (1948), 38–9. **21** This unpublished deed is quoted by kind permission of Lord Talbot. **22** It is probable that, in many cases, the *campus* of our medieval deeds means furlong, as it evidently does here, rather than field. There are only a few medieval Anglo-Irish deeds which give clear evidence in their descriptions of boundaries of strips running at right angles in adjacent furlongs – for instance one of 1293 in *COD*, i, no. 313. **23** These deeds are quoted by permission of IMC from the calendar now in the press [EN. *Dowdall deeds*, nos. 16, 173]. **24** *Reg. Gormanston*, pp 55–6.

to lie in the open fields, since the land of the lord of Slane is given as the western boundary of two of the strips. A further point of interest is the field name New Land, which suggests a fairly recent extension of tillage.

In Co. Dublin, we may quote deeds from Dundrum, Rathcoole, Crumlin and Swords. A grant of 1346 concerns nine acres in the manor of Dundrum, of which six lie scattered in the field of Kylgeman, and three lie in detached parcels in the north part of the town of Balyfynch.[25] In Rathcoole, a deed of 1318 grants two acres of arable in 'le Brodefeld': they lie in four separate half-acre strips.[26] In Crumlin, a deed of 1468 grants 25 acres in twelve parcels: an acre and a half near Biggeslie called le Hollowcrofte (which must mean that it was enclosed); an acre and a stang of meadow and another stang near the said Crofte; two acres of land in le Stonywayfeld; an acre and a half in le Yoghillfeld; an acre in a park (an enclosure) at Minganesborres called le Langheres; half an acre in le Kingesfeld; five acres in le Camyshefeld; an acre and a half in le Coilaghfeld; two acres and a half in le Firrewode; seven acres in le Cuokefeld; half an acre in a park near Lawles is place; an acre in Cuokefeld atte the Popell.[27] In 1490, four acres of arable land in the fields of Swords lay in three parcels, and here we may be tolerably certain that the lord's land lay in the open fields, since one acre lies between the land of the archbishop of Dublin, S. and N.[28]

The accidents of survival have left us among the Ormond deeds a large body of evidence for Co. Kilkenny, of which a few examples may be quoted. A number of thirteenth-century deeds relating to Corbali, which seems to be in the modern parish of Tullaroan, barony of Crannagh,[29] are particularly explicit. Thus a grant, *c.*1277, of eight acres says that two lie together in the moor between the land of William Casse and the land of Nicholas Brabezun, and six lie in four different places in the field that lies between the mansion that was Walter Cor's and the land that was Nicholas Brabecun's.[30] A late thirteenth-century deed from Villa Trenedyn (par. Traddingstown, bar. Gowran) is of particular interest, as it appears to relate to a complete holding. Roger Samson and Agnes his wife grant to Warin le Deveneys, burgess of Kilkenny, and his heirs, 47 acres in Villa Trenedyn, of which 15 lie in the field of Waytesameshulle, 15 in the field of Slabachsesfeld, 15 in the field of Cnochsynnach and 2 in the park of Holdewalles.[31] Here we see the holding equally divided between three fields and probably widely scattered in each of them, though no further details are given. In Dunnamaggan in 1293, one and three-quarter acres of arable lie in three different fields.[32] In Kells in Ossory in 1306, five and a half acres of arable lie *in diversis campis*.[33] A deed of 1320 relating to small scattered holdings in

25 *Calendar of the ancient deeds and muniments preserved in the Pembroke Estate Office* (Dublin, 1891), no. 33. 26 Smyly, 'Old deeds – pt 1, *Hermathena*, 66 (1945), p. 37. 27 Smyly, 'Old deeds – pt 4', *Hermathena*, 70 (1947), p. 19. 28 Smyly, 'Old deeds – pt 5', *Hermathena*, 71 (1948), 45–6. 29 *COD*, i, no. 174, note at p. 74. 30 Ibid., i, no. 206. 31 Ibid., i, no. 267. 32 Ibid., i, no. 313. 33 Ibid., i, no. 407.

Beled and Jonstoun may be noted, as it refers expressly to common of 'Gortinnerry and Gortinnotry and Gortingown and Mullanis McGillekewyn at the open time [L. *tempore aperto*]', which seems a clear reference to the communal servitudes of the openfield system.[34] A Carrickmacgriffyn deed of 1321 is worth quoting: it refers to seven acres of arable in three parcels, of which one, consisting of two acres, lies in breadth between grantor's land on both sides.[35] Clearly, the grantor's land was here being cultivated in separate units or this division would not have been made. In Haketestoun in 1353, we have a grant of 2¼ acres of arable in the field called le Mocheporte, two acres in the field called le Pyttelonde and half an acre in le Woweacris, together with common of pasture of the whole tenement.[36] A deed of 1447 refers to ten acres of arable in Callan, lying in five parcels: two acres are in the field called le blak rathe (a field name repeated in the sixteenth-century list of church property in Callan referred to earlier) between the earl of Ormond's lands, E. and W., which seems another clear instance of the lord's lands lying in the open fields.[37]

The list might be greatly prolonged, but I shall give only two more instances, from other parts of the country. A deed of *c.*1260 from Arklow grants six continuous acres in the southern part of the great field.[38] In Tipperary, we have a grant of 1330 concerning an acre and a half in Rathcool in the field which is called Glamegaddi, in width between the land of William Brit on one side and grantor's land on the other.[39]

The process by which this system broke up has not yet been worked out. In a few places, indeed, it lasted into the nineteenth century. As late as 1825, the strip holdings of the Middle Ages remained more or less unaltered in the village of Rathcoole, Co. Dublin, in Dalkey and in Saggart, while in Clondalkin they lasted well into the second half of the eighteenth century.[40] The map (map 2) is from a survey of the lands of Dalkey made in 1765 and copied in 1830, when conditions seem to have been still unchanged. The furlong organization which certainly existed in Rathcoole does not seem to have existed in Dalkey, no doubt because of the nature of the ground, but the long narrow strips, the dispersion of holdings, the meadow land and common are clearly shown, as well as irregularly shaped fields, probably representing late medieval and early modern enclosures, on the outskirts. The lands of the lord, the archbishop of Dublin (numbered on map 2), lay together between the tenants' lands and the common. The total area involved was 123 acres 34 perches (plantation measure) of common, and 152 acres 36 perches of arable. Of the arable, including meadow and gardens, 49 acres 13 perches were held by the archbishop, and 7 acres 31

34 Ibid., i, no. 548. 35 Ibid., i, no. 552. 36 *COD*, ii, no. 19. 37 *COD*, iii, no. 171. 38 *Reg. St John the Baptist*, no. 359. 39 Ibid., no. 475. 40 Longfield maps in the National Library of Ireland. A map of Rathcoole, *c.*1825, showing strip holdings and furlongs, is reproduced by John Hooper Harvey, *Dublin: a study in environment* (London, 1949), p. 65.

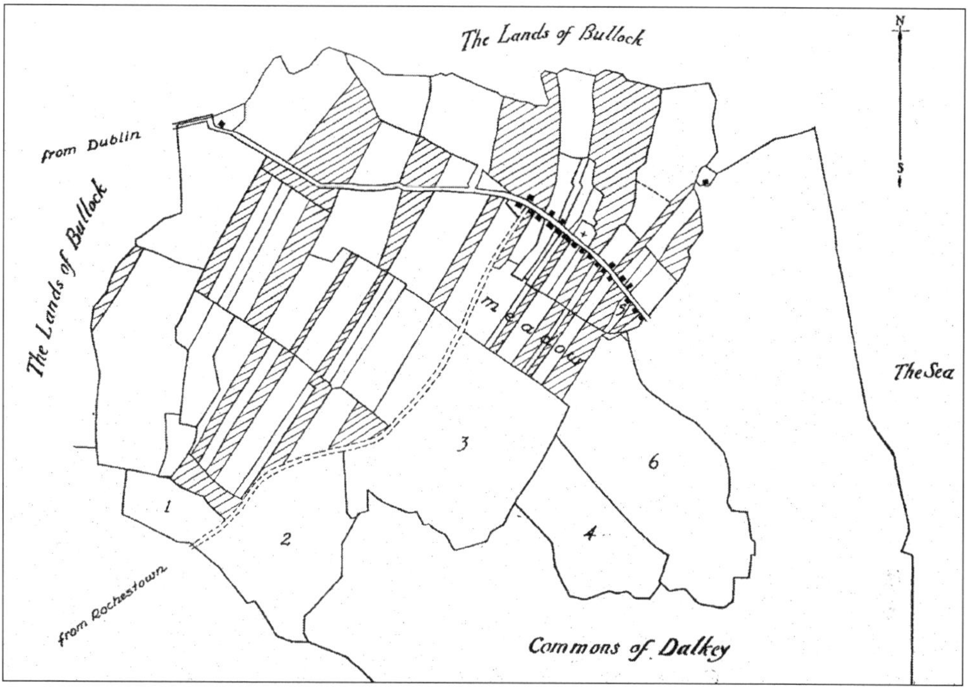


Map 2. Strip holdings in Dalkey, *c.*1830 (adapted from NLI, Longfield maps, Co. Dublin, iii, no. 77). © Royal Society of Antiquaries of Ireland.

perches in twelve separate parcels by a tenant under the dean and chapter of Christ Church. The remainder was in two holdings, all let to subtenants, of 67 acres 3 roods and 26 perches in forty-four parcels, and 28 acres and 4 perches in twenty-eight parcels respectively. The land of the latter holding has been shaded to illustrate the dispersion of strips. The largest separate parcel in this holding was just over 4 acres; many of the strips are less than an acre in size. The meadow was clearly held in strips originally only a rood in area, though here and elsewhere in the fields there had clearly been some consolidation of adjacent strips. Our only medieval account of Dalkey, in 1326, shows 40 acres leased to tenants at will, and 9 lying waste, no doubt substantially the area shown as held by the archbishop on our map, while the remainder was held by 39 burgage tenants, who were probably mostly fishermen. On the archiepiscopal lands north of Dublin, some traces of the medieval organization seem to have survived till late in the nineteenth century.[41] But it is only on the archiepiscopal

41 Longfield maps, Co. Dublin, iii, no. 77; *Reg. Alen*, p. 195; 'Miscellanea', *JRSAI*, 20 (1890), 81–2 (Mr R. Romney Kane (MRIA), Ailesbury Road, Dublin, to Rev. Dr G.T. Stokes, 4 Jan. 1890).

lands that we find these survivals, and only in the Pale that the conditions which made them possible existed: elsewhere, the exodus of the rural population of which we have so many complaints in the later Middle Ages, combined with Irish reconquest, must have swept away the arrangements made in the late twelfth and early thirteenth centuries. And even in the Pale, a distinct tendency to make enclosed fields is apparent in the fifteenth century, when we begin to find a large number of references to parks, or enclosures.[42] Usually, the documents speak only of the completed park, but a rare deed allows us to see it in the making, as in Malahide in 1495, when Thomas Balle was leased 'four acres more or less of tilling land to make a park'.[43]

The system of cultivation adopted by the Anglo-Norman settlers in Ireland is known to us almost entirely from the records of the greater estates. The extents of Ormond property contained in the Red book of Ormond, which cover manors scattered throughout the south-east, and the records of ecclesiastical property near Dublin all show a three course rotation of the type common in England: winter corn (wheat or rye), spring corn (oats) and fallow. The areas under each were approximately equal, though there were not necessarily only three fields. The Ormond manor of Lisronagh, where the lord's demesne was apparently quite separate from the lands of the tenants, had its demesne lands divided into twenty-six denominations, containing 358 acres and 1¼ stangs;[44] and at Carkenlis, Co. Limerick, in 1300, the demesne arable was in twelve denominations.[45] At Turvey, Co. Dublin, and at Cloncurry, Co. Kildare, however, there were apparently only three fields in the early fourteenth century.[46] It is possible that, in some places, a two course rotation was that first used by the settlers: by 1326, there were three demesne *seysona* of roughly equal area in the archbishop of Dublin's manor of Cullen, 50 acres under wheat, 48 under oats, and 68 fallow; but an undated valuation inserted at the end of the *Liber Niger* states that the demesnes of Cullen are 246 acres of arable, 92 in the field called Shanbalymore, and 74 in the field called Balymaregan and Barlycroft. The remaining 80 acres are not accounted for, but were no doubt in the hands of farmers, as they were in 1326.[47]

Labour services played a comparatively small part in the working of these demesnes. The week-work of the English manor seems to have been unknown in Ireland. The typical unfree tenant in Ireland was obliged to plough an acre for wheat and an acre for oats if he had a complete plough-team, and, if not, to join his neighbours in doing so; to reap for one or two days in harvest; perhaps to cart the corn to the haggard; to do one or two days hoeing, or to help with the hay; while, not uncommonly, he had to cart fuel as well. In addition, he paid a money rent, usually the same per acre as that paid by other classes of tenant on

42 For instance at Crumlin in 1468 (above, p. 279). 43 Quoted by kind permission of Lord Talbot. 44 *Lisronagh rental*, pp 42–3. 45 *Red bk Ormond*, p. 155. 46 Ibid., pp 27, 28. 47 Mills, 'Notices of the manor of St Sepulchre, Dublin', pp 37–8.

the same manor. It should be observed that the smaller free tenants and tenants holding by lease were commonly obliged to perform labour services of much the same type as those performed by betaghs, the equivalent of the English villein tenant.[48] The heaviest services I have noted were at Balybothy, Co. Tipperary, in 1415–16. Here each tenant must plough an acre for wheat and an acre for oats, and in addition owed the lord five days reaping, five days weeding and five days carting grain. But nowhere do we find anything resembling the hundred days work or more in the year which the English villein was commonly obliged to perform on his lord's land – a difference which can probably be explained, at least in part, by the problem of attracting settlers and the difficulty of retaining the betagh when, in many parts of the country, he could easily flee to the unconquered Irish districts taking the cattle, which seem to have been his chief property, with him.[49]

Clearly, every Norman-Irish lord who worked his demesnes himself must have employed a regular staff of paid labourers, nor was the work of the customary tenants at times of special pressure always sufficient to supplement this. The detailed accounts of the Christ Church property at Clonkeen (Kill of the Grange, Co. Dublin) for the harvest of 1344 show that out of a total of 562 days' work performed by reapers, 471 were done by labourers hired by the day and only 91 by the customary tenants.[50] The permanent staff of this manor was a bailiff, a serjeant, a carter, two ploughmen, two plough drivers, a door keeper, a woman 'drying malt and doing other necessary work within the manor', and a cowherd. Other labour was hired by the day as required.[51] The customary tenants on this manor did two separate ploughings, one in winter seed time and the other the spring ploughing, with fourteen ploughs.[52] Unfortunately, we do not know what the extent of the demesne at Clonkeen was, but the amount of wheat produced in 1344 was 113 crannocs 3 pecks, which – if the figure of 2¼ crannocs per acre in ordinary years given for the Ormond manor of Cloncurry, Co. Kildare, in 1304, may be taken as applicable – would give between 40 and 50 acres under wheat. Again, taking the Cloncurry figure of 5 bushels of wheat to sow an acre, the 27 crannocs 1¼ pecks of wheat allowed for seed this year would represent roughly the same area. On the same basis, there would appear to have been something like 30 acres under oats and a small area sown with barley, peas and beans – a total under the plough in any one year of some 80 acres. If the tenants' ploughs ploughed the usual acre apiece at each ploughing, this would leave 52 acres to be ploughed by the two demesne ploughs, and we may observe that the Cloncurry extent says that a plough of eight oxen well managed can plough 25 acres a year *quamlibet seysona*.[53]

48 For the different classes of tenant, see below pp 284–6. 49 *Lisronagh rental*, p. 47; *Red bk Ormond*, pp 123, 157 and passim; *Account roll Holy Trinity*, pp 189–98; *CDI*, passim. 50 *Account roll Holy Trinity*, pp 64–7. 51 Ibid., p. 62 and passim. 52 Ibid., pp 58, 78. 53 *Red bk Ormond*, p. 28; *Account roll Holy Trinity*, pp 77–82. A crannoc of wheat was

Though it is reasonably clear that nowhere in Ireland were labour services of really considerable importance in the economy of the manor, they continued to be stipulated for in leases to the end of the Middle Ages. In 1352, a lease of Tipperstown for sixteen years provided that, in addition to a money rent, the tenant should plough the demesnes at Clonkeen for one day at the winter sowing and one day at the spring sowing with his own plough, should reap for one day in harvest, and cart the corn for one day with his own cart or two cars.[54] As late as 1489, a lease of a messuage in the town of Malahide requires no money rent but nine harvest days, weeding days, rushes twice a year, ale silver, and a watch hen (that is, a render of a fowl, usually at Christmas) according to the custom of the town of Malahide. If the tenant falls in any contempt of the harvest days, the contempt to be 4*d.*, weeding days 1*d.*, rushes ½*d.* The tenant's heir was to be admitted on payment of 26*s.* 8*d.*, and the tenure appears to be very similar to English copyhold tenures.[55]

We may now consider the different classes to be found on the Anglo-Irish manor. At the top of the social scale come the free tenants, a term which is practically equivalent to tenant by military service, liable to the usual feudal incidents and generally paying, in addition, a money rent which seems to be connected with the relationship of the original grantee to his lord rather than with the area involved. In such exceptionally large manors as the Butler manor of Thurles, a free tenant might hold what was, in effect, a large sub-manor with a number of substantial free tenants under him.[56] The holdings of free tenants on the normal manor varied from perhaps 1,200 acres of arable (such a holding would not, of course, be involved in the fields of any village immediately dependent on the lord of the manor, but would be a separate entity with its own organization) to as little as one acre, and the smaller free tenants were sometimes required to perform labour services.[57] But whatever the services required of a free tenant, he held in fee and inheritance, and his services were fixed forever by his charter. The free tenant was usually, but not invariably, of English origin.[58] In a great many manors, an important class parallel to, but distinct from, the smaller free tenants, was that of the burgesses, the privileged inhabitants of a nucleated village given the elements of a town constitution.[59]

Next to the free tenants come the farmers. These were rent-paying tenants, holding for a term and on conditions fixed by their leases. Their holdings were usually small and they were sometimes the smaller free tenants who had not

equivalent to one English quarter, and a crannoc of oats to two. The eight ox team was apparently used throughout the thirteenth century (see *Pipe roll 14 John*, pp 38–40). 54 *Account roll Holy Trinity*, pp 207–9. 55 Quoted by kind permission of Lord Talbot. 56 *Red bk Ormond*, pp 35–9, 71. 57 Mills, 'Tenants and agriculture near Dublin', p. 59. The very large holdings were, of course, exceptional. It may be observed that the average size of the manor in Co. Dublin seems to have been less than elsewhere. 58 For names of obviously Irish free tenants see, e.g., *Red bk Ormond*, pp 20, 30. 59 See above, p. 275.

enough land of their own. They might be either English or Irish.[60] Below them were the gavillers, a term which seems to be peculiar to Ireland. At Lisronagh in 1326, their land is described as set to farm at the will of the lord; in the sixteenth century, Archbishop Alen described them as 'firmarii at will or by charter, not cotters or betaghs, but in the nature of copyholders'. In 1311, at Kilkea, Co. Kildare, they were described as tenants at the will of the lord.[61] They seem to have been mostly of English origin. It seems probable that they were, in fact, in much the same position as the English copyholder of the sixteenth century and that, though nominally they were tenants at will, in practice their holdings descended from father to son. They were clearly personally free.

The English villein was represented in Ireland by the betagh, personally unfree and always of Irish origin, though it is by no means improbable that, as the Middle Ages went on, men of English origin fell into this class.[62] Betaghs existed on most manors but not, apparently, on all, and their lands seem to have been separate from those of other classes of the agricultural community.[63] Judging by their surnames, where these are recorded, they lived in family groups. They paid a money rent for their land, which seems to have been held and cultivated in common, and were, in addition, bound to perform labour services, which were everywhere fixed by custom by the time we begin to get detailed information in the second half of the thirteenth century. There is some reason to suppose that these services tended to fall in amount in the later thirteenth and early fourteenth centuries,[64] and at the same time there was certainly a tendency in some parts of the country to replace them by a money payment: a common entry in inquisitions *post mortem* at the end of the thirteenth century is, 'here there are no works of betaghs because they are charged with rent'.[65] The typical labour services have already been described; in addition, they might be obliged to do other carting for the lord, to carry his letters concerning the affairs of the manor and other services of a similar kind.[66] Their heirs paid a heriot and, like the other classes of rural tenants except the burgesses, they were obliged to attend the lord's manor court.

Economically below the betaghs came the cottiers. These appear to have been of mixed origins: sometimes all bear English names (as at Lisronagh in 1326), sometimes Irish (as at Cloncurry in 1304). It is interesting to observe that no labour services are mentioned at Cloncurry. The cottier, however, normally performed labour services in addition to a small money rent: generally, two days

60 *Red bk Ormond*, passim. 61 Ibid., p. 13; *Lisronagh rental*, p. 43; Mills, 'Tenants and agriculture near Dublin', p. 55. 62 See, e.g., Nicholas Brymyngham, a *nativus* of the manor of Kilmainham in 1541 (*Extents Ir. mon. possessions*, p. 86). For the legal position of the betagh, see Otway-Ruthven, 'The native Irish and English law in medieval Ireland' (above, ch. 6). 63 See above, p. 277. 64 Mills, 'Tenants and agriculture near Dublin', p. 55. 65 *CDI*, passim. 66 *Lisronagh rental*, p. 47.

reaping and another two days in the year either hoeing or haymaking.[67] His holding was normally about half an acre.

Other aspects of the medieval Anglo-Irish manor closely resembled contemporary practice in England, though much work remains to be done on details. In particular, much work is needed on the details of agricultural practice, for which we have much more information than is commonly recognized, both in the sources already quoted, and in the still unpublished accounts of the Bigod lordship of Carlow in the late thirteenth century, which have been preserved in the Public Record Office, London. If I have succeeded in suggesting lines of approach to a subject much neglected among us, which is of fundamental historical importance, I have done all that I could hope.

67 Ibid., p. 48; *Red bk Ormond*, p. 33 and passim; *Account roll Holy Trinity*, pp 191–8.

CHAPTER 17

# The English and Ostmen in Ireland*

*Edmund Curtis*

As is well known, the adventurers of Norman and English blood who landed in Ireland in the years 1169–70 found themselves confronted not only by the Celtic natives, but also by a race who, like themselves, were Teutonic in blood and, as colonists and invaders, had preceded them by but a few hundred years. These were the descendants of Norwegian and Danish settlers who had blended now into a race, called by the generic name of Ostmen, both among themselves and by the English.[1] This race was practically an urban one. The Ostmen held five cities which they had founded and within whose walls they lived the lives of merchants, sometimes varied by acts of piracy – those cities being Dublin, Waterford, Limerick, Wexford and Cork. The first three were governed by petty kings, but it is uncertain whether the last two had dynasties of their own. Yet their colonies were not exclusively urban. The Dublin Ostmen had an indefinite rule and colonies extending over a district roughly corresponding to the modern Co. Dublin, stretching west to the modern Leixlip (the name of which indicates in Norse 'salmon-leap'), south to Wicklow and north over a much wider area extending to the borders of Meath, called by the Irish themselves Finegall, or 'boundary of the foreigners'. The whole formed a small kingdom called – in the Icelandic Landnámabók – 'Dyflinarski'. Waterford, a walled city in 1170, had probably rural settlements all along its fine harbour. A barony on the west side of the harbour, now called Gualtier, took its name from an Irish word, *gall-tir* ('foreigners' land') and has probably a like significance with Finegall. It is possible that the other three cities had a similar dependent district.

The circumstances of the conquest of these towns are well-enough known. It is sufficient to say that by the year 1200 all of them were in the hands of the English. What now happened to the Ostmen? It is probable that, of this powerful and numerous race, the greater part sailed off to the free Norse-land which remained in Man and the Scottish islands. Others, perhaps, went over to England to practise maritime trades. The pilots of the English seaports are

* First published in *EHR*, 23:90 (1908), 209–19. 1 Or rather by some form corresponding to the modern word Ostman. The Norse original was certainly Austmathr, 'Eastman'. Contemporary forms of the word are Oustmanni, Houstmanni, Eustmanni, Hostmanni etc. The modern 'Ostmen' has become accepted, but a good case might be made out for 'Ostmans' on the analogy of 'Normans' etc.

called Esturmanni in the documents of the thirteenth century. This itself is most certainly a Scandinavian word implying 'steersmen', and the pilots were probably mainly of Northman stock.[2] Here, then, was an occupation to which many of the Ostmen could turn. Those who remained were in the main practically excluded from those privileges, legal and commercial, which the English brought with them, though they received some favour not shown to the Irish.

In the first place, they were obliged to remove outside the walled towns. The idea was that 'cantreds', or 'hundreds', should be created for the Ostmen, outside of which they should not dwell. This kind of suburb was likely to be called after them. Thus, there was the well-known Ostmantown, on the north side of the Liffey, which afterwards became Oxmantown by corruption.[3] To this new town without the town, the Dublin Northmen were compelled to migrate. Similarly, there was a 'cantred' of the Ostmen near Limerick,[4] and near Waterford a 'vill of the Ostmen' was set up.[5] This compulsory migration took place either immediately after the cities fell into the hands of the newcomers or subsequently to a later rising of the older race, as, for instance, after the revolt of the Waterford Danes in 1174.[6] Of the land held by Ostmen far out in the country, probably most was confiscated or taken over, the owners having fled or been slain in the stand which the Northmen of Ireland had made. The royal race of Dublin had now for some time been designated by the Irish name MacTurcaill, a patronymic derived from that Torquil who was king of Dublin in 1133. The Asgall or Hasculf who was king in 1169, and whose attempt, by means of a viking rally, to recover Dublin ended in his own defeat and death, probably had all his lands confiscated. Yet various members of his family remained and much of their land in the neighbourhood of Dublin was granted away by the conquerors. Thus, Richard Strongbow granted to Walter de Ridlesford Brien and the land of the sons of Torquil.[7] Some of the family, however, received permission to keep their land on various tenures. Thus, Hamund Torquilson was allowed to keep Kinsaley (Kennsalich), near Portmarnock.[8] Yet, even this land was, by 1230, in the hands of Christ Church, Dublin;[9] for, in an inquest of that date, the church claims 'Ballyhamund' and the lands of 'Hamund' among its possessions. In the main, the Ostmen of Dublin confined themselves to Ostmantown, where they formed a wealthy class

2 See an order of Edward I to the Esturmanni of his dominions (*CDI 1293–1301*, p. 59). In Dugdale, *Monasticon*, vi, 1167, in a charter of William II, a certain Kytellus Estermannus of Chichester is mentioned. The names of the man and of his trade are both Scandinavian. 3 There are abundant references to Ostmantown in volume one of *CStM* and in the first two volumes of *CDI*. 4 'Cantred of the Ostmen and Holy City' (*CDI 1171–51*, p. 24). 5 'Vill of the Ostmen near Waterford' (*CDI 1252–84*, p. 426). 6 *Giraldi Cambrensis opera*, v, 313. 7 *RCH*, p. 4, no. 52. 8 M.J. McEnery (ed.), 'Calendar to Christ Church deeds, 1174–1684', *20th rep. DKPRI*, appendix 7, nos. 1–3. 9 Ibid., nos. 44, 364.

of merchants and landowners, continuing to hold and let valuable property; for instance, the municipal records of Dublin show an Englishman, Henry Tuche, holding land in the middle of the thirteenth century from Elicia, daughter of Athelstan, and Richard Peel holding a house of Arfinus Macardor, an Ostman in Ostmantown.[10] Yet, even here, land was apparently continually falling vacant, and we can only conjecture that there was a continuous exodus of the race back to the free Norse world. In the numerous grants of land in Ostmantown during the thirteenth century in favour of the church of St Mary's, Dublin, frequent reference is made to land 'formerly belonging' to persons of distinctively Norse names.[11]

A second feature of the fate of the Ostmen was that they were granted the special protection of the crown. Wealthy and defenceless, they were a fit subject for royal consideration. Also they had to be saved from English rapacity and prevented from joining the ranks of the Irish enemy. Hence the crown threw over the Ostmen the same invidious kind of protection which it accorded to the Jews in England. They were to become the 'king's Ostmen', and possibly the royal intention was to distinguish them from the English, who constantly sought charters and immunities, as a semi-subject class from which revenue might be obtained in return for protection from popular aggression. Thus, while the towns and the rest of the land were being incorporated or granted out in the usual feudal way, the Ostmen were placed in most cases under the crown. Thus King John, in granting the honour of Limerick to William de Breouse, declares: 'We keep the cantred of the Ostmen in our own demesne.'[12] Giraldus states that all south Munster was granted by Henry II to FitzStephen and Miles de Cogan, 'excepting however the city of Cork and the adjacent cantred of the Ostmen'.[13] But a better illustration is found in the charter of Henry II to the Ostmen of Waterford. This is preserved in the Lambeth Palace library, and has been thoroughly examined by Dr Alexander Bugge, who has done so much to make clear the early relations of Ireland and the Northmen.[14] The charter describes the Hostmanni of Waterford as 'the king's liege men'.

The mixed treatment of expulsion and royal favour which the old Ostman citizens received is well illustrated by what took place at Waterford on the landing of Henry II there. This is described in the course of a lawsuit concerning the legal rights of a reputed Ostman which took place in Waterford about the year 1310. One Robert le Waleys was charged of felony for having

10 Gilbert, *Hist. & mun. docs*, p. 480. 11 *CStM*, i, 477, land which Maurice le Manisk [(?) Manxman] formerly held. See also ibid., i, 474, 478. 12 *CDI 1171–51*, p. 24. 13 *Giraldi Cambrensis opera*, v, 347. 14 See his interesting article: Alexander Bugge, 'Nordisk sprog og nordisk nationalitet i Irland' in *Aarbøger for Nordisk Oldkyndighed og Historie*, 2nd ser., 15 (1900), 320. The charter which is given there begins, 'Henricus rex … Sciatis quod Hostmanni de Waterford homines mei legei sunt'. See also *CDI 1171–1251*, no. 2198.

killed one John MacGillemory. As he asserted that the deceased was an unfree Irishman, and the crown replied that MacGillemory was entitled to English law by charter of Henry III, the jury had to make an historical investigation. They found that, on Henry II's landing in Ireland, an attempt was made by the Ostmen of Waterford to prevent his entrance. For this they were expelled from the city. The king, however, assigned to them certain places outside the city, and here they constructed a town called 'Villa Oustmannorum'.[15] One Ostman, however, the ancestor of the deceased, on account of his exceptional loyalty, had been allowed to remain in the city, and afterwards was given the privileges for himself and his heirs of English law.[16] Not only the suburban but also the rural Ostmen of Co. Waterford were put into special relations with the crown. Thus, in Henry III's reign, there were in Co. Waterford some Norse tenants under the Norman lord, Johannes le Poer. These are called *Ostmanni domini regis*. There are also mentioned *Ostmanni alii domini regis*, who paid 6*s*. to the crown.[17] Again, on the outskirts of Waterford, Ostmen are spoken of in royal documents as *Custumanni nostri*, 'our Ostmen'.[18] In pursuance of its policy of protection, the crown also made an effort to secure for the older Teutonic race equal legal rights with the English themselves. The concession of privilege of English law to the John MacGillemory of the lawsuit would seem to imply that that law was denied to the rest of his Ostman neighbours. Yet it is evident, as we have seen, that Henry II granted the full rights of English law, at least locally, to the Ostmen of Waterford, and perhaps the privilege was intended to apply generally to other communities of that race. For more than a century they remembered this grant, as is attested by the frequent confirmations to petitioning Ostmen of 'English law as Henry FitzEmpress promised it'.[19] This was no small privilege in Ireland, where from the first the unhappy precedent was made of refusing to the Celtic natives all rights of law, except in the solitary concession of the same to the five 'royal bloods' of O'Neil, O'Brien, O'Connor, MacMurrough and O'Melaghlin.

But the English colonists strove to thwart this royal design. As always in Ireland, the crown's intention was good, but its effective power feeble. The English incomers got the bit between their teeth from the first, and the Ostmen suffered no less from their lawlessness than did the Celts. They were a small people, wealthy and pacific, unable to retaliate in tribal raids and, moreover, were tainted with that Celtic strain which the English always abominated before

15 Extract from Ir. justiciary roll, 3–7 Edw. II, m. 18 [EN. *CJRI 1308–14*, pp 185–8]. The text is given in Bugge, 'Nordisk sprog og nordisk nationalitet i Irland', pp 327–32. 16 Orpen, *Song of Dermot*, pp 278–9 (note to line 1506). 17 *35th rep. DKPRI*, p. 36 (Ir. pipe roll, 19–20 Hen. III, no. 2). 18 *CDI 1252–84*, no. 2134. *Custumanni* is the form given, but as the document refers to the MacGillemorys, who were Hibernicized Ostmen, and to Henry II's grant of English laws to that family, the word must be a mistake for, or variant to, *Oustmanni*. 19 *CDI 1252–84*, no. 2134 etc.

they themselves succumbed to it. In the main, the common English and perhaps local authorities seem to have denied them the promised participation in legal rights and to have treated them like rightless Irishmen. To enter an Irishman's house by force, to slay him, and occupy his lands and tenement as one's own was no felony. What could have been more tempting, then, than to treat the Ostmen offhand as Irishmen? For they possessed, to a large degree, the rich lands and tenements which the Irish among the colonists generally lacked. In short, the English colonists attempted to drive back the Ostmen solely to the enjoyment of the Brehon laws. The persistence of the Ostmen in claiming that they ought to be taken in all things for Englishmen is easily intelligible, and their petitions to the crown to save them from fraud and violence are very pathetic. Yet they seem to have had little effect. In Edward I's reign, a petition was forwarded to the crown from certain Ostmen which pointed out that it would be more useful to the king to have three hundred Englishmen, rather than that they should be made Irishmen by false inquisition and against the king's liberty.[20] This petition was granted, but such petitions were so numerous that the redress given by a distant potentate can have been of little effect.

The advantage to the English colonists of treating the older race as outlaws is obvious. They were the better enabled to do this successfully because, to the superficial eye of the law, the Ostmen were hard to distinguish from the rightless Irish. Separated from the great Norse world, few in numbers, the original Norsemen of Ireland had become in the course of three centuries more than half Hibernicized. It is evident that intermarriage between Irish kings and Dublin or other Northman princes had been complicated and numerous during the tenth and eleventh centuries, and the advantage was all on the side of the natives.[21] Intermarriage must have been as common among members of both races in the lower ranks. The extent to which the Ostmen had, by the end of the twelfth century, become Hibernicized is shown by the prevalence of partially Celtic patronymics among them and the common appearance of the Irish 'mac' in their surnames. The majority of petitioners and witnesses, etc., of that race whom we find in the state documents and grants are distinguished in this way: good instances are to be found in 'Philip mac Gothmond, an Ostman of Waterford'; and 'Gillecrist, William, and John macgillemory', of the same city, who petition at various times for English law; and in 'Hodo macfoyde' and 'Arfinus macardor', prominent house-owners in Ostmantown in the first half of the thirteenth century.[22] For the first time, Ireland had begun to exercise that magic fascination over Teutonic invaders which has resulted in the absorption

**20** *CDI 1285–92*, p. 306. **21** See appendices to J.H. Todd (ed.), *Cogadh Gaedhel re Gallaibh: the war of the Gaedhill with the Gaill, or, the invasions of Ireland by the Danes and other Norsemen. The original Irish text edited, with translation and introduction* (RS, London, 1867). **22** *CDI 1285–92*, p. 305 and no. 700; *CDI 1252–84*, no. 2134; Gilbert, *Hist. & mun. docs*, pp 149, 480.

of great masses of non-Gaelic settlers. And when we consider how universal Celtic patronymics had become by the time of the conquest among the Ostmen we can only conclude that they were already largely absorbed in speech and customs by Irish influence, and so found it difficult to make out a case for their own ancestry. The petition of the Philip mac Gothmond, alluded to above, illustrates well the grievances of the Ostmen, their state of partial Hibernicization, and the legal violence to which they were exposed by the English. In 1290, this man of mixed Norse-Irish name ('an Ostman and Englishman of Waterford') prayed a remedy against persons greedy of his demesne, for he was rich, who 'exact five marks payment when a man is killed' and 'wish, to prove that Philip and others of his race ... are Irishmen'. Evidently, English neighbours had not only denied him English law, as if he were an Irishman, but had also appealed to Brehon law when homicide was committed by his people and got him fined an *eric*, so that they gained immunity for their own misdeeds in the first case and compensation for his in the second.

A further feature of the treatment of the Ostmen was their exclusion from gilds and burgess rights. As we see, the numbers of this people must have been considerable, considering how few at first the English themselves probably were. In Waterford, Philip mac Gothmond had '400 of his race' about him. In the early part of the thirteenth century, there were in the Co. Wexford a hundred freeholders of this race, with their families; and yet, if we went by burgess rolls only and lists of the members of gilds, we should be almost left ignorant of the existence of a surviving Ostman race. It is clear that the English townsmen at once rigorously excluded these born traders from all participation in gild and borough rights. In the earliest burgess roll of Dublin, which dates from about the end of the twelfth century, out of many hundreds of names, only three seem to be of Norse origin: these are Cullin filius Seafani, Torsten utlag and Turstein filius Simundi.[23] In a list dated 1225–50, out of 114 names, only five seem to be those of Ostmen.[24] Again, in a roll of the Dublin merchant gild of the date 1226, out of 188 names, only five may be considered to be those of Ostmen, viz. Gillefintan, Liolf, William filius Turstein, Thomas Turcivil and Gunnig *forestarius*.[25] In a similar list of 1256–7, out of 178 names, there is only one which might be that of an Ostman: Stephanus Algar de Weseford.[26] On the other hand, a man whose name seems of undoubted Scandinavian origin rose to be mayor of Dublin in the early fourteenth century, one Ricardus Oluf.[27] We must consider, then, the Ostmen of Dublin as shut out at once from the walls and the privileges of Dublin citizens. And, from what we know of the early history of English Limerick, Waterford, Wexford and Cork, we must infer there a similar exclusion from the benefits of charters and trade associations.

23 Gilbert, *Hist. & mun. docs*, p. 3. 24 Ibid., p. 112. 25 Ibid., p. 82. 26 Ibid., p. 136.
27 Mayor of Dublin, 1316–17 (*CStM*, i, 511) [EN. cf. *NHI*, ix, 549].

The position of the rural Ostmen, and their treatment, is as interesting, but more obscure. The members of this race who held land in the counties around the cities they had built were probably considerable in number. In the level and fertile districts along the great rivers and harbours they must have settled early in that kind of free-farmer tenure which the Scandinavians established always in their colonies, and their numbers would be swelled by Ostmen excluded from the cities. We find some of them dwelling in the most inland or remote parts of Irish Munster. There was one of this race, Reginald Macotter (Ragnall son of Othere), so far inland as Tipperary in 1253; and another, Maurice Macotere, far away in Clonmel – 'at the world's end' – lived surrounded by three hundred of his people.[28] These solitary landholders in a tribal country had to be fitted into the feudal system which the Norman lords began to set up over as much of Ireland as they could reach. But they must have formed as puzzling anomalies to the establishment of the system as ever the *sochemanni* and *libere tenentes* of England formed for William the Conqueror's lawyers. We have enough evidence to show that they were exempted from the feudal regime and left as non-military tenants in an exceptional and privileged position.

An unpublished charter of the late thirteenth century throws an interesting light not only on the numbers and tenure of the Ostman landholders of Co. Wexford, but also on the mysterious disappearance of their race.[29] At the extinction in 1245 of the male line of the Marshall family, heirs to the estates of Richard Strongbow and lords of Leinster, their vast territories were divided among the five heiresses, of whom Joan obtained Wexford. She was given in marriage to Henry III's half-brother, William de Valence, who thus obtained the liberty of Wexford. In 1283, an inquisition was made by his orders upon the services and customs of the Ostmen of Co. Wexford. The finding of the jurors was favourable to the existing Ostmen, and the seneschal of Wexford issued in the name of his lord the following charter, reciting the terms of the verdict and giving effect to it:

> Omnibus has litteras visuris et audituris Robertus de Ymer senescallus Wesfordiae salutem. Noverit universitas vestra me ex mandato nobilissimi viri domini W. de Valence inquisitionem cepisse super redditibus, serviciis, et consuetudinibus Oustmannorum forinsecorum Com.

28 *CDI 1252–84*, no. 959; and *CDI 1285–92*, p. 306. 29 This Latin document is now in the PRO, London [TNA], and has been examined several times. It is given in Alexander Bugge, 'Bidrag til det sidste afsnit af Nordboernes historie i Irland', *Aarbøger for Nordisk Oldkyndighed og Historie*, 19 (1904), 312. My transcript is taken from another copy of the document in the possession of Mr G.H. Orpen, to whom I have to offer my warm thanks for lending it to me [EN. Another edition of this document (in record type, with English translation) appears in Herbert F. Hore, 'The Scandinavians in Leinster', *Journal of the Kilkenny and South-east of Ireland Archaeological Society* [*JRSAI*], 2nd ser., 1:2 (1857), 440–1].

Wesfordiae per iuratos subscriptos, viz. [here follow the names of twelve jurors].[29a] Qui iurati dicunt quod tempore Marescallorum Dominorum Lageniae fuerunt infra Com. Wesf[ordiae] quinquies viginti Oustmanni forinseci valde divites plura animalia habentes. Quorum quilibet suis temporibus reddere consueverat[29b] per annum praepositis Wesf[ordiae] ad duos terminos anni sex denarios pro corpore suo, scilicet ad Pascham et ad festum Sancti Michaelis, et duos denarios ad festum Sancti Petri quod dicitur ad Vinculum pro qualibet vacca quam habebat propriam, et quatuor denarios ad festum Omnium Sanctorum ne iret in exercitum. Et tres obolos in autumpno pro blado domini sui metendo apud Rosclar[30] per unum diem, et quatuor denarios pro quolibet affrenato et bove quem habebat in festo Sancti Martini vel arrare pro unoquoque affrenato et bove dimidium acrum terrae ibidem ad opus domini. Dicunt vero quod nunc non sunt infra dictum comitatum nisi quadraginta Oustmanni parum boni habentes et duodecim qui serviant Anglicis et aliis pro victu suo nichil in bonis habentes. Et dicunt quod tempore Marescallorum solebant praedicti Oustmanni terram tenere de quo domino volebant infra comitatum pro praedictis redditibus et serviciis domino Marescallo solvendis et reddendis. Et quod praedictus dominus horum Willelmus de Valence ipsos in eodem statu vel meliore pro salute animae suae et antecessorum suorum et successorum affectat tenere. Nec vult quod aliquis vivens generis portat vel sustentat mortuarium[31] nec pro mortuis distringatur. Praedictos Oustmannos nunc existentes ab omnibus oneribus, redditibus, et serviciis quae mortui solebant sustinere dum vixerunt ex mandato praedicti domini viri Willelmi de Valence in perpetuum clamo quietos, dans eisdem ex eodem mandato domini viri licentiam terram tenere de quo domino voluerint infra comitatum. Ita quod de caetero non distringantur pro aliquo redditu reddendo vel serviciis faciendis nisi pro ipsis qui vivi fuerint et secundum eorum facultates.
[Then follow the seals.]

This document throws a clearer light upon the position of the Ostmen after the conquest than any record we possess.

**29a** [EN. The names of the jurors appear in the document as follows: 'Henricum Wythay, Willielmum Marescall, Willielmum de Kadwely, Clemete [*sic*] Cod, Johannem le Styward, Robertum de Amera, Robertum de Arderne, David filium Ricardi, Johannem filium Philippi le Harpur, Johannem filium David le Harpur, David Cheure, et Adam Hay' (Hore, 'Scandinavians in Leinster', p. 440; Bugge, 'Bidrag til det sidste afsnit af Nordboernes historie i Irland', p. 312).] **29b** The transcript has *consueverint* [EN. This note by Edmund Curtis appears as n. 29a in the original version of the essay]. **30** The modern Rosslare, on Wexford harbour. **31** This, which is Dr Bugge's reading of the word, would mean some kind of duty payable at death.

It is not easy to explain why a hundred Ostmen at the beginning of the thirteenth century should, at the end, have dwindled down to forty. The free and non-military tenure by which the hundred held is, however, very interesting as being a relic of an early non-feudal land system set up in a tribal country. The phrase, 'they are accustomed to go with their land to whatever lord they will', might, indeed, come from our eleventh-century Domesday book as applied to some puzzling *sochemannus* or *libere tenens*, awkwardly free and useless to legal eyes. Yet, at the same time, these Ostmen had been forced to pay certain money dues to the reeves of Wexford, and had also submitted to some boon days on the lord's land. Such a tenure recalls those cases mentioned not infrequently in Domesday book of those freeholders who had the freedom of 'withdrawing themselves and their land'. And yet, like many of those English yeomen, though free from the more servile week work, these Ostmen had personal field labour to do on certain occasions for a lord.[32] Nothing more of moment is told us of such Ostman landowners as these who, with their racial stubbornness, had planted themselves out in the troubled open country. In the constant wars of Celtic clans and Norman adventurers, amid the universal decay of the English interest and the universal resurgence of the Irish tribes which distinguish the fourteenth and fifteenth centuries, such isolated communities must have failed to keep their footing. It was in the suburb of Dublin north of the Liffey to which they were forced to retire that the descendants of the founders of that city had the best chance of surviving and maintaining a racial distinctiveness. In Ostmantown, for a century and a quarter after the Norman invasion, these people remained distinct and apart, considerable in numbers and wealthy, judged by the amount of land and number of tenements which they held. In the early part of the thirteenth century, they were recognized by the crown as being both very distinct and worthy of equal credence with the English; witness an order by the crown that a jury composed of the Ostmen and English of Dublin should inquire into a right claimed by Holy Trinity.[33] Charters concerned with the transfer of land in this district in the early part of the thirteenth century are generally attested by a full list of Ostman witnesses; as, for instance, a grant of land in Ostmantown, proclaimed by Abbot Adam of St Mary's in 1205, which is attested by seven chief witnesses, to wit, Turkil 'Ostmannus', Arfin, Walter his son, Roger Anel, and Hamund Heraut (that is, 'Haralt').[34] In this same quarter of the century, we get many grants attested by Arfin mac Ardor, a very prominent Ostman, whose name indicates well the extent to which the old Northman population had been Hibernicized. The wealth and numbers of the

32 F.W. Maitland, *Domesday Book and beyond* (Cambridge, 1897), p. 72 and n. 33 *CDI 1171–1251*, no. 641. In 1215, the justiciary was to hold an inquiry by means of the Ostmen and English of Dublin upon claim of Holy Trinity to have a boat on the Anna Liffey. 34 *CStM*, i, 506.

race are well indicated in a long list of annual rents in Dublin which were transferred by the abbot of St Mary's to the city of Dublin in the years 1213–44.[35] In the section referring to Ostmantown are mentioned numerous Ostman landowners with such unmistakeable names as Cristinus, Yvor, Mathie de Trig de Man, Polyn and Thurkil. The decrease in the number of Ostman names appended to grants affecting Ostmantown, which is noticeable as the century went on, testifies to the gradual decay in numbers and importance of the people of this race.

Towards the end of the century such charters are attested by few or no Ostman witnesses; as, for instance, a grant made by Stephanus Blundus either in 1276 or 1283 (in which years the chief witness, Walter Unred, was mayor), the witnesses to which are all English, though the land was in Ostmantown.[36] The testator was, of course, English, but there seems to have been no objection to Ostman witnesses in the case of grants by Englishmen.Towards the end of the century, such evidences as the documents afford us as to the existence of a separate Ostman race begin to fail us. The Ostmen of Dublin practically disappear. English owners began to intrude into Ostmantown and to acquire property there. The best instance of this is seen in the various grants of land in that suburb made by Werburg, daughter of Thorkil, one of the old royal race, about the year 1270, in favour of Thomas de Lexinton, citizen of Dublin.[37] Most of this land was granted again at his death by the same Thomas to the church of St Mary, which gradually acquired most of Ostmantown.[38] Again, Ostmen began to grant or bequeath land extensively to churches. They possessed to the full that piety and passion for providing for their spiritual welfare which was always characteristic of the Norman race.[39] The anomalous position they held could not last. The wealthier would make good their claim to be 'Englishmen, and sharing in English law', and so would be absorbed by the newcomer.[40] The rest probably sank into the ranks of the broken Irish of the Pale. The records of the fourteenth century contain scarcely a trace of this isolated race, and suddenly and completely it vanished out of the history of Ireland.

35 Gilbert, *Hist. & mun. docs*, p. 474. 36 *CStM*, i, 499. 37 Ibid., i, 477, and also 489, 490, 492 etc. 38 Ibid., i, 480–2. 39 Ibid., i, 220, 233, 504 etc. 40 'Gylmhel mac Lotan fuit Estman et habuit legem Anglicorum', *c.*1244 (Gilbert, *Hist. & mun. docs*, p. 143).

CHAPTER 18

# The clan system among the English settlers in Ireland*

*Edmund Curtis*

The following document is copied from a transcript headed 'pro electione capitanei des Harolds' in the Harris *Collectanea*, in the National Library at Dublin.[1] These manuscripts contain materials gathered together by Archbishop King in the first quarter of the eighteenth century to serve for an ecclesiastical history of Ireland, a work which he never executed. The materials were added to by Walter Harris, the continuator of Ware, who drew up the valuable manuscript catalogue which forms part of the collection. The original of the present document has disappeared, and there is no mention of it in the published *Rotulorum patentium et clausorum cancellariae Hiberniae*.[1a]

> Irrot. in Canc. Hiberniæ.
>
> Memorandum quod Iohannes filius Henrici Harold, Mauritius filius Alexandri Harold, Iohannes filius Alexandri Harold, Willelmus filius Roberti Harold, Hugh filius Roberti Laghless, Petrus Howell, Richardus filius Michaelis Howell, Matthias Archbold, Elias filius Roberti Walsh, Robertus filius Galfridi Harold, et Rogerus filius Danielis Harold ibidem in praesentia Iusticiarii Hiberniae elegerunt super sacramentum suum Walterum Harold capitaneum progeniei des Harolds; qui quidem Walterus die et anno supradicto in praesentia praefati Iusticiarii tactis sacrosanctis evangeliis sacramentum praestitit corporale quod ipse in posterum bene et fideliter ad pacem domini Regis in omnibus se geret ut

* First published in *EHR*, 25 (1910), 116–20. 1 NLI, MS 2 [Harris], fo. 223. There are seventeen volumes of these *Collectanea*, reaching from the reign of Henry II to that of William III. They are neatly bound and in a good state of preservation. They have never been published either in part or whole, nor has any printed catalogue been made of them in spite of their importance for students of Irish history. The entries refer chiefly to ecclesiastical affairs, but the early volumes contain many copies of deeds, warrants, inquisitions and documents of general interest in Irish medieval history. The value of the collection is enhanced by the fact that many of the originals must have perished in the fire of 1711, which consumed the old Privy Council Chamber. A short description of the *Collectanea* is given in the appendix to the *Report of trustees of the National Library of Ireland for 1899*, p. 12 [EN. For a more detailed guide to the volumes in question, see Charles McNeill, 'Harris: *Collectanea de rebus Hibernicis*', *AH*, 6 (1934), 248–450]. 1a [EN. That is, *RCH*.]

pacifice se habebit, et si contingat quod aliquis de eius progenie aut parentela aut sibi adhaerens aliquam feloniam seu roberiam super fidelem populum ipsius Domini regis de caetero faceret, ipse Walterus iurat et fideliter manutenet capere corpus praedicti felonis pro posse suo et ipsum prisonae Domini regis mancipare cum notitiam inde habuerit et legitime requisitus. Aprilis 23$^{o}$ Ed. 3, vicesimo quarto.

Iohannes OBryn eodem anno electus capitaneus de OBryns iuratus etc. ut ante in memorando A.D. 1350.

Mattheus Archbold eodem modo electus capitaneus de Archbolds. A.D. 1350.

This writ for 'the election of the Harolds' supplies an early instance of the growth of Irish customs among the Norman-English landholders in Ireland. From the invasion of Edward Bruce onward, the Irish government found the feudal system of tenures breaking down and growing inadequate both from a military and a tenurial point of view. An alternative lay in legalizing the clan system and ratifying the election of 'captains of nations' among the Norman-English and Old Irish. The tide of Hibernicization was too strong to be resisted; the clan system offered a tenure and an agricultural order better suited to the country, while in the weakness of the government it was inevitable that private families should organize themselves on a patriarchal basis for purposes of defence and security. In this case, where chieftains of both Norman and Irish blood have their titles and election confirmed by the head of the Irish administration, we find one of the earliest instances of the government ratifying and surrendering to the Irish brehon system in its most characteristic form. In spite of the Statute of Kilkenny, this method of securing the loyalty of Irish and Anglo-Irish by ratifying tribal chieftainship was put into full practice in the sixteenth century. It was part of Henry VIII's policy of leaving the great Irish families undisturbed as long as they acknowledged the royal power in church and state. Under the Tudors, there are frequent instances in which the government legalizes the clan system generally in a treaty between the sovereign or lord deputy and the chief actual or claimant, the latter undertaking to act loyally, to pacify and Anglicize his country, and the government hoping to control the people through their native lord. Thus, in 1538, we find a compact between Lord Leonard Grey, the king's deputy, and Remund *alias* Jenico Savage, one of the 'degenerate Englishry' of eastern Ulster. The latter, 'having taken his oath of fealty, is to bear the name and have the honours of chief captain of his nation and of the country of the Savages otherwise Lecale'.[2] In the same reign, as in those of Edward VI and Mary, and in the early years of Elizabeth, grants of chieftaincy and tanistry to the purely Irish princes were

2 *CPR Ire.*, *Hen. VIII–Eliz.*, p. 45.

frequent. In 1554–5, Dermot M'Chair (that is, mac Cahir) Kavanagh was appointed captain and tanist of M'Amore's (that is, mac Damor's) country with attendance of twelve swordsmen. The grant recited that Queen Mary by letters patent in the first year of her reign had promoted his father, Charles (Cahir) mac Art Kavanagh, to the state of baron of Ballian for life and nominated him captain of his nation.[3]

The Anglo-Irish names mentioned in our document are those of families which acquired estates in the marches of Dublin and Kildare in the original enfeoffment of Leinster at the end of the twelfth century. The Harolds probably came into Ireland among the numerous immigrants of English burgess stock in the first fifty years after the invasion, although it is sometimes stated that they represent an original Scandinavian family. We find them holding the lands of Kilgobbin, or Kilgobban, south of Dundrum, Co. Dublin, under the Hakets from the early years of the thirteenth century.[4] In the fourteenth century, the tract of border country about Saggard, lying towards the Dublin mountains, became known from this family as Harold's Grange, while it was also called Grange of the Marches or Balgeeth.[5] As in the case of other Anglo-Irish families, they could not always resist the temptation to join in with the Irish against the colonists of their own blood. The annals of St Mary's abbey, Dublin, record one instance of their uniting with the Archbolds and the two great native clans against the settlers around Wicklow.[6] These two English names already represented 'septs' as early as 1315. The Harolds became of great importance on the borders of the Pale, being, in that most disturbed part of the island, semi-official guardians of the king's peace. During the sixteenth and seventeenth centuries, they suffered the common lot of forfeiture and dispossession along with many Anglo-Irish families whose religious sympathies led them into union with the Old-Irish. In 1536, Peter Talbot of Shankyll was made captain and governor of part of the marches of Co. Dublin called Harold's County to hold during pleasure in place of John 'Harrold'.[7] Among the forfeited proprietors of 1649, we find John Harold of Kilmakeoge in the half-barony of Rathdown, Co. Dublin.[8] The village of Harold's Cross, a few miles south of Dublin, keeps in memory this ancient Norman-Irish family.

The family of Lawless, or Laghles, acquired this significant designation at the beginning of the fourteenth century. In 1347, Robert Lawless and others were appointed guardians of the peace in the marches with power to assess and array its military force.[9] In 1389, the family of this name was seised of the

3 Ibid., p. 342. 4 See James Mills, 'The Norman settlement in Leinster – the cantreds near Dublin', *JRSAI*, 24 (1894), 166. 5 See John D'Alton, *The history of the county of Dublin* (Dublin, 1838), p. 722. 6 'Item, Otothiles et Obrynnes, Archibauldes et Haroldes conjurati fuerunt et villam de Wikelowe cum tota patria devastaverunt' (*CStM*, ii, 349). 7 *CPR Ire., Hen. VIII–Eliz.*, p. 26. 8 John O'Hart, *The Irish and Anglo-Irish landed gentry when Cromwell came to Ireland; or, a supplement to Irish pedigrees* (Dublin, 1884), p. 248. 9 Dalton, *History of the*

neighbourhood of Saggard, while in the fourteenth and fifteenth century it was in possession of Shanganagh and Kilruddery near Dalkey.[10] The Archbolds were, we have seen, a numerous race by 1315. At the end of the fifteenth century, they held the manor and lands of Much Bray and Little Bray (Moche Bree and Little Bree) in the south of Co. Dublin, which they retained in 1536–7.[11] In 1649, Morris Archbold of Kilmacud in the half-barony of Rathdown, Co. Dublin, was one of the forfeiting proprietors, while a Rowland Archbold also was deprived of the lands of Cloghran.[12] The Walshes were a family of Welsh origin with other branches in the counties Kilkenny and Mayo. They appear as considerable landholders in the country west of Dalkey, as we find in an extent made by the king's orders in 1256. By this, Elias le Waleys, deceased, was found to have possessed *Villa Walensis*, or Walshestown, with 99 acres *in capite* of the archbishop. Among the jurors appears one Philip Howell.[13] In 1609, James Walsh was seised of a castle and land in Shanganagh and Kiltuc from Peter Talbot in his manor of Rathdown, while, in 1654, it was found that this townland had been the property of John Walsh, rebel.[14] Howell, a name of Welsh origin, is early found among the settlers of the newer race who became so numerous in the district south of Dublin. Although persons of this surname do not appear as landowners of any importance, they meet us with the credibility of freeholders in lists of jurors and witnesses in this neighbourhood.[15]

These Norman-English families dwelt in the manors of Esker and Saggard on the borders between the city of Dublin and the independent Irish of the mountains. They had for neighbours the powerful fighting clan of the O'Byrnes – called OBroin by the Irish and, by the English settlers, OBryn – who had now become confined to the mountainous districts of the present counties of Dublin and Wicklow, where they held out till Tyrone's rising, 1594–1603. The John OBryn who makes his submission in this document is not mentioned in authentic O'Byrne genealogies as chief of that clan, nor indeed does the essentially Norman name John – in Irish Shane, Shaan or Seaghan – appear among their leaders till the end of the fifteenth century.[16] The chancery records, however, give a reference to one Shaan (John) OBryn, who is almost certainly the same person with the John who is here elected 'capitaneus'. In the Irish close rolls, 29–30 Edward III, there is recorded an affray between Adam Dodyng and other English, and the O'Byrnes, in which were killed or fatally wounded Ravenald McClorchan OBryn the elder and Mourth son of

*county of Dublin*, p. 25. **10** Ibid., pp 772, 900. **11** Ibid., p. 910 and *CPR Ire.*, *Hen. VIII–Eliz.*, pp 28–9. **12** Dalton, *History of the county of Dublin*, p. 910; *O'Hart, Irish and Anglo-Irish landed gentry*, p. 248. **13** *CDI 1252–84*, no. 1283. **14** Dalton, *History of the county of Dublin*, p. 900. **15** *CDI 1252–84*, p. 232 etc. **16** See the O'Byrne pedigrees in *AFM*, v, 1746–7, note *s.a.* 1580; Rev. John Francis Shearman, 'Loca Patriciana', *Journal of the Royal Historical and Archaeological Association of Ireland* [*JRSAI*], 4th ser., 3 (1874–5), 381 (pt 8),

McConghir Ravenald OBryn, while Shaan son of Donald Mór OBryn was taken and brought prisoner to Dublin castle.[17] The John who was captured in this fray of 1356 is not mentioned even in the most extensive genealogies. Donnchadh, or Donogh Mór (here called Donald by a natural mistake), is given as chief of the race about the end of the thirteenth century, while his son Murchadh, or Murkud, surrendered to the government in 1329. A Lorcan is also given as a son of Donoch Mór, while another son, Raghnall, is famous as having split the race in two and founded the Gavel Rannell or junior branch of the O'Byrnes.[18]

The John OBryn of our document gave little satisfaction to the government, for in 1359 this same John is mentioned as having been brought by James le Butler, earl of Ormond, before the justiciar, with whom he entered into terms of peace; he is described as 'captain of the OBryns and lately a rebel'.[19] He was evidently the younger and unconsidered son of a ruling chief, and as such may have made pretensions to the chiefship and secured election by a section of the clan. The Irish government, in ratifying his title and election, was perhaps not accepting the general will of the tribe. But in later days, it followed much the same policy in accepting Ferdorcha or Matthew O'Neill as representative of that family instead of the elder, and more legitimate, Shane. We have here, perhaps, an early instance of a policy similar to that which produced a 'queen's O'Neill' and an 'Irish O'Neill'.

487 (pt 9). 17 'Rex thesaurio ad peticionem Ade Dodyng pro se et sociis monstrantem qualiter ipsi ... congregati se de nocte armatos ad terram de les Bryns inter fortalicia eorum posuerunt ... sequenti die venientem quandam coniunctivam de ipsis Bryns viriliter sunt aggressi ... quosdam potentes de ipsis, viz. Ravenyld M^cClorcan Obryn seniorem letaliter vulneraverunt, Mourth filium M^cConghir Ravenyld Obryn in ipso conflictu occiderunt, et Shaan filium Donaldi Mor Obryn ceperunt [etc.]' (*RCH*, p. 59, no. 33). These confused names should be Raghnall son of Lorchan OBroin, Murchadh (or Morough) son of Connor Raghnall OBroin, and Shane son of Donogh Mór OBroin (see *CStM*, ii, 371). 18 Shearman, 'Loca Patriciana', p. 487. 19 *RCH*, p. 66.

CHAPTER 19

# The spoken languages of medieval Ireland*

*Edmund Curtis*

The first Norman invaders of Ireland, on their arrival here in 1169, found a Teutonic population strongly entrenched in the cities of the east and south, namely the 'Ostmen' (as they called themselves), men of Scandinavian descent, whose settlements had first begun about 850. The newcomers soon cleared these Irish Danes – such of them as did not abandon Ireland – out of the towns into the adjacent districts and, up to 1300, records show that they remained fairly numerous and important. But the race was soon absorbed either by the Norman-English or the Irish, and left little trace of itself.

As regards language, it is doubtful whether the Ostman population spoke Norse, even at the time of the English invasion. They had, since Clontarf, been steadily sinking into the mass of the native race; their royal races, such as the Macgillemuires of Waterford, had already Gaelic patronymics, and the Norman lords evidently treated them as little better than the Irish, to whom the conquerors refused all legal rights. The survivors of the race are found petitioning against this treatment: thus Maurice MacOtere (that is, 'son of Otir'), calling himself 'an Ostman dwelling at the end of the world in Ireland', petitioned the king in 1289 to grant to himself and his race, three hundred strong, English laws and liberties. This case and others show that, though the Ostmen knew their Teutonic origin, they were now so identified with the Irish in speech, habit and name that the English were on the face of things to treat them as such.

Many Scandinavian words are embedded in middle and even modern Irish. Bugge and Marstrander have shown that in all that relates to seacraft, for example, the loan-words in Irish and Scottish Gaelic are numerous; but it is clear that this element had already come in before the English invasion.

The Norman-French conquerors themselves and their men-at-arms were – from the point of view of language and race – a very motley crew. The Four Masters call the companions of Strongbow in 1170 'Flemings' (Ir. *Flemendaigh*), and it is well known that most of the first flight of conquerors came from south Wales and that part of south Pembrokeshire where Henry I had planted a colony of Flemings. Strongbow and de Lacy planted great numbers of their

* First published in *Studies: An Irish Quarterly Review*, 8 (1919), 234–54.

south Welsh retainers in the country, and 'Fleming' is still a common name among us; but, for all that, there is no evidence that the Flemish speech took root in Ireland. So it was with Welsh. Many of the common soldiers were pure Britons. The names Walsh, Barrett, Lynnot etc., are still borne by thousands of good Irishmen; and the troops used by the de Burgos in the conquest of Connacht were so largely Welsh that, from the settlers of this race in Mayo, 'the Welsh tribes of Tirawley' has become a familiar phrase. But numerous though the Welsh and Flemings were, they were soon absorbed on the one hand by the mass of Gaels or, on the other, by the English.

In effect, French, English and Irish were the three rivals for linguistic supremacy in medieval Ireland. I do not forget Latin, which as a common medium for law, literature and education was as familiarly used as in every other European land at that time, both by the colonists and the Irish. Stanyhurst (*Description of Ireland*, 1587) says: 'The Irish speak Latin like a vulgar language, learned in their common schools of leechcraft and law.' In Latin were also written those historical annals of Clyn and Grace which, apart from the Gaelic annals, are our main authorities for the history of these centuries.

But Latin was, after all, not a colloquial language. Of the three vernacular dialects, French (that is, Norman-French) was in Ireland, as in England, mainly an aristocratic language. The natural speech of the Fitzgeralds, Lacys, de Burgos, Marshalls and others of the first conquerors was that of the ruling caste in the country they came from. It is quite certain that they were not familiar with English; for it was not till the reign of Edward I, a century later, that the speech of the Anglo-Saxon population became a second language for the English aristocracy from the king downwards.

Within a century after Strongbow's landing, the Norman-French invaders had established themselves and their colonies over most of the south and east; and wherever they settled they brought with them their native tongue, which thus became one of the living languages of the island. As with the aristocratic class over all western Europe, they delighted in the vernacular epics of Arthur and Charlemagne, and Norman-French had a literary culture in Ireland second only to Irish itself.

We must remember also that the church, as in England, was staffed in its higher ranks mainly with Frenchmen or members of the French-speaking aristocracy, and that the lawyers among the colonists also made this language familiar; for in a debased form it was the vehicle of public law and justice. This was so in England, especially from 1275 till 1363, when by statute English took its place both for legal purposes and school instruction. In Ireland, French was first used in acts of parliament in 1310, and, alternated occasionally by Latin, goes on to 1472. French is the language of the Statutes of Kilkenny (1366). It is only after 1472 that English comes to be used in acts of parliament. It is probable that it was not then so familiar to the members of the Irish assembly as it was to those of England. The prospects of French surviving in the rural districts were not great; the tide of English on the one hand and of Irish on the other was too strong. Nevertheless, in the towns founded or rebuilt by the colonists this language was for a long time the one most affected by the ecclesiastics and the richer burgesses, who in origin were largely French or drawn from that English bourgeois class which had, some generations ago, followed William I into England.

For a couple of centuries after the conquest, French was the polite language, the language of commerce and civic government. Thus, if we take the statutes and ordinances of the cities of Dublin, Waterford, Limerick and Galway, we find French and Latin used at first, then from 1365 onwards Latin and English. Irish, however much it might be heard in the streets, was never an official language in these towns. English was the common and best-known tongue. French, though a polite speech, the *lingua franca* of trade and necessary as a legal jargon, was, in fact, not deeply rooted.

Even for these uses, French died out steadily after a couple of centuries and, though traveled persons or ecclesiastics might boast of an acquaintance with a speech which would carry you over most of Europe, French as spoken by them was enough to make a Frenchman stare.

Kilkenny, which, under the shield of the earls of Ormond, developed a real civilization of its own, possibly preserved French better than most towns. The red book of Ossory – that is, a collection of documents relating to the city and diocese – gives some interesting glimpses into the polyglot life of this city.

Richard Ledrede, who was bishop of Ossory (1318–60), was an episcopal reformer. He was greatly scandalized at the frivolous ways of the cathedral clergy, who along with monks and priests were numerous in the gay little city. He found that they and their clerks were given to using, on feast days, songs which were base, secular and only fit for mummers (L. *cantilenae teatrales, turpes et seculares*). Instead of these, he himself wrote some sixty hymns in Latin. He stole, however, airs of the songs he meant to supersede, acting on the principle of General Booth, who 'couldn't see why the devil should have all the best tunes'.

Bishop Ledrede gives the first line or two of the improper ditties above-mentioned; they are either in French or English, and are of interest as showing what were the popular songs of the day. Such are:

(1) Have mercie, frere, barfote that y go.
(2) alas hou shold y syng, yloren is my playing
hou shold y with that olde man
to leven and [forget] my leman
swettist of al thinge.
(3) harrow, ieo su trahy
par fol amor de mal amy.

(4) heu alas pour amour
qy moy myst en taunt dolour.

Some of these may have been imported from England; others, if not all, may have been the composition of local singers and thus may testify to the cultivation and use of English and French side by side in this Anglo-Irish town.[1]

In England, Norman-French has left a considerable body of literature. In Ireland also, it seemed about to become the literary vehicle of much secular verse and prose. Next after Giraldus Cambrensis, the Anglo-French *chanson de geste* called the 'Song of Dermot and the earl', composed by some follower of Strongbow, is the best authority for the conquest.[2] Later, in 1265, the founding of New Ross is the theme of a very spirited French ballad of the contemporary Michael Bernardi, a friar of Kildare, whose glowing picture of the glories of Ross makes his poem rather a romance than a historical document.[3]

But the flowering of French was brief here. After these pieces, we have but a few literary fragments extant. Possibly, much of this literature has simply perished. Among the nobles, French lingered longer than in the towns. Gerald, fourth earl of Desmond (1359–98),[4] wrote French verses still extant in the Book of Ross.

Among our Norman-Irish nobles, the FitzGeralds of Kildare were the most versed in the several languages of Ireland. Besides French and Irish and Latin, they used English freely in their communications with England and the government of the Pale. The ninth earl's library, found at Maynooth when Lord Grey took the castle in 1531, contained 112 books – a very considerable collection for these days. Of Latin there were 34, of French 36, of Irish 20, of English 22. Also a long medical treatise in Irish called *Lile na Heladhan Leighis* – a translation into Irish of Bernard of Gordon's *Lilium Medicinae*, written at Montpellier, in Latin, in 1303. The list testifies to the generous literary taste of this great house and shows how much at home they were in the four cultivated and spoken languages of their country.[5]

The modern Irish language shows proof of contact with the French of the conquerors. A great number of words, ending in *–áiste* (e.g., *páiste*, *bagáiste*), –

1 John T. Gilbert (ed.), 'Archives of the see of Ossory' in *10th rep. HMC*, app. 5, p. 242ff [EN. See Theo Stemmler, 'The vernacular snatches in the Red Book of Ossory: a textual case history', *Anglia*, 95 (1977), 122–9]. 2 *Song of Dermot* [EN. See also Evelyn Mullally (ed.), *The deeds of the Normans in Ireland: La geste des Engleis en Yrlande. A new edition of the chronicle formerly known as the* Song of Dermot and the Earl (Dublin, 2002)]. 3 [EN. For an edition of this poem, see Hugh Shields (ed.), 'The walling of New Ross: a thirteenth-century poem in French', *Long Room*, 12–13 (1975–6), 24–33.] 4 [EN. *Recte*, third earl of Desmond.] 5 Standish Hayes O'Grady (ed.), *Catalogue of Irish manuscripts in the British Museum*, (London, 1894), p. 154.

*iste*, and in *–un* (such as *garsún*), seem to be of French origin. So Dr Hyde thinks, while Dr Bergin and T.F. O'Rahilly consider that they were imported direct from English, which got them from Norman-French itself.[6]

However this may be, we certainly have in such words as *garsún* relics of a time when French-speaking nobles gave their commands to Irish-speaking retainers. French was too weak and too unlike in structure to affect the grammatical genius of the native language, as it did so emphatically in the case of Anglo-Saxon. But the survival of the particle *puinn* in Munster Irish (Ir. *níl puinn Gaoluinne agam* ['I haven't much Irish']) attests to a rather close effect on the language-structure, for this is the French particle 'point' and in Irish, as in modern French, had originally a negative force. There is a fascinating theory held by some scholars, but not yet worked out, that the well-known habit of speakers of southern Irish of throwing the accent on to the final syllable – as in *beannacht*, *turas*, etc. – is due to the Norman-French settlers, who were so numerous in Munster; but the whole question of French influence upon modern Irish has yet scarcely got beyond the stage of fascinating conjectures.

English, though it appears less on the surface than French, was the real rival of Irish in medieval Ireland. In the first century after the conquest, the English race and speech penetrated wide and deep into the country. What between the enfeoffments of the lesser tenants by the chief lords, the settlements of small freeholders and the foundation of towns, practically all the accessible and fertile lands of Meath, Leinster, east Ulster, Munster and even the fringes of Connacht were soon filled with an English-speaking population. The records of such widely separated urban communities as those of Cashel, Cloyne, Athenry and Ardee in the fourteenth and fifteenth centuries attest the existence there of a population as English-speaking as any in Cheshire or Gloucester. Blended with them or underneath them, and receiving little notice in the records, was, of course, a large mass of Irish-speaking villeins, small freeholders and burgesses, who survived among, or were indispensible to, the colonists.

But this strong English element ceased after a time to predominate. From the subject class and from the still unconquered clans, the Irish speech in the fourteenth century descended again into the plains and reached the town walls. The yeomen and small freeholders, the burgesses of the English towns, as the native race reconquered the soil, steadily forsook the land and emigrated either to England or to 'the Pale'. The great lords of English origin stood their ground, but at the expense of accepting Irish tenants, which they did willingly, and adopting the native speech and civilization. Nevertheless, English had a hold upon Ireland which it never lost, and even when Irish was most triumphant it has always been the second language of our country. Its strength

6 Douglas Hyde, 'On the terminations *–áiste*, *–iste*', *Gadelica: A Journal of Modern Irish Studies*, 1 (1912–13), 79–82; Thomas F. O'Rahilly, 'Miscellanea', ibid., pp 283–92.

was greatest in the walled towns; but it remained, though in lesser measure, to be the speech of certain rural areas of the south and east.

The towns of Ireland – Dublin, Drogheda, Dundalk and the rest, round the coast to Galway and Athenry – were in fact, and boasted themselves to be, strongholds of the English blood and speech. The purity of their blood was largely a fiction; but in heart and tongue they certainly remained true to their origins. The civic records are at first in Latin or French, later on in English and Latin, while the Gaelic language was never officially used or even recognized. The municipal records of Galway, which in the existing form begin in 1485 and are in English, contain only a few incidental Irish words connected with trade, such as *skeinghlac* ('a cut from the cow') and *baunlac* ('a measure of cloth'). Even in Athenry, a small and isolated walled town, the merchant oligarchy refused to adopt Irish officially. Thus, in some deeds and wills of the Blake family of this town, the language up to 1423 is Latin and, after 1430, English. The statutes of Waterford are in archaic English;[7] but this city was particularly loyal, as is attested by the long poem in English written about 1536 by Patrick Stronge, town clerk, which sums up the grants of former English kings and ends every seven lines with 'qui tu intacta semper manes'.

Kilkenny was an inland town and so should have succumbed to the Hibernicization which was the marked feature of the fifteenth century; but, protected as it was by the pro-English Ormonds, it remained an English enclave and, in 1608, its citizens boasted that they had always preserved the English language and laws.[8]

Naturally, Irish was heard in every one of these towns, probably in Dublin itself; for there was a resident Irish population which was not entirely deprived of rights, for from time to time the officials of Limerick, Waterford, Galway and other cities have obviously Irish names. Nevertheless, these places remained English, and when the Tudor officials began to visit them they found spoken in them a language which they recognized as a variety of their own. The towns were the *points d'appui* from which English speech and civilization spread again over the island, and the mixed race which dwelt in them and were acquainted well or ill with the native language were the instruments used by the new English in the Tudor reconquest.

A light on the survival of English as the common street and fireside speech of a large Anglo-Irish town is given in the story of Dame Alice le Kyteler. This

7 [EN. A new edition has recently appeared: *The great parchment book of Waterford: Liber antiquissimus civitatis Waterfordiae*, ed. Niall J. Byrne (IMC, Dublin, 2007).] 8 John T. Gilbert (ed.), 'Archives of the municipal corporation of Waterford' in *10th rep. HMC*, app. 5, p. 326; idem (ed.), 'Archives of the town of Galway' in *10th rep. HMC*, app. 5, p. 380; Roderic O'Flaherty, *A chronological description of west or h-Iar Connaught written A.D. 1684*, ed. James Hardiman (IAS, Dublin, 1846); *Lib. Mun. pub. Hib.*, i, pt 1, p. 21; Gilbert, *Facsimiles*, iii, pl. 10, 43.

woman was a native of Kilkenny and was prosecuted by the bishop for witchcraft and necromancy in 1325. One of the points against her was that she was wont to sweep the streets of Kilkenny between compline and curfew, driving the mire towards her son's house, and saying with conjurations:

> May all the welth of Kilkenny town
> Hie to the house of William my son.

The Kyteler case was one of the *causes célèbres* of medieval Ireland: the numerous and curious charges are an extraordinary comment on the superstitions of the age. Some of her accomplices were burned, others whipped; she herself disappeared. The immediate point is that her conjuration is in English – that is, the familiar tongue of the town – while we are told that the bishop's requisition at the court of the seneschal, that the accused should be taken and confined till the church should judge them, was repeated thrice aloud in English and French, so that all should understand.[9] But outside the towns, that is, in the rural parts of the colony and in the great lordships of Kildare, Desmond, Ormond and Connacht, the fortunes of the English language pursued another course. The outlying provinces became predominantly Gaelic; the nearer portion, later called 'the Pale', retained a portion of its English heritage.

The further away from Dublin, the less English were the Norman houses. In 1579, MacWilliam, head of the Clanrickard Burkes, knew no English, and from the middle of the fourteenth century the western de Burgos abandoned the Saxon speech, as they did attendance at the Dublin parliament and all communication with the government. But the Desmonds and Kildares, still more the Butlers, from 1400 onwards – that is the time when the aristocracy of England itself began to use English rather than their worn-out French – were acquainted with the common speech of the country of their origin. The FitzGeralds of Leinster were often justiciars and so had to deal with the English-speaking officials of Dublin and the Lancastrian kings, who made the native idiom once and for all the state language of England. They frequently intermarried with the noble families of that country. Thus Silken Thomas, though he apparently understood Irish, was the son of Elizabeth Zouche of Codnor, Derbyshire. The letters of his father, the ninth earl, to Henry VIII are in English. The two great rentals of the Kildare family – that is, the red book begun in 1503 and the rental begun in 1518 – are illustrative on the point of language. The earlier grants and deeds, which go back to 1300, are largely indentures made with Irish chiefs and tenants; the language of these is Latin and occasionally Irish. In the fifteenth and sixteenth centuries, they are still in Gaelic; but, for all other purposes, Latin is the earlier medium, English the later.

9 *ADowling*, pp 21–2; *CStM*, ii, 362–4.

We must, however, note that it was an Englishman or Anglo-Irishman, Philip Flattisbury, who drew up the rentals from 1518 onwards.[10]

The once-English gentry and lesser nobles, however, of the land outside the Pale, who fell into dependence on the great earls and contracted amicable relationships with their Gaelic neighbours, had few bonds with their mother-country and soon became Hibernicized in fashion and speech. But there were parts of the once wide-extended colony where English survived, not as an exotic or an accomplishment, but as the common fireside idiom of a plebeian rural community. A hundred years after the conquest, the Anglo-Saxon tongue had been widely diffused over all the lowland parts of the three southern provinces and east Ulster. But, from about 1320, it began to disappear, partly owing to the revival of the native race, the growing Hibernicization of the Norman lords and the migration back to England of the small tenantry who could not endure the oppressions of the magnates. This decay evoked the constant protest of the more English and plebeian colonists in parliament and elsewhere, and one of the few fragments of medieval Anglo-Irish verse we have, written about 1327, laments the ruin of the speech it is written in, and puts the blame on the government which favoured the great and connived at their Irish fashions:

> By graunting charters of peas
> to false English withouten leas
> this land shall be mich undoo.
> But gossipred and alterage
> and leesing of our language
> have mickly holp theretoo.[11]

By 1500, English had lost most of the ground to Irish. Munster had become Hibernicized, save for the larger towns, though it had been so well planted; and Co. Waterford – which was at first largely Danish and then so colonized under the le Poers that in Elizabeth's reign it was counted 'one of the most English shires of Ireland' – is today still one of the most Irish-speaking of our counties. By the time of Henry VIII, the true area of English, apart from the towns, was confined to south Co. Wexford and that part called the 'Pale' – a territory sixty

10 John T. Gilbert (ed.), 'Manuscripts of his grace, the duke of Leinster' in *9th rep. HMC*, pt 2, app., pp 265–93; see also H.F. Hore, 'The rental book of Gerald, ninth earl of Kildare, A.D. 1518', *Journal of the Kilkenny and South-east of Ireland Archaeological Society* [*JRSAI*], 5 (1858–9), 266–80, 301–10; ibid., 7 (1862–3), 110–37; ibid., 8 (1864–8), 501–18, 525–46 [EN. The complete text is now available in Gearóid Mac Niocaill (ed.), *Crown surveys of lands, 1540–41, with the Kildare rental begun in 1518* (IMC, Dublin, 1992)]. 11 Quoted in Sir John Davies, 'A discovery of the true causes why Ireland was never entirely subdued' in H. Morley (ed.), *Ireland under Elizabeth and James the first, described by Edmund Spenser, by Sir John Davies* [...] *and by Fynes Moryson* (London and New York, 1890), p. 298.

miles long and thirty broad, stretching from Dundalk and Ardee to Kilcullen and the Dublin Mountains. Stanyhurst (*Description of Ireland*, 1587) says: 'All the cities and towns of Ireland, with Fingall, the king's land, Meath, the counties of Kildare, Louth, Wexford speak to this day English … even so in all other places their native language is Irish.'

But even in this restricted area, Irish was encroaching upon English. A common religious sympathy and resentment at the policy of confiscation and persecution which the Tudor governments adopted drew together the Irish and the Old English, and the symbol of their unity was the Irish language. Stanyhurst says that 'Irish was generally gaggled in the Pale', and Barnaby Rich tells us that 'ten Englishmen would adopt Irish for the one Irishman that would adopt English habits'.[12]

The situation in the parts north of Dublin and along the east coast was curiously parallel, though in reverse order, to what we see in many parts of Ireland to this day. In the hills of Armagh and the bog lands of Roscommon, we may still find old men speaking a poor English but retaining in a pure form the Irish language which has died out all around them. So, in the sixteenth century, there were old people in Fingall and Wexford who still spoke a Chaucerian English which was crumbling away, and stammered in an imperfect Irish which was rapidly coming in. Those were not the days of leagues formed for the purpose of reviving dying languages but, by the end of another century, the activities of the government, the advent of fresh colonies and the defeat of the native party turned the tide decisively against Irish.

One strong reason for the decay of English was that the dialect imported by the first conquerors had almost lost touch with that of England. The early colonists spoke the English of Bristol and the south-western counties from which they were mainly derived, whereas by Tudor times the north-midland speech had become the generally accepted standard for all England. In Ireland, the Saxon speech – mixed as it was with Irish and Flemish words, and developing on its own lines – drew further and further away from the main English tongue, so that Elizabethan officials newly arrived listened with amazement and amusement to what was represented to them as good English.

In the sixteenth century, there were, apart from the towns, two areas and two only where a dialect of English was the predominant and general speech. These were, first, the district stretching from Dublin to Dundalk and Ardee and reaching inland to Trim and Maynooth; and, second, the southern parts of Co. Wexford. The former was the area generally called the Pale, and here in the early days of the conquest numerous settlements of English had been made. In the eastern portion of this – that is, Fingall ('the land of the Danes'), stretching

12 John Lynch, *Cambrensis eversus seu potius historica fides in rebus Hibernicis Giraldo Cambrensi abrogata*, tr. Matthew Kelly, 3 vols (Dublin, 1848–52), i, 182, 188.

from Dublin to Skerries – there had been an earlier Teutonic colony; and some place-names, such as Baldoyle ('the Danes' town') and Skerries, and some surnames, such as Sigerson, Sweetman (Suatgarman), Kettle and perhaps Segrave and Hamlet, still survive as witnesses to the old Northman settlement. How far any of the Scandinavian speech survived here we cannot tell, but certainly during the medieval period and up to modern times the local dialect was a form of English. Even in the seventeenth and eighteenth centuries, when Irish was the common speech of most of the common people, Fingall was notable for retaining the Saxon tongue. Thus, in a poem called the 'Battle of the Scalp' (Ir. *Bearna Croise Brighde*), Seán Ó Neachtain, a Gaelic poet of the early eighteenth century, while he makes the Wicklow combatants speak Irish, puts English into the mouths of the Fingall men.[13]

As to the speech of southern Wexford, we have better evidence. Here the two baronies of Forth and Bargy, an area of some 80,000 acres, were the home of a very distinctive colony brought in from south Wales and western England in the early days of the Norman conquest. It was a mixed population of Flemings, Welsh and English, the Flemings being especially strong; for Strongbow, FitzStephens and others of the first conquerors who came from south Wales themselves drew most of their fighting men from the Flemish colony which Henry I had planted at the expense of the Welsh in Pembrokeshire, especially in the peninsula of Gower, which is still so Teutonic as to be called 'little England beyond Wales'.

This was the original nest from which, in 1169, the first and main conquerors of Ireland took wing. 'There were three and a half hundreds', says the author of a *Description of Pembrokeshire* (1603), 'viz., the Rowse, Castlemartyn, Narberth and half of Dongledy which were planted with Normans, Flemish and Welsh, and their posterity remain there to this day and speak English.' Mixed with colonists from the southern shires of England, the immigrants from Pembroke planted in Ireland by Strongbow and his successors, the Marshalls, formed a separate and distinctive community, and the isolated character of the baronies cut off by rivers and mountains from the rest of Leinster allowed them to remain English when the rest of the English colonies had become Hibernicized. There is still a preponderance of Flemish, French and English names in this district – such as Fleming, Roche, Sherlock, Hay, Rossiter, Synnot, Cheevers, Prendergast – the majority of which have been traced to their original source in Pembrokeshire.[14]

13 BL, Egerton MS 165, fos. 91*r*–111*r* [EN. For an edition of this poem, see N.J.A. Williams, 'Cath Bearna Chroise Brighde', *Zeitschrift für Celtische Philologie*, 38 (1981), 269–337].
14 George Owen, lord of Kemes, *The description of Pembrokeshire (1603)*, ed. H. Owen, 4 pts paginated as 2 vols (Cymmrodorion Record Ser. 1, London, 1892), p. 38; Herbert F. Hore, 'On Irish families of Welsh extraction', *Archaeologia Cambrensis: The Journal of the Cambrian Archaeological Association*, new ser., 3 (1852), 127–49.

The peculiar speech of the baronies of Forth and Bargy lingered on till about 1860, and is now, save for a few words, extinct. It has been the subject of much conjecture, learned and unlearned, and has often been described as a mainly Flemish speech. But there can be no doubt that it was simply an early form of English derived from the western and south-western counties of England, from which Dublin, the towns and large parts of the colony were generally populated. Not even in Pembroke did the Flemish survive, and in Ireland, as was natural, the predominant tongue of English would absorb whatever Flemish, Welsh and other dialects might for a while obtain. Specimens of this Wexford speech can be seen in Jacob Poole's *Dialect of Forth and Bargy* – it was still alive when Poole died in 1827; and Barnes, the Dorsetshire poet who edited the book, claims that it was mere western English, and would have been readily understood in his own county where, as in Wexford, they turned the *s* into *z* and the *f* into *v*. Of the 1,200 words which Poole collected, about 40 appear to be pure Gaelic; but the Irish influence is slight.

This was the kind of English which, long isolated from the mother speech, strangely puzzled the Tudor officials and soldiers who brought with them that new midland English of London and the court which was destined to become the language in time of all Ireland. Stanyhurst tells an amusing story bearing on this point:

> There was of late days one of the peers of England sent to Wexford as commissioner … and hearing in affable wise the rude complaints of the country clowns, he conceived here and there sometimes a word otherwhiles a whole sentence. The nobleman, being very glad that upon his first coming to Ireland he understood so many words, told one of his followers that he stood in good hope to become shortly a well-spoken man in the Irish, supposing that the blunt people had prattled Irish all the while they had jangled English.

A curious backwash of fate swept many of these Flemish-English settlers oversea again to their original home. During and after the Desmond and Tyrone wars, great numbers of the Anglo-Irish of Leinster abandoned their unhappy country and settled in swarms about Milford Haven, Haverfordwest and in Pembrokeshire generally. But with their separate religion, their peculiar habits and even their strange English, they found themselves no longer at home in the place of their ancestors. The *Description of Pembrokeshire* says:

> As for the Irishmen, they are so powdered among the inhabitants of Rowse and Castlemartyn that in every village you shall find the third, fourth, or fifth householder an Irishman, and now of late they swarm more than in tymes past by reason of these late wars; these for the most

> part speak the English tongue … as many as come out of the county say that they understand no Irishe … neither loth anye well understand his [their] English.

Lewis, writing a century later on the same county, records the disappearance or absorption of these migrants: 'The county [of Pembroke] has got rid of its Hibernian swarm, but they have left behind them a pernicious taste of strong liquors in preference to the only beverage calculated for a British constitution – ale.'[15]

It is highly probable that, had the Tudor plantations not taken place, the Irish language would have become the general speech of all Ireland, for the Old English themselves were greatly attracted by it. Much as the Wexford folk boasted of their English blood and speech, their common parlance lost much of its purity. 'In our days,' says Stanyhurst, 'they have so acquainted themselves with the Irish as that they have made a mingle mangle or gallimaufreie of both the languages, as commonly the inhabitants of the meaner sort speake neither good English nor good Irish.'

As a written even more signally than as a spoken language, English failed to take deep root and flourish in this country between 1200 and 1500. No single considerable piece of prose or verse came out of the English colony.[16] The annals are all in Latin, French or Irish; but at the end of the period (about 1550) the book of Howth, based on Cambrensis and a Latin book once in the hands of the O'Neills, was produced in English. This is a real *chanson de geste*, full of vigour and feeling, and heralds the true beginnings of a great English prose in Ireland.

The true victor in the clash of languages was the native Gaelic. In 1250, it was only one of the several languages of the country; by 1500, it was almost without a rival in literary cultivation, in the extent over which it was spoken, in the attraction it had even for the colonists. It had swallowed up French and seemed about to make a final conquest of English. In the lands where the Norman lords ruled over a mixed population, its revival came soon and, though it took longer to penetrate the more thickly planted areas and longest of all the towns, its inherent vigour carried it into all the former strongholds of English. For, as a living speech, it had every advantage over the decaying English idiom and, as a medium of culture, it appealed to the Norman-Irish lords, the patrons

15 Owen, *Description of Pembrokeshire*, p. 40. 16 There are odd pieces, such as a poem on Sir Piers de Bermingham (d.1308), a satirical poem of Friar Michael of Kildare on the Dominicans, an English version of the *Secreta Secretorum* by James Yonge, *c.*1420 (Gilbert, *Facsimiles*, iii, pl. 4, 5, 36), and verses on the 'Pride of life' in the account roll of Holy Trinity, Dublin [EN. For a new edition of the poems in question, see *Anglo-Irish poems of the Middle Ages*, ed. Angela M. Lucas (Dublin, 1995), pp 66–73 ('Song of Michael of Kildare'), 150–7 ('Piers of Bermingham')].

of literature, and to the learned class afterwards represented by Keating. It was, in short, the one language in Ireland which, in the wealth of its vocabulary and the inspiration of its poets and scholars, was ever expanding and throwing out fresh buds.

The triumph of the native language was accelerated by the supremacy of the Geraldines (1460–1530), by a long period of self-government and native culture, and was confirmed later when the iniquities of the Tudor reconquest made the native Irish language the symbol of a nationalism dear to all the people of Ireland.

The Norman-Irish lords naturally were soon familiar with the language which they heard around them from childhood. When the Irish kings visited Richard II in Dublin in 1394, the earl of Ormond, though he was the most English of the magnates, interpreted the king's speech to them. The FitzGeralds themselves had a vein of poetry: the first earl of Kildare, who died in 1316, was remembered in the sixteenth century as a Gaelic poet; Gerald, the earl of Desmond, who died in 1398, has attributed to him some verses 'on womankind'; and his successor, Thomas, is credited with an extant Irish poem.[17] Other Norman-Irish gentlemen, even in the Pale, wrote exquisite verses duly preserved by the poets and copyists of the native race; nor were these mere literary *tours de force*, for by 1400 Gaelic was the language which came most instinctively and affectionately to the lips of the Old English. It was not till the settler renounced his English speech that the Gaels would take him to themselves. The Four Masters record that, in 1372, William son of Ulick de Burgo died, 'chiefest of the Burkes for polite manners' – a way of saying that he was a lover of the Irish language and culture. So far had the Hibernicizing of the once-Norman conquerors and their English tenants gone by Tudor times that, in the Dublin parliament which made Henry VIII king of Ireland, the earl of Ormond had to translate the speaker's address into Irish for the benefit of lords and commons, though these were mainly of Old English origin.[18]

The native cause had always been identical in the minds of the Gaelic race with the Irish language, and ignorance of it had always been a stumbling block to the would-be rulers of Ireland. This was especially reflected in the constant struggle of the native prelates and lower clergy against the Frenchmen and Englishmen whom the king and the pope thrust into Irish sees. In 1224,

17 C.W. Fitzgerald, *The earls of Kildare and their ancestors from 1057 to 1773* (3rd ed., Dublin, 1858), p. 28. See George Sigerson, *Bards of the Gael and Gall: examples of the poetic literature of Erinn done into English after the metres and modes of the Gael* (2nd ed., Dublin, 1907), for a verse translation of the fourth [EN. *recte* third] earl of Desmond's verses (at p. 224) and other Irish poems of the Old English. For Earl Thomas, see James Hardiman, *Irish minstrelsy, or bardic remains of Ireland with English poetical translations*, 3 vols (London, 1831), i, 365.
18 Philip Wilson, *The beginnings of modern Ireland* (Dublin, 1912), p. 247.

Marianus Scotus, archbishop of Cashel, had to resign because he was ignorant of the native language; and, in 1285, the Dublin officials advised the king that no Irishman should ever become archbishop or bishop because they preach against the king and fill benefices with Irishmen, so that an election of bishops may be made to maintain their language. The mendicant orders especially favoured the native speech: in 1229, the bishop of Kildare, an Englishman, fulminates against 'certain fanatics who spread in the Irish language the seeds of rebellion'; and when, in the Bruce invasion, the native race made its most desperate effort up to that time to throw off the English yoke, the Franciscans were foremost in upholding the national cause, so that a papal mandate was, in November 1317, directed to the Irish archbishops bidding them in the royal interest order 'friars preachers and other mendicants to desist from stirring up the people of Ireland to resist the King's authority'.[19]

In the parliament of 1366 in which the famous Statutes of Kilkenny were passed, the use of the Irish language was forbidden to the English of Munster and Leinster. But this provision failed so signally that, in 1495, Poynings' parliament repealed it, so admitting the complete triumph of the native tongue, even in the English Pale. This return of Irish into the eastern province continued unto our own times: the counties of Louth, Meath and Dublin were, up to sixty years ago, largely Irish-speaking; and, as late as 1908, there were old men about Slane, only twenty-eight miles from the capital, who still spoke Irish.[20]

The towns were the last to give way to the floodtide of the native language. The ruling classes in these had always boasted of their English blood and affections; whatever literature was produced in English was written within their walls, and they spoke of the people about them as the 'Irish enemy'. But the break in religion and their trading intercourse with Spain alienated them from their ancestral country; their relations with the Irish became more human and they felt the general resentment against the confiscations and wars by which the old Norman houses were ruined. So, when the Elizabethan officials and the like began to visit the Irish towns, they found to their astonishment that the high dignitaries of English descent who received them with little good will were obstinate papists, preferring the Irish language to the English, attached to Irish dress and habits, and giving little token of their ancient nationality. Tudor travellers in Ireland were greatly struck with the extent and recent spread of Irish in the Pale and the towns. Fynes Moryson, whose *Commonwealth of Ireland* was written at the beginning of James I's reign, found that the English-descended townsmen of Ireland had both Irish tongues and Spanish hearts:

**19** A. Theiner (ed.), *Vetera monumenta Hibernorum et Scotorum historiam illustrantia* (Rome, 1864), p. 23 (for M. Scotus); *CDI 1252–83*, p. 10 (for 1285); *CDI 1284–95*, p. 239 (for 1299); *CPL 1305–42*, pp 127–8, 148. **20** J.J. Lloyd [Seósamh Laoide], *Duanaire na Mídhe* (Dublin, 1914).

> The English-Irish and the very citizens, excepting those of Dublin where the Lord Deputy resides, though they could speak English as well as we, yet commonly speak Irish among themselves, and were hardly induced by our familiar conversation to speak English with us.

He observed the citizens of Waterford and Cork, having wives that could speak English, 'chide them bitterly when they speak English with us'. Also the townspeople of Waterford were 'degenerated from English to Irish, or rather to Spanish, and were no less alienated from the English than the very mere Irish, as in one particular case of their community of language with the Irish'.

The contempt and enmity which the Tudor and Stuart officials and settlers openly displayed for the native language roused men to defend and praise it who came from the original English stock themselves. Among such literary champions of the Gaelic culture, the foremost were Keating and Lynch. The latter – author of that long and spirited vindication of Ireland, *Cambrensis Eversus* – in repelling the charge that Irish was a seditious language, says that 'it has no peculiar aptitude for treasonable machinations', and as a cultured and vigorous tongue he puts it with its combined excellencies above all living languages. 'It surpasses', he says, 'in gravity the Spanish, in elegance the Italian, in colloquial charm the French, and equals, if it does not surpass, the German itself in inspiring terror.'

But such whole-hearted eulogies of the native language, which had won triumph upon triumph against the imported speech of Norseman, Frenchman and Saxon up to this time, were in reality but its funeral dirge; for at the very moment its decline had begun and was to continue for three centuries till, in our own day, it has completely vanished from the greater part of our country.

CHAPTER 20

# The problem of the frontier in medieval Ireland*

*James Lydon*

Medieval Europe during the period between the twelfth and the mid-fourteenth centuries underwent a profound change from what has been called an open to a closed society. Barriers of one kind or another developed – political, social, economic, linguistic, even religious – which fragmented society and turned it in upon itself by means of dividing lines which became ever more fixed. New territorial frontiers appeared, in part the result of advances from the east and south-east, or of expansion from the west eastwards. The emergence of these frontiers was, in its own way, no less significant in its results than was the later American frontier with which we are all familiar. And though so far no Turner has appeared to put forward a coherent and all-embracing thesis, the growing emphasis on comparative studies may enable us in the future to make the kind of generalizations upon which such a thesis must rest.

One manifestation of the open, expanding character of European society in the twelfth century was the Anglo-Norman invasion of Ireland during the reign of Henry II. But, by a curious paradox, it is also true that this same event produced in turn a manifestation of the great change which was occurring in Europe to a closed or contracting society. For the incastellation of Ireland by the invaders produced what was to be one of the first systematically fortified frontiers in Europe. Indeed, one of the most fascinating aspects of medieval Ireland is the clash which occurred at this time between an essentially tribal society which was on the brink of breaking free from the archaic social and political system which had stifled it for so long, and a feudal society which was politically more sophisticated and militarily more advanced. One result of the conflict was to drive Gaelic society into the past – in on itself, as it were – and to make it retain its more archaic features for centuries to come. But the other result, and the one on which I wish to concentrate here, was to create a frontier which persisted for centuries and which indeed is only now, in some of its aspects, in the last stages of eradication. Ireland, then, was traversed by the frontier between the feudal and non-feudal worlds, and presents a good example of the kind of frontier problem which was manifesting itself all over Europe. I do not propose, however, to look at this problem in its general European

* First published in *Topic: A Journal of the Liberal Arts*, 13 (1967), 5–22.

context, but merely to examine some aspects of it in its local, Irish context; for the subject is vast and we will have to content ourselves with a very broad treatment, entering into detail on a few selected topics which I believe are of special importance.

Our starting point should be the treaty of Windsor, which attempted, however unsuccessfully, to fix a territorial frontier between Anglo-Norman and Gaelic Ireland. Negotiated in 1175 between Henry II and the high king, Ruadhri, as between two sovereigns, the treaty is one of the first of its kind sealed by a king of England.[1] Ruadhri was motivated mainly by fear. Having failed to dislodge those who had invaded Ireland, he now hoped by means of this treaty to confine them to the parts of the island they now occupied. The price he had to pay was acceptance of the overlordship of Henry II, which was the price already paid before this by nearly all the important kings in Ireland. Indeed, they too seem to have acted out of fear for the safety of their lands and, if we are to believe Gervase of Canterbury, had sent an embassy to Henry asking him to come to Ireland and protect them from the land-grabbing invaders.[2] At any rate, one of the points agreed to in the treaty of Windsor was the division of Ireland into two areas: one area, already occupied by the settlers, was marked off as Anglo-Norman, in which the high king had no rights; the rest of the country was to be Gaelic, held of the king of England, but through the high king. Here, then, was a definite frontier, created by agreement between two sovereign representatives of Anglo-Norman and Gaelic Ireland. But it was quickly apparent that the treaty was going to be unworkable. Apart from anything else, the high king proved quite incapable of carrying out his part of its provisions, especially the collection of the tribute to be paid to Henry II by the other kings of Ireland. It is not surprising, therefore, that its terms were soon broken in Ireland by both sides.

As an attempt to delimit a frontier in Ireland, the treaty of Windsor was bound to be a failure, even if Henry II had been genuine in his attempts, and sufficiently interested, to uphold it – a matter of considerable doubt. For the Anglo-Normans who came to Ireland were not very different to their cousins in Italy and the Middle East and proved impossible to control or hold in check. They were a conquering race, flushed with success, rapacious for land, and with all the advantages which military and political superiority gave them. They had already proved sufficiently independent and defiant to force the Angevin king to come to Ireland in person, with a great army, to establish their subordinate position in relation to himself as lord of Ireland. They had clearly frightened the native Gaelic kings to such an extent that they voluntarily accepted the

1 A convenient translation of the text of the treaty will be found in *IHD*, pp 22–4. 2 *The historical works of Gervase of Canterbury*, ed. William Stubbs, 2 vols (RS 73, London, 1879–80), i, 234–5.

overlordship of a foreign king in return for protection in their lands. In the splendid speech which he puts into the mouth of Robert Fitzstephen on the eve of the battle of Dublin, Giraldus Cambrensis rather naively makes him declaim that the Anglo-Normans had come to Ireland to restore Diarmaid MacMurrough, the deposed king of Leinster, to his rightful lands: 'We are not come as pirates or freebooters, but to reinstate this illustrious, generous and liberal prince in his own territories, of which he has been despoiled by the treason of his followers. We have compassion on the distressed, we succour the oppressed, we restore the destitute to his country and his inheritance.' But in the same address Fitzstephen is also made to say:

> [Since] we are not only brave, but well armed, can it be supposed that an unarmed multitude and mere rabble are able to resist us? … It may be the consequence of this enterprise that the five portions into which [this land] is divided may be reduced unto one, and the dominion of the whole kingdom devolve on our posterity. If the victory be won by our prowess, and MacMurchard be restored, and the realm of Ireland be secured by our enterprise for us and our heirs for ever, how great will be our glory, how worthy of being achieved even by the loss of life and the contempt of death.[3]

This spirit of conquest was behind John Courcy's unlicensed invasion of Ulster. The same dream of dominion made it impossible for the absent lord of Ireland to contain his Anglo-Normans subjects in Ireland. Expansion was rapid and irresistible, and so the absent lord gave way to the inevitable. Charters were issued, granting away the lands of the Gaelic Irish, by Henry II, by the Lord John and even, long afterwards, when the age of expansion seemed to be over, by Edward I. The conquest of Connaught was successfully undertaken. Settlers were introduced, even into places as far distant as Kerry. All authorities are now agreed that, by the last quarter of the thirteenth century, about three quarters of the island had been conquered and, to one degree or another, settled. The sword, followed by incastellation, won and held all the land for the Anglo-Normans. An efficient administrative system, of a kind never conceived by the Gaelic Irish, protected the king's interests in this wide area of land.

This period of expansion and conquest meant a constantly shifting frontier which posed problems and tensions in the localities. For one thing, Gaelic Ireland was never fully subdued, the conquest was never completed. Cowed by the knight on his heavy charger, tasked by the Welsh archer, the Gaelic rulers

3 The quotation is from Giraldus Cambrensis, *Expugnatio Hibernica.* I have used the translation in Thomas Wright (ed.), *The historical works of Giraldus Cambrensis* (London, 1863), pp 200–1.

retired before the invader and let him take over the open country in many places. But the heavy knight was useless in densely wooded or boggy country, much less in the mountainous areas; and so large enclaves of Gaelic land survived in many parts of the island. These the settlers proved incapable of mastering and from them the Gaelic chieftains were able to make sorties on the settled lands. From the beginning, therefore, the problem of defence against the natives was one which preoccupied the government in Dublin, the magnates on their lands and local communities nearly everywhere as they developed. Each shared the responsibility in varying degrees at different times. On the whole, it was the local communities which bore the greater burden. Local taxation, to meet the cost of local wars, became a permanent feature of life in the localities. There were other burdens, too, occasioned by the needs of local defence – purveyance, for example, which meant the seizure of food (usually without payment) to feed the armies, or the seizure of horses, carts, boats, or anything else which might be useful to the commissariat for transportation. And, to make matters worse, all this gave plenty of opportunity for graft and peculation by the local government officials – the sheriffs and their underlings, the petty tyrants of the age. The magnates who were given charters to lands as yet unconquered, and therefore the task of pushing forward as well as defending the frontier, had to be allowed the means of doing this. They had to be allowed the right to maintain private armies, both for conquest and for garrisoning castles to hold down the land after conquest – dangerous weapons which could be turned against the king, as both King John and Henry III discovered. A blind eye had to be turned towards the practice of taking over extra-feudal rights held by the Gaelic rulers in lands which were conquered.

On the whole, however, this age of expansion did not give rise to any insoluble frontier problem. The castles, especially after the period of the simple motte-and-bailey earthworks, seem to have coped very well with the task of keeping the native Irish out, so long as they were well garrisoned and supplied. Safe behind the frontier, the settled lands enjoyed a stability and prosperity which they had never known before, with a boom in agriculture and a great expansion in trade and commerce. The rapid proliferation of fairs and markets, the mushrooming of boroughs everywhere, the growth of monastic and manorial settlements, all argue for an era of comparative peace and order which G.H. Orpen liked to call the *Pax Normannica*.[4] By the time the age of expansion had come to an end with the reign of Edward I, it seems clear that a stable frontier had been established, the problem of defending it had been adequately coped with, and Anglo-Norman Ireland seemed sufficiently well protected to allow further developments in the arts of peace to take place. No wonder Orpen could call the thirteenth century, 'a great age, great in its performance but even

4 Orpen, *Normans*, ii, 323.

greater in its promise'.[5] For it looked, indeed, as if greater developments were to take place in the future.

However, the unexpected happened when this apparent stability was undermined and began to collapse, as demonstrated most vividly in the events of the Bruce invasion during the early fourteenth century. The frontier began to contract and it went on contracting during that century of war, plague and famine. More and more land was lost to Gaelic Ireland as the frontier was pushed back in almost every part of the island. Nothing seemed able to check this contraction, not even armed intervention from England which reached a climax at the end of the century with the two expeditions of Richard II: by then, it was too late and Gaelic Ireland was in many areas gaining the ascendancy. This remarkable Gaelic revival – the 'Irish rally', as Eoin MacNeill called it[6] – posed a frontier problem of colossal dimensions to the English government in Ireland, a problem which defied solution in the Middle Ages, until the English area was confined to the narrow coastal strip in the east which was subsequently called the Pale, and to a few towns elsewhere.

In the opinion of Eoin MacNeill, who wrote what still remains the best, if very inadequate, account of this revival, the principal factor in causing the tide to turn in favour of Gaelic Ireland was 'national sentiment, intensified and supplied with a more definite political form under a sense of national oppression'.[7] It is easy to show that national sentiment of the kind conceived by MacNeill did not and could not have existed in Ireland at that time or indeed for long afterwards. But a 'sense of oppression' there certainly was, and I have no doubt that MacNeill was right in the importance he attached to this. One has only to look at the so-called 'remonstrance' addressed to Pope John XXII in 1317 to see this clearly. Whatever the truth of the many accusations against the *Gaill* ('foreigner') in this remarkable document – and on many counts these accusations can be shown to be false – there can be no doubt that the 'remonstrance' expresses a deep sense of grievance because of oppressions suffered.[8] And in the opinion of those who penned this appeal to the pope, this oppression was sufficient to justify rebellion against their liege lord, the king of England, and the revival of the high kingship of Ireland in the person of Edward Bruce, brother of Robert I of Scotland.

This attempt to revive the high kingship – an institution which, it was believed, went back beyond the dawn of history – is a remarkable example of the tenacity with which Gaelic Ireland clung to the past. Clearly, it was incapable of succeeding unless most of Gaelic Ireland was willing to support it and it is easy to show that this was not the case. There was nothing 'national' about this new monarchy. Like the two previous attempts to revive the high

5 Ibid., iv, 298. 6 Eoin MacNeill, *Phases of Irish history* (Dublin, 1919), ch. 12. 7 Ibid., p. 325. 8 *IHD*, pp 38–46.

kingship, this one too was largely an Ulster affair and was inspired by O'Neill pretensions to power in the north. When Brian O'Neill was given 'supreme authority' (as the annalists put it) in 1258 and styled himself 'king of the kings of Ireland',[9] he had little effective backing outside his own territory in Ulster. And though he seems to have grown strong enough to pose a serious threat in the north for a time, so that troops had to be rushed from Dublin for its defence, he was in the end easily defeated at the battle of Downpatrick in 1260 and his monarchy perished with him. An invitation to King Haakon of Norway, shortly afterwards, to accept the high kingship came to nothing and it wasn't until Edward Bruce arrived in 1315 that another attempt at revival took place. Bruce's high kingship rocked Anglo-Ireland to its foundations and came within an ace of permanence. Resurgent Gaelic Ireland was in many parts of the country successful; many Anglo-Irish jumped on the bandwagon; the Dublin government seemed powerless for lack of adequate resources and direction. Had Bruce been as good a statesman as he was a soldier, had he possessed the skill and determination of his brother Robert, he must have succeeded. But his rashness, his obvious contempt for his Gaelic allies, his inability to accept wise counsel and to act with moderation, above all his scorched earth policy which produced famine and death, led to his downfall and the collapse of his enterprise. His death at the battle of Faughairt (near Dundalk) finished the Irish high kingship for all time. But the damage had been done. The frontier everywhere was collapsing and was contracting. The Gaelic Irish were in the full flood of their resurgence and the *Gaill* were in retreat.

It would be a mistake, however, to attribute this mainly to the effects of the Bruce invasion, for it is quite clear that already in the thirteenth century the weakness of the Dublin government and its failure to adequately maintain defences along the frontier had allowed the native Irish to halt the expansion of the settled area and then slowly begin to drive the settlers back. The battle of Credran of 1257 halted Geraldine expansion into Donegal and secured the independence of O'Donnell lands; the battle of Callan in 1261 checked expansion into Desmond and preserved MacCarthy lordship over a large part of Kerry. These were great local victories, independent of any movement to revive an all-Ireland monarchy, and they typify the Gaelic revival in its most successful phases in the localities. For it was here that the real Irish rally took place, in hundreds of local battles, fought by local chieftains usually acting in isolation, though sometimes, and especially in the fourteenth century, forming alliances with other chieftains and even rebel English.

The success of this Gaelic revival in the localities naturally meant that the frontier began to break up. And while it is true that this is a phenomenon which

9 A letter from Henry III to his son Edward, written in 1260, remarks that O'Neill 'presumptuously bears himself King of the Kings of Ireland' (*CDI 1252–84*, no. 661).

is most discernible in the fourteenth century after the catastrophe of the Bruce wars, so that our attention tends to be focussed on that period as the age of decline of the English settlement – a decline which is epitomized for many by the statutes of the Kilkenny parliament of 1366 – it would a mistake to suppose that its real beginnings belong to that century. For there is ample evidence from the records of the second half of the thirteenth century to show that the frontier was beginning to crumble in places even then, despite the undoubted stability and prosperity which still were manifest in the greater part of settled lands. *Hibernici inimici* ('Irish enemies') is a constantly recurring phrase now; so is *fideles Anglici* ('loyal English'), which clearly implies the existence of not so loyal English – the 'English rebels' as they were to be called by later generations. The distinction between a *terra pacis* ('land of peace') and a *terra guerre* ('land of war'), which in the earlier period was clear-cut and easily marked throughout the island, now tends to become more blurred and less easily identified as more and more marchlands, or border areas, appear on the map. The roll of 'expenses of journies to divers parts Ireland' of John Sanford, keeper of Ireland, in 1288–90, gives a very vivid picture of how serious the Gaelic breakthrough had already become by then. On every membrane, he is described as parleying with Gaelic chieftains, making provision for guarding marches in many parts of the settled area, mounting expeditions against local chieftains.[10] On 9 September 1288, for example, he journeyed to Kildare and reviewed a muster of the feudal levies of Leinster. The record tells us:

> Having been duly passed in review by the keeper, it was provided that the seneschal of Kildare should guard the marches of Offaly, Totemoy, Rathymegan, and Kildare, as far as Kilross; the seneschal of Wexford, the marches of Kilross by le Ryban to Moyrath; the seneschal of Carlow; from Moyrath to Calcet of Leye; and the seneschal of Kilkenny, from Calcet of Leye by those marches to Dunselach, and that so long as the service should last they should remain in those parts, which were then very hostile.[11]

All these places were in the heart of what had been one of the most heavily settled parts of Ireland. Again and again during his perambulations through the country, the keeper was told how hostile the local Gaelic chieftains had become. Details are given of wars which have broken out in many parts, some of which the local communities found impossible to support. The keeper wrote a special memorandum on the Gaelic Irish of Leix and Offaly, 'rebels and enemies of the king', and says that they 'remained so hostile that no peace could be established in the marches of Leinster, but the king's lieges were daily killed, their houses

10 *CDI 1285–92*, no. 559, contains the full account. 11 Ibid., no. 559, at pp 265–6.

burned, and intolerable depredations were made'. Despite all his attempts, 'he could not draw them to the king's peace'.[12]

'Losses, depredations, burnings' – this was now to become a constant refrain of complaint by the settlers. One result of this was that people began to leave the country. At first, the emigrants were landholders. Even before the end of the thirteenth century, these absentees were already a problem to the extent that one of the earliest pieces of parliamentary legislation from Ireland, from the parliament of 1297, is partly concerned with them:

> The magnates and others who reside in England or elsewhere out of this land, who cause the profits of their land to be transmitted to them from this land, leaving nothing here to protect their tenements or the tenants thereof, shall from henceforth permit a competent portion at least to remain in the hands of their bailiffs, whereby their own lands may be sufficiently saved and defended, if it happen that war or disturbance of peace should be excited there by any persons.[13]

In the fourteenth century, there is a regular series of statutes and ordinances which attempt to force absentees to return to their lands in Ireland or else to provide the means for their defence, leading up to the famous statute of absentees of 1380, which was the basis for all future legislation on the subject.[14] On many occasions, vigorous attempts were made to enforce this legislation, but always without lasting effect. To the end of the Middle Ages, the absentees remained a problem, a source of complaint by those who remained in Ireland, who said that neglect of their lands by absentees was a source of weakness, an invitation to Gaelic chieftains to take over the lands, placing an intolerable burden of defence on the magnates and communities of Ireland. A good illustration of this a petition which was sent to the Irish council in 1393 by Thomas Butler, son of the earl of Ormond. This was the period during which the chieftains of Leinster were gradually gaining control of the river valleys, which made people like Art MacMurrough of Leinster such a menace to the settlers in Carlow, Kildare, Kilkenny and even Dublin itself. Control of the network of rivers which drained Leinster and Munster was imperative if the frontier against the Gaelic areas was be maintained. This was precisely the kind of argument used by Butler in his petition.[15]

But it wasn't only landholders, great and small, who migrated to England, but artisans and labourers as well, apart from a steady stream of clerks. Now this exodus to England in the fourteenth century was undoubtedly the result, in part, of the Black Death in Ireland; but a more potent cause was the breakdown

12 Ibid., no. 559, at pp 271–2. 13 *Stat. John–Hen. V*, p. 201. See also ibid., p. 199. 14 Ibid., pp 476–7. 15 *PKCI*, no. 183.

of the frontier with the success of the Gaelic revival. For instance, in the first half of the century it is possible to trace in places a flight of the settlers before resurgent Gaelic chieftains, moving away from the dangerous areas into the land of peace. This trend continues into the later period. There is an interesting petition to the Irish council from the town of Carlow in 1392 which illustrates this.[16] It explains that the 'town, houses and all the corn and other goods were burned, wasted and destroyed by McMorough, Okarroll and all the other Irish of the parts of Leinster and Munster', so that most of the inhabitants 'have gone from the said town to divers other parts, to the very great injury of the entire land of Ireland, and great comfort of the said enemies, and those who tarry there have it in mind to go and better themselves'. The council made a grant of money available, to be divided among 'those who are willing to reinhabit the town there, each in proportion to his building'. But as the land of peace contracted, so that less and less of Ireland remained safe for those who wished to find refuge from places like Carlow, there was a tendency for people to leave Ireland altogether and migrate to England. A petition from the commons in the Irish parliament of 1421 pointed out that

> day to day [we are] burdened with divers intolerable charges and wars, so that the ter-tenants, the artificers and labourers of the said land daily depart in great numbers from your said land to your kingdom of England and remain there, whereby the husbandry of your said land is greatly injured and disused, and your said lieges greatly weakened in their power of resisting the malice of your said enemies.[17]

Depopulation, which can easily be shown from many of the surviving manorial extents of the fourteenth century, became so serious that, before the end of the century, a number of proposals were made for introducing new colonists from England: one of the stipulations made by the duke of Surrey in 1398, when he was made lieutenant of the king in Ireland, was that he should have out of every parish, or every two parishes, in England a man and his wife for Ireland, 'to inhabit the said land where it is wasted on the marches'.[18] But schemes like this came to nothing and it was not until the sixteenth century that new colonization, or plantation, was seriously undertaken.

This emigration, and the depopulation which followed, left large parts of the original colony to the Gaelic chieftains. Some towns were swallowed up by them, especially in more distant places; others survived, little islands in a Gaelic sea, difficult of access and sometimes cut off altogether. Many of these were, naturally enough, on the coast – places like Galway, Waterford or Carrickfergus,

16 *PKCI*, no. 5. 17 *Stat. John–Hen. V*, p. 569. 18 The terms stipulated by Surrey are printed in full in Gilbert, *Viceroys*, pp 560–1.

which were normally accessible by sea even if the land routes were closed. But, even by sea, access was not always possible and was frequently hazardous when the piratical activities of Bretons, Flemings, Scots and French made sea journeys a dangerous undertaking. On the whole, however, such towns managed to survive intact, safe behind strong walls, trading with the Gaelic areas in their hinterlands and maintaining a delicate balance between their loyalty to the English king on the one hand – for which they were regularly well compensated – and their relations with the local Gaelic chieftains or the local rebel English on the other. The inland towns found it much more difficult to survive, unless they enjoyed the patronage of a powerful local protector. For some of these communities, the only resort left was often the payment of what was known as 'black rent' to the local Gaelic chieftain, a device which was very like the 'protection money' racket of American gangsters of our own day.

The overall impression one gets, then, is of a complete collapse of the frontier in many parts of the country as the Gaelic chieftains, or the rebel, degenerate English, take over land almost everywhere. Many towns are left isolated as outposts, especially on the coast; other pockets of English settlers survived where the settlers have managed to retain a hold on their lands because they have learned how to exist with the natives, though the cost of this was very often cultural and linguistic assimilation. In the fifteenth century in particular, we can see a new frontier emerging in the eastern part of the island; parts of the four loyal counties of Dublin, Meath, Kildare and Louth are treated as a unit for most purposes. The subsidies which came regularly now from England for the defence of Ireland – this in itself was another result of the Gaelic resurgence, because with the contraction of the land of peace the revenues available to the Dublin government sharply declined, so that the English exchequer had to meet a large part of the costs of the defence of Ireland; and these costs, of course, rose in proportion to the success of the Gaelic revival – are spent more and more on the defence of these four shires and rarely on mounting expeditions outside that area. But even the cost of defending that particular area proved too much in the end. So the real frontier contracted once again to the limits of what was known as the Pale, the small area marked off by a ditch, frontier castles, towers and wards and heavily defended bridges and fords.[19] Behind this Pale – so like the Pale of Calais, after which it was named – the English interest survived intact, often in a state of virtual siege by Gaelic chieftains or rebel English, and once or twice a danger spot to shaky dynasties on the English throne. It was an answer of sorts to the frontier problem, but it

19 The earliest mention of the Pale that I have found comes from 1446–7: Hugh Roe McMahon in his submission promises, 'to carrie nothing owte of the inglishe pale contrarie to the statutes' (E.P. Shirley, *Some account of the territory or dominion of Farney in the province and earldom of Ulster* (London, 1845), p. 24).

could only be a temporary answer if Ireland was ever to be secured for the English interest. It was the Tudors who first faced up to the frontier problem in a realistic way and saw that a conquest of Ireland was the only real answer: this time a complete conquest and not the haphazard, incomplete conquest of the twelfth century, which had sown the seeds of a dangerous frontier problem in the later Middle Ages. There was another kind of frontier, psychological more than anything else, which in its own way was just as important as the territorial frontier and which certainly created as much of a problem. It stemmed from a policy of racial segregation, which tried to set up a barrier between the races in Ireland. Basically, this official policy was founded on the belief that the Gaelic race was inferior, so that, in the terminology of the time, the settlers who were assimilated to Gaelic culture, in whatever degree, were 'degenerate'. The treatment of the native race, their general exclusion from the common law, for example, is one aspect of this policy. But what I want to concentrate on here is the more pernicious side of it, which can be seen in the deliberate policy of the Dublin government of setting up a cultural barrier which it tried to make impassable to the settlers in Ireland.

Before we look at this policy of apartheid, it might be as well first of all to ask a simple question. Was the policy necessary? We all know, having heard it a thousand times, that many of the settlers in Ireland became *Hibernicis ipsis Hiberniores* – more Irish than the Irish themselves. That trite phrase, so common that it hardly bears repetition, has too often been taken as adequate. But how much does it really tell us? What do we really know of the scope and degree of this Irishizing process? Practically nothing. And yet how important it is that we should know, if we are ever to understand the malaise which was a constant threat to the 'liege folk' of Ireland, a source of complaint by them to the king and his parliament, a continuous menace to the Anglicized areas, sufficiently real and sufficiently dangerous to necessitate a policy of race division. Professor Kelleher of Harvard has recently complained of the lack of communication between workers in the different areas of the field of Irish studies and has justly condemned historians in particular for taking too little account – he might well have said for being totally ignorant – of recent developments and discoveries in Irish literary history.[20] Here is a case in point. For too long, most historians with an interest in medieval Ireland have ignored altogether, apart from a passing nod at the annals, the Gaelic literary sources of the period with the result that when we come to talk of the way in which many of the settlers went native, to one degree or another, we have to fall back on generalities. I have not the expertise or range of knowledge to take myself out of that 'nodding' class of historians and deal adequately with this problem; nor can I hope to say much in the short space available here. But at the same time

20 John V. Kelleher, 'Early Irish history and pseudo-history', *Studia Hibernica*, 3, (1963), 114.

some statement is in order, so as to illustrate the feeling of insecurity and even danger which fraternization with the native Irish could produce.

It is clear that, from the beginning, intermarriage with Gaelic families took place, which is not altogether surprising considering that so many of the invaders were as much Welsh as Norman and were therefore susceptible to the peculiar Celtic charms of the women of Ireland. Strongbow married the daughter of the king of Leinster; de Lacy married the daughter of the high king. It is usually the more important people we hear about in this context; but it is plain that the more humble settlers often followed the example of their betters in contracting marriages of this kind. With marriage came the adoption of the Irish language and Irish customs – fosterage, for example, which was always regarded as a particularly dangerous abuse and was roundly condemned by successive governments down to the time of Sir John Davies in the seventeenth century. For fosterage, perhaps more than anything else, led to the Irishizing of generations of settlers. No wonder it was picked out as the most pernicious custom of all by Spenser, the famous sixteenth-century poet, in his *View of the state of Ireland*:

> [F]or first the child that sucketh the milk of the nurse must of necessity learn his first speech of her, the which being the first inured to his tongue, is ever after the most pleasing unto him, insomuch as though he afterwards be taught English, yet the smack of the first will always abide with him; and not only of the speech, but also of the manners and customs.[21]

The earl of Ulster, who patronized Gaelic poets and had a Gaelic elegy written on his death in 1326, represents a process of Irishizing which had been going on since the first invaders landed.[22] It was to an ancestor of this earl that a famous Gaelic court poet fled in the early thirteenth century when he was looking for refuge from an irate O'Donnell. This was Muiredach O'Dálaigh, and clearly he expected that Richard de Burgh of Connaught would give him asylum. And he paid for his sanctuary by means of a typical praise-poem of the kind in which the Gaelic nobility delighted, in which he said: 'The king of Assaroe has unfairly threatened me: I will turn my mouth to the Saxon hawks because of their promises to me.'[23] The poet may have been as cynical in this service as was a more famous descendant of his, Godfraidh Fionn O'Dálaigh,

21 H. Morley (ed.), *Ireland under Elizabeth and James the first, described by Edmund Spenser, by Sir John Davies* [...] *and by Fynes Moryson* (London and New York, 1890), p. 106. 22 Standish Hayes O'Grady and Robin Flower (eds), *Catalogue of Irish manuscripts in the British Museum*, 3 vols (London, 1926–53), i, 338. 23 David Greene, 'The professional poets' in Brian Ó Cuív (ed.), *Seven centuries of Irish learning, 1000–1700* (Thomas Davis Lectures: Dublin, 1961 for 1958), p. 47.

who addressed a poem to an earl of Desmond in which he said: 'A sovranty they never get we promise to the Gaels in our odes; you need not take any notice of this, it is our custom.' And later: 'There are two kindreds for whom poetry is composed in Ireland of the cool springs – the Gaels, known to fame, and the English of Britain's dewy isle. In poetry for the English we promise that the Gaels will be banished from Ireland; in poetry for the Gaels we promise that the English shall be routed across the sea.'[24] As Professor David Greene has pointed out: 'the foreigners would not have bought these poems unless they had been thoroughly integrated both linguistically and culturally. Those who had been found this praise poetry heady stuff.'[25] One might see in the career of the rebellious first earl of Desmond, with his grandiose schemes for a revival of the high kingship in his own person, how far such flattery could lead an attentive and gullible patron. Certainly, the poets were prepared to pander to the aspirations of their Anglo-Irish patrons and say the sort of thing the nobility liked to hear. In a panegyric hailing a Richard Burke of Connaught in the fifteenth century his poet proclaims: 'The charter of the sword – what better one is there? – is Richard's charter to Rath Raoileann [Ireland].'[26]

In many other ways, one can see how the settlers were at least partially assimilated to the Gaelic Ireland they found all around them. For example, we notice the influence of Brehon law, part of which was adopted in many areas, in relation to homicide or the inheritance of land, for example, and which produced that peculiar amalgam of Brehon and common law known as march law. Or, in the careers of many of the great magnates, one can trace the same process of assimilation at work. Perhaps the outstanding example in the fourteenth century is the third earl of Desmond, of whom a Gaelic writer had this to say:

> A nobleman of wonderful bounty, mirth and cheerfulness in conversation, charitable in his deeds, easy of access, a witty and ingenious composer of Irish poetry and a learned and profound chronicler; and, in fine, one of the English nobility that had Irish learning and professors thereof in greatest reverence of all the English land.[27]

His poems have recently been edited and they demonstrate in a very vivid way how thorough his cultural assimilation had been.[28] That an earl of Desmond should write poetry in Irish in the fourteenth century is remarkable; that he should write such good poetry is astonishing. Here was a man who was so Irishized that he was one of the finest Gaelic poets of his generation. But he was

24 Eleanor Knott, *Irish classical poetry: commonly called bardic poetry* (Dublin, 1957), p. 60. 25 Greene, 'Professional poets', pp 47–8. 26 Knott, *Irish classical poetry*, p. 59. 27 Robin Flower, *The Irish tradition* (Oxford, 1947), p. 144. 28 Gearóid Mac Niocaill (ed.), 'Duanaire Ghearóid Iarla', *Studia Hibernica*, 3 (1963), 7–59.

also a man who was deeply involved in the government of Ireland at the time, attending parliaments and councils of the king in Ireland, regularly accepting office, in one capacity or another, in the south-west, and even acting as justiciar and head of the Irish government. At the same time, he was trying to live on good terms with his Gaelic neighbours, with whom he had strong ties of friendship and, with some, the even stronger ties of fosterage. He spoke their language, he adopted their customs, he was assimilated to their traditions. But he was in an impossible position, occasionally forced through circumstances to make war on these same friends and neighbours – forced, as it were to forswear the Gaelic part of him. This clash between his two personalities is vividly illustrated by his poetry. To the king and his government in Ireland, people like Desmond demonstrated the dangers of cultural assimilation. He could not be trusted all the time. In his Irish guise, he, and others like him, patronized Gaelic poets and travelling minstrels who very often were thus able to penetrate the land of peace and to act as spies for chieftains in their raids on the settled areas. Even wandering friars, and especially the Franciscans, who found a welcome in many an Anglo-Irish friary or manor, could and did spy the land and carry back information to Gaelic leaders. There was real danger here: the more the Anglo-Irish 'degenerated' (as the government put it) into Gaelic habit, speech and custom, the greater the danger that incursions by 'Irish enemies' would follow. Indeed, later Tudor commentators, like Spenser or Gerrard or Campion, were convinced that one of the main reasons for the failure of the English settlement in medieval Ireland was, as Gerrard expressed it, that 'the quiete of the land began to decay [because] the English degeneratinge become Irishe'.[29] There were other dangers which this degeneracy occasioned, so that the so-called *degenerate* English became all too often the *rebel* English, defying the authority of king and government alike, and riding roughshod over the rights of the local communities everywhere.

Enough has been said to show that the process of Irishizing was a very real problem and, as the Burkes of Connaught or the Powers of Waterford demonstrate so well, was full of danger to the English interest in Ireland. No wonder, then, that a policy of separating the races and driving a cultural barrier between them was instituted. This policy is best exemplified in the Statutes of Kilkenny of 1366. But the legislation of 1366 had been anticipated in almost every detail by a host of earlier enactments from 1297 onwards: bans on Irish dress, language, games and so on, on marriage with the Gaelic enemy, on making treaties with them, on keeping rhymers or brehons, on trading with the Gaelic areas – none of this was new in the mid-fourteenth century. But it was given a new form, a new life at Kilkenny; and certainly later generations, to

29 Gerrard, 'Notes', pp 93, 121. Gerrard pointed out that, in his own time (1577), 'if Irishe speache, habit and conditions made the man Irishe, the moste parte of the Englishe [of the Pale] were Irishe' (ibid., p. 122).

judge from the frequent confirmations of these statutes or reference to them in the records of the later medieval period, regarded the Statutes of Kilkenny as the best and most authoritative summary of the so-called 'anti-Irish' legislation of the medieval Irish parliament.

This legislation and the policy underlying it was, on the whole, a complete failure, as some of the examples I cited earlier suggest and as the frequent breaches of the statutes prove. The Butlers continued to keep their brehons and court poets; the Geraldines still married and fostered with Gaelic families. Two great fifteenth century Gaelic compilations – the book of Fermoy and the *Saltair* of MacRichard – were assembled for Anglo-Irish families and, indeed, the latter one was so highly valued that it formed part of the ransom handed over by Butler to Fitzgerald after the battle of Pilltown in 1462. The library of the eighth earl of Kildare contained a large number of Gaelic books, side by side with volumes in English, Latin and French. But there is no point in multiplying examples which would all show the same thing: the way in which the Statutes of Kilkenny and similar legislation was ignored and the policy of creating a racial frontier a failure. Traffic with Gaelic Ireland continued and cultural assimilation went on virtually unchecked. The only cure, and that a drastic one, was new settlers from England in sufficiently large numbers to prevent their being swamped. In other words, what was needed was plantation – the very policy initiated in the sixteenth century when the answer to the frontier problem, conquest, was undertaken.

In the end, then, the answer to the frontier problem proved to be conquest and plantation. It was beyond the resources of medieval governments to supply this answer: the money was not available and I doubt if the interest in a solution was sufficiently strong in England either. But under the Tudors, Ireland became a danger, a threat to their security on the English throne. She became what a later generation was to call 'the back door to England'. This was a new factor in the situation and one which could not be ignored. It was then, therefore, that a solution to the medieval frontier problem was sought and found.

CHAPTER 21

# The middle nation*

*James Lydon*

In 1317, at the height of the Bruce invasion of Ireland, Donal O'Neill, calling himself 'king of Ulster and by hereditary right true heir of the whole of Ireland' (L. *Rex Ultonie, ac tocius Hiberniae hereditario jure verus heres*), sent a famous remonstrance to Pope John XXII in his own name and that of the 'kinglets and magnates and the people of Ireland' (L. *reguli et magnates ac populus Hiberniae*). Its purpose was to defend the Irish support for the Scots and to present a case against the lordship of the English king in Ireland. Listing grievances against the English of Ireland, the author of the remonstrance wrote: 'For the English inhabiting our land, who call themselves of the middle nation, are so different in character from the English of England and from other nations that with the greatest propriety they may be called a nation not of the middle, but of the utmost perfidy' (L. *Anglici enim nostram inhabitantes terram que se vocant mediae nacionis, sic sunt ab Anglicorum de Anglia ceterarumque nacionum moribus alieni, quod non mediae, sed extremae perfidiae, nacio propriissime possunt appellari*).[1] So far as I know this was the first, and the only, time that the term 'middle nation' (L. *media natio*) was used in this way and, while it can be argued that the real author was a Scot, there seems no reason to doubt that the document did in fact emanate from O'Neill and that it does genuinely reflect contemporary Gaelic attitudes. There are, therefore, two observations which may be made immediately. First of all, the author clearly states that the English of Ireland call themselves of the middle nation (he in fact uses this term twice in the course of his argument)[2] – that is, that the Anglo-Irish[3] saw themselves

* First published in James Lydon (ed.), *The English in medieval Ireland: proceedings of the first joint meeting of the Royal Irish Academy and the British Academy, Dublin, 1982* (Royal Irish Academy: Dublin, 1984), pp 1–26. 1 *IHD*, pp 38, 42. The Latin text is in Thomas Hearne (ed.), *Fordun, Scotichronicon*, 5 vols (Oxford, 1722), iii, 908, 916; Walter Goodall (ed.), *Johannis de Fordun Scotichronicon*, 2 vols (Edinburgh, 1759), ii, 259–60, 263. A diplomatic text is badly needed [EN. For a diplomatic edition, see D.E.R. Watt (ed.), Scotichronicon *by Walter Bower*, vi: *books XI and XII* (Aberdeen, 1991), pp 385–405, with notes by J.R.S. Phillips, ibid., pp 465–83]. For a discussion of the text in the context of contemporary canon law, see James Muldoon, 'The remonstrance of the Irish princes and the canon law tradition of the just war', *American Journal of Legal History*, 20 (1978), 309–25. 2 L. 'propter continuam perfidiam Anglicorum mediae nacionis' (Hearne, *Fordun, Scotichronicon*, iii, 921; Goodall, *Johannis de Fordun Scotichronicon*, ii, 265; tr. *IHD*, p. 44).

as a nation apart; and secondly, that the Gaelic Irish, in so far as this remonstrance does represent their views, accepted this concept and clearly distinguished between them, the Anglo-Irish and the English of England.

If this term 'middle nation' is peculiar to the remonstrance, the idea itself is much older. It was first voiced in the late twelfth century by Gerald of Wales, in a famous speech which he put into the mouth of Maurice fitz Gerald in 1170, during the siege of Dublin:

> What are we waiting for? Surely we do not look to our own people for succour? We are now constrained in our actions by this circumstance, that just as we are English as far as the Irish are concerned, likewise to the English we are Irish, and the inhabitants of this island and the other assail us with an equal degree of hatred.[4]

This may be a sentiment peculiar to Gerald, though I believe that it is more likely to represent an attitude of frustration which he encountered among his Geraldine relations in Ireland, whom he always depicted as a distinct group. There is a remarkable parallel to this a century later when the burgesses of a small borough in Anglesey complained that 'in Wales they were regarded as Englishmen and in England as Welshmen'.[5] People living in frontier regions were likely to find themselves in this middle position and therefore to acquire the characteristics of what the remonstrance called a middle nation.[6]

Before proceeding further, it is necessary to examine the term 'nation' and how it was applied in late medieval Ireland. It would probably be more in keeping with contemporary terminology to speak of middle nations, rather than of a single nation as such. For the term *natio* continued to be used in the older sense of *familia* or *gens* – the sense in which it used in a famous example from the Canterbury Tales, when the Wife of Bath laments:

> Allas! that any of my nacioun
> Sholde ever so foule disparaged be![7]

3 I propose to use this term, rather than the more cumbersome 'English of Ireland', even if it does beg the question. 4 Giraldus, *Expug. Hib.*, p. 81. 5 R.R. Davies, 'Race relations in post-conquest Wales: confrontation and compromise', *Trans. Hon. Soc. Cymmrod.* (1975 for 1974), 44, quoting G.O. Sayles (ed.), *Select cases in the court of the king's bench* (Selden Soc. 58, 1939), p. cxxiii. The petitioners emphasize the consequence: 'ita quod non habent statum Anglicorum nec eciam Wallicorum, set quod deterius est de utroque'. 6 I have dealt with some aspects of this in my paper, 'The problem of the frontier in medieval Ireland' (above, ch. 20). 7 W.W. Skeat, *The complete works of Geoffrey Chaucer: the Canterbury tales* (Cambridge, 1894), p. 351, lines 1068–9. The words, in fact, are given to the knight in her 'tale'.

It is in this sense that we find it used in Ireland, not just in literary sources such as the Anglo-Irish annals, but in government records; and not just about Gaelic clans, but about Anglo-Irish families. When Clyn records the death of Gerald fitz Maurice in 1287, he calls him 'captain of the Geraldines' (L. *capitaneus Geraldinorum*); and when he writes that his nephew John fitz Thomas was his heir, he added: 'This John was the first of this nation [L. *primus de hac natione*] to be made earl of Kildare.'[8] An earlier Kilkenny chronicle, in noting the murder of the first earl of Louth, says that he was killed with sixteen and more 'both of his nation and family' (L. *tam de natione quam familia*); it also records the death of Philip Talun with his son and 'about twenty-six of divers nations' (L. *circiter 26 diversorum nationum*).[9] Sometimes in official records, the phrase *natio et cognomen* or *nationes et cognomina* is used, as if the terms were interchangeable. Most commonly, however, the term nation is used on its own. A few examples will suffice to illustrate the point. In 1352, an Irish exchequer account describes the justiciar, Thomas Rokeby, going to Munster, 'to pacify divers English nations' (L. *diverse nationes Anglice*); a message to Henry IV from the Irish council in 1399 said that 'the English nations who are rebels in all parts of the country, such as Butlers, Powers, Geraldines, Berminghams, Daltons, Barrets and Dillons, are not amenable to the law'; a petition of 1416 from the commons of Ireland to the English parliament refers to the 'Geraldines, Burkes, Powers and other great nations of the land'; and, as late as 1525, a William Copinger of Cork could style himself 'captain of his nation'.[10]

It should be clear from such examples that, to the end of the Middle Ages, family, rather than nation in the wider sense, was the most important grouping in Ireland, as indeed elsewhere in Europe at that time. When the Kilkenny parliament of 1310 made each 'chieftain of great lineage' (F. *chekun cheif de graunt lygnage*) responsible for errant members of his family – a statute which was repeated in the parliament of 1324 – it was using a terminology (F. *lineage*) which is currently in fashion among historians.[11] It is necessary to stress here

8 *AClyn*, p. 10. 9 Robin Flower, 'The Kilkenny chronicle in Cotton MS. Vesp. B XI', *AH*, 2 (1931), 337, 339. 10 E 101/244/13; *PKCI*, p. 264; *PPC*, ii, 49; Charles McNeill, 'Reports on the Rawlinson collection of manuscripts preserved in the Bodleian Library, Oxford', *AH*, 1 (1930), p. 164 [EN. The record referred to here as dating from 1416 (*PPC*, ii, 49) has been attributed convincingly to *c.*1421. See Elizabeth Matthew, 'The governing of the Lancastrian lordship of Ireland in the time of James Butler, fourth earl of Ormond, *c.* 1420–52' (PhD, University of Durham, 1994), pp 149–50]. 11 *Stat. John–Hen. V*, p. 266. A good example of lineage in action can be seen in 1290 when Eustace le Poer assembled his *leygnage* and swore before the sheriff of Waterford to seize his guilty cousin, Robert le Poer (H. Cole (ed.), *Documents illustrative of English history in the thirteenth and fourteenth centuries* (RC, London, 1844), p. 71; *CDI 1285–92*, pp 307–8). In 1290, when Geoffrey de Geneville sought a papal dispensation for his son to marry his cousin, he emphasized that 'he requires many kinsmen and friends by marriage … to keep the peace and retain the inhabitants in obedience' (*CPL 1198–1304*, p. 513). The importance of lineage is elucidated in Frame, *Eng. lordship*, and in

that in the lordship of Ireland family, lineage, was of fundamental importance. When John fitz Thomas and John Cogan, in April 1297, sealed two important agreements with each other, saving clauses were inserted referring to 'those who are of the family and kin of both' (L. *de cognomine utriusque parentale*) and 'cousins of the family and kin of both' (L. *consanguinei de cognomine utriusque parentale*).[12] Loyalty to one's own nation, or lineage, came first.

But the remonstrance of 1317 makes it clear that larger groupings called nations were recognized. Writing about his ancestors, the kings of Ireland, Donal O'Neill says that 'it was they, not the English nor others of any nation, who eminently endowed the Irish church'.[13] There is plenty of evidence to show that 'nation' was used in this more modern sense. The 1191 foundation charter of St Patrick's in Dublin refers to the 'unlearned simplicity of the Irish nation'.[14] The 1325 proposals for the reform of the Irish church distinguish between two nations in the lordship, the English and the Irish, and even specifically refers to the *gentes Hibernie nationis* ('families of the Irish nation').[15] And, most interesting of all, King Robert I of Scotland wrote a letter to 'all the kings of Ireland, the prelates and clergy, and to the inhabitants of all Ireland, our friends', in which he said:

> Whereas we and you, and our people and your people, free in times past, share the same national ancestry and are urged to come together more eagerly and joyfully in friendship by a common language and common custom.

He urged that 'the special friendship between us and you' should be 'maintained and strengthened, so that, God willing, our nation may be restored to her former liberty'.[16] Here the deliberate linking of Scots and Irish into one nation is for political purposes; but it does show that the concept of nationality was even then capable of being exploited on the basis of common ancestry and language. It is also a reminder to us that, by the early fourteenth century, a strong sense of nationality, distinct from English nationality, had developed in Scotland.[17] In England, this sense had developed even earlier.[18]

Robin Frame, 'Power and society in the lordship of Ireland, 1272–1377', *P&P*, 76 (1977), 19–21. 12 *Red bk Kildare*, pp 42, 45. 13 *IHD*, p. 39. 14 William Monck Mason, *The history and antiquities of* [...] *St Patrick's* (Dublin, 1819), p. 445. 15 J.A. Watt, 'Negotiations between Edward II and John XXII concerning Ireland', *IHS*, 10:37 (1956), 16. 16 R. Nicholson, 'A sequel to Edward Bruce's invasion of Ireland', *SHR*, 42:133 (1963), 38–9. It is translated in G.W.S. Barrow, *Robert Bruce and the community of the realm of Scotland* (2nd ed., Edinburgh, 1976), p. 434; but he gives a reading of 'your nation' for *nostra natio*, which completely alters the meaning. 17 Barrow, *Robert Bruce*, pp 92, 119. 18 F.M. Powicke, *England in the thirteenth century, 1216–1307* (2nd ed., Oxford, 1953), p. 528. For the growth of a sense of nationality in England, see Barnaby C. Keeney, 'Military service and the development of nationalism in England', *Speculum*, 22:4 (1947), 534–49.

The concept of a middle nation, therefore, as applied to the Anglo-Irish, is not too far-fetched in the context of the early fourteenth century. But had the concept any reality? Is there any evidence to support the view that the Anglo-Irish were somehow apart from the Gaelic Irish and, more important, the English of England? Obviously generalization in this area is especially dangerous. Ireland was a highly fragmented society and any attempt to supply an artificial unitary character is bound to lead to misunderstanding. Nevertheless, there are hints of attitudes which were general and these must not be ignored just because they fit uneasily into a pattern which is shaped by local interests and loyalties. The conceptual framework which governments in London and Dublin imposed on the lordship, based on current ideas of social behaviour, may have been inappropriate to circumstances prevailing in any given locality in Ireland. But it was a framework that was accepted and even exploited, and it had its own validity. When men in England and Ireland tried to articulate principles which they accepted, they could do so only in the concepts of their own time. There are three main questions which will help to test the concept of a middle nation: what was the attitude of Gaelic Ireland to the Anglo-Irish; how were they seen from England; and, most important of all, how did they see themselves?

Gaelic attitudes are not only complex, they are far from uniform. Depending on circumstances they range from the vituperation of the remonstrance of 1317 ('their arrogance and excessive lust to lord it over us' is one of the milder complaints), or a letter of Donal O'Neill of the same year (where they are said to be 'worse than the inhuman Danes themselves', proceeding 'by foxlike fraud and deceit'),[19] to the almost affectionate note struck in a prose tract written for Eoghan O'Madden around the same time. The lines are now famous:

> And in his time Scottish foreigners less noble than our own foreigners arrived; for the old chieftains of Erin prospered under those princely English lords, who were our chief rulers, and who had given up their foreignness for a pure mind, their surliness for good manners, and their stubbornness for sweet mildness, and who had given up their perverseness for hospitality.[20]

The language may border on the purple, but it contains something which was to remain the constant feature of the Gaelic attitude towards the Anglo-Irish to the end of the medieval lordship: they were foreign (Ir. *Gall*). When the O'Madden tract talks about 'English lords' it uses the term *flath-ghallaibh* and

19 *IHD*, p. 44; Herbert Wood, 'Letter from Domnal O'Neill to Fineen Mac Carthy, 1317', *PRIA*, 37, C:7 (1926), 143 [EN. The latter document has since been shown to be a forgery: Diarmuid Ó Murchadha, 'Is the O'Neill–McCarthy letter a forgery?', *IHS*, 23:89 (1982), 61–7]. **20** John O'Donovan (ed.), *The tribes and customs of Hy Many, commonly called O'Kelly's country* (IAS, Dublin, 1843), p. 136.

it draws a clear distinction between them and the Scottish foreigners, who are called *allmaraigh*.[21] Put in a cruder way, the Anglo-Irish may be foreign, but they were not so foreign as other foreigners.

Gaelic literary sources are consistent in this attitude. In the annals, the term *Gall* is regularly used. But it is contrasted with English of England. For example, when the annals of Inisfallen refer to the wife of Peter Bermingham in 1305, she is called *in Gaillseach Shachsanach*.[22] Similarly, when Richard II comes to Ireland in 1394, other annals call him *righ Sagsan* and describe his army containing English and Welsh (Ir. *etir thSagsanaib ⁊ Bretnachaib*).[23] *Gall*, or Anglo-Irish, are clearly distinct from Saxon, or English. Nowhere is this contrast more evident than in the early fifteenth-century version of the *Expugnatio Hibernica* of Gerald of Wales. It is remarkable enough that Gerald should have been made available in Irish, presumably to satisfy the historical curiosity of an Irish patron, or even an Anglo-Irish lord who was more at home in the Irish language than in English. For our purposes, however, the most interesting feature of this text is the use of these same terms, *Gall* and *Sasan*.[24] The distinction cannot be clear-cut, since the author is dealing with the period of the first invasion; but one can see that he tries to be consistent in using *Sasanaigh* ('English') where he is writing about the people actually participating in the invasion or their contemporaries in England, and *Gall* ('foreigner') for those who have settled here. Naturally, he is frustrated in the effort, but he does try. More than a century later, when Richard Stanyhurst wrote his description of Ireland, he revealed that Gaelic Ireland still made this same distinction between the Anglo-Irish and the English:

> For the Irishe man standeth so much upon his gentilitie, that he termeth any one of the English sept, and planted in Ireland, Bobdeagh Galteagh, that is, English churle; but if he be an Englishman borne, then he nameth hym Bobdeagh Saxonnegh, that is, a Saxon churle.[25]

From the Gaelic perspective, then, the Anglo-Irish were a middle nation, not wholly English and certainly not really Gaelic. So when the third earl of Desmond died, a famous poet in Irish and still known in Gaelic tradition as Gearóid Iarla, he was praised by the annalists for his skill in composition, his scholarship, his generosity, his love of Irish learning and its professors – but it was as one of the noble Galls, who in all ways was the best of 'all the Gall of Ireland'.[26]

21 Ibid., pp 139, 140, 142. Once only (at p. 135) is this term applied to the Anglo-Irish. 22 *AI*, p. 394. 23 *AMisc*, p. 153. 24 Whitley Stokes, 'The Irish abridgment of the "Expugnatio Hibernica"', *EHR*, 20:77 (1905), 77–115. That the *Expugnatio* was circulating among Gaelic *literati* seems clear; it was used, for example, by the compiler of Mac Carthaigh's book (*AMisc*, p. x). 25 Liam Miller and Eileen Power (eds), *Holinshed's Irish chronicle* (Dublin, 1979), p. 112. 26 *AFM*, iv, 760–1; *AClon*, pp 319–20.

From the English perspective, the view of the Anglo-Irish seems consistently uncomplicated and unaltering, at least as revealed by official records. They were English, liegemen of the king, bound by his statutes and the same common law as his subjects in England. Yet a closer examination soon reveals ambiguities and suggests that, across the Irish Sea, not all Englishmen, even in the royal administration, were clear in their minds about the Anglo-Irish. The wardrobe clerk who in 1303 referred to the earl of Ulster and other Anglo-Irish who came to fight with King Edward in Scotland as *Hibernici*, must have classed as Irishmen all who lived in Ireland.[27] This was a common enough attitude. It can be seen most clearly at Oxford, where the Anglo-Irish were classed as *Hibernienses* ('Irish') among the nations which made up the university. They were involved in riots and faction fights as a national group, especially with the northerners. In 1252, an attempt was made to impose peace between the two groups by imposing oaths that they would not in future disturb the peace and that, if the chancellor were to be suspected of bias in settling future disputes, he would have two northerners and two Irish as assessors to help him. The agreement which was drawn up was sealed by twenty-eight *Hibernienses* and of them at least twenty-five, and possibly twenty-six, were Anglo-Irish.[28] Some Irish were also involved in the most famous riot of the thirteenth century, which occurred in 1238 when the papal legate was attacked and almost killed. The riot only became serious after an irate Italian cook threw a cauldron of boiling broth on a poor Irish chaplain who had been begging for food at the kitchen door of Oseney abbey, where the legate was staying. Among the leaders of the students who laid siege to the abbey was a teacher of law named Odo of Kilkenny, an Anglo-Irish name if ever there was one.[29]

English chroniclers virtually ignore Ireland and Irish affairs during the Middle Ages. But when they do mention the Anglo-Irish, they can reveal the same tendency to classify them as Irish. Adam of Usk, for example, calls all men born in Ireland *Ibernienses*, when he is recounting how they were ordered to return to Ireland in 1413.[30] Adam, in fact, is using the same term as the English statute of 1422 used when it ordered 'all people born in Ireland' to leave England within a month.[31] In this case, it is evident from the licences of

27 E 101/10/30. They are called *Hibernienses* in E 101/11/20. In 1311, Richard Wodehouse was paid for leading to Scotland *Hibernicos*, who were in fact Anglo-Irish (E 159/84, m. 103 [KR, memo. roll, 5 Edw. II]). In 1341, the English chancery similarly used 'Irish' when referring to royal ministers in Ireland: 'it would be better to be served in that land by English ministers [L. *per minstros Anglicos*] ... than by Irish ministers [L. *per Hibernicos ministros*]' (*Foedera*, ii, pt 2, p. 1171). 28 Aubrey Gwynn, *Anglo-Irish church life, 14th and 15th centuries* (Dublin, 1968), pp 15–16. There was another fight between the northerners and the Irish in 1273 in which some of the latter were killed (H.C. Maxwell-Lyte, *A history of the university of Oxford to 1530* (London, 1886), p. 130). 29 Maxwell-Lyte, *History of the university of Oxford*, p. 34. 30 *Chronicon Adae de Usk, 1377–1404*, ed. E.M. Thompson (2nd ed., Oxford, 1904), pp 131, 120. 31 James Hardiman (ed.), *A statute of the fortieth year of King Edward*

exemption issued that it was Anglo-Irish who were concerned in the statute. That chroniclers could sometimes appreciate that the people whom they called Irish might be different from the Gaelic Irish can readily be seen in the way in which Walsingham described the 1394 order that absentees should return home to Ireland. He first of all says simply that the *Hibernici* were ordered to go back to Ireland and glosses this by adding that many of them had come to England 'because the mere Irish, rivals of the Anglo-Irish' (L. *Anglicorum Hibernicorum aemuli*) had wasted their lands.[32] When Richard II came on his first expedition to Ireland, one chronicler wrote that he came to aid the *Hibernici veri Anglici* (or 'the true Irish English') against the *puros Hibernicos* ('pure Irish').[33]

That such an awareness of the distinction between the Anglo-Irish and Gaelic Irish could co-exist with designating them together as Irish shows that the position of the Anglo-Irish in England could often be ambiguous in the Middle Ages. At a time when contempt for foreigners was rife,[34] it was understandable that Anglo-Irish visitors, with their peculiarly archaic English which made them unintelligible, should be regarded as Irish and treated as such. Technically, they were not foreigners and legally could not so be treated. In 1443, for example, men and women born in Ireland, Wales and the Channel Islands were specifically exempted from a subsidy levied on alien householders in England.[35] But it might be expedient to buy a charter of denizenship, as if one were a foreigner, as John Alysaunder, 'born in Ireland', did in November 1441.[36] In 1441, the Irish council had to ask that Englishmen born in Ireland might have the same rights in England as Englishmen born in England.[37]

With such confusion, it is small wonder that an Irish petitioner in 1416 had to point out that there were two nations in Ireland: that of the petitioner, 'English and of the English nation'; and 'the Irish nation, enemies of our lord the king'.[38] But the confusion persisted, with both nations being classed as Irish and with the Anglo-Irish suffering as a result. When a petitioner, in 1422, pointed out that some students were 'lieges of our lord the king born in Ireland', and distinguished between them and others who were not lieges of the king, 'but enemies of our said lord the king and of his realm, by name Wylde

*III., enacted in a parliament held in Kilkenny, A.D. 1367, before Lionel, duke of Clarence, lord lieutenant of Ireland* (IAS, Dublin, 1843), p. 24n. 32 H.T. Riley (ed.), *Ypodigma Neustriae a Thoma Walsingham, quondam monacho monasterii S. Albani, conscriptum* (RS, London, 1876), p. 367. I owe this and the following reference to Dr Dorothy Johnston. 33 F.S. Hayden (ed.), *Eulogium historiarum sive temporis. Chronicon ab orbe condito usque ad annum domini 1366, a monacho quodam Malmesburiensi exaratum. Accedunt continuationes duae, quarum una ad annum 1413, altera ad annum 1490, perducta est*, 3 vols (RS, London, 1863), iii, 370. He added that parliament enacted that 'omnes nativi de Hibernia in Hiberniam remearent, dicens paucos Hibernicos esse ibidem, quare puri Hibernici praevalent ibidem'. 34 John Scattergood, *Politics and poetry in the fifteenth century* (London, 1971), p. 42 and ch. 3. 35 *CPR 1441–6*, p. 155. 36 Ibid., p. 36. 37 Otway-Ruthven, *Med. Ire.*, p. 370. 38 *Rot. parl.*, iv, 102.

Irishmen',[39] he was employing a fashionable designation (the term 'wild'), with the older classification of enemy, in order to distinguish sharply between the two nations. That he had to do so is a measure of the contemporary English attitude towards the Anglo-Irish, where they were definitely regarded as neither English nor Irish but something in between – a middle nation in fact.

In 1357, in a wide-ranging 'ordinance made for the estate of the land of Ireland', Edward III and his council referred to the problem of the 'divers dissensions' between 'those English born in Ireland and those born in England and dwelling in Ireland', so that 'many evils have heretofore happened'. But for us the really significant feature of this ordinance is that, in describing how these dissensions arose, it was said to be 'by reason of race', as if they were two different races indeed.[40] In June 1364, Edward III made precisely the same distinction when he wrote of the 'hurt and peril' which had happened in Ireland in times past because of the same divers dissensions 'between the English born in our kingdom of England and the English born in our land of Ireland' (L. *inter Anglicos, in regno nostro Angliae, et Anglicos, in terra nostra Hiberniae, oriundos*).[41] Then, in a famous statute, the Kilkenny parliament of 1366 tried to deal with the problem, enacting that 'no difference of allegiance shall henceforth be made between the English born in Ireland and the English born in England, by calling them *Englishobbe* or *Irishdogg*, but that all be called by one name, the English lieges of our lord the King'.[42] Surely, the important point here is not that the one people call one another clown or dog, but that they use the terms *English* or *Irish* as terms of abuse.

Whatever the political reality which lay behind this development of antagonism between the Anglo-Irish and the English in Ireland in the middle of Edward III's reign, we can hardly doubt that it manifests on the part of the Anglo-Irish an awareness of being different. Such an awareness did not develop overnight; it was the result of a long process which had been affecting the settlers since first they came to Ireland. There were obvious influences at work, such as intermarriage, which had a profound effect on the second generation of settlers. Such influences were to make the Anglo-Irish identify more with Ireland; they came to regard it as their *patria*, as Arnold Power so vividly showed during the great debate in the Dublin parliament of 1324 when he tried to turn his Anglo-Irish peers against his enemy, the English Bishop Ledrede of Ossory, by reminding them that 'the disgrace of this country touches every one of us'.[43]

It is easy to see that in the early phase of conquest and settlement there was an acute awareness of, and seemingly easy acceptance of, racial differences in Ireland. Early charters show this well. In 1203, for example, in a charter to the

39 Ibid., iv, 190. 40 *Stat. John–Hen. V*, p. 417. The original Latin phrase is, in fact, *racione nationis* (*Stat. of the realm*, i, 363). 41 *Foedera*, iii, pt 2, p. 738. 42 *Stat. John–Hen. V*, pp 436–7. 43 Thomas Wright (ed.), *A contemporary narrative of the proceedings against Alice*

abbot and monks of St Mary's, Drogheda, King John addressed himself to all his 'faithful subjects, French and English and Irish of Ireland', and this same formula was widely used in royal charters up to then.[44] Private charters, too, employed the same address: that of Strongbow granting Wicklow to Maurice fitz Gerald, *c.*1176, is 'hominibus Francis, Anglicis, Hiberniensibus'.[45]

It is notable that Ostmen are not mentioned in such charters, as if they were already being accepted as English – that is, that they were given the legal status of Englishmen. But their presence in the Scandinavian towns is reflected in other evidence. In Limerick in 1201, an inquest was held into the lands held by St Mary's, Limerick, and presumably because the lands (or some of them) had been acquired before the conquest, the jury consisted of twelve English, twelve Ostmen and twelve Irish.[46] But by 1240, when the bishop and Gerald Prendergast were in dispute about some of these lands, they agreed that a new inquisition should be held, but this by 'loyal English and Irish men' only.[47]

The disappearance of the Ostmen is significant. So too is the inclusion of Irish jurors, because by the middle of the thirteenth century attitudes were hardening. They could still be ambiguous, so that Irish might be employed as mercenaries and even enter indentured service, as Cornelius Obruyn did with the earl of March in the mid-fourteenth century.[48] Even the government, at the very time it was articulating the official attitude towards the Irish as enemies, could continue to employ them, as the Mac Murroughs of Leinster illustrate so well. It is hard to imagine them fulfilling a more important military role than did Donal Mac Murrough, 'captain of his nation', who came to Dublin in the summer of 1369 to inform William of Windsor and the council 'how and in what way war should be waged against the Otothills and other Irish enemies and rebels then in a state of war'.[49] At the other end of the social scale, *c.*1280, the tenants of the royal manor of Saggart, 'tam Anglici quam Hibernici', could petition in common for help from the king.[50] But even by that early date, it was

*Kyteler* (Camden Soc., 1st ser., 24, 1843), p. 17: 'nunc autem venit quidam alienigena de Anglia ... et quia infamia istius terrae personas omnium nostrum tangit, decet ut vos omnes partem faciatis contra ipsum'. It is significant that he refers to Ledrede, an Englishman, as a foreigner. The same 'patriotism' can be seen in 1447, when the Irish parliament enacted that because 'this land is entirely slandered and still is in such slanderous matters as were never known in this land before, as in ruining or destroying any man by sorcery or necromancy', the king should be informed 'of the truth in this matter, in avoidance of the slander of this land in common, asserting that no such art was attempted at any time in this land' (*Stat. Hen. VI*, p. 101). 44 Fr Colmcille, 'Seven documents from the old abbey of Mellifont', *JLAHS*, 13 (1953), 36. A similar address, in a charter of 1185–6, is at ibid., p. 41. See also *Chart. privil. immun.*, p. 1. 45 *Reg. Gormanston*, p. 193. For another example, in a charter of Walter de Lacy, see *Reg. St Thomas*, p. 11. 46 *Black bk Limerick*, pp 25–9. 47 Ibid., pp 111–2. 48 NAI, RC 8/30, p. 25 (Ir. memo. roll, 42–3 Edw. III). He was in fact employed by the earl on the manor of Trim 'pro custodia tenentium Hibernicorum nostrorum ibidem' (NAI, RC 8/30, pp 50–3 [Ir. memo. roll, 35–6 Edw. III]). 49 TNA (PRO), E 101/245/3, no. 151. 50 *Affairs Ire.*, no. 41.

becoming more normal for the Irish to be regarded as enemies, in fact or potentially, as another petition of about the same date shows. The mayor and city of Cork asked that 'a certain Irishman', Stephen Brendan, should be removed from the office of customer, to which he had been appointed by the Lombard merchants, 'because the Irish race [L. *Hibernica lingua*] is an enemy to you and yours'. As for his replacement, the mayor said that they did not care of what race or status he be, Lombard or English, 'so long as it is not an Irishman who is assigned to the said office'.[51] The holding of inquisitions was also a matter for reliable Englishmen. No longer are Irishmen formally addressed in charters as had been the case in earlier days. This is because the Irish living in the land of peace were in a depressed state. They were for the most part outside the common law, many being reduced to unfree status, and most firmly under the control of the settlers.

At the same time, there is evidence that the settlers had begun to adopt Gaelic characteristics which were to help to mark them off from pure English (L. *meri Anglici*) in the future. In the early days of the conquest, latimers – or professional interpreters – had to be widely employed. Familiarity with the Irish language soon made them redundant and they gradually disappeared.[52] But before that happened ignorance of Irish created many problems for the settlers, not least the church. In 1217, for example, Pope Honorius III accepted the fact that a shortage of Irish-speaking priests in the archdiocese of Armagh could lead to a possible miscarriage of justice in a case which was appealed to him.[53] And in 1224, Michael Scot, who had been provided to the metropolitan see of Cashel, resigned because he said that he 'was ignorant of the language of the land'.[54] To some extent, this always remained a problem. As late as 1485, a parliament in Dublin had to license the archbishop, Walter fitz Symond, to collate Irish clerks to benefices in this diocese, 'situated among Irish enemies', because, it was said, 'divers English clerks, who are enabled to have cure of souls, are inexpert in the Irish language'.[55]

During the thirteenth century, however, the settlers were becoming bilingual and, in those areas where the settlement had been most effective, they seem to

51 Ibid., no. 35; previously pr. Gearóid Mac Niocaill, *Na buirgéisí, XII–XV aois*, 2 vols (IMC, Dublin, 1964), ii, 351, n. 77. 52 Constance Bullock-Davies, *Professional interpreters and the matter of Britain* (University of Wales, 1966). 53 M.P. Sheehy (ed.), *Pontificia Hibernica: medieval papal chancery documents concerning Ireland, 640–1261*, 2 vols (Dublin, 1962–5), i, no. 109. 54 Ibid., i, nos. 167–8. 55 NAI, 7/1 [Ir. stat. roll, 2 Ric. III], quoted in Hardiman (ed.), *A statute of the fortieth year of King Edward III*, p. 47n. In 1418, it was claimed as an achievement that Robert de Mulfield, the English-born bishop of Killaloe, had learnt Irish and 'understands sufficiently and can speak the language of those parts as well as English' (*CPL 1417–31*, p. 8). Ignorance of Irish could equally pose a serious problem in the royal administration, not least in transcribing names for record purposes: in the mid-fourteenth century, an exchequer clerk could not enrol 'nomina diversorum personarum ibidem in obsequio nostro laborantium … eo quod eadem nomina in lingua nostra non possunt bene

have adopted a more relaxed attitude towards the Irish among them. In Leinster, for example, by the first quarter of the thirteenth century, the great houses must already have become sufficiently tolerant of the Irish population to be able to take pleasure in the mini-epic which we know as the *Song of Dermot and the earl*, the great hero of which was Dermot Mac Murrough, former king of Leinster. It is almost as if they had adopted him as part of their own heroic tradition. That they were able to enjoy Gaelic literature is well known. It seems that, by the end of the thirteenth century, its influence was already superseding French. The collection of poems which now resides in the British Library as Harley 913, produced in a Franciscan house in Ireland, is important as showing what a well-educated Anglo-Irishman might be reading in a religious community.[56] The contents include pieces in Latin as well as English, many of them well known internationally, such as the blasphemous parody *Missa de potatoribus* ('Mass of the drunkards') or the English *Abbot of Gloucester's feast*. Even some of these, however, show their Irish provenance. Others, such as the satire on the people of Kildare, were composed in Ireland. But more interesting for us is the well-known *Land of Cokayne*, which shows a familiarity with the Gaelic satirical tradition which reached great heights in the celebrated twelfth-century *Vision of Mac Conglinne*.[57] That *Cokayne* is satirizing Gaelic Cistercian life and is particularly savage about some of the more wonderful aspects of Gaelic hagiography (such as the ability of monks to levitate at will) is beside the point here. It could only have been written in Ireland by someone at home in the Gaelic literary tradition and yet familiar with the current literary fashions in England and France. It represents, then, the kind of blending of traditions that was to make the Anglo-Irish neither wholly English, nor yet Irish, but something in between.

Here we come to the matter of assimilation, or gaelicization, to use a term which seems acceptable nowadays. This is a fact of prime importance in any attempt to assess the sense of identity which marked the Anglo-Irish in the Middle Ages. It is, therefore, something which cannot be ignored. But it is a huge subject, still largely unexplored in detail.[58] In general, however, it is true that all of the settlers, in greater or lesser degree, were partially assimilated to Irish culture. Even if they never became 'more Irish than the Irish themselves' (a phrase whose origin is lost in the romantic nationalism of an earlier age), they

scribi' (NAI, RC 8/30, p. 242 [Ir. memo. roll, 47–8 Edw. III]). **56** W. Heuser, *Die Kildare-Gedichte: die ältesten mittelenglischen Denkmäler in Anglo-Irischer Überlieferung* (Bonn, 1904). For a general description, see St John D. Seymour, *Anglo-Irish literature, 1200–1582* (New York, 1970), chs 5–7. **57** P.L. Henry, 'The land of Cokaygne: cultures in contact in medieval Ireland', *Studia Hibernica*, 12 (1972), 120–41. **58** I have discussed this briefly in Lydon, *Lordship*, pp 179–88, 282–5, and Lydon, 'Problem of the frontier' (above, ch. 20). See now, Art Cosgrove, 'Hiberniores ipsis Hibernis' in Cosgrove and Donal McCartney (eds), *Studies in Irish history presented to R. Dudley Edwards* (Dublin, 1979), pp 1–14.

absorbed enough to make them so much at home in the language and literature of Ireland that they were hardly to be distinguished, in that respect at least, from their Gaelic contemporaries.

The degree to which the leading Anglo-Irish nobility had been assimilated can be quickly appreciated by taking one example, which concerns the most important families in late medieval Ireland: the Butlers and the Geraldines. When the 'white' earl of Ormond – who had ruled his great lordship through a mixture of English and Irish customs for the best part of half a century – died in 1452, his sons were in England and so the Butlers of Polestown took their place, one of whom eventually succeeded to the earldom. The head of this Polestown branch was Edmund Butler, better known, significantly, as Edmund mac Richard Butler. The year after the death of the earl (that is, 1453), this Edmund commissioned the writing of the book now classed as Laud Miscellanea 610 in the Bodleian in Oxford.[59] It is a collection of Irish literary and historical matter of the kind which any educated Gaelic Irishman with literary tastes might find interesting. So anxious was Edmund to have his book and enjoy it that he kept the scribes close by him until they had finished the copying; and so impatient was he that he insisted on work being done on Sundays, or even during the Christmas season:

> May God forgive him who makes us write on a Sunday night, namely Emunn Buitller.
> May God forgive Emunn for colouring this book on a Sunday night.
> Today is the Friday before Christmas, and there is heavy rain now as night falls.[60]

There is no doubting how eager Edmund was to have his book, and we may take it as a sign of how much he prized Irish *senchas*. He had been fostered by Richard O'Hedigan, archbishop of Cashel, on whose soul a blessing is invoked in another marginal entry.[61] The scribes complained about being pushed so hard, writing their grievances on the margins of the parchment in exactly the same sort of way as Irish scribes working in continental scriptoria hundreds of years earlier. But these marginalia reveal an easy intimacy with their patron, with a concern for his person ('I do not like Emund to be sleeping in front of the window on the windy side' is typical of many),[62] and an impatience at his absences:

> Good luck to the owner of this book, Emann Butler, for he has gone away from me today, and he thinks it a high price to pay for protecting his

**59** Myles Dillon, 'Laud Misc. 610', *Celtica*, 5 (1960), 64–76; 6 (1963), 135–55. **60** Dillon, 'Laud Misc. 610', *Celtica*, 6 (1963), 143, 151, 153. **61** Ibid., p. 151. **62** Ibid., p. 147.

> country that his scribe should be without him. And may God grant him to come home tonight.[63]

The cynic would say that the scribes expected their patron to read such marginalia when the book was finished; but this merely shows how deep the relationship was between them and him.

When Edmund Butler was put to the test in 1462, he showed that, for all his interest in things Gaelic, he was still loyal to the man he believed to be his true lord, the Lancastrian king, Henry VI. He joined with his English cousins when they led a desperate invasion of Ireland and suffered defeat and subsequent attainder with them after the battle of Pilltown near Carrick.[64] The victor of that occasion was the earl of Desmond. When Edmund Butler came to make terms for his release with Desmond, part of the ransom was this very book and another known as the 'Book of Carrick'. Another marginal entry explains that

> this Psalter was the Psalter of Mac Richard Butler, i.e. Emainn Buitiler until the rout of Baile in Phuill was inflicted on the Earl of Ormond and Mac Richard by Thomas, earl of Desmond, and this book and the Book of Carrick were taken in ransom for Mac Richard.[65]

They remained in Geraldine hands for over a hundred years. The earls of Desmond, too, valued the so-called Psalter highly and had faded passages – themselves evidence of much use – lovingly restored.[66] Like the Butlers, they were deeply interested in Gaelic literature. A famous ancestor had been that Gearóid Iarla we have already mentioned. When the seventh earl, Thomas, the victor of Pilltown, died in 1468 – he was, in fact, executed by the new chief governor, the earl of Worcester – he was praised by the annals almost as if he were a Gaelic lord: 'bountiful in bestowing good gifts on both laity and clergy and on all the learned, both antiquaries, poets and *aesdanas* of all Ireland.'[67]

At the highest level, then, the Anglo-Irish nobility had been at least partly assimilated and identified themselves with the culture of their Gaelic predecessors. They displayed an easy familiarity with, and obvious regard for, the literature and history of Ireland. But that is not to say that they ever denied their Englishness fully, or ever identified themselves with those Irish whom they consistently, to the end of the medieval lordship, regarded as enemies. Even before the end of the thirteenth century, the need to proclaim one's Englishness, almost like a badge, was recognized. Every student of medieval Irish history is familiar with the legislation of the 1297 parliament, because it reveals so vividly what were the most pressing problems besetting the lordship. One important

63 Ibid., p. 145. 64 Otway-Ruthven, *Med. Ire.*, p. 385; Curtis, *Med. Ire.*, p. 326; Gilbert, *Viceroys*, pp 377–8. 65 Dillon, 'Laud Misc. 610', *Celtica*, 6 (1963), p. 151. 66 Ibid., pp 137, 139. 67 Curtis, *Med. Ire.*, p. 333, quoting *AMacFirbis*.

feature of this parliament is that it was widely representative of the settled area – so much so, in fact, that an earlier generation of historians was able to call it Ireland's 'model parliament' and to compare it proudly with the English parliament of 1295. One famous statute is that which condemned the Anglo-Irish who 'attire themselves in Irish garments and having their heads half-shaved, grow and extend the hairs from the back of the head and call them *Culan*, conforming themselves to the Irish as well in garb as in countenance'.[68] What is most interesting about this statute is the term chosen by the parliament to describe such Anglo-Irish: *degeneres* – meaning that they had departed from their race.

Elsewhere in this same body of legislation, there is another revealing term used, this time about the Irish. In describing how they are 'stirred up to war', the parliament blamed settlers who were led 'some by covetousness, others from motives of revenge, envy, or of taking pledges', to attack Irish living in the king's peace. This is a rare occasion when Dublin was willing to admit that the Irish were not always at fault; but the real insight is provided by the explanation that such Irish, when unjustly attacked, 'rush instantly to war' because they are *leves* – that is, not capable of controlling themselves as reasonable beings, capricious, fickle, excitable.[69] The same attitude, if not the same term, was used in a letter of *c.*1331 from the Irish council to the pope, when the Irish were described as *gentes indomitas* ('ungovernable', 'wild').[70] The notion was an old one, as old as Gerald of Wales, who said that they were 'a race consistent only in their fickleness', 'unreliable', 'of unstable temperament', as well as being 'wild' and, of course, 'barbarous'.[71] Stephen of Lexington, a more sober observer, wrote in 1228 that the Irish were uncivilized, unable to act reasonably, backward, *gentes bestiales* ('a bestial people'), meaning that emotion rather than reason ruled them – *leves*, in another word.[72] Interestingly enough, the very term *bestialis* was used by Edward II nearly a hundred years later when he was answering the Irish remonstrance of 1317: he told the pope that much of the diocese of Cashel was situated among the Irish who were *homines bestiales et indoctos* ('bestial and uneducated').[73] This kind of attitude was typical of the superiority felt by conquering races everywhere and is not really surprising. It is well matched by the Irish attitude in the remonstrance, which had the nerve to say that 'the holy and dove-like simplicity' of the Irish people had been 'surprisingly altered into a serpentine craftiness through daily life with them [Anglo-Irish] and through

68 *Stat. John–Hen. V*, p. 211. 69 Ibid., p. 206. For a similar description of the Welsh, see *CCR 1330–3*, p. 150, and *CCR 1337–9*, p. 542 (for which references I am indebted to Prof. R.R. Davies). 70 Watt, 'Negotiations between Edward II and John XXII concerning Ireland', p. 19. 71 Giraldus, *Expug. Hib.*, pp 135, 249; Giraldus, *Topog. Hib.*, pp 84, 85. 72 B.W. O'Dwyer, 'The impact of the native Irish on the Cistercians in the thirteenth century', *Journal of Religious History*, 3 (1965), 295. 73 *Foedera*, ii, pt 1, p. 294.

their bad example'.[74] Indeed, so superior did the Gaelic Irish feel that it was not until the seventeenth century that they thought it necessary to defend themselves or their culture: that they were superior was self-evident.[75]

This notion that the Irish were wild (or *sauvage*, the term used by Richard II)[76] was given wide currency in the later Middle Ages. It was used in the *Libelle of Englyshe polycye*, for example.[77] Official records use it so frequently that it came to be almost a normal adjective associated with Irish. A wild Irishman was, almost by definition, dangerous and an enemy. When Nicholas Hogonona was imprisoned in the autumn of 1401, it was because an Austin friar to whom he had lent money 'went to certain people of London and made an untrue suggestion, submitting that he was *un wilde Irisshman* and an enemy of our lord the king'.[78] When a 1422 petition was presented in parliament against students from Ireland coming to Oxford, it distinguished between those who were lieges and others who were not lieges, 'but enemies to our lord the king and to his realm, by name wild Irishmen'.[79] This reflects official attitudes both in Dublin and London, where record sources show clearly that *inimicus* ('enemy') became the normal term to apply to those Irish who were outside the king's allegiance, even though they were not in open war. The very fact that the term 'land of war' (L. *terra guerre*) was synonymous with what was later called the Irishry, while 'land of peace' (L. *terra pacis*) was reserved for the Englishry, is indicative of official attitudes in the thirteenth century. In the early fourteenth century, the term 'felon' was still commonly applied to the Irish in the land of war, sometimes in association with 'enemy'.[80] But when 'the religious of Ireland' petitioned Edward III early in his reign that 'the Irish born and dwelling in the land of the king's peace' might be admitted to religious houses among the English, they excluded any 'Irish born in a land of war, an enemy of our lord the king'.[81] By the fifteenth century, the two terms – Irish and enemy – were constantly linked, almost as if they were interchangeable. So the concept of 'natural enemy' had developed and, in 1537, an official record could refer to 'Iryshe men, our naturall enymyes'.[82]

This association of *Hibernicus* with *inimicus* was not confined to official sources. Even churchmen could make it, almost instinctively. The Dublin provincial council of 1366 enacted:

74 *IHD*, pp 40–1. 75 F.J. Byrne, '*Senchas*: the nature of Gaelic historical tradition' in J.G. Barry (ed.), *Historical Studies IX* (Belfast, 1974), p. 154. 76 Curtis, 'Letters from Ric. II', p. 287. 77 *Libelle Eng. polycye*, lines 687, 691, 721, 725. 78 I.S. Leadam and J.F. Baldwin (eds), *Select cases before the king's council, 1243–1482* (Selden Soc. 35, 1918), pp 85–6. 79 *Rot. parl.*, iv, 190. 80 See the terminology used in J.F. Lydon (ed.), 'The enrolled account of Alexander Bicknor, 1307–14', *AH*, 30 (1982), 29–33. 81 James F. Ferguson, 'The "mere English" and the "mere Irish"', *Transactions of the Kilkenny Archaeological Society* [*JRSAI*], 1 (1849–51), 511. 82 *SP Hen. VIII*, ii, pt 3, p. 481.

> We command and decree that for the future ordinands of pure Irish nationality of our diocese and province shall be presumed to have lived continuously among evil people and to have come from an evil background until witnesses or letters are brought to prove the contrary.[83]

In 1389, a bishop of Killaloe could be referred to as *merus Hibernicus et de natione inimica* ('pure Irish and of an enemy nation').[84] On a more private level, the same attitude prevailed. As natural enemies, the Irish were to be hunted out and destroyed, which may help to explain some of the more horrific murders committed in the name of preserving the peace. When the annals of Inisfallen made Peter Bermingham say, after the multiple murder of the O'Connors in 1305, 'that he was not aware that there was a Gall in Ireland who had not undertaken to slay his Gaelic neighbour, and he knew that they would slay, as he had slain',[85] it was no more than reflecting contemporary opinion. From the Anglo-Irish side, this finds expression in the poem eulogizing Bermingham after his death: he was most deserving of praise because 'to Irishmen he was foe', hunting them 'as hunter doth the hare'.

> For when they thought best
> In the wilderness to have rest,
> That no man should them see,
> Then would he drive a quest
> Anon to their nest
> In the place where they would be.
>
> From sleep he would them wake,
> For terror they would quake
> And try to skulk away.[86]

Not the most elegant of poetry, but the whole poem shows the savage attitude which could prevail among the Anglo-Irish.

A century later, that attitude had not changed. The Dublin notary, James Yonge, was asked by the earl of Ormond, *c.*1420, to translate for him 'some good boke of governaunce of Prynces out of latyn othyr Frenche in-to your

83 J.A. Watt, *The church and the two nations in medieval Ireland* (Cambridge, 1970), p. 206. 84 *Foedera*, vii, 643 (a reference I owe to Dr Dorothy Johnston). 85 *AI*, pp 395–7. A passage in the remonstrance of 1317, which has more than a ring of truth about it, echoes the same attitude: 'there cannot now be or henceforward be established, sincere good will between them and us in this life. For we have a natural hostility to each other arising from the mutual, malignant and incessant slaying of fathers, brothers, nephews and other near relatives and friends so that we can have no inclination to reciprocate friendship in our time or that of our sons' (*IHD*, p. 44). 86 This is the translation in Seymour, *Anglo-Irish literature*, p. 84. The original is in Heuser, *Kildare-Gedichte*, p. 162.

modyr Englyshe tonge'.[87] Why Ormond should require such a book raises an interesting question: about thirty years previously, a treasurer of Ireland had produced a shorter Latin version of part of the *Secreta secretorum* – a pseudo-Aristotelian work of great importance and the very work which Yonge chose to translate under the title of *The governaunce of prynces.*[88] A century earlier, the Irish Dominican, Geoffrey of Waterford, had produced the famous French version of the same tract. That there was an Irish tradition of interest in this work is undoubted, suggesting perhaps a more sophisticated attitude towards politics among the Anglo-Irish than we have hitherto suspected. But, for our purposes here, the real interest of Yonge's version is his advice to Ormond on how to treat Irish enemies: 'Whan they fallyth into youre handis, Raase ham all out of rote, as the good gardyner dothe the nettylle.'[89] In the section on justice, he castigates 'dyvers Englyshe captaynys' for their 'neclygence in non-Punyshinge of hare nacionys' (that is, the Irish); and, in the section which advises that 'a prynce should not truste to his enemy', he warns Ormond that his Irish enemies and their ancestors were not 'trewe to you or to youre fadyer', except when 'ye were strongyr than thay'.[90]

With such an attitude towards the Irish, it is hardly surprising that the Anglo-Irish should try to assert and preserve their Englishness. At Limerick in 1295, a Richard de Wodeford was imprisoned because he defamed William the merchant by calling him an Irishman.[91] A Waterford bye-law of 1382 also enacted that to call an Englishman an Irishman was defamation.[92] In 1441, no less a person than the dean of Holy Trinity in Waterford, John Collyn, had to prove in a Kilkenny court that he was 'a true Englishman and of the English nation, namely of the Colleyns and in no way of the Conllaynes' (L. *verus Anglicus et Anglice nacionis videlicet de 'les Collynes' et nullo modo de 'les Conlleynes'*). Perhaps the most extreme example is the case of William Power who, in 1371, was sent to gaol in Waterford, 'because he could not speak English'. He made a fine of forty silver pence with the king to be released and his pledges had to undertake that he would apply himself diligently to learning English.[93]

87 Steele, *Secreta*, p. 122. 88 Jean-Philippe Genêt (ed.), *Four English political tracts of the later Middle Ages* (Camden Soc., 4th ser., 18, 1977), pp 22–39. Yonge used this same tract (*De quadripartita regis specie*), which shows a continuing Dublin interest in such texts (M.A. Manzaloui, 'The *Secreta secretorum* in English thought and literature' (DPhil, University of Oxford, 1954), p. 365). For Yonge, see esp. Alan Bliss, 'Language and literature' in Lydon, *Eng. in med. Ire.*, ch. 7, and Seymour, *Anglo-Irish literature*. 89 Steele, *Secreta*, p. 164. 90 Ibid., pp 160, 166. 91 *CJRI 1295–1303*, p. 18. For another case, see *CJRI 1307–14*, pp 102–3. For a similar law in Wales, see Davies, 'Race relations', p. 46. 92 John T. Gilbert (ed.), 'Archives of the municipal corporation of Waterford' in *10th rep. HMC*, app. 5, p. 292: 'if ony man duellyng within the lyberte of the same citie shal curse, diffame, or despice ony citsayn of the saide citie in calling him Yrishmann [...]'. 93 Cambridge University Library, Add. MS 3104, fo. 29 (I am indebted to Dr Philomena Connolly for a transcript).

To thus emphasize their Englishness did not mean that the Anglo-Irish identified less with Ireland. When James Yonge was writing for the earl of Ormond, he was constantly reminding him of Irish history, making good use, of course, of Gerald of Wales. This pride in their own history among the Anglo-Irish is something which goes back to the thirteenth century. In collecting their records and especially in copying, abbreviating and translating the work of Gerald of Wales, the Anglo-Irish were showing a self-awareness by the end of the thirteenth century.[94] There is a clear line in their historiography through the versions of Giraldus, Yonge, the historical matter in the book of Howth, to Stanihurst in the sixteenth century. It can leave us in no doubt that they had a pride in their own nation and an awareness that they were apart from both the English of England and the Gaelic Irish.

This, of course, had implications politically and, as we would say, constitutionally. Reading Yonge's *Governaunce*, one cannot fail to notice his resentment at the ineptitude of those whom he calls 'divers English captains of Ireland', identical to the resentment expressed by Gerald of Wales on behalf of his relatives and friends many generations earlier. Yonge even goes so far as to say that it was 'perelos to reherse' the matter further and says that he will leave off 'leste y sholde be shente [killed]'.[95] Similar resentment was expressed by the justiciar, Stephen Fulburn – himself a career civil servant and an Englishman to boot – in 1281, when he wrote to the king complaining of English sheriffs who returned to England and, out of malice, turned friends against him and vilified him.[96] Whatever the reason – personality clashes, material gain, hunger for power – there is no doubt that, regularly throughout the later Middle Ages, the Anglo-Irish resented and sometimes resisted interference in their affairs from England. They were not only prepared to defy the king's nominated chief governor – as they did with Lord Grey in 1478, when they refused to recognize his appointment under the privy seal, barred him from access to Dublin castle and the royal treasure, refused to hand over the Irish great seal, and finally summoned a parliament which continued to sit despite the fact that Grey summoned his own in the king's name – they even went so far on one occasion as to crown a king of England, when the great earl of Kildare crowned Lambert Simnel in Christ Church cathedral in May 1487.[97] They resented being bound by English statutes and, in a famous statute of their own in 1460, proclaimed Ireland to be

94 Robin Flower, 'Manuscripts of Irish interest in the British Museum', *AH*, 2 (1931), 310. 95 Steele, *Secreta*, pp 160–1. 96 SC 1/17/190. The calendared version (*CDI 1252–84*, no. 1881) completely distorts the meaning. I am grateful to Dr Philomena Connolly for checking the original letter for me in London. 97 *Ir. parl.*, pp 264–6; Otway-Ruthven, *Med. Ire.*, pp 398–9, 403; Gilbert, *Viceroys*, pp 404–6, 428–9; Bryan, *Great earl*, pp 33ff, 106–7.

> corporate of itself, by the ancient laws and customs used in the same, freed of the burden of any special law of the realm of England, save only such laws as by the lords spiritual and temporal and the commons of the said land had been in great council or parliament held, admitted, affirmed and proclaimed, according to sundry statutes thereof made.[98]

This may display a shaky knowledge of constitutional history and may even (though I do not believe this myself) be more the work of the duke of York than of the Anglo-Irish themselves. But who can doubt that it defines the independence of Ireland from English statutes and that it does so in sophisticated terms which echo a tradition of Anglo-Irish self-reliance and argue for a tradition of political thinking of long standing?

There is no time to develop this most important aspect of the middle nation further.[99] It is but one manifestation of the extent to which the Anglo-Irish identified with Ireland.[100] They showed this identification in many ways, not least in adopting local saints, spreading their cult, composing new offices for their feast, even translating relics to a newly built church. They did this not only with great saints of the past – such as Patrick, Bridget, Columba or Finian of Clonard (at whose tomb in Clonard miracles were conveniently being performed when Meath was being settled by Hugh de Lacy) – but they were also willing to cultivate a more recent saint like Laurence O'Toole of Dublin.[101] But, for all that, they remained true to what they saw as their English heritage, as can best be seen in the writings of Stanihurst at the end of the medieval period.[102] Even in their charity, they could remain true to form. When Dean

98 *Stat. Hen. VI*, p. 645. The Anglo-Irish, of course, wanted the best of both worlds. Not only did they regularly request help of one kind or another from the king, they were not slow to inform him (as they did in 1474) that he was bound to defend his land of Ireland because it 'ys oon of the membres of his moost noble corone' (Bryan, *Great earl*, p. 22). There was nothing inconsistent in repudiating an English parliament – which, by the fifteenth century, had an authority of its own – to which they were not summoned, while accepting the lordship of the king. **99** Frame, *Eng. lordship*, has re-assessed Anglo-Irish relations in the first half of the fourteenth century in a way which shows the Anglo-Irish community finding a political voice which not only expressed the mind of the resident nobility, but forced Edward III to listen. **100** Even though the official sources were still using the term 'English' for the Anglo-Irish at the end of the Middle Ages, they could qualify it by adding the adjective 'native'. A 1485 statute, for example, refers to the 'native English subjects of the king [F. *natiefs englois subgittez le Roy*] in this his land' (NAI, 7/1 [Ir. stat. roll, 2 Ric. III]). **101** Kathleen Hughes, 'The offices of S. Finnian of Clonard and S. Cianán of Duleek', *Analecta Bollandiana*, 73 (1955), 342–6; Aubrey Gwynn, 'Provincial and diocesan decrees of the diocese of Dublin during the Anglo-Norman period', *Archivium Hibernicum*, 11 (1944), 82–3; Katherine Walsh, *A fourteenth-century scholar and primate: Richard FitzRalph in Oxford, Avignon and Armagh* (Oxford, 1981), pp 190, 308; J.C. Crosthwaite (ed.), *The book of obits and martyrology of the cathedral church of Holy Trinity* (IAS, Dublin, 1844), pp xliii–li. **102** Colm Lennon, *Richard Stanihurst the Dubliner, 1547–1613* (Dublin, 1981).

John Aleyn of St Patrick's made his will in December 1505, making provision for the poor in a house to be maintained out of his estate, he wrote: 'The poor to be received and preferred in the said house are not any poor whatever, but faithful catholics of good repute, honest life and English nation.'[103] Archbishop fitz Ralph of Armagh had been shocked and dismayed at the hostilities he discovered when he returned to take over his diocese and, in a sermon which he preached before Pope Clement VI at Avignon in August 1349, he did not mince words: 'The two nations are always opposed to each other from a traditional hatred.'[104] It is surely significant that in 1488, when Sir Richard Edgecom was sent on a special mission to Ireland by Henry VII and tried to get the assembled Anglo-Irish nobility to accept certain conditions of pardon which they found impossible, they declared, we are told, with one voice that they would sooner turn Irish every one.[105] That was still the ultimate threat – to turn Irish!

We must therefore be careful not to take at their face value the more hysterical reports to come out of Ireland at the end of the Middle Ages, such as the one sent to Henry VIII in 1536:

> Your highness must understand that the English blood of the English conquest is in manner worn out of this land, and at all seasons in manner, without any restoration is diminished and enfeebled ... And, contrarywise, the Irish blood ever more and more, without such decay, increaseth.[106]

The Anglo-Irish community still preserved its distinction. It was John Dymmok, writing in 1600, who proposed a classification of the inhabitants of Ireland when he wrote in his *Treatise of Ireland*: 'The inhabitantes generally are of fowre sortes. English Irish, meer Irish, degenerate Englesh, and wilde Scotts.'[107] The English Irish (our Anglo-Irish) were still a distinct community, as were the pure Irish. Those who had assimilated to Gaelic Ireland were now clearly designated as degenerate, though it is significant that they were classed as English, as if there was still some hope that they might be recovered for civilization. Clearly, the notions of nation and race, which had been so dominant in the Middle Ages, were still vital and were to help to shape the new Ireland which was to emerge from the upheavals of conquest, plantation and religious revolution. The middle nation of medieval Ireland had preserved its separate identity into the new age.

**103** *Reg. Alen*, p. 259. The relevant section is printed in full in Latin in Crosthwaite, *Book of obits*, p. xxxiv. **104** Aubrey Gwynn, 'The black death in Ireland', *Studies*, 24 (1935), 31. **105** Walter Harris, *Hibernica, or some ancient pieces relating to Ireland* (Dublin, 1770), pt 1, p. 32 ('they wuld in no wise be bound in the said bond of *nisi*, and rather than they wuld do it, they wuld become Irish every of them'). Note, too, that the author calls Kildare and the others 'Irish lordes' (ibid., p. 30). **106** *SP Hen. VIII*, ii, pt 3, p. 338. **107** Richard Butler (ed.), *A treatice of Ireland by John Dymmok* (IAS, Dublin, 1842), p. 7.

FURTHER READING

# Government, war and society in English Ireland, 1171–1541: a guide to recent work

*Peter Crooks*

Late medieval Ireland is a small but dynamic research area. The following is a selective guide designed to direct the reader to some of the more significant developments of recent years in subjects addressed by the Lecky professors in this volume. Where the Irish material is particularly exiguous, I have made some suggestions from the secondary literature further afield, which I hope may help stimulate comparative ideas on the Irish evidence.[1]

## BIBLIOGRAPHIES AND GUIDES TO SOURCES

The essays printed in this volume represent merely a fraction of the published output of Curtis, Otway-Ruthven and Lydon. For comprehensive bibliographies of their work, see T.W. Moody, 'The writings of Edmund Curtis', *IHS*, 3:12 (1943); P.W.A. Asplin, 'The writings of Prof. A.J. Otway-Ruthven to 1980' in Lydon, *Eng. & Ire.*; P.W.A. Asplin, 'Bibliography of J.F. Lydon [to 1993]' in *Colony and frontier*. For general purposes, P.W.A. Asplin, *Medieval Ireland, c.1170–1485: a bibliography of secondary works* (1971), with its excellent index, is a useful starting-point despite being over three decades old. Indeed, its value today lies chiefly in the fact that it reflects the fashions of a former era. It must, however, be read alongside the magnificent bibliography Asplin prepared for *NHI*, vol. 2, the second impression of which includes a supplement listing secondary works mostly published between 1986 and 1993. Recent developments can be traced through the Royal Historical Society online bibliography.[2]

Approaching primary sources has become less daunting due to the publication of a number of valuable research guides. Philomena Connolly, *Medieval record sources*, Maynooth Research Guides for Irish Local History, no. 4 (2002), is indispensable. Its counterpart – *Medieval Gaelic sources* by Katharine Simms – is soon to be published in the same series. For invaluable guides to

1 Unless otherwise indicated, the place of publication is Dublin. 2 RHS bibliography: http://www.rhs.ac.uk/bibl/bibwel.asp.

manuscript material in Britain, see B.C. Donovan and D. Edwards, 'British sources for Irish history before 1485: a preliminary handlist of documents held in local and specialised repositories', *AH*, 37 (1998); and P. Dryburgh and B. Smith (eds), *Handbook and select calendar of sources for medieval Ireland in the National Archives of the United Kingdom* (TNA, 2005).

## PART 1: GOVERNMENT

### *Chapter 1: Ireland and the English crown, 1171–1541*

This essay would once have been described as an exercise in 'Anglo-Irish' history; today, it is more likely to be characterized as a contribution to the 'new' (now decidedly mature) British history, a sparkling historiographical introduction to which is S. Duffy, 'The British perspective' in S.H. Rigby (ed.), *A companion to Britain in the later Middle Ages* (Oxford, 2003). Among Irish medievalists, the 'British' approach is the distinctive calling card of Robin Frame, many of whose essays (collected in Frame, *Ire. & Brit.*) explore the interwoven histories of the two islands. Of these, 'England and Ireland, 1171–1399' in Frame, *Ire. & Brit.*, is closest in theme and scope to this chapter. For the end of the medieval period, the work of S.G. Ellis is fundamental: 'Crown, community and government in the English territories, 1450–1575', *History*, 71 (1986); idem, 'Tudor state formation and the shaping of the British Isles' in Ellis and S. Barber (eds), *Conquest and union: the fashioning of a British state, 1485–1725* (London, 1995); 'From dual monarchy to multiple kingdoms: unions and the English state, 1422–1607' in A. McInnes and J. Ohlmeyer (eds), *The Stuart kingdoms in the seventeenth century: awkward neighbours* (2002).

Revisionist interpretations of Ireland's relationship with the English crown have themselves been extensively revised in recent years. J. Gillingham, 'The English invasion of Ireland' in idem, *The English in the twelfth century: imperialism, national identity and political values* (Woodbridge, 2000), argues persuasively that 'English' is the adjective that distorts our understanding of the invasion least; how and why the invaders were repackaged as 'Norman' by historians is a subject Gillingham investigates in 'Normanizing the English invaders of Ireland' in H. Pryce and J. Watts (eds), *Power and identity in the Middle Ages: essays in memory of Rees Davies* (Oxford, 2007). W.L. Warren's sympathetic account of the English crown's dealings with Gaelic Ireland – first glimpsed in his readable biographies of *King John* (1961) and *Henry II* (1973), and later elaborated in an accumulation of essay-length studies[3] – is

3 W.L. Warren, 'The interpretation of twelfth-century Irish history' in J.C. Beckett (ed.), *Historical studies VII* (London, 1969); 'The historian as "private eye" ' in J.G. Barry (ed.), *Historical studies IX* (Belfast, 1974); 'John in Ireland, 1185' in J. Bossy and P. Jupp (eds), *Essays presented to Michael Roberts* (Belfast, 1976); 'King John and Ireland' in Lydon, *Eng. & Ire.*

systematically demolished by Seán Duffy in 'King John's expedition to Ireland, 1210: the evidence reconsidered', *IHS*, 30:117 (1996); 'John and Ireland: the origins of England's Irish problem' in S.D. Church (ed.), *King John: new interpretations* (Woodbridge, 1999); and 'Henry II and England's insular neighbours' in C. Harper-Bill and N. Vincent (eds), *Henry II: new interpretations* (Woodbridge, 2007). Warren also takes hard knocks for his centralist portrayal of the workings of English political society in R. Frame, 'Historians, aristocrats and Plantagenet Ireland, 1200–1360' in C. Given-Wilson, A. Kettle and L. Scales (eds), *War, government and aristocracy in the British Isles, c.1150–1500* (Woodbridge, 2008).

A clutch of recent works re-examine relations between the king and his English lieges in Ireland. The period *c.*1171–1315 is now relatively well served: C. Veach, 'Henry II's grant of Meath to Hugh de Lacy in 1172: a reassessment', *Ríocht na Midhe*, 18 (2007); R. Frame, 'Henry III and Ireland: the shaping of a peripheral lordship' and 'Ireland and the barons' wars', both in idem, *Ire. & Brit.*; B. Smith, 'Irish politics, 1220–1245', *Thirteenth Century England*, 8 (2001); P. Crooks, ' "Divide and rule": factionalism as royal policy in the lordship of Ireland, *c.*1171–1265', *Peritia*, 19 (2005); B. Hartland, 'The household knights of Edward I in Ireland', *HR*, 77 (2004); B. Hartland, 'English landholding in Ireland', *Thirteenth Century England*, 10 (2005); B. Hartland, 'English lords in late thirteenth and early fourteenth century Ireland: Roger Bigod and the de Clare lords of Thomond', *EHR*, 122:496 (2007). The later fourteenth and fifteenth centuries await sustained scrutiny: for an overview, see P. Crooks, 'Factions, feuds and noble power in the lordship of Ireland, *c.*1356–1496', *IHS*, 35:140 (2007).

### *Chapter 2: The chief governors of medieval Ireland*

The chief governorship of Ireland continues to generate scholarly interest, though sadly much of the best work remains unpublished. For specific chief governorships (listed here by the date of tenure), see P. Dryburgh, 'The career of Roger Mortimer, first earl of March (*c.*1287–1330)' (PhD, University of Bristol, 2002); R. Frame, 'The justiciarship of Ralph Ufford: warfare and politics in fourteenth-century Ireland', *Studia Hibernica*, 13 (1972); R. Frame, 'Thomas Rokeby, sheriff of Yorkshire and justiciar of Ireland', *Peritia*, 10 (1996); P. Connolly, 'Lionel of Clarence and Ireland, 1361–1366' (PhD, University of Dublin, 1977); S. Harbison, 'William of Windsor and Ireland, 1369–76' (MLitt, University of Dublin, 1977); B. Blacker, 'Thomas of Lancaster, duke of Clarence, 1388–1421: the consolidation of the Lancastrian dynasty' (PhD, University of Dublin, 1996). For an intensive examination of the office in first half of the fifteenth century, see E.A.E. Matthew, 'The governing of the Lancastrian lordship of Ireland in the time of James Butler, fourth earl of Ormond, *c.*1420–52' (PhD, University of Durham, 1994), ch. 1, 'The crown and the chief governorship'. For a slightly earlier period, the work of Dorothy Johnston is useful, esp. 'Chief governors and treasurers in the reign of Richard II' in *Colony and frontier*, which includes an edition of Edmund Mortimer's indenture of 1379 (KR, memo. roll, E 159/194, Trinity *communia*). A glimpse of the horse-trading that underlay appointments to office is provided in D. Johnston, 'The draft indenture of Thomas, duke of Gloucester, as lieutenant of Ireland, 1391', *Journal of the Society of Archivists*, 7:3 (1983). It is no coincidence that the intellectual lineage of each of these authors can be traced back to either Otway-Ruthven or Lydon (or both).

For the holders of the office in its earliest days, see M.T. Flanagan, 'Household favourites: Angevin royal agents in Ireland under Henry II and John' in A.P. Smyth (ed.), *Seanchas: studies in early and medieval Irish archaeology, history and literature in honour of Francis J. Byrne* (2000). The judicial activities of chief governors can be followed using P. Connolly, 'Pleas held before the chief governors of Ireland, 1308–76', *Ir. Jurist*, 18 (1983). The difficulties faced by English-born chief governors in negotiating the divisive internal politics of the colony is the theme of P. Crooks, 'The "calculus of faction" and Richard II's duchy of Ireland, *c.*1382–9' in N. Saul (ed.), *Fourteenth Century England V* (Woodbridge, 2008). S.G. Ellis has demonstrated that the near-monopoly on the office held by the earls of Kildare in the last phase of the medieval lordship was a pragmatic solution to the problem of governing Ireland that allowed the area administered directly by the central government to expand: Ellis, *Reform and revival: English government in Ireland 1470–1534* (Woodbridge, 1986); idem, *Tudor frontiers and noble power: the making of the British state* (Oxford, 1995). Dublin castle – the seat of English governance in Ireland, whose history was first exposed in snapshots in Gilbert, *Viceroys* – is examined in J.F. Lydon, 'Dublin castle in the Middle Ages' in S. Duffy (ed.), *Medieval Dublin III* (2002).

*Chapter 3: William of Windsor and the Irish parliament*

Military interventions funded after 1361 primarily by the English exchequer form the background to this essay. An excellent analysis from an administrative viewpoint is P. Connolly, 'The financing of English expeditions to Ireland, 1361–1376' in Lydon, *Eng. & Ire.* Ireland receives an honourable mention in Holmes, *Good parl.*, ch. 4. The interconnection between affairs at court and Ireland is further elaborated in S. Harbison, 'William of Windsor, the court party and the administration of Ireland' in Lydon, *Eng. & Ire.* P. Crooks, 'Negotiating authority in a colonial capital: Dublin and the Windsor crisis, 1369–78' in S. Duffy (ed.), *Medieval Dublin IX* (forthcoming) is less sympathetic to Windsor's policies. New evidence concerning Windsor's notorious wife is brought to light in W.M. Ormrod, 'Who was Alice Perrers?', *Chaucer Review*, 40:3 (2006).

The chief governorship of Sir William Windsor is merely a prism through which Lydon views the development of the Irish parliament. This field has been left fallow in the decades since. The chapters on the medieval parliament by F.X. Martin and A. Cosgrove in B. Farrell (ed.), *The Irish parliamentary tradition* (1973) are insubstantial and derivative. For a more sophisticated analysis, see A. Cosgrove, 'Parliament and the Anglo-Irish community: the declaration of 1460' and S.G. Ellis, 'Parliament and community in Yorkist and Tudor Ireland', both in A. Cosgrove and J.I. McGuire (eds), *Parliament and community: historical studies XIV* (Belfast, 1983). The anniversary of the famous Dublin parliament of 1297 was marked by a symposium, but, of the participants, only Lydon specifically addressed parliament as an institution. His essay, 'Parliament and the community of Ireland' in Lydon, *Law & disorder*, advances an interpretation first put forward in his work on Sir William Windsor, which in turn was indebted to the views of J.G. Edwards. Thus, the starting-point for all research on the medieval Irish parliament remains Richardson and Sayles, *Ir. parl.*

By contrast, English parliamentary studies are in the midst of a renaissance. The essays in R.G. Davies and J.H. Denton (eds), *The English parliament in the Middle Ages* (Manchester, 1981) provide crucial reassessments, but research has advanced rapidly since the appearance of J.S. Roskell, L. Clark and C. Rawcliffe (eds), *The house of commons, 1386–1421*, 4 vols (Stroud, 1993), while the monumental new edition and translation of the medieval rolls of parliament – C. Given-Wilson (ed.), *The parliament rolls of medieval England, 1275–1504*, 16 vols (Woodbridge, 2005) – will doubtless provoke an avalanche of monographs.

Some recent work has taken account of Irish evidence. A critical edition of the much-controverted Irish version of the parliamentary treatise, *Modus tenendi parliamentum*, is provided in N. Pronay and J. Taylor (eds), *Parliamentary texts of the later Middle Ages* (Oxford, 1980). Both the English and Irish versions of the *Modus* are considered in a stimulating article by K. Kerby-Fulton and S. Justice, 'Reformist intellectual culture in the English and Irish civil service: the *Modus tenendi parliamentum* and its literary relations', *Traditio*, 53 (1998). The authors dismiss the controversial view of G.O. Sayles that the 'Irish *Modus* lay behind the English *Modus*' (Sayles, 'The *Modus tenendi parliamentum*: English or Irish?' in Lydon, *Eng. & Ire.*). An important addition to our knowledge of parliamentary procedure was made with the discovery of a document (E 163/7/12) published by A.J. Otway-Ruthven under the title, 'The background to the arrest of Sir Christopher Preston in 1418', *AH*, 29 (1980). A stray membrane of this same document is appended to P. Crooks, 'The background to the arrest of the fifth earl of Kildare and Sir Christopher Preston in 1418: a missing membrane', *AH*, 40 (2007): the accompanying commentary suggests that Otway-Ruthven's reading is overly pessimistic and argues that the document provides striking evidence of the sophistication of English political culture and the vibrancy of 'parliamentary traditions' in early fifteenth-century Ireland, an interpretation earlier recommended by the sketch of parliament in R. Frame, 'English political culture in later medieval Ireland', *The History Review*, 13 (2002).

*Chapter 4: The medieval Irish chancery*

This remains the standard account of the development of the Irish chancery, although reference should also be made to S.G. Ellis, *Reform and revival: English government in Ireland, 1470–1534* (Woodbridge, 1986), esp. ch. 6, 'The seals and the secretariat'; and idem, 'The privy seals of chief governors in Ireland, 1392–1560', *BIHR*, 51 (1978). Otherwise, the literature on the Irish chancery is limited in the extreme. In this respect, the most positive development of recent years is the award of funding in 2007 to the TCD-based 'Irish Chancery Project' by the Irish Research Council for the Humanities and Social Sciences. The 'Chancery Project' was the brainchild of Otway-Ruthven, who intended to spend her retirement working on a new calendar of the medieval Irish chancery rolls that would supplant the inadequate Latin calendar published by the Irish Record Commissioners in 1828 (*RCH*). Illness intervened, but the project proceeded slowly throughout the 1980s under the direction of James Lydon,[4] and a trial reconstruction of a single close roll was published in 1992: E. Dowse and M. Murphy (eds), 'Rotulus clausus de anno 48 Edward III: a reconstruction', *AH*, 35 (1992). The new phase of the project – also based at TCD and directed by Katharine Simms – seeks to produce an electronic calendar of the Irish chancery rolls by June 2011, as well as new lists of the personnel of the Irish chancery.

As well as making accessible in English an invaluable corpus of primary material, the new calendar of Irish chancery rolls will allow researchers to examine the institutional development of the Irish chancery in light of the most recent research on its counterparts elsewhere. The development of medieval chanceries in Britain and France was the theme of a conference held at Montréal in September 1995, the proceedings of which have been published as K. Fianu and D.J. Guth (eds), *Écrit et pouvoir dans les chancelleries médiévales: espace Français, espace Anglais* (Louvain-la-Neuve, 1997). The essays contained therein on the English royal chancery are particularly relevant to Irish administrative developments, esp. D.A. Carpenter, 'The English royal chancery in the thirteenth century'; W.M. Ormrod, 'Accountability and collegiality: the

4 See Elizabeth Dowse and Margaret Murphy, 'The chancery project in the medieval history department, Trinity College, Dublin', *Humanities Communication Newsletter*, 11 (1989).

English royal secretariat in the mid-fourteenth century'; T. Haskett, 'The juridical role of the English chancery in late-medieval law and literacy'. Lists of administrative officers are relatively complete for the period up to 1377 (see *Admin. Ire.*) and have stimulated some innovative work on the character of royal government (see esp. Frame, *Eng. lordship*, ch. 3). Updated lists for the post-1377 period will facilitate further prosopographical studies. The rich returns that should result from such an approach are suggested by C.W. Smith, 'Some trends in the English royal chancery, 1377–1483', *Medieval Prosopography*, 6:1 (1985); D. Biggs, 'A Plantagenet revolution in government? The officers of the central government and the Lancastrian usurpation of 1399', *Medieval Prosopography*, 20 (1999); M. Richardson, *The medieval chancery under Henry V*, List and Index Soc., special ser., vol. 30 (1999).

*Chapter 5: Anglo-Irish shire government in the thirteenth century*

The most accessible review of the development of the shire system is now G. McGrath, 'The shiring of Ireland and the 1297 parliament' in Lydon, *Law & disorder*, which complements, but does not supplant, Otway-Ruthven's account. A number of good studies of individual counties exist, but none is better than Otway-Ruthven's examination of 'The medieval county of Kildare', *IHS*, 11:43 (1959). See also C.A. Empey, 'County Waterford, 1200–1300' in W. Nolan and T.P. Power (eds), *Waterford: history and society* (1992). On the development of the cantred, see P. MacCotter, 'Functions of the cantred in medieval Ireland', *Peritia*, 19 (2005). The cantred boundaries within certain regions are delineated in C.A. Empey, 'The cantreds of medieval Tipperary', *North Munster Antiquarian Journal*, 13 (1970); idem, 'The cantreds of the medieval county of Kilkenny', *JRSAI*, 101 (1971); and P. MacCotter, 'The cantreds of Desmond', *JCHAS*, 105 (2000).

Astonishingly little work has been done the men who served as sheriff: an exception is C. Parker, 'Local government in county Waterford in the thirteenth and fourteenth centuries, I-III [*c.*1208–1420]', *Decies*, 50 (1994); 51 (1995); 52 (1996). The subject of commissioners of the peace may be pursued through an early essay by R. Frame, 'The judicial powers of the medieval Irish keepers of the peace', *Ir. Jurist*, 2:2 (1967), revised in Frame, *Ire. & Brit.* The same author has published comprehensive lists of keepers of the peace: 'Commissions of the peace in Ireland, 1302–1461', *AH*, 35 (1992). The untapped potential of these lists to open up the subject of the growth of a lesser nobility, or 'gentry', in certain regions of English Ireland is clearer than ever in light of P. Coss, *The origins of the English gentry* (Oxford, 2003), esp. ch. 7, 'The explosion of commissions and its consequences'. Another approach to county histories that has been co-opted successfully from English historiography is B. Smith, 'A county community in early fourteenth-century Ireland: the case of Louth',

*EHR*, 108 (1993); and, in more detail, idem, *Colonisation and conquest in medieval Ireland: the English in Louth* (Cambridge, 1999).

The importance of liberties to the governance of the English king's dominions in the later Middle Ages is demonstrated in S.G. Ellis, 'The destruction of the liberties: some further evidence', *BIHR*, 54:130, (1981); and the essays in M. Prestwich (ed.), *Liberties and identities in the medieval British Isles* (Woodbridge, 2008). For individual Irish liberties, see C.A. Empey, 'County Kilkenny in the Anglo-Norman period' in W. Nolan and K. Whelan (eds), *Kilkenny: history and society* (1990); 'The Norman period, 1185–1500' in W. Nolan and T. McGrath (eds), *Tipperary: history and society* (1985); 'The Butler lordship', *Journal of the Butler Society*, 3 (1970–1). The liberty of Kerry receives some attention in P. MacCotter, 'Lordship and colony in Anglo-Norman Kerry, 1177–1400', *JKAHS*, 2nd ser., 4 (2004). Both documents and artefacts are used to good effect in M. Potterton, *Medieval Trim: history and archaeology* (2005), which includes chapters on the liberties of Meath and Trim, as well as appendices with lists of liberty officers. For Trim as a prized facet of a wider aristocratic network of estates, see B. Hartland, 'Vaucouleurs, Ludlow and Trim: the role of Ireland in the career of Geoffrey de Geneville (*c.*1226–1314)', *IHS*, 32:128 (2001). The unique arrangements for the governance of the Butler lordship are explored in C.A. Empey and K. Simms, 'The ordinances of the white earl and the problem of coigne in the later Middle Ages', *PRIA*, 75:C8 (1975); and, for a later period, D. Edwards and C.A. Empey, 'Tipperary liberty ordinances of the "black" earl of Ormond' in D. Edwards (ed.), *Regions and rulers in medieval Ireland: essays for Kenneth Nicholls* (2004). R. Frame, 'Lordship and liberties in Ireland and Wales, *c.*1170–*c.*1360' in Pryce and Watts (eds), *Power and identity in the Middle Ages*, is a refreshing attempt to move beyond the institutional approach pioneered by Otway-Ruthven and to interrogate the Irish evidence *à la* Davies: cf. R.R. Davies, *Lordship and society in the March of Wales, 1282–1400* (Oxford, 1978); and idem, 'Kings, lords and liberties in the March of Wales, 1066–1272', *TRHS*, 5th ser., 29 (1979).

### *Chapter 6: The native Irish and English law in medieval Ireland*

On the extension of English law to Ireland, see P. Brand, 'Ireland and the literature of the early common law', *Ir. Jurist*, 16 (1981). Otway-Ruthven's views on the status of the native Irish sparked considerable debate: G.J. Hand, 'The status of the native Irish in the lordship of Ireland, 1272–1331', *Ir. Jurist*, 1 (1966); Hand, *Eng. law*; B. Murphy, 'The status of the native Irish after 1331', *Ir. Jurist*, 2 (1967); R. Frame, 'The immediate effect and interpretation of the 1331 ordinance, *Una et eadem lex*: some new evidence', *Ir. Jurist*, 7 (1972); G. Mac Niocaill, 'Aspects of Irish law in the late thirteenth century' in G.A. Hayes-McCoy (ed.), *Historial Studies X* (Galway, 1976); and K.W. Nicholls, 'Anglo-

French Ireland and after', *Peritia*, 1 (1982). On the proposed 'purchase' of English law, see A. Gwynn, 'Edward I and the proposed purchase of English law for the Irish, *c.*1276–80', *TRHS*, 5th ser., 10 (1960); and, more recently, J.R.S. Phillips, 'David MacCarwell and the proposal to purchase English law, *c.*1273–*c.*1280', *Peritia*, 10 (1996). A different aspect of the relationship between Gaelic and English law is examined by Gearóid Mac Niocaill in his studies of the cross-fertilization between the two legal cultures, esp. 'The contact of Irish and common law', *Northern Ireland Legal Quarterly*, 23 (1972), and 'The interaction of the laws' in Lydon, *Eng. in med. Ire.*

The development of judicial institutions in the English colony is a subject that Paul Brand has made his own: 'The early history of the legal profession of the lordship of Ireland, 1250–1350' in D. Hogan and W.N. Osborough (eds), *Brehons, serjeants and attorneys: studies in the history of the Irish legal profession* (1990); 'The birth and development of a colonial judiciary: the judges of the lordship of Ireland, 1210–1377' in W.N. Osborough (ed.), *Explorations in law and history: Irish Legal History Society discourses, 1988–1994* (1995); 'English royal justices in the lordship of Ireland, *c.*1300' in H.B. Clarke and J.R.S. Phillips (eds), *Ireland, England and the continent in the Middle Ages and beyond: essays in memory of Friar F.X. Martin, o.s.a.* (2006).

## PART 2: WAR

### *Chapters 7–8: Knight service and royal service in medieval Ireland*

S.G. Ellis, 'Taxation and defence in late medieval Ireland: the survival of scutage', *JRSAI*, 107 (1977), adds to the evidence presented by Otway-Ruthven for the late medieval period. Two key essays on knight service in England whose findings are pertinent to the Irish experience are J. Gillingham, 'The introduction of knight service into England', *Anglo-Norman Studies*, 4 (1981), and J.C. Holt, 'The introduction of knight-service in England', *Anglo-Norman Studies*, 6 (1983). Robin Frame adopts a less overtly institutional approach to the militarism of colonial life in 'War and peace in the medieval lordship of Ireland' and 'Military service in the lordship of Ireland, 1290–1360: institutions and society on the Anglo-Gaelic frontier', both in Frame, *Ire. & Brit.*; and Frame, 'The defence of the English lordship, 1250–1450' in T. Bartlett and K. Jeffery (eds), *A military history of Ireland* (1996). The patterns of Gaelic warfare are brought to life in K. Simms, 'Gaelic warfare in the Middle Ages' in Bartlett and Jeffery (eds), *Military history of Ireland.* Critical editions of a number of seigneurial instruments of Irish provenance – by means of which English lords retained men (both English and Gaelic) in their service – appear with a useful commentary in M. Jones and S. Walker (eds), 'Private indentures for life service in peace and war, 1278–1476', *Camden Miscellany XXXII* (Camden Soc., 5th ser., 3, 1994).

Any discussion of feudalism – whether combined with the qualifier 'military' or otherwise – must now take account of debates on the supposed 'tyranny' of that construct. The key works are E.A.R. Brown, 'The tyranny of a construct: feudalism and historians of medieval Europe', *AHR*, 79:4 (1974); and S. Reynolds, *Fiefs and vassals: the medieval evidence reinterpreted* (Oxford, 1994). The latter tome is heavy in every sense and, seemingly, more discussed than read; a convenient crib is S. Reynolds, 'Fiefs and vassals in Scotland: a view from outside', *SHR*, 82:214 (2003), whose views on the Scottish evidence are especially relevant to Ireland. As Otway-Ruthven's approach is undoubtedly Stentonian, D. Bates, 'Re-ordering the past and negotiating the present in Stenton's *First century*' (The Stenton lecture, 1999: Reading, 2000), is useful in providing an appraisal of the work of the great man. Otway-Ruthven's cool analysis of 'military feudalism' is relatively unproblematic on its own terms; more insidious are underlying assumptions (characteristic of her generation) about feudalism's supposedly illegitimate successor. Aspects of the enormous secondary literature on 'bastard feudalism' are discussed, with reference to Ireland, in P. Crooks, 'Factions, feuds and noble power in the lordship of Ireland, *c.*1356–1496', *IHS*, 35:140 (2007), but see also D. Crouch, 'From Stenton to McFarlane: models of societies of the twelfth and thirteenth centuries', *TRHS*, 6th ser., 5 (1995); and P. Coss, 'From feudalism to bastard feudalism' in N. Fryde, P. Monet and O.G. Oexle (eds), *Die Gegenwart des Feudalismus* (Göttingen, 2002).

### *Chapters 9–12: Ireland's participation in English military activities*[5]

Edward I's campaigns in Scotland are discussed in M. Brown, *The wars of Scotland, 1214–1371* (Edinburgh, 2004); and M. Prestwich, *Plantagenet England, 1225–1360* (Oxford, 2005), ch. 9. Among more detailed studies, James Lydon has made another valuable contribution to the history of military logistics in 'The Dublin purveyors and the wars in Scotland, 1296–1324' in G. Mac Niocaill and P.F. Wallace (eds), *Keimelia: studies in medieval archaeology and history in memory of Tom Delaney* (Galway, 1988); while, Edward I's campaign of 1303–4 is re-examined in M. Haskell, 'Breaking the stalemate: the Scottish campaign of Edward I, 1303–4', *Thirteenth Century England*, 7 (1999).

A goodly proportion of the recent literature on Ireland and Scotland has focussed on the Bruce invasion. Robin Frame has made some revisions to his

5 Chapters 9 to 12 are considered here together because of the overlap in subject matter. The title for this section of further reading is suggested by the thesis from which much of the material is drawn: James Lydon, 'Ireland's participation in the military activities of English kings in the thirteenth and fourteenth centuries' (PhD, University of London, 1955).

classic essay, 'The Bruces in Ireland, 1315–18' in Frame, *Ire. & Brit.* J.R.S. Phillips subjects the famous 'remonstrance' of the Irish princes to acute analysis in 'The Irish remonstrance of 1317: an international perspective', *IHS*, 27:106 (1990), and 'The remonstrance revisited: England and Ireland in the early fourteenth century' in T.G. Fraser and K. Jeffery (ed.), *Men, women and war: historical studies XVIII* (1993). The sequence of events during the Bruce invasion is revised in S. Duffy, 'The Bruce invasion of Ireland: a revised itinerary and chronology' in idem (ed.), *Robert the Bruce's Irish wars: the invasions of Ireland, 1306–29* (Stroud, 2002). The latter volume reprints articles by G.O. Sayles and Ranald Nicholson, as well as three essays by James Lydon: 'The Bruce invasion of Ireland: an examination of some problems' [1st pr. G.A. Hayes-McCoy (ed.), *Historical Studies IV* (London, 1963)]; 'The Scottish soldier abroad: the Bruce invasion and the galloglass' [1st pr. G.G. Simpson (ed.), *The Scottish soldier abroad, 1247–1967* (Edinburgh, 1992)]; 'The impact of the Bruce invasion, 1315–27' [1st pr. *NHI*, vol. 2]. The same volume also includes Seán Duffy's essay, 'The Bruce brothers and the Irish Sea world, 1306–29', whose reconstruction of the links between Ulster and Scotland departs markedly from the account in A.A.M. Duncan, 'The Scots' invasion of Ireland, 1315' in R.R. Davies (ed.), *The British Isles, 1100–1500: comparisons, contrasts and connections* (Edinburgh, 1988). Much of this literature is synthesized and amplified in C. McNamee, *The wars of the Bruces: Scotland, England and Ireland, 1306–1328* (East Linton, 1997).

All this work can be seen as contributing to the history of the irruption of the English state across Britain and Ireland and indigenous reactions to that process – a subject that has been surveyed with unparalleled insight and eloquence by R.R. Davies, esp. *Domination and conquest: the experience of Ireland, Scotland and Wales, 1100–1300* (Cambridge, 1990), and *The first English empire: power and identities in the British Isles, 1093–1343* (Oxford, 2000). The limits of English expansion are revealed in M. Prestwich, 'Colonial Scotland: the English in Scotland under Edward I' in R. Mason (ed.), *Scotland and England, 1286–1815* (Edinburgh, 1987); R. Frame, 'Overlordship and reaction, *c.*1200–*c.*1450' in idem, *Ire. & Brit.*; and, more recently, B. Smith, 'Lordship in the British Isles, *c.*1320–*c.*1360: the ebb tide of the English empire?' in Pryce and Watts (eds), *Power and identity in the Middle Ages*. P. Crooks, 'State of the Union: perspectives on English imperialism in the late Middle Ages' (forthcoming), argues that the political and cultural infrastructure of the medieval English 'empire' was more durable than has been allowed and that the story should be extended geographically to include the continent and chronologically to (at least) the fall of Bordeaux in 1453.

*Chapter 13: Richard II's expeditions to Ireland*

In this article, Lydon plugs a hole in Curtis' account of Richard II and Ireland, which T.F. Tout criticized for its neglect of the wardrobe accounts that shed light on the military side of the first royal expedition.[6] On the English interventions of the later fourteenth century that form the backdrop to this essay, see now D. Green, 'Lordship and principality: colonial policy in Ireland and Aquitaine in the 1360s', *Journal of British Studies*, 47 (2008); and S. Harbison, 'William of Windsor and the wars of Thomond', *JRSAI*, 119 (1989). These enterprises reached a climax with Richard II, whose two expeditions have been exhaustively examined in a series of articles by D. Johnston: 'Richard II and the submissions of Gaelic Ireland', *IHS*, 22:85 (1980); 'The interim years: Richard II and Ireland, 1395–1399' in Lydon, *Eng. & Ire.*; 'Richard II's departure from Ireland, July 1399', *EHR*, 98:389 (1983). Robin Frame takes issue with Lydon's portrayal of the first expedition as a 'military triumph' in Frame, 'English officials and Irish chiefs in the fourteenth century' in idem, *Ire. & Brit.*; and Frame, *Eng. lordship*, 'Conclusions: past and future'. See also the same author's analysis of the relationship between the crown and the Irish of Leinster: Frame, 'Two kings in Leinster: the crown and the MicMhurchadha in the fourteenth century' in *Colony and frontier*. The most insightful discussion of the 'diplomatic triumph' (the phrase is Lydon's) represented by the submissions of the Gaelic chiefs will be found in R.R. Davies, 'Lordship or colony?' in Lydon, *Eng. in med. Ire.*

Of late, English historians have begun to take heed of Ireland's role in the events of Richard's reign and his evolving ideas of kingship. M. Bennett, 'Richard II and the wider realm' in A. Goodman and J.L. Gillespie, *Richard II: the art of kingship* (Oxford, 1999), opens up the subject in a stimulating way that has influenced the chapter on Ireland by Richard's most recent biographer: N. Saul, *Richard II* (London, 1997), ch. 12. Richard's policy of knighting Gaelic chiefs is discussed in the context of more general chivalric ideals in J.L. Gillespie, 'Richard II: chivalry and kingship' in idem (ed.), *The age of Richard II* (Stroud, 1997); and idem, 'Richard II's knights: chivalry and patronage', *Journal of Medieval History*, 13:2 (1987). N. Saul, 'Richard II and the vocabulary of kingship', *EHR*, 110:438 (1995), argues that the terms of the Gaelic submissions encouraged the king's exalted conception of his own 'majesty',

6 T.F. Tout, review of Curtis, *Ric. II & Ire.*, in *EHR*, 43:169 (1928): 'His [Curtis'] subject is not really "Richard II and Ireland" so much as Richard's relations to the Irish chieftains, up to and during the period of his first Irish expedition. Beyond this his curiosity does not seem to extend. Neither the military details of the expedition, nor the extensive wanderings of the king, nor the personnel of Richard's following are brought out so exhaustively as the texts would have allowed. And beyond those texts our editor has refused to go. There are sources in the Record Office [PRO] which would have helped to answer questions which he dismisses as hopeless.'

something that came to the fore during his final years of tyranny. The knighting ceremonies and other 'civilizing projects' colourfully recounted by Jean Froissart are analyzed in C. Sponsler, 'The captivity of Henry Chrystede: Froissart's *Chroniques*, Ireland, and fourteenth-century nationalism' in K. Lavezzo (ed.), *Imagining a medieval English nation* (Medieval Cultures ser., no. 37, Minneapolis, 2004). Richard II's tyranny and his disastrous final expedition to Ireland are now best approached via M. Bennett, *Richard II and the revolution of 1399* (Stroud, 1999). The impact in Ireland of the Lancastrian revolution of 1399 requires further study, but the work of Alastair Dunn touches on Ireland and particularly the vast transmarine estates of the Mortimer family, a subject that is otherwise strangely neglected for this period: see A. Dunn, 'Richard II and the Mortimer inheritance' in C. Given-Wilson (ed.), *Fourteenth century England II* (Woodbridge, 2002), and idem, *The politics of magnate power: England and Wales, 1389–1413* (Oxford, 2003).

## *Chapter 14: Richard, duke of York, as viceroy of Ireland, 1447–1460*

The standard account is P.A. Johnson, *Duke Richard of York, 1411–1460* (Oxford, 1988), but, on the duke's career in Ireland, see also J.L. Gillespie, 'Richard, duke of York as king's lieutenant in Ireland: the white rose a-blooming', *The Ricardian: Journal of the Richard III Society*, 5:69 (1980); V. Gorman, 'Richard, duke of York, and the development of an Irish faction', *PRIA*, 85:C6 (1985); and T.B. Pugh, 'Richard Plantagenet (1411–60), duke of York, as the king's lieutenant in France and Ireland' in J.G. Rowe (ed.), *Aspects of late medieval government and society: essays presented to J.R. Lander* (Toronto, 1986). E.A.E. Matthew, 'The financing of the lordship of Ireland under Henry V and Henry VI' in A.J. Pollard (ed.), *Property and politics: essays in later medieval English history* (Gloucester, 1984), presents a picture of the administration of Lancastrian Ireland that is more optimistic than the gloomy accounts in Otway-Ruthven, *Med. Ire.*, and Lydon, *Lordship*. The interface between the archdiocese of Armagh and the Uí Néill – which was crucial to York's success in Ireland – is analyzed by K. Simms in 'The archbishopric of Armagh and the O'Neills, 1347–1471', *IHS*, 19:73 (1974); 'The concordat between Primate John Mey and Henry O'Neill (1455)', *Archivium Hibernicum*, 34 (1976); and '"The king's friend": O Neill, the crown and the earldom of Ulster' in Lydon, *Eng. & Ire*. See also J. Watt, '*Ecclesia inter Anglicos et inter Hibernicos*: confrontation and coexistence in the medieval diocese and province of Armagh' in Lydon, *Eng. in med. Ire*. On the events of 1460, see A. Cosgrove, 'Parliament and the Anglo-Irish community: the declaration of 1460' in Cosgrove and McGuire (eds), *Parliament and community*; J. Moore MacDowell, 'The devaluation of 1460 and the origins of the Irish pound', *IHS*, 25:97 (1986); J. Lydon, '"Ireland corporate of itself": the parliament of 1460', *HI*, 3:2 (1995).

Much of Curtis' account is taken up with a recital of events in England before and during the Wars of the Roses. Consequently, there is an ocean of relevant literature available, much of which is usefully synthesized and surveyed in C. Carpenter, *The wars of the roses: politics and the constitution in England,* c. *1437–1509* (Cambridge, 1997). Insightful chapters on Ireland punctuate R.A. Griffiths' magisterial *Reign of Henry VI* (2nd ed., Stroud, 1998), although his picture of aristocratic violence and disorder is unduly negative. One aspect of English affairs that impinged directly on Lancastrian and Yorkist Ireland was the question of the Mortimer claim to the English throne, a matter that has received a good deal of notice due to the publication of a hitherto-unknown document in M. Bennett, 'Edward III's entail and the succession to the crown, 1376–1471', *EHR*, 113:452 (1998). Further to this, see C. Given-Wilson, 'Legitimation, designation and succession to the throne in fourteenth-century England' in I. Alfonso, H. Kennedy and J. Escalona (eds), *Building legitimacy: political discourses and forms of legitimation in medieval societies* (Leiden, 2004), and I. Mortimer, 'Richard II and the succession to the crown', *History*, 91:303 (2006).

## PART 3: SOCIETY

### *Chapters 15–16: Norman settlement and Anglo-Irish agriculture*

Otway-Ruthven's pioneering contribution to the historiography of European colonization is assessed in J. Gillingham, 'A second tidal wave? The historiography of English colonization of Ireland, Scotland and Wales in the twelfth and thirteenth centuries' in J.M. Piskorski (ed.), *Historiographical approaches to medieval colonization of east central Europe: a comparative analysis against the background of other European inter-ethnic colonization processes in the Middle Ages* (New York, 2002). Robert Bartlett integrates the peripheries (sometimes at the expense of the core) into his stunningly original analysis of Europe's 'Europeanization': *The making of Europe: conquest, colonization and cultural change, 950–1350* (London, 1993). That he could draw so heavily on Irish evidence is in no small part a tribute to Otway-Ruthven, whose work on settlement has been highly influential and embraced by many disciplines, among them archaeology and historical geography. A notable success-story in interdisciplinarity is K.J. Edwards, F.W. Hammond and A. Simms, 'The medieval settlement of Newcastle Lyons, County Dublin: an interdisciplinary approach', *PRIA*, 83:C14 (1983). The historical geographer's approach to manorial settlement is nowhere better summarized than in A. Simms, 'The geography of Irish manors: the examples of the Llanthony cells of Duleek and Colp, Co. Meath' in J. Bradley (ed.), *Settlement and society in medieval Ireland*

(Kilkenny, 1988). Among records-historians of settlement, Otway-Ruthven's pupil, C.A. Empey, is pre-eminent: 'Medieval Knocktopher: a study in manorial settlement', *Old Kilkenny Review*, 2:4–5 (1982); 'The settlement of the kingdom of Limerick' in Lydon, *Eng. & Ire.*; 'Conquest and settlement: patterns of Anglo-Norman settlement in north Munster and south Leinster', *Irish Economic and Social History*, 13 (1986); 'The Anglo-Norman settlement in the cantred of Eliogarty' in J. Bradley (ed.), *Settlement and society in medieval Ireland*. T.B. Barry, *The archaeology of medieval Ireland* (London, 1988) is a standard introduction to the archaeological evidence, but account must also be taken of K.D. O'Conor, *The archaeology of medieval rural settlement in Ireland* (RIA, 1998); T. O'Keeffe, *Medieval Ireland: an archaeology* (Stroud, 2000); and the essays collected in T.B. Barry (ed.), *A history of settlement in Ireland* (London, 1999), and J. Lyttelton and T. O'Keeffe (eds), *The manor in medieval and early modern Ireland* (2004).

The most thorough examination of the manorial economy in Ireland is M.C. Lyons, 'Manorial administration and the manorial economy in Ireland, *c.*1200–*c.*1377', 2 vols (PhD, University of Dublin, 1984), which sadly remains unpublished. The best (albeit rather dry) survey in print is K. Down, 'Colonial economy and society in the high Middle Ages' in *NHI*, vol. 2, which is complemented by K. Nicholls, 'Gaelic society and economy' in the same volume. These surveys are brought up to date by Brian Graham in his précis of the principal issues, 'Ireland: economy and society' in Rigby (ed.), *Companion to Britain in the later Middle Ages*; while Richard Britnell includes chapters on Ireland in his broad-brush survey of insular economic and social developments across half a millennium: *Britain and Ireland, 1050–1530: economy and society* (Oxford, 2004). Of more detailed work, H. Jäger, 'Land use in medieval Ireland: a review of the documentary evidence', *Irish Economic and Social History*, 10 (1983), is useful; while for an excellent localized analysis, see D.N. Hall, M. Hennessy and T. O'Keeffe, 'Medieval agriculture and settlement in Oughterard and Castlewarden, Co. Kildare', *Irish Geography*, 19 (1985). M. Murphy, 'The profits of lordship: Roger Bigod, earl of Norfolk, and the lordship of Carlow, 1270–1306' in L. Doran and J. Lyttleton (eds), *Lordship in medieval Ireland: image and reality* (2008), throws a flood of light on estate management in a profitable English lordship at the height of the agrarian boom, using the unpublished accounts of the Bigod lordship of Carlow referred to by Otway-Ruthven. Generally speaking, Otway-Ruthven's anatomy of the colony's social strata has not been superseded, but G. Mac Niocaill, 'The origins of the *betagh*', *Ir. Jurist*, 1 (1966), is now the definitive study of its subject. The subject of demography remains in its infancy, but see Gearóid Mac Niocaill's 1981 O'Donnell lecture, 'Irish population before Petty: problems and possibilities' (1981).

The pace of work is inevitably faster further afield, where an abundance of evidence and a labour surplus make for a plentiful historiographical harvest. Demesne cultivation in England is discussed in forensic detail in B.M.S. Campbell, *English seigniorial agriculture, 1250–1450* (Cambridge, 2000). For the crises of the fourteenth century, see the same author's substantial essay, 'The agrarian problem in the early fourteenth century', *P&P*, 188 (2005). Developments in economic theory can been followed in J. Hatcher and M. Bailey, *Modelling the Middle Ages: the history and theory of England's economic development* (Oxford, 2001); while those with a Marxian bent (a rare breed in medieval Irish studies) may wish to consult C. Wickham, 'Memories of underdevelopment: what has Marxism done for medieval history, and what can it still do?' in idem (ed.), *Marxist history-writing for the twenty-first century* (Oxford, 2007).

*Chapter 17: The English and Ostmen in Ireland*

Curtis returns to the subject of the Norse population of Dublin in 'Norse Dublin', *Dublin Historical Record*, 4 (1941–2), repr. H.B. Clarke (ed.), *Medieval Dublin: the making of a metropolis* (1990); the latter edition includes a bibliographical note by H.B. Clarke on the literature to 1990. After nearly a century's silence, a spurt of new essays on the Ostmen of Dublin from the pen of Emer Purcell is extremely welcome: 'The expulsion of the Ostmen, 1169–71: the documentary evidence', *Peritia*, 17–18 (2003–4); 'Land use in medieval Oxmantown' in S. Duffy (ed.), *Medieval Dublin IV* (2003); 'The city and the suburb: medieval Dublin and Oxmantown' in S. Duffy (ed.), *Medieval Dublin VI* (2005). The development of Dublin as an 'English' city is traced in S. Duffy, 'Ireland's Hastings: the Anglo-Norman conquest of Dublin', *Anglo-Norman Studies*, 20 (1998); J. Lydon, 'Dublin in transition: from Ostman town to English borough' in S. Duffy (ed.), *Medieval Dublin II* (2001); and S. Duffy, 'Town and crown: the kings of England and their city of Dublin', *Thirteenth Century England*, 10 (2003). For the Ostmen further afield, see J. Bradley, 'The interpretation of Scandinavian settlement in Ireland' in idem (ed.), *Settlement and society in medieval Ireland*; B. Colfer, 'Medieval Wexford', *Journal of the Wexford Historical Society*, 13 (1990–1); J. Bradley and A. Halpin, 'The topographical development of Scandinavian and Anglo-Norman Waterford' in Nolan and Power (eds), *Waterford: history and society*; C. Parker, 'The Ostmen in post-Norman Waterford', *Decies*, 49 (1994).

*Chapter 18: The clan system among the English settlers in Ireland*

The first serious consideration of the lineages of south Dublin appeared nearly a century after this study by Curtis: C. Maginn, 'English marcher lineages in south Dublin in the late Middle Ages', *IHS*, 34:134 (2004). On lineages in

Ireland more generally, see R. Frame, 'Power and society in the lordship of Ireland, 1272–1377' in idem, *Ire. & Brit.*; Frame, *Eng. lordship*, ch. 1; and K.W. Nicholls, 'The development of lordship in county Cork' in P. O'Flanagan and C.G. Buttimer (eds), *Cork: history and society* (1993). C. Parker, 'Paterfamilias and *parentela*: the le Poer lineage in fourteenth-century Waterford', *PRIA*, 95:C2 (1995), provides a full-scale analysis of one lineage, although his genealogical reconstruction of the le Poer family must be treated with caution; cf. P. MacCotter and K.W. Nicholls (eds), *The pipe roll of Cloyne: Rotulus pipae Clonensis* (Cork, 1996), index, s.n. 'Power'.

The pre-conquest Welsh community of Dublin is a subject that Curtis investigated further in 'The Fitz Rerys, Welsh lords of Cloghran, Co. Dublin', *JLAHS*, 5:1 (1921). Building on these foundations, see M.T. Flanagan, '*Historia Gruffud vab Kenan* and the origins of Balrothery, Co. Dublin', *Cambrian Medieval Celtic Studies*, 28 (1994), whose conclusions are modified in S. Duffy, 'The 1169 invasion as a turning-point in Irish–Welsh relations' in B. Smith (ed.), *Britain and Ireland, 900–1300: insular responses to medieval European change* (Cambridge, 1996). See also the penetrating review article, S. Duffy, 'Ostmen, Irish and Welsh in the eleventh century', *Peritia*, 9 (1995).

A quarter-centenary celebration and the wanton destruction of Carrickmines castle have together conspired to make the Dublin marchlands a hot topic during the last decade: see K.W. Nicholls, '*Crioch Branach*: the O'Byrnes and their country' and E. O'Byrne, 'The rise of the Gabhal Raghnaill', both in *Feagh McHugh O'Byrne: the Wicklow firebrand. A volume of quartercentennial essays* (Rathdrum Historical Society, no. 1, 1998); E. O'Byrne, 'A much disputed land: Carrickmines and the Dublin marches' in S. Duffy (ed.), *Medieval Dublin IV* (2003); E. O'Byrne, 'Cultures in contact in the Leinster and Dublin marches, 1170–1400' in S. Duffy (ed.), *Medieval Dublin V* (2004); and L. Simpson, 'Dublin's southern frontier under siege: Kindlestown castle, Delgany, County Wicklow' in Duffy (ed.), *Medieval Dublin IV*. In more general terms, see E. O'Byrne, *War, politics and the Irish Leinster, 1156–1606* (2003); J.F. Lydon, 'Medieval Wicklow: "a land of war"' and L. Simpson, 'Anglo-Norman settlement in Uí Briúin Chualann', both in K. Hannigan and W. Nolan (eds), *Wicklow: history and society* (1994). E. Curtis, 'Janico Dartas, Richard II's "Gascon squire": his career in Ireland, 1394–1426', *JRSAI*, 63 (1933), narrates the career of a soldier who became entrenched in Ireland after receiving lands in the march of Leinster by royal grant; the essay should now be read alongside S. Walker, 'Janico Dartasso: chivalry, nationality and the man-at-arms', *History*, 84:273 (1999). Further to Curtis' closing point, K. Simms, 'Relations with the Irish' in Lydon, *Law & disorder*, shows that 'double chieftaincies' were already characteristic of relations with Gaelic Ireland in the final decades of the thirteenth century, when the English colony was at its height.

*Chapter 19: The spoken languages of medieval Ireland*

This chapter is a product of its time, but its significance is clear from the fact it was still deemed worthy of attack in the 1980s. See A. Bliss, 'Language and literature' in Lydon, *Eng. in med. Ire*, and also the chapter by Bliss and J. Long, 'Literature in Norman French and English to 1534' in *NHI*, vol. 2. The latter volume also includes a useful introductory chapter on Gaelic literature by J. Carney, 'Literature in Irish, 1169–1534'. E. Bhreathnach and R. Ó Floinn, 'Ireland: culture and society' in Rigby (ed.), *Companion to Britain in the later Middle Ages*, provides a valuable overview of cultural developments in Irish, French and English. For the spoken languages of Ireland in a later period, see V. Carey, '"Neither good English nor good Irish": bilingualism and identity formation in sixteenth-century Ireland' in H. Morgan (ed.), *Political ideology in Ireland, 1541–1641* (1999); and A. Bliss, *Spoken English in Ireland, 1600–1740* (1979).

On the literature in French, see J. Long, 'Dermot and the earl: who wrote the *Song*?', *PRIA*, C (1975); W. Sayers, 'Anglo-Norman verse on New Ross and its founders', *IHS*, 28:110 (1992); E. Mullally, 'Hiberno-Norman literature and its public' in Bradley (ed.), *Settlement and society in medieval Ireland*; and E. Mullally (ed.), *The deeds of the Normans in Ireland: La geste des Engleis en Yrlande. A new edition of the chronicle formerly known as* The Song of Dermot and the Earl (2002). Katharine Simms has been instrumental in unlocking the mysteries of bardic poetry for historians: 'Bardic poetry as historical source' in T. Dunne (ed.), *The writer as witness: literature as historical evidence. Historical Studies XIV* (Cork, 1987); 'Literary sources for the history of Gaelic Ireland in the post-Norman period' in K. McCone and K. Simms (eds), *Progress in medieval Irish studies* (Maynooth, 1996); 'Literacy and the Irish bards' in H. Pryce (ed.), *Literacy in medieval Celtic societies* (Cambridge, 1998). For a later period, see M. O Riordan, *The Gaelic mind and the collapse of the Gaelic world* (Cork, 1990). Our knowledge of the Latin annals produced within the English colony has made strides forward of late due to the work of Bernadette Williams, esp. 'The "Kilkenny chronicle"' in *Colony & frontier*, and 'The Dominican annals of Dublin' in S. Duffy (ed.), *Medieval Dublin II* (2001). B. Williams (ed.), *The annals of Ireland by Friar John Clyn* (2007), contains not only a new edition with translation of this chronicle (cf. *AClyn*), but also a substantial introduction. A new edition and translation of 'Pembridge's annals' (formerly ed. J.T. Gilbert in *CStM*, vol. 2) is in preparation by Dr Williams and is eagerly anticipated. As long ago as 1967, Otway-Ruthven noted that 'we have no critical edition of the chronicle of Henry Marlborough'.[7] That situation, alas, remains unchanged.

7 A.J. Otway-Ruthven, 'Thirty years' work in Irish history (I): medieval Ireland (1169–1485)', *IHS*, 15:60 (1967), 362.

Of the literary evidence for the languages he discusses, Curtis devotes least attention to English, but the subject is well served elsewhere. J.L. Kallen, 'English in Ireland' in R. Burchfield (ed.), *The Cambridge history of the English language,* v: *English in Britain and overseas: origins and development* (Cambridge, 1994), may be consulted by way of introduction and for its substantial bibliography; but the literature continues to grow. Of recent works, R. Hickey, 'The beginnings of Irish English', *Folia Linguistica Historica*, 14:1–2 (1993), and idem 'Dublin and Middle English' in P.J. Lucas and A.M. Lucas (eds), *Studies in English medieval language and literature* (Frankfurt, 2002), are of particular importance. On the dialect of Co. Wexford, see R. Roche, 'Forth and Bargy: a place apart' in Whelan (ed.), *Wexford: history and society*; and J. Poole, *The dialect of Forth and Bargy, Co. Wexford, Ireland*, ed. T.P. Dolan and D. Ó Muirithe (1996). The English verse produced in the colony is translated in A.M. Lucas (ed.), *Anglo-Irish poems of the Middle Ages* (1995); while T. Turville-Petre, *England the nation: language, literature, and national identity* (Oxford, 1996), ch. 5, offers a stimulating analysis of these poems in the context of burgeoning national sentiment in fourteenth-century England. Appreciation of the changing status of English as a spoken and written language in the metropolis is crucial for an understanding of the role of the language in the colony. On this question, see W.M. Ormrod, 'The use of English: language, law, and political culture in fourteenth-century England', *Speculum*, 78:3 (2003); J. Catto, 'Written English: the making of the language, 1370–1400', *P&P*, 179 (2003); A. Ruddick, 'Ethnic identity and political language in the king of England's dominions: a fourteenth-century perspective' in L. Clarke (ed.), *The fifteenth century VI: identity and insurgency in the late Middle Ages* (Woodbridge, 2006). The relevance of these works to the colonial situation is clear from recent studies of cultural transmission across the Irish Sea in the later fourteenth and early fifteenth centuries: K. Kerby-Fulton and S. Justice, 'Langlandian reading circles and the civil service in London and Dublin, 1380–1427' in W. Scase, R. Copeland and D. Lawton (eds), *New Medieval Literatures*, 1 (1997); R.R. Davies, 'The life, travels, and library of an early reader of *Piers Plowman*', *The Yearbook of Langland Studies,* 13 (1999); K. Kerby-Fulton and D. L. Despres, *Iconography and the professional reader: the politics of book production and the Douce* Piers Plowman (Minneapolis, 1999).

### *Chapter 20: The problem of the frontier in medieval Ireland*

Lydon's seminal contribution to the idea of the medieval frontier in Ireland explains the choice of 'frontier' as one of two key themes for the *Festschrift* presented to him upon his retirement (*Colony & frontier*). It would be interesting to revisit Lydon's invocation of the American 'frontier thesis' in light of the enormous literature that was generated around the centenary of Turner's infamous essay in 1993: see, for instance, W. Cronon, 'Revisiting the vanishing frontier: the legacy of Frederick Jackson Turner', *Western Historical Quarterly*, 18:2 (1987); and J. Adelman and S. Aron, 'From borderlands to borders: empires, nation-states and the peoples in between in North American history', *AHR*, 104:3 (1999). The relevance of Turner's thesis to medieval Europe is explored in R.I. Burns, 'The significance of the frontier in the Middle Ages' in R. Bartlett and A. MacKay, *Medieval frontier societies* (Oxford, 1989). The latter volume is now a classic; two comparative studies therein that draw on Irish evidence (though written by 'outsiders') are particularly outstanding: R. Bartlett, 'Colonial aristocracies in the high Middle Ages', and R.R. Davies, 'Frontier arrangements in fragmented societies: Ireland and Wales'. R. Bartlett, 'Heartland and border: the mental and physical geography of medieval Europe' in Pryce and Watts (eds), *Power and identity in the Middle Ages*, pursues the theme of periphery and core with all the author's customary panache.

Among Irish historians, too, the idea of 'frontier' has played well. For regional case studies, see B. Smith, 'The concept of the march in medieval Ireland: the case of Uriel', *PRIA*, 88, C (1988); idem, 'The medieval border: Anglo-Irish and Gaelic Irish in late thirteenth and early fourteenth century Uriel' in R. Gillespie and H. O'Sullivan (eds), *The borderlands: essays on the history of the Ulster–Leinster border* (Belfast, 1989); and C. Ó Cléirigh, 'The problems of defence: a regional case study' in Lydon, *Law & disorder*. The subject has also been taken up by archaeologists and historical geographers, most successfully in P.J. Duffy, 'The nature of the medieval frontier in Ireland', *Studia Hibernica*, 22–3 (1982–3). J. Morrissey, 'Cultural geographies in the contact zone: Gaels, Galls and overlapping territories in late medieval Ireland', *Social and Cultural Geography*, 6:4 (2005), seeks to update frontier studies by exporting the idea of a 'contact zone' to medieval Ireland through a brief case study of Kilnamanagh, Co. Tipperary. For a more traditional archaeological perspective, see T.B. Barry, 'The last frontier: defence and settlement in late medieval Ireland' in *Colony & frontier*.

Lydon's essay is broad in thematic content and touches on many factors that have become closely associated with the decline of the colony from the fourteenth century. The impact of famine and plague is now treated in M. Lyons, 'Weather, famine, pestilence and plague in Ireland, 900–1500' in E.M. Crawford (ed.), *Famine: the Irish experience* (Edinburgh, 1989); and M. Kelly, *A history of the black death in Ireland* (Stroud, 2001). On the Scottish mercenaries who played a key role in the military resurgence of Gaelic Ireland, see a new collection, *The world of the galloglass: kings, warlords and warriors in Ireland and Scotland, 1200–1600*, ed. S. Duffy (2007): the contribution of Kenneth Nicholls to that volume ('Scottish mercenary kindreds in Ireland, 1250–1600') is of particular importance. Robin Frame queries whether tracking 'decline' is the most useful approach to the history of the later medieval colony in Frame, 'The "failure" of the first English conquest of Ireland' in idem, *Ire. & Brit.* A case in point is absenteeism. The first serious study was Frame, *Eng. lordship*, ch. 2; recent work by Beth Hartland has followed this in adopting a less fatalistic approach than was hitherto traditional: 'Reasons for leaving: the effect of conflict on English landholding in late thirteenth-century Leinster', *Journal of Medieval History*, 32 (2006), and 'Absenteeism: the chronology of a concept', *Thirteenth Century England*, 11 (2007). On that iconic, if under-studied, frontier – the Pale – see S.G. Ellis, *The Pale and the far north: government and society in two early Tudor borderlands* (Galway, 1988); idem, 'An English gentleman and his community: Sir William Darcy of Platten' in V. Carey and U. Lotz-Heumann (eds), *Taking sides? Colonial and confessional* mentalités *in early modern Ireland: essays in honour of Karl S. Bottigheimer* (2003); and, from an archaeological perspective with a whiff of Turner, T. O'Keeffe, 'Medieval frontiers and fortification: the Pale and its evolution' in F.H.A. Aalen and K. Whelan (eds), *Dublin city and county: from prehistory to present* (1992).

*Chapter 21: The middle nation*

The identity of the English colonists in later medieval Ireland is perhaps the most contested issue in the historiography of recent decades. Lydon further elaborates his ideas in 'Nation and race in medieval Ireland' in S. Forde, L. Johnson and A.V. Murray (eds), *Concepts of national identity in the Middle Ages* (Leeds, 1995). This post-dates a vigorous debate on colonial identity that became ensnared by a controversy concerning 'historical revisionism' in Ireland (for which, see Brady, *Revisionism*). The key essays are S.G. Ellis, 'Nationalist historiography and the English and Gaelic worlds in the late Middle Ages', *IHS*, 25:97 (1986), and B. Bradshaw, 'Nationalism and historical scholarship in modern Ireland', *IHS* 26:104 (1989);[8] and Ellis, 'Historiographical debate. Representations of the past in Ireland: whose past and whose present?', *IHS*, 27:108 (1991). Art Cosgrove's entry into the fray is less constructive due to its recapitulation of the familiar: 'The writing of medieval Irish history', *IHS*, 27:106 (1990). Subtleties are sometimes lost when arguments are tailored for a popular audience; consequently, a spat between Steven Ellis and Kenneth Nicholls from 1999, though it makes for good reading, should be handled charily, since the impression of extreme polarization is typical neither of the authors, nor of historical opinion more generally: S.G. Ellis, 'More Irish than the Irish themselves? The "Anglo-Irish" in Tudor Ireland', *HI*, 7:1 (1999); K.W. Nicholls, 'World's apart? The Ellis two-nation theory on late medieval Ireland', *HI*, 7:2 (1999).

The combatants in this debate restricted their discussion for the most part to the late medieval and early modern periods. R. Frame, ' "Les Engleys nées en

8 Both repr. Brady, *Revisionism*.

Irlande": the English political identity in medieval Ireland' in idem, *Ire. & Brit*, traces the sharpening sense of Englishness among the colonists 'in the century and a half between Magna Carta and the Statutes of Kilkenny'. A contrasting picture of English lords immersed in Gaelic culture emerges from K. Simms, 'Bards and barons: the Anglo-Irish aristocracy and the native culture' in Bartlett and MacKay (eds), *Medieval frontier societies*. The two interpretations are probably consonant with each other. Whereas Frame's concern was with the *political* identity of the colonists, Simms explored *cultural* identity as revealed in bardic poems commissioned by English lords. To some extent the gap has been narrowed by Frame's recent foray, 'Exporting state and nation: being English in medieval Ireland' in L.E. Scales and O. Zimmer (eds), *Power and the nation in European history* (Cambridge, 2005), which reaffirms the resilience of 'Englishness' in Ireland, but does so by mustering evidence from (among other things) bardic poetry. He thereby allows for considerable cultural variegation among those settlers who described themselves as 'English'. An attempt to break the deadlock from a different angle is P. Crooks, ' "Hobbes", "dogs" and politics in the Ireland of Lionel of Antwerp, *c.* 1361–6', *Haskins Society Journal*, 16 (2005), which explores the discrepancies between what political actors *said* and what they *did*.

Some of the most exciting work of recent years has been in answer to Seán Duffy's plea for a study of 'English and Anglicized Ireland' (S. Duffy, 'The problem of degeneracy' in Lydon, *Law & disorder*). Acculturation is a cardinal theme of Simms, *Kings*, but more detailed studies of how English culture (in the broadest sense) operated upon Gaelic lordship are now appearing as a result of the research of Freya Verstraten: 'Both king and vassal: Feidlim Ua Conchobair of Connacht, 1230–65', *JGAHS*, 55 (2003); 'Naming practices among the Irish secular nobility in the high Middle Ages', *Journal of Medieval History*, 32:1 (2006); 'Images of Gaelic lordship in Ireland, *c.*1200–*c.*1400' in Doran and Lyttleton (eds), *Lordship in medieval Ireland*.

'Identity' is a master concept that will continue to be theorized. Many 'theoretically-informed' studies suffer from a lack of empirical grounding. James Muldoon, *Identity on the medieval Irish frontier: degenerate Englishmen, wild Irishmen, middle nations* (Gainesville, 2003), is a case in point, although it presents some fascinating comparative ideas that deserve to be properly worked out. For sound judgments and useful reviews of the term (and related concepts) in an extended chronological framework, see K. Stringer, 'Social and political communities in European history: some reflections on recent studies' in C. Björn, A. Grant and K. Stringer (eds), *Nations, nationalism and patriotism in the European past* (Copenhagen 1994), and R. Bartlett, 'Medieval and modern concepts of race and ethnicity', *Journal of Medieval and Modern Studies*, 31:1 (2001). R.R. Davies, 'The peoples of Britain and Ireland, 1100–1400 [pts I–IV]', *TRHS*, 6th ser., 4–7 (1994–7), is an exhilarating whirlwind tour of insular identities. A similar approach to the period after 1400 is R. Griffiths, 'The island of Britain in the fifteenth century: perceptions of the peoples of the British Isles', *Journal of Medieval History*, 29 (2003); and (somewhat derivatively) A. Goodman, 'The British Isles imagined' in Clarke (ed.), *The fifteenth century VI*. There is little to suggest that scholarly fascination with the subject is subsiding. For the latest crop of articles, see S.G. Ellis, 'Frontiers and identities in the historiography of the British Isles' in idem and L. Klusáková (eds), *Frontiers and identities: exploring the research area* (Pisa, 2006); idem, 'Integration, identities and frontiers in the British Isles: a European perspective' in H. Gustafsson and H. Sanders (eds), *Vid gränsen: integration och identiteter i det förnationalla Norden* [*At the border: integration and identities in the pre-national Nordic countries*] (Göteborg [Gothenburg] 2006); R.A. Griffiths, 'Crossing the frontiers of the English realm in the fifteenth century' in Pryce and Watts (eds), *Power and identity in the Middle Ages*.

# Index

Members of English ruling dynasties are normally indexed under their forenames (e.g., 'Edward I', 'Lionel of Antwerp'). Other titled English lords are listed under family names (e.g., 'Butler'). A family name such as 'de Burgh' is entered under 'B'; 'de' is omitted from the index for individuals active after *c.*1307. An exception is made for members of the Geraldine family, who normally appear under 'Geraldines' in their various branches. The distinction between a patronymic ('fitz Gerald') and surname ('FitzGerald') is indicated by spacing. Married women are normally indexed under their maiden names.

Gaelic names appear most commonly in an Anglicized form in this volume: consequently, the Anglicized form is indexed first, followed in square brackets by alternate spellings and the Irish form of the name. The lower-case 'mac' indicates a genuine patronymic as opposed to an element in a surname.

Where a principal officer in the Irish administration is found in the text acting in that capacity, the office is entered in the index after his name.

Place-names in Ireland are identified by the modern county ('Co.'). Entries followed by 'county' refer to the medieval shires of Ireland.

Bold type indicates chapters and tables. Italics indicate post-medieval personalities, antiquarians and historians. The following abbreviations are used:

| | | | |
|---|---|---|---|
| *a.* | ante [before] | Ir. | Irish |
| (a)bp(ric) | (arch)bishop(ric) | Ire. | Ireland |
| apptd | appointed | K. | keeper |
| C. | chancellor | KP(s) | keeper(s) of the peace |
| clk | clerk | kg(dom) | king(dom) |
| Co. | county [modern] | l. | lord |
| dau. | daughter | parl. | parliament |
| dep. | deputy | sh. | sheriff |
| dk | duke | T. | treasurer |
| e. | earl | w. | wife |
| Eng. | England | | |
| G. | chief governor (i.e. *custos*, justiciar, governor, lieutenant, lord deputy etc.) | | |